THE STORY OF BRITAIN

SIR ROY STRONG

THE
STORY
OF
BRITAIN

FROMM INTERNATIONAL PUBLISHING CORPORATION
New York

FIRST FROMM INTERNATIONAL HARDCOVER, 1997

Copyright © 1996 Oman Productions ltd.

Designed by Douglas Martin
Picture research: Diana Phillips
Indexer: Douglas Matthews

LIBRARY OF CONGRESS CATALOGING-IN-PUBLICATION DATA

Strong, Roy C.
The Story of Britain / Sir Roy Strong.
p.   cm.
Includes index.
ISBN 0-88064-178-9
1. Great Britain--History   I. Title.
DA30.S77   1997
941--dc21   96-49409

Typeset by Textype Typesetters
Cambridge, England

Printed in Hong Kong
by C&C Offset Printing Co., Ltd.

10 9 8 7 6 5 4 3 2 1

CONTENTS

Preface, ix

A people without history
Is not redeemed from time, for history is a pattern
Of timeless moments. So, while the light fails
On a winter's afternoon, in a secluded chapel
History is now and England.

T.S. Eliot LITTLE GIDDING from *Four Quartets*

PREFACE

THIS book was the idea of my literary agent, Felicity Bryan, whose daughter Alice could not be parted from *Our Island Story*, a book which introduced more than one generation to the subject of British history. The present publication, when it came to be written, took on a life of its own once I started. In fact it was unique in my writing career in almost telling me as I went along the direction it wanted me to go in. So it evolved into what one hopes might be an introduction for anyone of any age to the history of the island which the Romans first designated as Britain. In it, I hope, the reader will find his bearings in what has been conceived as a sustained narrative whose imperative has been less when and how than why.

Such a publication cannot ever be anything other than idiosyncratic. No writer can wholly shed his predilections and prejudices however hard he tries. So far as I can I will define these so that when and if encountered, they can be discounted. By the time this book is published I shall be sixty, which means that my earliest memories are those of the Second World War and of the fervent patriotism necessary for a nation under siege. I would describe myself as a conservative with a small 'c' by instinct, and a practising Christian of a variety which might be labelled progressive Anglican Catholic. My education took me to the Warburg Institute whose orbit is the history of the classical tradition, so I am firmly a European in both my intellectual make-up and by political conviction. I am also a product of my own age, a lower middle class boy who made his way upwards through hard work and scholarships to join the ranks of the professional classes who now control the destiny of the country.

There is nothing particularly original about this book. Its span is so enormous that it could never be anything other than a synthesis of syntheses. It is built with gratitude on the work of others and where they disagree, as all academics do, I have inevitably, for a book of this general and introductory nature, had to settle on a compromise. Only in the case of the modern period have I indicated that historians are divided in their views. All I have attempted to achieve is to present a fair and balanced picture of successive ages bound together by a strong narrative which encourages the reader to turn the page and read on.

For those periods in which human beings emerge as distinct personalities with influence over events I have introduced the occasional biography in an attempt to set people within time. Up until Chaucer biography is virtually an impossibility, apart from kings, saints and statesmen, and even then it is difficult. In our own century I was equally defeated until I recalled Sir Isaiah Berlin once saying, "No great people any more." That indeed may be true in what is the age of the common man, but it may equally reflect my own inability to find them. The choice of the biographies is mine, but I have tried to alight upon people who changed the direction of things.

This is the first time that I have read the entire history of Britain since I was an undergraduate in the 1950s, having inhabited in my academic work the cultural pasture land of Tudor and early Stuart England. British history has changed enormously since then, particularly by widening its terms of reference beyond the confines of politics and economics. That wider vision has been enriching and I have attempted to incorporate it, and indeed in doing so found the occasional biography a wonderful vehicle for demonstrating how the cultural and intellectual history of this country cannot be separated from the tide of political events. But I have avoided compiling a bibliography of the huge number of books I read and consulted, since any such list in a book of this nature is bound to be unhelpful for specific purposes.

History and its teaching has been very much in the public eye as I have been writing but I have avoided becoming entangled in things like the national curriculum, preferring to pursue my own solitary path. In the same way I have deliberately avoided reading any other general history of Britain for fear of any influence on my own pen. The guiding light has been the belief that a country which is ignorant of its past loses its identity.

The project has been a shared passion, fired and urged ever onward by my editor: An author is blessed by few remarkable editors in a lifetime but Julia MacRae is one of them. My voyage down the centuries has not been a lonely one. Whenever I have shown signs of flagging she has picked me up and put me firmly back at the prow of the ship of British history and urged me to sail on. Words cannot express my sense of gratitude to her. Publishing is teamwork and in the case of a large project like this must call for a commitment and vision in which everyone has a part to play. I am deeply grateful to all of them. Douglas Martin, the designer, has been obsessed as we all have with ensuring that the book is put together not only to look handsome in terms of design but above all to entice the reader to read.

Over the illustrations, the initial picture research I undertook myself as I went along choosing images which were not merely illustration but evidence, filling out the text and making the reader aware that what he was reading about was all around him or could be seen in museum and gallery collections. That initial selection has been hugely refined and improved by Diana Phillips, who has taken my guiding principles and gone on to look for the unusual and less familiar. The modern period in particular, which suffers from a surfeit of images, is her own.

It is one thing to write an introductory history of this kind. It is quite another thing to find someone not only knowledgeable across the whole canvas covered but sympathetic to the book's aims. We were fortunate to alight upon Keith Perry, Head of History at St Paul's School. He has saved me from many an error and too sweeping a generalisation and, in the case of the eighteenth century, a period whose politics I have always found difficult, his advice has been invaluable. Nor should I wish to forget the hard work in terms of editing put in by all Julia MacRae's colleagues.

This project, I decided, demanded either two or twenty years. Alas, I have not got twenty to spare. In fact from initiation to publication it will add up to four. That decision to opt for the shorter period may have been foolhardy but it is one which has ensured a sense of pace, movement and energy. As I wrote the book I was intensely aware of the fact that the very idea of Britain was being deconstructed. Perhaps, I thought, this introductory history might make a younger generation of islanders give thought as to what it is which binds them together as being British.

ROY STRONG   Herefordshire

Chapter One

THE ISLAND

BRITAIN is an island and that fact is more important than any other in understanding its history. Only twice has it ever been conquered, once in 55 B.C. (before Christ) by the Romans and again in 1066 by the Normans.

The conquerors always had to have a dialogue with the conquered, producing, sooner or later, a mixed society with elements from both. In the main, however, the country was invaded piecemeal by those resilient enough to brave the rough waters of its encircling seas. Because of that difficulty the numbers which came, whether they were tribes from the Rhineland, Romans from the Mediterranean south, Anglo-Saxons from Germany or Vikings from Scandinavia, were always small. Once here they were absorbed into the existing population.

This simple fact, that anyone who came had to make a storm-tossed journey in a boat, accounts for two dominant characteristics of the British as a people: they are both inward and outward looking. The British still cherish their island as a domain separate and inviolate from the rest of the world. Arriving by air today does not remove the sense of entering something cut off. Even a tunnel running under the Channel does not eradicate the sense of a filter against the outside world which, once passed through, has moulded what is immediately recognisable as Britain in the way of attitudes, style and ideas. Unlike other European countries the boundaries of what was to be Britain were drawn at the outset by its geographical formation.

At the same time this has made the British people voyagers and travellers, for in order to learn about the world outside they had to leave the island sanctuary. Scholars and pilgrims have traversed Europe and the Middle East, men of God have crossed the globe to convert the unbeliever, discoverers have sailed the furthest oceans in search of new lands, and thousands of its inhabitants have emigrated to found new countries. Hemmed in by its waters Britain has produced a people who have had to be, and on the whole still are, tolerant of each other's differences. The British by nature are in love with what they regard as the security of their island and the tranquillity of life which that engenders. It explains their innate conservatism, their ability to compromise, their pragmatism as well as their quite revolutionary voyages of the

The earliest map in which Britain appears in recognisable form. Dating from the second quarter of the eleventh century this is a medieval world map or *Mappa Mundi*. These were made according to a rigid framework prescribed by the Church. Geographical accuracy was of little concern, the purpose being to educate the viewer as to the principles of a Christian world whose centre was Jerusalem, scene of the Crucifixion and Resurrection of Christ. In this scheme Britain, top left, was on the very fringes of Christendom.

mind. Island claustrophobia must also account for the great geniuses of our history, a William Shakespeare or an Isaac Newton, for example, whose minds explode beyond island confines in search of universal truth.

If the reality of being an island is central to its history so is Britain's terrain and climate. It is a country divided into highland and lowland zones. To the north and west rise hills and mountains, some as high as two thousand feet, with poor soil, high rainfall and cold conditions. Even today such parts of the country remain remote and difficult of access, but in earlier centuries they were all but cut off. On the whole they were poor but they held wealth in the form of minerals: lead in North Wales, Derbyshire, Yorkshire and Anglesey, gold in Wales, tin in Cornwall and iron in the Forest of Dean. To the east and south stretched the lowlands with rich fertile soil, a far gentler climate with river valleys and a domain which made communications much easier. Its wealth was of another kind, abundant cornfields, and lush pasturage for sheep and cattle which produced meat, leather and, above all, wool.

From the very beginning Britain's geography also defined the central theme of its internal history: the tension between the highlands and lowlands, between Scotland and Wales and the midlands and the south. Time and again that drama was to be played out over centuries. The lowlands, however, were far more exposed to settlers than the rest of the country, for geographically they faced the Channel across which nearly all the settlers came. When Julius Caesar finally decided to conquer the island in 55 B.C. he was to bring with him the civilisation of an empire which spanned the known world. He looked across the Channel at a very different, far more primitive culture, that of the Celts, the last of a long line stretching back over three hundred thousand years to when the country had not been an island but physically part of Europe, where a few hunters had strayed, and then found themselves severed by the massive land change which created the Channel.

For four hundred years Britain was to be part of the great empire of Rome until, at the beginning of the fifth century, the Romans withdrew their legions and the island was left to seek its own salvation in the face of the raids of barbarian tribes from the north. That union of Britain with parts of continental Europe was to be the dominant theme in her history for the next thousand years. Later, in the eleventh century, a second invasion by the Normans united England with a large part of what is modern France. That empire expanded and contracted for five hundred years until in 1558, the last remaining outpost, the port of Calais, surrendered to the French king.

By then America had been discovered and men could look west for the first time. Before that only Ireland lay beyond the island of Britain and man's gaze was fixed firmly eastwards. These were centuries when Britain lay on the very edge of what was the known world, one whose focal point during the pagan ages was Rome and in the Christian ones that followed, Jerusalem. Its remote geographical position, however, was no index of its importance, for it was invaded for a reason. It was wealthy and had the potential of being a power base to sustain empires beyond its watery frontiers. In the Middle Ages the kings of England were to run the most advanced state in Western Europe. But when the Roman legions set sail to conquer the island of Britain all that lay in the future.

The most famous pre-Roman religious monument, Stonehenge, is set in the middle of Salisbury Plain, near Amesbury, Wiltshire. Its use remains a mystery but the stones were set to act as some kind of observatory whereby to measure time through the movement of the sun and stars. What we see today is the monument in its final stage; the present ring of great sarsen stones from the Marlborough Downs was erected c. 1500 BC.

Chapter Two

BRITANNIA

THE island enters written history for the first time in a passage which records the visit to the Cornish peninsula of a Greek sea captain, Pytheas of Marseilles, about 320 B.C. He describes how the natives mined tin and transported it in wickerwork boats covered in hides to what is now St. Michael's Mount where it was sold to foreign merchants, in the main from Gaul. Pytheas went on to circumnavigate the whole island, a remarkable achievement, giving the civilised Greek world a glimpse of the country the Romans were to call Britannia. The natives, he records, lived in wattle or wooden huts, storing their grain in underground silos and drinking a brew made from corn and honey. They were ruled by many kings and chiefs and, if they did fight, they rode into battle in chariots.

Thereafter silence descends and Britain becomes again a land of mystery, only dispelled by the coming of the Romans. That mystery was lifted because the Romans, like the Greeks, could read and write and it is largely from what they wrote that we are able to tell the island's history. But it is history from their viewpoint, for they were the victors over a people who were illiterate and left no written records. We only know the Roman side of the story. The Celtic one would no doubt have been very different.

Pytheas was giving us a glimpse of that society. The Celts were tribes from the upper Danube who radiated outwards from there, eventually settling in Italy, Spain and Britain. They were an agricultural people who lived in farmsteads or villages tending their pigs, goats, sheep and cattle and cultivating the soil, by means of a shallow plough, to produce corn which they stored in underground pits. Such settlements could be large. They were surrounded by defensive palisades or earthbanks such as the famous one which still survives at Maiden Castle, near Dorchester. The Celts were, in fact, an advanced people. They could spin and weave and also make pottery, besides being skilled in metalwork. Some of their artefacts which have been excavated are of great beauty making use of bold abstract forms. They arrived in Britain from about 700 B.C. quickly taking over from the primitive peoples who were already there.

The Celts were of striking appearance, tall with fair skin, blue eyes and blond hair.

Their everyday dress consisted of a tunic over which they wore a cloak fastened by a brooch. They loved brilliant colours and gold jewellery. Each tribe dominated an area of the country such as the Iceni in the north-east or the Brigantes in the north. Each too had its own king, below whom the people were divided into three classes. There were the nobles, together with their retainers, whose prime task was to fight. They rode into battle on horseback or in chariots, uttering horrendous cries and wielding iron swords in such a way that any enemy was terrified at their approach. Next there were the Druids. They were drawn from the noble class and their role was to act as judges and teachers but, above all, deal with the gods by means of charms, magic and incantations. The Celts were dominated by the super- natural in the form of the spirits of woods, rivers, sea and sky. Religious rites and ceremonies took place in sacred groves in which, when the gods were angry, propitiation was offered in the form of burning men alive encased in wickerwork cages. Below the nobles and the Druids there was the vast mass, little more than slaves working the soil. The Celts were a people with powerful traditions handed on from one generation to the next by word of mouth.

Hill forts for defence and protection proliferated during the Iron Age. Maiden Castle, near Dorchester, Dorset, is the most famous. It was no defence, however, against the Romans. In 44 AD. the second legion, led by the future Emperor Vespasian, conquered it. The mutilated bodies of those they massacred were discovered during excavation.

For about six hundred years they were left unmolested until, in the middle of the first century B.C., Julius Caesar decided to conquer them. What inspired him was the knowledge that another tribe of the Belgae, whom he had just conquered in Gaul, was in the south-west of England and that they had had contact with their defeated brethren in north-west France. On 26 August, 55 B.C., some ten thousand men and five hundred cavalry set sail from Boulogne and landed somewhere between Dover and Deal. The highly efficient Roman army had little difficulty in routing the local Celtic chieftains. Caesar carefully noted the way that they fought and how quickly they surrendered, and determined to return the following year. On 6 July, 54 B.C., an even larger army set sail, this time with five thousand legionaries or foot soldiers and two thousand cavalry in some eight hundred boats. They landed in the same area as before and again defeated the Britons but, as their fleet had been wrecked in a storm, they were forced to return to the beach and repair it. In the meantime the British tribal leader, Cassivellaunus, rallied the Britons. Then the Romans began to push northwards, crossing the river Thames and conquering the whole of the south-east. The approach of winter meant that they had to make the crossing to Gaul before the really bad weather set in and so peace was made with the British chiefs, who handed over hostages and promised an annual ransom.

Nothing is then heard for a century. The reason for this is a simple one, for during these years the tempestuous events which led to the creation of the Roman Empire took place. While the battles raged which led up to that event, an island on its fringes was an irrelevance. Four centuries later, when the Romans abandoned Britain, that was to happen again, the army being needed this time to support the empire in its heartlands. During the intervening years the Celtic kingdoms became much more organised with tribes like the Atrebates whose capital was at Silchester, the Catuvellauni centred on Prae Wood near St. Albans, and the Trinovantes at Camulodunum later Colchester. Beyond these, in the south-west peninsula and in the mountains of Wales and Scotland, lived tribes whose existence was extremely primitive.

It was only ever a matter of time before the Romans would return to the subject of the island. Its conquest had always remained on the agenda, but it was not until 40 A.D. (*Anno Domini*, 'in the year of Our Lord') that an army was poised to invade. That invasion was in fact called off at the last minute, but four years later everything came together for a massive attack. The warring tribes within the country had called on the Romans to intervene. More important, the Romans realised the potential of the island in terms of its mineral wealth and corn production. They knew too that until Druidism was wiped out in Britain it would continue to flourish in Gaul, with all the

Wherever the Romans conquered they built forts as self-sufficient outposts for their troops. Each fort was laid out in an identical manner and included within its defences everything necessary for everyday living. The view here is of the remains of the granary at Housesteads in Northumberland constructed in the second century AD.

appalling human sacrifice which they abhorred. Last, but by no means least, there was a new emperor, Claudius, who was in urgent need of a great military victory to secure his power over the empire.

In late April or May four legions, forty thousand men in all, led by Aulus Plautius, crossed the Channel and landed at Richborough in Kent. From there they proceeded across the river Medway and defeated the Britons. To achieve this the Roman soldiers had to swim the river in full equipment and then engage in a battle which lasted two days. The Britons retreated and the Romans continued their advance, crossing the Thames. There was then a short pause to allow time for the arrival of the emperor who brought elephants with him to overawe the enemy. The campaign could then restart. The Romans advanced on Camulodunum which they stormed and took, making it the capital of a new province of the Roman Empire which they called Britannia. At this point many Celtic kings surrendered and the Emperor Claudius, after having been in the country only sixteen days, left for Rome where he was accorded a mighty imperial triumph. The Romans erected arches to commemorate such victories, and the one dedicated to Britain bore an inscription which ran: 'He subdued eleven kings of Britain without any reverse, and received their surrender, and was the first to bring barbarian nations beyond the ocean under Roman sway.'

Aulus Plautius had been left in Britain as its first governor with the task of continuing the conquest. Three legions set off in three different directions: one north, one to the midlands and one westwards. The Celts believed their strength to be in their hillforts with their great earthwork ramparts but they were to prove no safeguard against the Roman soldiers whose artillery battered the defences and burnt down the gates. In this first campaign the Romans conquered up to a line which ran from Exeter to Lincoln. In 47 A.D. Aulus Plautius retired and was succeeded by Publius Ostorius Scapula who renewed the Roman advance pushing far north and west.

The Celts were not without their heroes. One was Caractacus, king of the Catuvellauni, who resisted the Romans for nine long years being driven to seek refuge first with the Silures in South Wales and then move northwards to the Brigantes, where he was defeated and handed over to the Romans by their queen. He and his family were transported to Rome and made to walk through the streets of the city. Such was the admiration of the populace for the courage and bearing of this Celtic prince that Caractacus and his family were pardoned.

More serious was the resistance of the queen of the Iceni, Boudicca. By then a new governor, Suetonius Paulinus, had come and the Romans had begun seriously to set about colonising the country. The towns of Camulodunum (Colchester) and Verulamium (St. Albans) had been founded and the sacred groves of the Druids on the isle of Anglesey had been wiped out. The Britons were reduced to being a subject people forced to pay large sums to the Romans. In the case of the Iceni, their land had been annexed, their queen, Boudicca, scourged and her daughters violated. Such actions by the Romans unleashed a savage rebellion led by Boudicca, a woman of strong character. A Roman historian describes her thus:

> 'In stature she was very tall, in appearance most terrifying, her glance was fierce, her voice harsh; a great mass of tawniest hair fell to her hips; around her neck was a large golden torc [choker]; she wore, as usual, a tunic of various colours over which a thick mantle was fastened by a brooch.'

The Iceni joined with the Trinovantes and other tribes and took the new Roman capital of Camulodunum, butchering its inhabitants. They defeated part of the IX Legion which had hastened south from Lincoln to meet the crisis. Verulamium and London too fell to Boudicca and in all some seventy thousand people were massacred. But Paulinus at last rallied his legions and somewhere near either Coventry or Lichfield the Britons were defeated, Boudicca taking poison.

In 77 A.D. Cnaeus Iulius Agricola arrived as governor and it was to be under him that Britain took on its character as a province of the empire. Agricola springs to life thanks to a biography of him by his son-in-law, the historian Tacitus, who wrote: 'You would readily have believed him to be a good man, and gladly to be a great one.' Agricola was born in Gaul. His father was a Roman senator. Educated at Marseilles in rhetoric and philosophy, he actually began his career in Britain during the peaceful part of Suetonius Paulinus's governorship. Thereafter he worked his way up the ladder serving in various parts of the empire including Britain until, at last, he was appointed its governor, a position he occupied for the unprecedented period of seven years. During that time he advanced and conquered Scotland. For the first time the whole island was under single rule and to celebrate this a vast triumphal arch was built at Richborough whose foundations are still visible today. But trouble in the mainland empire led to the abandonment of Scotland so that, as Tacitus wrote, 'the conquest of Britain was completed and immediately let go'.

In the long run this retreat from Scotland was to prove a major reason for the collapse of Roman Britain. All along it was realised that the country could only flourish if the wild tribes were kept firmly out. Initially it was the three great fortresses of York, Chester and Caerleon which were built to house the legions upon which this depended but in 122 the Roman Emperor Hadrian came to Britain and ordered the

Before the invention of mercurised glass, looking glasses were of highly polished reflective metal. This bronze mirror catches the sophistication of Celtic metalwork with its use of swirling harmonious pattern. It was made just before the Roman invasions and was found near Birdlip, overlooking Gloucester.

building of a wall eighty miles long, stretching from the Tyne to the Solway. It was a stupendous project and much of it still stands. It was never less than eight feet thick and fifteen feet high. Every fifteen miles there was a fort and between each fort there were two watch towers. In addition there were sixteen really major forts. On the enemy side there was a ditch as protection and a second on the Roman side to facilitate transportation of supplies. No less than nine thousand five hundred men were needed to man the wall.

In this way Roman Britain was created and existed in peace and security for several hundred years. Tacitus describes how that was achieved:

'In order that a people, hitherto scattered and uncivilised and therefore ready for war, might become accustomed to peace and ease, Agricola encouraged individuals and helped communities to build temples, fora, and houses . . . Further, he trained the sons of the chiefs in the liberal arts and expressed a preference for British natural ability over the trained abilities of the Gauls. The result was that the people who used to reject the Latin language, began to aspire to rhetoric. Further, the wearing of our national dress came to be esteemed and the toga came into fashion. And so little by little, the Britons were seduced into alluring vices: arcades, baths and sumptuous banquets. In their simplicity they called such novelties 'civilisation', when in reality they were part of their enslavement.'

The Romans were to leave a mighty legacy which was to change the face of the island and its history.

A Celtic gold torc or collar made about 50 B.C. fashioned from eight strands of twisted wire and with a coin of the period inside of the terminals. A Roman historian describes Boudicca, queen of the Iceni, wearing just such an ornament. This one was found at Snettisham, Suffolk, close to the area over which she ruled.

Chapter Three

ROMAN BRITAIN

EVERYWHERE the Romans went they took their civilisation with them, one which had evolved in the warm south of the Mediterranean. Although mostly sensitive to the peoples that they conquered, they nonetheless superimposed upon them a whole way of life. The ruins of their cities and villas which we can still visit today are remarkable, above all, for the fact that, whether they are in Africa, the Middle East or Britain, they are all the same, both in their planning and use of classical architecture. And these were not the only things which were uniform: so was the structure of government the Romans imposed upon their empire, and its language, both spoken and written, which was Latin.

For four centuries Britain was one province of the greatest empire the world has ever known. That the Romans could transform the Celts with such speed was due to the fact that their army was also their civilisation on the move. Among the thousands of soldiers there would be those who knew how to read and write, plan cities and design buildings. There were others who could construct roads and waterways or possessed skills such as medicine. Without these abilities such a rapid transformation could not have taken place, one which saw a scattered rural society change itself into a society whose focus was to be something quite new, the town.

The army combined strength with knowledge, and Roman Britain was to burgeon and prosper as long as it remained. The province called for fifty-five thousand men to maintain it, initially as an army of occupation but later as one defending what had become Romano-British society. These soldiers were divided into two groups, the first being made up of legions all of whose members were Roman citizens. Citizenship could be granted by the emperor to anyone and gave that person not only certain rights but status within society. Legionaries came from all over the empire, not only from Italy but from places like Spain and Gaul. Each legion was made up of five thousand five hundred men, a hundred and twenty of those being cavalry, and each, in the early days of empire, was commanded by a Roman senator, a member of the governing body, with fifty-nine senior officers or centurions below him.

There was a second group called the auxiliaries. They too could come from any-

where but were unlikely to be Roman citizens, a privilege which was only extended to them later. These men were employed for various specialist purposes such as archers, slingers or skirmishers. To both these groups of land forces must be added a fleet, probably based in Dover whose main task was to patrol the seas against any potential invaders.

The Romans conquered Scotland and then were forced to abandon it. The tribes within it were kept at bay by an eighty-mile long wall stretching from the Tyne to Solway. The section here at Housesteads is one of the most spectacular surviving parts.

   Roman soldiers looked very different from the Celts they defeated. They wore metal helmets and articulated plate armour and carried shields of wood and leather with a sword and dagger suspended from a belt. Each legionary had to carry two javelins which, on going into battle, were hurled at the enemy after which the sword and dagger came into play in hand-to-hand combat. Their life was one of unremitting discipline, with a nineteen-mile march and drill twice a day, every day. A high degree of fitness was demanded so that a legionary could leap fully armed onto a horse or swim with all his equipment across a river.

Dotted across Britain the legions were established in forts sited to achieve maximum strategic defence. These forts were all laid out to a uniform pattern, rectangles of fifty acres or more housing upwards of six thousand men. In the centre of the enclosure was the general's headquarters with a road crossing in front dividing the site into two, and a second road leading up to it. In this way the area was divided into three blocks containing barracks, hospitals, granaries, storerooms, bath houses, stables and workshops. Outside the confines of the fort there were private houses for the soldiers' families, temples for worship and an amphitheatre for sports and entertainment.

The army, after its initial conquest of the island, spent the majority of its time in peacetime tasks. The most important of these was governing the country. At its head was the governor, appointed directly by the emperor for a period of between three and five years. He was always chosen from among the most outstanding of the legionary commanders. The governor resided in London which by 60 A.D. had become the administrative capital of Britain, something which it has been ever since. The governor was complemented by a second official of almost equal power and independent of him, the procurator, again appointed by the emperor. He was the civil servant in charge of finances, seeing that taxes were collected and that the army was paid.

The system of government was not only made up of a network of garrisons stretching over the country but also of towns connected by roads. Roads were constructed by the legionaries as they conquered the country, and were essential for ensuring the swift movement of goods and commerce. These great highways, some twenty to twenty-four feet wide, were carefully built up in several layers of sand, gravel and stones and subject to constant maintenance. They are easily

Tombstone of a Roman centurion of the Twentieth Legion. Marcus Favonius Facilis, buried at Camulodonum, present day Colchester. The attire is that of a soldier with cuirass, sword, and javelin in his right hand.

recognisable today in any stretch of straight road connecting two towns whose origins were Roman. The network was not haphazard either for they all converged on London, giving it a primacy which has never been lost.

The greatest change of all, however, was the introduction of towns. To the Romans, urban life was the only one they recognised, something totally alien to the Celts who dwelt in scattered enclosures, often on hilltops. From the very outset the Romans began erecting towns of a kind which incorporated all the features which were to be found in the towns of their native Italy. They were all laid out to a similar pattern, a rectangular grid of streets covering anything between a hundred and three hundred acres. At the centre there would be a group of public buildings: a forum surrounded by a colonnade which acted as a civic centre with a marketplace either in or near it; on one side there would be the basilica or town hall from where the town was governed and where the law courts were situated. These headed a long list of other communal buildings which embodied the Roman way of life, to which the Celts were successfully converted. Each town had its own public baths, often several of them, with elaborate changing rooms, a gym, cold baths and rooms which ranged in temperature from tepid to hot. The Romans were masters in handling water, everything from aqueducts to bring it from rivers and springs outside a town to the drainage and sewerage within.

Each town also had its own amphitheatre on the outskirts, a large oval area surrounded by tiered wooden seats where races, combats, beast hunts and bear and bull-baiting could take place. Some also had theatres which were similar in construction but D-shaped where the citizens could enjoy plays, pantomime, singing and recitation. Both inside and outside the built-up area there would be many temples dedicated to the gods, not only the Roman ones, such as Jupiter, Juno and Minerva, but also to the emperor as a living god. At Camulodunum there was the headquarters of the imperial cult, with a huge temple which was the setting for ceremonies acted annually by delegates from all over the island. Over the centuries, shops which began as being of wood set on a stone base gradually became ones entirely built of stone. Initially the towns were constructed without walls but later, as the threats of invasion multiplied, they were added.

For the Romans, towns were an essential element of the pattern of government which they introduced. Each town had what was called a senate, an assembly of its most important citizens. Four magistrates were elected annually, two to act as judges and two others to control finance and building. In this way, fanning out from London along the roads, the decrees of the emperor and the orders of the governor and the procurator reached the furthest boundaries of the island.

The Romans brought their culture with them. Few aspects of that have survived better than the rich mosaic floors of their villas. This one is from a vast villa covering twenty-six acres at Woodchester in Gloucestershire dating from the fourth century. The wide range of local stones contributed to the quite exceptional colour and variety of mosaics executed in Britain.

Unlike the small Celtic rural communities, towns were by no means self-sufficient, for they depended on foodstuffs being brought into the marketplaces along the roads by cart from the countryside. The countryside, too, underwent a reorganisation in the form of the villa, a change which was far less revolutionary to the indigenous population. Villas began as the main farmhouse of an estate around which the old Celtic native huts clustered. They were simple but comfortable structures with central communal rooms and wings projecting at either end, and verandahs around them. Only the most splendid were of such a size as to form a complete courtyard. As time passed they became more luxurious with comforts like underfloor heating, mosaic floors and wall paintings. Occasionally, as at Fishbourne, they could almost be palaces. That villa covered no less than five acres with a colonnaded courtyard at its heart, and walls adorned with imported marble.

These villas presided over an agriculture which was not so very different from that practised by the Celts. The Romans, however, introduced new vegetables such as the cabbage, peas, parsnips and turnips, and new fruits too, apples, plums, cherries and walnuts. Better varieties of cattle were imported and the domestic cat arrived. Flowers such as the lily, rose, pansy and poppy were brought not only for their medicinal properties but for their decorative ones as well. For the first time men made gardens.

From the farms the produce not only went to the towns but, in the case of grain, to the ports for export to the mainland. Tin, copper, lead and, above all, iron ore, were excavated. Stone was quarried for building. Bricks and tiles were manufactured and jewellery, pottery and glass were made. With an abundance of wool, a textile industry developed.

Roman Britain was held together by a strong system of government. The creation of towns and villas formed a ruling class, one which could, and indeed did, include Celts who were Romanised, lived in towns and spoke Latin. In the country Celtic survived as the language of the peasantry. This new governing class was also in part held together by worship of the emperor, and through that gained allegiance to the whole idea of the Roman Empire.

The Romans, however, were tolerant in matters of religion, except in the case of cults which involved human sacrifice. That was why they eradicated the Druids. Otherwise the gods of the Celts lived on side by side with those introduced by the Romans. Later came new cults such as that of the Persian god, Mithras, or the Egyptian goddess, Isis. Christianity, too, reached Britain. As early as the beginning of the third century it was written that 'parts of Britain inaccessible to the Romans have been subjected to Christ'. Its early history is extremely obscure until, at the beginning of the fourth century, Christianity became the official faith of the Roman Empire. In

391 the Emperor Theodosius ordered the closure of all pagan temples. By then the British church was highly organised, sending its bishops as delegates to the great councils held on the mainland.

At its height in the third and early fourth century Roman Britain must have been spectacular, with its bustling, prosperous towns adorned with handsome public buildings and its countryside dotted with gracious villas. Life seemed full only of certainties, abundant food, ease of travel and increasing wealth. Little thought was given to the savage tribes which lived on the other side of Hadrian's wall, let alone those which could cross the seas. Even if these wild peoples did erupt from time to time to disturb the imperial peace, they were soon put to flight by the military might of the legions. Everything worked as long as those legions were in place. When circumstances arose which would lead to their withdrawal the civilisation of Roman Britain was seen to be hanging by a thread.

Finds at the Roman fort of Vindolanda, modern Chesterholm, in Northumbria. One is a betrothal medallion carved from Whitby jet, probably in York, and the other a letter written in pen and ink, probably to a soldier sending him socks, sandals, and underpants.

The only surviving body of what is likely to have been a Briton from the late Roman period found preserved in peat near Wilmslow in Cheshire. It is likely that he was clubbed to death, then garrotted, having his throat cut also as part of a ritual sacrifice. The fact that his finger nails were carefully manicured indicate that he was civilised.

Chapter Four

DARKNESS AND DAWN

ROMAN BRITAIN was a fragile civilisation on the fringes of a mighty empire. When that empire began to break up, the legions were called back from its frontiers to cope with threats at its heart. Britain had always depended for its existence on the legions to keep at bay the barbarians on the other side of Hadrian's wall, and on the fleet which had patrolled the Channel warding off invaders from the continental mainland. The country looked to Rome also for its system of government, law and order, one which stretched downwards from the emperor through his governor and procurator to the officers who ran the towns scattered across the country. Once the army and the fleet were gone Britain was left unprotected and devoid of any central authority. The inhabitants had not been trained to meet that need when it arose, which made them even more vulnerable when the attacks from outside began.

All of this, however, did not happen at once. In dramatic contrast to the Roman conquest, that by the barbarians was to be a long drawn-out process which dragged on for two hundred years. It was only by the sixth century that a different map of Britain began to emerge, one made up of a series of small independent kingdoms which bore little relation to what the Romans had created. These centuries are known as the Dark Ages, dark because a whole civilisation disintegrated, dark also because our knowledge of what actually took place is very fragmentary. It has to be pieced together from the very few written accounts compiled a long time after the events which they describe, and from what has been discovered through archaeology (the digging up of the past).

The threats from outside were there from the beginning, but from the third century they began to be serious. There would be sudden attacks, but these were often followed by deceptively long periods of peace which lulled the Britons into a false sense of security. By the beginning of the fourth century, however, the raids accelerated and it was clear that this time there was to be no rest. Invaders came from every direction. There were the Scots from Ireland who attacked the west, the Picts from the far north who crossed Hadrian's wall and penetrated south, and the Anglo-Saxons who landed in the south-east and East Anglia. The Anglo-Saxons were made up of various tribes who came from an area stretching between the mouths of the rivers Rhine and Elbe. In the long run they were to be the dominant force in forging what was to be Anglo-Saxon England. A group of them was called *Engle* and from that came the word England.

When the raids first began the Romans responded by constructing a series of fortresses along what they designated the Saxon Shore, an area of coastline running from Brancaster to Portchester, near Portsmouth. Soon the Romans could no longer maintain a fleet and the country's defences dwindled to what legions remained. In 367 there was an appalling attack, so severe that even London was besieged. The problem was that it was impossible to fight on every frontier. The south-east was defended only at the expense of leaving the north unprotected. Indeed gradually the north was abandoned and a series of small border kingdoms emerged, whose task it was to ward off the Picts. That signalled the opening phase of the disintegration of what had been Roman Britain.

In 410 the Emperor Honorius told the British that they must fend for themselves. The Romans abandoned Britain and the last of the legions departed. The rich towns and gracious villas stood unprotected, easy prey for the barbarians who now arrived annually. Each spring they came from across the seas for a season of plundering and looting, burning and sacking the villas and destroying towns. Each autumn they returned home until gradually they chose instead to settle. The Britons were faced with a cruel choice, either to flee or to come to some kind of agreement with them. Some did leave the country, burying their valuables in the hope of returning in happier times. But most remained. Their solution was to give land to the barbarians in return for military service in their defence.

By the middle of the fifth century there were settlers all over the country. By then the villa life of the Romans had had to be abandoned. Most of the towns carried on within their walls. As the attacks became even more severe, there was sometimes a retreat to more easily defended hilltop sites. All around them the Britons saw the way of life they had taken for granted gradually grind to a halt. Pottery and glass, for example, ceased to be made. Then the coinage stopped which meant the collapse of trade and commerce. While this was happening the Christian religion thrived and the church, in spite of the troubled times, sent representatives to the great councils which took place on the continental mainland. To many it must have seemed that the end of the world was at hand. One such was a British priest, Gildas, who, looking back from the mid-sixth century, gives us an impression of the atmosphere of the age. He describes how 'loathsome hordes of Scots and Picts eagerly emerged from coracles [a form of boat] that carried them across the gulf of the sea like dark swarms of worms.' Monasteries and churches were pillaged and pitiful appeals were made to Rome for help: 'The barbarians drive us to the sea; the sea drives us to the barbarians; between these two means of death we are either killed or drowned.'

The Romans always called anyone who was not Roman a barbarian. However violent the Anglo-Saxons, they were a people with their own rich traditions. They were pagans who worshipped gods such as Woden, Thunor or Frig whose names were to be the origin of our Wednesday, Thursday and Friday. They had no interest in the Roman way of life. Their society was very differently structured. At the top came the nobles who fought, next the *ceorls* who farmed and, at the bottom, slaves. The Anglo-Saxons were not town-dwellers, living instead in wooden villages in clusters of huts around a large central hall. Unlike the Britons their whole existence was war. Fighting bound them together in ties of loyalty to their leaders. Loyalty was seen as the greatest of human virtues and, as a consequence, the most detestable of all crimes was the betrayal of a king. In their own way they were civilised, producing an heroic poetry and a magnificent art summed up in the splendid objects found in an early seventh century king's tomb known as the Sutton Hoo treasure, which is now in the British Museum. Beneath a vast mound of earth the king lay in a huge ship surrounded by weapons and jewels, a helmet, shield and purse, all objects of great beauty and skilful workmanship, rich with the figures of birds, animal heads and dragons. The ship called for forty oarsmen to row this chief to the next world.

Sooner or later these two groups of people with two divergent ways of living were destined to clash. One account of how this happened describes how most of lowland Britain came under the rule of a man called Vortigern who, in 449, invited a group of Anglo-Saxons led by Hengist and Horsa to settle in Kent and fight on his behalf. But not long after they rose in revolt, leading to a long series of battles for the remainder of the century. During this period there emerged a British hero called Ambrosius Aurelianus and there was a great victory over the Anglo-Saxons at a place called *Mons Badonicus*. But nothing is known about this hero beyond his name, not the precise date of the decisive battle. After it there followed half-a-century of peace. Everything is shrouded in mystery, so much so that several centuries later a British hero was invented. He was King Arthur.

Although the British victories delayed the Anglo-Saxons, by the close of the next century Roman Britain had vanished piecemeal, bit by bit eroded as chiefs landed in various parts of the country and carved out small kingdoms for themselves. In the south-east there was the kingdom of Kent and the south Saxon kingdom. In the east

At Sutton Hoo in east Suffolk the grave of a Saxon king from about 625 was uncovered. The vast burial mound concealed a great open rowing ship with space for forty oarsmen and a steersman.

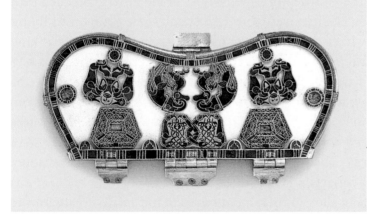

Into the wood cabin amidships had been placed the king's treasure including his helmet made of iron and covered with tinned decorative plates, the features gilded.

Also found were golden shoulder clasps and a purse, all set with garnets and *mille fiori* glass. The king is likely to have been Raedwald, king of East Anglia.

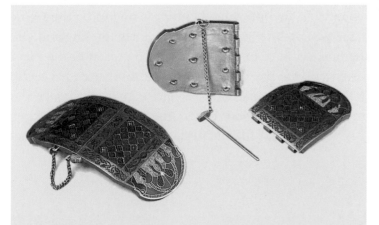

there was the kingdom of the East Saxons, the East Angles and that of Lindsey. In the midlands there was the kingdom of Mercia and in the north that of Northumbria. Finally in the south-west there was that of Wessex. It took a hundred years for all these gradually to take shape. Their relationship with one another was in the main one of war. In 577 the Anglo-Saxons took the three great Roman towns of Bath, Cirencester and Gloucester. Those who could fled either into Wales or into the south-west peninsula called the kingdom of Dumnonia.

England was now made up of a series of small warring kingdoms. All that held them together was a tradition whereby one of those kings was recognised as having some kind of supremacy over the others expressed in the title, *bretwalda*. This was a turbulent age during which first one kingdom was dominant and then another. Early in the seventh century it was Northumbria under Edwin until he was killed in battle by the British. Then it was the turn of Mercia under Offa. What is so striking is that with these barbarian kings the memory and tradition of the Roman Empire still lingered. Offa's coinage imitates that of a Roman emperor and even more startling he built his own version of Hadrian's wall, a great earthwork or dyke of a hundred and fifty miles along the Welsh border. Finally in 825 Mercia was defeated by Wessex.

Amidst all this confusion and seemingly unending destruction there emerged a remarkable civilisation. By the eighth century, men whose grandfathers had been heathen barbarians had not only been converted to Christianity but gone on to found churches and monasteries which were to be centres of art and learning of a kind which was to act as a beacon shining out across the rest of Western Europe. This revolution came about by the action of the head of the church, the pope, Gregory the Great, in sending in 597 a mission to convert the Anglo-Saxons. That had been inspired many years before in Rome when he had seen a group of fair-haired youths and asked who they were and their country of origin. He was told that they were *Engles* or Angles, in Latin *Angli*. The pope is said to have remarked that he saw them not as *Angli* but *Angeli*, that is, angels.

What is so surprising about the old British church is that it made no attempt to convert the invaders. In the fifth century St. Patrick had set about converting the Irish and establishing the Celtic church. In the following century it was to be the Celtic church which was to send missionaries to evangelise the north of England. St. Columba set up a base on the tiny island of Iona from which to preach to the Picts. The real turning point, however, was the papal mission to the south-east led by St. Augustine. The king of Kent, Ethelbert, was married to a Christian Frankish princess who practised her faith within the royal household. When Augustine landed the king, fearing magic, insisted that his meeting with the missionaries take place beneath an

The Saxon tower of the church of St. Mary the Virgin at Sompting, Sussex. Built c. 1040-60 it is among the most famous of Anglo-Saxon churches and the only surviving example with a steeple of a type which may have been quite common. Its style came from the churches of the Rhineland.

open sky. Out of this came the grant of a place in Canterbury in which they could live and had permission to preach. Soon there were many converts and old churches began to be restored and new ones built. After a year Ethelbert himself became Christian. Augustine was consecrated Bishop and later Archbishop of Canterbury. He began to construct on the ruins of the old Roman Christian church a new one whose descendant is our present cathedral.

That mission was only the beginning of the conversion of the Anglo-Saxons, a task which took most of the seventh century to achieve. It was accomplished by the Roman missionaries from the south going north and the Celtic missionaries from the north moving south. There were huge set-backs. On the death of Ethelbert the mission was almost extinguished but somehow it survived. When Ethelbert's daughter had married Edwin, king of Northumbria, he too converted but Christianity foundered when he was killed. A later Northumbrian king, Oswald, turned to Celtic monks to re-Christianise the country. In 635 St. Aidan settled on the island of Lindisfarne and began his work of conversion. At about the same time Wessex became Christian and then, later, Mercia.

Everywhere churches and monasteries sprang up as the Celtic and Roman missionaries triumphed, but they also clashed. The problem was that the Celtic church followed the old British church which in its isolation had developed traditions which were different from those of the Roman missionaries. They celebrated Easter on a different day, for instance. Their bishops, too, were free-roaming whereas the Roman bishops each had a diocese, a fixed area of the country over which they presided. Their monasteries were also different, for the Celts could have ones for both sexes together. In 664 a meeting was held to resolve these differences, the Synod of Whitby, in which the Roman case representing universal practice elsewhere carried the day. Six years later the pope sent a great archbishop, Theodore of Tarsus, whose arrival signalled the golden age of the Anglo-Saxon church.

For a century the church was the focus of huge enthusiasm attracting members of royal and noble families to enter the monastic life. Anglo-Saxon kings often went on pilgrimage to Rome. Monks crossed from England to convert those who still lived in the lands their ancestors had come from. Along with the Christian faith they carried also the fruits of a great cultural renaissance which had taken place in England, stemming from Rome and the Celtic church. And Theodore brought the learning embod-

Page from the Lindisfarne Gospels which were written and illuminated about the year 698 at the island monastery of Lindisfarne by a monk called Eadfrith who later became its bishop. Each of the four gospels is prefaced by what is known as a 'carpet' page, an elaborate abstract pattern incorporating a cross. The manuscript is among the world's greatest works of art, one in which Roman, Celtic, and Anglo-Saxon influences are fused.

ied in the writings of the ancient world of Greece and Rome as they had survived through the Dark Ages along with the great works of early Christian scholars and theologians. Monasteries such as Canterbury and Malmesbury became centres of teaching where both Greek and Latin were taught, together with what were called the Seven Liberal Arts, subjects which for over a thousand years were regarded as embracing the sum of human knowledge: the *trivium*: grammar or the art of writing, rhetoric or the art of speaking, and dialectic, that of reasoned argument; and the *quadrivium*, which consisted of arithmetic, geometry, astronomy and music. Combined, these seven topics were all seen as essential for expounding the mysteries of the scriptures.

The most famous of all these scholars was the monk Bede (c.673–735) who celebrated this age in the following way:

> 'And certainly there were never happier times since the English sought Britain; for, having very powerful and Christian kings, they were a terror to all barbarous nations, and the desires of all were bent on the joys of the heavenly kingdom of which they had recently heard, and whoever wished to be instructed in sacred studies had masters at hand to teach them.'

Opening page of King Alfred's translation into Anglo-Saxon of Pope Gregory the Great's *Pastoral Rule* in which the attributes and duties of the clergy are described. This is the copy sent by him to the Bishop of Worcester, Waerferth, vivid evidence of the king's policies in acton. Such translations were among the very first steps in the creation of a vernacular literature in English.

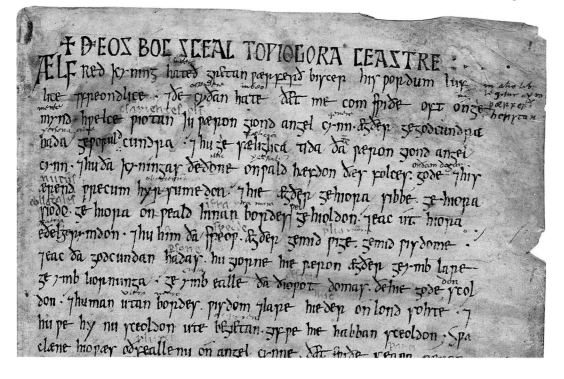

Ruins of the monastic church at Reculver, Kent. The church was built in 669 by Bassam, a follower of St. Augustine. The aerial view delineates the first church and the eighth century enlargements to it. The altar was in the curved chancel at the east end and the nave had small rooms off it which often housed tombs. The two west front towers are later, Norman, c.1170.

It was in Northumbria that this civilisation reached its greatest flowering. We can still see the monumental stone crosses adorned with vine-leaf decoration and figures of Christ and the saints which were set up to proclaim the faith. Nothing comparable with these was being produced in Western Europe at the time. Even more remarkable are the Lindisfarne Gospels written about the year 700 in the great monastery on Holy Island off the coast of Northumbria. This is what is called an 'illuminated manuscript', one in which the pages are of vellum, that is prepared animal skin, painted with pigments whose effects could be enriched with burnished gold. It was the work of the bishop and in it we see complex inter-laced ornament woven into a many-coloured network of astounding freshness and delicacy of colour.

So it was that by the eighth century a new society, deeply Christian, had come into being. One of the ironies of history is that this had emerged from the destruction of Roman Britain. Now it too was to face the same fate when new invaders from beyond the seas, the Vikings, began to attack. In 793 Lindisfarne, where this miraculous Gospel-book was compiled, was sacked and once more a civilisation was faced with the possibility of extinction.

Chapter Five

ALFRED
AND THE VIKINGS

THE Vikings terrified the Anglo-Saxons as much as they themselves had terrified the Britons centuries before. From beyond the seas the island was exposed once more to wave after wave of invaders, bent on pillage and plunder and destroying yet again a fragile civilisation. The story of this is dramatically told in the only history of the period, the *Anglo-Saxon Chronicle*, which traces how these raids accelerated during the second half of the eighth century:

'843.   King Aethelwulf [of Wessex] fought at Carhampton against the companies of thirty-five ships, and the Danes [who were Vikings from Denmark] had the power of the battlefield.

851.   Ealdorman Ceorl, with the men of Devon, fought with heathen men . . . made great slaughter and took the victory. The heathen men stayed over the winter, and that year three hundred and fifty ships came to the mouth of the Thames; they ruined Canterbury, put to flight Brihtwulf the Mercian king and his troops . . .

866.   The [Viking] army went from East Anglia over the Humber's mouth to York in Northumbria. There was great discord in this people amongst themselves; they had overthrown their king, Osbriht, and had taken an unnatural king, Aelle . . . The kings were both killed and the survivors made peace with the force . . .

870.   . . . In that year, St. Edmund the king [of East Anglia] fought against them and the Danes took the victory, killed the king, and overcame all the land. They destroyed all the churches they came to . . .

874.   The force went from Lindsey to Repton and took winter quarters there. They drove the king [of Mercia], Burhred, over the sea, twenty-two years after he had had the kingdom; and they overcame all the land.'

These entries tell us how one by one the kingdoms of the Anglo-Saxons were wiped out until there was only Wessex left, where a young man called Alfred came to the throne in the year 871. During his reign which lasted almost thirty years, the advance of the Vikings was halted and the foundations of what was to become the kingdom of England were laid.

Alfred was born at Wantage in Berkshire in 849, the youngest son of King Aethelwulf, by his first wife Osburh. He had four elder brothers, all of whom became kings of Wessex before him. Alfred was a favourite child and although 'ignorant of letters' until later in life he was brought up both listening to and learning the poems loved by the Anglo-Saxons, poems which recited the brave deeds of warrior princes of the kind he would have aspired to become. Devoutly loyal to the church, Alfred was sent to Rome when he was only four where he was received with great honour by Pope Leo IV. Two years later he travelled there again, this time with his father, stopping on the return journey at the court of Charles the Bald, king of the Franks.

Throughout Alfred's early life there was constant disagreement about the succession to the kingdom of Wessex, for the crown did not automatically pass from father to eldest son. Who became the next king depended both on the power of the existing monarch and on the strength and competence of the contenders, be they his sons or brothers. But by the time that Aethelwulf's fourth son became king, it was agreed that his children should be passed over in favour of Alfred. By then the Viking menace was very great indeed, threatening Wessex with extinction.

The Vikings were not altogether the pagan savages that those writing the *Anglo-Saxon Chronicle* would have us believe. They were a people from Scandinavia, mainly Norway, Sweden and Denmark, whose life was working the land and fishing but who went on to attack and later settle in Britain, Northern France, Russia, Iceland and Greenland. They are even believed to have reached America. One of the key reasons for their restless voyaging was that their homelands no longer produced enough to support them. Another was the nature of their society which was one which glorified fighting. The Vikings were pagan, and believed that the gods rewarded fighters above all and that bloodshed and death in battle were the true paths to wealth and happiness. As a people they were endowed with a stupendous energy which made them fearless seafarers searching for trade and plunder across vast oceans. Each year bands of Vikings put out to sea, seeking out richer lands than their own to pillage, bringing home gold, silver and jewels. Their leaders were either kings or 'jarls' whose key role was to see that their followers were handsomely rewarded with booty.

And this indeed was what drew them to the British Isles wiping out as they went churches and monasteries, towns and villages, carrying from them any kind of valuable from a sacred vessel to a horse. Gradually, as they burnt and sacked the country, there was nothing left for them to take except the land. Their leaders began to divide that up among their men, who then settled. In the main it was Norwegians in Scotland, Ireland and the Western Isles, while in England it was the Danes. At first they put in puppet Anglo-Saxon kings but gradually they began to replace these with kings of their own. We can easily trace where the Danes settled, areas of the country known as the Danelaw, by the endings to the place names. Whereas the Anglo-Saxon endings were 'hams' and 'tuns', that is 'homes' and 'towns', the Danes had their 'bys' and 'thorpes'.

The Danes had already made ferocious attacks on Wessex by the time Alfred succeeded his brother but in 878 they launched what they believed to be their final assault, which, if successful, would have meant that virtually the whole island would be in their hands. To achieve this they planned a surprise attack in winter when no one usually fought. The *Anglo-Saxon Chronicle* takes up the story:

' . . . the [Danish host] went secretly in midwinter after Twelfth Night to Chippenham, and rode over Wessex and occupied it, and drove a great part of the inhabitants oversea, and reduced the greater part of the rest, except Alfred the king; and he with a small company moved under difficulties through woods and into inaccessible places in the marshes.'

This was on what was the Isle of Athelney near Taunton in Somerset. Protected by the swamps and floods which surrounded it, the king was able to plot his campaign. Messengers were sent out summoning the 'fyrd' or militia from Somerset, Wiltshire and West Hampshire, men who were all 'fain of him'. On the appointed day they met and defeated the Danes under their king, Guthrum, at Edington, going on after to lay siege to their fortress at Chippenham which they took. For the first time the Danish king sued for peace, swearing to depart from Wessex, and Guthrum and twenty-nine of his followers were baptised. This was the first turning of the tide.

The Danes, of course, held the north and East Anglia, but the kingdom of Wessex now gradually expanded to embrace all the southern Anglo-Saxons. In 886 Alfred captured London, which had been a part of the old kingdom of Mercia, putting it in the charge of Ethelred, an earldorman of the Mercians, who married Alfred's daughter. It was written of Alfred that 'all the English people that were not under subjugation to the Danes submitted to him.' In the peace Alfred made with Guthrum that year English and Danes were accepted as equals and for the first time there is reference to 'all the English race'. The Viking threat had created a common identity and a common cause which found expression in a common leader, the king of Wessex, who now began to be referred to as 'king of the Anglo-Saxons'.

Alfred was a man of quite extraordinary vision. He inherited the traditions of Anglo-Saxon Christian civilisation from the great age of the seventh century and re-

A tenth century cross from
Middleton, Yorkshire,
incorporating a pagan Viking
warrior with his shield, helmet
and axe. This is one of a series of
crosses in Anglo-Scandinavian
style.

launched them as the foundations of what in the following century was to be the kingdom of England. He realised
that to create a realm which was stable, peaceful and civilised depended first on having good laws, which should
apply to all the English, even those who were subjects of
the Danes. He studied the laws made by the great Anglo-
Saxon kings, including Offa of Mercia, and then issued his own:

The Alfred Jewel, inscribed
with Alfred's name, possibly
the handle to a pointer used
for following manuscript text.
These were distributed by
King Alfred with his copies of
Pope Gregory's *Pastoral Care*.

> 'Then I, King Alfred, collected these together and ordered to be written many
> of them which our forefathers observed, those which I liked; and many of
> those which I did not like, I rejected with the advice of my councillors, and
> ordered them to be differently observed.'

Uniquely too, he believed that such a society needed not only good government,
but learning of a kind which would not only be for clerics but for lay people. He himself was taught to read Latin late in life and he set up a school at his court for young
nobles to learn to be literate so that they could play their role in the state. This was a
great innovation. The need arose from the terrible devastation wrought to the country by the Danes when all the libraries and places of learning were destroyed. Alfred
recounts:

> 'So completely had learning decayed in England that there were few men this
> side of the Humber who could apprehend their [Latin] services in English or
> even translate a letter from Latin into English, and I think that there were not
> many beyond the Humber. There were so few of them that I cannot even recol-
> lect a single one south of the Thames when I succeeded to the kingdom.'

Alfred summoned scholars to his court from Wales, France and Ireland and
together they set about translating some of the treasures of ancient Christian litera-

ture into Anglo-Saxon. The king himself translated four books, including Pope Gregory the Great's *Pastoral Care*, a copy of which was sent to every bishop. This work described both the qualities and the duties of the clergy.

Laws and learning marched hand in hand with new measures to ensure the defence of the kingdom. Alfred realised that the Anglo-Saxons must develop sea power and so he ordered the construction of warships'. . . nearly twice as long as those of the Danes, and swifter and steadier and higher, some with sixty oars, some with more; not built after the Frisian manner nor after the Danish, but as seemed best and most useful to the king himself.'

Even more important was the building of a network of defended enclosures, 'burhs', in which men could seek safety along with their goods and cattle. These were strategically placed and were either on the site of old towns or carefully chosen to be new ones. We can trace many of them today in place names which end in 'borough'. No village was to be further than twenty miles from such a safe haven. The king also reorganised the militia, or 'fyrd', on a rota system so that half the men came at a time while the other half stayed behind to tend and harvest the crops.

Most of these reforms were in place by the time the next Viking army landed from the Continent in 892. During the previous decade Alfred had secured his position as 'king of the Angles and of the Anglo-Saxons'. This was celebrated in the biography which was written of the king's life and in the publication of the *Anglo-Saxon Chronicle* in which all the Anglo-Saxons were seen as sharing somehow a common history uniting them against the enemy, the Danes.

When they began their new attack on Wessex the Danes found that they could not succeed as before. Everywhere they went their army was impeded by the 'burhs' and by the Anglo-Saxon army which now remained active all the year round. For four years the Vikings harassed the English but they failed to achieve victory. In the end they were forced either to settle in parts of the country already occupied by the Danes or to leave.

Alfred died at about the age of fifty in 899. Little is known about his last years but they were no doubt spent in consolidating what he had begun and impressing on his son, Edward, the necessity that he should continue to build on his father's foundations and reconquer the land which was now called the Danelaw. It was not until seven hundred years later that Alfred began to be accorded the title 'the Great'. No one at the time regarded him as any better than any of the other outstanding Anglo-Saxon kings. Today, however, we can see more clearly than his contemporaries how much Alfred deserved the epithet accorded him by subsequent centuries.

Chapter Six

THE KINGDOM OF ENGLAND

THE tenth century was to be the last one of Anglo-Saxon England, for the dynasty which descended from Alfred was first to reconquer and create a united kingdom of England and then collapse in ruins. By the turn of the year 1000, when many believed that the world would end, a new wave of Vikings, the Norsemen, scourged the country, this time one of their number becoming king of England. But beneath all these dramatic sagas of victory and defeat there was slowly emerging a society whose framework began to be one we would recognise today. It was during this period, for instance, that all the English shires and counties took shape. They, in turn, were divided into a series of smaller units called hundreds, each one of which had a 'moot' or court in which presided someone appointed by the king who, along with those who lived in the area, meted out justice. This meant that the running of the country in terms of right and wrong rested at grassroots on a dialogue between the king or his representative and ordinary people.

This dialogue between ruler and ruled was to be a fundamental thread which was to run down through the centuries fashioning how the country was to be governed and justice administered. At its highest level it was reflected in the fact that Anglo-Saxon kings were always elected from a member of the royal dynasty. That was the task of the great magnates, both nobility and upper clergy, who made up the king's council or Witenagemot. In spite of the tempestuous events, the status and mystique surrounding the monarchy continued to grow through the century, by the end of which an added dimension was bestowed on the wearer of the crown, that of coronation in a church. In this ceremony it was not, however, the crowning by the bishop which was the most important act but the anointing of the king with holy oil in the same way in which priests were anointed. This act set him apart from ordinary men. Everything, however, depended on the personality of the king. A strong one could achieve much, a weak one little, but that never eroded the respect people had for their ruler.

During this century also came the first signs that government was becoming literate, that kings no longer relied wholly on word of mouth, but began to record their decisions on paper as formal documents. Charters, royal grants of land or privileges, were the first such documents to emerge. These were always in Latin. Then came a form of royal letter called a writ which contained in writing the king's instructions. These, in contrast, were written in Anglo-Saxon and could be read out at once to everyone by the king's representative. To prove that these documents came from the king, a wax seal containing an impression of his image and name was attached to them. Everyone then knew that this could only have come from the king's royal writing office called the chancery. This was the department of the royal household which staffed the royal chapels and was made up of priests who were monks who could read and write.

King Edgar offering his charter to the New Minster at Winchester. Dated 966 this is the earliest manuscript in the style associated with the monastic community at Winchester. Ultimately inspiration came from the art of late classical antiquity, but via carlingian France. To this style English artists added brilliant colours, ornamentation and pattern with a vivid use of line drawing to indicate action. The text is in gold on purple vellum.

At the same time a system of universal taxation gradually began. This was the direct result of the attacks by the Norsemen who were shamefully bought off with large sums of money called 'Dane-geld'. Everyone had to contribute towards this; the money was collected from all over the country in carts and delivered to the king's treasury at Winchester. Although these taxes were the result of a crisis they set a precedent: everyone should be taxed to meet certain definite common needs such as war. But for centuries taxation was to be exceptional, for the kings of England were expected to live 'of their own', that is from the income from the vast estates which they held as the country's richest landowner.

All of these developments were to be passed on as part of the Anglo-Saxon inheritance. No one, however, could have foreseen that when King Alfred died his dynasty was to end in disaster and ignominy. In fact most of his immediate successors indicated far otherwise. His son Edward the Elder, his grandson Athelstan and his great-grandson, Athelstan's nephew, Edgar, were all great kings who took up where Alfred had left off the task of creating and consolidating the new kingdom of England.

From the first Edward the Elder was styled 'king of the Anglo-Saxons' and this indeed was what he set out to be. Under him his father's defensive war turned into an offensive one. In 909 he opened hostilities which lasted a decade and ended with him in control of the whole of the country south of the Humber. The king was a brilliant military tactician. In his campaigns he had the support of Ethelred, ealdorman of Mercia, who was married to his sister, Aethelflaed, 'Lady of the Mercians'. Year by year they edged further into the Danelaw territory, each time securing another area by building a 'burh'. In 917 the city of Colchester fell signalling the passing into his hands of the whole of East Anglia and the eastern midlands. The *Anglo-Saxon Chronicle* writes:

> 'And many people who had been under the rule of the Danes in East Anglia and in Essex submitted to him; and all the army in East Anglia swore agreement with him, that they [agree to] all that he would, and keep peace with all whom the king wished to keep peace, both at sea and on land.'

Edward wisely accepted the Danes as his subjects letting them live under him according to their own system of law.

The next turning point came after the deaths of both his sister and brother-in-law when he was formally elected king of Mercia: 'And all the people who had settled in

St. Dunstan, Archbishop of Canterbury, kneels in adoration before Christ. By tradition this is a self-portrait by the saint when he was Abbot of Glastonbury. Above him one of the Latin verses reads: 'I pray thee, Christ, protect me Dunstan.' Dunstan was the prime mover in the cultural revival of the tenth century. He was himself a skilled calligrapher, painter and player of the harp.

Ałb Aller :D:D:

NE·D·2·19·
(2176)
Bod. 578.

Dunstanum memet clemens rogo xpe tuere
Tenarias me non sina sorbsisse procellas;

Mercia, both Danish and English, submitted to him.' By 920 he had reconquered England as far as the Peak District.

'And then the king of Scots and all the people of the Scots . . . and all who live in Northumbria, both English and Danish, Norseman and others, and also the king of the Strathclyde Welsh . . . chose him as their lord and father.'

When Edward the Elder died on 17 July 924 he bequeathed to his eldest, Athelstan, a mighty achievement.

Athelstan was to be like his father, a victorious leader in the field of battle. But he was also to take his place as one of the great kings then ruling in Northern Europe, one whose court was famous for its splendour. During his reign the Norsemen invasions renewed, time and again attempting to set up a northern kingdom based on York. In 927 Athelstan defeated them and not only re-established his rule in that part of the country but at the same time received the submission of what was left of the pre-Viking Northumbrian kingdom which centred on Bamburgh, along with that of the kings of Scotland, Strathclyde and Gwent. Athelstan had to return the following year to defeat the Norsemen yet again, and shortly after that even the Welsh kings did him homage.

Athelstan saw himself as king of England in the grandest sense casting himself in the following terms in documents: 'I, Athelstan, king of the English, elevated by the right hand of the Almighty, which is Christ, to the throne of the whole kingdom of Britain.'

His task was to weld together a people made up of West Saxons, Mercians, East Anglians, Danes, Norsemen and Northumbrians. This he did by being an active law maker and also by introducing a single currency for the realm. In the year that he died, 937, he was once again victorious in battle at a place called Brunanburgh, defeat-

Coin of Athelstan. The use of the profile follows classical precedent.

ing an alliance of the Norsemen with the kings of Scotland and Strathclyde.

Athelstan's greatest legacy was the establishment of the notion of a single king ruling both north and south. His death was followed by a period of twenty years during which three kings reigned and a Norse kingdom based on York kept on reasserting itself. This was the prime problem which beset Athelstan's brothers, Edmund and Eadred, both of whom followed him as king in succession. Both of them were successful in driving the Norsemen out of York, Eadred dealing with the last of the Norse adventurers, Eric Bloodaxe, whose death in 954 was to usher in twenty-five years of peace.

On Eadred's death, Edmund the Elder's son, Eadwig, was elected king. Short though the previous two reigns had been, both kings had been outstanding. Now there succeeded one who demonstrated the weakness of the system, for he was feckless and defiant, upsetting everyone around him. So deficient was he in the qualities needed to rule that both Mercia and Northumbria defected and chose his younger brother, Edgar. If Eadwig had not died in 959 there would have been revolution, but his death made way for another great king.

Edgar was only sixteen when he succeeded. He died at thirty-two leaving behind him a legend of having been instrumental in giving England a golden age of peace. In achieving that he was aided by three quite outstanding churchmen, Dunstan, Archbishop of Canterbury, Oswald, Archbishop of York and Aethelwold, Bishop of Winchester. They played a crucial role in the conduct of affairs of state but at the same time carried through a radical reform of the church, introducing a new set of rules to govern monasteries based on those used on the Continent at the great abbey of Cluny. This close relationship of church and state was reflected in another significant development, the introduction of the ceremony of crowning and anointing the king. This rite was performed when Edgar was thirty and shortly after, it is said, it was followed by the homage of his subject kings, who rowed him from his palace to the church at Chester while he tended the prow.

By the time Edgar died in 975 the kings of England had come to occupy a position as among the leading rulers in Western Europe. Then followed forty years in which it seemed nearly everything they had achieved was thrown away. But not quite, for the idea of the single kingdom was so strong that it was able to survive decades of rule by two unworthy occupants of the throne. The first of these, Edgar's eldest son Edward, was only fifteen at his accession. He was violent, so much so that within three years he was deliberately murdered in a plot which involved his stepmother, brother and his servants. The tragedy was that Ethelred, his brother, was to be no better.

The name Ethelred means 'noble counsel' but later he was to be labelled 'unraed' or 'no counsel', worse even, for it could mean 'evil counsel' or even 'treacherous plot'. Ethelred came to power as the result of a crime. He remained always a guilty and insecure man. He was the first Anglo-Saxon king to fail in the duty to lead his men in battle. During a reign of thirty-eight years he only led them thrice. When he succeeded to the throne, England was a rich, powerful and renowned country. By the time he died it had been over-run by enemy forces. Ethelred's reign coincided with a

Emma of Normandy, queen of Ethelred and Canute, receiving the *Enconium*, a tribute to her in her second widowhood, written about 1040 to press the claim of her son, Harthacanute, to the throne. This is a rare instance of the biography of someone who had no claims to sainthood, the work of a monk of St. Omer in Normandy who presents Emma with his book. Behind stand her two sons, Harthacanute and the future Edward the Confessor.

new wave of attacks by the Norsemen, ones which were spurred on by the fact that the country was once again worth plundering and was also an easy prey, for it had a weak ineffective king who had disbanded the fleet.

The characteristic of this reign was inertia. Both king and government stood by, letting the Norse invaders march the length and breadth of the land without doing anything much to stop them. Even worse, they embarked on a policy of appeasement, buying off the Norsemen with huge payments of gold, the infamous 'Dane-geld'. In 991 Ethelred bought peace for the sum of 22,000 pounds in gold. So inept was the government that in 1002 the king ordered the massacre of the long-settled Danes believing them to be abetters of the Norsemen, when they were not.

By then the Norse attacks had taken a far more serious direction, the conquest of the kingdom. In 1009 Sweyn, king of Denmark, landed at the head of a vast army and by 1013 '. . . all the nation regarded him as full king.' Ethelred fled into exile. But then Sweyn died and in the confused period which followed Ethelred died too, followed not long after by the death of his son Edmund and the election by the Witenagemot of Sweyn's son, Canute.

In this way England entered the eleventh century as part of a huge Scandinavian empire which embraced Denmark and Sweden and part of Norway. Canute, who had begun his life as a bloodthirsty Norse warrior, transformed himself into an ideal Anglo-Saxon king. He married Ethelred's widow, Emma of Normandy, and chose as his model, King Edgar. For Canute England was the jewel in his crown. He became a great lawgiver realising that in order to govern successfully he must be true to his contract with his people. His greatest innovation was to divide the entire country into four great earldoms each presided over by an 'earl' or 'jarl'. Canute was the most powerful king in Western Europe and when he went to Rome for the coronation of the Holy Roman Emperor by the pope he wrote back describing how they 'all received me with honour, and honoured me with lavish gifts.'

Canute, however, failed to make any provision as to what would happen after his death. He left two sons, one by Emma, Harthacanute, and another, Harold Harefoot, by his mistress. Harthacanute rushed off to Denmark while Harold seized power and had himself proclaimed king. He reigned for five calamitous years, dying when Harthacanute was about to land at the head of an army to reclaim the kingdom. Harthacanute now took over but regarded England as little more than a source of money to maintain his Scandinavian empire. The *Anglo-Saxon Chronicle* sums him up: 'And he did nothing worthy of a king as long as he ruled.' After two years he died and was succeeded by his half-brother, Ethelred's son, Edward.

Chapter Seven

1066

On the night of 24 April 1066 a comet appeared in the night sky. Today we know it to have been Halley's comet but to men at the time such a fiery portent presaged dire and dramatic events on earth. And in the case of England, this was to prove true for by the close of that year, Harold, the last Anglo-Saxon king, had perished on the field of battle and William, Duke of Normandy, had become king.

It was the outcome of a train of events which went back to the reign of Edward the Confessor. Edward, who came to the throne in 1042, was a competent and wise monarch, ruling England for twenty-four years and leaving a united country to his successor. He was a man of deep piety and his greatest legacy was to be the construction of Westminster Abbey. Although Edward was childless this was not a problem, for Anglo-Saxon kings did not succeed by primogeniture, the succession of the eldest son. They were elected by the assembly of nobles, the Witenagemot, and any noble who was of royal blood could be chosen. It was through the ceremony of anointing with holy oil and coronation that the man chosen became king. When Edward the Confessor lay dying on 5th January 1066 he nominated Harold, Earl of Wessex of the House of Godwin, as his heir. After Edward's death, Harold was duly elected by the Witenagemot.

Harold's somewhat tenuous claim to royal descent was through his mother, a Scandinavian princess. His sister had been Edward's queen. He was a man of strong character and a brilliant soldier. The earls of Wessex were the most powerful in the land and Harold's father, Earl Godwin, had been instrumental in putting Edward the Confessor on the throne. But the relationship was never an easy one. Edward, who had been brought up in exile in Normandy, tried to assert his independence of the House of Godwin by appointing Normans to positions in his government. For a time the earl and his two sons were exiled but eventually they returned, supported by a fleet, and were reconciled to the king. Therefore, when Edward died and Harold succeeded, everything seemed to indicate that the Anglo-Saxon kingdom would continue as before.

1 Edward the Confessor enthroned in his palace entrusts Harold, his brother-in-law, with a mission. Harold and his party then set sail and are driven ashore in France and handed over to Duke William of Normandy.

William I was to claim later that Edward the Confessor had chosen him as his heir but it is likely that this was embroidery after the event, when William needed to stress his rights to a throne he had taken by force of arms. William claimed that Edward had promised him the crown in 1051 but there is nothing to prove this beyond his assertion. Even more mysterious is what happened in 1064 when Harold visited William in Normandy. No one knows why he went or what exactly happened but William stated that it was for Harold to swear his allegiance to him as future king of England.

The Bayeux Tapestry was embroidered during the decade 1070-1080, almost certainly commissioned by William the Conqueror's half-brother, Odo of Bayeux. Odo was also Count of Kent where the embroidery was executed, most probably at Canterbury. It is 70 metres long and 50 centimetres wide and it is stitched in woollen yarn in eight colours onto fine linen. Both as a work of art and an historical document it is unique.

2 While in Normandy Harold swears, touching two reliquaries, fealty to William. In the oath Harold *probably swore that he would not oppose William's claim to the English throne.*

William's claim was extremely remote, for he was only Edward's second cousin once removed, a great-nephew of his queen. A much more important factor was the nature of the duke and his people. The duchy of Normandy was only a century old, a creation of William's grandfather, a Viking who had conquered this part of northern France. William himself was illegitimate, the son of the daughter of a tanner and Duke Robert. He succeeded when he was only seven years old and during the following twenty years was to emerge as an experienced and able ruler, administrator and commander. He was tough, cruel but not tyrannical, endowed with huge energy and motivated by an overweening ambition. He was a capable and brave leader of his men in the field and did not hesitate to share their rigours to the full. He was also a devout

3 Harold violates the oath by accepting the crown on Edward's death. Astrologers tell Harold of a comet in the sky, an evil omen foreboding disaster for the oath-breaker.

and fervent supporter of the church. All of these personal qualities explain why he was so successful when he conquered England.

But it does not explain why he did it. This needs to be set in the broader framework of the Normans as a people. At the close of the eleventh century they had a vitality other peoples lacked. At the same time that they were to conquer England and Wales they conquered southern Italy and Sicily. A little later they were to play a major role in the first Crusade to rescue the Holy Land

Although the tapestry records the conquest of England, its purpose was a religious one, to show that perjury following an oath taken over relics, as had been done by Harold, drew retribution on that person and his kinsmen. In this way the invasion and the defeat and the death of Harold are presented as Acts of God. That story is told with 626 characters, 202 horses, 41 ships and 37 buildings besides an abundance of detail about life in the eleventh century.

AD PEVENE SAE :•

from Moslem control. Compared with Normandy England was a rich country, and it promised ample rewards to
anyone who joined the army William began to assemble.

*4 William lands at Pevensey, his
ship bearing the banner bestowed by
Pope Alexander II.*

William was also a master of diplomacy and propaganda. He succeeded in persuading both the Holy Roman Emperor and the pope of the justice of his cause.
Indeed the latter even sent him a banner as a symbol of his support.

While William was gathering his army and building his fleet Harold was faced
with another invasion by another claimant, Harold Hardrada, king of Norway, who
had the support of Harold's brother, Tostig. In response to this, Harold summoned
his army and his fleet in preparation to repel this assault from the north. For four
months they waited and it never came so Harold dispersed the army and sent the fleet
to London. No sooner had this been done than news came that the king of Norway
with a fleet of three hundred ships had landed in the north. The Norwegians marched

ADERVNT ꝉ SIMVL:ANGLI ꝉ ET FRA

5 *The Battle of Hastings in action, 14 September 1066.*

on York and defeated the Earls of Mercia and Northumbria. This presented Harold with an appalling problem for he was threatened on both sides, an army actually in the north and a second one ready to cross the Channel. Was it possible for him to march north, defeat the Norwegians and return south in time to meet the Normans? Harold gathered his troops and marched them north. On 25 September he gained one of the decisive victories of the age at Stamford Bridge. The king of Norway and Tostig were both killed and what was left of the invading army took to their ships. They were never to return.

Luck, however, was against Harold for while he was in the north the wind changed direction enabling the Normans to set sail and land at Pevensey on 28 September. As Harold was in the north, the fleet in London, and the militia disbanded, William was unopposed. Harold and his mounted housecarls came south in less than

thirteen days. Scraping together what infantry he could, his aim was to surprise the Normans as he had the Norwegians by his speed. But this time his army was

6 Harold dies after being shot in the eye with an arrow.

exhausted. Surprise he did achieve and through it the choice of battle site, a hilly stretch of land flanked by marshy streams not far from Hastings where William had made his headquarters.

Harold formed his soldiers into a wall of shields at the brow of the hill. They fought on foot armed with axes. William's army was made up of archers and knights on horseback wielding swords. These he divided into three, reflecting exactly the freebooting nature of the expedition: to the left Bretons, to the right mercenaries, with the Normans in the centre. Both armies numbered about seven thousand but the invading army was not only the more seasoned and experienced but the less tired. The Battle of Hastings began at 9 a.m. on 14 October. The duke's first attack up hill was driven back and if Harold and his men had then seized the offensive there is a chance that they would have won the battle, but they did not. Instead a second and then a third attack followed. The last was fatal, for Harold was felled by a mounted knight with a sword. When the Anglo-Saxons saw that this had happened they fled. Harold's body was buried in unconsecrated ground on a cliff. Thus perished the last Anglo-Saxon king.

The Battle of Hastings was to be the opening chapter in the story of the death of Anglo-Saxon England. Soon the whole of the south-east surrendered to William. The army advanced on London, sacking and pillaging on its way. At Berkhampstead the Anglo-Saxon nobility capitulated, swore fealty to William as their king, and parted with hostages. On Christmas Day William was anointed and crowned in Westminster Abbey. Soon after he returned to Normandy.

The conquest of England was not achieved overnight. At first William declared his intent of being king within an existing system respecting the Anglo-Saxon people, their laws and customs. But within a few years that policy was abandoned in favour of reducing England to the status of a province of Normandy.

When William left he appointed two regents. *The Anglo-Saxon Chronicle* records: 'Bishop Odo [William's half-brother] and Earl William [fitzOsbern of Hereford] were left behind here, and they built castles far and wide throughout the land, oppressing the unhappy people, and things went ever from bad to worse.'

The result was that constant rebellions broke out all over the country in the following four years. They were rigorously put down, especially the one in the north which, from 1069-70, was given over to a reign of terror. The city of York was sacked, the monasteries were pillaged, churches burned to the ground and the land laid waste. It was recorded that:

'William in the fullness of his wrath ordered the corn and cattle, with the implements of husbandry and every sort of provisions, to be collected in heaps and set on fire until the whole was consumed and thus destroyed at once all that could serve for support of life in the whole country lying beyond the Humber.'

For three years the wretched inhabitants struggled against famine, misery and death. It was to take a decade for the north to begin to recover. Already by 1071, five years on from the invasion, William's ruthless and efficient military machine had made the Norman Conquest an irreversible fact.

Chapter Eight

THE CONQUEST: LOSS AND GAIN

NOTHING was quite the same after 1066. The chronicler Odericus Vitalis summed up the effect of William I's conquest of England thus: '... the native inhabitants were crushed, imprisoned, disinherited, banished and scattered beyond the limits of their own country; while his own vassals were exalted to wealth and honours and raised to all offices ...'

In this way the writer put his finger on the greatest change of all, the creation of a new ruling class. By the end of William's reign, the old English aristocracy had gone. In its place was a new foreign nobility made up of Normans, French and Flemings, men who had come over with the Conqueror. Between them they were to own half the territorial wealth of the kingdom. The result of this was to reduce the existing inhabitants to the status of a subject people.

As soon as it became clear that the king's initial desire to work with the old Anglo-Saxon aristocracy had failed, he set out to create a new one of followers who would be loyal to him and ensure his position as king of England. That was secured by two things: castles, and knights to man them. Castles were built at strategic points throughout the land, deliberately designed to subdue local communities. Initially these castles were constructed of wood with a mound called a 'motte' with a ditch around it and a tower on the top. There would also be a fortified area below which was called a bailey. Gradually these wooden castles were replaced by ones of stone many of which, such as Pevensey and Chepstow, stand today, albeit in ruins. The most famous of all was the Tower of London designed to hold the city in subjection to its new king.

The king needed five thousand knights to man these castles and it was that very practical need which contributed to the emergence of a system which later ages called feudalism. It eventually became more formalised but it began purely as a means whereby William could man his strongholds. He solved the manning problem by granting the confiscated lands of the defeated English aristocracy to his followers in return for their guarantee to supply armed knights. William granted lands to a hundred and seventy of his followers who became thereby his tenants-in-chief. Only in the case of the earls who guarded areas of the country open to external attack, such as the Welsh borders, were grants of lands made forming a single unit. Usually they were scattered through several shires. Collectively each group of lands was called an honour and each honour consisted of several smaller units called manors. These in their turn were either held directly by the tenant-in-chief for his own use, and therefore part of what was known as his demesne, or granted by him to one of his followers in return for some specified service. The result was that each of the tenants-in-chief had two groups of knights on which to call for service to the king, one consisting of those who were permanently part of the tenant-in-chief's household and a second of those who came in return for land. William was a strong king who chose his tenants well and so the system worked. The trouble was that with a weaker ruler the system was to break down, leading to private castles and armies.

The same revolution was applied to the Anglo-Saxon church. In Normandy William had controlled all the appointments of bishops and abbots, filling them with his own friends and relations. Exactly the same thing was to occur in England as bishops and abbots from before 1066 either died or were deposed. They were replaced by Normans and, like the nobility, they had to render the king rent in the form of armed knights. Together the tenants-in-chief, bishops and abbots made up the new ruling class, for the higher clergy, being educated, were essential for the running of the government. In these changes William was aided by a new Archbishop of Canterbury, Lanfranc, who replaced the deposed Anglo-Saxon, Stigand. Together they set about reorganising the English church, moving sees to more populous areas such as Shrewsbury, Chester and Salisbury. Both believed that priests should be celibate and gradually the toleration by the Anglo-Saxon church of married bishops and clergy ceased. More significant for the future was the creation of special courts to deal with church cases only.

All of this activity precipitated a wave of new building in the handsome monumental style called Norman. This was an age of cathedral building with Durham, started towards the end of the reign, as its supreme masterpiece. Apart from architecture the Normans were culturally inferior to the people they had conquered whose sculpture, metalwork, embroidery and illumination were of European renown. Anglo-Saxon civilisation came to its end, a fate made worse because the language which had produced a remarkable literature was now deemed inferior. The new ruling class used French and Latin and made no attempt to learn Anglo-Saxon.

Women, too, found their status diminished. In Anglo-Saxon England they had

more or less enjoyed an equality with men. That was now taken away and St. Paul's attitude to women as being inferior prevailed. Women were subject first to their fathers and then, after marriage, to their husbands. Only when a woman became a wealthy widow did she gain any form of independence.

All these changes brought order and peace to the country through strong government. But it is a history which inevitably can only be written from the evidence of the winning side. This has left us one of the greatest of all documents in English history, the Domesday Book. In 1085 William feared invasion from Denmark; needing to find out the wealth of his kingdom in order to extract the maximum in taxation, he ordered this mighty survey to be undertaken. He '. . . sent his men all over England into every shire to ascertain how many hundreds of hides [a unit of land] there were in each shire and how much land and livestock the king himself owned in the country and what annual dues were lawfully his from each shire. He also had it recorded how much land his archbishops had, and his diocesan bishops, his abbots and his earls . . . what and how much each man, who was a landowner here in England, had in land and livestock, and how much money it was worth.'

This amazing compilation, of a kind achieved by no later medieval king, was put together with great speed in a huge document of four hundred double-sided pages. At the same time the king summoned his tenants-in-chief and all other major landowners to a court held at Salisbury where they were made to swear an oath of allegiance to him. In these two great acts William reasserted his power over his new realm.

Domesday Book gives us a unique panorama of English society as it was at the end of William I's reign, twenty years after the Conquest. It paints a picture of a country where virtually the entire population was engaged in agriculture with little or no industry or commerce, and few towns. Apart from heathland, scrub and the royal forests (protected by law for the king's hunting and the source of deep resentment) all of the land was either under the plough or pasture. Arable farming centred on villages from which the peasants set out to work in the surrounding fields, which were divided into strips belonging either to the landlord or rented to the peasant in return for his labour. Sheep farming focused on scattered hamlets housing shepherds who tended the flocks. Life for nearly everyone rarely rose above subsistence level, a never-ending cycle of toil to produce corn for bread, barley for ale, sheep for wool, goats for milk and pigs for meat.

Within these small rural communities the classes

The Conquest led to a prodigious outburst of building. Nearly every cathedral and abbey church in England was rebuilt in a new style, the Romanesque, typified by grandeur of scale and making use of massively thick walls, huge columns and lofty vaults to achieve a new spaciousness. Durham Cathedral was begun in 1093 and completed in 1130. Today it is recognised as the supreme masterpiece of the style.

The chest in which the Domesday Book was kept from the early seventeenth century onwards. Lined and bound with iron it has the remains of three locks, the keys to which were held by three different officials, thus controlling access to it. Initially Domesday Book was kept at Winchester and later in the Palace of Westminster.

were divided forming what were the lower sections of the vast social pyramid which culminated in the king. There were firstly the freemen who owned their land but yet were expected to attend the lord's court, assist him at busy seasons of the year and pay him a levy. Next came the smallholders who made up two-fifths of the population paying rent for farms of up to thirty acres. Then there were the cottagers with up to three acres who worked, for example, as shepherds, blacksmiths or swineherds. Lastly there came the lowest of all, those who were slaves devoid of any land or rights. Together these four groups made up the subject native population, one which the Normans were steadily to grind down.

For the invaders, and for William I, the conquest of England was a remarkable achievement. It was to be an enduring one, for unlike the preceding centuries, no other invading force was to be successful until 1688 when another William crossed the Channel, this time from the Low Countries. For the native population it was a cruel and humiliating defeat which swept their civilisation away. The new aristocracy saw its first loyalty not to the land they had conquered but to Normandy. England was taxed and exploited in the interests of what was a smaller, poorer and far less cultured country. Henceforward too, for better or worse, English kings were also to be continental rulers and for four centuries the wealth of England was expended in wars aimed at acquiring, defending and sustaining a mainland empire whose final foothold was not to be lost until 1558.

The Tower of London was one of a vast network of castles built by William I to subject England. A temporary stronghold was erected soon after 1066 to be followed by the present massive structure of the White Tower completed by 1100. The rooms were stacked one on top of each other to increase security, with storage below and living quarters above. By the close of the thirteenth century concentric rings of defence had been added. The Tower had the dual function during the Middle Ages of acting as a royal palace and a fortress to overawe London.

Chapter Nine

THE NORMAN KINGS

HE state which William I created called for strong kings to exercise power over it. Fortunately he was succeeded by two of his sons who were just such men, but disaster was to strike later when his grandson seized the throne. As in the case of the Anglo-Saxon kings there was no such thing as primogeniture, the automatic succession of the eldest son. The crown passed firstly to the king's second son, William Rufus, next to his third son Henry I, and finally to his grandson, Stephen. Both on the first and second occasions it should have gone to William's eldest son, Robert, and on the last to the Conqueror's granddaughter, the Empress Matilda and her son, the future Henry II.

When he died in 1087, William left Normandy to Robert, and chose his second surviving son, William, to rule England. He was later nicknamed Rufus, most likely on account of his red hair. Many of the nobles consequently found themselves serving two masters, having lands in both countries. This decision of the Conqueror to split his inheritance was not liked and soon after his accession William Rufus was faced with a rebellion led by Bishop Odo of Bayeux designed to put Robert on the throne. It was crushed. Indeed William Rufus was even more savage than his father. He was a monarch who lived entirely for the battlefield, on which he was fearless. Greedy and immoral, he meted out strong justice and eliminated anyone who defied him. He exacted from his tenants-in-chief everything he could: large fines on the succession of an heir to an estate, the right to custody of that heir and his lands if he was not of age and also the right of disposing of any heiress in marriage. All of these measures were used to exact money.

William's deadliest foe was the church for which he had little time, being, unlike his father, far from pious. When a bishop or an abbot died, William, instead of appointing a new one, left the post vacant and took over the revenues for the crown. As a result the church denounced him as a monster. But under him the Norman rule of England was consolidated. When he was accidentally killed while hunting in the New Forest in August 1100 it was seen by many, not surprisingly, as the judgement of God on a wicked tyrant.

William Rufus never married and on his death the crown should have passed to his elder brother, Robert, but that did not happen. William's younger brother, Henry, happened to be part of the fatal hunting party, and within days he seized the royal treasury and had himself crowned king. During his reign the system created by William I reached its climax. And once again, that it did so was a direct reflection of the qualities of the king, for he too was a cruel and violent man who spent his life either fighting or hunting. When he snatched the crown he issued a charter promising the barons that he would make amends for the deeds of his brother, but it meant nothing. To win the English he married an Anglo-Saxon princess descended from Alfred, but that too meant little. Henry continued his brother's policy of exacting everything he could from his vassals, above all money to pay for his expensive continental wars. When his brother Robert invaded England he bought him off with a pension, but in doing this he was only buying time for it was his intention that Normandy should be his too, and in 1106 he defeated his brother at the Battle of Tinchebray. Henry took over the duchy and put Robert in prison, where he died.

Despite his shortcomings Henry could be a skilful administrator. His reign also saw the development of the 'exchequer', when a committee met during the king's frequent absences abroad to oversee and audit accounts.

Henry, however, was afflicted by a major problem. His only son William was drowned at sea crossing to Normandy. Although he had married again there was no son, so that he was left only with a daughter, Matilda, who was married to the Holy Roman Emperor, Henry V. Henry I's last years were clouded by all the problems of securing his daughter's succession. Firstly her husband died, and she was left childless. She returned to her father's court, where Henry summoned all his tenants-in-chief and made them swear to acknowledge her as his successor. His hope was then to obtain a grandson and so he married her off to a man ten years her junior, Geoffrey Plantagenet, Count of Anjou. Matilda herself was arrogant and by no means popular with the king's vassals. To this unpopularity was now added a man who ruled over a state which was Normandy's enemy. The Angevins and the Normans had always fought each other and now the latter were faced with the possibility of the leader of their traditional foe being their king. They did not like it.

All of this explains why, when Henry I died in December 1135, no one opposed the crown being seized by Stephen, the son of the Conqueror's daughter, Adela, Countess of Blois. Stephen had always been a favourite of his uncle, who made him the greatest landowner in England, but he lacked the attributes of a strong king. Affable, popular and generous, he was a good knight but he did not know how to wield the rod of iron which was essential to keep the unruly barons in order. The

58

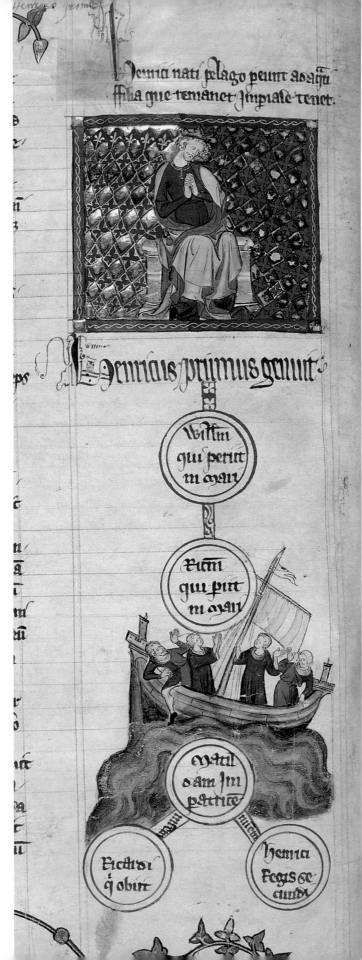

Henria nati pelago pereunt adaisu
filia que remanet imperiale tenet.

Henricus primus genuit

Willm
qui periit
in mari

Ricm
qui piit
in mari

Matil
dam im
patrice

Ricard
q obiit

Henria
regis se
cunda

A fourteenth century royal family tree depicts Henry I with, below, an inset scene of the loss of his son, William, in the White Ship which foundered on its journey to England in November 1120. When told, the king fell senseless to the ground with grief.

result was anarchy. Some of the barons went over to Matilda, others were loyal to Stephen. Worse, in the absence of firm royal power, the barons began to fight private wars with each other. A monk records what this meant for the people of England:

'When the traitors saw that Stephen was a good-humoured, kindly, and easy-going man who inflicted no punishment then they committed all manner of horrible crimes. They had done him homage and sworn oaths of fealty to him, but not one of their oaths was kept. They were all forsworn and their oaths broken. For every great man built him castles and held them against the king; and they filled the whole land with these castles; and when the castles were built, they filled them with devils and wicked men . . . Never did a country endure greater misery, and never did the heathen act more vilely than they did . . .'

For over two decades England was devastated. Stephen had lost control.

In the end the barons began to look with more and more favour on the Angevins and in 1144 Geoffrey, Count of Anjou, conquered Normandy. Five years later he passed the duchy onto his son by Matilda, Henry. The new Duke of Normandy was both shrewd and intelligent. On his father's death he gained Anjou and then, the following year, he married a great heiress, Eleanor, who brought Aquitaine. At the age of nineteen Henry was already the ruler of a large part of western France. Next he began to threaten Stephen by attacks on England. Stephen's own son died and, bowing to the inevitable, he adopted Henry as his heir a year before his own death in 1154. Henry came to the throne as the first of a new dynasty, the Plantagenets.

Over sixty years divide the death of William the Conqueror from that of Stephen. A rigid structure had been seen to work well and then fall apart depending on the character of the king. That was to apply until well into the seventeenth century. But by 1154 much else had changed. Two generations had passed since the Conquest and the invaders had become natives. Now all English society had to respond to changes which were affecting every country in Western Europe.

The Anglo-Saxon and the Norman church had been at the service of the state. The kings were sacred beings set apart like the priesthood who led their people in devotion to the church and also appointed both bishops and abbots. The king presented them on appointment with a staff and a ring, symbols of their office. The staff, called a crozier, symbolised their role as the shepherd of their flock. They then did homage to the king and received their lands in the same way as any of his lay tenants-in-chief. By the close of the eleventh century the church was undergoing a revolution, asserting the dignity of the priestly office and the power of the popes as direct successors of Christ through St. Peter. Bishops and abbots were henceforth to be appointed for their spiritual leadership and not because they would be capable royal officials running the government. They were no longer to purchase their positions. All of this struggle to separate the church from the control of the state was to become focused on the one act of the king giving the office holder his staff and ring.

Even before 1066 the pope had forbidden this but it was to take many years before his decision was to become fact. In England it first surfaced in 1093 when William Rufus, thinking he was dying, filled the vacant see of Canterbury with a learned and saintly man, Anselm, abbot of the monastery of Bec in Normandy. Anselm refused to be invested by William and both king and archbishop appealed to Rome, beginning what was to be a never-ending series of disputes. In the reign of Henry I a compromise was reached: the king no longer gave the cleric his ring and staff but retained the right to receive his homage. But neither side was happy. When Anselm died in 1109 Henry left the see empty for five years.

At the same time that the battle lines were being drawn between clergy and laity, the church was undergoing other dramatic developments. This was a golden age for monasticism. Between 1066 and 1154 the number of religious houses rose from forty-eight to nearly three hundred with most belonging to the new reforming orders. Of these the Cistercians were to leave the imposing monuments we see today in the ruined abbeys, for example of Tintern or Fountains. The Cistercians were reformers who sought out the most desolate and remote valleys where they farmed the land and built their austere churches. In contrast to the rich splendour of the Benedictines, the interiors were devoid of decoration and the emphasis was on simplicity. The monks were 'dressed as angels might be' in habits of undyed wool, and lived a life of poverty. Simultaneously with this passionate revival of monastic life celibacy was enforced upon the clergy. Both before and after the Conquest priests had often been married but now this was banned, reinforcing those who took holy orders as a caste apart from ordinary men.

More monasteries meant more learning for they were centres of teaching. They were international, as they belonged to orders which had houses all over Europe and spoke and wrote the common *lingua franca*, Latin. The twelfth century was an age of intellectual ferment which saw the emergence of universities. Learned men moved around with as much ease as today. One such was Adelard of Bath who lived through the period from William Rufus to Henry II. He was a student at two great French cathedral schools, Tours and Laon; then he travelled in Greece, Asia Minor, Sicily, south Italy and probably Spain. He knew Latin, Greek and Arabic and spent his life translating books on philosophy and science which were to open up new avenues of thought. Not only were universities such as Oxford emerging as centres of learning, but also grammar schools for members of the laity. Soon it was realised that to be

educated not only opened up a career in the church but increasingly elsewhere.

Neither the king nor his nobles learned to read or write for they kept secretaries. As the government became more complicated, it called for men who were educated. What were parts of the royal household gradually began to take on the character of what were later to be government departments. The royal chapel provided church services for the court but as its clerics were literate they, under the chancellor, did the paperwork of government. The chamber included the private and sleeping apartments of the king and came under the chamberlain and the treasurer. The king still kept some of his money under the royal bed but most of it was in the treasury. The accounts were done twice a year in the exchequer called after the chequerboard, a table resembling a chessboard on which addition and subtraction could be demonstrated. Afterwards the accounts were written up on a huge roll of parchment. The earliest surviving one is from 1130 and the system continued almost until Queen Victoria's time.

Royal government was active in the form of justices on tour holding court all over the country, the direct ancestor of our assize courts. In each shire the king was represented by a sheriff whose duty it was to see that taxes were collected and delivered to the exchequer. The country was in fact becoming more prosperous. By royal grant, fairs began to be held and as trade and industry developed guilds were formed in the cities and towns. By 1130 weavers' guilds existed in London and four other towns reflecting the importance of the wool trade, particularly the export of wool itself to Flanders where it was woven into fine cloth.

It was during this period too that the warrior became first and foremost the knight. This was a society about and for men, in which women did not figure beyond influence, although they could be highly educated. A knight was a man of gentle birth trained in the martial arts whose role was devotion to Holy Church and to justice. War was his profession but it was war fought according to a complex code of rules. No one was allowed to fight during Lent or at Christmas. The likelihood of actually being killed was remote, for the aim was always to take knights of the opposing side captive and exact a large ransom for their release. The people who did suffer were the ordinary population. If the knights were not engaged in campaigns they staged tournaments, combats exactly like a battle but minus any killing. The chronicler Odericus Vitalis describing a battle in 1119 catches the atmosphere of this age of knights:

'For they were clad entirely in iron, and they spared each other for the love of God and for the sake of their fellowship. Nor did they seek to kill the fugitives but rather to take prisoners. Christian soldiers do not thirst to spill their brothers' blood, but, God willing, rejoice in lawful victory for the good of the Holy Church and the peace of the faithful.'

It was this atmosphere which made it possible for knights from all over Europe to unite in the crusade, with the common cause of delivering the holy city of Jerusalem out of the hands of the Infidel. In England the knightly ideal was coloured too by the romantic stories of King Arthur and his Knights of the Round Table which gained currency during this period, providing a pattern of behaviour for men to emulate for the next five hundred years.

Oxen drawing a plough, an illustration from an eleventh century calendar for the month of January. Behind the ploughman follows a sower scattering seed.

Chapter Ten

THE FIRST PLANTAGENET

W HEN Henry II came to the throne in 1154 a new era began, for he was the first of thirteen kings, the Plantagenets, who were to rule England for three hundred years. Their name by tradition came from the sprig of broom which his father, Geoffrey of Anjou, wore in his hat, in Latin: *planta genista*. They were an extraordinary family with a deep love of power, people of compelling fascination and charm but, at the same time, often unattractive and strangely unnerving. Subject to wild and unpredictable rages, they were yet endowed with remarkable application. Whatever they did, whether good or evil, was done with their whole might. All these traits were present in the life of perhaps their greatest member, Henry II.

Henry was that rare figure in English history, a man of European stature. That he owed not just to the extent of the empire over which he ruled, but to the fact that he was universally respected for being a just and wise king. So much so that twice he was called upon to act as judge and mediator between his fellow rulers, once in 1173 between those of Toulouse and Aragon and again in 1177 between the kings of Navarre and Aragon. Through his children's marriages his family connections spread through the whole of Europe. His daughters became queens of Sicily and Castile and Duchess of Saxony. Two of his grandchildren were Holy Roman Emperors, Otto IV and Frederick II. For half a century England was to be part of the greatest territorial empire seen in Western Europe since Charlemagne four centuries before, one held together almost solely by the strength of character of its king.

Henry II would have been an extraordinary figure in any age. Grey eyes darted out from a freckled fiery face framed by short red hair. Red hair and fits of temper often go together, and Henry was the first of a long line of Plantagenets noted for their irrational outbursts of rage. His head was large, hinting at the formidable brain power within, for he was a noted linguist able to understand all the many languages used in his domains: English, North French, Provençal, Welsh and Latin. He was also the first post-Conquest king to be literate, being able both to read and to write. Henry knew a great deal about law and even sat himself as a judge. He was a man blessed with a phenomenal memory, never forgetting a face. Stocky and athletic in build, he was frugal in his diet and unostentatious in his dress. His energy was unmatched and he was constantly on the move across an empire which stretched south to the foot of the Pyrenees and west to the Atlantic seaboard. Most of modern France was ruled by him. To his contemporaries he was restless and cunning but at the same time trusted and feared.

Peter of Blois, secretary to the queen, gives a vivid picture of what life was like with the king. If he said that he was staying somewhere 'you may be sure that the king will leave the place bright and early, and upset everyone's calculations in his haste . . . But if the prince has announced that he is setting off early to reach a particular place, beyond doubt he will change his mind and sleep till noon.' If he indicated what his route was to be he was sure to change it 'to another place, where there may be a single house, and no food for anyone else. And I believe our plight added to the king's pleasure.'

For thirty-five years Henry II held together the enormous empire which he either inherited or which came to him through marriage: England, Normandy, Brittany, Anjou and Aquitaine. Modelling himself on his grandfather, Henry I, he set out to restore the power of the crown and in so doing not only reactivated and recaptured that king's achievements but went on to lay the foundations of a system of government which was to last for centuries. These developments came about partly because the king, having always to be on the move, needed to leave officers he could trust behind him, who could run this or that part of his empire while he was somewhere else. So successful was he in the case of England that he was able to absent himself for several years at a time, and yet order and justice were maintained. This he also owed to the fact that he had a genius for choosing the right men, all, that is, except one—Thomas Becket.

When Henry came to the throne his main aim was to turn the clock back to 1135, the year Henry I died. There was a vigorous campaign to restore royal power. Castles illegally constructed by the barons were demolished. Those they had taken from the crown were returned. The towns and lands granted away by Stephen were taken back by the king. The reign thus opened with this dramatic return to order. Later Henry was to build and expand on this. In 1166 an act of government called the Assize of Clarendon laid down provisions for the maintenance of public order in a way hitherto unknown. Ten years after that the role of the itinerant royal justices was greatly extended. Six groups of three justices each became responsible for four to eight coun-

Bronze knocker dating from c. 1180 from the sanctuary door of Durham Cathedral. By grasping it a wrongdoer sought the protection of the church, accepting whatever penalty was imposed.

ties. Henceforward royal justice was a reality. As a result law and order replaced disorder and lawlessness.

This gave the peace and security which brings prosperity. The king never over-taxed his subjects and throughout his reign the royal revenues rose steadily. Men at the time realised the magnitude of Henry's achievement. As one chronicler, William of Newburgh, wrote:

'In his exalted position in the state, he was most diligent in defending and pro-moting the peace of the realm; in wielding the sword for the punishment of evildoers, he was a true servant of God.'

That is how Henry II would have been remembered if it were not for one man, Thomas Becket. When the king came to the throne he had appointed Becket to the major administrative post of chancellor. Becket had been archdeacon of Canterbury and the right-hand man of the archbishop. But he was not a priest. He and the king became great friends. Becket was a smart young man-about-town, witty, extravagant, even flamboyant. He combined glamour and efficiency. Riding through London one cold midwinter's day the king spotted a beggar freezing in rags. Turning to Becket, who rode at his side, he said, 'Would it not be a meritorious act to give that poor old man a warm cloak?' The chancellor assented, not guessing what was to follow. 'Yours be the merit then,' said the king, seizing Becket's splendid fur-lined cloak and throwing it to the man.

In Becket the king saw a means of tidying up relations between church and state. He believed that with his friend as Archbishop of Canterbury the situation could return to how it had been just after the Conquest, before the church had embarked on its campaign to free itself of lay control. In 1161 the opportunity came with the death of the existing archbishop. The king asked Becket to take on the role. 'How religious and saintly is the man you want to appoint to that holy see!' Becket exclaimed, pointing to his rich dress. The king persisted, and in doing so made the one fatal misjudgment of his entire reign.

On 2 June 1162, Thomas Becket was ordained priest and on the following day he was appointed Archbishop of Canterbury. No one has ever been able to explain the total reversal of character which then took place. Becket at once resigned all his secular offices and suddenly changed his style of life from one of indulgent splendour to one of self-denial and humility. The scene was set for a tremendous clash of wills when Henry set about re-establishing his authority over the church, failing to recognise not only that times had changed but that his old friend had been trained in the new canon law in which the clergy were exempt from lay interference.

Henry gathered all these 'royal customs' into a document known as the Constitutions of Clarendon presented to a meeting of the great council in January 1164. The king's intention was a reasonable one, to improve the standards of justice, in this instance in the ecclesiastical courts. Five of the provisions, however, were seen by Becket as infringements of the rights of the church. Attention was focused especially on the one whereby a clerk was to be brought first of all before a lay court, where he pleaded what was called 'benefit of clergy'. This meant that the case was then transferred to the bishop's court. If the man was then found guilty he was handed back to the lay court for sentencing. The worst sentence the church court could give was to defrock the clerk which meant that murder could be got away with. Becket, however, stood firm on the ground that 'God judges no man twice in the same matter.' He therefore refused to put his seal to the document.

The king was enraged. Nine months later Becket was summoned to be tried for contempt. Henry set out to humiliate the archbishop in every way he could. In a terrible final scene, when sentence was about to be pronounced on him, Becket, holding his processional cross in his hands, defied the court: 'Such as I am, I am your father, and you are magnates of the household, lay powers, secular persons. I refuse to hear your judgement.' He swept out of the room, fled the same night, and took a boat into exile.

For six years there followed endless attempts to bring

The murder of Thomas Becket in Canterbury Cathedral on 29 December 1170 from a thirteenth century manuscript.

about a reconciliation. The quarrel was made worse by Henry having his eldest son, also Henry, crowned as his successor by the Archbishop of York. Becket had already excommunicated many of the king's supporters, cutting them off from the sacraments of the church; now he threatened to put the country under interdict which meant closing all the churches. As a result of this, in July 1170 Henry was forced to give in, and Becket returned to England. His first act was to excommunicate all the bishops who had taken part in Henry's son's coronation. When the king was told, one of the bishops said, 'My lord, while Thomas lives, you will have no peace, nor quiet, nor prosperity.' The king was seized with fury: 'What idle and miserable men I have encouraged and promoted in this kingdom, faithless to their lord, who let me be mocked by a low-born clerk.' At this four knights slipped out of the room, crossed the Channel and made their way to Canterbury. On the afternoon of 29 December they murdered the archbishop in his own cathedral. When the news reached the king he gave way to a paroxysm of grief, neither eating nor speaking for three days.

Henry had lost. The shock waves crossed Europe. Becket's tomb became a shrine at which miracles occurred and, soon after, the pope canonised him. On 12 July 1174 the king himself did penance, walking barefoot through the streets of Canterbury and after that gave himself over to being flogged by his bishops and monks. The Constitutions of Clarendon became a dead letter it seemed, but in reality most of what the king wanted was implemented.

Box or Châsse containing relics of St. Thomas Becket. Over forty-five of these survive, mainly dating like this one from the thirteenth century. Such relic boxes were exhibited on a beam over the altar. They were enamelled with scenes from the life and death of the saint.

The tragic story of Henry II and Becket cast a shadow over the reign. So too did another incident which fell over its closing years, for the king's love of power was so great that he could part with none of it. The result was a dynastic quarrel in which Henry's queen sided with his sons. Eleanor of Aquitaine was a remarkable woman in her own right, a child of the warm south, impetuous and passionate. She presided over a court of troubadour courtiers at Poitou. They contributed to a new cultural milieu which centred on the idealisation of the knight's relationship to his lady, something which accorded women a far more important status in society. But when, in 1173, she joined her sons in rebellion against her husband, Henry II shut her away for fifteen years.

The king had four sons: Henry, Richard, Geoffrey and John. They were fated to disagree. 'Dost thou not know,' Geoffrey once wrote to his father, 'that it is our proper nature, planted in us by inheritance from our ancestors, that none of us should love the other, but that ever brother should strive against brother, and son against father?' For over a decade there was sporadic war between them, all attempts at reconciliation failing. Then, in 1183, the eldest son died and Henry redivided his empire: Richard was to have Normandy, Anjou and England, Geoffrey Brittany, and John Aquitaine. But Richard refused to let John have the latter and the war was renewed.

Henry died in the castle at Chinon on 6 July 1189 during a war in which his sons had taken sides with his deadliest enemy, Philip Augustus, king of France. The king's last words were: 'Shame, shame on a conquered king.' The truth was far different. Henry II was the greatest of all the Plantagenet kings. His bequest was good government in terms of peace, law and order on a scale unknown to any other country in Western Europe at the time. It was a splendid inheritance.

Pilgrim souvenirs of St. Thomas Becket. Visitors to the saint's shrine would have purchased one of these badges to wear. They were mass-produced from moulds.

Chapter Eleven

THE END
OF AN EMPIRE

ENRY II had left a great empire but within twenty-five years virtually all of it had gone. That loss was to haunt the Plantagenet kings for three hundred years. Time and again they tried to recover it, for, to them, the continental territories were in many ways closer to their hearts. Like their Norman predecessors, the Plantagenets had their roots not in England but in France, in their case in Aquitaine which they were to retain. This was an age when there was no sense of any national or cultural divide. The ruling classes were united by a common language and culture. The only divide was the feudal one of fealty either to the king of England or France. If the abilities of Henry's heirs had been different England could have remained the power-base of a lasting Angevin empire. As it was, their short comings precipitated its collapse.

Nothing is more striking than the stability of England with its strongly centralised government established by the Normans. So strong was it that it could withstand the fact that the new king, Richard I, who ruled for a decade, only visited the country twice, once for three months and a second time for only two. Richard I remains the troubadour monarch whose adventures were to make him the romantic hero of legend. He combined his father's shrewdness and physical strength with his mother's grandeur and passion. Homosexual by nature, he was both a poet and a musician, even conducting his own chapel choir. His knowledge of every aspect of warfare and of the art of fortification was universally recognised. Dubbed *Coeur de Lion* or Lion-hearted, in tribute to his dare-devil bravery, he was also known as Richard Oc e No or Yea-and-Nay, meaning that whatever he said, that he did, never breaking the word he gave. But he was selfish. England was looked upon as little more than a source for money to pay for the Crusade upon which he embarked in August 1190. Travelling via Italy, Sicily and Cyprus to the Holy Land, each port of call gave him an opportunity to act out to the full his role as the valiant crusading knight. Disaster struck,

however, for, on his homeward journey, he was ship-wrecked and eventually fell into the hands of enemies, firstly the Duke of Austria and then the Holy Roman Emperor. Once again it was to be England which was to be the loser, for the enormous sum of 150,000 crowns had to be raised in taxes as a ransom.

Two mid-thirteenth century tiles celebrating the victory of Richard I over a turbanned Saladin who drops his curved sword as his horse collapses. It is likely that these tiles were made for a royal palace, possibly for Henry III.

When he had left the country the provision he had made for its government had not been satisfactory. His instincts were right in trusting neither of his two brothers. The youngest, John, he showered with lands. Geoffrey, who was illegitimate, he caused to be elected Archbishop of York. Simultaneously he banished both of them for a period of three years, in this way hoping to avert any mischief making. Unfortunately he chose the wrong man to govern the country in his absence. William Longchamp, Bishop of Ely, was made royal justiciar, chancellor, besides being papal legate. He was one of those administrators of humble origins who had risen to eminence as one of the officials who ran the Angevin empire. But he was tactless and very unpopular.

Richard relented, and allowed John to return to England, with the result that the inevitable happened and the barons turned to him. In 1191 Geoffrey defied his banishment and landed in England. Longchamp promptly had him seized at the altar of the priory in which he was staying. This gave John precisely the opportunity he needed and he summoned Longchamp to stand trial at a council of bishops and barons. Longchamp dared not go and the meeting promptly excommunicated him and ordered his immediate arrest. Eventually he fled the country. On 8 October, at the same meeting, John was made regent 'by the common deliberation of the king's vassals'.

In fact this was to mean government by the council itself. When news reached England that the king was a prisoner, John attempted to seize power but failed. Although the king's absence had put a tremendous strain on the system of government inherited from Henry II, it was able to withstand such an attempt and remain loyal. When Richard returned in 1194 he wisely did not reinstate Longchamp but this time selected a man of quite outstanding abilities, Hubert Walter.

Like Longchamp, Walter's background was service in Henry II's government. He had accompanied Richard on the Crusade and was elected Archbishop of Canterbury in 1193 and made justiciar. When the king left England for the last time in May of the following year Walter was left as virtual ruler of England until his death in 1205. From the king's point of view his main task was to raise money to pay for war. But his real achievements lay elsewhere. In 1196, for example, standard weights and measures were introduced. Before then they had differed according to each region of the country. He used the itinerant justices for the first time, not only as judges but as an arm of government charged, while they travelled, to inquire as to whether royal policy had been carried out or not and to report back their findings. For the first time too the knights of the shire, those knights that is who were landholders, began to be used as instruments of government. They were called upon to act in all manner of local disputes such as quarrels over boundaries.

But perhaps the greatest revolution of all was the advent of keeping government records. By the end of the twelfth century more and more people could read and write. Government was also becoming more complicated. The long absences of the king made it necessary for records to be kept of what had been done. In 1199 the chancery, which was the administrative headquarters of government, began to record its annual activities on pieces of parchment made from sheepskin. These were sewn together and kept not as a book but in the form of a huge roll which was the direct ancestor of our modern filing system. Documents henceforward became an accepted part of business. Soon the judges followed suit in the law courts and then the bishops began to keep records in their dioceses. From the beginning of the thirteenth century the history of England can be written from such records.

Richard meanwhile was engaged in defending his continental empire against the

French king, Philip Augustus. In the south there stretched a network bound together by family connection. His queen was Berengaria of Navarre, his sister was queen of Castile and his widowed sister Countess of Toulouse. Richard's nephew was the new Holy Roman Emperor and a new pope, Innocent III, was also his ally. As a consequence of this and his own military skill, he was victorious in his wars against Philip Augustus. And then, in his forty-ninth year, as a result of a misplaced fit of bravado, he was killed. In a dispute over the ownership of some treasure he besieged the small town of Châlus in the Limousin. A crossbowman took aim at him. Richard paused to mock him a moment too long. The bolt pierced his left shoulder. Gangrene set in and he died of blood poisoning on 6 April 1199.

The king of legend was childless and the Angevin Empire passed to John. This time it was a far from glorious legacy: war with an increasingly potent French king, financial breakdown in an England sucked dry of money to pay for it, plus the late king's Crusade and ransom money. To that can be added years of famine. Whatever Richard's shortcomings had been he was respected and evoked loyalty. No one, however, quite trusted John. His father had nicknamed him Lackland, for, as the youngest son, at first he had no share in the family inheritance. He was spoiled and wayward, in love with the good life: rich clothes and jewels, good food, abundant drink and women. While the word of both his father and brother had been taken as law, with anything John promised, men began to look for confirmation in writing.

Nothing, therefore, boded well in the new reign. It was not helped either by John breaking rules of conduct which feudal society regarded as sacrosanct. The first was to take as his bride a woman who was already betrothed. In 1200 John had his marriage to Isabella of Gloucester annulled in order to marry the heiress of Angoulême, another Isabella. The man to whom she had been betrothed appealed to his overlord, Philip Augustus of France. In this instance the French king was overlord of John too. The court condemned the English king to the forfeiture of all the lands he held as a vassal of the French king, the Angevin Empire minus England. Normandy, Anjou and Brittany soon fell into the hands of Philip Augustus. During the war John had captured his brother Geoffrey's son, Arthur, whom Richard had once designated his heir. Once again John offended the feudal code of correct conduct by having him covertly murdered. To kill a foe in open single combat would have been acceptable but to dispose of him secretly was quite another matter. All that was now left of the Angevin Empire was Aquitaine, commercially held fast to England by the wine trade.

These disasters were followed by a seven-year struggle with the pope over the choice of a new Archbishop of Canterbury. When Hubert Walter died in 1205 the monks went ahead and elected a new archbishop with no reference to the king. They left for Rome to seek the pope's confirmation of their choice. John, enraged, forced the monks who remained to elect his choice and they also proceeded to Rome. Pope Innocent III declared both of the elections void and the monks under his direction went on to elect an Englishman who was a member of the papal court, the theologian Stephen Langton. John was furious and refused to admit the new archbishop. The pope in reply excommunicated the king and laid the country under an interdict. For seven years the churches remained closed except for infant baptism and deathbed confessions. Only when John was preparing for a major offensive to recover his lost continental lands did he make peace with the pope and admit Langton to England. In 1214 John reopened the war against Philip Augustus but the campaign was a total failure.

He returned to find not only an empty treasury but an enraged baronage who could take no more of the king's endless excuses to extract money from them. The Angevin system of government was breaking down. John was faced with rebellion and, in May 1215, he was forced to admit that he was beaten. A month later he put his seal to what is still looked upon as a landmark, the Great Charter or Magna Carta.

The Great Charter contained over sixty clauses putting into writing an agreed body of laws covering every aspect of government and of the relationship of the king to his subjects. What it really represented was the fact that under the Plantagenets government had developed

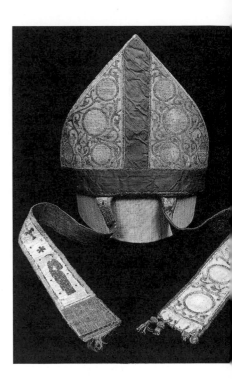

Bishop's mitre of white silk embroidered with silver thread made some time between 1160 and 1220, an example of medieval English embroidery, *opus anglicanum* whose fame was European.

The opening lines of Magna Carta presented to King John at Runnymede in 1215.

without consultation, piecemeal as expediency demanded. That development was not rejected but put down accompanied by guidelines which both sides should observe. This was the beginning of the idea that people ought to be consulted and in the long term it was to lead to Parliament. For the first time the king was beginning to be seen as answerable not only to God but to the law.

The Charter's most famous clause implied such a view:

'No freeman shall be arrested, or kept in prison, or disseised [of his freehold], or banished, or in any way brought to ruin . . . unless by lawful judgment of his peers or by the law of the land.'

In short, every man should be tried before sentence was given. Other clauses guaranteed the freedom of the church from royal interference and the privileges of the newly emerging boroughs, above all the City of London.

That the Great Charter was to be such a landmark only emerged over the centuries. No sooner was it agreed than John got the pope to declare it invalid and, gathering his forces, the king took to arms against the barons. They, in turn, called in the heir to the French throne, the dauphin, and it was in the midst of this chaos that John died in October 1215 and was succeeded by his son, Henry.

After these momentous changes the thirteenth century opened with a very different perspective. With the loss of virtually all the continental empire in 1214, for the first time since 1066 the monarch became firmly based in England. For a hundred and fifty years the kingdom had been ruled by peripatetic kings who often spent more of their time on the other side of the Channel. England had been one piece of a larger mosaic. After 1214 that ceased with tremendous consequences. The Channel was no longer a river dividing the same country, far easier to cross than the Alps. It had to become instead a moat of defence and John indeed established a navy, realising that henceforth there would be great battles fought at sea. England was set on the path to become the inviolate island kingdom, no longer a part of, but set apart from, Europe.

Chapter Twelve

THE GOTHIC AGE

Henry III was nine when he came to the throne. He was to rule England for fifty-six years and effectively for most of the thirteenth century. This was an age of enormous change and growing prosperity for the country, caught in a new architectural style imported and adapted from Northern France, the Gothic. All over England churches and cathedrals were rebuilt in the new manner reflecting the confidence and wealth of a society secure in its Christian faith and in the order of things, not only in this life but in the one to come. Clusters of small columns soared heavenwards forming pointed arches and windows inset with stone tracery and filled with stained glass, culminating in elaborately ribbed vaults. This was medieval England at its apogee, as one province of a Christendom held together by a common faith, with its focus in Rome and its head the pope, the successor of St. Peter. The clergy moved across what was to them a Europe without boundaries speaking and writing a *lingua franca*, Latin. The noble classes too had most things in common, bound together by their acceptance of the conventions of feudalism and by the etiquette of chivalry. The loss of most of the Angevin Empire did not mean that England became insular. The English kings saw themselves as players on the international stage and the aristocracy shared the language and lifestyle of their peers across the Channel.

Against this backcloth of a united Christendom with shared ideals the events acted out in each area of Europe assume a different perspective. In England it revolved around the consequences of the Great Charter inherited from the king's father's reign. In Henry's case this was to become acute, for his idea of kingship was extremely elevated and from that sprang the periodic clash of king and barons, for the barons naturally desired to control or curtail the king's powers, constantly invoking the Great Charter in their support.

Henry III lacked the most important attribute essential for any medieval king: he was not a soldier. As a consequence he failed to do the two things which the barons most looked for: lead them into battle and shine in the tiltyard. Instead he expressed his kingship through art and pageantry, in both of which fields he was a master.

Extravagant, petulant, suspicious, obstinate and sharp-tongued, he had only one aim, to ensure that he was absolute monarch.

Henry's aspirations for the monarchy were summed up in one building, Westminster Abbey. In 1245 he took the decision to rebuild the old Anglo-Saxon abbey replacing it with a magnificent building in the French Gothic style which he had seen in Paris. The new abbey was to provide a setting for priest-like kings who were vicars of God on earth and lords of all men, lay and clerical. Their sanctity was emphasised by the royal saint, Edward the Confessor, who was given a splendid new shrine behind the high altar around which there was to be a royal burial place for the kings of England. The regalia was kept in the new church which was also the setting for the ritual of coronation in which each king, through being anointed, became set apart and above ordinary men. It was even believed that the king could heal by touch those suffering from a disease called scrofula.

Such grandeur reflected exactly how Henry III viewed his position and, although his father had lost most of the Angevin inheritance, this did not lessen the son's desire to compensate for it in other ways. The fact that both attempts to re-establish the Plantagenets as rulers on the mainland again ended in disaster should

The shrine of St. Edward the Confessor in Westminster Abbey. The illumination shows pilgrims waiting their turn to creep into one of the apertures in the base to make their petition. A custodian stands to the right reading out the saint's miracles. The richly decorated casket above, called the feretory, contained the bones. On the pillar to the right a statue of the king looks towards a vision he saw of St. John the Baptist.

not obscure the king's ambition. In 1254 he accepted the crown of Sicily for his younger son, Edmund, but that failed. Three years later his brother, Richard of Cornwall, was elected king of Germany. That too was doomed. As a result Henry, in 1259, was finally forced formally to renounce his rights to Normandy, Anjou and Poitou to Louis IX of France.

The barons were always against these expensive entanglements and the mountain of debt they incurred eventually ensured that their view of the king's position, as being one with some constraints, gained increasing support. For the first thirty years of his reign, however, Henry was able to rule more or less as he liked. The unease developing in the mind of the barons was partly due to the king's arrogance but partly also due to something else, government was becoming increasingly complicated. A century before, the chancery and the exchequer were merely parts of the royal household dealing with administrative and financial affairs. By the middle of the thirteenth century they had moved out and become separate departments, each with its own highly organised officials and records. The barons were suspicious and began to want a voice in the choice of the chancellor and the treasurer and even, on occasions, of the royal justiciar. Their means of achieving such control was through meetings of the Great Council which included all the lay and clerical leaders of the nation, but whose composition was by no means fixed. The king, however, made use instead of his own Royal Council consisting of men of his own choosing. The barons objected to this. Henry would have survived these challenges to his rule if his choices had been wiser and his government more effective. As it was, both tended to be ineffective and muddled.

The barons found a leader in the king's brother-in-law Simon de Montfort, a man of energy and vision, and their opportunity came with the collapse of the king's foreign adventures. For almost ten years, between 1257 and 1265, king and barons were locked into a succession of crises in a struggle for control. At first the king was forced to submit to the kingdom being governed by a Council of Fifteen of the barons' choosing headed by Simon de Montfort. Thereafter followed reversal and counter reversal as first one side and then the other was able to impose its will on government. The eventual result was civil war. At the Battle of Lewes the king was defeated and, a year later in 1265, at the Battle of Evesham, Simon de Montfort was not only defeated but killed.

Henry III had seemingly won but that was not altogether true, for during these crisis years recourse had been made again and again to meetings of the Great Council. To these now came, in addition, knights to represent the shires and, on one occasion, burgesses to represent the towns. Never before had meetings been held including so many different classes of those who made up the realm of England. The meetings were called 'parliaments' from the French word *parler*, to speak, because they were conferences or parleys between the king and his subjects about affairs of state. Gradually the idea that the king should consult the magnates and representatives of the kingdom on certain subjects like taxation gained currency as something to be expected. No one in 1272, when Henry III died, could have foreseen that these sporadic parleys would lead to our modern Parliament.

What they did reflect was a very different society from that which had existed immediately after the Norman Conquest. In spite of the periodic outbursts of fighting between king and barons, England was remarkably stable. Medieval warfare in any case was rarely more than a localised and seasonal event affecting only a small area of the country. As the king pursued a policy of peace with France, expensive wars with their high taxation were avoided. Peace meant prosperity, so that both trade and agriculture could flourish without dislocation. This was the age when the wool trade began to develop on a large scale as international big business. Its organisation changed as English merchants learnt how to export wool across Europe. Initially this had been handled by Italians living in England who had come to collect the taxes due to the pope, but increasingly English merchants began to take over from them, particularly in the case of the huge export trade with Flanders where the wool was woven into fine cloth. It was woven in England too, which meant increasing numbers of weavers, fullers and dyers. Skilled tradespeople were more and more in evidence as not only the wool trade grew but so did other industries based on lead, tin, coal, iron and salt. Everywhere towns were burgeoning: ports like Bristol which prospered on the wine trade from Gascony, Lynn with its short crossing to Flanders, or Newcastle which exported to Scandinavia. Above all London, not only because it was next to the seat of the court and government at Westminster, but because it was the focal point of the country's road system and, as a consequence, was the major port for all transactions with the continent.

In the long term these entrepreneurs were to be the future but they sit uneasily within medieval society which was seen as consisting of only three groups: men of prayer, made up of those who had taken religious vows, men of war, embracing the feudal nobility and knights, and, finally, the men of toil or the peasants: in Latin: the *oratores*, *bellatores* and *laboratores*. The *oratores* belonged to the international fraternity of the Church of Rome with its hierarchy stretching across Europe bound in obedience to the pope and subject to canon law. In England the church was headed by its two archbishops of Canterbury and York, each with a network of dioceses below them, three in the north and eighteen in the south. Some, like Durham and Winchester, were amongst the richest in Christendom. Others, such as Bangor or Exeter, were poor. The church had won its freedom and even had the last say in the choice of the clergy who worked in some nine thousand five hundred parishes. These owed their living to the tithe, a tenth part of the produce of the land of each parishioner. Then there were the monasteries: the old Benedictine foundations going back before the Conquest, those which had been founded in the previous century including about two hundred and fifty Augustinian houses and some hundred Cistercian. The wealth of all these varied according to their endowment but collectively the church offered a rich source of patronage not only at the disposal of the bishops but of the king and nobles. But the thirteenth century was the age of two new orders, that of St. Francis of Assisi and St. Dominic, the grey and the black friars. Unlike the earlier orders the members of these were out and about, especially in the towns, preaching, teaching and hearing confessions. They produced men of great learning who added to the lustre of the new universities at Oxford and Cambridge.

This was the great age of church building, especially of cathedrals, a movement which began in 1174 with Canterbury Cathedral and reached its climax with Salisbury. In 1220 the old Salisbury Cathedral was abandoned and the one we see today arose during the following fifty years. Churches, whether great or small, were the grandest of all medieval buildings for a very simple reason: every day the Eucharist, the liturgy of the mass, in which bread and wine became the body and blood of the Son of God, was acted out in them. They were built therefore to house God and, in addition, the bones and relics of holy people, God's saints. All these cathedral rebuildings included re-siting a saint's shrine behind the high altar. Such shrines were venerated and visited by people who came on pilgrimage. Sometimes the saint would intercede and heal the sick or avert a catastrophe. Each cathedral belonged to its saint or martyr.

The belief in the supernatural, in miracles, strange coincidences and of constant visible evidence of the invisible, was universal. People moved out of their wood, wattle and mud houses and, on entering the church, crossed into a world which mirrored exactly to them the Heavenly Jerusalem to come in the next life. Light, the symbol of the divine, poured in through windows peopled with the figures of saints. Everywhere, both inside and out, was covered with paintings and sculpture of the inhabitants of heaven whose prayers aided those on earth. Now only the glass retains its colour but then every wall and statue would have been brilliantly painted and gilded. Through the

The nave of Lincoln Cathedral built between 1209 and 1235. All over England cathedrals were rebuilt in the thirteenth century in the new Gothic style imported from France. In 1220 Bishop Hugh, who died in 1200, was canonised, attracting crowds of pilgrims to Lincoln. Sixty years later in 1280 his bones were moved to the angels' choir, an event attended by Edward I and his queen.

church building each community expressed its identity and its wealth, for it was the setting for the great spiritual events which punctuated man's earthly pilgrimage: baptism, confirmation, penance, communion and burial. The church provided the back-cloth too for processions on holy days and for courts, judgements and performances. It could even house a school.

The men of war or *bellatores* were a fluctuating group as great families rose and fell. Nobility was bestowed by birth and expressed by success in arms. Mass knightings of young nobles were staged on feast days of the church and at battles. A knight traditionally had to be able to equip himself with a horse and all the trappings of a cavalry-man. In addition he and all his class from earls to the lowliest knight of the shire were bound by the conventions of chivalry. The church's view of the knight cast him into a role as the defender of Holy Church and the weak. In its secular context stress was laid on three great virtues: bravery, loyalty to liege lord and lady and, most of all, on generosity. This accounts for the increasingly lavish living style of the baronial classes who supported huge retinues in attendance upon them. Wealth came through good management of their estates and from the king, who was the fount of patronage and the bestower of gifts in the way of heiresses or lands. The knight's role was to fight or to train for his role as defender through a favourite pastime, the tournament. These began as miniature pitched battles but during the thirteenth century evolved into feats of skill in which two knights charged against each other with lances along a bar-rier, the lists, and scored points for their skill. In this they displayed prowess not only in honour of their lord but in tribute to their lady who watched from a nearby gallery.

That was some sign that the status of women was slowly changing but they were still devoid of power and had few legal rights. Their role as a humanising influence and as the object of a knight's veneration accelerated a changed attitude beyond that of a chattel. The status of a wife also improved as succession to estates now depended on legitimacy. But the only occasion when women could stand firmly on their own was as widows, when they became highly desirable acquisitions.

At the bottom of this pyramid toiled the *laboratores* or peasants. There had been a huge population growth, and by the year 1300 the population had grown to between four and five million. Agriculture failed to keep pace with the new numbers to be fed and there was widespread poverty and near famine conditions. The peasants' lifestyle had hardly changed from the post-Conquest period. Some were wholly or partly free but the vast majority were villeins, unfree by birth and tied to the land of their lord's manor. For their few strips they continued to pay him in kind through their labour. They still lived in mud and wood one-room dwellings with a central hearth, animals and men together. Their virtually static existence is a reminder that the boundaries of

A knight kneels in homage to his king. Drawing from the middle of the thirteenth century.

the majority of Englishmen in the thirteenth century were literally those of the immediate landscape beyond which they rarely if ever travelled.

This ordered view of society was unquestioned and seemingly immutable. It was viewed as God-ordained, for, above and beyond, it was mirrored in the structure of the universe. This descended, it was believed, in the form of concentric circles downwards from heaven to earth. At the top was heaven presided over by God. Below that extended hierarchies of angels and below them, in turn, the seven planets which circled the earth and whose influence affected everything on it from political events to a man's physical condition. The earth was flat. Jerusalem, the Holy City, stood at its centre while England lay on the fringes of its known extent. Everywhere man looked in medieval England he would have moved with ease from earth to heaven in his thoughts, such was the constant interplay between the two. No wonder that when the great mosaic floor, on which the kings of England were henceforth to be crowned, was laid out for Henry III before the high altar of Westminster Abbey it took the form of the universe in diagram. In the king's view God reigned over the cosmos in the same way that he, as His representative on earth, ruled over the realm of England. It was a view which was to remain unchallenged for the next three hundred and fifty years.

Chapter Thirteen

TOWARDS A UNITED ISLAND

ALTHOUGH the waters of the English Channel were never a barrier but rather a highway, in the governing of a kingdom dramatic changes in land level most certainly were, in an age when transport was either on foot, on horseback or by cart. The realm of England which the Normans conquered consisted of the lowlands, the south-east and west and the midlands. Beyond these lay the Celtic lands, Wales, Cumberland and Scotland, all regions in the highland zone whose layers of defence depended on ranges of hills and mountainous terrain. They were inaccessible and within them lived the old British populations held together by a shared heritage of language, traditions and trade, pursuing a different, harsher life of dairy farming, sheep grazing and a lighter, scattered arable farming suitable to its soils. At the close of the thirteenth century the relationship of these peoples to the English monarchs was a distant one based on their overlordship of the Welsh princes and the Scottish kings. However, when Edward I succeeded his father Henry III in 1272 his ambition was to extend his rule to embrace the natural boundaries of the island.

What is so striking is that this had not been attempted before. Had William I conquered both Scotland and Wales the history of Britain would have been very different. Such a conquest would have imposed over the whole island at an early date a centralising uniformity in administration, law, language and commerce which knew no barriers. Leaving these regions virtually untouched for two centuries strengthened their

sense of individual identity and independence both politically and culturally. By the time that Edward I set out to subjugate them, his attack only increased regional loyalties leaving a pattern of tension which is still alive today.

By the close of the thirteenth century there was also a new sense of identity within England. The king's name, Edward, in honour of his father's favourite saint, Edward the Confessor, was making use of an English name not favoured by the Anglo-Norman aristocracy. Imperceptibly, however, since 1066 intermarriage had created a more united society no longer easily divided into French speaking nobility and Anglo-Saxon speaking middle classes and peasantry. English began to emerge as a language spoken by every class, one which took into its structure and vocabulary much Anglo-Norman French. The upper classes were bilingual and the king himself spoke French, Latin and English.

Edward was in nearly every sense of the word an ideal medieval monarch. Over six feet tall (when his tomb was opened his skeleton measured six feet two inches) he was majestic in presence, a fearless warrior both on the battlefield and in the tiltyard. His childhood had been idyllic with loving parents and to this he was to add a happy marriage to Eleanor of Castile. So devastated was he when she died in 1290 that he ordered magnificent stone crosses, three of which survive, to be built wherever her coffin had rested on its journey south from Lincoln to Westminster Abbey. Edward also inherited the full Plantagenet spleen, given to fits of rage, on one occasion tossing his daughter's coronet into the fire.

When his father died in 1272 Edward was on Crusade and, as an index of the stability of the English government, it was not until two years later that he reached England. Edward shared his father's strong belief in the sanctity of kingship and had led the royalist forces against Simon de Montfort at Evesham. When he came to the throne a new era dawned, for with him a new generation sprang into prominence. His first act was to set in motion a whole series of reforms, reached in consultation with meetings of Parlia-

Labours of the months from a calendar in a fourteenth century manuscript depicting typical events like threshing, reaping, sowing and drying off wet boots.

ment and embodied in what were called statutes which were to become a new means of making law. Through them the king was able to remedy grievances over land tenure, see to the maintenance of law and order and stem gifts of land to the church. But his major policies concerned the unification of the island under one sovereign by conquering first Wales and then Scotland.

William I had established the great border earldoms of Shrewsbury, Chester and Hereford along the Marches. There was little incentive to subject Wales because, unlike England, it was a very poor, backward coun-try geographically divided into a series of princedoms which only occasionally came together under one single ruler. The princes paid homage to the English kings or not as it politically suited them but, by the thirteenth century, the English had penetrated quite far into the principality. This was the result of an unchanging pattern of periodic campaigning in which first the English feudal force invaded, then the princes withdrew to the hills, no battle would be fought and, at the close of the season, the English returned home again.

These spasmodic forays were now succeeded by a policy of conquest. This involved three major elements. The first was money, raised from Italian bankers and re-paid out of the customs on the wool trade. Money meant that an army could be supplied and that, following conquest, massive castles could be built to subjugate the Welsh in the same way that William I had the Anglo-Saxons. Finally, following the same precedent, a new governing class had to be established. Everything connected with Edward's Welsh policy proved to be a brilliant success as

When Eleanor of Castile died in 1290 her body was carried from Lincoln to Westminster. The king was so devoted to his wife that he commissioned twelve crosses, each erected on a site where the funeral procession rested. This elegant figure of the queen comes from the one erected at Waltham Cross and is the work of Alexander of Abingdon in 1291-92.

much as his parallel programme for the Scots was to prove a disaster.

Wales was then ruled by Llywelen ap Gruffyd styled 'Prince of Wales' who gave Edward just the excuse he needed by refusing to pay him homage. In 1277 a massive force was assembled, so powerful that Llywelen submitted without even fighting. Five years later he was to lead a rebellion and be killed, the Welsh proving no match for English cavalrymen and archers. As a result, by 1295, the principality of Wales had ceased to exist. New counties were created and English administration was introduced. English people were encouraged to settle and bring with them their skills. They felt no shame in subjecting the Welsh and the idea that they embodied a civilisation would not have crossed the English minds. To them the Welsh were lawbreakers devoted to murder, robbery and rape.

Edward at this time had the resources to carry the war to its conclusion and impose his rule once and for all on a disunited and disorganised people. That took the tangible form of a massive series of castles which incorporated the latest techniques in fortification, designed to overawe the walled towns which nestled below their many towers. Ten in all were built which in their time were unrivalled in Latin Christendom as marvels of military engineering. All of them were constructed by the King's Works, the department devoted to building and maintaining royal residences, and designed by James of St. George, a Savoyard architect. Most of these castles still stand, providing a parallel series of magnificent secular buildings equal in their way to the Gothic cathedrals arising at the same time. The castles were not houses of God, but strongholds to dominate a people. Usually they were sited on inaccessible promontories or above rivers, and incorporated cunning sequences of gates, walls and passages to defy any assailant. The new means of holding off the enemy was by way of concentric defences: an outer moat, then a low wall followed by a second taller one punctuated by towers. The grandest of all the castles was Carnarfon, which was to be the king's seat of government. It was built on the site where it was believed was buried the father of the first Christian Emperor, Constantine. To emphasise this imperial legacy Edward I had its splendid polygonal walls and towers endowed with stripes of

masonry to echo the walls of the capital of the Eastern Empire, Byzantium. The figures of three eagles, imperial symbols, were placed on the turrets of the castle's greatest tower to emphasise Edward's triumph.

Scotland, however, was to be a very different story. Unlike Wales, by the close of the thirteenth century it had already developed into a kingdom of its own, directly modelled on the Anglo-Norman one. Scotland had begun, like Wales, as a land of many kingdoms but, by the close of the eleventh century, had attained unity under kings who recognised those of England as their over-

Harlech was the most perfect of the castles built by Edward I to secure his conquest of Wales and was designed by James of St.George. Its layout represents the high-water mark of thirteenth century military architecture. Perched on a rocky outcrop overlooking the sea it was virtually unassailable from the west. A great ditch was hewn from the solid rock to secure it from the south and east, a triumph of engineering.

lords. David I, who ruled in the middle of the twelfth century, had been brought up at the English court and set out to create a kingdom on the English model with its power base in the Lothian area of the Lowlands. During his reign castles were built, dioceses were established and north-west Scotland and the Western Isles brought under his sway. The thirteenth century was a settled period with close connections with England, for sisters of both Henry III and Edward I were queens of Scotland. But, in 1286, the opportunity to alter all that came when Alexander III died leaving no immediate heir.

Edward I saw this as a means whereby he might bend Scotland to his will and

make it share the fate of Wales. As the overlord, he was called upon to preside over the court which had to decide which out of thirteen claimants should be the next king in what was called the Great Cause. Edward only undertook this on the understanding that whoever was chosen would pay him homage along with the Scottish barons. Out of the two leading clamaints, John Balliol and Robert Bruce, Edward chose the former. At first everything went well but when it became apparent that Edward intended to reduce Scotland to utter dependency there was revolt. Edward then planned for conquest along the lines of Wales, intending to build castles and introduce English officials, administration and law. The Scots resisted but they were defeated by Edward's campaign in 1296 when he was so victorious that he was able to carry off the Stone of Destiny, on which the kings of Scotland were crowned, from Scone to Westminster Abbey.

But Edward's Scottish plan was not to succeed. The reason for this was twofold. In the first instance the Scots had a sense of collective identity and loyalty far stronger than the Welsh. More serious was the king's financial plight as successive Parliaments proved increasingly reluctant to meet his demands. He was even reduced to seizing the money in church treasuries destined for the Crusade. This lack of financial resources meant, for instance, building castles of wood and not stone.

The Scots turned to Robert Bruce as their king and found a leader in William Wallace, a brilliant and ruthless exponent of the art of guerilla warfare. The tide began to turn when he defeated the English at the Battle of Stirling Bridge. Thenceforth, year in and year out, a major campaign was fought each summer. Eventually William Wallace was captured, brought to London and barbarously executed. As the war dragged on Edward became more and more vindictive. In 1305 he abolished the kingdom of Scotland altogether and declared it merely a 'land' subject to him. In defiance the Scots crowned Robert Bruce. The year after, 1307, Edward died setting out to campaign once again. He instructed his servants not to bury him but to carry his bones with the army until such time as the Scots were defeated. His son, Edward, disregarded his father's dying commands and he was buried in Westminster Abbey.

Chapter Fourteen

AN INCOMPETENT KING

E DWARD II's coronation foretold in ritual the catastrophe to come. In the procession a handsome young Gascon knight, Piers Gaveston, recently created Earl of Cornwall, carried the crown of St. Edward. In his robes of purple velvet embroidered with pearls, Gaveston outshone every other noble present. For a newly created earl to take one of the leading ceremonial roles on such an occasion was seen as a calculated affront. It was one which Gaveston made worse by deliberately dressing to eclipse his peers all of whom wore the traditional cloth of gold. Envy and resentment set in and he was never to be forgiven. For the first time the natural balance of crown and nobility was seriously put out by a new phenomenon, the royal favourite, someone with whom a ruler was so infatuated that he not only showered that person with riches and honours but would listen to him and to him alone.

Although medieval history records the clashes of king and barons, for the majority of the time they worked together in harmony governing the state. That harmony was achieved by the king keeping a rigorous check on the distribution of rewards and benefits known as patronage. To obtain the support of his nobles the king had vast resources which he could call upon: grants of land, the bestowal of rich heiresses, the allocation of wardships of heirs to great estates, besides positions at court. Edward I had been brilliant at this, having even more to give away to the barons as a result of his successful Welsh campaigns. His son, Edward II, still had much at his disposal, but the problem was that what he had he gave to the wrong people, men who were greedy, ruthless and ambitious. In the end this was to ruin him.

But none of that could be foreseen when Edward came to the throne in 1307 amidst a surge of optimism. He was then twenty-three. Tall, good-looking, with fair curly hair, muscular in build, he was a keen addict of the open air life, not only hunting but other forms of sport, such as boating and swimming, which were then viewed as being unkingly. That was not, however, his only unkingly trait, for he loved to spend time on menial work of the type undertaken by peasants, like hedging, ditching and plastering. In common with all his family he was subject to wild fits of temper, but that was less damaging than his inclination to laziness and lack of decision. His real

undoing, however, was his passion for male favourites. Although the father of four children by Isabella of France, 'a most elegant lady and beautiful woman', Edward was homosexual by nature, something viewed then as a mortal sin on the level with heresy. All of this combined dramatically to lower respect for the monarchy.

Head of Edward II from his tomb in Gloucester Cathedral. Constructed at the behest of his son it was conceived as one for a martyr with prayer niches for pilgrims to use. The cult of Edward as a saint was to be short-lived. The effigy of the king was carved from alabaster.

In the eyes of the king, Piers Gaveston could do no wrong, and he was showered with rewards which made him more and more envied and disliked. He was far from tactful. After the coronation he went on to unhorse and defeat many of the greatest nobles at the tournament staged to celebrate the event. His biting, witty tongue mocked and derided them. To each of the great earls he accorded a nickname. Gloucester was 'whoreson' or 'cuck-old's bird', Lincoln 'broste belly', Leicester 'the fiddler' and Warwick 'black hound of Arden'. 'Let him call me hound,' the earl exclaimed. 'One day the hound will bite him.'

The king's relationship with Gaveston went back a long way. Indeed his father had been so enraged with his son that he had torn out great handfuls of his hair from his head in anger over it. Soon after Edward came to the throne the earls met, anxious to curb what they regarded as the growing power of the king and to curtail the influence of his favourite. They agreed to act to secure the reform of 'things which have been done before this time contrary to his [the king's] honour and rights of the crown'. When Edward was crowned there was an additional phrase added to the coronation oath, in which he promised to obey 'the rightful laws and customs which the community of the realm shall have chosen'. Both of these moves represented their unease and their deep distrust of Piers Gaveston whose exile the earls obtained.

But Edward could not live without Gaveston, and soon afterwards he returned. So wildly unpopular was he that the king began to lose the support of barons who had always been loyal to the crown. What made matters worse was that Edward failed to create any new group to replace those who joined the opposition. In 1311 he was presented with a long list of demands by the barons called the Ordinances which included Gaveston's exile. This the king refused to accept. Both the king and his favourite went north. Gaveston was besieged by the barons in Scarborough Castle and was forced to surrender, albeit promised safe conduct. He was led south, when an even greater disaster befell him. He was captured by his deadliest enemy, the man he had jeeringly named the 'black hound of Arden', the Earl of Warwick. Warwick had only one thing in mind, vengeance. He took Gaveston off to Warwick Castle, where he was tried and convicted by the earls. The favourite was executed a mile north of the town amidst scenes of mob enthusiasm and blowing of horns. When the king heard the news he said, 'By God's soul, he acted like a fool. If he had taken my advice he would never have fallen into the hands of the earls.'

During the next decade the earls found a leader in the king's cousin, Thomas of Lancaster. His power was enormous, having inherited five earldoms, maintaining a huge retinue and having as many armed knights in his services as the king. Unfortunately, like Edward, he too was lazy, lacking vision and direction. During these years the barons dominated the king whose position was pathetically weak. His only chance to retrieve the situation failed. In 1314 he led the largest army against the Scots since his father's campaigns. On 23 and 24 June the English suffered defeat at the Battle of Bannockburn, their armoured knights floundering in the bog which the Scots had deliberately chosen as the site for combat. Victory could have restored Edward's fortunes. Defeat only hastened his ruin.

The same year was marked by heavy rains which returned again the next year. It poured down from the skies seemingly without ceasing. Even if seed did germinate

The Battle of Bannockburn in
June 1314 as depicted in a
fifteenth century Scottish
manuscript.

the grain rotted on the stalk. This meant that following defeat in battle came hunger and starvation. The price for what little food there was rocketed. The huge households of the nobility were drastically reduced in size, which only added to the numbers of the distressed. As there was little with which to feed the cattle, disease set in. Fewer cattle meant fewer oxen with which to plough the fields. It also meant less meat, cheese and milk. These were years of utter misery for the whole population.

The responsibility for much of this was laid at the door not of the king but of Thomas of Lancaster and the earls. Edward began to form a new group of favourites but once again the barons demanded and obtained their removal. Then, when the Scots took Berwick, it was seen even more as the fault of the earls. By then Edward had a new favourite, Hugh Despencer, who, like Gaveston, was greedy and ambitious. Despencer's aim was to build up a huge estate in South Wales and in doing so he upset the lords of the Marches who seized his lands and demanded and got his exile. This time, however, the king rallied his forces against the barons and defeated them under the leadership of Thomas of Lancaster at the Battle of Boroughbridge. At last, ten years on, the king was able to have his revenge for their treatment of Piers Gaveston. Just as Gaveston had been mocked and jeered at before his execution so Thomas of Lancaster was forced to ride to his on a 'lean white palfrey' with a tattered and torn hat put on his head. It was winter and the crowds lining the route pelted him with snowballs. As it was alleged that he had looked to the enemy, Scotland, to help him he was made to kneel facing northwards to be executed.

That was the signal for a bloodbath on a scale not seen before. On the advice of the young Despencer and his father, a reign of terror followed aimed at wiping out the opposition. Twenty-five nobles were executed, others went to prison or into exile. Many were forced to buy their freedom by means of crippling fines. The Ordinances of 1311 were annulled. The Despencers now grasped at everything they could in the way of money and lands. Men were made to pay them fictitious debts. Rich heiresses and widows were harassed until they parted with their estates. Royal funds paid for the Despencers' every whim. The opposition to all of this came from a most unexpected quarter, the queen, now seen no longer as that 'most elegant lady and beautiful woman' but as that 'she-wolf' of France. Edward had already abandoned Isabella. As he came to realise just how strong-willed she was he vowed that, if he had no other weapon, he would crush her with his own teeth.

The queen left England with her son Edward, the Prince of Wales, for France where he was bethrothed to the daughter of the Count of Hainault. There Isabella was joined by many exiles from England including Roger Mortimer, who had been condemned to death but who drugged the guards in the Tower of London at the banquet he gave on the eve of his execution and escaped. He became the queen's lover and, together with a small band of mercenaries from the Count of Hainault, they landed in Suffolk in September 1326. So unpopular was the king that members of his household fled. London threw open its gates in joy. In the face of this, Edward and the two Despencers panicked and left for Wales. Horror now piled on horror. The elder Despencer was caught up with at Bristol and this time it was the turn of the barons to exact revenge. He was tried and hanged, drawn and quartered amidst the cries of the townspeople. Meanwhile the king and the younger Despencer set sail from Chepstow and landed in Glamorgan. Their fate was to be even more appalling, for they were captured by Thomas of Lancaster's youngest brother, Henry. Despencer was carried to Hereford and barbarously executed.

The king was taken to Kenilworth castle. He refused to attend Parliament which, when it met, was told in a sermon by the Archbishop of Canterbury that Edward, by consent of the magnates, clergy and people, was no longer king. A deputation, including representatives of all these groups, was sent to Kenilworth to inform him. Edward fainted with grief and then begged for mercy, agreeing to resign his throne on condition that his son succeed him.

No one knows the fate of Edward II. It remains one of the great mysteries of British history. Roger Mortimer certainly plotted his death but did he succeed? One account would lead us to believe that he did. According to this the king was deliberately imprisoned in squalor and finally murdered at Berkeley Castle. Another account is so extraordinary that it could be true. In this Edward succeeds in escaping by killing the porter. He journeyed first to Ireland, then to France, where he was received by the pope at Avignon, and finally to Italy, where he became a hermit. Whatever his fate a splendid tomb was erected to him in Gloucester Cathedral.

The triumph of Queen Isabella and Mortimer, now Earl of March, was by no means one of right over wrong. In fact all it meant was that one group of ruthless and greedy people had replaced another. For three years these two ruled England disastrously, until, once more, an opposition formed to remove them. That failed, but their fate was to be sealed by the young Edward III. Unlike his father, Edward had a knack for choosing the right associates. In 1330 he and his friends gained entrance to Nottingham Castle, by way of underground tunnels, and confronted the queen and Mortimer. Isabella begged, 'Good son, good son, have pity on gentle Mortimer,' but none was forthcoming. He was taken to London, tried and executed. The queen went into an enforced retirement, spent reading romances and eventually becoming a Franciscan nun.

The real reign of Edward III now began but with a terrible legacy. For twenty-five years the country had been ruled by an incompetent king challenged by incompetent nobles. There had been defeat in war, and famine. Never had there been such horrendous and cruel bloodshed as revenge took its toll. Beneath this melodrama real problems were fought out about the relationship of king and barons. The barons wished to limit the king's power, his right to select ministers and grant lands to whom he thought fit. They viewed the royal household as a sink of iniquity peopled by shifty and unsavoury characters out to get what they could. Despicable as the king was he had, nonetheless, a case for his rights as an efficient way of running the country. When one earl said to him, 'King, if you destroy your barons, you indeed make light of your own honour,' he replied, 'There is no one who is sorry for me; none fights for my rights against them.'

In the midst of these struggles Parliament grew in importance, almost by accident, for it gave either side a means of making it seem that they had popular support. With a strong king, like Edward I, Parliament was used to show that the nation backed his aggressive policies. With a weak one, like Edward II, those who came together ceased meekly to assent to the king's proposals, and began to initiate ones of their own. As both king and barons wished to demonstrate that they acted on behalf of the whole country, the two sides were anxious that representatives of the shires and the towns were always included. The magnates were summoned by royal writ. The knights of the shires and the burgesses of the boroughs were elected in response to writs. The task of the magnates was to advise and debate great policy matters. The knights and the burgesses were there to sanction taxes to pay for that policy. The Scottish war gave them more and more power which they used as a lever to get what they wanted before agreeing to confirm the taxes. When they returned home their task was to tell everyone what had been decided. In this way, more and more people became involved in the process of governing the country.

Never had the monarchy sunk so low in public esteem as during the reign of Edward II. The fact that the king was a failure did not in any way, however, shake people's belief in the sanctity of the crown and its position at the summit of the social pyramid. With the accession of a more than capable king, everything was to go into reverse and its glory was to return.

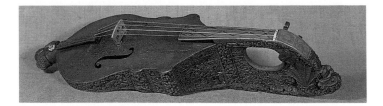

An early fourteenth century gittern, an instrument which would have been played like a guitar. The instrument was carved from a single piece of wood.

Chapter Fifteen

THE HUNDRED YEARS WAR

THIS king Edward,' wrote the chronicler Froissart, 'was forsooth of a passing goodness, and full gracious among all the worthy men of the world.' For over half a century Edward III was to rule England as an ideal king until old age and the loss of his beloved queen began to erode the powers which had made him great. Like his grandfather, on whom he modelled himself, Edward was supremely endowed with all the attributes looked for in a medieval king. He was a brave general in battle, a born leader of men in time of peace, generous too, with an abundance of charm and good humour which endeared him to all with whom he came into contact. Edward set out to make himself a paragon of the chivalrous virtues, living out to the full the exploits of King Arthur and his court as they were recorded in the romances which were the fashionable reading of the age. Indeed he transformed Windsor Castle into his Camelot, a haven of chivalrous endeavour to which knights flocked from all over Europe in tribute to his fame. Pageantry and splendour were the order of the day from a ruler who was to be a mighty patron of architects, painters and musicians. Under Edward III the crown regained its vanished lustre.

Edward married Philippa of Hainault in 1328 and for forty years she stood by his side as a steadying influence, one which could curb the notorious Plantagenet rages, as when she interceded after the siege of Calais for the lives of its good citizens. She provided the king with no less than twelve surviving children, presiding over a royal family which was unique in being both united and happy. Unlike former reigns none of the king's sons plotted or revolted against him in old age.

That is a fair indication of the character of the man, one which ensured his widespread popularity with his people. It is caught too in this anecdote, recorded by Froissart, describing him on board ship shortly before a naval battle:

' . . . the king stood at his ship's prow, clad in a jacket of black velvet, and on his head a hat of black beaver that became him right well; and he was then . . . as merry as ever he was seen. He made his minstrels sound before him

on their trumpets a German dance that had been brought in of late by Lord John Chandos, who was there present; and then for pastime he made the said knight sing with his minstrels, and took great pleasure therein. While the king thus took his pleasure . . . the watch cried: "Ho! I see a ship coming, and me thinks it is a ship of Spain!" Then the minstrels held their peace . . .'

Sir Geoffrey Luttrell, Lord of Irnham, in Lincolnshire together with his wife, Agnes Sutton, in a miniature in his psalter executed about 1325 to 1335. The manuscript is filled with marginal scenes depicting everyday life in the early fourteenth century.

As the enemy fleet appeared the king ordered wine and 'then he laced on his helm, and the rest did likewise.' The English then won a resounding victory.

What is striking about his reign is its political and social stability in the face of a major war and the horrors of the plague known as the Black Death. The king owed his success at home to the fact that, unlike his father, he realised the importance of the correct use of patronage in keeping the nobles loyal and contented with his rule.

He created new earls, granting them lands, and even married some of his daughters into the nobility, thus forging further ties of loyalty to the crown. But the greatest binding factor of them all was to be the war with France known as the Hundred Years War, one which, in fact, lasted one hundred and fifteen years in all.

The causes of this war were complex. In 1328 a new dynasty succeeded to the throne of France, the Valois. In that country the right to succeed could only pass through men and never through a woman, a principle which was called the Salic Law. That was not true in England where women could succeed to the crown. If such had been the case in France Edward III would have had the greater claim to be king of France because of his mother Isabella, than Philip VI, the first Valois king. But Edward initially never queried his right and indeed paid the new king homage for his French lands.

As time passed, however, relations between the two countries began to deteriorate sharply. There were squabbles over boundaries, legal disputes and commercial rivalry. There were above all clashes in the Netherlands which were crucial for the English wool trade. In the Channel French and English ships came to blows. Then there was Scotland, whose alliance with France meant entry to England through the back door. Add to that Edward's desire to take up the torch from his warrior grandfather and all the ingredients for a major conflict were in place.

Legend has it that at a great feast there was set before the king a heron, chosen deliberately as the most cowardly of all the birds, a fit dish in the eyes of the host for a monarch who had failed to claim his rightful inheritance. Not long after this, Edward asserted his right to the French crown and, in 1340, assumed publicly the title of king of France, quartering onto his coat of arms the lilies of France which remain there to this day. As a consequence this war was to be different from all its predecessors, for it was no longer to be vassal versus overlord but true king against usurper.

This was a war undertaken with all the fervour of a crusade. That God was perceived to be the ultimate judge of the victor was reflected in the repeated challenges to single combat hurled at each other by the two kings. These never happened but every campaign and battle was fought with the full panoply of chivalry. Edward III played his role to the full, riding at the head of his troops into battle, rallying them on the eve with a speech. His son, Edward of Woodstock, called the Black Prince probably on account of his black armour, was even more celebrated than his father, being hailed as 'the flower of chivalry of all the world'. At the age of sixteen he was already leading part of the English forces into the battle.

The war united every class behind the king. The nobles and knights lived out a chivalrous ideal, vowing to their ladies that they would not do this or that until such time as they had fulfilled this or that feat of arms. Edward rallied his knights even in time of peace by holding spectacular tournaments, arenas for training young knights in how to fight and in the rules of chivalry. He rebuilt Windsor Castle as a setting for the great festivals of chivalry which he staged. In 1348 he founded a special fraternity or order, the Knights of the Garter, whose motto challenged anyone who dared oppose the English claim to the French crown: *Honi soit qui mal y pense* (Shame to him who thinks evil of it).

To nobles and knights alike the war was not only acting out a role, it was also highly profitable. After each English victory there would be huge ransoms to be paid for captured French knights, so huge that whole castles were built from the proceeds. Not only that but the ordinary soldiers, men-at-arms and archers, also did well. The chronicler of Walsingham wrote: 'There were few women who did not have something from Caen, Calais and other overseas towns; clothing, furs, bedcovers, cutlery. Tablecloths and linen, bowls in wood and silver were to be seen in every English house.' More to the point such men were better paid and equipped than ever before. The skilled English archers were now deployed to devastating effect as their arrows rained down on the enemy from both sides. Armour too had developed, so that knights were better protected than ever. Cannon made their earliest appearance, heralding the age of gunpowder. On top of that, the wars against the Scots had taught the English a great deal about tactics, particularly the value of the plundering raid during which whole villages would be destroyed, the countryside laid to waste and the population slaughtered. For decades the French war was to be hugely popular with all sections of society, for the king was also a master of public relations, sharing with his people the justice of his cause and his victories by way of speeches in Parliament, sermons in the parish pulpit, and the circulation of newsletters.

For over two decades the English won victory after victory. In 1339 the French fleet was routed at Sluys. Seven years later there came an even more famous victory at Crécy thanks to the king's skill as a general and the abilities of the archers. That was followed by the siege and surrender of the port of Calais which was to remain in English hands for two centuries. Edward evacuated the starving citizens, giving them a square meal as they left, and later repopulating the town with English settlers. Ten years later came another legendary battle, Poitiers, in which the young Black Prince was the hero, and the French king was captured. As an index of the chivalrous code of the time the prince waited on his regal captive at table. The French king was taken to England, making an entrance into London during which he was showered with golden leaves. He was consigned to a luxurious prison in the Tower of London.

That glorious phase of the war came to an end in 1360 when peace was made and

the vast ransom of three million pounds was paid for the French king. The English lands in France were enlarged as they now included Calais, and they were all held in

A 14th century document depicts the granting of Aquitaine to the Black Prince, who kneels before his father, Edward III.

full sovereignty. Although the war was renewed again in the 1370s it was never as successful. By then Edward was old and the Black Prince ill. He was to predecease his father. The Valois kings shrewdly avoided battle and gradually re-established themselves, for the brutal savagery of the English to the French had not increased support for Edward III's rule. Any idea of giving the French justice and good government was remote from his mind. The war meant profits. There was to be no return to the continental empire of Henry II.

Behind all the pomp and pageantry attending these triumphs, however, lurked the figure of the money-lender. The king went bankrupt twice. There were the wages of the soldiers, once paid at twice the going rate, there was the cost of transport and victuals, besides the huge financial subsidies he gave to allies abroad to send in armies. As a result Edward fell into the hands of Italian money-lenders who in the end went bankrupt themselves. Then he turned to English merchants. Parliament was perpetually being pressed for funds and, as a result, gradually secured greater and greater control of the purse strings. However hostile or critical Parliament became over the cost of the war, Edward's hold always managed to ride it out.

Criticism became sharper as the king moved into old age. When his queen died in 1369 a restraining hand was removed. Increasingly Edward grew indolent, falling under the influence of his greedy mistress, Alice Perrers, who was out for every penny she could get. At a great tournament held at Smithfield she appeared as the Lady of the Sun decked out in the late queen's jewels. As Edward lay on his deathbed she is said to have pulled the rings off his fingers and fled.

Edward died at the age of sixty-five and was buried in Westminster Abbey. On his tomb we see his effigy in bronze, not that of the golden-haired young knight but resembling rather an Old Testament prophet with flowing locks and beard. By him lies his beloved queen, Philippa, and around the sides of the tomb stand his twelve children, who were, with their descendants, to be the ruin of the house of Plantagenet. In retrospect the reign of Edward III was soon to be seen as a golden age in which the fortunes of the late medieval monarchy reached their heights both in terms of popularity and achievement.

Weepers from the tomb of Edward III in Westminster Abbey. These depict three of the king's sons.

Chapter Sixteen

THE BLACK DEATH

NOTHING quite so terrible as the Black Death had ever been experienced in England before. William of Dene, a monk of Rochester, records what happened in his part of Kent:

'To our great grief the plague carried off so vast a multitude of people of both sexes that nobody could be found who would bear the corpses to the grave. Men and women carried their own children on their shoulders to the church and threw them into a common pit. From these pits such an appalling stench was given off that scarcely anyone dared even walk beside the cemeteries.'

So many people died in the household of the Bishop of Rochester, which was a small one, that 'nobody was left to serve him in any capacity'; in all four priests, five esquires, ten attendants, seven young clerics and six pages died. All over the country the story was more or less the same, as the plague claimed between a quarter and a third of the entire population.

To people at the time this could only be the judgement of God on their sinfulness. Supernatural warnings of the coming disaster had been sighted all over Europe. Astrologers scanned the heavens for portents of doom and were rewarded by a really evil conjunction of the stars which took place on 20 March 1345: the planets Saturn, Jupiter and Mars were in the house of the zodiacal sign Aquarius, the water bearer. Saturn and Jupiter spelt death and destruction. Mars and Jupiter with Aquarius signalled a pestilence which would be spread through the air. And it was believed that such diseases travelled through the atmosphere, drifting like mists or clouds across the sky out of the east, and then mysteriously descending to engulf a city or a whole region.

When the plague arrived in 1348 no one knew what it was. Everyone was stunned both by the speed with which it travelled and by that with which it killed. Men were said to fall down and die with only a glance from a victim. In no time the symptoms were familiar, boils which could be the size of an apple in the groin, armpits or neck, then the rapid spread of the disease through the rest of the body, producing black spots on the skin. Those who spat blood died in three days, the rest in five. It came to be known in Latin as *pestis atra* or *atra mors* which translated into English meant the 'dread', 'terrible' or 'black' pestilence or death.

Today we know that this was almost without doubt bubonic plague, a contagious disease usually found in remote areas of the world, like West Arabia or North India, which could and did from time to time escape and travel west. The middle of the fourteenth century was the occasion for just such an escape, one which, in the case of England, was not finally to leave its shore until after the Great Plague of London in 1665. And it was not carried by mysterious mists and clouds but by black rats, who carried the fleas with the germ as they migrated along the trade routes from the east through Baghdad, Armenia and the Crimea and then on by boat across the Mediterranean into the ports and from thence across country. And it was not just bubonic plague but two other ghastly forms as well, one in which the lungs were attacked resulting in bloodspitting, and a second which fatally infected the bloodstream within hours. All three were lethal. All were unpleasant diseases, filthy, unsightly, odious, evoking fear and panic in everyone who came in contact with a victim. In the countries of mainland Europe the plague produced outbreaks of mass hysteria as people implored heaven to bring these horrors to an end.

Nothing quite so dramatic happened in England but the results were as devastating. It seems the plague arrived first by way of the port of Melcombe Regis in Dorset towards the end of June 1348. At first it spread only slowly but by late July and August it was moving fast across the West Country, striking the two cities of Exeter and Bristol. It then moved on towards the Thames Valley which it reached by March. By July it was heading northwards, although by then it had been gaining entry through other ports. Those cities and towns which believed that they could remain immune by closing their gates were wrong, for the black rats got in through the ditches and sewers.

Nowhere was its impact more catastrophic than on the capital, London. In one of the two huge new cemeteries created outside the walls to receive the dead an inscription read:

> 'A great plague raging in the year of our Lord 1349, this churchyard was consecrated; wherein . . . were buried more than fifty thousand bodies of the dead . . . whose souls God have mercy upon. Amen.'

The more likely figure was half that amount but no one can blame them for the exaggeration, stunned as they were by the daily sight of the long procession of carts piled high with corpses. London was ripe for the plague. It was crowded. Everyone ate and slept together. The narrow lanes were deep in mud and filth and sanitation was primitive, in the main tipping or draining everything which had to be disposed of into the Thames.

An illumination to a text of the mass to be said in times of pestilence.

The plague spared no one, rich or poor, clergy or laity. Indeed the clergy suffered badly for, as they ministered to the sick and dying, they had a much greater chance of being infected. But that was not how it was seen at the time. The poor thought that the rich got off lightly, seeing them close their houses and leave for what they thought was the safety of the country. The clergy who were remembered were not those who bravely stayed behind, but those who abandoned their flock. As one monk wrote: 'In this plague many chaplains and hired parish priests would not serve without excessive pay.' But all over the country the impact of the plague was different. Some areas fared well, others very badly.

1349 was not the only year the plague ravaged. The Black Death haunted the late fourteenth century. It was to come back time and again to claim its victims. Over ten years later, in 1361, it returned, this time being called the 'mortality of infants', for mostly children and babies died. It was to come back yet again in 1369 and 1375.

William of Wykeham founded
New College, Oxford, in 1379 to
train clergy to fill the places left
by the Black Death. By tradition
the college was built on the
site of the city's plague pit.

Every time this happened the population shrank and so did the amount of land under
cultivation. At the same time those few who were left untouched could charge more
for their work so wages went up. So scarce was labour that at times livestock wan-
dered in the fields untended, and at harvest-time the crops perished, for there was no
one to bring them in. Henry Knighton's chronicle, the most complete contemporary
account of the epidemic, vividly paints a picture of England in the aftermath:

'After the pestilence many buildings both great and small in all cities, towns and boroughs fell into total ruin for lack of inhabitants; similarly many small villages and hamlets became desolate and no houses were left in them, for all those who dwelt in them were dead, and it seemed likely that many such little villages would never again be inhabited.'

The greatest loss, however, was probably sustained by the church. Not only did the behaviour of many of the clergy lose them respect but death wiped out virtually half of those in orders. The result was that many of those ordained in haste to fill the gaps lacked a sense of true vocation and brought the church into disrepute. As a consequence colleges were founded both in Oxford and Cambridge to train clergy to meet the dramatic need for men of real quality. William of Wykeham, Bishop of Winchester, founded New College in Oxford in 1380 with a garden on the site of what had been the city's largest plague pit.

The Black Death left men with a sense of spiritual crisis to which the church in its existing form failed adequately to respond. It gave rise to a sense of deep unease and overwhelming gloom as all through the decades down to 1400 danced the figure of Death, claiming his victims, bishop and abbot, parish priest and monk, noble and knight, merchant and craftsman, freeman or villein, rich and poor, young and old. Over all of them his menacing scythe hovered, waiting to strike.

Even in an age accustomed to infant mortality and death by the age of forty as the norm, the suddenness of the plague brought judgement day almost into the present. This was the era when around the chancel arches of the parish churches what was called a Doom was painted, the terrible Last Judgement when men would be called to account. Those who had led the good life would be gathered up by the angels and led to paradise but those who had sinned would be seized by the talons of devils to be cast into everlasting torment. The Black Death signalled that the day of reckoning was indeed at hand.

A fifteenth century jewel depicting the Trinity and with the word 'Anazapta', a charm against the plague.

Chapter Seventeen

THE GREAT REVOLT

When Adam delved and Eve span
Who was then a gentleman?

THIS was the couplet used by the priest John Ball when preaching to the thousands of peasants gathered outside London who made up the Great Revolt. What he spoke about was social revolution:

'In the beginning all men were equal: servitude man to man was introduced by the unjust dealings of the wicked. For if God had intended some to be serfs and others lords, He would have made a distinction between them at the beginning.'

There had never before in England been such an eruption of the lowest and most deprived classes of society. It threatened everything that the medieval world held as God-ordained, a structure descending in pyramid form with the king at the top to lord, knight, squire, burgess and freeman. All of these, however, were represented in Parliament and their voices could be heard in the government of the realm. Below them was the vast mass of the population, the poor villeins and wage-earners, who had no such voice. For a few months, during the summer of 1381, the governing classes were stunned into shock and inaction when this underclass all but succeeded in toppling them from power.

The revolt occurred four years into the reign of the new king, Richard II, son of the Black Prince and grandson of Edward III. He was only ten when he came to the throne in 1377 so that many quoted the biblical verse: 'Woe be to thee, O land, when thy king is a child.' Richard was tall and delicately featured, with wavy fair hair and blue eyes. His every gesture was regal and his coronation was staged as a great spectacle designed to impress on everyone the sanctity of an anointed king. But in fact for many years real power lay in the hands of the great lords and magnates and in those of his mother, Princess Joan, known when young as 'the Fair Maid of Kent'. The policy they pursued was the ruinous one of war with France.

The Great Revolt was triggered off by the need for money to continue that struggle. In 1380 Parliament imposed what was called a poll-tax on the whole adult population of the kingdom. The amount was one shilling. Men like carters, ploughmen and shepherds only earned about thirteen shillings and four pence a year. The average monthly wage for a man and his family was just about a shilling. The poll-tax was a monument to the greed and selfishness of those in Parliament, for they deliberately pushed the burden of taxation onto those who were unrepresented. When it came to collection, there was widespread evasion. So large was the shortfall that in the spring of 1381 government officials were sent out into the shires to force its collection. The result was open revolt, for the tax was the final straw in a list of grievances which had lain smouldering over several decades.

There is no chronicle which tells us the story of this revolt from the viewpoint of the revolutionaries. They were illiterate and often inarticulate men whose lot in life cannot be described as anything other than wretched. The villeins led an existence just short of animal. They were tied to their lord's manor, receiving in return for service strips of land scattered over what might be several large fields. They lived in huts of wattle and daub, together with their animals and fowls. The floor was mud, and there was no chimney. From dawn till dusk they laboured in the fields, three of those days working on the lord's land, tending and shearing his sheep, feeding his swine, and sowing and reaping his crops. There was no escaping the lord of the manor for they were bound to take their grain to his mill for grinding and their flour to his bakehouse for bread. Sometimes the miller and baker were dishonest. A villein could not even marry without his lord's permission and when he died the lord took his best beast.

The second best beast was taken by the church. The priest in fact took a tenth of everything a villein produced, which was called the tithe. This included all his crops whether in the fields or the kitchen garden, honey, milk, and firewood too. The villeins of England were slaves in all but name.

But in the late fourteenth century things were changing due to the effects of the Black Death. As the population fell dramatically, labour became expensive and villeins, growing prosperous, could sometimes buy their freedom. Most, however, were refused it and the result was bitter frustration. This frustration was made even worse by the Statute of Labourers in 1351 which laid down that wages had to remain the same as they were before the plague. Any villein caught being paid more or, worse, leaving his lord's manor to be better treated elsewhere, was punished either by fine, imprisonment, the stocks or pillory. They had no rights. The attempt to freeze wages not only aroused bitterness in the country; in the towns, too, it affected craftsmen who were wage-earners, people like weavers, tilers and tailors. There it was a case of employers versus employed.

The most conservative and unbending of all the landlords was the church. No wonder then that the ordinary people listened intently to what was said by some priests in their pulpits when they denounced the sinfulness of the clergy. In particular they would have heard such things from the followers of John Wycliffe, known as the Lollards, who believed that the role of the church was a spiritual and not a temporal one, criticising its great riches and power, and believing that these should be taken away.

What was so remarkable about the Great Revolt was its speed and suddenness, evidence of a widespread network working in unison. On the very last day of May there were simultaneous risings in Kent and Essex. In Kent the peasants stormed and took Rochester Castle and later Canterbury. In Essex they took Colchester, Brentwood and Chelmsford. The discontented massed in thousands and soon their leaders emerged, Jack Straw in Essex and Wat Tyler in Kent. Everywhere they went they released prisoners but above all they burnt documents: court rolls and tax lists, anything which recorded serfdom. Landlords were seized and forced to give their villeins charters of freedom. Everyone was asked to swear loyalty to 'King Richard and the true Commons', for they did not blame the king but his wicked advisers.

By 12 June both groups had converged on London, the Essex men at Mile End and the Kentish men on Blackheath. They then sacked Southwark and the Archbishop of Canterbury's palace of Lambeth. The government was panic-stricken and powerless. The army was at Plymouth, about to embark for France. So the king and his mother took refuge in the Tower. Richard was only fourteen but he agreed to meet Wat Tyler on the banks of the Thames. On 13 June he and members of his council took barge for Greenwich. The king called to the rebels: 'Sirs, what have you to say to me? Tell me, I came here to talk to you.' The rebels shouted back, bidding them land, but those attending the king were so paralysed with fear that they ordered the barge to row back to the Tower.

Through treachery, the rebels gained admittance to the city, inside which they had many supporters. There were terrible scenes. They hated the king's uncle, John of Gaunt, so his splendid palace of the Savoy was sacked and burnt to the ground. Next they turned to the Temple in the Inns of Court, seat of the equally hated lawyers. That was plundered and then the mob advanced on the Tower, threatening to kill everyone in it unless the king met them. The Council was divided, but many urged what was in fact to happen, to grant the rebels everything and then later rescind it on the grounds that it had been exacted by force. It called for exceptional bravery by the young king who agreed to the meeting which was to take place at Mile End outside the city.

On 14 June it was recorded that Richard rode forth 'like a lamb among wolves' to face sixty thousand peasants attended by only a few nobles. He was fearless, and bravely rode into their midst, proclaiming: 'Good people, I am your lord and king. What do you have to say to me?' They petitioned for the abolition of villeinage, 'so that we shall never again be called serfs and bondmen.' The king agreed that their former service to their lord be replaced by an annual payment of four pence per acre. Thirty clerks were also ordered to draw up pardons for the rebels. They then started to disperse homewards, and the king and his attendants began to return to the Tower.

There, in his absence, scenes of untold horror had taken place for someone had stupidly left the drawbridge down. The mob invaded the palace, seizing the archbishop and others and executing them all. Princess Joan was carried by the mob to the Queen's Wardrobe, a repository near St. Paul's, where the king joined her. Anarchy then reigned in London.

The rebels gained access to the Tower of London where they murdered several of the king's ministers, including the Archbishop of Canterbury. An illumination from Froissart's *Chronicles*.

A second conference was arranged, this time in the square at Smithfield, but on this occasion the king and his entourage, fearing violence, wore steel beneath their clothes. The king began by asking William Walworth, Lord Mayor of London, to summon Wat Tyler. Tyler came forward but showed no deference to the king who asked, 'Why do you not go home?' Another set of conditions followed which included the total abolition of serfdom and the confiscation of all church property to which the king agreed. Then, suddenly, a member of the king's train denounced Tyler as the most notorious thief in Kent. Tyler attempted to stab the man. Richard then ordered Walworth to arrest Tyler. A scuffle ensued in which Walworth was saved by his chain mail from being wounded by Tyler and a squire ran the rebel through with his sword, killing him.

A terrible moment then followed. The rebels drew their bows on the royal party but the king advanced towards them saying, 'Sirs, will you shoot your king? I will be your chief and captain, you shall have from me that which you seek. Only follow me to the fields without.' He then led them in the direction of Clerkenwell. Walworth meanwhile returned to the city, swiftly mustered seven thousand men and advanced to where the king and the rebels had gone, bearing Tyler's head on a lance. Richard, however, would not permit a massacre, and dismissed the rebels who thanked him for his clemency. They then swarmed off towards the country. The king returned to the Wardrobe where he was met by his mother in tears: 'Ah, fair son, what pain and anguish have I had for you this day!' Froissart relates she said. 'Certes, Madam,' he replied, 'I know it well. But now rejoice and praise God, for today I have recovered my heritage which was lost, and the realm of England also.' Such was the bravery of Richard of Bordeaux.

But that was not quite the end. The rebellion had to be crushed wherever it had taken place all through the country. In London the rebels, including their leader Jack Straw, were rounded up and executed by Walworth. In the country they were hunted down, hanged, drawn and quartered. The king's new Chief Justice browbeat juries to condemn rebels to death or imprisonment. But in terms of the age the treatment was not over-cruel. The Great Revolt was a failure, for villeinage went on and only died a slow death through the following century. What the governing classes learnt once and for all was never again unfairly to transfer the burden of taxation from the rich onto the poor.

The encounter of Richard II and Wat Tyler at Smithfield, the occasion when Tyler was killed, as depicted in Froissart's *Chronicles*.

Chapter Eighteen

THE FATE
OF RICHARD II

RICHARD II has been called the last medieval king. He was certainly the most complicated. His court set new standards of taste and magnificence. It was the royal cook who wrote the first English cookery book, *The Forme of Cury*, from the Latin *curare*, meaning to dress food. The king's palaces at Kennington, Sheen and Eltham were the wonders of the age. They had every luxury; at Sheen there were even baths with huge bronze taps giving hot and cold water. Richard was a connoisseur of architecture, sculpture, books, music and painting. He loved splendid clothes, embroidery and jewels. He even invented the handkerchief. Special pieces of material were provided for him on which he blew his nose. Up until then no one had bothered with such a thing. All of this did not mean that he would make a successful king.

In order to rule Richard needed the support of some of the most powerful lords. His grandfather, Edward III, had permitted the lords to raise private armies for the French war. These they retained, even in time of peace. England was dominated by a few great families such as the FitzAlans, Mowbrays, Beauchamps, Staffords, Percys and Nevilles, who had vast lands, castles and manors, making a series of states within a state. Even more powerful were the king's uncles, sons of Edward III, above all John of Gaunt, Duke of Lancaster. He was arrogant and boastful but he had huge energy and ambition. Through his second wife he claimed the throne of Castile. Richard always remained suspicious of his uncle but as king he had no choice other than to work with one group or other of the nobles. At the same time he sought to create men who depended wholly on the crown; this was resented both by the lords and by Parliament which they largely controlled. Parliament only met when the king summoned it, and that he did only when he needed money. Taxation was never popular and the Commons, abetted by some of the lords, used Parliament in order to criticise the king and his court. Every time the lords saw the king becoming more independent of them they set out to destroy his followers, sending them to exile or death. The tragedy of Richard II was that he was alone.

Richard II at about the age of thirty. The earliest portrait from life of a king of England, it has always hung in Westminster Abbey. It is likely that Richard commissioned this portrait to represent his perpetual presence in the choir of the Abbey, where he and his queen had worshipped. It would originally have been placed at the back of the king's pew.

The king also parted company with the great magnates in being a peacemaker. He realised that the long war with France which he inherited was ruining the country. The great lords always pressed for the war to be renewed, for through it they profited by plunder and ransoms. By wanting peace, Richard was also seen to be at odds with what the people believed a king should be, a brave knight and leader of the nation on the field of battle. In this he fell short of his hero father, the Black Prince, cherished as the ideal for him to follow. Instead the king, although fearless, was not physically strong and only took part once in the tournaments which were at the heart of court life. His view of what made a king depended not on battle but on the fact that he had been set apart from ordinary men at his coronation when he had been anointed as the chosen of God. The ceremony and etiquette of his court emphasised this, so that by the end of his reign it is recorded that:

> '. . . in solemn days and great feasts, in the which he weared his crown, and went in his royal array . . . and made in his chamber, a throne whereon he was wont to sit from after meat unto evensong speaking to no man, but over-looking all men, and if he looked on any man, what estate or degree that ever he were of, he must kneel.'

And kneel not once but three times. All through his life Richard clung to what was known as the royal prerogative, those rights which set him above everyone.

As a man Richard was intelligent, cultured, and passionately loyal to his friends. Like all the Plantagenets he was subject to sudden rages, and he became more neurotic as he grew older. He never forgot or forgave, nursing grudges until the opportunity arose to take vengeance. He was devoted to his queen, Anne of Bohemia, whom he married in 1382. She was sweet-natured and shared his interest in the elegancies of life. The fact that there were no children did not make for stability, for the succes-

The Wilton Diptych. This was a portable altarpiece almost certainly commissioned by the king himself for his own use. Its outside is decorated with emblems personal to Richard II but it opens to show the king being presented by three saints to the Virgin and Child attended by angels. Richard is said to have dedicated himself to the Virgin before riding out to face the Peasants' Revolt. Although painted about 1396-97 it shows the king as he was at his accession. At his breast he wears a jewel of a white hart, a favourite badge of his, which is also worn by the angels. From left to right behind him stand three saints whom he venerated: St. Edmund, the young Anglo-Saxon king of East Anglia, St. Edward the Confessor and St. John the Baptist. The king has just presented the Virgin with the island of Britain as her dowry. The island is painted on the globe atop the banner of St. George, held by one of the angels.

sion was always in doubt. When she died in 1394 his second wife, Isabella of France, was only eight. He was devoted to her too.

From his earliest years, following the defeat of the Great Revolt, the king tried to form his own circle of trusted advisers, men like his tutor, Sir Simon Burley, and Robert de Vere, Earl of Oxford, both of whom shared his love of the arts. Burley was always held to be one of those most responsible for Richard's exalted idea of kingship. Richard was able to pursue his policy of peace and truces were made with both France and Scotland. Inevitably those who were excluded from the king's inner circle gradually came to form an opposition. In 1385 one of the king's uncles, the malicious and vengeful Duke of Gloucester, together with the Earls of Warwick and Arundel, used Parliament to attack the king, demanding the removal of his ministers. 'I will not dismiss the meanest of my scullions at Parliament's command,' was his reply. Gloucester reminded his nephew of the terrible fate of Edward II and the young king was forced to give in. His friends and advisers were either dismissed or imprisoned. Parliament then appointed others in their place.

But the king knew that in capitulating, his royal prerogative had been infringed; he turned to the judges for their opinion and they agreed. As a result, by the end of the year both sides took to arms. The royal forces were defeated and their leader, Richard's friend, Robert de Vere, was forced to escape to France. The victors, now styled the Lords Appellant, took their revenge by means of what was called the Merciless Parliament. One by one the king's advisers were condemned without a trial. They were brutally executed or sent into exile. The queen even went on her knees to Arundel begging for the life of her husband's old tutor, Simon Burley, but he was callously executed. In one huge bloodbath the king lost almost everyone he most loved and trusted.

Richard never forgot this and he in his turn plotted revenge. It was to take him over a decade to achieve it. A year later he began to turn the tables on the Lords Appellant by the simple means of asking them how old he was. Gloucester answered that he was past twenty. Then the king said, 'Therefore I am of full age to govern myself, my household and my realm . . .' And so he dismissed Gloucester and appointed his own officers and advisers assuming himself the reins of government. Peace was once more made with France and then he turned his attention to Ireland, spending eight months there meeting the Irish chiefs and ordering those in England who had Irish estates to return to them. Few English kings have had such an enlightened interest in Ireland.

Meanwhile Gloucester and his allies plotted against Richard but they were foiled and arrested. In December 1397 Parliament was summoned but this time it was one in fear of the king, who surrounded it with his own army of loyal archers wearing his badge of the white hind. Gloucester had already been taken to Calais Castle where he was murdered. He was posthumously condemned for treason. Then came Arundel and Warwick. Arundel was sentenced to death and executed on the same spot on Tower Hill where Richard's beloved tutor had met his end. A death had been paid for by a death. Warwick, now old, was banished for life to the Isle of Man. Richard seemed triumphant. He celebrated by using his father's badge of the rising sun. At last at the age of thirty it seemed that he was truly king. But that was to prove a mirage.

The trouble with such actions was that it made the nobility feel unsafe. If Gloucester and his cronies could be treated in this way so could all of them. And the treatment of two more confirmed their suspicions. The dukes of Norfolk and Hereford fell out and it was agreed that their differences should be settled by trial by battle. This was a fight to the death, for whoever lost the fight was led away to be executed. Both men were famous for their prowess. Hereford, better known as Bolingbroke, was the king's cousin and heir to John of Gaunt, Duke of Lancaster. He was not only cultured and politically astute but a superb man-at-arms, athletic and strong, possessing the qualities people looked for in a medieval king. The cousins did not like each other.

On 16 September 1398 the whole court gathered at Gosforth just outside Coventry to watch the encounter. There were thousands of onlookers from all over Europe. The trumpets sounded for the combat to begin. The tents of the contestants were taken away and Bolingbroke placed his lance on his thigh, made the sign of the cross and began to advance. Suddenly the king, splendidly enthroned on high, stood up and cried, 'Ho! Ho!' throwing his staff down and stopping the fight to the consternation of the onlookers. He then banished Norfolk for life and Bolingbroke for ten years. Norfolk was to die in Venice but Bolingbroke's sentence was reduced to six years with the guarantee that he would inherit his father's huge estates.

On 2 February 1399 John of Gaunt, Duke of Lancaster, died. Richard broke his word and seized the estates. No one now felt safe. The great lords of the north, the Percys, protested and Richard ordered their arrest, but they fled. For Bolingbroke it was the final straw. He was persuaded to invade England but not at first with the idea of seizing the crown. Landing on 4 July in Hull, close to his Lancastrian castles, he soon found all the great magnates were flocking to his standard.

In the meantime the king had made a fatal mistake. He went again to Ireland. When he returned at the close of July it was already too late. There had been mass desertion to the enemy. By the time he reached Conway Castle even his own army had deserted him. When he sent emissaries to Bolingbroke they were taken hostage. Bolingbroke then sent his own to Richard. The king was to be guaranteed the throne but

Bolingbroke was to have the Lancastrian lands and the office of seneschal of the king-dom. The king, trusting in what he had been offered, then rode out of the castle. Six miles from it he was seized. He had been tricked.

From then on, everything was disaster. The king was humiliated and imprisoned. Parliament met and Bolingbroke claimed the throne by conquest and by his royal descent from Henry III. A group of 'sages in law' was set up who said that the king could be deposed on account of his 'perjuries, sacrileges, unnatural armies, exactions from his subjects, reduction of his people to slavery, and weakness of rule'. Richard was allowed no trial. On hearing what had happened he cried: 'My God: a wonderful land is this and a fickle – which hath exiled, slain, destroyed, or ruined so many kings, rulers and great men . . .' On 30 September his forced renunciation of the throne was read out to Parliament and Bolingbroke stepped forward and claimed it. A fortnight later he was crowned as Henry IV.

Richard II was taken northwards to the Lancastrian castle of Pontefract. He was never seen again and was dead by 14 February 1400, it seems deliberately starved to death or murdered. He was given a magnificent funeral by the new king just to ensure that everyone knew that Richard II was no more.

In this manner ended the reign of one of the most brilliant and flawed of all medieval kings. Much of his vision was far-seeing. He knew that peace with France was what was needed but the struggle was to continue for another hundred and fifty years. He realised too that no king could rule while he was at the mercy of the greed of the great magnates with their vast wealth and private armies. As long as the crown was isolated it was always in danger of becoming the victim of the double-dealing, cruelty and treachery of the nobles. Richard's failure to overcome that set the scene for the Wars of the Roses.

The transportation of the body of Richard II to London from Pontefract. Great show was made of the embalmed body, so that people should realise that the king was dead. An illumination from Froissart's *Chronicles*.

Chapter Nineteen

THE FATHER
OF ENGLISH POETRY

When in April the sweet showers fall
And pierce the drought of March to the root . . .
Then people long to go on pilgrimages
And palmers long to seek the stranger strands
Of far-off saints, hallowed in sundry lands,
And specially, from every shire's end
Of England, down to Canterbury they wend
To seek the holy blissful martyr, quick
To give his help to them when they were sick.

THIS is the opening of one of the most famous of all English poems, *The Canterbury Tales* by Geoffrey Chaucer, written during the reign of Richard II. Known as the Father of English Poetry, Chaucer was the first poet to be buried in what was later to be called Poets' Corner in Westminster Abbey. His poetry was the result of a great change. For the first time English began to be widely used. Before then, the nobles spoke French, and the church and the law used Latin. Only the ordinary people spoke English. As a result of the Black Death, however, there were not enough teachers to teach French and so it was recorded that: 'In all the grammar schools of England, children leaveth French and construeth and learneth English.'

Chaucer was a Londoner. His father was a rich vintner or what we would call a brewer. London, the largest city in the kingdom, lay on the north bank of the river Thames surrounded by thick walls, the country outside so close that a citizen could smell the haymaking. Inside there was space for gardens but the streets were very narrow with tall houses on either side, made of stone, or wood and plaster, with thatched roofs. There were no less than eighty-five parishes with a hundred churches, whose bells were always ringing. The largest church was St. Paul's Cathedral which towered above the skyline. The streets bustled with people, horses and dogs. In the public squares hung the corpses of criminals, fly-bitten and pecked by birds. There was only

one bridge across the river, London Bridge, over the gateway of which the heads of wrongdoers were stuck on spikes as a warning. Secure within its great walls, with the Tower at its eastern end, and the Strand leading to Westminster and the court at its western, London was the most important city in the realm.

Chaucer's father, John, lived in a fine house in Thames Street. There was no such thing as privacy and every room was shared. In the garden there were fruit trees and a pen for pigs. Chickens were kept inside. The house had a kit-chen and bakehouse for cooking, a larder, buttery and cellar for stores, and a laundry for the washing. The main room was the hall in which everyone ate. Then there were the bedrooms with several people sleeping in a bed. The floors were covered in rushes and straw, filthy from spilt drink, spit, food, and worse. There were no chairs or tables. People sat on benches or trunks, and tables were set up from trestles and planks of wood for meals.

Chaucer's London, a panorama looking over Tower Hill, to the right, towards the Pool, the arcaded warehouses of Billingsgate and part of London Bridge with its chapel of St. Thomas and double row of houses. The small boats are a reminder that the Thames was the main highway both for passengers and goods. Beyond the city skyline is punctuated by the many towers of its churches. The view, from a late fifteenth century illumination, somewhat distorts the topography.

The house was cold and dark. Each night the fires had to be put out at a set time, the curfew, and no one dared go out after that for fear of murder or robbery.

Chaucer was born about 1340, just eight years before the Black Death, when Edward III was still on the throne. His mother and father were very ambitious for him, so he was brought up to speak French, the language of the court. At seven he started school, learning how to read and write Latin. He next studied what was called the *trivium*: grammar, logic and rhetoric. Grammar taught him how to read and write properly, logic how to argue well, and rhetoric how to speak sensibly. Although only a merchant's son he gained a post in the household of Elizabeth, Countess of Ulster, wife of the king's third son, Lionel.

The earl and countess lived the customary life of a great aristocratic family, moving from one castle to another across their vast estates. This was because their household had so many people that it had to move on whenever the food ran out. Everything travelled with them: tapestries, furniture, clothes, silver, armour and weapons for hunting. The castles were set in the midst of huge parks for the chase, and elegant gardens in which to walk. The life they lived was rich and splendid. Besides the sport of hunting there were tournaments in which knights fought against each other for prizes and to show their skill. The earl and countess would look on from a gaily decorated box as the knights, escorted by their servants, all in magnificent attire, made their entry into the arena. Such an occasion would have included acrobats, jugglers, clowns and dancers.

On holy days there would be a banquet. The food was made in the form of castles, woods, rivers and fields, like a landscape spreading across the table. During the feast there would be music and spectacle.

Sometimes whole forests seemed to come into the hall, filled with singing birds, or a mechanical horse strode around the room, or artificial wild animals such as lions and elephants would parade. On other occasions a minstrel would sing or, as young Chaucer would have noted, a poet would read to the feasters, making them laugh and cry.

It was indeed the setting for poetry. In castles and houses up and down the kingdom, members of the household would gather during the long winter evenings to hear someone read to them. Books, of course, were very rare, written by hand and often illuminated in the same way as the Bibles and service books used in churches and monasteries. The most popular reading of all were romances of chivalry, fabulous adventure stories, especially about King Arthur and his knights. In these stories knights encountered not only other knights in deadly combat, but the infidel, monsters, and evil spirits. For the fourteenth century listener they reflected the ideals of his own time, of the knight and his duty both to God, his king and his lady.

While in the countess's household Chaucer met another of the king's sons, John of Gaunt, Duke of Lancaster, who was to become a life-long friend and the sister of whose last wife he was to marry. The old king's mistress, Alice Perrers, was also a friend. Soon Chaucer became a trusted royal servant and was sent by the king with messages abroad. In this way he learned about all that was new in French and Italian poetry.

But a poet had to make a living. Writing poems earned him the favour of the court and in the end brought him a job. When the young Richard II came to the throne, John of Gaunt saw that Chaucer was made controller of customs and subsidies. His office was at the port of London checking all the taxes paid by merchants to the king, an important post, for the tax paid on wool brought the money needed to pay for the long wars with France. For this he got a handsome rent-free house and an annual allowance. He continued, however, to travel abroad 'on the king's secret business' and later in life was given the even grander job of looking after Richard II's two favourite palaces, Eltham and Sheen. Chaucer, in fact, became rich.

Chaucer lived through all the appalling events of the second half of the fourteenth century, and never lost favour with the court, being called upon to read his poems before the king and his guests. Sometimes he must have read to them love stories like the *Romance of the Rose* or *Troilus and Cressida*. On other occasions he would have made them laugh with *The Parliament of Fowls*. Above all he would read to them from his masterpiece, *The Canterbury Tales*. The setting for this long poem was a pilgrimage to the shrine of St Thomas Becket at Canterbury. People went on pilgrimages then much as we would go on a holiday today. A pilgrimage was offered as a penance to God for sin or to give thanks for recovery from a grave illness or indeed to seek a cure for one. The pilgrim went on a journey to the tomb of a holy person, a saint, to ask for his prayers and give thanks to God. It was usual to travel in a group because it was safer, but also because of the good company.

Chaucer describes how his pilgrims met at an inn in Southwark on the south bank of the Thames. He chooses his characters in a way which gives us a brilliant panorama of his England. Some of them, like the rich merchant, came from the town, some, like the poor priest, from the country. There are both men and women, clergy and lay people, high and low. And there were also those who were no better than they should be like the much married wife from Bath and the greedy friar.

Chaucer would have met young men like the squire with his curly hair at the Countess of Ulster's house:

Chaucer reading *Troilus and Cressida* to the court.

Singing he was, or fluting all the day;
He was as fresh as is the month of May.
Short was his gown, the sleeves were long and wide;
He knew the way to sit a horse and ride.
He could make songs and poems and recite,
Knew how to joust and dance, to draw and write.

His merchant stepped out of the London he knew:

This estimable Merchant so had set
His wits to work, none knew he was in debt,
He was so stately in administration,
In loans and bargains and negotiation.
He was an excellent fellow all the same;
To tell the truth I do not know his name.

He writes of people with all their virtues as well as their vices:

There was a Monk, a leader of the fashions;
Inspecting farms and hunting were his passions . . .
The Rule of good St Benet or St Maur
As old and strict he tended to ignore;
He let go by the things of yesterday
And took the modern world's more spacious way.

And the monk he contrasts with the humble parson:

Wide was his parish, with houses far asunder.
Yet he neglected not in rain or thunder,
In sickness or in grief, to pay a call
On the remotest, whether great or small
Upon his feet, and in his hand a stave.

The women are as strongly drawn. There was the nun who not only 'spoke daintily in French' but:

. . . used to weep if she but saw a mouse
Caught in a trap, if it were dead or bleeding.
And she had little dogs she would be feeding
With roasted flesh, or milk, or fine white bread.

There was also a rich widow:

> *Her hose were of the finest scarlet red*
> *And gartered tight; her shoes were soft and new.*
> *Bold was her face, handsome, and red in hue.*
> *A worthy woman all her life, what's more*
> *She'd had five husbands, all at the church door . . .*

So Geoffrey Chaucer set the scene, painting a glowing picture of the England of Richard II. Then the pilgrims set off, each one promising to tell two tales on the way there and two more on the way back. There would have been over two hundred and twenty stories if he had ever finished it. But he never did. Geoffrey Chaucer died 25 October 1400, leaving his great masterpiece incomplete.

A page from Chaucer's *Canterbury Tales* as it was first printed by William Caxton in 1475. They were written in the very last years of the fourteenth century.

Chapter Twenty

THE VICTOR OF AGINCOURT

N ow is a good time, for all England prayeth for us; and therefore be of good cheer, and let us go to our journey.' With these words ringing in their ears the English soldiers advanced on the French to achieve a famous victory at the Battle of Agincourt. They were spoken by King Henry V, who saw himself as his great grandfather, Edward III, leading his army in conquest of his rightful inheritance, the realm of France. Henry V was to unite his country in seemingly glorious victories, which remain part of national myth, but he was to do it at a price.

Such unity was much needed when Henry came to the throne in 1413. His father, Henry IV, had proved to be a lacklustre ailing monarch whose whole reign was dogged by rebellions, both in the north and, more seriously, in Wales, which the English had treated badly. In comparison the short nine-year reign of his son was to be like a meteor erupting and skimming its way across a night sky. Unlike Richard II, Henry V was to give his subjects what they wanted, war with France.

The king was twenty-four when he came to the throne. He was a born leader of men, a natural soldier and a skilled tactician. He had enormous vitality and physical charm, with his long oval face, straight nose, high cheekbones, full red lips, deeply cleft chin and large expressive hazel eyes. He had a zest for life and was hugely athletic. At the same time he was a man of intellect and careful consideration, a good listener, well educated with an ability to read and write English, French and Latin. He was perfectly endowed for his role as king, a role he intended to play to the full.

From the moment of his accession, Henry voiced his territorial claims to France, along with one for the hand of the French king's daughter. On the other side of the Channel he was seen initially as little more than a figure of fun. The French nobles said 'that they would send Henry, king of [the] English, since he was a youngster, little balls to play with and soft cushions to lie upon, until he had grown to manly strength later on.'

Thomas Occleve presenting his poem *De Regimine Principum* to Henry V. There is no doubt that this was intended to be a portrait.

Such comments the French were shortly to regret, for the king had already made up his mind to invade and lay claim to his lands as Duke of Normandy, a part of France which the English had lost two hundred and fifty years before. Henry supervised the expedition in every detail. He realised that an army needed a constant supply of food and weapons to be successful. It also needed equipment to assault walled cities: towers and scaling ladders, engines for battering walls, guns and artillery. Then there were the soldiers; firstly, the men-at-arms, mounted knights, each man bringing with him as many as four horses tended by grooms and pages; secondly, the archers, both mounted and on foot; and finally the gunners, miners, smiths, painters, armourers, tent makers, carpenters, fletchers, bowyers, farriers, carters and cordeners. The king himself took most of his household as well, including his minstrels, for he loved music. No less than nine thousand people in all crossed the Channel in one thousand five hundred ships. It was a masterpiece of organisation and the king had supervised every detail. But it was expensive, and had to be paid for by raising huge loans on items like the royal jewels.

Henry's plan was to capture the port of Harfleur and use it as a base to re-establish English rule in Normandy. The moment was right; Charles VI, king of France, had periods of insanity and the French nobility was divided into warring parties. The English fleet crossed on 11 August 1415 and laid siege to Harfleur, which was protected by strong battlements, ditches and towers. The attackers had to fill in the ditches in order to get their guns close enough to strike so the siege was slow, and it was not until 22 September that Harfleur capitulated. By then Henry had lost a third of his army through sickness. There was to be no looting or plundering, but two thousand citizens were expelled to make way for colonisation from England. Henry really believed himself to be the rightful Duke of Normandy but he was to learn that the clock could not so easily be put back.

After this victory no one seemed to know what to do next, until the king decided to return via Calais. A garrison was left in Harfleur and the army began what was believed to be an eight day march, covering some one hundred and twenty miles. What had not been anticipated was that the French would destroy the bridges and fords across the River Somme. As a result the English army found itself making a huge detour upriver so that in all the soldiers marched two hundred and fifty miles in seventeen days. On 19 October they were at last able to cross the river and face the French army on the opposite bank. The next day the French issued a challenge to battle.

The battle was fought on a piece of open ground

The Battle of Agincourt 25 October 1415 as recorded in Froissart's *Chronicles*. The rival armies can be identified by their heraldic banners, either the lions of England or the lilies of France.

close to the village of Agincourt on 25 October. The French army was three or four times the size of the English one, but it was largely made up of knights in heavy armour, with very few archers. They hoped to win purely on numbers; indeed they went into the fight assuming that the victory was theirs. But they lacked two things: archers and, above all, leadership. The English had both, together with another unexpected advantage, the weather, for on the eve of battle it rained hard, turning the ploughed field into a quagmire.

The key factor proved to be the archers, for they could decimate the French with their arrows at a distance of two hundred yards. And this was the distance to which they advanced before driving stakes into the ground to face the French cavalry. When the French charged, it was chaos. The horses were caught on the staves. There were so many French that they fell over each other. Others turned back causing further panic. As the enemy lay unable to get up in the mud, the English cut their throats. Arrows meanwhile rained down on the rest. By then a large number of prisoners was taken when the king, sighting a third wave of the French army about to advance, ordered their slaughter. This was against all the rules of chivalry and the men-at-arms refused, so that Henry was forced to command his archers to carry out the massacre. The battle was a great, if disgraceful, victory and destroyed the flower of the French nobility.

Both king and army returned to England in triumph. When they entered London the city staged splendid pageantry. Figures depicting St. George, the Apostles, angels, and the king's regal ancestors, hailed him as victor. English pride was restored and the king proceeded to plan a second invasion, intending to return not only as Duke of Normandy but as France's future king.

The marriage of Henry V to Katherine of Valois, 1420. A drawing from a series made c. 1485-90 called *The Pageant of the Birth, Life and Death of Richard Beauchamp, Earl of Warwick.*

During the next year the English were again victorious, this time over the French fleet. Meanwhile Henry not only mustered his army, but gained two allies in the Holy Roman Emperor, Sigismund, and the Duke of Burgundy. In August 1417 the army crossed again to France. The town of Caen fell, then Falaise and finally, in the August of the following year, the English lay siege to the capital of Normandy, Rouen. This was a long cruel siege lasting six months. Food ran out in the city and twelve thousand women, old men, and children were pushed out of its gates. Normally they would have been allowed safe passage through the English lines but Henry left them to die of starvation in the ditch between the city walls and his own troops. On 19 January Rouen surrendered and the whole of Normandy was in Henry's hands.

By then the French were in complete disarray, and one wholly unexpected event gave Henry V everything he aspired to. In September the Duke of Burgundy was murdered at a meeting with the heir to the French throne, the Dauphin. So great was the reaction to this that the French sued for peace, Charles VI agreeing to disinherit his son and recognise Henry, married to his daughter Katherine, as 'heir of France'. Henry V entered Paris in triumph and when he and his bride returned to England there was universal rejoicing. The child of this marriage would be destined to rule over the dual monarchy of France and England. On the surface no king of England had restored the nation to such glory. But it was an illusion.

The greatest difficulty was that the treaty with the French stated that Henry could be king of the country, but that he would have to pay for the conquest of it first. He returned to France in June 1422 to begin the long and arduous task which in his case was cut short, for he died on 31 August of the disease which had racked his own army at Harfleur, dysentery. By then the vision had clouded. The war was costly and Parliament began to complain about taxation. The conquest of Normandy was not working and it was proving impossible to administer. And, just as the French war had united England behind Henry, so, in defeat, it was uniting the French behind the Dauphin. Within a few years Joan of Arc appeared to inspire a new loyalty to the French crown and, with Henry dead, the English had lost their commander.

In many ways if Henry V had not revived the French war he would have been a greater king. At home he restored the fortunes of the monarchy and was revered by his subjects for his unswerving devotion to justice. But his belief in his rights led him to take his country into a war which could never be won. He left his heir to face the defeat which would have been his had he lived longer. Before long, the dual monarchy had vanished, and within thirty years England was reduced only to its old foothold of Calais.

Chapter Twenty-One

THE WARS OF
THE ROSES

H ENRY VI was only nine months old when he came to the throne but by the age of three he had opened Parliament (where he 'shrieked and cried and sprang'), and at ten he was crowned in Paris as Henry II, king of France. Although a child king always presented problems there seemed no reason to fear disaster, for the king's two uncles, Humphrey, Duke of Gloucester and John, Duke of Bedford, guided the state. Both were politically astute and cultured, and Bedford was a successful regent of France. But in 1435 he died. Then, when the king reached the age of twenty, Gloucester fell from favour.

What no one had foreseen was that Henry VI was to grow up a simpleton. The whole running of the country depended on having a forceful and intelligent king.

The birth of Henry VI on 6 December 1421. A drawing from a series made c. 1485-90 called *The Pageant of the Birth, Life and Death of Richard Beauchamp, Earl of Warwick.*

Henry inherited his father's name without any of his abilities. John Blacman, a Carthusian monk who was one of the king's chaplains, described him thus:

> 'A diligent and sincere worshipper of God was this king, more given to God and devout prayer than to handling worldly and temporal things . . .'

A medieval king had to lead both in peace and war.

Richard Beauchamp, Earl of Warwick, known as the Kingmaker was entrusted with the upbringing of the young Henry VI. Here he holds the infant monarch crowned and carrying the orb and sceptre in his arms. A drawing from the *Rous Roll*, c. 1480-85.

Henry did neither. He was a saint in the making, pious, peace-loving, easily influenced, a faithful husband and a loving father – but a hopeless king. He went to battle not to fight but to stand clutching his prayer-book ready to be taken by whichever side won. After a nervous breakdown in 1453 he became the pawn of whoever seized power, the victim of the rival parties who took sides in what we call the Wars of the Roses.

These civil wars would never have happened if the character of Henry VI had been otherwise. Law and justice at the time depended on the king making effective use of his nobles, because there was no army or police force. To make the system work, the king had skilfully to choose the right allies within the ranks of the nobility and reward them with titles, lands and offices. His failure to do so meant that people could no longer look to the crown for the exercise of law and justice and, as a result, were forced to turn to the next best thing, the great lord whose power in the locality in which they lived would protect them. In return they would wear his livery and badge and, if necessary, fight for him. This meant that gradually the whole of England became divided up into groups loyal to this or that lord; in turn the lords themselves became split into factions supporting this or that party at court. To this must be added local feuds and rivalries between families. The north, for instance, was divided between the Nevilles and the Percys, the south-west between the Courtneys and the Bonvilles. The collapse of the crown meant that law and justice were gradually perverted and criminals were not brought to book because they had the protection of some great lord. Worse, all this set the scene for civil war. The prize was control of the crown and government, with all that that meant in terms of power and rewards.

The only real solution to the country's problems was to get rid of the king; and it is surprising how long it took for that to be done. Men in the Middle Ages devoutly believed that a king was a sacred being set apart at his coronation. It took thirty years for someone to seize the throne, but even then the nobility were uneasy. It was only after forty years and Henry's murder that a new and strong king, Edward IV, could successfully rule.

There was no lack of claimants to the throne, because Edward III, the king's great grandfather, had so many sons. Henry VI was descended from his third son, John of Gaunt, Duke of Lancaster. When he became of age, the king made the terrible mistake of excluding from the government the one man who had perhaps a better claim than he did, being descended from both Edward's second and fourth son. He was Richard, Duke of York, a man of immense ambition. In 1450 Richard began to demand a place in the government of the kingdom. At first he failed to get it and then, when the king fell ill, he was made Protector of England and set about exerting power.

This inaugurated the long period of instability known as the Wars of the Roses during which the government became the victim of whoever could wield enough strength to seize control. There were those who had been in power earlier in the reign headed by the king's strong-willed queen, Margaret of Anjou. Henry had married her in 1445. She was by nature tempestuous and the first to resort to arms in defence of her husband and of her only son, Edward, Prince of Wales. On the other side there was York and those who had been excluded like the Nevilles. Both could muster armies and when the king recovered his health in 1455 the Yorkists had to take to arms and capture him at the first Battle of St. Albans to re-establish their hold on government. That hold, however, was to be short-lived for royalist forces not long after regained it. There then followed a tumultuous period in which first one side and then the other gained control of this pathetically weak king, but ending finally in the defeat of the Yorkists who were forced to flee the country.

During a period of twenty-five years the crown was to change hands no less than six times. The great break came with the decision that the king should be replaced.

That only came slowly. When Richard, Duke of York, landed at Chester in 1460 it was clear that this time he had come to claim the throne, and he marched on London with that intent. When he got there, the most the lords would do was recognise him as heir apparent, passing over Henry VI's own son. York's triumph was short-lived for the Lancastrians defeated him at the Battle of Wakefield Bridge, the duke being killed and his head cruelly adorned with a paper crown and set on the gates of the city of York. But he had an able, energetic and handsome heir in Edward, Earl of March. He led a new Yorkist army to victory at Mortimer's Cross, during which three suns prophetically appeared in the sky, and after which he marched on London and was installed as King Edward IV.

It was, however, to take him ten years to establish himself as king. That was due not only to renewed efforts by the Lancastrians to restore Henry VI but because Edward's greatest ally, Richard Neville, Earl of Warwick, known as 'the kingmaker', was to prove treacherous. Edward was driven into exile again and owed his restoration as much as anything to his brother-in-law, the Duke of Burgundy. In March 1471 he landed in England eventually reaching London which opened its gates. There then followed a whirlwind campaign. At the Battle of Barnet in April Warwick was slain. A month later at Tewkesbury the Prince of Wales was killed. Soon after Henry VI was murdered and Margaret of Anjou eventually went into exile in France. This wiped out the Lancastrians and signalled the real end of the Wars of the Roses.

Today we see these wars through Shakespeare's plays written over a century later in the reign of Queen Elizabeth I. It was natural then, of course, to depict the previous century as a turbulent one from which her grandfather, the Lancastrian Henry VII, had rescued the country by defeating the tyrant Richard III and marrying the Yorkist princess, Elizabeth. In this way writers in the sixteenth century re-wrote the history of the previous one, presenting it as a bloody battlefield littered with dead in thousands, fought over by two parties whose badges were the white rose of York and the red one of Lancaster. The reality of fifteenth century England was very different. A French chronicler records:

'England enjoyed this peculiar mercy above all other kingdoms, that neither the country nor the people, nor the houses were wasted, destroyed or demolished; but the calamities and misfortunes of the war fell only upon the soldiers, and especially upon the nobility.'

Livery badges were a feature of the Wars of the Roses, worn by followers of particular persons as expressions of loyalty. The white swan was the badge of Henry VI's queen, Margaret of Anjou. This jewel would have been worn by someone of rank and was found near the site of the Battle of St. Albans.

In short, normal life went on. Towns and cities tried to keep out of the war by avoiding taking sides or hedging their bets. In fact they were so little affected that they rarely bothered to repair their walls and certainly did not build new ones. Trade continued as usual. Many of the officers of government stayed in their posts regardless of who was in power. Most of the country in fact saw no fighting at all. The war was also remarkable in that on only one occasion was there plunder and pillaging.

Surprisingly, there was a new sense of security which was reflected in building. Castles became transformed into houses with large windows to let in the light, where comfort and not defence was the key consideration. Large numbers of beautiful churches were built all over the country in the delicate airy style named Perpendicular. Eton College Chapel, Windsor, and King's College Chapel, Cambridge, are two of the most famous.

So the bewildering changes of who was or was not in power and the long list of battles gives a very misleading picture of the age. There were only thirteen weeks of real fighting during thirty-two years. Numbers killed ran into hundreds and not thousands. As the same French chronicler wrote:

'It is a custom in England that the victors in battle kill nobody, especially none of the ordinary soldiers, because everyone wants to please them . . .'

The reason why there was no such thing as a prolonged war was because no one knew how to keep an army supplied. In addition, apart from the professional soldiers, the army was made up of people like farmers and yeomen who worked on the land and were always anxious to get home to their crops. The war was also indecisive because like was fighting like.

Both sides had cavalry, foot soldiers, archers and artillery. Due to the fact that the arrows killed the horses the knights would dismount and fight on foot with swords, maces or battle axes. Even this they found difficult because their armour was so heavy and hot in summer. The huge loss of life by the nobility was due to their role in battle, that of leading their retainers. Attended by their standard bearers they stood out as targets to be cut down.

What really brought the main period of the Wars of the Roses to an end was everyone's realisation that a strong king was needed. As the war progressed the nobility gradually came to be aware that little was to be gained by this perpetual turmoil in which the lives of members of their families were lost and their lands taken from them by the rival party. More and more they avoided joining either side. The growth of that attitude was to ensure the success of the rule of first Edward IV and later that of Henry VII.

Chapter Twenty-Two

RETURN TO ORDER: EDWARD IV

AFTER his return to power in 1471 Edward IV ruled for twelve years as a tremendously successful and popular king blessed with nearly all the attributes men looked for in a monarch. Well over six feet tall he was renowned for his good looks and exquisite manners but he also possessed that rare gift, the common touch. This is how an Italian, Mancini, described him:

A manuscript being presented to Edward IV, one he commissioned while he was in exile in Flanders in 1470-71. It is likely to depict him actually during his residence in Bruges and the second figure from the left wearing the Order of the Garter may be intended for the future Richard III.

'Edward was of a gentle nature and cheerful aspect . . . He was easy of access to his friends and to others, even the least notable. Frequently he called to his side strangers . . . He was so genial in his greeting that if he saw a newcomer bewildered at his appearance and royal magnificence he would give him courage to speak by laying a kindly hand upon his shoulder.'

Much to the horror of the nobility he would give hunting parties for rich London merchants. If he had any weaknesses they were food (he became fat as he grew older), and women, for his mistresses were many; a particular favourite was Jane Shore, the widow of a London grocer, who was an influence for the good. According to Sir Thomas More:

'Where the king took displeasure she would mitigate and appease his mind; where men were out of favour she would bring them in his grace. For many that had highly offended she obtained pardon . . .'

She was clearly hugely intelligent and attractive and More goes on to say about her: 'For a proper wit had she and could read well and write, merry in company,

ready and quick in answer . . .'

All over Europe, as the fifteenth century drew to its close, men looked more and more to rulers as the focus for holding a state together. During the last twelve years of his life Edward was able to put the monarchy back once again at the centre of the country's life. This called for acting the part to the full which he did, always dressing magnificently in the height of fashion unlike Henry VI who wore an old blue gown. Edward also ceremonially wore his crown on great festivals before the assembled court. The royal household was put into good order, not only in the interests of efficiency and value for money but to provide regal splendour aimed at impressing both his subjects and visitors from abroad. When, for example, a great Flemish nobleman visited Windsor

The family of Edward IV as recorded in contemporary stained glass between 1475 and 1483 in Canterbury Cathedral. From left to right the figures are: Richard, Duke of York, Edward, Prince of Wales, Edward IV, Elizabeth Woodville and, in the furthest two panels, five of her seven daughters. The heads of the two princes are modern replacements.

he was led to three 'rooms of pleasance'. In the first there was a bed with a counterpane of cloth of gold furred with ermine, in the second a bed hung in white and in the third two baths within tents. There were elaborate processions, banquets and dancing as well as rich gifts. The nobleman would have returned to his master, the Duke of Burgundy, whose court set style for every other, and told him of the splendour of that of England.

Edward realised even more the importance of money and knew that the shortest route to unpopularity was to ask Parliament to grant taxes. There was then no distinction between the public and private revenue of the crown and when Edward announced his intention to 'live of his own' he meant he would attempt to pay the costs of running the country from his own wealth. That involved making the king the richest person in the country. He began by creating a new financial department called the King's Chamber so that he could keep an eye on expenditure, so much so that later in the reign he was accused of being a miser. The royal estates were put in order to produce more income and they also grew in size. When the king's younger brother, the Duke of Clarence, was condemned for treason, his lands passed to the crown. Edward's second son married the heiress to the Duke of Norfolk and when she died most of her lands came too. As Edward's rule brought peace, trade prospered, and he made certain that the large customs dues were collected by 'men of shrewdness'. And he did not stop at entertaining merchants, he was one himself, investing in both the import and export trade and making handsome profits. On the only occasion he set out to invade France and renew the war he allowed himself to be bought off by the French king for a pension of fifty thousand crowns a year. As a result Edward IV was the first king not to die in debt for nearly three hundred years.

A king had to have money in his coffers but he also needed to establish his authority over remote parts of the country, which he would rarely if ever visit. Firstly Edward sent his infant son, Edward, Prince of Wales, to Ludlow and set up a council there to govern the Welsh Marches in his name. His brother, Richard, Duke of Gloucester, went to his castle forty miles from York to represent the king in the north. Other members of the king's family were despatched elsewhere. Through this not only was order restored, but justice too. Indeed Edward himself sat from time to time as a judge.

His queen, Elizabeth Woodville, produced no less than ten children. These were valuable assets, for through marriages the king could enhance the position of the

King's College Chapel, Cambridge, one of the supreme achievements of the Perpendicular style. The College was founded by Henry VI in 1441, building works being interrupted first by the poverty of the crown and later by the hostility which Edward IV showed to what was a Lancastrian foundation. Building was resumed at the close of his reign and it was completed by Henry VII.

house of York through Europe. As a result one princess was to become queen of France, a second queen of Scotland, while others were destined to marry into the royal and princely houses of Spain and the Low Countries. Indeed it was during this period that England's relationship with the latter was at its closest, for the king's sister was Duchess of Burgundy.

Both the king and the queen patronised the arts and learning, regarded as important for adding lustre to the crown. St. George's Chapel, Windsor Castle, is Edward's most famous surviving monument. It was built to add greater splendour to the annual ceremonies of the Order of the Garter and also to act as a mausoleum for the dynasty. He was a lavish benefactor of Henry VI's foundations, King's College, Cambridge and Eton, while his queen, in her turn, gave to Queen's College, Cambridge. Edward delighted in books, especially histories and romances, creating a royal library filled with gorgeously illuminated manuscripts executed for him in Bruges, many of which can be seen today in the British Library.

There were, however, to be two fatal flaws to the brilliant success of Edward's rule, one which he could, and the other which he could not, have foreseen. No one could have predicted that he would have died in his fortieth year leaving a child of twelve to succeed, with all the problems that would entail. What he should have made provision for was the consequences of his marriage. This was an affair of the heart.

Elizabeth Woodville was the widow of a knight, Sir John Grey, and already had two sons. The match with the king was made in secret and only became public when there was pressure for the king to make a suitable dynastic marriage with a foreign royal princess. It was then that he was forced to admit that he was already married. The Woodvilles were not liked. They were regarded as 'low' and Edward was faced with providing for his queen's large and greedy family. This involved titles, estates and marriages to rich heiresses. The Woodvilles quickly came to be bitterly resented but, worse than that, they were actually hated by Edward's brother, Richard, Duke of Gloucester. Edward must have known that and yet he made little effort to provide for the problems which could arise if he died early. When the king did so, on 9 April 1483, he therefore left the Yorkists divided amongst themselves with terrible consequences.

In spite of that, Edward IV saved the country, bringing it from dereliction and disaster to great prosperity. Although he led one campaign into France and was forced into a war with Scotland, all his instincts were for peace. As a result, for the first time in decades, the monarchy had become again the guarantee of order and justice in the land and the fount of political power. The tragedy that followed this triumph was to turn Edward into one of England's great forgotten kings.

Chapter Twenty-Three

VIOLENT INTERLUDE: RICHARD III

WHEN Edward IV died he left a son aged twelve. The usual arrangements were set in motion by the Council to govern the kingdom during the king's minority. Conflict amongst members of the Council there certainly was but no one anticipated that the late king's brother, Richard, Duke of Gloucester, would stop at nothing to seize the crown. No one guessed this at first, and only gradually did it dawn on people what Gloucester had in mind. At what exact moment the duke took his final decision is not known, but by the time he did, it was already too late to stop him, for he had arranged the deaths of anyone who stood in his path.

Richard was a man of delicate build and athletic, despite having shoulders which were slightly uneven. He had his brother's charm but much more energy. He was hugely able, generous to his friends, pious indeed, but none of those characteristics could quite conceal a man who was also ruthless, ambitious, and wholly treacherous. He had been loyal to his brother while he was king, holding the north for him. At the same time he had built up huge estates by exerting pressure on heiresses and persuading frightened old ladies to part with their inheritances. But none of this would have made anyone suspect quite what was to happen after his brother died.

To achieve the crown Gloucester needed to eliminate his enemies and secure allies. He had support especially in the north and could equally rely on all those who had been out of favour in the previous reign, particularly those who resented the queen's family, the Woodvilles. Gloucester's allies were headed by the Duke of Buckingham, by John Howard soon to be Duke of Norfolk, and the Duke of Suffolk who was married to Gloucester's sister. Their first objective was to gain control of the king.

As Gloucester rode south, the king left Ludlow with his uncle and guardian, the queen's brother, Lord Rivers. On his journey Gloucester joined the Duke of Buckingham, and together they met Lord Rivers and the king. That was on 30 April 1483, when the three noblemen passed the evening in revelry. What happened the next morning was something very different. Richard took control of Edward V, and arrested Lord Rivers and others sending them to be imprisoned in the north. This was his first great strike. When news of it reached the queen she and her daughters and youngest son, the Duke of York, sought sanctuary in the Abbey of Westminster.

Gloucester had got rid of the Woodvilles. Outwardly there was no sign yet that the young king was to enjoy the same fate. On 4 May the two dukes escorted him into London, and between a week and a fortnight later he was taken to the Tower, the normal place of residence for a monarch prior to his coronation. Pending that event the Council made Gloucester Lord Protector of England.

Then came the second strike. The queen wisely refused to leave sanctuary, but she was then accused of plotting against Gloucester. This was used as an excuse to arrest three of the late king's most important ministers, executing without trial Lord Hastings, whom Gloucester up until that moment had cultivated as a friend. Some have argued that this was the moment when the duke had definitely made up his mind to usurp the crown. What happened next confirms this view. Three days later the infant Duke of York was taken from Westminster to join his brother in the Tower. They were never to be seen alive again, murdered at some unknown date it seems on the instructions of Gloucester after he became king. It is believed that they were suffocated to death in their beds.

In order for Gloucester to become king, however, he still had to prove that he had a better claim to the throne than the princes in the Tower. On 22 June a sermon was preached at St. Paul's telling the Londoners that the princes were not legitimate because, it was falsely claimed, Edward IV's marriage to Elizabeth Woodville was not valid. Two days later Gloucester struck again, ordering the execution of those whom he had imprisoned in the north. It would appear the opposition had been wiped out, and Buckingham publicly urged Gloucester to take the throne. On 26 June those who had assembled for Parliament duly elected Gloucester as Richard III. A few days later he was crowned.

Richard III came to the English throne by way of a pathway soaked with the blood of his victims. He succeeded because no one suspected his real motive until it was too late, and each and every one of his victims had walked like lambs to the slaughter. He was a master of cunning and deceit. But he made one fatal mistake. What he had not reckoned with was that as people recovered from the appalling shock of these events they would begin to draw together to form a united opposition. The revulsion against the new king was widespread in the south leading to rebellions in the autumn. By then Richard had fallen out with the man who had

Richard III. A late sixteenth century portrait which is based on one painted during the king's lifetime. Even at a later remove the intelligence of the man is captured.

RICARDVS · III · ANG · REX ·

helped him to the throne. Buckingham rebelled and he too was executed.

The royal arms of England supported by Richard III's badge of a boar from a charter of 1484.

Richard III had done two things which everyone then regarded with deep abhorrence as utter wickedness; the first was to violate inheritance and the second to commit child murder, infanticide. He was seen as Herod who had ordered the Massacre of the Innocents. Richard had been the princes' protector and yet he had had them killed. Everyone was outraged.

From then on nothing went right. Richard toured areas of England hoping to win popular support but failed. Northerners were brought south and given positions which caused widespread resentment. He lost the support of the Yorkists in the south of England with results which were fatal. His queen died and so did his heir. It was even believed that he had murdered his wife so as to be able to marry his niece, Elizabeth of York. As a result all through 1484 a new alliance was formed, one which saw the way forward as a marriage between Elizabeth and the minor claimant of Lancastrian descent, Henry Tudor.

Henry was in exile in Britanny, where everyone had flocked who wished to see the overthrow of Richard III. In August 1485 Henry Tudor, Earl of Richmond, landed at Milford Haven in Wales and marched via Shrewsbury to meet the royal army near Leicester at Bosworth. The Battle of Bosworth on 22 August was to be one of the decisive battles in the history of England. Richard III's army was much larger, but many who fought were reluctant and some even went over to the other side. The king fell on the field of battle and the victor was proclaimed Henry VII.

Richard III remains a unique figure whose crimes at the time were considered so repugnant that even the customary respect for his dead body was absent. This is how he ended:

'In the mean time the body of king Richard naked of all clothing, and laid upon an horse back with the arms and the legs hanging down on both sides, was brought to th'abbey of monks Franciscan at Leicester, a miserable spectacle in good sooth, but not unworthy for the man's life, and there was buried two days after without any pomp or solemn funeral.'

His death was to usher in the Tudor age. Over a century later, in the reign of the last Tudor, Elizabeth I, William Shakespeare was to write his play *Richard III*. By then the king had been transformed from the heartless criminal of his own time into the evil hunchback we recognise on stage today. Richard III, however, is one of the rare characters in British history who still arouses strong passions both in his condemnation and defence. Like the fates of Edward II and Richard II no one knows precisely what happened to the two princes while they were in the Tower. How long they actually remained alive and how they were done away with continues to attract lively debate which for many leaves open the option that Richard was in fact not responsible. The finger has even been pointed at his successor, Henry VII. What remains unchallenged is the fact that Richard failed to build up enough support to maintain himself in power. Even if one day he were proved to be innocent of infanticide he would remain a failed monarch.

A bronze processional cross, which had been in the possession of the Comerford family for about 70 years, and is reputed to have been dug up on the field of Bosworth in 1778.

Chapter Twenty-Four

WILLIAM CAXTON: PRINTER

THE arrival of printing in England was to be of far more importance than any of the changes of ruler during the Wars of the Roses. Up until this time books had been copied out by hand by scribes in monasteries or other workshops, a long and laborious process. As a result books were rare and very costly. Printing by machine meant that they could be cheap and plentiful. The knowledge books contained could also be spread far wider, reaching new audiences, as more people than ever before learned to read. When William Caxton set up his printing presses in the precincts of Westminster Abbey in 1476 it was to be a landmark in the history of the English language and literature, daily life and culture.

England was, in fact, quite late in receiving the new art of printing. The invention and use of moveable type had happened in Germany in the 1430s and was brought to perfection by Johann Gutenberg. From there it spread up the Rhine and into the Low Countries, besides travelling south to Italy. Caxton was to learn the craft from an unknown printer in Cologne when he was already in his fifties, a considerable age for a man to start a second career in the fifteenth century. His life captures vividly what it was like to live through the Wars of the Roses. He emerges, above all, as resilient. Fortunately for us, Caxton was a compulsive writer who reveals his character through his writings. Here was a man who had gusto, was sharp in his business dealings, pious in his faith, and totally loyal to the Yorkist cause. And that was both to make and break his career.

'I was born and learned my English in Kent in the Weald,' he wrote. That must have been in the reign of Henry V. Caxton came from a Norfolk family whose connections with the wool trade took them into both London and Kent. William's life followed a pattern which was standard at the time for boys of the merchant and trading classes. The most important City company to deal with the export of English woollen cloth was the

William Caxton presents the first book printed in English, his *Recuyell of the Historyes of Troye*, to Edward IV's sister, Margaret, Duchess of Burgundy.

A printer's shop in the late sixteenth century. It would not have changed much from Caxton's day. To the right there sits a type-setter while to the left someone prepares to ink the blocks for the printing press.

Mercers, and so he was apprenticed, a little before 1438, to the mercer, Robert Large. Large was an important businessman in the export of cloth to Flanders and was to become Lord Mayor of London. The Mercers, too, were Yorkists. Caxton trained in his household for anything between seven and ten or eleven years taking an oath to obey his master, serve him well, keep his trade secrets and do no business on his own account. Towards the end of that time it was customary for any promising young man to be sent to spend a year or two abroad representing his master. And this is what happened to William Caxton, who was sent to Bruges.

Bruges at this time was one of the greatest of European cities in terms of its wealth, magnificence and culture. It formed part of the dominions of the most elegant and extravagant court in Northern Europe, that of the Dukes of Burgundy, whose aim was to create a kingdom for themselves in that area of the Low Countries. Duke Philip the Good lived with unmatched splendour in a style which kings of England, such as Edward IV and Henry VII, copied. Bruges was a centre for the trade in luxury goods: figs, oranges, lemons, pepper, wax, quicksilver, satins, carpets, parrots and monkeys. Their own products included rich silks, jewellery, candles and illuminated manuscripts. Here booksellers and manuscript illuminators had their highly organised workshops with a thriving export trade all over Europe.

But Caxton was no part of that. He began by being a member of the English colony who lived in a communal residence in English Street, in a way a little like an Oxford college. Here he stayed, probably to avoid the civil wars at home and, in 1462, was made Governor, a full-time occupation involving looking after the interests of English merchants in the city. He held this post for nine years until he lost it during the short period when the Lancastrian king, Henry VI, was restored to power. Caxton, the loyal Yorkist, had to find a new career.

He was not, however, without important friends. In 1468 Edward IV's sister, Margaret, had married the Duke of Burgundy. She was a great patron both of authors and of the scribes and artists who produced beautifully illuminated books. She loved to read romances of chivalry and also books of religious devotion. Caxton became her part-time adviser and business agent, for she too dabbled in the wool trade. Already he had begun to translate a book of just the kind which the duchess liked to read, *The History of Troy*. She asked to see it, he tells us, and 'she anon found a fault in mine English, which she commanded me to amend . . .' More importantly she ordered him to finish the translation.

Caxton was first and foremost a businessman. In September 1471 he had finished the translation of what he knew had already been a bestseller at the Burgundian court. The duchess would certainly want several copies and there would be a large demand in England. It was precisely at this moment that he went on a mission to Cologne on behalf of Edward IV where he saw the answer to his problem, the printing press. He stayed there eighteen months learning how to print, and on his return to Bruges he began to set up his own press. He must have brought men with him from Cologne for there were many operations involved in producing a book: setting the type, working the presses, assembling and binding the pages. At the end of 1474 or early in the new

William Caxton's printer's mark which appeared on all the books he published.

year he at last produced *The History of Troy*, the first book ever to be printed in English. He wrote about this event with great pride:

'I have practiced and learned at my great charge and dispense [expense] to ordain this book in print after the manner and form as ye see here, and is not written with pen and ink as other books be, to the end every man may have them at once . . .'

Probably as many as four or five hundred copies were printed. It would have taken many scribes and several years to have written them all by hand. Caxton, however, was careful to see that his printed pages resembled as closely as possible the handwritten books which the court used. A woodcut shows him presenting his book to the duchess. He is only just admitted into her throne room to kneel before her while around her gather ladies in waiting with elaborate wimple headdresses, courtiers chattering, and a pet monkey.

Many of Caxton's copies would have been exported to England. His decision to move back there came in 1476, when the Duke of Burgundy was defeated and the whole country thrown into chaos. Late in that year Caxton opened his shop next to the chapter house of Westminster Abbey. This was an ideal location for it was on the path linking the palace to the church. Along that route would bustle courtiers, nobles, lawyers, churchmen, government officials and those who came to London for Parliament. Caxton knew what Edward IV and his court liked. They wanted to read what was fashionable at the court of Burgundy. So he began to print a long series of books which reflect the interests particularly of the queen and her relatives, the Woodvilles. Some were even translated by her brother, Lord Rivers. They included romances, school textbooks, a phrase book for travellers, lives of the saints, a history of England and, the most famous of all, Chaucer's *Canterbury Tales*.

The business prospered and soon he had new premises at the sign of the Red Pale which stood where the glass office block of the Department of Trade and Industry stands today in Victoria Street. But then things began to go badly wrong. Under Richard III his chief patrons, the Woodvilles, fell from power. Caxton remained loyal to them for as long as he could, producing books which owed their inspiration to the queen and her family, in which he included hidden references to them for fear of offending the usurper. But, by the spring of 1484, Caxton was forced to come to terms with the new regime and dedicate a book to Richard III. Alas, the result was that when Henry VII came to the throne the following year Caxton lost royal favour which he was not to regain for several years. But he did live long enough to achieve it, dedicating books both to the new king and his heir. He died in 1491 leaving his business to his chief assistant, Wynkyn de Worde.

Chapter Twenty-Five

RETURN TO ORDER: THE TUDORS

W HEN, in August 1485, the twenty-eight year old Henry Tudor stood as victor on the field of Bosworth it was by no means the dawn of a new age. For men at the time it merely marked yet another twist of fate in the long struggle of two rival dynasties to gain the throne. Half-a-century later, in the reign of his son, Henry VIII, the perception of that event had radically changed. By then the accession of the Tudors was accepted as the beginning of a new era. That transformation had been brought about by two things. The first was the success of Tudor rule, son had succeeded father without bloodletting, and the second was the promotion by the family itself of the idea. Those who wished to flatter them naturally vilified Richard III, glossed over the achievements of Edward IV, and magnified the horrors of the Wars of the Roses. In this way there was created the legend of the Union of the Roses, the red of Lancaster with the white of York, to form the one Tudor Rose.

The truth was very different, for the reign of Henry VII, and the first twenty years of his son's, were in reality a continuation of what had gone before. Henry VII was a reversion to Edward IV, a king who knew how to work and adapt the existing system to his advantage. But, unlike Edward, he was devoid of personal vices rendering him as a consequence a somewhat colourless monarch, one wholly devoid of the sexual bravura which made Edward IV and Henry VIII such compulsive personalities. Henry VII, however, was endowed with qualities which made for successful kingship: industry and application, patience and powers of organisation, and a firm belief in the splendour of the crown. Under him that conviction was to increase as it compensated for what he lacked most, a good claim to the throne. Henry's was extremely remote, dependent on one side on the marriage of his grandfather to the widow of Henry V and, on the other, descent from one of the children of John of Gaunt by his mistress, a line which had specifically been excluded from succession to the crown.

That sense of dynastic weakness was to haunt Henry VII for the greater part of his reign making it essential for him to establish the Tudor family as the rightful rulers of

England, recognised not only at home but also abroad. At the same time he had to ensure ordered government and a revived respect for royal power. On his accession he was all too well aware of this weakness; shrewdly, he never even argued his case for the crown, telling Parliament that it was his by inheritance and by divine judgment in battle. He then began the long task of eliminating rival claimants. These had arisen because of the intermarriage in the previous century of the royal family with members of the aristocracy. A great change takes place therefore, under the Tudors. Gradually, there is a deliberate distancing of the monarchy from the nobility. But it did not happen at once.

Henry began by marrying the Yorkist heiress, Edward's daughter Elizabeth. In September 1486 she gave birth to a son, who was named after the legendary British king, Arthur. From this moment the theme was that of the Union of the Roses of York and Lancaster. The problem was that there were several other white Roses, both genuine and spurious, who, for the next seventeen years, would attempt to gain the throne. One such claimant, Edward, Earl of Warwick, son of Edward IV's brother Clarence, was already held in custody in the Tower. Henry thus had under his control the one eligible male of age, which meant that the Yorkists had to fall back on impostors. The first of these was a harmless youth called Lambert Simnel, passed off by an Oxford priest first as one of the murdered princes and then as Edward, Earl of Warwick. Henry VII paraded the real earl through the streets of London, but to no effect. Simnel was taken to the Netherlands where he was supported by John, Earl of Lincoln, a son of Edward IV's sister, Elizabeth. The pretender sailed to Ireland and was crowned Edward VI in Dublin, after which both he and Lincoln landed in Lancashire. On 16 June 1487 they were defeated at the Battle of Stoke. Lincoln was killed and Simnel, a victim of the king's sardonic humour, was relegated to the royal kitchens as a scullion.

More dangerous was the second pretender, Perkin Warbeck, who for eight years maintained a role as the younger of the two princes in the Tower, Richard, Duke of York. Warbeck, the son of a Tournai boatman, was persuaded to take on the role in the autumn of 1491. He was enormously assisted by the diplomatic situation, for it suited foreign rulers at odds with Henry to entertain and recognise a rival claimant. The first to do so was the king of France but, when France wished for peace with Henry, Warbeck was forced to move on to the Netherlands where he was taken up by the ruler of the Low Countries, the Archduke Maximilian, who paraded him

Henry VII's Chapel, Westminster Abbey, built in 1503-1512 to house the tombs of the new Tudor dynasty. It represents the final flowering of the Middle Ages with its magnificently vaulted Perpendicular ceiling. The king's tomb within it, however, was to be the work of an Italian sculptor in the new Renaissance style, the first signal of a massive change of taste.

around Europe and, in 1495, financed a feeble invasion of England. A few hundred followers landed near Deal in Kent and were promptly massacred, Warbeck moving on to Ireland, where he failed to take Waterford, and then to Scotland. James IV received 'Prince Richard of England' and gave him an aristocratic bride. There was another attempted invasion of England from the north which was a disaster and, in 1495, yet another, this time from the south-west. Once more it was a catastrophe. On the advance of the royalist army towards Exeter Warbeck fled and sought sanctuary, later throwing himself on the king's mercy. Warbeck joined Warwick in the Tower. The story did not quite end there. Two years later fear of yet another plot led Henry to execute both of them.

Focus then shifted to the remaining sons of Edward IV's sister Elizabeth, Edmund, Earl of Suffolk and his brother Richard. Suffolk fled the country fearing the worst and was eventually handed back to Henry VII in 1506. Seven years later Henry VIII had him executed. Suffolk's brother Richard was to fall at the Battle of Pavia in 1525. Although this ostensibly wiped out all claimants, the Tudor family remained obsessed by anyone with a claim to the throne, however remote. Henry VII's grandchild Elizabeth was to reign for forty-five years refusing to recognise or even name a successor.

Henry VII followed Edward IV in sharing a firm belief that sound finances were one of the keys to successful rulership. When the king died after a reign of twenty-four years, an Italian wrote that he was 'the richest lord that is now known in the world'. That was an exaggeration for the truth was that he had died only just solvent, but that in itself was a major and rare feat, achieved through capitalising on what was his due as monarch in the way of income from crown lands, customs, and fees paid in connection with feudal rights. As the victor of Bosworth, Henry was able to pass acts of attainder against his enemies and thus take over their estates. What was unusual was that he held on to these estates, so that the income from them more than trebled. His avoidance of expensive foreign wars meant that trade flourished, and the amount which came in through customs went up. He also insisted on all his feudal dues, which made those who rigorously collected them very unpopular. Like Edward IV he saw that these revenues did not go into the cumbrous Exchequer but into his Chamber. There he himself took part in auditing the accounts, carefully putting his initials at the bottom of each page.

The monarchy needed to be rich, very rich, to rule successfully. It also needed good advice drawn from a broad spectrum of people, and it was during Henry's reign that the centre of regal power became based in the Council. This consisted of up to a hundred and fifty councillors in all, peers, lawyers, household officials and ecclesiastics. They rarely met all at once but formed a fluid group of support available to the king, embodying expertise covering every aspect of government. As time passed, some of these groups began to fulfil specific functions, such as the councillors who dealt with poor men's petitions, and gradually became known as the Court of Requests.

The monarchy also needed support throughout the country and many of the councillors occupied key posts outside London, in the north or on the Welsh Borders, for example. But far more important was the enhanced status given to members of the gentry, who were appointed by the crown to fill the role of Justice of the Peace. Through the century of Tudor rule they were fundamental instruments for the execution of royal policy in the countryside. The only weakness in the system was that they were unpaid. But the Tudors were brilliant at sensing the pulse of grass roots opinion, rarely asking officials to carry out a policy to which there was overwhelming opposition.

All of these things signalled what was to be the keynote of Tudor rule, the concentration of power in the hands of the dynasty. This changed the nature of power which became something no longer supported by armed retainers but exercised instead through wealth and political influence at court. Men now attached themselves to a great lord who enjoyed the king's favour, seeing this as the only way to preferment. Attendance at court and an office in the household therefore became the summit of ambition for the aristocracy. The Tudor kings saw this as a means of control and elaborated the role of the king, one already mystical in the Middle Ages, so that by the close of the sixteenth century the ruler enjoyed almost semi-divine status. What was known as the royal prerogative, an indefinite reserve of power vested in the will of the king, was universally accepted as sacrosanct and crucial to the working of the state. All of this was achieved by means of a steady escalation in the ceremonial and spectacle of the monarchy, whose every manifestation gradually took on an outward surface of unmatched magnificence. Under Henry VII the king became 'his Grace' but under his son the king became 'his Majesty'.

Henry VII's later years were overshadowed by the tragic death of his eldest son, Arthur, whose marriage in 1501 to the daughter of a newly-united Spain, Catherine of Aragon, had set the seal of international recognition on the dynasty. When Henry died at the age of fifty-two on 21 April 1509, he was succeeded by his second son, then aged only eighteen, who promptly married his brother's widow. On the surface no change could have seemed more dramatic, for Henry VIII had all the out-going characteristics his father had so singularly lacked. He was a handsome golden-haired youth, educated to be both an academic as well as an athlete. He was a talented musi-

Henry VII's tomb in Westminster Abbey was by a Florentine sculptor, Pietro Torrigiani. His work signalled the tentative arrival in England of the renaissance in Italy.

cian, could hold his own in a theological debate, and loved both the arts and learning. At the same time he was a skilled horseman, imbued with a devotion to chivalry, determined to shine as a man-at-arms not only in the pageantry of the tiltyard but on the field of battle. Henry had one fatal flaw: he disliked the business of government. For most of the first twenty years of his reign he found a solution to his disinterest in a person of exceptional application and brilliance, Thomas Wolsey. Wolsey was to rule England for the king, able to fulfil his every whim, taking from him the unwelcome burden of running the state, so that he could indulge in one long festival.

Behind the scenes, the system remained untouched but instead of being directly controlled by the king it was worked by his great minister. That soon bred resentment, especially among the older noble families. Wolsey was the son of an Ipswich butcher and cattle dealer and had risen rapidly through the church. He entered Henry VII's service in 1507 and in the new reign ascended with the speed of a meteor: Bishop of Lincoln and Archbishop of York in 1514, Lord Chancellor and Cardinal the year after. As the Archbishop of Canterbury refused to die Wolsey got himself appointed by the pope *legatus a latere*, that is, a special residential legate whose powers extended over the whole English church. No previous prelate had ever held such extensive powers or had such a devouring passion for work. But Wolsey was proud, and his splendid style, which included building Hampton Court, aroused envy in those who looked on. His gentleman-usher, Thomas Cavendish, gives a memorable impression:

'There was . . . borne before him, first the great seal of England, and then his cardinal's hat, by a nobleman or some worthy gentleman, right solemnly, bare-headed . . . Thus he passed forth with two great crosses of silver borne before him; with also two great pillars of silver, and his sergeant-at-arms with a great mace of silver gilt. Then his gentlemen-ushers cried and said: "Oh, my lords and masters! Make way for my Lord's Grace!"'

Wolsey's prime task was to fulfil the king's wish to make England a major player on the stage of European politics, where the position was very different from that of the preceding century. Everything on the mainland had come to focus on the great struggle between the Valois kings of France and the Habsburg rulers of most of the rest of Western Europe. In this confrontation, Wolsey believed that England could play a crucial role as peacemaker. Alas, that was to prove to be an expensive delusion. It was, however, to provide the *raison d'être* for a succession of spectacular diplomatic meetings. The most famous of these, known as Field of the Cloth of Gold, was held in 1520 between Henry and the French king, Francis I, an event whose extravagance has passed into legend. Over five thousand persons attended Henry and his queen, and over six thousand laboured on constructing a small temporary town of gorgeous tents and pavilions, whose centrepiece was a glittering palace of painted canvas and wood. England was virtually emptied of precious fabrics and jewels to decorate this palace.

As usual, Wolsey took care of every detail, right down to worrying about whether there would be enough beer and wine, green geese, rabbits, storks, quails and cheese to feed everyone. This was typical of the relationship between king and minister which was to remain undisturbed until Henry VIII's whims took a more dangerous direction, one which Wolsey could not follow. In the spring of 1527 Henry decided that his marriage to his brother's widow was sinful and sought for it to be annulled. That single decision was to precipitate the greatest changes England had undergone since 1066. It was also to bring about the fall of Wolsey.

The famous meeting of Henry VIII and Francis I, the Field of Cloth of Gold, in 1520 was one of the most spectacular pageants of the age. Here its splendour is evoked by a painter later in the reign who brings together in one picture several of the events. To the left the king makes his entry into Guisnes with Cardinal Wolsey at his side. To the right is the fantastic temporary palace which was built to accommodate the royal party, its walls of wood and painted canvas. In the centre above, the two kings meet while, to the right, they watch a tournament. One of the spectacles was a firework dragon, seen top left, which flew across the sky during mass on 23 June. To the right a small army of kitchen staff apply their skills to feeding the vast assembly of people.

Chapter Twenty-Six

REFORMATION AND REVOLUTION

WHEN Henry VIII informed Wolsey that he wished his marriage to be annulled by the pope, it was at a time when the experience of going to church was as it had been for centuries. The congregation gathered in the nave to hear the Latin mass. The walls and windows of the church were bright with paintings and stained glass depicting the gospel stories and the lives of the saints. There were carved images of the Virgin and saints before which candles were lit as prayers were said asking for their intercession in heaven. The nave was divided from the chancel by a screen beyond which the laity did not pass, and above which was suspended a life-size image of Christ on the cross flanked by the Virgin and St. John, known as the rood. Beyond lay the chancel, the area of the church sacred to the priest, with a stone altar against the east end. Sometimes near the altar there would be relics of saints exhibited, bones or fragments of clothing, kept within a container of some precious material. The altar was adorned with rich hangings which were changed according to the season of the church's year, white for Easter or red for the feasts of martyrs. The altar was the focus of the entire church, for on it was re-enacted in the mass each day the sacrifice of Christ on the cross. The priest wore embroidered vestments, incense was burned, and at solemn moments bells were rung. Above the altar a small piece of consecrated bread, the host, was exhibited within a suspended container called a pyx, covered by a veil or cloth. In this way, even outside the mass, Christ's body was perpetually present, heaven came down to earth. Medieval Catholic Christianity was a vivid faith approached through things seen and the senses.

Half-a-century later that experience was to be very different. Although the stained glass might still remain because of the expense of replacing it with plain glass, the interior was virtually stripped bare, every painted or sculpted image either painted over, taken away or defaced, the walls whitewashed and

Henry VIII at prayer in the royal closet, a specially canopied enclosure within the Chapel Royal. The illumination dates from the middle of the 1530s and appears in the borders of a manuscript recording the activities of the Order of the Garter.

adorned only with biblical texts. Over the rood screen instead of the cross there was the royal arms. Within the chancel the stone altar and pyx had gone. Instead there was a wooden table used only very occasionally when Holy Communion, the service which replaced the mass, took place, when it was taken down into the body of the church with only a linen cloth laid over it. The priest was no longer attired with vestments but a surplice. On most Sundays the service would have been one of morning prayer, said not in Latin but English, and in which the congregation took part. Lessons were read from an English Bible, and the main focus was no longer the chancel but the pulpit from which the sermon was delivered. A Christianity which had appealed to the eye had been replaced by one whose prime organ was the ear and whose aim was to hear and receive the word of God.

In terms of the people of England that was to be the greatest change of the century. No one in 1527 could have foreseen that this would be the long-term consequence of what began as the king's marital problems. This huge change needs also to be set against the broader backcloth of the movement known as the Reformation which swept across Europe. Up until the beginning of the sixteenth century the Catholic church had remained one, with the pope at its head ruling through his bishops. For centuries the church had gone through good and bad periods, yet always managing to respond to reform in time to avert schism and division. Always, that is, until this century, when the response came too late, reinforcing, instead of lessening, the divisions. The result was the breakup of Christendom into Catholic and Protestant, between those who remained loyal to Rome and Catholic Christianity and those who rejected Rome and embraced a form of Protestantism. This caused a catastrophic division across the whole of Western Europe, one which affected not only families but whole countries, leading to bloody persecution and war.

By the time that Henry VIII wanted his divorce from Catherine of Aragon this great movement was well established in Germany under the leadership of Martin Luther, whose ideas were already reaching England. These ideas anticipated much of what was eventually to happen during the coming decades: the rejection of papal authority, the abolition of religious orders, the ability of priests to marry, the right of the laity to receive the wine as well as the bread at mass or communion, the use of the vernacular for church services and the sweeping away of the cult of the Virgin and saints, pilgrimages and relics. The medieval church had preached seven sacraments, baptism in infancy, confirmation in childhood, matrimony and holy orders, penance and the Eucharist to cleanse and feed the soul, and anointing to comfort the sick and dying. Luther only preached two: baptism and the Eucharist. The theological debate over what happened at the latter raged furiously, the reformers seeing it more as a commemoration than a literal transmutation of the bread and wine into Christ's body and blood. As if all of this were not enough, the reformers redefined man's relation with God in such a way that much of what the church had laid store by – good works, pilgrimages, pardons, formal penances, masses for the souls of the departed – was rendered redundant. Returning to St. Paul the reformers proclaimed his words that man could be justified or saved by faith alone. Such beliefs changed the nature of the clergy; they ceased to be a caste set apart acting as intermediaries between God and man.

In 1527 Henry's queen was forty and past child-bearing. Her only surviving child was one sickly daughter, Mary. The king saw this as a judgment for marrying his brother's widow, something which the Bible explicitly forbade and which had only been made possible by a special dispensation from the pope. Henry wanted a son and he was now deeply in love with a lady of the court, Anne Boleyn, young enough to bear one. Anne was an ambitious, educated woman whose time at the French court had left her sympathetic to the reformers. Wolsey's task was to obtain a divorce from the pope so that she and the king could wed, something which he failed to do, not only because the pope saw no reason to grant one but also because during that time he was under the control of the queen's nephew, the Emperor Charles V. The cardinal's attempts dragged on for two years until, in 1529, the pope saw a way of prolonging the saga even further by setting up a court in England presided over by Wolsey and an Italian cardinal. It sat for five months through the summer of 1529 achieving little, when the pope suddenly revoked the case to Rome.

Cardinal Wolsey's public appearances began to rival in splendour those of the king. Before him were carried massive silver crosses and his cardinal's hat.

The king was furious. And here, for the first time on any scale, emerges that personal characteristic which was to dominate the rest of the reign. Henry VIII made people but he also broke them if they crossed his path. Wolsey was to be his first major victim, one who evoked little sympathy due to his unpopularity. He was a failure with enemies on all sides. The cardinal was indicted of *praemunire*, that is of exercising an unlawful jurisdiction in this country, alluding to his legatine powers. Deprived of his office of chancellor he set off to visit his See of York. A year later he was arrested and was escorted south, but he was ill and sought shelter in the abbey of Leicester where he died, thus avoiding the executioner's axe. Some of his last words were: 'But if I had served God as diligently as I have done the king, He would not have given me over in my grey hairs.'

Events now began to take a sharper turn. The king appointed a new chancellor, Sir Thomas More. But of far greater importance was the summoning of Parliament which met in November 1529. This was to prove a turning point in its history. Henry needed support. Parliament consisted not only of the lords but more particularly representatives of the towns and shires. It was thus a means whereby the monarchy in its war against Rome could be seen to be at one with the country. The great statutes which it was shortly to pass demonstrated a new partnership which set a pattern for the future. The king was also fortunate, for he was able to benefit from the strongly anti-clerical mood of the Commons. People were envious of the wealth of the church which held a third of all the country's land. They resented paying tithes and also ecclesiastical courts. They were disgusted at the corruption of many of the clergy, typified by the worldliness of Wolsey. What was to play into the king's hands even more in this opening phase was the clergy's resentment of Rome, the result of having been ridden over roughshod by Wolsey with his legatine powers.

So the scene was set for acts which were to bring about the greatest changes to England since 1066. These began with an onslaught on the church. In December 1530 the whole clergy was indicted of *praemunire*, that is, like Wolsey, charged with having exercised an unlawful jurisdiction. Two months later Henry pardoned them in return for a huge fine and the recognition of the king 'as far as the law of Christ allows supreme head of the Church in England'. In this way the gauntlet was thrown down to the pope who ignored it and forbade the king to remarry.

In December 1531 these opening shots were given a new impetus through the admission to the inner circle of the Council of Thomas Cromwell. He, like Wolsey in whose service he had been, was of humble origins. Brilliant but also cold and calculating, he was endowed with a first-rate mind together with the attributes of a cunning tactician who knew how to manipulate Parliament. In Cromwell, Henry had alighted upon the one man able to mastermind his will and offices were showered upon him. He was made Chancellor of the Exchequer and Principal Secretary.

Events began to move more swiftly. Parliament attacked the ecclesiastical courts. In a panic the convocations of York and Canterbury put them into the hands of the king in an act known as the Submission of the Clergy. Henry was now in control of the church. Early in 1533 he married Anne Boleyn secretly. She was already pregnant. In March Parliament passed the Act in Restraint of Appeals severing the church from Rome, in effect creating the Church *of* England as against the church *in* England. The preamble to the act proclaimed that 'this realm of England is an empire . . . governed by one Supreme Head and king'. In one mighty gesture England was severed from the Universal Church, the king replacing the pope with himself.

Meanwhile the old Archbishop of Canterbury had died allowing Henry to appoint one sympathetic to his plight but who was also a reformer, Thomas Cranmer. He granted the king his divorce, Henry remarried and, in September, the new queen gave birth to a daughter, Elizabeth. The year after the severance from Rome was wound up in the Act of Supremacy which transferred to the king as 'Supreme Head of the Church of England' all ecclesiastical dues formerly sent to the pope. In those days everything depended on precedent and the king claimed that he was doing no more than putting the clock back to the days of the early church. In his view the new power he exercised, to administer and tax the church, control its laws and courts and even define doctrine and lay down ritual, were those which had been enjoyed by Roman emperors before they had been usurped by the popes.

What is surprising is how little opposition this revolution evoked. Perhaps people thought that this was merely a temporary dislocation which would later be patched up, but they were wrong. Those who realised the full implications and protested were savagely treated. A nun, Elizabeth Barton, who predicted a dire fate for the king if he pursued these policies was rounded up with her accomplices and executed. More victims followed after the first Act of Succession demanded an oath from every adult recognising that the king's first marriage had been invalid and that his heir was to be a child by Anne Boleyn. A handful of monks of the strictest order, the Carthusians, were cruelly tortured, hanged, drawn and quartered for refusing to swear it. Two saintly men, John Fisher, Bishop of Rochester, and Sir Thomas More were sent to the scaffold. But on the whole the revolution which destroyed the medieval church in England was a bloodless one.

There was, however, to be no let up. In January 1535 Cromwell, in his new capacity as vicar-general of the Church of England, sent out commissioners to report on the state of the monasteries. Their findings could have been guessed even before they

to enjoy his elevation for long. Henry's eye had fallen on the lascivious niece of the conservative Norfolk, Katherine Howard. Soon after Cromwell found himself in the Tower and executed. Thus ended the life of a man who was hated and yet whose impact on the history of the country was incalculable.

After Cromwell's demise the conservatives were in the ascendant, even though the new queen's notorious past came to light and she too went to the scaffold. Henry then made his sixth and last marriage to Catherine Parr. By this time he had become the gross monster of popular legend but she reunited him with his children and had a significant influence, seeing that Edward and Elizabeth were educated by those who favoured reform. Henry VIII died at the age of fifty-seven on 27 January 1547.

Not since the Norman Conquest, five hundred years before, had England undergone such dramatic changes imposed from above on her people. The victims still excite our sense of compassion but they were few when set against the enormity of what had been done. Church and state had been welded into one. A new alliance had been forged between the monarchy and the nobility and gentry who had co-operated in the destruction of the medieval church. The powers of the crown had been exalted to unprecedented heights. A new political identity had been established: the commonweal of England. What is surprising is how that survived the disastrous decade that followed. So far the interiors of the churches had barely been touched. Although there was an English Bible issued under royal auspices in 1536, the Latin mass remained unchanged. Henry VIII was barely buried before the intrusive hand of Tudor government began to touch the everyday religious life of England in a far more dramatic way.

Title-page to the English Bible. The translation was made under the aegis of Thomas Cromwell and appeared in April 1539. The first, by Miles Coverdale, was published in 1536. The advent of a Bible in the English language was to have immense influence on the English people and later their colonial offspring in the New World. Henry VIII hands it simultaneously to the Archbishop of Canterbury and to Thomas Cromwell and from them it spreads downwards to rich and poor, young and old, men and women.

Chapter Twenty-Seven

A MAN FOR ALL SEASONS

To those caught up in it, the Reformation was to bring a conflict of loyalties of a kind not witnessed before. Men were forced to choose between loyalty to the king or to the Universal Church. As the century progressed this polarity was to develop into one between rival faiths. But that had not yet happened in the 1530s when the dilemma claimed its first victims. Of these the most famous was Sir Thomas More, Henry VIII's scholarly and saintly Lord Chancellor.

More was born in the last year of the reign of Edward IV, the son of John More, a barrister of Lincoln's Inn, one of the Inns of Court, the London headquarters of the legal profession. As was the custom he was placed in a noble household, in his case that of the Archbishop of Canterbury, Cardinal Morton. There his precosity was immediately recognised, the cardinal saying: 'This child here waiting at table whosoever shall live to see it, will prove a marvellous man.' It was the archbishop who saw to it that young Thomas was sent to Oxford with an eye to his entering the church. Throughout his life More remained a man of intense piety, even secretly wearing a hairshirt next to his skin as a form of perpetual penance. Although he considered the religious life he realised that it was not his true vocation, and was called to the bar in 1502. By then he had become one of the most accomplished classical scholars of his generation in Latin and Greek, for he grew up precisely during the period when England, on the distant fringes of Europe, was responding to the great cultural revival known as the Renaissance.

That movement had originated in Italy over a century before. It began with scholars called humanists who turned their attention to the writers of Greece and Rome, whose works had often been corrupted during the Middle Ages, or indeed been lost and were now recovered. The humanists turned to these in order not only to re-establish a purity of style in writing but also to recover lost knowledge and ideas. It was a passionate quest out of which sprang a new learning and a new art whose focus was man as God's image, but occupying a very different position in the scheme of

FAMILIA THOMÆ MORI ANGL: CANCELL:

Thomas Morus A⁺.50. Alicia Thomæ Mori uxor A⁺.57. Iohannes Morus pater A⁺.76.Iohannes Morus Thomæ filius A⁺.19. Anna Grisacria Iohannis Mori Sponsa A⁺.15.Margareta Ropera Thomæ Mori filia A⁺.22.
Elisabeta Damea Thomæ Mori filia A⁺.21. Cæcilia Heroina Thomæ Mori filia A⁺.20. Margareta Giga Clementis uxor Mori filiabus Condiscipula et cognata A⁺.22. Henricus Patensonus Thomæ Mori morio A⁺.40.

Thomas More, his father and his household in 1527-28. This was a drawing made by the great German artist Hans Holbein which was sent to More's friend, the humanist Erasmus. It records what the first family group in British art looked like as it was being painted, with notes of proposed alterations to the composition. It depicts a room in More's Chelsea house.

things from his medieval predecessor. In his new role man could atune himself to God's universe through the study and discovery of its underlying principles, ones believed to be expressed in number and proportion. These were reached through an examination of its physical phenomena and by its inheritance, both written and visual, from the ancient world. One aspect of that return was the search for the earliest and therefore the truest texts of the great works of the past, above all those of the Bible and of the early Christian writers. To achieve a pure uncorrupted text of the New Testament from the original Greek was, they believed, a means whereby to get closer to the word of God. The greatest exponent of this north of the Alps was Erasmus, who became one of More's greatest friends. Typically they wrote to each other letters in the new elegant Latin modelled on authors like the Roman Cicero, and not in the bastardised Latin of the Middle Ages.

When More was twenty-six he married Jane Colt, the daughter of an Essex gentleman. By her he became the father of three daughters and a son but she died young. Within a month of her demise More, anxious about the care of his young family, married a widow, Alice Middleton, 'aged, blunt and rude', as she was described at the time, but he loved her. The household they ruled over was a pious one, besides being a monument to the new values of humanist learning. More was a pioneer of women's education and his children were schooled in both religion and the classics, 'for erudition in women,' he wrote, 'is a new thing and a reproach to the idleness of men.' So they were taught Latin, Greek, philosophy, theology, mathematics and astronomy. The More family lived first in the City and later in the mansion which he

Thomas More's gift to Henry VIII of five poems celebrating the king's coronation in 1509. Elegant Latin verses salute the dawn of a new age and extol the king's beauty, learning and nobility. The borders of the manuscript are decorated with flowers including red and white roses symbolising the union of York and Lancaster.

built himself at Chelsea on the banks of the Thames. The famous German painter, Hans Holbein, who was to bring the new humanist art of portraiture to England and who was to paint More and his family, described it as 'dignified without being magnificent.'

In 1516 More's most famous work was published, *Utopia*, which describes an imaginary nation as recounted by a traveller who had voyaged to America, discovered only thirteen years before. More uses this account to attack the greed and pride of his own society but also goes on to include extraordinary premonitions of things to come: attacks on hunting, euthanasia, religious tolerance, cremation of the dead, as well as women priests and soldiers. It is the only one of his writings still read today.

The year before it appeared he had entered Henry VIII's service and rapidly rose to be a member of the Council. His charm and wit entranced the king who constantly called for his attendance, even inviting him up onto the roof of the palace 'to consider with him the diversities, courses, motions and operations of the stars and planets.' The king too would come to Chelsea. William Roper, who married More's eldest daughter, Margaret, describes one such visit:

'For the pleasure he took in his company, would His Grace suddenly sometimes come to his house in Chelsea, to be merry with him; whither on a time unlooked for, he came to dinner with him, and after, in a fair garden of his, walked with him by the space of an hour, holding his arm about his neck.'

More was showered with royal favours being knighted, made under-treasurer of the Exchequer and Speaker of the House of Commons.

Soon he was called upon to defend the church against the ideas arriving in England from Germany during the 1520s. Such ideas had even percolated his own household and he was upset to find his son-in-law Roper convinced 'that faith only did justify, that the works of man did nothing profit. . .' More was appalled by the spread of false doctrine, that is heresy, deviations from the teaching of the Universal Church, and attacked the reformers vigorously in a long series of writings. Then, as Lord Chancellor, he had to mete out to those heretics who believed such things the fate laid down for them by legislation, burning at the stake.

It was with great reluctance that he accepted the office of Lord Chancellor in succession to Wolsey, making it conditional that at no point would he be called upon to act in any way in the divorce. More accepted totally the ruling of the church, that Henry's first marriage was valid and that Catherine of Aragon could not be set aside.

Hans Holbein's woodcut of Utopia in the Basel edition of 1518. The visitor, Hythlodaeus, bottom left, points past his ship to the island itself with its own town of Amaurotum or Dream Town.

As the events of the 1530s unfolded he looked aghast at the statutes which were being passed by the Reformation Parliament, ones severing England from the Universal Church. On the day after the clergy acknowledged the king as the Supreme Head of the Church he gave up the seal of office and with it the majority of his income. His family were horrified. 'We may not look at our pleasure to go to heaven on feather beds,' he told them, 'it is not the way.' The king was irked that this brilliant minister would not publicly support him, and when More refused to go to Anne Boleyn's coronation the new queen's family were out for his blood. They did not have to wait long.

The nun of Kent, who predicted that the king would die a villain's death if ever he put Catherine of Aragon away, had mentioned More as one of her supporters. When she was rounded up More was questioned but successfully defended himself. The king then increased the pressure by stopping his salary as a councillor. In March 1534 the first Act of Succession was passed. It laid down that every adult had to take an oath recognising that the king's first marriage had been invalid and swearing loyalty to a succession by way of children born to Henry and Anne. Anyone who even spoke against these things was guilty of treason for which the punishment was forfeiture of goods and death. On the day that More was summoned to take that oath he knew that it would be the last time that he would see his family together. Instead of letting them escort him to his barge on the Thames, where he used to kiss each of them farewell, he left them at the garden gate and got into the boat alone with his son-in-law Roper 'with a heavy heart.' Suddenly, as the boat was propelled along the water, he turned to Roper and said in his ear, 'Son Roper, I thank Our Lord, the field is won.'

Twice More was induced to take the oath and refused. He was imprisoned in the Tower. His family were distraught, above all his wife, Dame Alice, who failed totally to understand his refusal. Visiting him she upbraided him for all that he had thrown away. More's son-in-law, William Roper, records the exchange:

> 'After he had a while quietly heard her, with a cheerful countenance he said unto her, "I pray thee, good Mistress Alice, tell me one thing."
> "What is that?" quoth she.
> "Is not this house," quoth he, "as nigh unto heaven as my own?"'

So far he had faced imprisonment and the loss of his goods, but Parliament passed a new Act of Treason in which death was prescribed if ever anyone as much as denied the Royal Supremacy of the church before a witness.

It was now only a matter of time. Four months later More was cross-examined by Thomas Cromwell and other members of the Council. Once again he succeeded in evading the issue. Shortly after, the pope made John Fisher, Bishop of Rochester, who was in the Tower for the same offence, a cardinal. Henry was furious: 'Let the pope send him a [cardinal's] hat when he will. I will so provide that whenever it cometh he will wear it on his shoulders, for head shall he have none to set it on.'

A little later, Fisher was tricked into denying the Royal Supremacy and executed on Tower Hill. Something similar happened to More. In July he was at last brought to trial. He defended himself gallantly, but the judgment was a foregone conclusion. Just before sentence was passed he at long last broke his silence and spoke of his commitment to a Universal Church whose powers neither prince nor Parliament had any right to usurp as they had been entrusted by Christ to St. Peter and his successors as popes.

As he left Westminster Hall and made his way to Tower Wharf his eldest daughter, Margaret, knelt and received his blessing. She pushed her way through the crowds and guards 'and there openly in the sight of them all, embraced him, took him about the neck and kissed him.' More wrote to her for the last time from his cell in the Tower: 'Farewell my dear child and pray for me, and I shall pray for you and all your friends that we may merrily meet in heaven.'

The following morning, 6 July, before nine o'clock More was beheaded on Tower Hill:

> 'Going up the scaffold, which was so weak that it was ready to fall, he said merrily to Master Lieutenant, "I pray you Master Lieutenant, see me safe up, and for my coming down let me shift for myself."'

He obeyed the king's command that he should say but little, 'protesting that he died his good servant, but God's first.' His body was thrown into a traitor's grave and his head, as was the custom, was impaled and exhibited on London Bridge. Later his daughter Margaret rescued it and gave it burial.

More's execution evoked horror through the whole of Western Europe. He was one of the earliest victims of the English Reformation. As the decades passed these multiplied from both sides of the divide. More passionately believed that Henry VIII in divorcing his wife had acted against God's law over which Parliament had no sway. Neither the king nor Parliament have any right, he believed, to rend asunder the seamless robe of the Universal Church. More is one of those rare figures who occupied a great office of state and never compromised what he believed in. No one since has failed to be moved by this story of a man who died for his principles meeting the event neither with silent resignation, nor with a pious homily, but with a joke.

Chapter Twenty-Eight

THE TURBULENT
DECADE

HENRY VIII left three pale-faced and fair-haired children, Edward, aged nine, who succeeded as king, Mary, who was thirty-two, and Elizabeth, who was fourteen. All of them inherited their father's strength of will, his pride and his arrogance but they were divided by religion. And that division was profoundly to affect the middle years of the century as one by one the children succeeded to the crown, each time taking the country in a different direction. Edward, who had the makings of a theological prig, was an ardent, indeed extreme devotee of the Protestant cause; Mary, her faith shaped by the cruel fate of her mother, yearned for a return to Middle Ages Catholicism; while Elizabeth dwelt somewhere between, hankering for things as they had stood on her father's death, Catholicism without the pope.

But changes in religion were not the only things which were dramatically to affect everyone during these years. There were others which, added to religion, were cumulatively to lead to social unrest, riots and even open rebellion on a scale which threatened established order. One was roaring inflation. For over a century prices had been more or less stable. Then, during the first half of the century, they doubled. No one at the time understood why and blamed it on greedy landlords. As prices went up, the government naturally needed more money and decided, late in Henry VIII's reign, to take a short cut by making what was soon realised to be a disastrous mistake, debasing the coinage, that is reducing the amount of silver in each coin. By 1550 the silver content was a sixth of what it had been in 1500. To begin with debasing made the government richer because there was more money but soon everyone realised that the coinage was in reality worth less, so they put up their prices.

If people put up their prices then naturally everyone needs more money in order to live. Not only do the poor at the bottom of the social scale get poorer but so do the rich. Both were under pressure for money and this triggered change. At the summit was the crown which as the century progressed became poorer and poorer, because it relied for its income on rents which were fixed. As a consequence it had to seek other ways of raising cash or turn to Parliament, which no ruler enjoyed doing. Lower down the scale landowners also had to seek ways to increase revenue. One was by increasing large-scale sheep-farming. Its labour costs were low, just a shepherd and a boy to

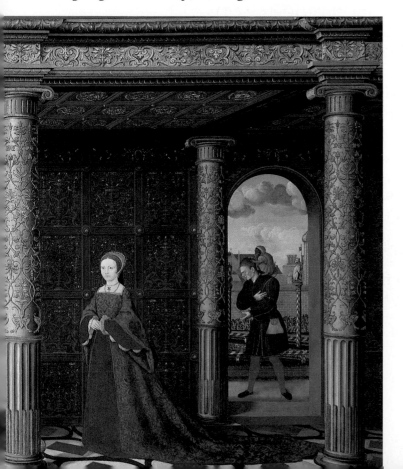

The family of Henry VIII at the close of his reign. The king sits enthroned with the Tudor arms on a canopy above him, his son Edward VI, to his right, and his third wife, Jane Seymour, to his left. To the left there is his eldest daughter by his first wife, Catherine of Aragon, the future Mary I. To the right his daughter by his second wife, Anne Boleyn, the future Elizabeth I. The richly gilded interior records the reality of Tudor palace decoration, while through the two arches the garden of Whitehall Palace is seen.

tend the huge flocks. But to do this called for areas of pastureland very different from the old system of land division into strips. Some owners began to consolidate as much of their land as they could, evicting peasants and even demolishing whole villages, beginning to create the enclosed fields with fences, hedges and ditches which we recognise as the pattern of the countryside today. They even went on to enclose the common land, used by everyone for grazing for their animals. Enclosures could be as much for cattle as for sheep. Where they could the owners raised rents; where men could not pay they lost their land, and faced the option of either becoming wage-earning labourers or taking to the open road as vagabonds. The centuries-old system of peasants with strips of land for which they paid by tending the lord's demesne began very gradually to disappear. But it was to be a prolonged process stretching over the next three hundred years. The gainer from all this was the landowner, and the most enterprising of the labouring classes, who became leasehold farmers. The losers became landless labourers. A pattern of rural life was thus established which was to last into the twentieth century, and only to vanish with mechanisation.

Large-scale sheep-farming was one response to the pressures of inflation. But there were others. Landowners with estates which had natural resources such as coal or zinc-ore began to exploit them. Merchants responded by opening up new markets. This was often done by means of what was called a joint stock company, which was a group of men, not only merchants but gentry, even courtiers, who pooled money to finance an enterprise and then shared out any profits. As the century progressed merchants were looking for outlets for English goods in Africa, India, Russia and the Levant. The great houses which are the glory of the Tudor age began to arise from the proceeds.

In this way the successful landowner was the winner in every sense of the word. He could be an aristocrat or a gentleman, and the passage from one to the other was in the hands of the monarch who could knight and ennoble. Successful is the key word, for families rose and fell for any number of reasons from political to financial incompetence. But none of this could erode the fact that there were more landowners than ever. They were the people who sought and held office at court and in government, were Justices of the Peace in the shires, and were elected as members of Parliament to the Commons. They were a broad spectrum of people: nobility, gentry, merchants, lawyers, even yeomen.

Collectively, they now had power as never before. In order to carry through the Reformation the crown had sought an alliance with them, and that they never allowed any subsequent wearer of the crown to forget. As a result the landowning classes were to set the political agenda for the nation until the reign of Queen Victoria. No monarch could successfully rule without their support. In the Commons they had their means of voicing dissent and increasingly they were to assert that as a right.

These profound changes reached a pitch during the middle years of the century when their effects were aggravated by a long series of disastrous harvests. So bad were the harvests of 1555 and 1556 that someone wrote: 'The scarcity of bread was so great in so much the plain poor people did [eat] of acorns and drink water.' To add to the misery of these years, there were terrible epidemics. Many of the consequences of all this could have been avoided if government had been competent, but it was not. For a decade everything that Tudor rule had stood for was under threat. The strength of that earlier achievement can be measured by the fact that their rule survived these years and emerged virtually unscathed to pass once more into competent hands when the last Tudor came to the throne in 1558.

The events of the 1530s had effectively re-ordered the power structure in the country though not much had actually touched the rhythm of ordinary daily life. But that was to happen more and more. The *Chronicle of the Grey Friars of London* records two events which changed a centuries' old way of life. The first occurred in September 1547: '*Item* the V day in September began the king's visitation at [St.] Paul's, and all images pulled down . . . and so all images pulled down throughout all England at that time, and all churches new white-limed, with the [Ten] Commandments written on the walls. . .'

Under Edward VI the attack on images began resulting in the mass destruction of a heritage of medieval painting and sculpture, of which today only fragments remain. The churches were stripped bare and whitewashed.

Then, a year later: '*Item* after Easter began the services in English at [St.] Paul's and also in diverse other parish churches. . .'

The first changed the appearance of every parish church in the country as images of the Virgin and saints were either taken out and burnt if they were of wood, or smashed to bits with hammers if they were of stone. The multi-coloured wall paintings telling the stories of the gospels and of the saints vanished beneath whitewash upon which biblical texts were now written. The second entry signals services in English, no longer Latin. By the end of Edward VI's reign the old Latin mass had been swept away and replaced by the services of Holy Communion enacted at a table which stood in the nave of the church. But that was to happen only occasionally, for the main form of worship came to be Morning Prayer whose focus was on psalm singing and the sermon from the pulpit. English religion gradually assumed a pattern which was to last into the twentieth century.

As in the 1530s it was change from the top. Throughout the century there lingered a hankering after the old way of worship. The rites and rituals of medieval Catholicism did not vanish overnight. The fact that nearly everyone went along with the changes, albeit with resignation, reflected the overwhelming respect and fear which the Tudor rulers evoked, even if, as in the case of Edward VI, that ruler happened to be a child and an unattractive one at that.

Like his sister Elizabeth, Edward was intellectually precocious. In addition he was self-righteous and downright cruel, characteristics of his father, and, a trait of childhood, he was easily dominated. Due to his upbringing he was devoted to Protestantism and fascinated by all forms of theological debate. Where religious change had stood still late in Henry VIII's reign, the new king wished to move it on, and in this he found allies in the two men who effectively governed the realm for him. The first of these was his uncle, Edward Seymour, Duke of Somerset, a brave and brilliant soldier, who was made Protector of the Realm. Somerset was a poor politician, having a visionary streak which extended to caring about the fate of those who suffered from the enclosures. Sympathy for the poor and oppressed was not an attribute for a Tudor politician. That sympathy in the end was to be his undoing for it alienated the landowners, who should have been his power base. All they saw as a result of his few years of rule was a threat to themselves in the form of rebellion and riot from below.

But the reign began ostensibly well with the Protector winning a resounding victory over the Scots at the Battle of Pinkie. Bans on religious debate were lifted and reformers flooded into the country turning it into a Babel of conflicting religious opinions. The chantries, foundations for saying masses for the souls of the dead, were dissolved and their lands and treasure confiscated for the crown. That was the first of a series of changes to hit every man, for it wiped out simple actions like the lighting of candles in church to mark a prayer of intercession. Soon came the order to remove images, a decree which was progressively amplified and extended until, by 1551, everything was to be obliterated. The churches assumed that empty stripped appearance which was to last until the Victorian age. The clergy were then given permission to marry and the laity to receive the wine as well as the bread at communion. Meanwhile Thomas Cranmer, Archbishop of Canterbury, compiled a *Book of Common Prayer* to replace the old service books. It was in English and retained much of Catholic practice, including the use of ritual and vestments. In June 1549 Parliament passed an Act of Uniformity imposing its use in every church.

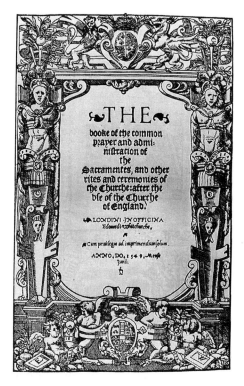

The title-page of the 1549 Prayer Book, the first and more conservative of the two issued in Edward VI's reign.

Although there had already been unrest and riots in the south-west and the midlands the year before, the new service triggered off a major uprising in Cornwall. To the consternation of the government the rebels began to march east but then, fortunately, changed their minds and laid siege to Exeter. In August an army was sent, and they were wiped out. At the same time there was an even more serious uprising in East Anglia, led by a yeoman called Robert Kett, which began in July, when rebels took the city of Norwich. This time the grievances were not religious but social, fuelled by resentment of enclosures. The initial attempt by the government to cope with this insurrection was a fiasco and it was not until an army was sent under John Dudley, Earl of Warwick, that the fate of the rebels was sealed by a bloodbath both in battle and in the subsequent executions.

The Tudor ruling classes feared the overthrow of established order more than anything and two years of Somerset's government had eroded any confidence in him. The king had never liked Somerset, nor had he friends in the Council which ran the country with him. In October he was arrested and sent to the Tower. Power now passed to a very different kind of person, Warwick, who, two years later, became Duke of Northumberland, and who saw that Somerset in time was duly executed. Northumberland was a man who had no scruple and whose ambitions knew no bounds. It is difficult indeed to disentangle a single redeeming feature in his character. What now happened was a return to the style of the previous century, when powerful magnates struggled to gain control of the king, and hence political power, which they exercised solely in the interests of their own personal greed. Northumberland dominated the boy king. Religious reform now went further than ever before. A second *Book of Common Prayer* was imposed in 1552, this time laying down penalties for anyone who failed to use it. In this virtually any lingerings of the old Catholic mass were eliminated. What little treasure was left in the parish churches was confiscated. Protestant bishops were appointed and each appointment was an excuse to exact their lands from them.

This descent into money-grabbing and malpractice accelerated when it was known that the king was fatally ill with tuberculosis. By the summer of 1552 it was clear that his chances of survival were negligible. With the king's death, Northumberland realised his own power would be gone, for the succession was laid down by statute to pass to the Catholic Mary. So together the king and Northumberland illegally set about altering the succession in favour of the descendants of Henry VIII's sister, Mary, Duchess of Suffolk, and in particular her granddaughter, Lady Jane Grey. Northumberland saw to it that she was married to his eldest son. The Council was extremely unhappy at this violation but they were bullied into submission, Northumberland acting 'in a great rage and fury', the king 'with sharp words and angry countenance.'

So it was that on 6 July 1553 Edward at last died, and Jane Grey was proclaimed queen four days later. It was a wildly unpopular move even with the Protestant Londoners. It went against two deeply held convictions, the sanctity of the legal succession of heirs and the veneration in which the Tudor dynasty was held. Both were so strongly felt that they far outweighed any consideration as to Mary's commitment to the old faith. On hearing of Northumberland's coup, she fled to Suffolk where she was proclaimed queen and soon had crowds flocking to her support. Northumberland, who advanced to confront her, found his supporters melting away as he rode. In the end, even he was forced to declare for her, await arrest and eventual execution for treason.

Mary thus came to the throne on a wave of popular sentiment which she then proceeded to squander by misreading. 'The bonfires were without number,' it was reported, 'and what with such shouting and crying of the people, and ringing of bells, there could no man hear what another said.' The new queen was a strong-willed Tudor who had suffered twenty years of humiliation and ill-treatment for loyalty to her mother and to Catholicism. It had left her looking prematurely old. But she had a charm and graciousness of manner and a childlike innocence of the ways of the

Although painted in his sister Elizabeth's reign, this picture records how in retrospect the reign of her brother, Edward VI, was viewed. Their father, Henry VIII, lies on his deathbed pointing to his son as his successor. To Edward's left stands Edward Seymour, Duke of Somerset, in his role as Lord Protector during the king's minority. Next to him sits John Dudley, Duke of Northumberland, and Thomas Cranmer, Archbishop of Canterbury. This is a triumph of the Protestant faith with the open Bible at the king's feet crushing the pope and two monks, while through a window Rome, cast as the wicked Babylon, goes up in flames and soldiers destroy images of the saints.

world. The tide which had swept her back to power she read as one longing for a return to pre-Reformation England. Nothing could have been further from the reality but with a characteristic Tudor wilfulness she set about to achieve precisely that, along with according honour to her mother's family, the Spanish Habsburgs. She knew that at thirty-seven she was almost past child-bearing and the need for a male heir was urgent. Alas, she would hear of no other as a bridegroom than the Habsburg Emperor Charles V's son, Philip.

There was huge opposition but the queen was set on her course, an unwise one, for her subjects saw England reduced to being yet one more province of the vast Habsburg Empire and themselves ruled by a Spanish king. Although Parliament passed the legislation to restore religion to where it had been in 1547, a first step to reunion with Rome, it opposed her match with Philip. The Protestant bishops were deprived of their sees but any attempt to set in reversal the huge change in land ownership met with a blank wall. In even suggesting this Mary began to lose the support of the classes which could hold her in power.

So fiercely was the Spanish match resented that it provoked rebellion. Sir Thomas Wyatt and three thousand men advanced on London from Kent. Mary just managed to rally the Londoners to her cause and the uprising was suppressed but she failed to respond to the warnings the unrest gave. One of the crueller consequences was the execution of Jane Grey and her husband. Mary pressed ahead. In July 1554 Philip

Two illuminations of Mary I capture the sanctity of the monarchy which was endowed with healing powers. Both were inheritances from the medieval kings of England. In the first the queen touches for the King's Evil, or scrofula, by laying her bare hands on the sufferer who is presented to her by a monk. She would then make the sign of the cross on his sores holding a gold coin in her hand. This the patient subsequently wore. In the second she takes part in the ceremony in which rings were rendered talismanic and able to cure muscular pains or spasms, and, more especially, epilepsy. The rings were called cramp rings and here the queen kneels before the altar with two golden dishes filled with them. As she prays she takes the rings one by one and rubs them, after which they were sprinkled with holy water. Her sister Elizabeth I continued with the first practice but discontinued the second.

landed, and they were married at Winchester. Soon she believed she was pregnant and England would have an heir. That was to prove false. But in November all she strove for seemingly reached fulfilment when her cousin, Cardinal Pole, who had lived for decades in exile, arrived as papal legate. Parliament repealed the acts of the Reformation Parliament, and England was formally reconciled to Rome. Pole was installed as Archbishop of Canterbury in place of the deprived Cranmer. But all of this was to prove a hollow success.

On the whole people had been happy with her initial return to the religion of 1547. If Mary had left it there she might have been more successful. Instead she brought back the pope which revived the strong anti-clericalism of the people, and made those who had benefited from the spoliations of the church feel vulnerable that what they had gained in the last twenty years might well in the long run be taken away.

Mary made things even worse by her revival of the heresy laws. From January 1555 onwards there began the long series of public burnings which were to give the future Church of England its martyrs. No policy of hers did more harm to the fragile Catholic cause than this. By the time Mary died, some three hundred men and women had been burned at the stake for their beliefs, among them men of outstanding integrity such as the former Archbishop of Canterbury, Thomas Cranmer. Nothing was to erase this horror from the popular imagination. It reinforced attitudes which were to dominate the English mind for centuries in which the Protestant faith and independence of a foreign power were inextricably linked.

There was one final blow to come. England was dragged into war with France in her new role as one of the Habsburg domains. The war was not only unpopular, it was catastrophic. In January 1558, after centuries of being England's last outpost on the mainland, Calais fell to the French. National humiliation could go no further. Mary died on 17 November a broken woman, followed, twelve hours later by Cardinal Pole. Henry Machyn, a London undertaker, records in his diary that 'all the churches in London did ring, and at night [men] did make bonfires and set tables in the street, and did eat and drink; and make merry, for the new queen.' Thus ended what was a tragedy.

Mary's short reign had been a total failure for she had lost the co-operation and support of the very people who had brought her to power. In refusing to accept the status quo, and turning back the clock too far, she ensured that they now saw a Protestant settlement as the only possibility which would offer them security. Her persecution of Protestants and dalliance with Spain helped create the myth of England as the New Jerusalem. Under her the blood of the martyrs had run freely and the country had been subject to foreign domination not only by the pope but also by Spain. Everything therefore was set in place for the accession of a new queen, one whose Protestant sympathies were well-known. Her advent was to be presented as an act of divine deliverance. What was really fortunate was that the young woman destined for that role accepted the part, playing it for all it was worth for nearly half-a-century, thus leaving behind her a legend.

Chapter Twenty-Nine

A NEW IDENTITY

ELIZABETH I was twenty-six when she came to the throne, a tall young woman of commanding presence with auburn hair and piercing grey-black eyes. She was to reign longer than any other Tudor, forty-five years in all. That lay in the future. In 1558 what the people saw was an inexperienced unmarried woman assume control of the vanquished fortunes of England. As in the case of her sister, Elizabeth's childhood had been far from happy and indeed fraught with dangers when, as Mary's heir, she had been suspected of involvement in plots. All of this made her overlay what was an intellect of striking clarity of perception with a quality of evasiveness. The new queen always left room to manoeuvre herself out of the tightest political corner. But her judgment was sound, supremely so in the case of people. Her selection of officials could rarely be faulted and, as a consequence, there gradually emerged a cohesive group of educated and highly intelligent officials who gave the kingdom a sustained stability. Most of them were chosen from the ramifications of her mother's family or that of her principal minister, William Cecil.

Cecil was the son of a Northamptonshire gentleman who had served both Somerset and Northumberland but who lost office under Mary. But, like Elizabeth, he conformed in the matter of religion. On her accession she appointed him her Principal Secretary and over a decade later he became Lord Treasurer. The history of her reign is the story of this alliance between a great queen, sagacious, brave, tolerant as far she dare, if at the same time vain and capricious, with a minister who shared her conservative instincts, believing also in caution and that in matters of religion a window should not be opened into men's souls. It was a great partnership which lasted forty years and whose main purpose was no longer revolution but consolidation, to bring peace to the country by building on the foundations laid by Elizabeth's father in the 1530s.

There was never any doubt that England would revert to being Protestant. The question was: of what kind? And that is where the queen's impact was to be so significant, for her wish was to return to matters as they stood shortly after Henry VIII's death. Her problem lay in the fact that those whom she needed on her side wanted a far more extreme form of Protestantism. During her sister Mary's reign the opinion formers had lived in exile on the continent where they had come into contact with a far more radical variety of Protestantism than anything yet seen in England, one which banished bishops and replaced them with a system of ministers and elders chosen by the congregation. These were the type of men who got themselves elected to Elizabeth's first Parliament in 1559. Unfortunately for the queen all changes in religion since her father's reign had been achieved by way of statute. She had no choice but to follow the same course, and in the process found herself having to accept a far more extreme form of faith than she wanted. She was to spend the rest of her reign preventing any further moves in that direction. By doing so she, more than anyone else, was responsible for the emergence of the Church of England.

Initially she had hoped to embark on religious changes piecemeal but after peace was made with France in the spring of 1559, the government was able to proceed with a religious settlement. Elizabeth could not look to her sister's bishops for support. They resigned, and she had to fall back on appointing men who were more radical than she liked. She wanted to return to the moderate, and still largely Catholic, prayer book of 1549 but she was forced to concede to the restoration of the far more radical version of 1552, although she saw to it that some of its more extreme attitudes were eliminated or watered-down. Vestments and church interiors were to be as they had been in 1548 and people were to receive communion kneeling. The queen herself was no longer supreme head but governor of the church. And, as on previous occasions, the acts enforcing these changes came from above.

England in reality was still Catholic. What became the Anglican Church slowly emerged as the reign progressed. It was shaped and sharpened by political events and gradually defined as its intellectuals appeared and asserted its midway position

It was customary for the monarch to wash the feet of as many poor people as their age each Maundy Thursday, thus emulating Christ washing those of the disciples before the Last Supper. This ceremony, which emphasised the sanctity of the ruler, continued after the Reformation. Here, early in her reign, the young Elizabeth I, wearing a long apron, advances towards a row of seated old ladies. This rare record of court life was painted, in the form of a miniature, by a woman, Levina Teerlinc.

between Catholic and what was called Puritan, made up of those people who wished to 'purify' or further reform the church. The queen's position was crucial, for she resisted Parliament's repeated attempts to interfere and also saw to it that the stringent acts which laid down penalties on Catholics were not rigorously enforced. Although there were to be victims of persecution on both sides, they were few compared with the bloodbaths over religion which took place across the Channel in France and the Netherlands.

The Catholics during the first decade of the reign stood abandoned by the pope. Most of them occasionally conformed to the Church of England and, as there was no pressure on them to take the Oath of Supremacy, they were not faced with any dilemma of choice. This suited the temper of the queen's government, for by the time that the pope began to act, a huge number had already drifted into Anglicanism by default.

In 1570 all that was suddenly to change, for in that year the pope excommunicated the queen, that is, he declared her a heretic and as such unfit to wear the crown, therefore absolving her subjects from any need to obey her. Catholics had now to choose between pope or queen. Most chose the latter. Those who did not were inevitably seen as enemies of the state, and Parliament demanded heavy penalties. The queen resisted. In the middle of that decade, priests trained in special seminaries began to arrive from abroad, so that those who had remained loyal to Rome now had their faith rekindled. Then, in the 1580s, priests of a very different kind came, members of the Society of Jesus called Jesuits, trained in a fervent revived Catholicism known as Counter-Reformation. For them loyalty to the pope was paramount. Although priests were told to avoid any pronouncement on the queen's status, if they were caught they were unable to dodge the implications of the papal bull. Parliament, strongly Protestant, put up the fines for recusancy (non-attendance at church) to twenty pounds a month and declared conversion treason. Spain, by then England's greatest enemy, spearheaded the Catholic cause. In the face of this the Elizabethan government had little choice and so the martyrdoms began. About two hundred and fifty Catholics suffered imprisonment or execution for their faith. Nothing could have been further from the queen's tolerant intention.

The legend of Elizabeth I as the Virgin Queen was created in her own lifetime through public appearances of the kind seen in this imaginary triumphal procession at the close of her reign. Young courtiers support a canopy over the queen while ahead of her walk some of the greatest noblemen including, second from the left, the hero of Armada, Charles Howard, Lord Howard of Effingham, later Earl of Nottingham.

By the year she died the Catholics had settled down to being a small, closely-knit, albeit from time to time beleaguered, community. Their faith eliminated them from public office and from the universities. This exclusion was not reversed until the nineteenth century. Almost without exception they were loyal to the queen and state, yet they suffered much from the rudimentary equation of their faith with England's enemies abroad.

In the queen's eyes the Puritans posed an even greater threat, for they worked within the fabric of the established church and Parliament to change it. They had powerful allies at court, including the queen's favourite, Robert Dudley, Earl of Leicester.

Polarisation, however, was gradual. As the 1560s progressed, the queen's new archbishop, Matthew Parker, began to enforce conformity insisting, for example, that copes and surplices were worn and the sign of the cross used at baptism. As a consequence the Puritans began to form their own groups within the church and press for changes through Parliament, changes which would have not only abolished the bishops but any trace of ritual reminiscent of Rome. Time and again, the Commons, basing themselves on their claim to free speech, tried to initiate legislation to effect change. And time and again the queen vetoed any discussion of the topic as infringing her royal prerogative, power sacred to a monarch alone. For this offence one member, Peter Wentworth, was sent twice to the Tower. These skirmishes between the queen and the Commons laid the foundations for far more serious conflicts in the next century.

The Puritans in effect failed and in the long run were forced, like the Catholics, out of the Church of England, particularly later in the reign when an ecclesiastical court was set up to stamp out nonconformity. In spite of this, the new church began to emerge as remarkably comprehensive with an identity which claimed to be at once Catholic yet reformed, beginning with the rudimentary statement that membership of the state equated with that of the church. As before the Reformation, there was still an ecclesiastical hierarchy but members were appointed by the queen and a degree of Catholic ritual and colour survived: the use of copes and surplices, organs and music. Its worship and beliefs became enshrined in three works which were to be familiar to all Englishmen for nearly four centuries, profoundly affecting how they thought and regarded the world around them. All three were written in the vernacular, and two of them still rank amongst the great classics of the English language. Their significance cannot be overestimated, for they were read and used in every parish church and home.

The first was Thomas Cranmer's *Prayer Book* which contained the liturgy of the

Church of England, those services familiar to everyone who went to their parish church. The nobility of its prose has never been surpassed and it remains in use even to this day. The second work was to come only a few years into the reign of Elizabeth's successor, James I. *The Authorised Version of the Bible* still figures among the glories of English literature. Both were to affect the minds and hearts of generations of English people not only in their native country but wherever they voyaged and settled around the globe. Both, too, were foundations of a piety which was Anglican, one which combined a strong sense of dignity and order in public worship with an equal commitment to the inner spiritual life, often finding its truest expression in flights of poetic revelation.

The last of this trinity gave ordinary people a view not only of their church as being a true continuation of what had existed before the Reformation but also of their own history and their place within it. Its influence was to last until our own century. John Foxe's *Actes and Monuments* or *Book of Martyrs* as it was commonly called, not only narrated the sufferings of Protestants under Mary but went on to cast England and the English into an heroic role, that of the chosen nation of God which had thrown off the shackles of Rome. The whole of human and English history was cast into a dramatic story in which light overcame darkness, Protestantism Catholicism, and the valiant kings of England the wicked popes of Rome. Its climax was the accession of a virgin queen. In Foxe's eyes, the advent of Elizabeth the deliverer was the culmination. As time went by and the rule of the queen fulfilled these prognostications, what had begun as a pious hope became a reality. And never more so than in the aftermath of the defeat of the great Armada sent by Spain.

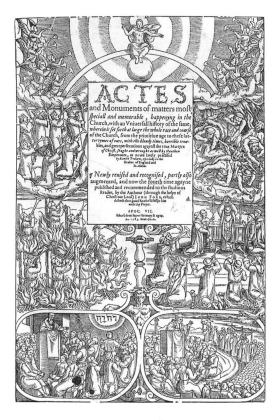

For three centuries this book was to be familiar to every Englishman. John Foxe's *Actes and Monuments*, 1563, cast the English as God's chosen people and Elizabeth I as their deliverer. Copies were placed in every parish church. Its vivid text and illustrations celebrated the martyrs of Mary's reign and fuelled a fear and hatred of Catholicism which was to be part of the British heritage into the present century. The title-page presents a crude contrast between the two faiths, one in which Protestants are seen as listening to the Word of God, dying for their faith and taking their place in heaven, while Catholics wallow in a welter of ritual and images and are condemned to hell.

Chapter Thirty

ARMADA

THE Church of England split the religious issue and avoided the horrendous bloodshed which occurred elsewhere in Europe as Catholic fought Protestant. It laid the ground for a new sense of national identity, one which was to be further consolidated by threats from outside. The effect of such threats is always to draw together rival parties in opposition to the common external enemy. That was to be Spain, until Elizabeth's reign the Tudors' key ally abroad. It was still England's ally in 1558, but thirty years later was to send an army of conquest, the great Armada, to subject the country, dethrone the queen and re-establish Catholicism. The defeat of that invasion, the embodiment of the might of the vast Spanish Empire which stretched around the globe, by the navy of a tiny island kingdom was to send shock waves across Europe. Elizabeth assumed an aura of almost cosmic grandeur and the country emerged with a new sense of mission and purpose.

At the opening of the reign, however, the enemy remained the traditional one of France, a situation made worse by the fact that its king was married to the ruler of Scotland, Mary Queen of Scots, who, because of her descent from Henry VII's daughter, Margaret, was heir to the English throne in the event of Elizabeth having no children. Mary was also Catholic. Fortunately for the English government the threat from France suddenly lessened, for the French king died and Mary was forced to return to her native kingdom. Mary Queen of Scots was a beautiful and passionate woman who inspired deep personal loyalty, but she was also wilful and politically inept. She found her own country in the throes of the Reformation, and her reign was one long disaster, so much so that in 1568 she was forced to flee over the border into England and seek succour at the hands of her cousin, Elizabeth.

Elizabeth was faced with an appalling problem, although she swiftly realised that Mary returned either to France or Scotland could be an even bigger one. When she fled to England, the Scottish queen stood accused of complicity in the murder of her second husband, Lord Darnley, and an investigation of this charge was staged, inconclusive enough to leave Mary tainted with enough guilt to justify confining her in a series of fortress-houses in the midlands for almost the next twenty years.

Nonetheless Mary, as both Elizabeth's heir and a Catholic, remained a perpetual threat. Over the years the Scottish queen was to be the focus of a whole series of plots aimed at replacing Elizabeth with Mary. The first of these followed hard on what was the only significant uprising against the new government, the 1569 rebellion. This plot involved the Duke of Norfolk and the two northern earls of Westmorland and Northumberland, all Catholic and all deeply resentful of the power of William Cecil and others who made up the new regime. Norfolk was sent to the Tower before he could act, but the two others attempted to raise the north. The plot was a total failure, one which the plotters paid for not only with their own lives but those of eight hundred other people, as the north was once more subjected to the full might of Tudor rule. Behind the scenario of the rebellion had been the intention that Norfolk should marry the Scottish queen and reign jointly. That scheme was re-enacted two years later in an intrigue known as the Ridolfi Plot, which this time involved the Spanish ambassador. Norfolk was executed for his part in this, but it set the pattern for the long series of plots against Elizabeth which followed, all involving the Queen of Scots.

The rule of Elizabeth was very fragile in its early years but it was to benefit from two things. The first was the quality of her government which put down sure foundations and built up widespread support across a broad section of society and, in addition, ensured financial stability after the roaring inflation of the middle years of the century. The second was the disintegration of England's continental neighbours into long-lasting civil wars. In France there were three decades of civil war between Catholics and Protestants, or Huguenots as they were called. The queen from time to time would aid the Huguenots, until the might of Spain grew so overpowering that France and England became allies. In the Low Countries, England's most important commercial link, there was an uprising against the rule of the king of Spain. Once again Elizabeth was able cautiously to intervene in aid of the rebels, but she always carefully avoided anything which would lead to a direct confrontation with Spain.

This was to work well for over twenty years, valuable years during which the Elizabethan state established itself, gained confidence and attracted deep loyalty from its people, but in the 1580s things changed dramatically with a series of events which precipitated the sailing of the great Armada. Spain was indeed a world power. Philip II ruled over the whole Iberian peninsula, having conquered not only Portugal but also most of Italy, the Low Countries and all of South America. Other members of his family, the Habsburgs, dominated Germany and Central Europe. Up until the 1580s the greatest enemies of Philip's far-flung empire were the French and the Turks. Then, quite suddenly, the English became far more serious on many counts. A new generation of bold maritime adventurers, headed by Sir Francis Drake, increased their attacks on the convoys of gold and silver from the New World upon which the Spanish Empire depended. Worse, Spanish domination of the New World was threatened by English attempts to found a colony named Virginia in honour of the queen. Finally in 1585, Elizabeth actually signed a treaty with the Low Countries' rebels, the Dutch, and sent an English army under the leadership of her favourite, the Earl of Leicester. During the same period she supported and encouraged the attacks made by the claimant to the Portuguese throne on Spanish colonies. All of this led Philip to conclude that his reputation had been gravely impaired and that England and her queen should be wiped out and become a province of the vast Habsburg empire. That conclusion was reinforced when, in the aftermath of yet another plot, Mary Queen of Scots was brought to trial and executed in February 1587.

Mary was immediately billed as a martyr to the Catholic cause and this touched the vital nerve which, more than anything else, drove the king on to seek revenge. For Philip II the vast fleet and army he assembled was a crusade. The men recruited to take part in it prepared for the conquest of England in the same way that they did for battle against the infidel Turk. Most of Catholic Europe, headed by the pope, contributed ships, men and money to the Armada. He even blessed the banner which adorned its flagship. Prayers were said in the monasteries of Spain for the success of this holy war. From the outset, Philip never doubted but that God was on his side and that it was his duty to depose a heretic queen and restore England to the Catholic faith.

Such a powerful threat called for an equal fervour of purpose on the English side. The queen, a superb actress, was presented to her people as the chosen vessel of God, a virgin – for by now it was clear that she would never marry – sacred and set aside to lead the Protestant cause, not only on the part of England but Europe. By the 1580s the anniversary of her accession to the throne, 17 November, had become a national holiday in which court and country joined in celebrating what was seen as the years progressed as a God-ordained deliverance from the joint yoke of Spain and the pope. The splendour of the monarchy and the magnificence of the queen replaced the spectacle of the pre-Reformation Catholic church and provided a new potent focus of loyalty. When, in 1588, the great Armada finally sailed, much of the future destiny of Europe was seen to be embodied in the confrontation.

Philip's great fleet was one part of his strategy against England. Its main purpose, however, was to enable a Spanish army to cross the Channel from the Low Countries and land. From the outset therefore the campaign was never seen as a sea battle but as an invasion followed by an advance on London. That had always been the scheme from as far back as 1586 when Philip had first made up his mind to invade. The fact that it took two years before the Armada eventually sailed reflected not only changes of plan and lack of money but even more the devastating effect of Sir Francis Drake's raid on the Spanish fleet in Cadiz harbour in April 1587 when thirty ships were sunk. When the Armada at last set sail in April of the following year it consisted of one hun-

Images of the Virgin and saints were replaced by those of the Virgin Queen. Courtiers wore jewels such as this one to express their devotion to the queen celebrated as both monarch and lady, the former expressed by the proud profile on the outside of the locket and the latter by the lyrical miniature of her inside by the court painter, Nicholas Hilliard. Within she is beauty's rose, without, the guardian of the church, symbolised by Noah's ark.

dred and thirty ships with some seven thousand sailors and seventeen thousand soldiers with a further seventeen thousand who were to cross from the Netherlands.

England was not then a great maritime power. There were thirty-four royal ships to which was added one hundred and ninety private ones which were requisitioned and fitted out for battle. There were, therefore, in terms of number more English ships than Spanish and, which was of far greater importance, of a different kind. They were much smaller and were thus able to manoeuvre more easily than the cumbrous Spanish galleons. In addition, English guns and gunnery was recognised as the best in the world, with artillery that could shoot at a great distance to deadly effect when the encounter came. At the end of 1587 Lord Howard of Effingham was put in charge of the fleet with Lord Henry Seymour as second in command. In June 1588, as the Armada approached, Howard and Drake waited at Plymouth with ninety ships while Seymour waited elsewhere with another thirty. Meanwhile on land there had been a similar mustering of forces to defend the realm. Fifteen years before the county militia had been set up, each county pledging to select and train men to fight with pike and musket. The signal for seventy-six thousand men to muster was given through a series of beacons set on high points along the coast. When the time came on 30 July and the Armada was sighted, the beacons blazed along the Cornish coast proclaiming its approach.

The *Ark Royal* was the flagship of the Admiral of the Fleet, Lord Howard of Effingham. It was built in 1587 for Sir Walter Raleigh but acquired by the queen before it was launched.

Meanwhile London had been put in readiness with thousands of men to defend the queen. Not far away at Tilbury, under the Earl of Leicester, an army of seventeen thousand soldiers was camped. There Elizabeth, arrayed like an Amazon with a breastplate, reviewed her troops and delivered the greatest speech of her reign casting herself as the beloved ruler of her people fearlessly leading them into war for God and country.

> '. . .I come amongst you. . . being resolved in the midst and heat of battle to live or die amongst you all. To lay down for God and for my kingdom and for my people my honour and my blood even in the dust. I know I have the body of a weak and feeble woman but I have the heart and stomach of a king, and of a king of England too. . .'

Although no one knew it at the time, her speech was delivered when the danger had already passed. The first shots had been fired off Plymouth in July but they had been indecisive. On 1 August the Armada advanced in what looked to the English fleet like a mighty crescent. More fighting ensued and on 6 August the Armada reached Calais where it waited for news of the Spanish army which was to cross the Channel from the Low Countries. Unknown to the Spaniards it had been blockaded by the Dutch rebels. Then came the English master-stroke. Fire ships were sent in at night amongst the ships of the Armada, forcing them to weigh anchor and drift northwards, thus renewing the battle and, at the same time, rendering impossible any link-up with troops crossing from the Netherlands. Now came the main battle off Gravelines with huge losses on the Spanish side. By the end of that day the Armada was in danger of being driven by winds on to the sandbanks unless it headed into the North Sea. The Spanish in their battered ships had no other choice. They were forced into making a terrible voyage all around Scotland. There had already been large losses of men and there were few victuals left. The weather was bitterly cold, something for which they were totally unequipped. Worse, one by one ships were either lost or wrecked on the coasts of Scotland and Ireland. Over eleven thousand men perished and what survived and reached Spain was the wreck of a fleet.

Richard Hakluyt, the chronicler of England's mar-

A gold pendant set with rubies in the form of a salamander recovered from one of the Spanish ships, the *Girona*, wrecked on its homeward journey off the west coast of Ireland. Such a jewel would have been worn by one of the highest-ranking officers.

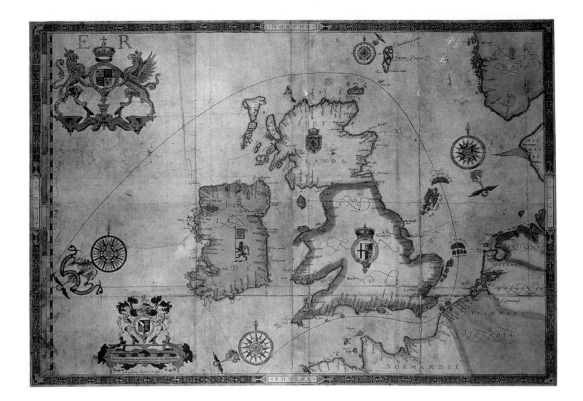

The homeward journey of the Spanish Armada. A contemporary coloured engraving records the defeat at Gravelines and the route northwards which the Spanish fleet was forced to take via Scotland and the west coast of Ireland. Many ships were unable to follow course and foundered.

itime enterprise wrote: 'Never was any nation blessed of JEHOVAH with a more glorious and wonderful victory upon the seas, than our vanquishing of the dreadful Spanish Armada, 1588.' To England and Protestant Europe this was seen as God's judgment and his handmaiden went in triumph through the streets of London to St. Paul's Cathedral to give thanks amidst the acclamations of her people. Elizabeth became a legend within her own lifetime. In a sense she became England. The defeat of the Spanish Armada made a reality of what her government had striven to achieve, a united people held together by the crown, Protestant, patriotic, fearless in defence of queen and country. Although in political terms the victory may have changed little and the country was to remain involved in a costly war for the rest of the reign, in moral ones it gave a confidence and creative energy to what was in essence a new civilisation and society, that of the England of Elizabeth I.

Chapter Thirty-One

GLORIANA'S ENGLAND

WHEN Elizabeth died in 1603 she bequeathed to her successor a very different country from the one her grandfather had taken over in 1485. After the northern rebellion of 1569 there began the long period of the Elizabethan peace in which the prime aim of government was to achieve stability. This was an age whose whole stress was on order, rank and degree and a deep fear of anything or anyone who might upset it. Obedience to higher powers was its watchword. It was in many ways a deeply conservative and authoritarian society, which penalised those who did not think and act as government decreed that they should. What is so surprising is that this did not impede its unrivalled energy which created a new and vigorous secular culture whose influence still radiates through the centuries.

At its apex stood the queen. Although Elizabeth had been assiduously courted for years by foreign princes, in the end she never married, thus averting the possibly disastrous consequences of the wrong husband. What may have been for her a personal tragedy was turned to an advantage as the reverence accorded a Virgin Queen was deliberately built up over the decades, elevating the monarchy to semi-divine status. Every section of society paid her tribute: the young nobility cast themselves as knights of romance fighting in defence of a 'Faerie Queene', the poets hymned her as their lady of the sonnets, while the clergy roared forth their belief that the country had been blessed with a ruler fit to rank alongside those in the Old Testament. Elizabeth responded to all these roles with equal enthusiasm exhibiting herself to her people in splendid ceremonial. Moreover she was blessed with the common touch, always casting herself in her speeches as the embodiment of her beloved people. The impact of the monarchy reached across the country as never before. Although most of her subjects never saw her in person, each Sunday in church they could look at her enthroned on the engraved title page of the Bible and see her coat of arms hung over the chancel arch. In the nearby great house her portrait was the first to be hung, a glittering bejewelled icon, as the focus of the newly fashionable long galleries.

The monarchy was essentially London-based, with the court moving from palace to palace along the river Thames: Whitehall, Greenwich, Richmond and Hampton

Court. The year assumed a set pattern which was to continue after her death. It began early in November when the queen entered London in splendour in time for the celebration of her Accession Day each 17 November when all the bells across the country were rung. It was the occasion for a service and a sermon in every church, and, at court, for a magnificent fancy-dress tournament. A month later came Christmas and the revels which ushered in the New Year. In the spring the court moved to other palaces and then, in June, set off on progress for several months. This called for hundreds of carts and horses to transport everything and everybody. The queen stayed in the newly-built great houses of her subjects, but these were rarely big enough and those who could not be accommodated had to sleep outside in tents. Everywhere she went the bells rang and people came out to greet her.

The countryside through which she travelled had changed character from what she would have remembered as a child. Where once the landscape had been punctuated by castles and monasteries, now it was dotted with great houses. There was a building boom as aristocracy and gentry outvied each other in erecting residences fit to receive the queen. Such houses dominated the land around, often being sited on hilltops. No longer built for defence, they boasted huge areas of glass, so that from a distance they caught the eye as they sparkled in the sunshine. Within, their spacious rooms and galleries reflected a new luxury of living, while outside elaborate gardens in which to stroll were laid out for the first time. Henceforth the rich lavished their money not in the hope of buying a place in the next world, by erecting a chapel or bequeathing money for masses to be said for their souls, but on display and comfort in the present. The only addition they made to the church would be a tomb, aggressive and gaudy in style and built often as not where the medieval altar would once have stood.

The way to the top after all was no longer via the church. Indeed no churchman held an office of state any more. Advancement now lay by way of a great lord who enjoyed favour at court. Education at the university was of less importance than a few years spent at the Inns of Court in London learning the rudiments of law. The ideal now was to be a gentleman in the new, Renaissance, sense of the word. For this a man had to be educated and widely read in both the classics and foreign languages. He should, in addition, have travelled to observe foreign lands and peoples. He had not only to be a man-at-arms as in the Middle Ages but also endowed with all the courtly accomplishments, to dance, play a musical instrument and sing. All of these attributes set him apart from the lower classes, although it remained a fluid society. Families rose and fell according to ability and political favour, but, for the first time, there emerged an enduring interconnected establishment class: the Cecils, Careys, Knollys,

Cavendishes, Dudleys and Devereux. The way up the tree was through ability, royal favour, office and marriage to an heiress. Women also played their part, for upper-class women were often highly educated. They too could rise like Elizabeth Barlow, a yeoman's daughter, through a succession of marriages to be the notorious 'Bess of Hardwick', Countess of Shrewsbury, the grandest lady in the kingdom next to the queen.

A great Elizabethan lady at her toilet. Elizabeth Vernon was Maid of Honour to the queen and secretly married the Earl of Southampton in 1598 to the queen's rage. This is a rare glimpse of a grand lady in the act of getting dressed showing her corset and embroidered petticoat which is covered with gauze for protection. Her ruff with jewels attached to it has been pinned to a curtain while her jewel box disgorges a magnificent array of pendants and necklaces. The amply filled pin-cushion is a reminder that much of her clothing and jewellery would have been pinned into position by her maidservants. Her rank as a countess is recorded in the ermine-lined crimson velvet mantle behind.

Nor was it a society closed to the merchant classes, for both the aristocracy and gentry put their money into trade and did not hesitate to marry a rich city heiress. Towns were booming. London grew at a phenomenal speed benefiting from the dislocation of the port of Antwerp due to the wars in the Netherlands. The population of London by 1600 was over 200,000, spilling out beyond its walls and over onto the south bank to Southwark. No other city matched London, and most appeared little more than overgrown villages. In terms of population Norwich came next with 15,000 citizens, and then followed places like York, Exeter and King's Lynn. By the time that the queen died one person in ten was living in a town. Once again there was a change in the way they spent their money, for now corporate pride was no longer expressed in enriching parish churches but in fine civic buildings: market places, hospitals, town halls and almshouses for the poor and old.

London was the home of the printing presses. Although government censorship was strict it did not impede the huge outpouring of books and pamphlets. A small library was soon the prerogative of any educated person, unknown a few decades earlier. It was not Oxford or Cambridge which became the dynamic centre of learning but London. In 1596 the will of the queen's financier, Sir Thomas Gresham, came into operation, founding Gresham College. The subjects taught there were forward-looking, practical ones in the applied sciences, subjects directly useful in the real world of commerce, such as mathematics needed for good accounting or navigation essential for mariners exploring new trading routes.

Elizabethan society was more divided than its predecessor with the gaps widening between one layer and the next. Some classes were more important than they had been in the past. At the top still stood the nobility, a static class, just under sixty in all, of which half were only barons. Elizabeth saw to it that there were few additions. Most of her officials never rose beyond the rank of knight. As a result the nobility, though still grand, diminished in power and by the close of the reign the vast trains of retainers, typical of the era of the Wars of the Roses, had become a thing of the past. But the nobility had to be seen to maintain their social position and this was expensive, leading to debt and sales of land in order to raise capital. The greatest change was that they were no longer important in their own right. They only became important if they enjoyed the favour of the queen.

In sharp contrast there was a vast burgeoning of the gentry classes. They expanded in number hugely between the 1540s and 1580s. By 1600 the pattern that each village had its squire was well in evidence. Land was the real measure as to whether someone could claim to be a gentleman. Add to that education. These were men who sought grants of arms and built large houses amidst parkland for the hunt.

Such houses were meant to impress, with private rooms for the family, huge fire-places, ornate plaster ceilings, panelling and rich furnishings. The gentry lived off the rents from their estates, dabbling also in industry and even more in maritime enterprise. But such families could come and go. Their survival depended on injections of money through marriage to heiresses, and sons to inherit. Daughters only spelt ruin as the estate was divided between the sons-in-law.

Below them came another class on the make; in the countryside the yeoman farmers, and in the towns the master craftsmen. In both cases their prosperity was

Embroidery was one of the great arts of the Elizabethan age produced by professionals, as in this instance, as well as by ladies in households. The Bradford table carpet is thirteen feet long and almost six feet wide with four hundred stitches to every square inch. Its borders are vibrant with scenes of contemporary life: here a horseman hunts boar, gentry engage in the hunt, a fisherman is about to net his catch.

also expressed through building and their houses, many still standing, reflect new-found comfort, solid oak-framed or brick buildings with many rooms and fireplaces, and glass in windows. Their greatest status symbol was the chimney. These were men who had built up substantial farms or who were rich merchants as the result of what was becoming a consumer society. Wool and the manufacture of cloth remained the staple industry. But there was the new phenomenon of the joint stock company in which capital, subscribed from many sources, combined for enterprises such as opening up a foreign market or colonisation, in return for a share of the profits of success.

The thrusting gentry, yeoman and merchant classes embody the forward-looking energy of the age, the forces and agents of change. None of this dynamism should obscure the fact that much remained unchanged. Most of the population continued to be engaged in subsistence farming, somehow eking out a living from as little as fifteen acres of land. It was mixed farming, for the pastoral farms needed oats for fodder and barley for brewing and the arable farms relied on livestock to fertilise the fields on which the corn was grown. Often, to make ends meet, they took on spinning and weaving. Then there were the poor villagers who grew their own vegetables and kept a cow. Although there had been enclosures and deforestation, the fields were still mainly cultivated in strips and the overwhelming impression was of woods and greenery. For the first time surveys and maps were made evoking a countryside which was an entrancing mosaic of coppices and commonland, open-field ploughland and little hedged pastures, common meadow and gracious parkland.

The fundamental unit remained the parish. Whereas before the Reformation people had come together in religious fraternities, now they met under the aegis of the church wardens to discuss how to look after the poor or mend the roads, appoint a schoolmaster or settle local disputes. From 1538 onwards all births, marriages and burials had to be recorded, thus for the first time creating for each community an archive of its own, establishing a sense of corporate identity. Every Sunday the villagers met in the parish church to hear the word of God. Attendance was compulsory. Only the very rich could afford the fines for not going. The clergyman continued to receive his tithes but now he was more often than not a married man with a wife and children to support. He was far better educated than his medieval predecessors, probably having been to a university, and he would have a study with books. His status was that of a yeoman.

The role of the Justice of the Peace continued to be expanded as the prime agent of local administration and the enforcement of government statutes. In particular the poor laws of 1597 and 1601 entrusted them with running a system of relief and welfare which was to last for two centuries. Two overseers of the poor were appointed in each parish to collect the poor-rate which financed relief, took care of the sick, and provided work for the unemployed. But the prevailing attitude to the poor was that they caused the problem by their own idleness, so that their treatment was often brutal.

It is against this tapestry that we must set the last fifteen years of the reign, ones racked by war abroad and famine, plague and inflation at home. England after 1588 was perpetually on the alert against invasion. There was an army in the Low Countries, another from time to time in France and yet a third attempting to subject Ireland, apart from the fleets sent against Spain. All of this took a terrible toll. War was expensive and Elizabeth was forced to call Parliament no less than six times to ask for subsidies which they granted. Even then she had to sell crown lands, raise loans and grant monopolies, that is the exclusive right over a particular commodity. These actions stored up trouble for her successor. At the same time it was a period of bad harvests with four of the wettest summers in human memory after 1592. The result was famine and inflation, all made worse by soldiers returning from the wars, poor, sick, wounded and unemployed.

These were the clouds which dimmed the radiance of 1588. And one by one the great men who had made the age passed on: the queen's favourite, Leicester, died in 1588, the maritime hero, Drake, in 1596 and her chief minister, Cecil, in 1598. Everyone sensed the end of an era, for the queen herself was over sixty, then a great age. But her judgment was undiminished, choosing Cecil's brilliant second son, Robert, as his successor.

Her last years were troubled by her fascination for a glamorous young aristocrat, Robert Devereux, Earl of Essex. Handsome and endowed with an abundance of charm, he enchanted the ageing queen. Yet, shrewdly, she realised that he was politically inept, and resisted his attempts to secure a place in the government of the kingdom. Casting himself as Gloriana's knight he took part in the campaigns against Spain both on land and sea, and finally headed the army in Ireland. For a whole century the English had struggled to conquer that country, now seen to be doubly dangerous as the back door into England for Spain. Rarely had control extended further than an area around Dublin, known as the Pale. Beyond that the wild Irish tribes led a life which had changed little for centuries, one of tribal warfare, blood feuds, raids and killings. But in the 1590s the conquest of Ireland was taken seriously and indeed by the time the queen died had been achieved. But it was to ruin Essex, for he disobeyed her instructions and, worse, fearing his enemies at court, crossed to England to plead his cause. He even burst into the queen's bedchamber as she was being dressed by her ladies. His reward was confinement. Then followed a rapid downward spiral which led Essex and his followers, early in 1601, to attempt to raise London and seize power at court. It was a disaster. Essex was brought to trial and executed.

In Essex, there was reflected all the restlessness of a new generation, tired of the old queen's seemingly unending reign. But, to the last, Elizabeth retained her magic. In the same year the earl went to the scaffold, she received a deputation from the Commons. It was the occasion of her last public speech, one which became so famous it was known as the 'golden speech'. She spoke as the living embodiment of the nation:

> 'Though God hath raised me high, yet this I count the glory of my crown, that
> I have reigned with your loves . . . Though you have had and may have many
> mightier and wiser princes sitting on this seat, yet you never had nor shall have
> any that will love you better. . .'

She went on to tell them of her faith in them and of her gratitude, and then, in one final gesture, bade them come forward one by one to kiss her hand. In this tableau of the Virgin Queen, a frail yet magnificent old lady receiving the homage of her subjects, is caught the true greatness of her spirit.

She died in her seventieth year on 24 March 1603. In spite of all the problems of her last years nothing can detract from her achievement. When Elizabeth came to the throne England was a defeated, bankrupt and demoralised country. When she died, forty-five years later, it was well on the way to being a major power. More even than that, her rule had given birth to a great civilisation.

Elizabeth I died on 24 March 1603 and her funeral took place on 28 April. One poet wrote: 'Her hearse (as it was borne) seemed to be an island swimming in water, for round it there rained showers of tears.'

When those lining the route saw the coffin with its effigy of the queen on the top a groaning and weeping went up 'as the like hath not been seen or known in the memory of man.'

Chapter Thirty-Two

IMMORTAL SHAKESPEARE

I F THE monarchy and the new Church of England were two forces welding society into a new identity based on shared assumptions and ideals, a third was to be the cultural renaissance of the age. Before the Reformation culture had been centred primarily on the church as both a patron of the arts and learning. In the new post-Reformation society the focus was to shift to the court, the aristocracy, and above all London. Although Latin remained a language essential for any educated person to know, this was the age when English asserted itself as never before. There was no such thing as standard English. The language remained fluid and regional, but it emerged as one of an unsurpassed beauty and richness, taking into its vocabulary a huge number of borrowings from Latin, French and Greek. Sunday by Sunday English now resounded in the parish churches instead of Latin, and the printing presses fed a far more widely literate public with a flood of reading matter from practical manuals to sermons, from political tracts to poetry.

The new humanist renaissance culture extolled the role of the patron as befitting a prince and a gentleman and went on to esteem it worthy for both also to write. The queen wrote poetry and so did many of her courtiers, Sir Philip Sidney and Sir Walter Raleigh among them. They also knew and patronised the great poets of the day such as Edmund Spenser whose unfinished romantic epic *The Faerie Queene* celebrated Elizabeth as Gloriana. The new literature gradually created its own classics which the educated classes shared as part of a common identity. For the first time something akin to a national literature emerged. At the same time something else occurred which had no parallel in the rest of Europe, the emergence of a popular theatre with a repertory of plays as much in demand at court as they were with the young London apprentices. This was the achievement of an extraordinary galaxy of playwrights who laid the foundations of the English theatrical tradition, writers including Christopher Marlowe, Ben Jonson, but supremely William Shakespeare.

Shakespeare was born in the Warwickshire town of Stratford-upon-Avon in April

1564, the son of John and Mary Shakespeare. John was the son of a tenant farmer from nearby Snitterfield who had made his career as a glover but who also dealt in wool. His wife came of superior yeoman into gentry stock, for she was an Arden of Wilmcote, a family which could trace its ancestry back before the Norman Conquest. Mary Arden brought with her an inheritance which quickly enhanced John Shakespeare's status and by the time that William, his third child and second son, was born, he was borough chamberlain and four years later its bailiff or mayor.

The Shakespeares were to have four more children, the last in 1580, by which time John had ceased to attend the town council meetings due to financial difficulties. There are indications that the family, although conforming to the government's religious settlement, may have been out of tune with it. During the 1560s this did not present a problem. Government did not press hard for conformity and English Catholics were cut adrift from any instruction from Rome. But as the reign progressed, the religious lines sharpened. The young Shakespeare would have passed his childhood in a household where belief pulled in more than one direction, both forwards and backwards. His own writings are full of references to the Book of Common Prayer and to the Bishops' Bible read in every church, so there is reason to believe that Shakespeare drifted the way of most of the population.

Nothing is known of his education, but as the son of the town's chamberlain he would have been entitled to a free one at the King's New School. Here he would have learned the alphabet, the catechism, the 'Our Father' and how to write. He would then have moved on to study Latin and the classics. He next appears with certainty in November 1582, aged eighteen, being granted a special licence to marry Anne Hathaway. She was already pregnant by him, for she gave birth only six months later to their first child, a daughter called Susanna. Anne was the daughter of Richard Hathaway of Shottery, and eight years Shakespeare's senior. It is clear that he had got her into trouble and had little option other than to marry her. Three years later they had twins, Hamnet and Judith. True to the conventions of the age a marriage was indissoluble, but there is no indication that the match was much more than an enduring formality. Shakespeare's wife seems never to have left Stratford and she was to outlive him by seven years. His own life, however, was to take a very different direction.

Nothing more is heard of him until 1592, by which time he was twenty-eight, when he surfaces in London as an actor in one of the leading companies of the day. How this came about there is no way of knowing, but somehow he had become attracted to, and caught up in, one of the great cultural explosions of the age: popular theatre. In 1576 the first public theatres were built in London, the Curtain and The Theatre; built to the north in the fields beyond the city walls in order to be firmly out-

Shakespeare used Raphael Holinshed's *Chronicles*, 1577, as a source for a number of his plays including *Macbeth* written with James I in mind. Here a woodcut shows Macbeth's famous encounter with the three witches.

side the jurisdiction of the City Fathers. They, being Puritan, loathed the playhouses – 'To which places . . . do usually resort great numbers of light and lewd disposed persons' – and would use any excuse to close them. In this they failed, for not only were the theatres enormously popular but they had support from aristocratic patrons and the court. So successful were they that they spread, eleven years later, to south of the river, to Bankside in Southwark where the Rose opened.

The theatres were circular or polygonal in shape, with galleries looking across and down onto a stage which faced south-west in order to catch every shaft of light, for the plays were performed in the afternoon. The stage itself was a raised platform and the central ground level enclosure was filled with standing spectators. Here is how a Swiss visitor, Thomas Platter, describes the experience of going to one:

'And thus every day at two o'clock in the afternoon . . . two if not three comedies are performed, at separate places, wherewith folk make merry together, and whichever does best gets the best audience. The places are so built, that they play on a raised platform, and everyone can well see it all. There are, however, separate galleries and there one stands more comfortably and moreover can sit, but one pays more for it.'

As time passed these open-air theatres became increasingly elaborate with painted decoration making the pillars look like marble. Over the stage there was a gallery, so that the actors could stage scenes on more than one level. The costumes were rich and the effects became more complex. The plays however were easily adaptable to being staged in other venues, such as a great hall at court or in a noble house, or even in an inn yard when the company went on tour.

These theatres in the main were related to particular companies of actors who enjoyed the patronage and protection of a great lord, essential, bearing in mind the hostility of the civic authorities who regarded the playhouses as dens of iniquity. Shakespeare is likely to have learned his craft in the company of the builder of the The Theatre, James Burbage. His company had a succession of very powerful patrons including the queen's favourite, the Earl of Leicester, and, later, her cousin, Lord Hunsdon. In the reign of Elizabeth's successor they rose to the summit becoming the King's Men. Although the Puritan authorities were so hostile, regarding actors as little more than disturbers of the peace, the life of the average player had to be an extremely disciplined one. No less than six different plays could be performed in one week and up to thirty in a period of six months. Every play had to be learnt, actors having to double up with more than one part, then rehearsed, all of which demanded high powers of energy and concentration. Each production called for detailed direction, for costumes and props to be made, music and sound effects to be supervised, apart from the front-of-house duties, from running the box office to ensuring the supply of refreshments for sale during a performance.

By the time that Shakespeare was certainly in London he had already been acting and indeed writing plays. More to the point, he proved himself capable of writing plays which were huge box office successes, like the innovative popular history plays which presented a panorama of the reign of the ill-fated Henry VI. Through the decade a whole succession of plays followed and the company's success was such that in 1595 they were called upon to perform before the queen at Christmas. Those performances at court must have been a success, for they were summoned back the next year, the traditional occasion upon which Elizabeth was so delighted with the character of Sir John Falstaff that she bade Shakespeare write a play about him in love. *The Merry Wives of Windsor* was the result, thought to have been staged on the occasion of the creation of new Knights of the Garter in the spring of 1597.

By 1600 Shakespeare had become extremely prosperous. His father had applied and been granted a coat of arms which meant that both he and his son were gentlemen, and entitled to be addressed as 'Mr'. Shakespeare then purchased the second largest house in his native town, New Place, and later went on to purchase extensive land in the vicinity. In addition he had shares in the new theatre which opened on Bankside in 1598, the Globe.

All this paints an outwardly simple story of the life of a successful entrepreneur actor-playwright who was able to produce precisely what his audiences wanted. But other aspects of Shakespeare remain a total mystery. At the same time that the plays were enjoying their popularity he established himself as a poet, dedicating, in 1594, his poem *The Rape of Lucrece* to the young Earl of Southampton. To that young aristocrat, one of the circle centred on Elizabeth's last favourite, Essex, it is thought he wrote a series of sonnets, but it cannot be proved. Nor can the identity of the lady to whom yet more sonnets were written, the Dark Lady with her notorious black hair, black brows and black eyes. (These mysteries still remain to be convincingly unlocked, although many scholars have tried.) But one senses the company was somehow on the fringes of the Essex set, for a group of his followers paid for a performance of Shakespeare's *Richard II*, including the scene of the king's deposition, banned by the authorities, to be

A panorama of Bankside shortly before 1644 by Wenceslas Hollar showing the Globe Theatre. This was the second Globe, the first having been burnt down during a performance of Shakespeare's *Henry VIII*, which opened in 1614. The flag means that a performance is in progress.

performed on the eve of the earl's attempt to raise the Londoners. Southampton, Shakespeare's patron, received the death sentence, one which was commuted to life imprisonment. But none of this seems to have affected the company, which continued to play at court.

The Globe Theatre was a huge success. In the new reign James I proved an even greater lover of the drama than Elizabeth had been, doubling the number of plays performed at court. All of this meant that Shakespeare needed to increase the repertoire and write in response to the tastes of a new era. The king's obsession with witches was met in *Macbeth* and the court's increasing taste for visual fantasy in plays like *Pericles*. In response to this fashion a new indoor theatre was constructed at Blackfriars seating a mere seven hundred against the Globe's three thousand. To this came a far more exclusive audience hungry for plays lit artificially and for the first time making use of special effects and machinery. For them Shakespeare provided the transformations and wonders which enliven his late plays such as *The Winter's Tale* and *The Tempest*.

In June 1613 the Globe was burnt down during a performance of what was arguably Shakespeare's last play *Henry VIII*. By then, or even earlier, he seems to have moved back to his native Stratford where he died on 23 April 1616. In his will he left virtually his entire estate to his eldest daughter, Susanna, wife of Dr John Hall. His only son had died decades before and his second daughter was left little, the result of having made a bad marriage. His wife he never even referred to in his will by name, leaving her only a bed and its hangings.

Shakespeare is one of those enigmatic figures who cross the pages of history and give away nothing. Six of his signatures exist but not a single line of his own writing. Although his career as a successful businessman and writer is there to trace, the inner voyage of his mind remains opaque. Who were the young man and the Dark Lady to whom he wrote the sonnets? What were his religious beliefs? What was his exact relationship with his family and his patrons? What is the true chronology of his plays? All of these questions still remain unanswered giving rise in our own age to a massive academic industry.

It is clear that his work was admired in his own lifetime, but yet he remained only a common playhouse poet. It is fortunate that after his death the two remaining members of his company sensed that there was a heritage to impart, and embarked on a project to publish his complete works. This began during the summer of 1621 and finally appeared two years later. The *First Folio* transmitted to posterity 'Mr. William Shakespeare's Comedies, Histories & Tragedies'. The thirty-six plays are prefaced by a eulogy from his contemporary, Ben Jonson:

Triumph, my Britain, thou hast one to show
To whom all scenes of Europe homage owe.

For that decision to publish the whole world must never cease to give thanks.

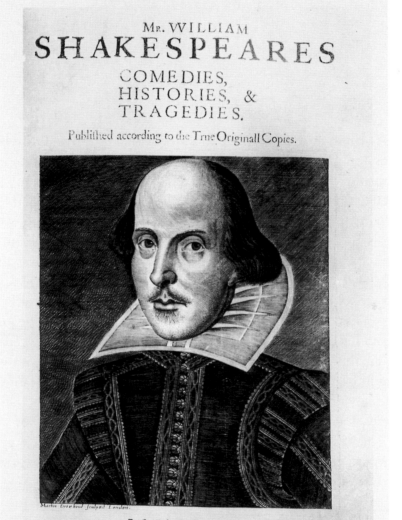

The title-page to the *First Folio*, the collected plays of Shakespeare published in 1623 adorned with an engraving of the playwright after a portrait painted about a decade earlier.

Chapter Thirty-Three

AN UNTRUSTWORTHY DYNASTY

A BARREN virgin queen gave place to a king with a queen and three children. For the first time in half-a-century the succession was to present no problem. The population received the king with adulation, keenly anticipating changes after years of stagnation. Elizabeth had nominated James VI of Scotland, son of Mary Queen of Scots, as her successor on her deathbed. Her minister Robert Cecil, during the last years of her reign, laid down all the lines of communication necessary to ensure a smooth succession. James I of England, as he became, was thirty-eight in 1603. He had been king of Scotland almost from birth and had learnt his statecraft in the rugged school of Scottish politics during the late sixteenth century. For years his eyes had been cast longingly southwards to the promised land. As he journeyed into England from his backward, poverty-stricken northern kingdom the contrast cannot have been anything other than dramatic, as the aristocracy vied with each other to receive him in houses of a splendour unknown to him. When he came into possession of the late queen's many magnificent palaces James must have pondered on his good fortune. He had inherited all Elizabeth's glories but in reality they were a mirage, screening a flawed legacy. What the country desperately needed was a reforming monarch. What it got was one content to enjoy the many creature comforts which had so fortuitously come his way after years of spartan deprivation.

The biggest problem James inherited was how to pay for the government. Running the kingdom was becoming more and more expensive. The king was still expected to live 'of his own', that is, on the revenues from crown lands and other dues settled in the main hundreds of years before during the feudal ages, asking for money from Parliament only to meet the expenses of

James I in robes of state, crowned and bearing the orb and sceptre as monarch by Divine Right. The picture records an architectural revolution for through the mullioned windows there is a view of the new banqueting hall of Whitehall Palace designed by Inigo Jones in the classical style which was still being built when the picture was painted. The king hated sitting for his portrait.

war. This system was already under severe strain by the close of Elizabeth's reign. During that of James and his son, Charles I, the strain was to reach breaking point. Money to run government could come from two sources and both were to be explored during the forty years that preceded the collapse. One way forward was for Parliament to recognise the need for regular taxation in time of peace, in order to pay for the daily running of government, the salaries of officials and the costs of the great organs of state, the law courts, the treasury, the army, the navy, as well as the expenses of the royal court. In return for such recognition the king would cease to raise money by way of the many outmoded and unpopular ways which were hangovers from the Middle Ages, such as fining people of a certain income if they refused to be knighted or if they infringed forest laws made centuries before. The second way forward was to dispense with Parliament, something which would have been in tune with what was happening all over the rest of Europe at the time, and develop to the full the royal Divine Right to impose various taxes and dues. There were precedents for each method in the past, so that king and Parliament could both equally claim that right was on their side.

With goodwill a resolution could perhaps have been reached. The fact that it was not reflects the one big change that did come with the new dynasty, the progressive erosion of trust between the monarchy and the people. All of the Tudors, even Mary at the outset, had enjoyed the deep trust of the majority of the nation. Even during the difficult last decade of Elizabeth's reign, when troubles were gathering thick and fast, that had not faltered. But now that trust gradually began to be eroded. That it was can be attributed to the characters of the first two Stuart kings.

Of the two kings James I was by far the less disastrous, although even under him significant cracks began to appear. He was a shambling, ungainly man, a pedant with a brilliant if sometimes wayward and prickly brain. His passions were theology, the hunt, and handsome young men, for he was basically homosexual. He had a deep dislike of public appearances. The contrast with the Tudors, virtually all of them superb actors on a public stage, could not have been greater. But there was a worse canker. Although by the close of the century the Tudors were accorded virtually semi-divine status, they never claimed it. James I, in sharp contrast, stated both in his writings and public speeches that kings were God's lieutenants on earth, a belief enshrined in what

The title-page to the *Authorised Version of the Bible*, the new translation instigated by James I and published in 1611. This was to have an enduring impact wherever the English language and Anglican Church spread, until the second half of the twentieth century. Two prophets, Moses left and Aaron right, stand within the wall of the Old Testament which supports the four Evangelists above, behind whom stand the Apostles. At the top the radiance of the Tetragrammaton, the four-lettered Hebrew name of God, outshines both the sun and the moon.

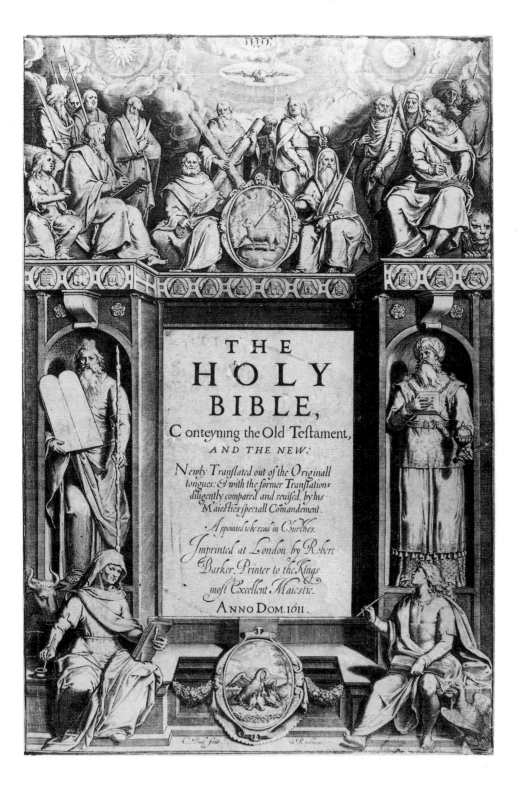

was referred to as the Divine Right of Kings. Such an exaltation would not have been so bad if James had not kept lecturing Parliament on this fact, or if his court had retained his predecessor's splendid sobriety. Instead the court became a byword for extravagance and corruption as the king showered offices, titles, lands and money on his favourites. Such prodigality made it difficult to persuade Parliament to vote regular taxation when all they saw was money seemingly being frittered away. More serious was the relationship of the court to the country as a whole. Elizabeth had always retained around her officers whose views were widely differing. She had favourites, but she was always careful to advance only those with real abilities. Under James that changed. He too had favourites, beautiful certainly, but politically inept. Nonetheless he advanced them to office and power, and thus did lasting damage. What he did retain, however, was Elizabeth's balance of varied interests around him, thus preserving a wide network of support and communication across the country.

So in spite of it all, the old machinery of Tudor government creaked along into the new century. James opened his reign by making peace with Spain which immediately brought a much needed surge of economic activity. In the same year, 1604, he summoned a theological conference at Hampton Court, so that the Puritans could voice their demands for further reformation of the Church of England. Although the event itself was a failure James, like Elizabeth, maintained the comprehensive nature of the national church. Indeed the situation under him was in some ways easier, for he had been brought up a Calvinist, that is a follower of the reformer John Calvin whose extreme Protestantism as practised in Geneva had been the basis of the Puritan movement in England. During James's reign more and more clergy were university graduates equipped to be active 'godly ministers', preaching, reading and expounding the Scriptures. The Puritan life was one of the faith in action, with a strong line on public morality and order. There were few pressures to upset its ability to exist side by side with an Anglicanism whose focus was very different, and which retained many beliefs and practices from the medieval Catholic church, such as regarding the church as an institution with a hierarchy, in particular, bishops, and maintaining the importance of decent ritual in worship with a faith whose mainspring was the contemplation of Christ as exemplar. Only towards the close of the reign was this peaceful coexistence to be disturbed.

The Catholics went on as before in spite of what would seem to have been an enormous set-back, the consequences of the Gunpowder Plot. In 1605 a group of Catholics plotted to blow up Parliament at the very moment it was being opened by the king. In one huge explosion the Lords and Commons and most of the royal family were to have been wiped out; then one of the king's children was to be put on the

A Dutch view of the Gunpowder Plot of 1605. Above, the conspirators, depicted as country gentlemen, converse, while below they meet their savage fate. Several of the conspirators, including the most famous Guy Fawkes, were dragged from the Tower to Westminster, where they were hanged, drawn and quartered.

throne and married to a foreign Catholic prince. The fact that this conspiracy was betrayed by a loyal Catholic peer is indicative that the scheme did not have the support of the broad mass of those who remained loyal to the old religion. For a time Catholics were fined and imprisoned and then the clouds blew over and there was a reversion to the norm. Peace with Spain, and James's passionate wish to act as a peacemaker in Europe by marrying one child to a Protestant and another to a Catholic, made it easier for them. What was unfortunate about the Gunpowder Plot was the king's decision that it should be turned into an annual commemoration each 5 November with a special service in every parish church, a practice which continued until the middle of the reign of Queen Victoria. This annual event fixed in the minds of most of the population what had begun in Mary's reign and been consolidated with the Armada: the rudimentary interpretation of public affairs in terms of king versus pope and Protestant versus Catholic. It bred an atmosphere of fear and suspicion which it was to prove easy to play upon.

James was fortunate in inheriting Robert Cecil, whom he ennobled as Lord Salisbury. Salisbury set about the only major attempt to put the government's finances in good order via Parliament. He started with a reform of the crown lands where rents which had remained fixed for decades were surveyed, and new leases introduced at a higher price. But he went beyond this to propose to Parliament the sweeping away of all the old feudal sources of revenue. The 1610 Parliament was offered the abolition of these in return for £600,000 to wipe out the existing royal debts plus the guarantee of a regular income of £200,000 p.a. In the end, negotiations for what was called the Great Contract broke down. Parliament refused to come to terms with the reality of paying for running government. The crown now had no other choice but to look elsewhere for revenue. Already the ground had been prepared when, in 1606, the courts ruled that duties imposed for the regulation of commerce were part of foreign policy, and anything to do with foreign policy pertained to the royal prerogative. And it was on that decision both James and more particularly Charles were to build.

Salisbury died in 1612, the same year in which the king's eldest son, Henry, died. After these two deaths there was a lurch downhill. No one of Salisbury's calibre replaced him and James's second son was no substitute for the dynamic Henry. The court began to be tarnished with scandal, above all with the notorious case of the murder of Sir Thomas Overbury, political adviser to one of James's early favourites, Robert Carr, whom he created Viscount Rochester. In 1611 Rochester began his affair with Frances Howard, wife of the young Earl of Essex. She was beautiful, with innocent childlike features masking an evil malignity within. Frances was a member of the Howard family whose members held the most important offices at court. They saw

The king that never was. James I's eldest son, Henry, died of typhoid fever in his nineteenth year in 1612. He was a young man of exceptional promise with a passionate interest in the arts and a commitment to revive the vanished glories of the previous reign. His death was a tragedy. Here, attended by the Earl of Essex, he is about to slay the stag at his feet in a picture painted in the first year of his father's reign, 1603.

her as a means to secure further their influence over the king. In order to marry Rochester, Frances had to obtain a divorce from her husband, Essex, something virtually unheard of at that period. Frances, however, had an enemy in Overbury, who opposed her. James also disliked Overbury, who was consigned to the Tower where he died shortly after. This freed the way for the divorce and in December 1613 Rochester married Frances amidst a blaze of courtly spectacle. The triumph was to be short-lived, for soon afterwards it emerged that Overbury had been poisoned and the lines of accusation and evidence all led to Frances and her accomplices. As a result she and her husband were the subject of a sensational trial. Although her accomplices were hanged, Frances and Rochester, thanks to the king, were sent to the Tower and then allowed to live in seclusion. But the whole sordid saga had exposed the court as rotten and the king as abetting a perversion of justice.

Rochester's fall, was hastened deliberately by the faction at court opposed both to him and to the Howards. They knew that the only way to dislodge them was to replace Rochester in the king's affections with another man, and alighted upon an impoverished younger son of a Leicestershire gentleman, George Villiers. He was reckoned to be the handsomest man of his age. The opposition deliberately groomed him to attract the king's eye and they succeeded. Villiers's rise was meteoric: Viscount Villiers in 1616, Earl of Buckingham in 1617, Marquis in 1618 and, finally, Duke in 1623. Buckingham was more dangerous than his predecessors, for he combined political aspirations with political ineptitude. But James gave him office, indeed as he grew older became so besotted with him that he could take no decision without him. Buckingham was astute enough to realise that the king was old, and that if he was to survive he needed also to capture the heir to the throne with his charm. In this he was successful, and Buckingham therefore came to dominate the decade, uniting the two reigns until his death in 1628.

Buckingham's tragedy was the same as the king's. He was not a reformer but like James, he knew how to keep the existing system creaking along, although he made far more enemies along the way. This was due to the fact that he was one of a large family, each member of which had to be rewarded with titles, splendid marriages, grants of money and lands, which only added to people's perception of the court as a sink of iniquity. Something could have been salvaged from the wreckage if James had not embarked on war with all the appalling financial problems that entailed. He had begun his reign with every intention of pursuing conciliation. His daughter Elizabeth had been married to the leading Protestant in the Holy Roman Empire, Frederick, Elector Palatine. Frederick had been elected king of Bohemia, thus threatening the Catholic Habsburg domination of Central Europe. An army was sent into Bohemia; Frederick was defeated and forced to flee into exile, an event which triggered off the European conflagration called the Thirty Years' War, an horrendous and bloody politico-religious power struggle involving at one time or another virtually all the European powers.

Many in England, particularly the Puritans, wished to join the Protestant cause, but James believed that a settlement could be reached by means of diplomacy. He continued his policy of conciliation, negotiating with Spain for the marriage of his son to an Infanta, a wildly unpopular proposal. James was forced to summon Parliament to ask them for a subsidy to make war. The Commons agreed on condition that the war was against Spain and that the marriage negotiations were broken off. James was furious, informing the members that they existed by his grace alone. The behaviour of the king led the Commons to define their own status in the form of a Protestation which stated that an elected Parliament was 'the ancient and undoubted birthright' of every Englishman. So enraged was the king by this that he tore the document out of the Commons' journal in which they recorded their proceedings. In the same Parliament, the House of Lords, responding to what they saw as corrupt minis-

The High and Mighty Prince Charles, Prince of Wales, &c.
The Manner of his Arriuall at the Spanish Court, the Magnificence of his Royall Entertainement there: His happy Returne, and hearty welcome, both to the King and Kingdome of England, the fifth of October, 1623. Heere liuely and briefely described, together with certaine other delightfull passages, obseruable in the whole Trauaile.

A popular print captures the public rejoicing at the return of the Prince of Wales from Spain without a Spanish Catholic bride in 1623. Hats are thrown into the air with joy and bonfires blaze.

ters, revived the fifteenth century practice of impeachment, in order to purge the Lord Chancellor, Francis Bacon from the government. If James had been wiser both developments could have been averted. As it was they left a dangerous legacy for the future.

The Spanish marriage project ended in disaster, with the consequent desire to appease the damaged honour of the heir to the throne by making war on Spain. This meant asking Parliament for money when the country was in the grip of the worst economic depression of the century. War on the Continent had contributed to a huge slump in the export of broadcloth. At home there were failed harvests, followed by famine. Nonetheless Parliament, which met again in 1624, voted some £300,000 towards a joint land and sea attack on Spain with the Dutch.

Parliament, suspicious of James and even more of Buckingham's influence over him, laid down that the money was to be accounted for by treasurers of their own appointment. James, in fact, ignored what had been promised, and spent the money on subsidising foreign armies who might have re-established Frederick and Elizabeth in the Palatinate. But they failed.

James died on 27 March 1625. In one sense his demise caused no break in the flow of events under the dominating but fatal influence of Buckingham. In another sense it did, for it was his son's characteristics which were to accelerate even more significantly a breakdown of relations with Parliament. Under James the ship of state may have become progressively leakier but it just about managed to remain on course. Under his successor, it was to sink amidst a sea of recriminations.

Chapter Thirty-Four

THE KING'S ARCADIA

THE new king shared the beliefs but not the vices of his father. For Charles I the monarch was indeed a sacred being set apart, something which was emphasised by his austere and reserved manner and by his introduction of the rigid ceremonial he had seen at the Spanish court which he had visited to woo the Infanta. While his father had endured public appearances Charles rarely if ever made them, his court becoming a closed world from which he excluded those whose views did not coincide with his own. The result was gradually to cut the monarchy adrift from any popular support. The fact that Charles was shy and diffident with a stutter was no assistance either, to a man for whom the very fact that he was king endowed his every action and decision with a divine rectitude however wrong these actions and decisions might be. His Archbishop of Canterbury, William Laud, was to write of him that he 'neither knows how to be, nor to be made, great.' All of this boded ill in 1625, for his inheritance was far worse than his father's: royal credit was by then truly exhausted.

The country was still engaged in a war it could not afford. The distrust felt for the crown, and what was regarded as the malign influence of Buckingham, led to the first Parliament of the reign granting the customs dues known as tonnage and poundage for only one year. Every Parliament until then had automatically granted these for the lifetime of the monarch. The Commons then proceeded to attack Buckingham who was leading what proved to be a disastrous war. So the pattern began of Parliaments refusing to pay for mishandled wars over the course of which they had no control. On both sides this produced bitterness and recriminations leading to polarisation. In 1626 the crown jewels were pawned and, the following year, Charles made over to the City most of the remaining crown lands to pay off old royal debts and stave off the repayment of another loan. This act

Charles I with his queen, Henrietta Maria, and their two eldest children, the future Charles II at his father's knee and Princess Mary in her mother's arms. This huge picture was the first of the great series of portraits painted by the recently arrived court painter, Sir Anthony van Dyck, which were to immortalise the king and his court, The grandeur with which the artist endows his sitters was far removed from their physical reality. Both king and queen were unprepossessing in appearance, Henrietta Maria having protruding teeth.

represented the effective end of medieval kingship, for when the lands went the king no longer had anything 'of his own' by which to pay for government. The only way forward, if Parliament refused to co-operate, was to invoke the royal prerogative and raise taxes.

Once again Charles called Parliament. Those who were elected were hostile, and arrived from the shires with grievances against the war, which had lurched from one catastrophe to the next, and the means whereby the king had financed it. Charles had raised money by what were called forced loans. Five knights had refused to pay and been arrested. In short, by doing this they had challenged the king's actions, but Charles would not be drawn and refused to allow the legality of such loans to be tested in the courts. The judges supported him in so far as they agreed that the crown must have power of arrest. The result of all this was to drive the Commons to compile a list of grievances, the Petition of Right, condemning what they saw as the crown's innovatory methods of financing government. In their desire to return to the old Elizabethan status quo, they found themselves gradually taking on the role of defenders of what they saw as ancient liberties. The reality was that Parliament wanted government without paying for it. The crown was in fact more forward-looking in its policies. The tragedy was that the money raised by the crown was used to finance failure.

On 23 August 1628 Buckingham was assassinated. Both the populace and the Commons rejoiced, to the bitter grief of the king who had lost his closest friend. Far from resolving the tension between Charles and Parliament, it was to exacerbate it even more, for Buckingham, like James I, had shrewdly kept a foot in more than one camp. The king, with Buckingham removed, now pursued an unswerving path which allowed for no deviations. He was forced to accept the Petition of Right, which he did most ungraciously, and then promptly ignored it. Once more Parliament met and once again the result was an impasse. Charles realised that as long as he avoided war he could rule without Parliament. And that, in 1629, was what he decided to do, embarking on a decade known as the years of Personal Rule.

From the king's point of view the decision was a wise one. Seen through his eyes Parliament had become an irksome, old-fashioned institution which stood in the way of effective good government. It had failed to move with the times. Across the Channel similar representative bodies were disappearing as rulers ran their states far more efficiently without the encumbrance of dealing with meetings of elected representatives. In any case the English Parliament only existed by the grace of the king. Without him its actions had no binding legal status. Parliaments were called only in time of necessity and ten years of James's reign had passed without one. No one complained at the time for long sessions were expensive, calling for residence in London and absence from dealing with business in the country. But for two things, Parliament could have fallen into abeyance and disappeared. The first was that because of the war, which had gone on for several years, Parliament had almost become an annual event so that members got to know each other and a corporate feeling had emerged. Further, the king's actions had forced them to formulate Parliament's rights for the first time. All of this was not easily forgotten, but it could have been. The second factor was the recurrence of war. What in the end brought Parliament back again was something the king could never have foreseen – war within his own kingdoms.

But for over ten years Charles successfully ruled the country in person without Parliament. He made peace with both France and Spain, henceforth confining British influence abroad to the field of diplomacy. Buckingham was replaced in his affections by his Catholic French queen, Henrietta Maria, and together they set out to make their court a model in terms of virtue and good order for the rest of the country to emulate. After the immoral court of his father, that of Charles was a monument to sobriety. The sale of offices, for example, was strictly forbidden. The old Privy Council was reinvigorated, the judges were cast as agents for royal reform as they toured the country, and the gentry were encouraged to remain on their estates fulfilling their local obligations. Peace brought commercial prosperity and with that, income to the crown through customs dues which Charles levied as his right. Financially the king stretched his prerogative dues to their limit: fines for not being knighted, the imposition of ancient forest laws, and of the royal right to tax in order to create a fleet and naval defences in time of danger, a tax known as Ship Money.

Government had never been so stable since the days of the Cecils. The king, moreover, had two able ministers, Thomas Wentworth, who efficiently administered the north and then Ireland as Lord Deputy, and William Laud, Bishop of London, and then Archbishop of Canterbury, who carried through the royal religious policy. Both, like the king, were obsessed with conformity and good order. The trouble was that conformity to such a vision made enemies and also led to exclusion for those who would not do as they were directed. Prior to Charles's reign there had been room for manoeuvre, especially in matters of belief where ambiguity embraced divergence. Now there was none, and that was to prove the major rock upon which the monarchy foundered.

Charles I did not share his father's stance on religion. For him the Puritans were an aberration to be rooted out. He saw the Church of England as the old pre-Reformation Catholic church reformed, purged of abuses and superstition. That position, which Elizabeth I had shared but never enforced, now came into reality. Its adherents were called Arminians after a Dutch theologian called Arminius, but overall this was a specifically Anglican movement. The creed of the Church of England had been codified under Elizabeth in a document called the Thirty-Nine Articles. Although open to a Puritan interpretation they were by no means extreme in their Protestantism. This was an age of intense and passionate belief. As long as those who read the Thirty-Nine Articles in a different way were quiescent, no problems arose. But that began to change at the close of James I's reign when a new generation of clergy asserted the theological uniqueness of the English church as being independent not only of Rome but also of Geneva. There was a reassertion of the belief that what man did in this life actually contributed to the salvation of his soul, an attitude regarded with utter horror by the Puritans, who held that every human being was destined from birth either to heaven or hell. There was a reaffirmation also of the importance of the sacraments, in particular that of Holy Communion. To emphasise its sanctity the table which had been brought down into the nave for communion was now to remain in the position of the pre-Reformation altar, railed off in a sanctuary. The word 'altar' reappeared. As the movement developed, order and ceremony and the beauty of art were re-introduced into the churches: stained glass, crucifixes, candlesticks, bowing towards the altar, and vestments. In addition there was a commitment to stop the asset-stripping of the church and to restore its endowments.

The new Anglican movement mirrored the Puritan one, for it could also be not only fervent but aggressive. More important, it gained the support first of Buckingham and then of the king. Charles I changed virtually the entire episcopate and senior clergy, appointing only those who would carry through changes. His chief agent was William Laud who succeeded to Canterbury in 1633. Laud was tactless and querulous and pushed on relentlessly with the reformation, and the suppression of Puritanism. In the years before the king's Personal Rule, attacks in the Commons on the movement went hand-in-hand with those on royal finances. Members of Parliament were overwhelmingly Puritan. Without its meetings they had lost their mouthpiece.

On the surface, however, the king's long peace seemed like Arcadia. The country had changed greatly from the previous century. The south came to dominate more and more as London continued to expand as a port at the expense of the regional ones. As the home of the court (which no longer travelled), the government and the law, visits to London became obligatory for gentry from the regions who now began to acquire town houses. As a consequence, London became the great consumer of everything from food and coal to luxury goods. By 1640 it had some three hundred and fifty thousand inhabitants. Norwich, the country's second largest city, had a mere twenty thousand. Cities and towns elsewhere seemed little more than overgrown villages, whose streets quickly gave way to fields and country.

In spite of its appalling road system, England was a highly commercialised country in a manner only rivalled by northern Italy and the Low Countries. Although there had been a devastating recession many people were much better off, a fact reflected in their wills, which reveal that even quite humble families now ate off pewter and cooked in brass. The fluidity of the social structure inherited from the Tudors continued, something which set England apart from the mainland where the aristocracy became a caste. In England the nobility paid taxes, married commoners and engaged in commercial investment. The crown contributed to this fluidity by bestowing titles on those who had grown wealthy on account of their commercial endeavour. The aristocratic, gentry and yeoman classes followed the example of the crown in setting out to maximise profits from land. Their success can be seen in the proliferation of manor houses across the landscape. Merchants also prospered and set the pattern of turning that prosperity into land by setting up as country gentry. For the first time the professional classes, made up in the main of lawyers and clergy, took on an identity. The clergy now assumed the character of well-off yeomen, university educated and, being able to marry, founders of dynasties. Their rise in status was to make the rectory a fit residence for the younger sons of the gentry classes.

All of this formed a sharp contrast to what was an ever-widening gap between the classes which flourished and those doomed to swell the ranks of the migrant poor. Landless paupers grew and grew in numbers until it was reckoned that they made up one third of the population. More and more of them drifted towards the towns in search of work. Government became obsessed with seeing that the local poor rate was levied to cope with this burgeoning tide of poverty. So bad was it that it was to be the driving force which led to the earliest waves of emigration to New England during the 1620s.

This was the downside of early Stuart society which otherwise was remarkable for its volatility. People could move socially upwards if they were clever, and by 1640 about a third of the male population was literate. The educational drive sprang from Protestant and especially Puritan impulses, for a man needed to read in order to study the Scriptures. Puritanism was the religion of the literate. At the bottom of the social heap, access upwards was by way of apprenticeship and education in a grammar school. There was no lack of scholarships for the gifted. By the middle of the century most towns had a grammar school, many had several. The demand for education was not only driven by religion but by changes in business methods which now called for complex written contracts and book-keeping.

People were no longer static. Families, no longer tied to the land, moved around at every level of society either on account of marriage or the demands of work. Although there was no such thing as birth control, due to the high infant mortality rate the family unit rarely exceeded five in number. It continued to be a male-dominated society in which women could only gain status as widows with property. A woman's role was to preside over and serve the household, and as a consequence the need for women to be educated was removed. Theirs was a circumscribed existence; apart from work their only outlet was religion.

Britain, however, was not a united state. Although James I had proclaimed himself king of Great Britain reviving the ancient Roman name, he and and his son ruled over three very distinct kingdoms each with its own equally distinct traditions. Both Scotland and Ireland were poor, backward and neglected countries, the victims amongst other things of distance from Whitehall Palace. Neither James nor Charles went to Ireland, and Scotland was only visited under duress. This status quo would probably have continued if Charles I had not extended his obsession with order and uniformity to his other kingdoms. In the case of Ireland the king was fortunate in Thomas Wentworth, who carried through such administrative and religious reform with efficiency. When, however, Charles turned his attention to Scotland he had no such ally and was rudely jolted out of his dream world.

The Scots rightly felt marginalised at every level of society. The country had an extreme Protestant tradition stemming back to Calvin and Geneva via the great Scottish reformer John Knox. In Scotland there was no theological ambiguity as in the case of England. Nonetheless Charles, never deviating for an instant from his chosen path of imposing uniformity in his kingdoms, issued, in 1637, a version of the English

A series of ladies representing the four seasons provides a panorama of the 1640s with glimpses of the England of Charles I. Spring has a new country house with an elaborate garden laid out in the latest Italian style; Summer affords a

Prayer Book for use in Scotland. It was not even a version of that of 1552 but of the far more Catholic one of 1549. It was introduced without any consultation either with the Scottish Parliament or the church assembly. The result was riot and rebellion. Charles succeeded in uniting both nobility and populace against him and a Covenant was signed by the Scots to defend their church. They looked southwards and saw what they believed was the introduction of popery by the back door. The queen practised her Catholicism openly, indeed converts were made and the king even received a papal agent in residence at court. The transformation of the Church of England under Laud signalled to the Scots that the age of Antichrist had indeed come. They took to arms and marched across the border.

Everything that the king had striven to achieve depended on avoiding war. And now it had come, not from without but within. The only way Charles could meet the invasion without calling Parliament was to resort to the old medieval summons-to-arms of a king to his tenants-in-chief. The resulting assembly bore no resemblance to a modern army. An ill-clothed, ill-armed and ill-trained motley crew marched north and disintegrated in the face of the Scots. In June 1639 Charles was forced to buy time, and he signed the Treaty of Berwick. The Scots had the advantage in more senses than one, for in the south a major crisis was looming, one which they realised could only work to their advantage. In the midst of the crisis Charles turned to the one man who might know how to handle it, Thomas Wentworth. Now ennobled as Earl of Strafford, he returned to England and told the king that he must do the one thing he had striven at all costs to avoid, call Parliament.

view across St. James's Park to Inigo Jones's Whitehall Banqueting House; Autumn looks over the Thames towards a grotto, while Winter, a prostitute, plies her wares against the shops of Cheapside.

Chapter Thirty-Five

THREE KINGDOMS
IN CRISIS

IN A SENSE a civil war of a kind had already begun. Ostensibly it was the revolt of one kingdom against the policies of a king it shared with two others. But the Scots knew that they had allies south of the border. Grievances had been piling up with no means of voicing them, above all those of the Puritans, who shared the Covenanters' view that the king's religious policy was that of Antichrist. They saw in the new ceremony and beauty of Anglican worship the forerunner of a surrender to Rome. Saturated in the Bible, it needed little imagination for the aggrieved to believe that they were living through a fulfilment of the prophecies of the Book of Revelation.

So, when Parliament met in April 1640, the king was taken aback by the sheer deluge of complaints. They were not only religious, but also fiscal, bitter attacks on the king's use of his prerogative powers to raise taxes by what they regarded as devious means with no legal basis. They objected strongest of all to Ship Money. In the same year that the Scots rebelled, 1637, the king's right to levy this tax had been challenged in the courts but the majority of the judges declared in favour of the king. Five, however, did not: but what seemed a victory for the royal prerogative was to provide three years later the ammunition the opposition required to attack it.

So overwhelmed was Charles by the torrent of complaints that within three weeks he rashly took the decision to dissolve a Parliament which became known as the Short Parliament. No subsidy had been granted. The dissolution proved to be an incredibly short-sighted move, for this action only fuelled distrust at a time when, with a few concessions, the king could have gained the subsidy he needed to meet the challenge of the Scots. As it was, he was reduced once more to a feudal call-to-arms and a second even more ill-armed group assembled at Selby. The men en route had given vent to their Puritan sympathies by sacking any church which had been reordered in the manner prescribed by the archbishop. A wave of anti-popery swept through the army which was fed with fears of Catholic plots. When, in August, the Covenanters crossed the border the English army disintegrated for a second time.

The king, in yet a further attempt to bypass Parliament, revived from the Middle Ages a meeting of the Great Council of peers. This assembled at York and peace was made with the Covenanters but at a price: £850 a day. The crown was bankrupt and the peers insisted that Parliament was called. This time the king had no alternative.

No one on 3 November 1640 could have predicted that they were to be members of the longest Parliament in English history, the Long Parliament. When its members assembled they were interested in one thing only, achieving a return to what they now viewed as the golden age of Gloriana when ruler and country had been one. They wanted Laud's innovations swept away, along with Ship Money. There was no way that they were

A portrait by Lely of the shipbuilder, Peter Pett, with the *Sovereign of the Seas*. This magnificent vessel was launched in 1637 and was the largest and finest ship in the world at that date, the pride of the fleet paid for by the unpopular Ship Money tax.

going to grant Charles one penny with which to pay the agreed price to the Scots until he had met their demands. The king had not only alienated the Commons but also the Lords who were now united as one.

The Commons, led by John Pym, lived at fever pitch, its fears of Catholic plots fanned by Puritan preachers. A statute was passed decreeing that there should be no more than three years between Parliaments. The Triennial Act ensured no repetition of a decade of Personal Rule. Impeachment was then invoked to sweep away the agents of prerogative rule: Strafford, Laud, and the judges who declared for the king. In the face of this onslaught the king's Council virtually collapsed and, in an attempt to stave off retribution, Charles began to fill any gaps in government with nobles whom he had excluded from the court because their views failed to coincide with his own. The king, however, was still imbued with a deep belief in his own rectitude and his cause justified any means to which he might resort. He sought to raise money abroad and then attempted to use what was left of the army to release Strafford, who was imprisoned in the Tower. On 3 May news of this plot reached Parliament. Outrage against the king was unleashed on a scale not seen before. The Puritan London mob advanced on Whitehall Palace and the king began to fear for his own life and that of the queen. Going back on a promise he had given Strafford, he signed the warrant for his execution. On 12 May Strafford was beheaded.

The fact that the king had planned to use force, and would clearly do so again if he had the opportunity, opened the floodgates. Now the acts of Parliament came in a mighty surge, sweeping away everything which the decade of Personal Rule had stood for. Ship Money, forest rights and knighthood fines were abolished, then Parliament turned its attention to the organs whereby prerogative rule had been sustained. The Court of Star Chamber and the Court of High Commission were abolished. Religious fervour ran amok as the Puritans saw the Apocalypse loom: the Commons swept away every vestige of Laud's religious policy and then began to agitate for the abolition of the bishops.

These moves epitomised revolution and directly challenged the existing social order. The Lords drew back in support of the bishops who sat in the upper house alongside them. They stood by the Prayer Book. Although this defence of the bishops and the Prayer Book sent up a flare that there could be a potential split in the ranks, Lords and Commons continued united for the time being. The king announced his intention of going north. Once more fear seized the House as to what he might do, but northwards he went in August. Any form of royal control had already collapsed and Parliament, from merely passing statutes, now moved on towards actual control of the government.

A. Doctor VÎher, Lord Prʸte of Ireland,
B. the Sherifes of London,
C. the Earle of Strafford,
D. his kindred and Friend

The execution of Thomas Wentworth, Earl of Strafford on Tower Hill on 12 May 1641.

By late October, when Parliament reassembled after a recess, reaction against these events began to set in. The mob disorder seen in London had spread across the country, where there were violent sackings of churches. For a brief moment it seemed that affairs could turn in the king's favour as the established classes looked on in dismay at the drift towards anarchy. Charles was not to be so fortunate, however, for, although the Scottish army had been paid by Parliament and disbanded, a Catholic rising erupted in Ireland against the Protestant settlers. Nothing could have been more fatal. Rumour once again ran riot. Here was a second kingdom in revolt and an army needed to quell it. In view of recent events Parliament had no intention of voting the king money for an army which he would almost certainly use against them. Parliament therefore decided to take on itself the executive role.

Once this borderline had been crossed a very different kind of polarisation began to happen. Pym and his followers in Parliament pushed on regardless, drawing up a long indictment of the ills of the king's reign, the Grand Remonstrance. It was passed by only a narrow majority. Charles rejected it, and took his stand by the Church of England as it was enshrined in the Prayer Book. The king almost welcomed confrontation and continued to look towards ways of escape, by force if need be. London was wholly against him, its government given over to Puritan radicals who viewed Charles as untrustworthy and the court as a hotbed of popery.

In response to what the king saw as Parliament's violation of his sacred rights, on 3 January 1642 he sent down charges for the impeachment of the five most revolutionary members of the Commons, headed by Pym. The next day Charles himself came, attended by soldiers bent on securing their arrest but, as he said, the birds had flown. With this melodramatic encounter the king reached a point of no return. On 10 January he rode out of Whitehall Palace never to return until his execution seven years later. He went first to Hampton Court and then to York, endeavouring to gain control of arms and raise troops. Those moderates left in the House were in despair as the extremists mobilised the militia against what they saw as a 'popish malignant' enemy. Religious hysteria set in, leading to a total breakdown of the traditional role of Parliament as a mediator and bridgehead between crown and people. The moderates naturally turned towards the king while the Puritan sectarians who remained cast Parliament into a role it had never before occupied – as God's instrument with which to usher in the rule of the saints.

An unbending king who had violated any attempts to build bridges and who had refused to take one step towards the middle ground had contributed greatly to his own downfall. For those caught up in them, it seemed that these were events of the cataclysmic kind associated with the Second Coming. A bewildered population who had never wanted war was gradually forced to take sides as their consciences dictated. The printing presses, now out of government control, poured forth pamphlets casting these happenings as a struggle of light against dark, of true religion against false and of Christ versus Antichrist. No one who had lived through the mirage of the king's Arcadia could have anticipated such a terrifying retribution. The world was indeed upside down.

The Duke of Buckingham, like the king, was a patron of the arts and commissioned the greatest painter of the age, Rubens, to decorate the ceiling of his study at York House, his London residence, for which this is a sketch. Rubens was an exponent of the new baroque style with its use of light and movement to achieve illusion. He uses these to apotheosise the duke who is lifted heavenwards towards the Temple of Virtue by Minerva and Mercury.

Chapter Thirty-Six

THE BRITISH VITRUVIUS

THE KING'S departure from London signalled the end of an era in another sense, for it marked the dissolution of the most civilised court in Europe. Charles I was the greatest patron of the arts ever to sit upon the throne. During his reign all the fruits of the Italian Renaissance in the way of architecture, sculpture, painting and theatre reached England. This revolution, spearheaded by an isolated inward-looking king and court, was as significant in its own way as the one which overtook the monarchy. Nothing was to be quite the same after it, for it changed the direction of British civilisation. Houses, towns, theatres, sculpture and painting all actually looked different. That they did so was not only due to the support of the king but to the genius of the man who was his adviser on matters connected with the arts and who, in his office as Surveyor, was in charge of all royal building enterprises. So important was Inigo Jones that he became called the British Vitruvius, making him England's equivalent of the first century Roman whose book on architecture was the foundation stone of the new Renaissance style.

Thanks to the Reformation England had been cut off during the sixteenth century from direct contact with Italy, the fountainhead of the cultural revolution known as the Renaissance. There the passionate study of antiquity during the fifteenth and sixteenth centuries had given rise to the revival of architecture in the classical manner, the construction of theatres as men believed they had been in ancient Greece and Rome, sculpture directly in emulation of surviving classical examples, and painting in which major innovations, like perspective which defined space on a flat surface, were incorporated. England remained far removed from all this, severed by Henry VIII's quarrel with the papacy and eventually the pope's excommunication of his daughter, Elizabeth. Few English Protestants were able to visit Italy safely. The result of this was an amazingly idiosyncratic culture in which classical elements were made use of but not understood, deployed within a framework which was still essentially medieval, so that the great Elizabethan country houses have more in common with medieval cathedrals, concerned with exotic outline and shape from afar, by way of roof lines peppered with parapets and pinnacles and whose walls were shimmering sheets of glass.

All that came to an end with the deliberate introduction of the disciplined, restrained order laid down in the rules governing classical architecture, ones in which exact mathematical ratios governed the shape of a building both inside and out. There was no room for flights of fancy. That this rigorous restrained style of architecture was deliberately adopted by a king whose main obsession was order and discipline in the state cannot be a coincidence.

Inigo Jones started his life as an Elizabethan. Born in London in 1573 of a family engaged in the cloth trade, little is known about him before 1603. It is likely that he served an apprenticeship as a painter and he definitely visited Italy in the 1590s when, thanks to the end of religious war on the mainland, it became easier for Protestants to travel there. He probably went as part of the household of a great nobleman, but he was there long enough to master the language. He next turns up working for the king of Denmark who must have recommended him to his sister, James I's queen, Anne of Denmark. For her, in 1605, he staged the first of his revolutions.

He achieved this jointly with the poet and playwright, Ben Jonson, who wrote the text of *The Masque of Blackness* for performance at court on Twelfth Night. It was the

Costume for Henry, Prince of Wales in the masque of *Oberon, The Fairy Prince*, 1611. In this spectacle the young prince presented himself attired like a Roman Emperor as the heir to King Arthur.

James I's queen, Anne of Denmark, was a great patron of Inigo Jones. The picture by Paul van Somer features one of the gateways in the new classical style Jones built for her in 1617-18 just after his return from Italy. These were added to the old rambling Tudor palace of Oatlands in Surrey.

A design by Inigo Jones for an unknown masque in the 1620's. In this we see the birth of the picture-frame stage, a proscenium arch framing a scene, in this case a landscape. The drawing is squared-up to enable it to be enlarged by the scene painter. The rocks at the front would have concealed steps down which the masquers descended to dance their ballet.

first of a series of masques which Jones was to stage for the Stuart court over a period of almost forty years. A masque was an elaborate entertainment in which members of the royal family and of the aristocracy took part. The masques were a mixture of song and verse, mime and dance, held together by spectacular scenery and costumes. The formula never changed. Each masque was neatly divided into two parts. In the first, actors appeared dressed as monsters, fiends, or representatives of the ills of society, in settings which mirrored such disorder: hell mouths, ruins or a stormy sea. Then would come a transformation scene in which all this would be magically swept away to reveal the masquers in gorgeous costumes and jewels floating in a glory of light on a cloud or in a temple or aboard ship. The masquers never spoke, indeed they wore masks concealing their identity although everyone in the audience knew they were only the grandest people. After this initial breathtaking theatrical tableau, they slowly moved downstage and then descended by steps into an arena to dance a series of ballets before asking onlookers to join the dancing. It was Jones's task to design the costumes and scenery, direct and light the performance on stage and latterly to help to devise the plots.

The theme of these entertainments made clear to the spectators the godlike nature of royalty. No wonder Charles I not only danced in them but helped devise their plots with Inigo Jones. The masques vanished with the Civil War but their legacy was a revolution in theatre, the introduction of the proscenium stage, where the stage is at one end of the room surrounded by what looks like a picture frame, behind which, by means of painted shutters pushed on and off along grooves, scenery could be changed several times, evoking different locations. The settings made use of perspective, again something which was new, aimed at creating vistas into the distance. In addition, there was machinery whereby clouds could descend or mountains arise. In this way Inigo Jones brought visual spectacle to theatre, spelling the end of the open-air arena playhouses of Shakespeare's day. By the second half of the century theatre was an indoor experience, in which the audience peered at scene changes through a frame sited at the end of a horseshoe tiered with seats.

But that was only one of Jones's revolutions. The second came in architecture. In 1613 he set out again with a great nobleman, the Earl of Arundel, on another visit to Italy. He was then forty but the tour this time took him everywhere so that he was able not only to drink in every detail but to come back to England armed with the architectural drawings of the two greatest Venetian Renaissance architects, Palladio and Scamozzi. He returned in 1615 to take up the office of Surveyor in control of the entire royal building programme.

Jones was unique in one other way. He could draw. More importantly, he was the first Englishman to use drawing in the form of sketches and designs on a par with handwriting as a means to convey his ideas. And his first building was to be another revolution, the earliest Italianate villa in the classical manner ever erected in England, the Queen's House, Greenwich, started in 1616 for the queen, Anne of Denmark. This was to be the ancestor of hundreds of country houses. Three years later the room in which the court masques were staged, the Banqueting House of Whitehall Palace, was burnt to the ground and to replace this Jones built the first great example of classical architecture ever seen in the country. The new Banqueting House was a double cube modelled on an ancient Roman basilica and at the time must have created a sensation towering above the rambling, assymetrical red-brick palace of the Tudors.

Charles I was never rich enough to build as he would have wished. Inigo Jones drew endless schemes for a vast new palace but it was never built. The king, however, paid for a magnificent new portico for St. Paul's Cathedral. It too was in the classical style, standing fifty-six feet high with vast columns dominating the city as a symbol of the royal commitment to Anglicanism of a kind hated by the city's Puritan citizens. The city was fast expanding and here too Jones left his mark by designing the first London square, the piazza at Covent Garden, an elegant colonnaded enclosure with its focal point yet another innovation, the first church to be built in the style of a classical temple, St. Paul's.

Through his travels, Inigo Jones was familiar with the work of the great masters of the Renaissance. As a consequence he was intimately connected with the formation of the earliest collections of works of art in England, those of Prince Henry, the Earl of Arundel, and Charles I. The idea of having an art collection was in itself new, one in which the taste and knowledge of those of royal or noble birth was reflected in rooms filled with paintings, bronzes, antique coins and medals, miniatures, and all kinds of rarities. Charles I assembled the greatest art collection of any English monarch, filling the walls of his palaces with masterpieces and thus making people aware for the first time of the achievements of the Renaissance. This in its turn led Charles to patronise painters of international renown. The greatest painter north of the Alps, Peter Paul Rubens, was commissioned to paint the ceiling of the Whitehall Banqueting House with canvases glorifying James I. His pupil, Anthony van Dyck, immortalised Charles I, his queen and their children in a series of portraits which continue to radiate an unreal magical enchantment.

Unreal is perhaps the key word, for Inigo Jones's contributions to these revolutions in English civilisation cast them as art being used in the service of political power. No wonder that later the Puritans sold off the royal collections, which were filled with Catholic religious paintings of a kind that confirmed their view that the court was a nest of popery. The masques, in which the king and queen were presented as gods, were seen as cunning visual deceits and the Banqueting House as the 'queen's dancing barn'. Acting and dancing in any form was to them iniquity.

Inigo Jones was nearly seventy when civil war broke out, a great age. He was taken prisoner in 1645 at the siege of Basing House, a savage encounter in which the place was cruelly ravaged and left a smoking roofless ruin. Jones, by then seventy-two, was stripped by the soldiery and carried away from the scene in a blanket. Darkness enfolds his last years. He died six years later in London, a wealthy man, but he had lived to see the civilisation he had helped create seemingly destroyed.

Inigo Jones used drawing as a means of working out his ideas and presenting them to his clients. From time to time he looked in a mirror and sketched himself.

Chapter Thirty-Seven

WAR

EVERYONE was stunned when it was realised that the country was about to be plunged into a war no one wanted. In the counties, frantic attempts were made to remain neutral and keep out of the impending conflict. Sooner or later, however, all were forced to take sides. Lucy Hutchinson, wife of a leading Parliamentary commander, wrote: 'Every county. . .had the civil war within itself', for every part of the nation had adherents of both sides. The Civil War was to cut right through society, dividing the nobility, the gentry, the merchant and professional classes. It even tore families asunder, leading to tragic confrontations. The motives which drove people to choose one side or the other could be various but the overwhelming divide was the one of religion. This was to be England's only religious war, one fought not between Catholics and Protestants, as on the mainland, but between two interpretations of the Protestant tradition.

The Parliamentary side saw itself as fighting to preserve an institution whose powers were not only under threat but whose very existence had been in danger. The Puritan members of the Commons cast themselves as the godly engaged in a struggle against the forces of Antichrist, embodied in some tremendous hidden Catholic plot to take over England. They lived in an atmosphere of intense religious fervour committed to a further reformation of the church, sweeping away any traces of what they saw as the dregs of popery. What form that reformation would take remained unclear, and in the long run would lead to division, but that could not be seen at the outset. What they yearned for was a return to the old days when king and Parliament jointly embodied the unity of the nation. The England of Gloriana assumed a golden glow. Indeed throughout the war the Parliamentarians maintained they were fighting for a king who had been misled by evil counsellors.

The Royalists too were fighting for the king and for the preservation of the Protestant religion, the Church of England as it had been established under Elizabeth with its order and liturgy enshrined in the Prayer Book. They stood also for the existing scheme of things, for a hierarchy which stretched down from the monarch and in which each knew his place, and saw any threat to it as menacing social order and leading to anarchy.

This was to be a very different war from the Wars of the Roses which only affected a few people and a small part of the country. The Civil War was to be a bloody one of skirmishes, battles and sieges affecting virtually the whole country. It was a modern war, fought with firearms whose acrid smoke almost blinded the soldiers. By 1643 ten per cent of the male population was under arms. Over three and a half per cent of the population was to perish in one way or another and few families were unaffected. From the parish of Myddle in rural Shropshire twenty-one men had gone to fight. Of these thirteen did not return. Being killed while under arms was only one fate, for the war brought in its train disease and plague. No one involved in the siege of a town or castle was ever likely to forget the experience: the starvation of the inmates, the storming of the walls, the slaughter of those within, followed by the sacking and burning. Indeed the word plunder entered the English language at this period. A fifth of Gloucester was demolished, two thirds of Taunton destroyed and Birmingham, Bolton and Leicester were brutally plundered. Everywhere there was dislocation lead-

Part of a musket drill as recorded by Henry Hexham in his *The Principles of the Art Militarie* published in 1637. Hexham was a soldier for over forty years. His book is a manual for the most up-to-date techniques of his day, those used in the Civil War.

ing to hardship as rents fell and industry slumped. These were not the only side effects as the countryside had to face marauding armies ravaging crops, seizing cattle and horses and attacking those going about their daily work. The toll in taxes and the financial exaction on both sides was crippling. Most counties paid in a month as much as they had previously paid in a year in Ship Money.

Money and a means of raising it was the key to the war. The side which could raise most money efficiently was bound in the end to win because it could keep its soldiers not only paid but amply supplied in the field. The king began with the advantage of having the army, but for money he relied in the main on rich supporters, and that in the long run told against him. As the sole authority and source of command it would seem that he had another advantage, but he was indecisive and, worse, could follow contrary directions simultaneously. The Royalist side was divided also, between those who favoured an early return to peace, on the basis of back to 1641, and those, like the queen, for whom nothing less than the obliteration of the Parliamentarians would do.

When the war began the king's army was led by the Earl of Lindsey but the figure who was to capture the public imagination was the king's handsome nephew, Prince Rupert of the Rhine, General of the Horse. Son of Charles's sister, the widowed queen of Bohemia, Rupert brought to the Royalist cause all the latest skills in the handling of cavalry, cutting a brave and romantic figure on the battlefield. But he was arrogant. Collectively the Royalists came to be designated Cavaliers, a word used in scorn by those who saw them as little more then courtly gentlemen playing at being soldiers.

The opposition became labelled Roundheads, again a term of abuse referring to those amongst the godly who thought sobriety met by cropping their hair short. The Parliamentary side had one man of organisational genius, John Pym, leader of the Commons, who saw clearly the importance of a war machine. Under his direction Parliament created committees in the regions whose task it was to collect taxes and confiscate the lands of Royalists. Soon a sales tax, the excise, was introduced which was wildly unpopular but it meant that soldiers were paid. Although Parliament entered the war with only militiamen for its army under the Earl of Essex, the control of London with all its vast financial resources was to prove crucial to its success. Crucial also was the navy's declaration in Parliament's favour. From the first, however, the Parliamentary side was dogged by regionalism, for the troops from one region would not go to the assistance of those in another. Nor could a war be well run whose authority was divided amongst a series of committees. What was striking as the war progressed was how necessity forced Parliament effectively to take on the role of the king to act as the executive.

Van Dyck's painting of the eldest surviving sons of Charles I's sister, Elizabeth, Queen of Bohemia, to the left Charles Louis, Elector Palatine, to the right, Prince Rupert, the future royalist general at the age of eighteen. He was already then described as 'of a rare condition, full of spirit and action . . . whatsoever he wills, he wills vehemently.'

Although Charles raised the royal standard on 22 August at Nottingham the first battle was not fought until two months later. On 23 October the rival armies, both marching towards London, blundered upon each other at Edgehill in Warwickshire. It was a battle which set the pattern to be followed in others. The Royalists began by squabbling among themselves about tactics. The battle opened with Prince Rupert leading a brilliant cavalry charge, pursuing the enemy from the field, unaware that the rest of the Royalist army he had left behind was hard pressed, Lord Lindsey falling mortally wounded and the king himself in danger. In spite of this Parliamentary forces failed to carry the field, and the result was a draw. But the king then threw away his chances. Advancing on London the Royalists again confronted the Parliamentary army at Turnham Green but chose not to fight. Instead the king opted for a stately progress towards Oxford where he set up his court for the duration of the war.

Edgehill had left the Parliamentary side demoralised and weakened. The winter months, during which there was no fighting, again took on a set pattern, being dedicated to abortive peace negotiations. Parliament on its side demanded its privileges, the king his prerogatives. The result was always stalemate, for Charles would never give way on their demands for the abolition of the episcopacy and his control of the army or cede his right to choose his own ministers and veto legislation. The full consequences of this inability to compromise were to come even more sharply into focus when the war was over.

Parliament looked north to Scotland and to the army of the Covenanters for a solution. In return, the Covenanters demanded not only that Parliament pay its army but that the Church of England be transformed into an English equivalent of the Scottish kirk with ministers, elected elders and assemblies to govern it, quite free from any control by the secular authority. With this a divide began to set in between those in the House who wished to go along this path and those who decidedly did not. For the moment that impending division was neatly side-stepped by referring the problem to a body called the Westminster Assembly which Parliament had set up in 1642 to bring forward proposals for church reform. Parliament then swore a Solemn League and Covenant with the Scots.

Pamphlet describing the king's declaration of war at Nottingham where his standard was raised on 22 August 1642.

During the winter of 1642–43, the country began to divide geographically as counties fell under the control of whichever party happened to be the strongest. Parliament consolidated its control over East Anglia and the south-east, the Royalists the north and south-west. In the campaign of 1643 Prince Rupert took Bristol, giving the Royalists a major port. Another indecisive battle was fought at Newbury. Real change only came in the following year when twenty-thousand Covenanters crossed the border to attack the Royalist army in the north. On 2 July the most important battle of the Civil War was fought at Marston Moor in Yorkshire. Two Royalist armies faced three Parliamentary ones. Once again the Royalist cavalry, seemingly victorious, galloped off the field in pursuit of loot while the remainder of its army was left to face defeat. That victory was made possible by the action of the troops from the Eastern Association headed by a Huntingdonshire gentleman called Oliver Cromwell, who led the cavalry. Unlike the Royalist cavalry they did not leave the field but reformed and charged again. 'God made them as stubble to our swords' was how Cromwell vividly described the cutting down of the Royalist soldiers. A fortnight later York surrendered, the governor securing the best terms he could. 'Thus disconsolate we march,' he wrote, 'forc'd to leave our country. . . not daring to see mine own house, nor take a farewell of my children. . .' The king had lost the north.

The 1644 campaign was nothing like so dramatic with a Royalist victory in the south-west at Lostwithiel when Essex was defeated and a second encounter at Newbury which was again indecisive. But the Royalist cause was already faltering, and its fate was to be sealed in the spring of the following year when Parliament created the New Model Army, lampooned by the Royalists as the 'New Noddle'. Until then Parliamentary troops had been regionally based with strong local loyalties. Now a new national army was to be established, with Sir Thomas Fairfax as its commander and Oliver Cromwell as its Lieutenant General of Horse. On 14 June this formidable force defeated the Royalists in the second decisive battle of the war, Naseby in Northamptonshire. Numerically the Royalists were outnumbered by two to one and the king almost fell into the hands of the enemy. Catastrophic from his point of view was the capture of his correspondence revealing his negotiations with the Catholics and the Irish, both actions which made him the epitome of perfidy in the eyes of Parliament. A Roundhead wrote of the battle: 'I saw the field so strewed with carcasses of horses and men, the bodies lay slain four miles in length, but most thick on the hill where the king stood.' A month later what was left of the Royalist army was annihilated by the New Model Army at Langport in Somerset. Cromwell saw the victory as divine judgement: 'To see this, is it not the face of God?'

Bristol surrendered in September and in Scotland a Royalist rising led by the Earl of Montrose was defeated. The war was over. The king, realising that he was finished in military terms, had to surrender, but to whom? In London Parliament was in a state of outrage at his dealings with the Catholics, which only confirmed all their fears that Antichrist was in their midst. In April 1646 the king, with two men, slipped out of Oxford in the disguise of a servant. After wandering for a week he turned northwards, choosing rather to surrender to the lesser of the two evils by putting himself in the hands of the Scots.

Now a whole new phase was about to begin, for the war, far from deciding anything, had only made matters worse. Everyone had seen the established order of things turned upside down. The squire had been reduced to the level of a common fugitive driven from his estates, the parson had been ousted from his living, houses had been requisitioned for billeting troops, merchandise had been confiscated. Everywhere people looked they had seen rank and degree challenged and property rights

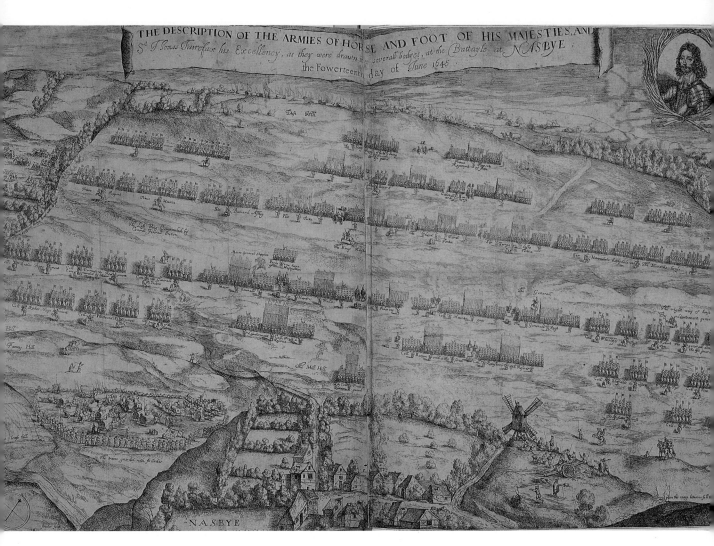

A panoramic view of the battle of Naseby, 14 June 1645. The two armies face each other with the king alone on horseback in the centre. To the far right of the Parliamentary army is 'The right wing of horse commanded by lieutenant general Cromwell'. The engraving conceals the fact that the Parliamentary army outnumbered the Royalist by two to one.

disregarded. Men had been uprooted from the fields and turned into soldiers in a national army marching to defeat those whom they saw and were told were the forces of Antichrist. They believed their victory would signal the dawn of the age of the saints in preparation for Christ's Second Coming. Censorship had gone and voices never heard before gave utterance, foretelling a society in which not only would there be no place for the king but no room for privately owned property or for doffing one's hat to any man.

Chapter Thirty-Eight

THE WORLD
UPSIDE DOWN

THE breakdown of government had meant the collapse of censorship. Up until the civil war everything printed had to be passed by the censor, thus ensuring that nothing attacking either the monarchy or the church ever appeared. If it did, it was either printed abroad or came from secret presses. In Elizabeth's reign the Puritans had just such a press, which produced a series of scurrilous attacks on the established church. But these were as nothing compared to the flood from the presses during the 1640s and 1650s. Literally thousands of news-sheets and leaflets poured out, giving voice to the views of sections of society never heard from before, artisans, craftsmen, and ordinary working folk, the normally silent half of the population. These were the views of people who could read and were therefore able to study the scriptures, finding in them a very different world from the one they lived in. The views of the illiterate classes also got into print for the first time. Both groups were in a state of high religious fervour, often ecstasy, believing that the Holy Spirit spoke to them direct. Such visions threw up demands for other forms of society, ones in which neither a king nor an aristocracy or an organised church had any place at all.

When the war ended in 1646 those who had fought for Parliament now formed two broad groups. There were those who still wanted to retain a national church, albeit reformed along Presbyterian lines, and there were those who had abandoned that idea. The latter were known as Independents, men who believed that membership of the state should be separated from membership of the church, and that religion should be free to take any number of forms provided it was neither Catholic nor Episcopalian. Parliament fast dismantled the Church of England as it had existed in 1642. Archbishop Laud was sent to the scaffold in 1645, signalling a long list of ordinances destroying the Anglican Church. The bishops were abolished and forced into exile, loyal clergy were driven from their livings. Cathedrals and churches were subjected to a wave of violent iconoclasm in which much of what was left in the way of stained glass and decoration was wiped out, and any of Laud's

The war unleashed a renewed wave of iconoclasm smashing everything which had not been torn down in the reign of Edward VI and even more demolishing any of Archbishop Laud's innovations. Here the chancel of a church which has been reordered, with communion rails, the communion table sited where the altar used to stand with a cross on it is dismantled.

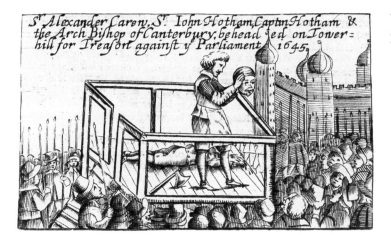

The execution of William Laud, Archbishop of Canterbury, on Tower Hill on 10 January 1645.

The sacking and burning of the contents of the queen's Catholic chapel at Somerset House, 23 May 1643.

Popular prints capture some of the dramatic events which marked the English Revolution.

innovations, such as rails dividing off the sanctuary, were smashed to pieces. In 1647 Parliament made the use of the Prayer Book and the celebration of Christmas, Good Friday, Easter and Whitsun a criminal offence.

It is one thing to sweep an institution aside, it is quite another to reach agreement as to what should replace it. Parliament was divided on this. Religious groups were many and various. The members of one, the Independents (later called Congregationalists) formed their own congregations, no longer based on the old parish system but one in which groups spontaneously came together to worship God in the way they saw fit. They believed in predestination, and indeed that those whom God had destined to be saved could be identified now. These chosen people, called the Elect, were alone deemed worthy of receiving communion, the rest of the congregation having to sit and look on. The Elect were regarded as saints and their advent, according to the Bible, was a signal that Christ's Second Coming, when he would reign jointly with them, was imminent.

One group which took such beliefs to their logical conclusion believed that political power now belonged not as of old to king, nobility and gentry, but to the saints. They were called Fifth Monarchists, and saw themselves as living during the last days when the final battle was being fought between the forces of Christ and Antichrist. In such a scheme of things rank and property, the basis of existing society, counted for nothing. The Fifth Monarchists therefore objected to the existing legal system which punished people heavily for offences against property, such as stealing, and demanded instead heavy sentences against any infringement of the moral code.

Another, and more important group, the Levellers, was a movement which attracted yeomen, small businessmen, craftsmen and, most vital of all, it later attracted followers from the rank and file of the New Model Army. They, too, questioned a society based on property-owning, wishing to 'level down' extremes of wealth, and demanding that the right to vote be no longer confined to those who had the right property qualification but extended to include everyone except servants and beggars. They saw themselves as victims of the Norman Conquest when William I had reduced the native English to servitude, in thrall to a foreign nobility. The Levellers also objected to a legal system obsessed with offences against property. They shrewdly realised that it was the law which kept in place the existing structure of society and campaigned for its change and also for the abolition of the House of Lords, the payment of tithes to the clergy, and the hated excise tax. They were asking in fact for many of the things which the middle classes were to get in the nineteenth and twentieth centuries.

Neither of these groups was to survive the 1650s but two others were to go on and make up the vigorous tradition of dissent and non-conformity allied to social radicalism which carried into the twentieth century. The Baptists saw the church not as an organisation but as a coming together of those who had undergone baptism as a conscious act of commit-ment. In this way they formed communities scattered through the country. The Quakers also looked to the spirit but in their case, as against that of the Baptists, much more of the social as well as the religious radicalism was to survive, accounting for the appalling persecution which they underwent. They were to deny all civil auth-ority or hierarchy, something expressed by their refusal to take their hats off to anyone.

These were not the only groups. There were in addition Ranters, Diggers, Seekers and Muggletonians, each of which had its own solution for the woes of England. During the years following the end of the war there was an unprecedented overturning, questioning and revaluing of everything which had previously been taken for granted. Old values, old beliefs, and old institutions were called into question as never before. All of this ferment was to run its course until those caught up in it became disillusioned, for Christ did not come with his saints to reign but instead England dissolved into anarchy, dissension and disorder. At the same time there still remained a strong body of opinion which yearned for the return of an established social order.

Broadsheet denouncing the independents, characterised here by various religious groups, Catholics, Anabaptists, Brownists and members of the Family of Love.

As if all of this was not enough, the man who held the key to the resolution of the country's problems, the king, remained also with a vision of faith and society from which nothing would budge him. He believed that the Royalists had lost the war as God's punishment of him for breaking his word to Strafford. Both monarchy and church became even more sacrosanct in his eyes, to the extent that he felt absolved and free to embark on any path, however devious, that might lead to their reinstatement.

With such immovable views it is hardly surprising that Parliament got nowhere in trying to formulate some form of peace. The country was in crisis. The army had to be paid. There was widespread depression, price rises and food shortages, as well as the ravages of plague. Heavy rains ruined the harvest and people began to refuse to pay taxes. The equivalent of eighteen pre-war subsidies was now exacted annually. All of this conspired to produce a profound longing for peace. The period of Charles I's Personal Rule must indeed have seemed now in retrospect not tyranny but Arcadia.

If the rocklike stance of the king was of little help, neither was the split which now opened wide within the ranks of Parliament. There were those who would make peace with the king on the basis of a Presbyterian Church of England and there were those, the Independents, who refused to trust him and demanded that the army be kept in being and that there be liberty of conscience. The resolution of this impasse was to come from a quite new political force which came to fill the vacuum, the New Model Army led by Oliver Cromwell.

That army was quite unlike any other army before or since. In number it was some 22,000: 6,600 cavalry, 1,000 mounted infantry and 14,400 ordinary infantry. It was a massive force to have in existence in peace time, moreover it was not made up of the usual motley crew of mercenaries, soldiers of fortune and conscripts, but the godly. Its generals were devout Puritans. The army lived in an atmosphere of religious fervour and active piety, fired by sermons, given over to regular prayer, fasting and Bible study and ruled by a strict moral code. It cast itself as the instrument of divine providence, sent by God to destroy Antichrist. Its leader, Oliver Cromwell, saw himself as much the agent of the divine will as did the king. Cromwell viewed each event as it unfolded as evidence of God's intent. As he pondered, he began to conclude that there were those in Parliament who were frustrating what he believed was the will of God.

Parliament and the army fell out. Parliament began to make moves to disband the army which, in its turn, seized what they regarded as the key to a settlement, the person of the king. In June 1647 the New Model Army drew up a solemn Engagement stating that it would not disband until such time as justice had been done. Soon after followed another document, the Representation, demanding the removal from Parliament of those regarded as corrupt, calling for parliaments lasting only for fixed periods of time and for liberty of conscience.

If the year 1647 had been one of progressive chaos, the following year was worse. The king, equally firm in his beliefs, had not hesitated to reach a secret agreement with the Scots. In return for introducing Presbyterianism in England they agreed to invade from the north. That invasion was to be one part of a pattern of widespread unrest that swept the country, uprisings by Royalists frustrated by the failure of what passed as government in London to reach a settlement. These were soon put down by the army which also wiped out the Scots at the Battle of Preston. Cromwell, always vigilant for signs from heaven, saw the victory as an act of God.

Political power now resided in a victorious army which already had its own programme for action. In the spring a three-day fast had been observed and it was agreed that after the army had finally vanquished its foes it would 'call for Charles Stuart, that man of blood, to account for that blood he had shed and mischief he had done.' This dramatic decision meant that they had rejected the belief that the king was God's viceroy on earth. They believed instead that the king held his power not from God but from the people as a sacred trust, a contract which Charles I had violated. For Oliver Cromwell and the army the king was a tyrant of the type they read about in the Old Testament, one on whom God cried out for vengeance. To Cromwell, Charles was a 'man against whom the Lord hath witnessed.'

Oliver Cromwell and officers from the army expelling from Parliament any member opposed to their policies in November 1648. The ninety-six who remained were known as The Rump.

To achieve any act of justice, the army needed to remove those whom they classified as corrupt members of Parliament. These included any who would deal with

Be gone you rogues
You haue Sate long enough

the king, who would disband the army, or who were against liberty of conscience. In November troops from the army surrounded the House and excluded every member opposed to its policies. Only ninety-six members of Parliament were left, and they became known as the Rump. On 29 December, they passed an ordinance for the trial of the king. As the law courts only existed to carry out justice in the king's name, such an act in itself turned the status quo upside down. Now the Commons, or what was left of them, had usurped the role of the monarch. A revolution as to where power lay in society was taking place.

On 6 January 1649 the court met to try the king. Charles naturally refused to recognise that it had any legal status. By now he was a tired, grey-haired, prematurely aged man, but he rose fully to play the role now offered him, for it was his turn to present himself as the champion of the liberty and freedom of the people of England. The outcome of the trial was a foregone conclusion, and on 27 January he was sentenced to death. Only fifty-nine signatories, however, could be found to sign the warrant for his execution.

Three days later the citizens of London were witnesses to an unheard-of spectacle, the execution of a king. For those who believed in the monarchy the act was one of blasphemy, the slaying of the Lord's anointed. For the army and its followers it was one of divine judgment against a tyrant. The scaffold was erected before Inigo Jones's Whitehall Banqueting House, the setting of the stately masques in which Charles had appeared to his court as a deity. Those now seemed but rehearsals for this ultimate apotheosis, his own execution. Fearing public unrest, the scaffold was hemmed in by soldiers. Attended by the Bishop of London, the king stepped out and said 'I go from a corruptible to an incorruptible crown, where no disturbance can be.' To the end he never doubted the righteousness of his cause. In this, the final scene of what was the masque of his own death, he had already cast himself as a martyr ascending to heaven. The terrible groan which went up from the watching crowd as his head fell at one stroke from his body signalled not the end of the monarchy but the inevitability of its return.

The execution of Charles I on 30 January 1649 before the Whitehall Banqueting House. King and executioner face each other across the picture. Below on one side Charles walks to his execution while on the other in its aftermath onlookers dip their handkerchiefs in his blood as relics of the royal martyr.

Chapter Thirty-Nine

A FAILED REPUBLIC

THE church had gone. The king had gone. To those in the vanguard of sweeping away these institutions such acts prefaced the new age of the spirit. The prophecies read about in Daniel and in the Book of Revelation were being fulfilled here and now, and Christ's kingdom on earth was imminent. His way, however, needed to be prepared with acts of government which would create a godly society, one which was upright, moral and devout. The extreme Protestant sects which proliferated during these years lived in an aura of perpetual expectancy of the Second Coming, or millenarianism, as it was called. All over the country ordinary people were caught up in waves of religious hysteria producing a society which was the reverse of that which the rule of Elizabeth I had striven to achieve half-a-century before, one which ensured stability and order in both church and state and in which each man knew his place.

As a consequence this was a decade not of hope but of fear. The lynch-pins of the old social structure in which king, nobility and gentry had shared power and office had gone. For the first time since the Peasants' Revolt the submerged remainder of the population raised its head, threatening both property and status. Much of the old infrastructure of ordinary daily life as it had been known to everyone had already been, or was about to be, swept away. Simple rustic pleasures such as May Day and the revelry of the Twelve Days of Christmas were forbidden.

All over the country society was dislocated leading to riots and disturbances. The general sense of despair was not helped either by the worst commercial slump of the century or harvests wrecked by torrential rain. Depressed, disillusioned, and often dispossessed, more people emigrated to the newly-founded colonies of New England than at any other period till the nineteenth century.

But for those at the centre of things it was a time for rejoicing as they hailed the dawn of a new age. Parliament was now free to set up whatever form of government it thought conducive to the rule of the saints. Those members still left, the Rump, had travelled a long way since they first met in 1641. What they still retained, however, was their allegiance to their class, the gentry, viewing with deep misgivings the widespread demands for social reform from the sects, fearing also an election because of its uncertain consequences. Their attitudes are caught early on in the suppression of the Levellers, and later the re-introduction of press censorship to stem the flood of what they regarded as subversive ideas. If they had a model towards which they looked it was Venice, a stable republic for centuries but of a very particular kind, one which made sure that the right to vote and hold office was confined only to a closed circle of rich mercantile families.

In February 1649 the monarchy and the House of Lords were abolished. On 13 February a Council of State was set up, elected from the Commons, to govern the country. In May, England was declared to be 'a commonwealth and free state' under God. A new constitution was now in place. What was lacking was a government which had a clear policy as to the direction in which things should go.

For the time being Cromwell's New Model Army, having seemingly achieved its political objective, was quiescent. In July it crossed the sea to deal with the Catholic Irish. To the army this was living the apocalypse. They were the forces of Christ sent to smite those of Antichrist. Pity or compassion of any kind had no place and the inhabitants of Drogheda and Wexford were mercilessly put to the sword. The devastation did not stop there, for the army went on, under Henry Ireton, to destroy every building and burn the crops in the fields, starving the country into submission. Almost half the population perished, and Cromwell left behind him a living legend of horror.

In the spring of the following year Parliament began to set about passing acts to create the society of the saints. The death penalty was introduced for fornication, adultery, swearing and blasphemy. The courts, however, never implemented it. Parliament then demanded that all adult males swear an oath of loyalty to the new regime, the Engagement. This was a gigantic blunder, for all over England people refused and lost office forming thereby a substantial group opposed to the new government.

The king in one sense never died and his heir, Charles II, now became the focus for those still loyal to the Royalist cause or who saw him as a means to bring down the new republic. Amongst these were the Scottish Covenanters who wished to impose their strict form of Presbyterianism on England. Charles II, like his father before him, loathed them, but the end justified the means. Cromwell and his army had no sooner returned from Ireland than they set off to defeat the Scots, which they did at the Battle of Dunbar in which three thousand Covenanters were slain and ten thousand infantry taken prisoner. The leader of the Scots, Alexander Leslie, was resourceful and retreated to defensive positions in the highlands. Charles II went on to be crowned king of Scotland and, in the following year, crossed the border with a Scottish army. He found little support along the way from a war-weary people faced with yet another Scottish army traipsing southwards. Devoid of the hoped-for Royalist uprisings Charles abandoned his march against London and headed westwards, towards the old Royalist heartlands. Cromwell, too, marched swiftly south and, on the anniversary of the Battle of Dunbar, routed the Royalist army at Worcester. The king narrowly escaped capture and eventually made his way into exile.

Given the composition of the Rump government and the expectations of it in the world outside it was doomed to failure. The Rump was made up of property-owning country gentry and lawyers, hardly likely to embrace with enthusiasm radical reforms which would threaten and change their own status so dramatically. Any extension of the franchise would erode their privilege. Equally, although a commission on legal reform produced many recommendations, they were not implemented. In the case of religion there was again inertia. Plans were made to re-draw the parish boundaries to ensure that everyone was within reach of a church every three miles, but again the proposals crossed too many vested interests. The Rump's only achievement was a commission set up to spread the light of the gospel in what was seen as Royalist and

Charles II escapes the Parliamentary army at Boscobel House on September 6 1651. The picture was commissioned by the king himself after his Restoration to commemorate his flight after the battle of Worcester and two of his hiding places, Whiteladies, left, and Boscobel, right, some miles apart, have been brought together in the painting. The army in pursuit is seen to the left. In the right foreground is an oak with two figures concealed within its branches. These are the king and a Colonel Carlos.

After the Restoration there was a card game based on the history of the Rump Parliament. Oliver Cromwell makes a pact with the Devil and the rest follows.

Catholic Wales and the north. But even this foundered within a few years, although the success of the Welsh venture can be measured by the long dissenting tradition. Indeed the only major reform carried through was due to pressure from the army in the aftermath of Dunbar, when an act established liberty of conscience and abolished compulsory church attendance each Sunday.

There was another reason for lack of policy, lack of money. In spite of the weight of taxation the government's financial plight was disastrous. All its funds were eaten up paying for the civil wars and the army. Everything that could be sold was sold: the cathedrals, the royal palaces, the king's fabulous art collection, what little remained of the crown lands, along with lands which had belonged to deans and chapters, to bishops and dispossessed Royalists. So bad was the financial situation that the excise tax was being anticipated four years in advance.

All of this was exacerbated by a foreign war with the Dutch. Next to agriculture anything to do with the sea or shipping was England's greatest industry. With their vast fleet, the Dutch were taking over the carrying trade both in the Baltic and in the American colonies. An act was passed laying down that henceforth all imports had to be either in English ships or in those of the country of origin. War broke out in 1652

zealous Puritan formed what was to prove to be an uneasy alliance with the landed gentleman. As time progressed the strain of having to reconcile the two began to show. Puritanism in the form he embraced, that of the Independents, took him in the direction of a political radicalism which called for everything from an extension of the franchise to a reform of the law. Birth and background as a member of the gentry classes dictated a defence of the status quo, an inbred conservatism and caution in the face of change and, most of all, a deeply held belief that property was the basis of society.

That duality was never quite resolved in Cromwell but it was to edge nearer towards the role of the gentleman as against that of the Puritan after a major series of debates had been held at Putney in the autumn of 1647 between the conservative elements in the army, the 'grandees' as they were called, and those who espoused the creed of the Levellers. In these debates Cromwell came down on the side of the 'grandees' who stood against any form of democracy other than one based on a property qualification to vote. Indeed, under the short-lived republic, Cromwell was to take part in hunting down the remaining army Levellers, shooting them at Burford in Oxfordshire in 1649.

The Instrument of Government drawn up by the army whereby Oliver Cromwell became Lord Protector was England's first written constitution. It laid down that there was to be no taxation or legislation without the consent of Parliament, that there was to be joint control of the militia and, in certain things, Cromwell could only act in concert with a Council of State. Whatever gloss could be put on this there could be no denying that it represented the first step back towards a monarchy, and the Protector accordingly created what amounted to a court. In an effort to win loyalty in the country, the Engagement, whereby men had been forced to recognise the abolition of the king and the House of Lords, was done away with. It was a gesture which had only a limited effect, for nothing was to conceal the perpetual unease which existed between the Protector and all of his Parliaments. In one sense the members had turned to him because he shared their loyalty to the landed interest, in another he embodied the institution they hated most, the army. Cromwell's greatest drawback was his power base, for it impeded any attempt to build up civilian support for his regime.

If he parted company with Parliament over the army, he did so equally in matters of religion, for to him toleration was a fundamental tenet. 'I had rather,' he said, 'that Mahometanism were permitted amongst us than that one of God's children should be persecuted.' The trouble was the proliferation of all kinds of sects brought not only varieties of religious experience and worship but also, in cases like the Quakers,

THE
Declaration and Standard

Of the *Levellers* of *England* ;
Delivered in a Speech to his Excellency the Lord Gen. *Fairfax*,
on *Friday* last at White-Hall, by Mr. *Everard*, a late Member of the
Army, and his Prophesie in reference thereunto ; shewing what will
befall the Nobility and Gentry of this Nation, by their submitting to
community ; With their invitation and promise unto the people, and
their proceedings in *Windsor* Park, *Oatlands* Park, and severall other
places ; also, the Examination and confession of the said Mr. *Everard*
before his Excelleney, the manner of his deportment with his Hat on,
and his severall speeches and expressions, when he was commanded
to put it off. Together with a List of the severall Regiments of Horse
and Foot that have cast Lots to go for *Ireland*.

Imprinted at *London*, for *G. Laurinson*, *aprill* 23. 1649.

In the aftermath of the execution of the king extreme sects looked for the fruition of their beliefs. One such group, the Diggers, an offshoot of the Levellers, occupied land near Walton-on-Thames and began a colony in which all goods would be held in common. One of their traits, recorded here, was their refusal to doff their hats to their superiors.

attitudes which challenged the existing social order. Although Cromwell never attempted to take the path of the Barebones Parliament and attack tithes and lay patronage of livings, his tolerance of each and every sect, however bizarre, left members of Parliament aghast. Officially the Presbyterian *Book of Discipline* replaced the *Book of Common Prayer* but the form worship took in each parish church was in fact determined by the minister and the congregation, and no longer by the government. To this had to be added a whole variety of sects which cut across all parish boundaries attracting whom they would, and forming their own networks. In the face of the mounting chaos the clergy drew together in an attempt to halt the slide into anarchy. No wonder that by the middle of the 1650s doubt and disillusion were setting in. In 1656 members of the Worcestershire Association reported:

'We find by sad experience, that the people understand not our public teaching, though we study to speak as plain as we can, and that after many years of preaching . . . too many can scarce tell anything that have been said.'

The Puritan movement was fast running out of steam.

But to the Protector the army and religious toleration were untouchables. So, when his first Parliament in the autumn of 1654 began to attack both, he dissolved it. Thereafter the rift was permanent. The Instrument of Government had, in fact, only provided for the rule of the Protector until such time as Parliament endorsed it, which it had refused to do. Throughout 1655 the Protector ruled without any authority and this began to be questioned in the courts. Royalist uprisings that year then led Cromwell to make his most disastrous mistake, the division of the country into eleven regions each ruled by a major-general. Local unrest was not his only motive, for the conjunction of sixes, an apocalyptic number, in 1656 and the imminence of 1666, another year whose figures signalled the fulfilment of yet more prophecies in the Book of Revelation, called for haste in preparing the country for the rule of the godly. Under the aegis of the major-generals there was a massive onslaught against immorality: Sunday sports were forbidden, alehouses shut, cock fighting and horse racing banned. In one part of Lancashire alone, Blackburn Hundred, two hundred alehouses were closed.

But it was not only these kill-joy policies which upset people. Perhaps even more important was the resentment of direct rule from Westminster, army rule at that, by outsiders often regarded as being of a lower class. Local interest was outraged. The decision to tax Royalists was also unfortunate, for it opened up old wounds which a wiser government would have sought to heal. It is hardly surprising therefore that the Parliament which met in September 1656 reflected how much the major-generals were loathed, along with the army and the burden of taxation. Cromwell was forced to give in, first on an issue of religious toleration, allowing the savage punishment of one, John Nayler, who had proclaimed himself the new Messiah and re-enacted Christ's entry into Jerusalem in Bristol. The major-generals were removed, but the tax on Royalists remained. Parliament then turned its attention to the constitution, throwing out the Instrument of Government and putting together its own, embodied in a document called the Humble Petition and Advice. This took the drift back to 1640 even further. In its initial form Cromwell was offered the crown, which he refused, but a second upper chamber was created nominated by the Lord Protector and consisting of aristocrats and army officers. Although he had declined to be made king it was implict that the Protectorship would be hereditary. In January 1658 this new Parliament assembled. Once again it fell out with the Protector and once again he dissolved it.

While the constitution was going through these successive changes, none of which worked, government somehow had to go on. The problems of Scotland and Ireland had to be dealt with, as well as England's place in the wider perspective of European politics. Through the constitutional changes both Scotland and Ireland lost their Parliaments, being given instead thirty seats each at Westminster. It was not popular. Nor was Cromwell's encouragement of Independency in Scotland as against the kirk, which provoked rebellion. In Ireland, his early brutal legacy was firmly built upon. Forty thousand Catholic landowners were forced to emigrate to the rocky west. Henceforward anyone who was Catholic was automatically denied the right to train or practise any urban trade or profession, or to hold office. Irish Catholics were deliberately reduced to the level of an underclass.

In the case of Europe, Cromwell's mind was filled with nostalgia for the age of the Armada, visualising a Protestant alliance which would defeat the Catholic Habsburgs and hammer at the gates of the papal Antichrist in Rome itself. Alas, the reality turned out to be far different. In April 1654, peace was made with the Dutch. Under Robert Blake, the English fleet secured the dominion of the narrow seas and, as a consequence, the rulers of Europe came to respect the Protector. He renewed the old Elizabethan policy of war against Spain with a catastrophic expedition against the Spanish Caribbean Empire, redeemed only by the capture of Jamaica. But it was an expensive policy and the protectorate lurched from one financial crisis to the next.

The sands of time had already run out. On 3 September 1658, the anniversary of his two greatest victories,

A miniature of Oliver Cromwell by Samuel Cooper. This was painted from life in the 1650s and was a pattern kept by the artist in his studio from which to make further copies. Cromwell insisted that in his portraits he be recorded 'warts and all'.

The Dutch waged a satirical war on Cromwell, here shown with horns springing out of his head.

OLIVIER CROMWEL
Protecckteur

Dunbar and Worcester, Cromwell died. Nothing could obscure the fact that his rule had been a failure. It had little support across the country and there was bitter hatred for the army and for the huge burden of taxation. Nonetheless it was to take another year before opinion finally swung decisively in favour of the return of the Stuarts.

The succession ostensibly went smoothly with Cromwell's son, Richard, becoming Lord Protector. He lacked, however, both his father's energy and his feeling for power. Worse, he did not have any hold on the army. The result was a series of almost nonsensical events. In January 1659 Parliament met and gradually moved to strip the army of its powers. The army, seeing this about to happen, forced Richard Cromwell to dissolve Parliament. Following that the army decided to reconvene the Rump which they themselves had ironically ejected in 1653. When that met, it too proved no more satisfactory to the military. Infuriated by their sterile debates, the army threw out the Rump for a second time in October and set up its own interim government.

What the army in London had not foreseen was that its brethren in Scotland, Ireland and Yorkshire would stand by the Rump. As a result the army was forced to disband its interim government and on 24 December the Rump reassembled yet again. Meanwhile General George Monck, who headed the army in Scotland, marched south. After three weeks he realised that a total impasse had been reached. The Rump was unpopular and the army was split. Amidst the mounting chaos, he concluded that the only alternative left was to put the clock back the whole way. On 21 February 1660 the members of Parliament purged by the army in 1648 were allowed to take their seats once more. They had been excluded for their moderate Royalist sympathies, and their return, or rather that of those still alive, meant that the republicans would certainly be outvoted. On 16 March the Long Parliament, which had first met in 1641 thereby earning its title, declared itself dissolved. Almost two decades of political and constitutional turmoil had come to an end.

In the aftermath, those who had lived through it must have asked themselves what, if anything, had been gained? One of the main causes of the war had been taxation by way of the royal prerogative, reflecting the central problem as to how government was to be paid for. Nothing in respect of this had changed at all. Taxation had been crippling, far in excess of anything experienced during the Personal Rule of Charles I. Both the republic and the protectorate, however, had continued to live in precisely the same way as the first two Stuarts, struggling from hand to mouth, and with a mountain of unpaid debt.

And what of religion? Where once there had been at least the semblance of uniformity, now there was fragmentation. During those heady years men and women

The Ranters Declaration,
WITH

Their new Oath and Proteſtation ; their ſtrange Votes, and a new way to get money ; their Proclamation and Summons ; their new way of Ranting, never before heard of ; their dancing of the *Hey* naked, at the white *Lyon* in Peticoat-lane ; their mad Dream, and Dr. *Pockridge* his Speech, with their Trial, Examination, and Anſwers : the coming in of 3000. their Prayer and Recantation, *to be in all Cities and Market-towns read and publiſhed* ; the mad-Ranters further Reſolution ; their Chriſtmas Carol, and blaſpheming Song ; their two pretended-abominable Keyes to enter Heaven , and the worſhiping of his little-majeſty, the late Biſhop of *Canterbury* : A new and further Diſcovery of their black Art, with the Names of thoſe that are poſſeſſt by the Devil, having ſtrange and hideous cries heard within them, *to the great admiration of all thoſe that ſhall read and peruſe this enſuing ſubject.*

Licenſed according to order, and publiſhed by M. *Stubs*, a late fellow-Ranter

Imprinted at London , by J. C. MDCL. *1650*

The Ranter's Declaration, 1650, a leaflet attacking this sect which was spreading widely. Here they are shown mocking the celebration of Christmas.

had really believed they were living through the cataclysmic confrontations described in the Book of Revelation, ones peopled by fantastic monsters and abounding in signs and portents in the heavens, but by 1660 all this had gone, for nothing predicted had actually come to pass. Neither Christ nor his saints had come to claim their kingdom. People were exhausted by years of religious controversy, and the mood of the country was swinging sharply towards a more ordered, quieter, faith and piety.

In 1642 the country gentry and lawyers who sat in the Commons had seen the monarchy as a threat to their property through the agents of prerogative rule. Those infringements by the crown must have appeared by 1660 innocuous compared to the ragings of the many-headed monster from below, sects who questioned property, rank and status. The post-Reformation state had been an alliance between the crown and the property-owning classes in the sharing of political power. The monarchy was now seen as the only guarantee that this could continue, and the threat from below be held in check. The state was now set for a strong reaction against everything which had taken place during the previous twenty years. The governing classes were to be reconciled to the crown as the one way of ensuring their sway over the country. This point of view was to prevail until the Victorian age, when reformers were to rediscover the rich legacy of ideas from the age of Cromwell, reactivating them to justify the claims of the new middle classes to a share at last in that political power.

Chapter Forty-One

THE SEARCH FOR STABILITY

O N 29 May 1660 a spectacular procession approached the City of London. It opened with a dozen gilded coaches which jolted their way forwards, escorted by horsemen wearing silver doublets. Then came a thousand soldiers followed by the City sheriffs in gold lace, and trumpeters in black velvet and cloth of gold. On it pressed, a seemingly never-ending cavalcade, numbering in all some twenty thousand and culminating in the solitary figure of a man whose thirtieth birthday it was, Charles II. Slim in build, with dark hair and saturnine features, Charles was soberly dressed, apart from the crimson plume waving in his hat which he raised 'to all in the most stately manner ever seen'. It took seven hours for the procession to pass through the London streets and reach Whitehall Palace. The diarist, John Evelyn, who stood in the Strand to see it pass, wrote: ' . . . it was the Lord's doing, and such a restoration never mentioned in any history, ancient or modern, since the return of the Jews from the Babylonish captivity.'

But not everyone who looked on shared his state of euphoria. 'A pox on all kings,' yelled one woman as the king rode by.

And that dissenting voice caught a reality which was also reflected in the king's remark to the crowds of fawning lords who awaited him at Whitehall: 'I doubt it has been my own fault I have been absent so long, for I see nobody that does not protest he has ever wished for my return.' The truth of the matter was that Charles II's return was a last-ditch attempt to re-establish an equilibrium, this time going backwards to 1642, and trying to wipe out the previous eighteen years, which had been so tumultuous in terms of events and ideas. It was not to be long before people realised the impossibility of such a task. Republicanism, and religious radicalism in particular, could not be blotted out. They either went underground or had to be tolerated, either outside or within the system. Nonetheless the deep-seated desire by the gentry classes for peace and social order after years of anarchy, chaos and military rule was such that a veneer of stability was achieved by what was known as the Restoration

On May 29 1660 Charles II made his entry into London, the climax of which was his reception by both Houses of Parliament in Whitehall Palace. The House of Commons received him in Inigo Jones's Banqueting House, towards which this procession rides, the very building from whose windows his father had stepped to be executed in 1649. May 29 was the king's birthday; it was to be made into an annual national festival celebrating the restoration of the Monarchy.

Settlement. But it was extremely fragile, so much so that within a decade king and Parliament were again at serious loggerheads in an encounter that had much in common with the one which had precipitated the civil war.

But in 1660 the king, the government, and the social élite joined forces to reassert their hold on political power. Once again the character of the monarch was to be an important contributory factor in ensuring its success. Charles II was an exception among the Stuarts in possessing the common touch, of the kind which had endeared the Tudor dynasty to its people. He was an affable, charming and easy-going man, a lover of women, for he was to have a notorious string of mistresses, and a devotee of the good life, anxious never again to go into exile. And, in spite of laziness, he was politically astute, if cynical, and a shrewd judge of men. Beneath the surface, however, lurked more mysterious thoughts which were only to surface as the reign progressed. How much they were there from the very beginning it is impossible to know. Some of Charles's years of exile had been spent in France, where Louis XIV ruled over the greatest state in Western Europe as an absolute monarch. His most famous remark sums up this position: 'L'etat c'est moi' or 'I am the state'. To see that his will was enforced there was a huge bureaucracy of paid royal officials and a mighty standing army. Hand-in-hand with Louis' absolutist rule, made manifest in his magnificent court at Versailles, went an unswerving devotion to the Catholic faith. Charles admired his French cousin and the system. His sister, Henrietta, was soon to be married to Louis' brother. In comparison Charles found himself ruling over a state which, apart from the Netherlands, was an exception in the Europe of his age, one whose officials were unpaid amateurs, where there was no adequate standing army, where the crown was impoverished, where there was not one faith but many, and where a representative assembly, Parliament, still existed to irk effective government.

But in order to regain the throne Charles had to accept these limitations, and forge ahead with the acts which made up the Restoration Settlement. This was to be the major work of his first two Parliaments, the Convention Parliament, which met in April 1660 and which had invited him to return, and the Cavalier Parliament of May 1661, which was to sit for most of the reign and more than half of whose members had fought or suffered for the Royalist cause. Together they forged, or rather failed to forge, the settlement.

Many of the acts that were passed were both pragmatic and prudent, those, for instance, which recognised the validity of legal decisions during the interregnum or pardoned all republicans except the actual regicides, but on the broader issues there were failures. Parliament, which for almost two decades had taken on the role of the executive, now reverted to its old advisory capacity and was made up once more of Lords and Commons. But the experience of the previous eighteen years could not so easily be forgotten, and the notion of semi-organised opposition to government was to resurface eventually in the precursors of our modern political parties. Looking back to 1642 meant a return to all those unresolved grey areas over which king and Parliament had fought. The royal prerogative returned, with its right to conduct foreign policy, control the executive, act in the interests of the security of the state, and prorogue or dissolve Parliament. Only a Triennial Act, decreeing that there must be no more than a three-year gap between Parliaments, offered any check on the sovereign ruling without it, but by the closing years of the reign Charles was able even to ignore that.

Nor was the financial settlement any better. Indeed finance had been one of the main causes of the civil war, the inability of Parliament to recognise that government had to be paid for. Although Parliament now assessed that cost, they failed to meet it. Even with the addition of the old excise tax and a new hearth tax (one paid by every householder) the amount fell drastically short of what was needed. Parliament feared making the king financially independent, in fact, for it would erode their own power. The result was mushrooming debt, eventually forcing Charles to become the secret pensioner of Louis XIV, in this way demeaning the country's status within Europe.

Both crown and Parliament were united in effecting the disbandment of the New Model Army, feared as the seedbed for radical social ideas. But it was replaced by an anachronism, a return to the locally raised militias under the control of the gentry, a hopelessly outmoded means of defending the realm. Reluctantly, as a result of a minor insurrection, Parliament agreed to a small standing army but it was minute compared with the military machine of the French.

Religion remained the most intractable problem of all. The king himself was liberal in outlook, anxious to achieve a compromise in which those of a Presbyterian persuasion (who had been instrumental in his return) might be accommodated within a revived Church of England. Once again the result was failure. The Presbyterians and the Anglicans could reach no agreement and all over the country loyalty to the old Anglican form of worship reasserted itself in a tidal wave. The Cavalier Parliament, which was full of Royalist Anglicans, passed an Act of Uniformity re-introducing the *Book of Common Prayer*. All ministers refusing to conform to its practice were to be deprived of their livings. As a consequence, over nine hundred left. They joined the ranks of the dissenters, the various sects against which Parliament passed a series of acts, known after the name of the king's chief minister, the Earl of Clarendon, as the Clarendon Code. The religious settlement bore no resemblance to 1642. For the first time an official split within Protestantism in the country was recognised. In spite of the efforts of the more tolerant bishops either to retain the Presbyterians within the Church or maintain an open door for their return, a new religious underclass was created, one which joined the Catholics, suffering persecution, harassment and social disabilities, such as exclusion from all public offices and the universities.

In this way the higher-ranking country gentry reasserted their old position as mediators between crown and people, occupying once more their accustomed roles as unpaid servants of the government in the shires, the officers who kept peace and order, administered justice, and controlled the militia. In return they received honours, offices and favours at court, besides gaining privileges for their local

The last page of Samuel Pepys's Diary, 31 May 1669. Pepys kept his diary from the closing months of 1659 using a system of shorthand, the key to which was only rediscovered in the last century, thus unlocking a unique source of both information and delight. To his contemporaries Pepys was an able and reforming naval administrator. To posterity he is known as one of the greatest of all diarists, providing a vivid and scintillating record of the England of the 1660s. He ceased to keep it in the mistaken belief that he was losing his sight.

communities. But what kind of society was it? England after 1660 likewise could not go back in time, for the country was about to embark on a major period of change which would leave it unrecognisable compared with the England of the 1630s.

That change was largely to stem from what has been called the Commercial Revolution, something which was to be of far more consequence than the Restoration itself. It led to a new prosperity which was founded largely on the Navigation Acts, setting limits on foreign shipping in English ports, which had been revived during the Commonwealth. By the close of the 1660s, England was rapidly developing the largest merchant fleet in Europe and was also emerging as the continent's *entrepôt*, that is, the centre for the re-export trade. The produce of the developing North American and West Indian colonies together with produce from the East, in particular India, was brought to England in return for home manufactures. Goods imported were then re-exported across Europe. Metals or textiles were exported to Africa in return for slaves who were taken to Barbados or Jamaica to work the plantations whose sugar then came to England. The American colonies of Virginia and Maryland produced tobacco, which was traded again via the mother country. The cloth industry too was to search out new markets in Asia Minor and in Spain and Portugal and their colonies in the New World. As the century drew to its close, no other country in Western Europe could rival England in terms of capital resources and potential investment. The wealth of its merchants and of the great trading companies, such as the East India, the Royal African and the Levant, was prodigious. By the 1680s cloth formed only about sixty per cent of the country's exports, something unthinkable in 1600.

In the countryside there was increased activity. Agricultural methods were improved to meet the needs of the developing towns for supplies of fresh meat, vegetables and fruit. There was a huge expansion in the coal industry, again to meet the demand for heating the homes of town dwellers. Protestant refugees from abroad brought new skills and techniques, which not only broad-ened the range of textiles but introduced whole new areas of manufacture: porcelain, lace, silk, fine linen, clocks and instrument making.

Even those deemed 'the poorer sort' were soon ob-

This picture, painted in 1670 and traditionally known as *The Tichborne Dole*, provides a unique panorama of rural society in the reign of Charles II. It depicts an event held annually on Lady Day, March 25, at Tichborne in Hampshire when the lord of the manor, in this case Sir Henry Tichborne, distributed bread to the poor. Before the old Tudor manor house stand assembled the family, their servants and retainers together with tenants and villagers providing in one image the whole social hierarchy of Restoration England. Sir Henry was a loyal supporter of the Stuarts.

served to have buckles on their shoes and ribbons on their hats. The standard of living of most classes rose steadily in the late seventeenth century. England was rapidly developing into a consumer society, with a huge growth in the domestic market, as more people than ever before had the comforts of life and could follow fashion. As a consequence, the social pyramid flattened. Although Charles II created forty new peers, around fifty per cent of all land belonged to the gentry classes whose number multiplied to include new forms such as the 'urban gentry'. As a class they became far more stratified, with baronets at the top, a title introduced by James I in 1611 recognising that a new title was called for, midway between a lord and a knight. After the baronets came knights, and then untitled gentlemen, some of whom could be far wealthier in terms of land than their titled superiors.

More important for the future was the emergence in a clearer form of the professions: law, medicine, the army, the church, the universities and teaching. For the first time those who passed their entire working lives in the service of government, later to be called civil servants, emerged as an identifiable group, men like the famous diarist, Samuel Pepys. In addition musicians, painters, architects and even men of letters attained a new standing. All of these professions became ways of social advancement for those from below. Their arrival was a reflection of a far more complex and highly literate society which had need of the services they could provide. And if we move down the social ladder a rung, there was an equal burgeoning of 'the middling sort', craftsmen, shop- and inn-keepers, vivid reflections of the reality of the Commercial Revolution as all shared in the new found prosperity.

All that is except, initially, the crown. As the 1660s progressed the government's position steadily worsened. England could not afford a foreign policy. The wars with the Dutch were renewed in 1665 and 1672 but with no real success. Then there were the twin disasters of the Great Plague of 1665, (the last echo of the Black Death of the fourteenth century) which killed thousands, followed, the year after, by the Great Fire of London which effectively destroyed the City. In the context of Britain's commercial endeavours the main enemy was the Dutch and their destruction was the prime objective of any foreign policy. In 1670 Charles signed the secret Treaty of Dover, the first of a series with France whereby he became a pensioner, albeit a modest one, of Louis XIV and, in the words of the treaty, sought jointly 'to humble the pride of The States General'. Few in 1670 could have foreseen that within twenty years France was to become Britain's enemy in a power struggle lasting over a century. The secret part was to be toleration for Catholics and the announcement of his own conversion. No one has been able to explain precisely the king's motives for this and even Louis XIV had reservations. Charles was in fact not to convert until his deathbed.

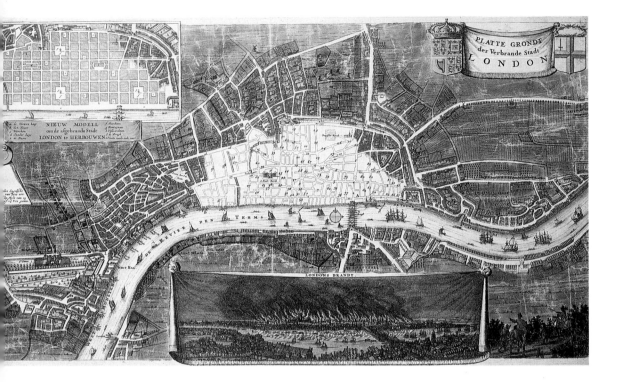

Such a foreign policy ran counter to an increasingly anti-French sentiment and a hostility to the flaunting of Catholicism at court, both by the queen, the king's mistress, and some of his ministers. Parliament viewed all of this with increasing suspicion. In 1672, as a step on the path to alleviating the position of Catholics, the king issued a Declaration of Indulgence, suspending the penal laws, including the notorious Clarendon Code against all non-Anglicans, allowing Catholics to hold

A Dutch engraving shows the extent of the City wiped out in the Great Fire of 1666. Effectively the London of Chaucer and Shakespeare went up in flames. Inset is a scene of the conflagration. Pepys wrote in his Diary: 'God grant mine eyes may never behold the like, who now saw above ten thousand houses all in one flame.'

services in private and Protestant dissenters to worship in places under licence. So strong was the reaction of the Anglican Royalists in the Cavalier Parliament that when they met in the following year they threatened to curtail the royal finances. The king was forced to withdraw the Declaration. Parliament then went on to pass the Test Act, which laid down that everyone holding any form of public office should swear loyalty to the Established Church and affirm their abhorrence of Catholicism. The effect of that was not only an exodus of Catholics from office but the revelation that the king's brother, James, Duke of York, was a convert. As Charles's wife, the Portuguese Catholic Catherine of Braganza, had failed to produce a child, James was the heir to the throne. Although Catholics formed only one per cent of the population, fear distorted that into a popular belief that what had been going on at court was part of some international plot whereby the country would be converted, if need be by force of arms, and a French style rule introduced.

And it was this atmosphere of hot-house intrigue which provided the fruitful ground upon which those who concocted what was called the Popish Plot built. Such a plot never existed outside the mind of its inventor, a devious and deceitful ex-Anglican cleric called Titus Oates. The political consequences of his fantasy were to be appalling, for they awoke in the English consciousness all of the irrational fear of Catholicism which stretched back to the burnings of Mary's reign, on through the Armada and the Gunpowder Plot, to the fears of Rome engendered by the dealings of the court of the king's father. Oates worked in tandem with another disreputable cleric, Israel Tonge, and together they fabricated the details of a plot which included firing the City of London, England being invaded by French and Irish forces (who would put to the sword anyone who refused to convert), and the murder of the king so that his Catholic brother might take over. The plotters claimed the whole scheme was financed by the pope and engineered under the auspices of the Jesuits.

Charles II, and many in the government, realised from the start that all of this was pure fantasy, and indeed it would not have led to anything but for two strokes of fate. Sir Edmund Godfrey, the magistrate to whom Oates had sworn the truth of his story, was found skewered by a sword, a death immediately attributed by the populace to the Jesuits. Next, letters were discovered by a former secretary to the Duke of York looking forward to the Catholic revival which would follow James's accession. Unfortunately, that man's name had been among those listed by Oates as being party to the plot.

No concurrence of events could have been more catastrophic for they seemed to confirm the truth of what Oates and Tonge had outlined. The Popish Plot unleashed anti-Catholic hysteria on a grand scale and led to the campaign by the Earl of Shaftesbury to exclude the Duke of York from the succession. This in turn precipitated the emergence within Parliament of recognisable parties. Already government had cultivated a group sympathetic to its interests known as a 'court' party, as against members who were opposed, a loose association of gentry making a 'country' party. But now in the face of the crisis these groups were to harden along far more definite lines and gain names, the Tories, those Anglicans who regarded the crown as sacred and inviolate, and the Whigs, who believed that sovereignty was a trust from the people which would be betrayed if a Catholic were ever allowed to succeed.

What was known as the Exclusion Crisis dominated the years 1679 to 1681. If Shaftesbury and the Whigs had won, it would have meant that Parliament could dictate the succession to the throne, in effect establish a form of elected monarchy. It implied, too, a limitation on regal power. When the Cavalier Parliament met in 1679 it began by attacking the king's chief minister, the Earl of Danby. Charles met the onslaught by dissolving Parliament and summoning a new one. That action was his greatest mistake, for the Parliament returned was elected when anti-Catholic sentiment was at fever pitch. For three years Charles weathered the assault by the only weapon in his armoury, the royal prerogative whereby he had the right to prorogue or dissolve Parliament. Every time Parliament came near to passing an Exclusion Act, this was what happened. In addition, he attempted to weaken the opposition inviting into the government as many Whigs as he could accommodate. The third and final attempt to exclude James took place in a Parliament deliberately summoned to sit in the Royalist stronghold of Oxford. Within a week the king dissolved it and Parliament was not to meet again in his lifetime.

The king had ostensibly won, but this encounter was to leave a significant legacy. The battle had given rise to organisation on a scale which constituted the creation of a political party. The Whigs had their leader, Shaftesbury, who, along with a committee, directed from the centre and organised propaganda not only in the metropolis but also in the shires. The alliance stretched across country, setting out to secure the election of members who would more or less support their political programme. To the Tories the royal prerogative was sacred, sovereignty in their view was vested in the crown, kingship came from God and not the people, whose only role was to obey or, at the most, passively resist. To the Whigs, in contrast, sovereignty was vested in the people (by which they meant some 200,000 adult males who had the right to vote), it rested in the final resort on consent embodied in a pact or agreement between governor and governed. If that pact was violated then the people had a right to resist.

For the moment this challenging ferment of ideas was to go into abeyance, because for the first time the royal finances, thanks to the commercial boom, a renewal of the French pension, and reforms at the Treasury, gave the king unprecedented independence. Many of the Whigs went abroad into exile. Indeed, Shaftesbury himself fled to Holland, and was to die there. Meanwhile, the monarchy in England embarked on precisely the path many had feared.

Chapter Forty-Two

THE UNEXPECTED
REVOLUTION

CHARLES II died on the morning of 6 February 1685 leaving fourteen illegitimate children, the progeny of a roll call of extravagant mistresses, but no heir by his wife. His last years had seen the monarchy resurgent. Although bound to summon a Parliament within each three-year period, 1684 had passed without one and no protest had been voiced. The year before a plot in which some of the more extreme of the Whigs had been involved, the Rye House Plot, had planned the assassination of both royal brothers, and generated another floodtide of devotion to the crown. There was little to suggest that the accession of James, Duke of York, as king would signal any dramatic change of direction. Indeed the Parliament which had to be summoned to vote the royal finances for the reign was Tory almost to a man.

James II, however, was a very different character from his brother. Where Charles had been dark, James was fair. Where Charles had been endowed with an endearing common touch, James was devoid of warmth and exuded a cold regal hauteur. In his portraits he looks down on, rather than out at, the spectator. As a military man and as Lord High Admiral he believed in iron discipline, and that the prime role of those below was to obey unquestioningly. In addition, he shared with his father an unswerving belief in the divinity of kings. Whilst Duke of York he had married a daughter of the Earl of Clarendon, Anne Hyde, by whom he had two daughters, Mary and Anne. Both had been brought up as Protestants but their mother, a year before her death, became Catholic, followed shortly after by her husband, the event which, when it came to light, had precipitated the Exclusion Crisis. James eventually let Louis XIV choose him a bride, an Italian Catholic princess, Mary of Modena.

James's overt commitment to the Catholic cause was to be his ruin. If he had remained Anglican, history would have taken a different direction, for a monarchy firmly in alliance with the Church of England and the Royalist Tories in the shires would probably have

The grand formality of royal portraiture in the baroque age reflects accurately the aloofness characteristic of James II.

succeeded in transforming the country along the lines of the French monarchy into an absolutist state. But such a transformation depended on support which, on account of his religious commitment, James progressively eroded. What is astonishing is that he was able to take his personal policy so far and that it was not to be until the spring of 1688 that matters came to a head. The reason for the delay was fear, fear of a repetition of the years after 1642. The monarchy had returned in 1660 as the only means to sustain social order and ensure the hold on power of the landed gentry classes. It was only when James ruthlessly proceeded to dislodge them from office in favour of Catholics and Dissenters that the spell was broken.

One thought above every other dominated the king – how to make England safe for Catholics and how, in the longer term, to convert the country back to Rome. To move things in that direction would have called for phenomenal tact and patience. Unfortunately the king was endowed with neither. What was more, anti-Catholicism had gone through one of its wildest irrational outbursts only five years earlier in the aftermath of the Popish Plot. In France, Louis XIV had expelled half-a-million Protestants in the interests of creating a wholly Catholic state. Many of them had come to England, not only bringing welcome commercial skills but also adding to the fear as to what could take place if James pursued a similar policy.

In order to achieve his objective James had to ensure that candidates of his own choosing were not only in control of central and local government but would be elected to Parliament. That process of royal infiltration had already been started by Charles II during his last years but under James it was to be all too visibly accelerated. Such a policy was a move in the direction of absolute rule and carried with it the demotion of the Church of England from its place of privilege. In addition, in order to achieve his religious ends, it meant removing from office the very people who had brought him to the throne, the Tory Anglican Royalists. It was fatally short-sighted of James.

Luck was with him at first. In 1685, an illegitimate son of Charles II, James, Duke of Monmouth, challenged his right to the throne as a candidate of the fallen Whigs. He landed in the south-west and attracted a large following amongst those who feared the king's popery. Although Monmouth took Taunton, the government doubled the size of the army and routed the rebels at Sedgemoor. They were savagely put down and Monmouth was executed. By James, this victory was read as the judgment of God.

The army was not dispersed but kept standing. It numbered twenty thousand in all. A large standing army was one of the chief mainstays of any absolute monarch and its continued existence provoked a sense of nervous unease. That might have evaporated if the king had not dispensed over sixty of its officers, who were Catholic, from submitting to the Test Acts, which prohibited Catholics from holding crown office. In one case that right was tried in the law courts. To meet such contingencies James had continued his brother's policy of removing all judges who would oppose the royal will. As a consequence the crown won the case, but it was clear to everyone that the law had been bent.

Gradually central government began to be purged of moderates and an inner Catholic ring of ministers and advisers was brought in. To the people, the erection of a spectacular Catholic chapel in Whitehall Palace to which both the king and queen went in pomp to hear mass, must have seemed quite astonishing. Until that time, the Catholic chapels of the Stuart queens had been discreet, hidden affairs. Now the Catholic faith in all its colourful baroque splendour was seen at the heart of the life of the court. Although Charles II had from time to time tried to use his royal right to dispense in attempts to introduce religious toleration for both Catholics and Dissenters, he had failed. James II was to use that right with far greater frequency to achieve precisely that end. In 1686 he used it to forbid clergy to preach anything controversial or seditious, by which he meant any attack on those outside the Church of England. When one cleric offended, Henry Compton, the Bishop of London, refused to suspend him. The king set up a special Commission for Ecclesiastical Causes, and it suspended both. James believed that the church was now silenced and would continue in its role of preaching obedience to the crown from the pulpit.

Having introduced Catholics into the army and into central government James's next move was to place them in the localities. In January 1687 five hundred new Justices of the Peace were appointed, over sixty per cent of whom were Catholic. Once again, the king made use of his dispensing right to remove from the Catholics any obligation to swear the Oaths of Allegiance and Supremacy. Three months later he issued a Declaration of Indulgence suspending both the penal laws against Catholics and Dissenters and the Test Acts. More and more people looked on aghast at the drift of events, but there was no sign of organised opposition.

The king had stated that he would gain parliamentary approval for the Declaration which meant that he had to be certain of a massive majority of members would vote in its favour. To achieve that meant a purge not only of local government, but also of the towns. By March 1688 some twelve hundred people had been removed from office and replaced by Catholics and Dissenters. There was, however, still no sign of public resistance. What the king would have read as acquiescence was in fact alienation. That meant that if there was a challenge of some kind whoever made it could rely on the passivity of the majority, who would not rise in the king's defence.

Obedience and non-resistance to the crown was part of the creed of the Tories. And James had lost their support. He had violated those who would have sustained him in power. The Church of England by the Declaration was seen to be reduced to the level of a competing sect. Worse, James had dissolved the alliance of monarchy and church by turning to those outside it, Catholics and Dissenters. Parliamentary powers had been reduced seemingly to an irrelevance by his use of the royal right to dispense. And all over the country there had been a repetition of what had happened under the Commonwealth, many of the most powerful men in each of the shires, knights and baronets, the old cavalier gentry, had been removed in favour of Catholics and Dissenters, often of inferior social status.

Everything was in place for a bid to be made to turn the tide but there was no thought as yet of replacing the king. His wife, Mary of Modena, had remained childless and his heir was his eldest daughter, Mary, staunchly Anglican, who had been married to the ruler of the Protestant Netherlands, William of Orange. No one in the spring of 1688 could have predicted that by the close of the year James would have fled, and that William and Mary would have replaced him as joint sovereigns. That was not in anyone's mind when members of the English nobility began to make overtures to William to intervene.

That request was to reach a crescendo during the summer. In April the king issued a second Declaration of Indulgence. Seven bishops headed by William Sancroft, Archbishop of Canterbury, refused to instruct their clergy to read it from the pulpit and went on to challenge its legality. The king ordered their arrest on 8 June. They were brought to trial and, on 30 June, were acquitted. The City of London, a bulwark of Protestantism, went wild with rejoicing. On that same evening a formal letter of invitation was sent to William of Orange asking that he invade the country. Even then it is remarkable how few of the nobility actually signed it. That letter was also prompted by the birth on 10 June of a Prince of Wales. For the first time it was clear that James's reign would not be an aberration but that he could be the first of a line of Catholic kings of Great Britain.

Across the Channel in the Netherlands a large army and fleet began to be assembled. It did not cross the minds of either James or his ministers that it was destined for England until the middle of August. They believed that it was in readiness for yet another phase in the struggle of the Dutch against Louis XIV. And in one sense they were correct, for William's interest in England was motivated by precisely that, the need for the country to play the role both Charles and James had abrogated, to lead Europe against France. That need for the wealth and power of England to be part of the coalition was the unwritten scenario behind William's

Declaration of 30 September in which he listed publicly his reasons for intervening. These included the removal of 'evil counsellors', that is the Catholics, the re-introduction of the Test Acts, the settlement of the problem of dissent and, above all, the election of a free and lawful Parliament. Among these reasons there was one statement which suggested that a change of ruler was in the air. The baby Prince of Wales, on no creditable evidence whatsoever, was declared an impostor smuggled into the queen's bedroom.

A Dutch satirical print on the birth of a Prince of Wales to James II and Mary of Modena. The propaganda machine of William of Orange built on the popular belief that the child was a miller's son smuggled into the queen's bedroom, hence the windmill in the child's hand.

In England panic at last set in, but it came too late. Luck was on William's side virtually the entire time during the bizarre events which ran their course through the autumn months. James refused help from the French, who completely misjudged the situation, and stood by while their pensioner forfeited his throne which passed to their deadliest foe. James too believed that William would never attack his own father-in-law, let alone send an army and a fleet across the Channel during the turbulent months of the onset of winter. So it was not until the end of September that the king accepted the fact that England was to be invaded. The result was a precipitate rush of concessions. Things like the Ecclesiastical Commission were abolished, and the campaign to gain control of the towns by means of new charters was thrown into the melting-pot. Even the writs for a general election were suddenly withdrawn. Government had lost its nerve and that was fatal, for the king was still powerful. In spite of the defection of some of the army the majority of it remained intact. Nor were there any signs of overt rebellion in the regions.

The invasion was held up on account of the weather. The original intention had been to land in Yorkshire and march south but instead the fleet landed in the south-west at Torbay. The royal army meanwhile had advanced on Salisbury. But instead of leading his troops directly into battle, James delayed, facilitating further desertions to the enemy. The king, who three years earlier had seen God as being on his side, now disintegrated. Physically wracked – from a violent nose bleed – he gave way to depression and returned to London without fighting. The result was disaster.

On his return James learnt that his second daughter, Anne, had deserted him. He sent commissioners to deal with William, who demanded the removal of all Catholics from office and that the king should summon a free Parliament. Meanwhile his thoughts turned to flight. That of his queen and son was the first to be achieved, and then on 11 December he fled Whitehall by means of a secret passage and made his way to the coast, where he was recognised and escorted back to London which had already opened its gates to William. James refused every proposal and was escorted to Rochester. On 22 December he made a second, and this time successful, attempt to flee the country, largely because at William's connivance no attempt was made to stop him. William of Orange was not yet king, nor was there any mention of it, but with James gone he alone

More Dutch propaganda prints telling the story of the invasion of William III and the flight of James II. The leaders of the Church of England had refused to read James II's Declaration of Indulgence permitting liberty of conscience in the churches. Seven of them, who petitioned the king to withdraw the order, were arrested and sent to the Tower of London. Here they are depicted as martyrs for the Protestant faith.

held all the cards ensuring the stability of life and property. In short, England had been conquered by a foreign army for the second time since 1066. The difference this time was that the conquest was to be a bloodless one.

A hasty election was then called and there was a replay in many ways of the events which prefaced the Restoration. Once again there was a Convention Parliament, for no monarch had summoned it. This met on 22 January when both Whigs and Tories discussed the implications of the king's flight. Once more fear of violence and rebellion was at the heart of what followed. No one wished for a recurrence of the 1650s. The problem was how to make legal William's seizure of power by force of arms. On 6 February Parliament voted that the throne was vacant and that the king, through fleeing, had abdicated. Shades of the Whig arguments from the period of the Exclusion Crisis now re-surfaced. A Catholic king and his heir were excluded and Parliament offered the crown to Mary and William jointly, although William had no claim to it whatsoever, except by dint of his marriage and military victory. By then William would accept nothing less. Together the new king and queen were presented to the nation as the country's saviours from popery and arbitary rule.

That it was a bloodless change of regime was due not only to James's failure to go to battle but also to the quiescence of the Anglican Tory gentry who may not have welcomed a foreign king but certainly saw him as the only option open to guarantee their continued hold on political power. The governing élite had reasserted their role in 1660. They had reasserted it again in 1688. It was to remain unassailed for almost a century and a half, despite the fact that 1688 also marked the beginning of the years of Jacobite threat. Gilbert Burnet, Bishop of Salisbury, who had accompanied William of Orange on his invasion of England rightly designated it 'the unexpected revolution'.

A popular double portrait of William III and Mary II on an English Delftware plate of 1690. English tin-glazed earthenware followed Dutch styles. The queen indeed set a fashion for blue and white Delftware in interior decoration.

Chapter Forty-Three

THE BIRTH OF A GREAT POWER

ILLIAM III was never a popular king. Cold and withdrawn, his manner stiff and formal, he was devoid of any attribute which would have endeared him to his new subjects. But he was a formidable statesman and general, and it was these aspects of the man which had brought him to England. William saw the island from a European perspective and, as a consequence, was to transform its status. Not since the Elizabethan war against Spain had England played such a major part in European politics. Under Charles II the country had been reduced to the level of being a satellite of France. Under James II it had opted for isolationism. Now all that was to be changed as England, with all her vast commercial, financial and naval resources, was to be deployed in the service of a Grand Alliance against France, designed to curb its expansionist policies and restore the balance of power, that configuration of states whereby no one state dominated all the others. When it began, the war was initially viewed as a short-term commitment. No one could have expected that it was to involve two huge wars and nineteen years of fighting on a massive scale. Nor could anyone have guessed that Britain would emerge from it as a world Great Power.

The war was to be one of two events which were to be instruments of change affecting the country until well into the eighteenth century. The other was the revolutionary settlement itself. That fundamentally altered the nature of royal power. William's claim to the throne was as husband of the rightful and lawful queen who had come to power partly because there was no other option. They reigned as joint sovereigns but power in reality lay with William alone. As one peer observed: 'I look upon this day's work to be the ruin of the monarchy in England, for we have made the crown elective.' William was never to acknowledge that his position was in any way different from that of his predecessors, but in truth it was. The Bill of Rights, which Parliament passed, enshrined a view that the monarchy now existed subject to conditions. The royal suspending power was declared illegal. The king could no longer maintain a standing army in peacetime without the consent of Parliament. All Catholics were henceforth to be excluded from the line of succession. Any hopes that the revolution would achieve greater comprehensiveness for the Church of England ended in failure as much as they did in 1660. The Toleration Bill passed in May 1689 offered only limited freedom of worship to Dissenters but did nothing to alleviate their status as second-class citizens.

1688 was to be presented by historians of the Whig cause in retrospect as a landmark in the evolution of a limited parliamentary monarchy. What is striking, however, is how little changed. Monarchy and government remained inseparable. Ministers continued to be chosen and appointed by the monarch. Indeed ministers could only remain in office as long as they retained royal favour. They depended too on the support in Parliament of those who received the benefits flowing from crown patronage. The king had at his disposal a huge array of offices, pensions and other perquisites which he was to retain into the nineteenth century. His control of foreign policy continued to remain virtually unassailable.

The two wars straddled two reigns, but unlike earlier periods, the accession of a new monarch heralded no alteration in policy. William and Mary were childless and, on his death in 1702, the crown passed to his sister-in-law, Anne. She was a stout, small-minded woman of thirty-seven with an obsession for tittle-tattle and card-playing. But she was not devoid of political acumen. Devoted to duty and the Church of England, she was seen to bathe in the reflected glory of the achievements of others. She shared with her brother-in-law an exalted view of the royal prerogative and firmly resisted any attempts at its erosion.

For thirty years, however, the country was dominated by a war which was a confrontation with the greatest military machine seen in Europe since the Roman Empire. Up to 400,000 men could be under arms, able to sustain the conflict on more than one frontier. Both of the wars, the Nine Years War, which lasted from 1689 to 1697, and the War of the Spanish Succession, which lasted from 1701 to 1713, were about curtailing French ambitions to dominate Europe, in particular by asserting claims to Spain and her empire on the demise of its last Habsburg king, Charles II. In 1688 Louis XIV had invaded Germany, and early in the following year the Dutch had declared war on France, a preface to the formation of the Grand Alliance of the German Emperor, England, Savoy and many of the states of Germany. England's enthusiasm had only been kindled when James II invaded Ireland.

That invasion triggered a surge of Irish Catholic nationalism causing the Presbyterians to flee for safety to Londonderry and Enniskillen. An English army relieved Londonderry in May but a second army sent in August ended in disaster. The following year William himself invaded the country and won a resounding victory at the Battle of the Boyne. Even then it was to take more than a year to complete the reconquest of Ireland. The English retribution for Irish insurrection was to leave a bloody inheritance stretching down the centuries. Parliament re-imposed the Anglican Test Acts on all office-holders, with the result that all Catholics and all Presbyterians were out-lawed from politics. Catholics in particular suffered sav-age legal penalties, which effectively wiped them out from the landowning classes. Ireland was callously reduced to colonial subservience under the rule of a repressive lan-ded minority, who subscribed to the Church of Ireland.

Ireland renders fealty to William III, 1690. Medals were part of the king's propaganda campaign along with prints. This one depicts William, crowned by Victory, giving the kneeling figure of Ireland the olive branch of peace. In this way the bitter defeat and repression of the Irish was presented as an act of benign pacification.

William remains a cult figure to this day among the Protestants of Northern Ireland, but to him the whole incident was a remote and tiresome sideshow, def-lecting his energies from the great battle against the French on the mainland. There the theatre of war was the Spanish Netherlands (the modern Belgium) and the pattern it took was one of annual summer campaigns, made up of indecisive battles and long sieges. William's campaigns were not particularly successful, but in 1695 he captured Namur. After that, Louis XIV was ready for peace and in 1697 the Treaty of Ryswick was signed. In it Louis abandoned all that he had taken since 1678, except for Strasbourg and part of Alsace. More important, Louis recognised William as king.

The peace settled little, for the succession to the Spanish throne was still an open issue. In the intervening years William and Louis reached two agreements as to what should happen, the Partition Treaties. When knowledge of these became public in 1700, public outrage was such that it began the erosion of foreign policy being a royal prerogative. William's popularity sank even lower. There was bitter resentment about his long absences abroad, the cost of the war, and the continuance of the army. The resentment was exacerbated by uncertainty about the succession for in 1700 Anne's only son died. As a result in 1701 the Act of Succession bestowed the crown on the descendants of James I's daughter Elizabeth, the Electors of Hanover. The same year the ailing Charles II at last died leaving his throne to Louis XIV's grandson, Philip of Anjou. The French king promptly ignored both Partition Treaties and ignored too his recognition of William as king in favour of recognising, on James II's death, his son as James III.

That reawoke in Britain a desire to rekindle the war but it was not this time to be led by William who was past his campaigning days. He appointed as commander-in-chief of the English forces John Churchill, later to become the Duke of Marlborough. William disliked him, although he realised his potential. The king never lived to see it, however, dying, unloved and unmourned, early in 1702. Churchill had been waiting in the wings for years and the advent of the new queen, whose closest confidant was Churchill's wife, only escalated his rise to prominence. The War of the Spanish Succession was to be the vehicle for the ablest soldier ever to command the British army. Endowed with grace, charm and courtesy, this handsome man was the perfect courtier. He was also flawed, for he brought with those attributes a ruthless self-seeking, greed and avarice. But he was a brilliant military commander and tactician and under his leadership the whole pace of the war dramatically changed. Marlborough believed in battles and set about manoeuvring his troops in order to surprise the French army and force it to give battle. There followed a series of legendary victories which made Marlborough the hero of Europe. In 1704 the French army suffered the first defeat for two generations at Blenheim sustaining 23,000 casualties and 15,000 prisoners, including the marshal. The queen created Churchill Duke of Marlborough and bestowed on him the royal manor of Woodstock on which arose Blenheim Palace as a monument to his glory.

Queen Anne presents the plans of Blenheim Palace to Military Merit, 1708. Blenheim Palace was the queen's gift to the Duke of Marlborough to mark his military defeat of the armies of Louis XIV. This is a sketch by Sir Godfrey Kneller for a much larger picture which was to be hung in the palace to commemorate the event. It was never painted as Anne and the Marlboroughs fell out.

This was to be the first of a long series of victories. Ramillies followed in 1706, leading to the surrender of the Spanish Netherlands. Two years later came Oudenarde, and Malplaquet in 1709. In Spain the war went less well, the British being defeated at Almanza, but by then the French were exhausted. Marlborough knew that France could only finally be broken by maintaining a stranglehold on all her many frontiers: Spain, Germany, the Netherlands and Italy. That Marlborough had been instrumental in achieving, but after the victories the allies began to quarrel and, fatally for him, war weariness set in at home. Queen Anne, on hearing the news of the battle of Oudenarde, had commented: 'Oh, Lord, when will all this dreadful bloodshed cease?' Marlborough was dismissed on a trumped-up charge and peace negotiations reached a successful conclusion at Utrecht in April 1713.

Two tapestries from the series ordered by the Duke of Marlborough in Brussels by Judocus de Vos, one depicting the duke surveying his troops at the Battle of Oudenarde on 30 June 1708 and the second the fall of Lille in December of the same year. De Vos was guided by the duke in their composition and had access also to plans of the battles and sieges as well as to portraits of those involved. The tapestries still hang in the State Rooms at Blenheim.

It was a turning point in the country's history, one owed to an unpopular king who saw the importance of Britain within the European arena. By the year that Queen Anne died, 1714, Britain enjoyed an international status unknown since the days of her greatest medieval kings. No European power could afford to ignore her, nor could Britain turn its back any longer on the continental mainland. The maintenance of the balance of power indeed became a central preoccupation of Britain's foreign policy throughout the eighteenth century. That that happened was not due solely to the whim of William III or the politicians, but to a growing awareness of the important place Britain occupied in Europe, an awareness largely brought about by the growth of the press. The lapse of the Licencing Act in 1695 meant that the case for and against involvement in the war had been fought out in print for every educated person to read, resulting in a public realisation that England could not stand aside from Europe and be certain that her commercial wealth, her sea power, or indeed the Protestant succession, would not be endangered.

In the Treaty of Utrecht Louis XIV was effectively checked, and he actually guaranteed in a secret clause that he would no longer aid the exiled Stuarts. It was also agreed that the crowns of France and Spain would never be united. Britain emerged with concessions which began to form a nascent empire: Hudson's Bay, Newfoundland, Nova Scotia, Arcadia, St. Christopher, Minorca and Gibraltar. The commercial advantages accrued, especially in respect of trade with the Spanish Empire, were immense.

Both wars had a tremendous impact on the nation. Britain had experienced nothing like them for two centuries. It was the first time since the fifteenth century that a British army was annually engaged in a campaign on the Continent. The war was long and very expensive. The geographical extent of the second war in particular was without precedent, involving military action in Spain, the Netherlands, Germany, Italy and the West Indies. At its peak, during the years 1706 to 1711, the British army, excluding officers, numbered some 120,000. James II's army, which had so alarmed the governing classes, had only been 20,000. Just as the army had expanded, so too did the navy, not only in the number of ships but in their quality and performance. By the close of the war the Royal Navy was the largest and strongest navy in Europe. Some index of the rising wealth of the country can be gauged by the fact that the overall cost of both wars was £140 million.

A war on such a scale called for the grass roots support of the nation. Only the backwoods Tory gentry were xenophobic, for both Whig and Tory showed no great divide in the matter of foreign policy. The wars may have begun on the initiative of the Dutch king but as they progressed they became more and more expressions of a national sentiment. Henceforward foreign policy had to have not only the endorsement of both the Cabinet and Parliament but, in addition, the support of the nation. When that waned, as it did in the years before 1713, policy had to change and peace be made.

Chapter Forty-Four

INSTABILITY AND CHANGE

THE 'unexpected revolution' in fact settled nothing. It ushered in thirty years of political instability on such a scale that it is surprising that civil war was averted. Society was split from top to bottom, Whig or Tory, court and country, a polarisation decisively reinforced by the revolution. Those who were Whigs supported what was called the Protestant Succession. The Whigs also stood for religious tolerance of a kind, and certainly drew support from the dissenting community. They firmly backed William III's war policy, seeing the necessity of countering the might of France and attaining a balance of power within Europe. The Tories were also made up of those who had been forced to accept the 1689 settlement out of necessity. But they saw James II as the rightful king though they felt no loyalty to a Catholic. They believed in the old scheme of things, the king as God's vice-regent on earth, in the union of church and state as one, defending the monopoly of the Church of England against any erosion by dissent. And they did not warm to the engulfment of the country in a European conflict which drained England of men and money.

Sharp divisions of this kind would have been enough even without the exacerbation that followed. The pressure of the war, with its constant need for funds voted by Parliament, was such that William, in 1694, accepted a Triennial Act, which meant that Parliament now had to be re-elected every three years. The king, however, retained the right of dissolution. As a consequence of this, during the next twenty-two years there were no less than ten general elections. Election fever had no sooner subsided than it needed to be relaunched, so that both Whigs and Tories were in a constant state of animation.

That sense of being engaged in perpetual battle was heightened after 1695 when the Licensing Act lapsed, thus fuelling political debate on a gargantuan scale, for both parties indulged in a war of words. Even more important was the emergence of newspapers. By 1700 there were some twenty of them which meant that the electorate was better informed both on home and foreign affairs than ever before.

But, as yet, there was no question of a government being formed wholly by one party, either Whig or Tory. Both William III and Anne would have regarded this as an infringement of their royal powers, so a selected handful of aristocrats acting on their behalf took on the role of 'managers', somehow putting together a government which was made up neither completely of one side nor of the other. One ministry succeeded another in bewildering confusion. Within each, however, certain ministers continued to hold office, providing a continuity which at first glance seems absent. During this period the country was governed by what today we would describe as a series of coalitions.

The late 17th century saw the development of more and more places of public assembly. The coffee house reached its zenith of popularity in the reign of Queen Anne, a fashionable meeting place where politicians, business and other professional people would gather: 'You have all manner of news there: you have a good fire, which you may sit by as long as you please; you have a Dish of Coffee; you meet your friends for the transack of Business, and all for a Penny, if you don't care to spend more.'

On the surface, it would seem that such a way of running the country could have led only to a total breakdown. The fact that these frequent reversals did not result in breakdown or worse was due not only to the fact that the moderates on both sides of the political spectrum held very similar views but also to the profound changes which were taking place, ones which in the coming century were to give Britain its unique and enviable stability. Although ministers may have come and gone with rapidity, due to the pressures of the war, both sides realised that government had to go on. For this to happen there had to be a large and efficient machine staffed by people, civil servants, who would work on, regardless of who was in power. During the thirty years after 1689 the civil service trebled in size. New kinds of civil servant emerged, like career diplomats, and whole new departments were created: the Post Office, the Navy Office, the Customs and Excise. These developments increased the power of the crown which had an ever-growing army of official posts in its giving. The men who worked in these departments were professionals and were often properly salaried officials, unlike their predecessors who made their living through fees and perks. They also began to run the government in a way which reflected the advances in the sciences which were taking place, making use, for example, of statistics for the first time.

Government thus became a profession. If that was a change, an even bigger one was to contribute towards stability, the financial revolution. All through the century there had still lingered the old medieval notion that the king should 'live of his own'. Parliament was reluctant to vote any monarch a sufficiency of income because it would, they believed, erode its power. The war with France was responsible for finally changing that notion, so that at long last the basic principle that government had to be paid for was finally accepted. In 1698 Parliament swept away the age-old differentiation between ordinary and extraordinary expenditure. Instead the king was voted for life what was called the 'Civil List', which comprised the expenses of his household and the cost of civil government. All other expenses had to be met by taxes raised and voted for by Parliament. To meet the unprecedented sum of five million pounds which was needed annually for the war, the first high-yield tax in British history was introduced, the Land Tax, a tax on the rents and produce of land and real estate.

At the same time the royal debts were converted into the National Debt, a system whereby Parliament raised money from the public for loan to the king's government. It was raised through lotteries, the sale of annuities, and loans from the leading trading companies. If that became one method by which the war was financed, another was the Bank of England which was founded in 1694. Those who backed its creation promised the loan of half its initial capital to the king in return for a royal charter. In this way the fruits of the Commercial Revolution supported, and in the end ensured the success of, the war. It was won on England's credit.

Both developments reflected the rise of the City in the way in which we know it today, as the nation's financial heartland, serviced, like government, by a new breed of professionals, money-men, bankers, brokers and stockjobbers, who practised new ways of handling and dealing with financial matters, such as fire insurance and bills of exchange. What the public still had yet to learn, however, was the difference between sound and unsound investment, a lesson which could only be learned through experience. That came in 1720 with what is known as the South Sea Bubble. The South Sea Company had held out the bait of substantial capital gains and attracted a stampede of purchasers of shares. The result was a financial madhouse, brought to a sudden catastrophic collapse in the autumn when foreign investors withdrew their capital. Panic set in, triggering off the company's ruin, and leaving hundreds of investors either with huge losses or bankrupt.

The emergence of the City signalled a shift in what people thought of as property. In the past that had always meant land which produced income. That definition, of course, continued, but the meaning was gradually extended to take in office-holding or an annuity, both of which guaranteed income, for instance, to army officers or urban professionals. The revolution of 1688 established the divine right of property owners; due to this redefinition and to the upsurge in national prosperity there were many more of them by 1720. That also meant that the electorate was expanding, and was now around 340,000 people, one in four or five of the male adult population, but after that date it was to decline in number. Elections after 1716 were in fact infrequent, and hard-fought contests the exception. The obsession with property caused a steady rise of offences against it and laws to protect it, which, if infringed, were punishable by death. As a consequence hanging, for instance, was a possible penalty for stealing goods worth only five shillings. Although the number of capital offences trebled down to 1800, the number of executions fell.

This growth in the propertied classes was one of the undercurrents which contributed in the long term towards stability. Other shifts within the social structure produced consolidation as against confrontation. Unlike earlier periods, there was a reversion to landowning on a vast scale, so vast in fact that it led to the number of dukes being multiplied to twenty-five to reflect the new reality. Their living style became increasingly grandiose, with country houses which were palaces of a hitherto unknown splendour, stuffed with treasures, and dedicated to display and to life in the grand manner.

The first home of the Bank of England, which opened its doors on 21 June 1694, was Mercers' Hall in Cheapside. By noon on the first day a loan capital of £1,200,000 had been deposited by those anxious to help the war against France and also obtain an 8% return on their capital. In 1734 the Bank built its own premises on its historic Threadneedle Street site where it remains to this day.

The gentry and the yeomanry meanwhile colonised the professions: the church, the law, the army and navy, and the civil service. At the same time population decline removed other pressures. That, combined with improvements in agricultural methods, ensured that the lower classes were better off than ever before. Britain had only a minute peasantry unlike any other country in Western Europe, except the Low Countries.

The Commercial Revolution begun earlier was both hindered and helped by the war. Hindered in the sense that it disrupted trading routes and markets, impeding the flow of raw materials. Helped in that, being victorious, trade with Spain, Portugal, Italy and the Levant was stronger than ever before. So too was that with the Spanish colonies. To these outlets were now added parts of Canada ceded by the French. Add to this the vast increase in size of the merchant fleet and the fact that the navy was henceforth never absent from Mediterranean waters, and the scene was set for commercial dominance.

The war engendered a far more widespread industrial base. Birmingham began its development, in response to its role in the manufacture of guns and swords for the army. The dockyards of Chatham, Portsmouth and Plymouth rapidly expanded as shipbuilding became a major industry. During these decades the foundations of the Industrial Revolution of the next century were firmly laid. Thomas Newcomen's steam pump, in use by the early years of the eighteenth century, was the most important technological advance of all, signalling the arrival of the age of the machine. Soon after, a Quaker ironmaster, Abraham Darby, discovered a method of using coal in the smelting of iron ore to produce durable and workable iron, a breakthrough of huge potential. And all over the country industry was becoming better organised, bringing together onto one site processes which had previously been scattered in people's homes and workshops.

This gave rise to the prominence of towns whose identity was a particular industry or activity: Bristol, Liverpool and Whitehaven as ports; Plymouth, Scarborough and Sunderland for shipbuilding; Leeds and Halifax as new centres for the clothing industry; and Wolverhampton, Walsall, Dudley and, especially, Birmingham and Sheffield, for metalworking. Collectively, these towns embodied a geographical shift away from the south-east and the arrival of the industrial midlands and north.

These industries were to become some of the major energies of the new century, a startling contrast to the fate of religion which had so dominated the previous one. During these decades the Church of England

Broad Quay, Bristol, in the early 18th century. Bristol was a thriving west country port due to trade with America, Africa and the West Indies. The city streetscape is still basically medieval.

INSTABILITY AND CHANGE 309

became disorientated and by 1720 politically marginalised. The Toleration Act officially recognised its failure to be comprehensive by allowing Dissenters, under licence, to build their own meeting houses for the first time. By 1700 over three thousand of these had been erected, making the schism all too publicly visible. Anglicans felt threatened by dissent seeming to flourish on every side. They were under threat again by the lifting of censorship, which opened the floodgates not only to debate between denominations but worse, literature which promoted ideas which were often heretical and anti-Christian, engendered by an age dedicated to the pursuit of the sciences and the rule of reason. The revolution itself had shaken the Church of England which had rested on the belief that church and state should be coeval and that the king was the Lord's Anointed. That world was never to return. Instead Anglicans were confronted with virtually an elected king who was a Calvinist and saw the man whom they regarded as the Lord's Anointed a Catholic exile. Some four hundred clergy including seven bishops could not accept William as king and left the church. Even those who remained often barely concealed their loyalty to the exiled Stuarts. It was inevitable that the church, particularly that part of it which was High, should fall into an alliance with the Tories, an association which was to prove fatal. William III understandably had little time for the church and refused to summon Convocation, the assembly of clergy of Canterbury and York. Under the first Hanoverian, George I, Convocation, which opposed the Whig hegemony, was finally suppressed. With traditional belief under attack, its hold over the laity dramatically weakened and its inability to respond to change, the Church of England felt dispirited and beleaguered. The strong reaction against forms of religious enthusiasm which had so dominated the century was also telling against it. Nonetheless, the pattern is not a consistent one. In many parishes the church retained vigour and the old view of a complacent, ineffective ministry lacking spiritual commitment cannot be sustained. The Georgian church had its saints. For the bulk of the population squire and parson were twin poles fixed in the firmament of life.

In Scotland the religious situation was very different, for as part of the revolutionary settlement Presbyterianism had been accepted as the country's official faith. Even though the monarch might style himself king of Great Britain the truth was that he remained king of three distinct kingdoms, England, Scotland and Ireland. The last could be discounted, becoming little more than a subject province, but Scotland retained its own system of law and government, including an active Parliament. The religious settlement of 1689 only increased division and faction and made William III determined to achieve full political union with England. In that he failed, but the idea remained on the political agenda to resurface later when the

Scottish Parliament refused to confirm the Act of Succession in favour of the House of Hanover. In 1703 it went even further, stating that a decision as to its future ruler would not be made until after Queen Anne's death. Such an act was viewed with dismay south of the border, for not only could it mean that the crown could pass elsewhere but, in addition, Scottish regiments could be withdrawn from the European conflict. In Scotland there was, however, a party in favour of the Hanoverians and this in the end led to negotiations. An Act of Union was eventually passed by both Parliaments and in October 1707 the Parliament of Great Britain met for the first time.

That was not to be the end of Scotland which retained its own legal system, nor could an act of Parliament wipe out centuries of separate political and cultural development. The pressures which had caused the union to happen in 1707 were at root economic. Scotland's economy was poor. Union with England was in the long run to reverse that, for, by abolishing the border between the two kingdoms, a new state was created which was to be the biggest free trade area in the whole of Western Europe.

The House of Commons in 1710. After the Union with Scotland in 1707 the old House had to be enlarged to take in the Scottish MPs. Sir Christopher Wren was called in to alter what had started life as St. Stephen's Chapel transforming it into an elegant galleried hall. 558 members were crammed into a space 60 by 26 feet but attendance was fortunately spasmodic. The picture records the time-honoured arrangement with the Speaker in his chair and visitors to the House confined behind a bar.

All of these diverse currents within society and the economy taken collectively were indicators of a stability to come, but that was not perceived at the time. The whole of the seventeenth century had been a long search for a new working relationship between the crown and its ministers on the one hand and the crown and Parliament on the other. Abroad, it must have seemed that other states had order, stability and tranquillity compared with the long sequence of civil war, revolution, rebellion and conspiracy that had punctuated the eighty years following the final breakdown of the old Tudor system of government. But, on the other hand, people valued the inheritance of those struggles: liberty, representative institutions, and the rule of common law, things virtually absent from the rest of Europe. The price that was paid was the constant change of government and fierce party warfare between Whig and Tory.

When Queen Anne died in 1714 those divisions were as bitter and as entrenched as ever and yet the succession went smoothly. That was partly due to the Act of Succession and the Whigs, and partly to the disarray of the Tory opposition. James II's son, recognised by Louis XIV as James III and known as the Old Pretender, had been urged to convert to Anglicanism but had refused. That refusal split the Tory party, leaving most of it inert as George I claimed Great Britain. A year later, however, the Old Pretender landed in Scotland and his supporters marched south as far as Preston before being finally crushed. Only with that defeat of what was a serious challenge to the new dynasty could the rule of the House of Hanover truly begin.

The arrival of George I saw a resolution within reach. Unlike both his predecessors, who felt their power would be eroded if ever they came down fully in favour of only one party or the other, the new king had no hesitation in cementing an alliance with one party, the Whigs. In 1716 there was another landmark, the Septennial Act, extending the life of Parliaments from three to seven years. This act contributed to the Whigs' ability to establish themselves firmly in power but took the heat out of party debate. Everything was in place for Sir Robert Walpole to perfect what was to be the most sophisticated patronage system ever constructed to ensure that the Old Corps of Whigs remained in power. The elements making for stability which underlay the turbulence typical of the three decades after 1688 were now at last to find political expression. The age of oligarchy was about to begin.

Chapter Forty-Five

FROM MAGIC TO SCIENCE: ISAAC NEWTON

ALL of these changes were as nothing compared with the greatest of them all, the one known as the Scientific Revolution. That transformation was epitomised in the life of a single man, Sir Isaac Newton, who was born in the year in which the Civil War broke out and who died in the one in which George II came to the throne. Newton's great works, *Principia* (1687) and *Optics* (1704) were to be looked back on as two of the greatest foundation stones of modern science. Both of them eventually changed the way people looked at the everyday world around them, and that of the sky above. These deeply erudite volumes were to affect how men thought about the universe and were to contribute to the great age of practical invention to come, which saw the construction of canals and roads for better transport, a revolution in agricultural methods, and inventions like the steam engine which signalled the Industrial Revolution.

All of these developments which found their expression in the practical world owed their initial impetus to voyages of the mind made in cloistered studies during the seventeenth century. And no voyage was to be greater than that made by Newton. The offspring of an illiterate yeoman family, he was slowly to become recognised as the greatest intellect of his age. And pure intellect he was. As a consequence he emerges as a lonely, tortured, self-absorbed, friendless man who, with increasing age, took on characteristics which can only be described as unpleasant: hatred of any form of criticism and an iron will to dominate and have his own way. Newton was accorded respect and admiration by his contemporaries but never affection. Indeed he barely emerges as human, and yet his polymathic mind left a legacy which was to blaze a trail still influential today.

Sir Godfrey Kneller's portrait of Sir Isaac Newton tidies up someone who was in appearance 'usually untidy and slovenly'. Bishop Atterbury wrote that: 'In the whole air of his face . . . there was nothing of that penetrating sagacity which appears in his compositions.'

Although he is referred to as a scientist, no such person existed until the nineteenth century when the word was invented to describe a new profession. What was to become science had its roots in the heritage of scientific literature from classical antiquity, especially from Ancient Greece. Just as the renewal of interest in, and study of, that inheritance triggered the Renaissance and, to a degree, the Reformation, so it was responsible for the advent of the Scientific Revolution. But in the case of science the story is a far more complex one, for there are no less than three distinct strands which each in its own way was to contribute to what in our day we categorise as science. No one at the time could judge any one of these strands as more correct than the other. That judgement could only be made with hindsight. Newton, however, stands at the bridgehead and is looked back upon as a founder of modern science. But he was a child of his own time and although many of his thoughts and discoveries belong to the future, to today's world, others belong to a past which we now discount as a world haunted by magic and superstition.

The first of the three traditions was the organic one which stemmed from the Greek philosopher, Aristotle. This gave the Middle Ages its world picture, one in which the earth was flat and around which revolved the sun and planets. On earth everything was subject to change and decay whereas the celestial world was immutable. Each phenomenon had its natural course whether it was an acorn which became an oak or a stone which, on account of its weight, fell downwards. The stars reigned over the destiny of men, and God as prime mover ruled over it all. It was a picture easily allied to the one depicted in the Bible and hence was fiercely defended by theologians on both sides of the religious divide, Catholics as well as Protestants. Indeed, to challenge it was seen to threaten Christian belief. In a Europe dominated until the late seventeenth century by religious fervour, this tradition enjoyed a revival and was firmly ensconced in all the great universities. It was not a sterile tradition either, for out of it came great discoveries like that by the physician William Harvey of the circulation of the blood.

The second tradition, the magical, was quintessentially a Renaissance one, for the Renaissance was also a time of magic, fed by the discovery of what were then believed to be the writings of ancient Egyptian sages. These gave a very different picture of the universe, one in which the earth was no longer at its centre and flat but was round and revolved with the other planets around the sun. In this scheme of things God was seen as revealing the mysteries of the universe through number. Pioneered by Copernicus, the impact of this through the sixteenth century was vast, for it led to the development of mathematics which were viewed as akin to, if not actually identical with, the workings of the mind of God. The learned men who adhered to these views

An orrery made by John Rowley about 1712 which belonged to the Earl of Orrey, who thereby gave his name to such devices, which depicted the working of the universe in model form. The structure of the universe here stems from the discoveries of Copernicus, the sun being at the centre with the planets revolving around it. Here the earth can be seen making its course with the moon in its turn circling around it. By the second half of the 17th century this embodied a mechanistic view of the universe in which God was the Great Engineer presiding over a machine.

were known as *magi* or 'wise men', deeply learned in the lore of the universe as they understood it, committed to sharing its secrets only with a privileged few. As a result of this and of the fact that their views contradicted the world as it was found in the Bible, magi were often regarded with deep suspicion, so deep that one of them, Giordano Bruno, was burned in Rome for heresy in 1600.

This magical tradition also opened up new worlds of discovery, and was responsible, for instance, for the great advances in astronomy, because a more accurate knowledge of the stars meant that it would be possible to cast better horoscopes. Overall, this was a view of the universe totally at variance with the organic one. It was one in which the 'wise man' or magus could, it was believed, through his knowledge of numbers and their working in terms of mathematics and geometry, actually harness both natural and supernatural forces. For them God was the greatest magician of them all.

It was to that tradition that Newton belonged, but he also straddled the third strand, the mechanistic, which was to be the one to triumph at the close of the seventeenth century and lead on to the scientist of the Victorian age. The mechanistic tradition was neither organic nor magical. It arose out of a renewed study of the Greek mathematician, Archimedes. For the followers of this tradition, God was the Great Engineer and the universe was seen as one huge machine, regular, permanent and predictable. They shared with those who belonged to the magical tradition an obsession with mathematics, not because numbers had any magical powers but because they provided the key to the workings of that machine, ones which could also be approached through practical experiment and discovery. It is hardly surprising therefore that many of their greatest contributions were in the fields of mechanics and engineering resulting, for instance, in the development of the mechanical clock. What occurred during the seventeenth century was that this tradition increasingly gained ground, and took over from the magical tradition a firm commitment to heliocentricity, that the earth revolved around the sun.

The spread of these new ideas was aided by an increase in the number of people who could work in what at the time was a new language, that of mathematics. All the great minds of the age were fascinated by it, for it made possible an intellectual sophistication which was quickly seen to outstrip all other forms of human reasoning, opening up new frontiers of knowledge. That the mechanistic and mechanical view of the world was to gain such currency in England was a direct consequence of the reaction against the religious excesses of the 1650s. And it was precisely during that period that Isaac Newton came of age.

Newton was born on Christmas Day 1642 at Woolsthorpe, seven miles south of Grantham in Lincolnshire. His father died when he was only six months old and his mother when he was three. But they left him money which paid for his education. He was an extremely precocious child, silent and apart from other children, in short, a swot. When he left the local grammar school the headmaster paid tribute to him as the most brilliant pupil they had ever had. In June 1661, one year after the return of Charles II, he went up to Cambridge, leaving rural life for good, and beginning what was to be a lifetime's voyage of the mind. Withdrawn and solitary, he quickly discovered that the university was an intellectual backwater and that he had to invent his own course of studies.

Newton's mind was extraordinary for it ran in so many directions which to us

In an old Latin exercise book from his grammar school days in Grantham, Newton recorded his expenses in going up to Trinity College, Cambridge. These include payments to the White Lion Inn at Cambridge, carriage to the college, and the purchase of a chamberpot for 2sh. 2d.

would seem contradictory but which in terms of the period were not particularly unusual. At one moment he would be searching for a universal language and at another he would bury himself deep in the history of Biblical prophecy. More and more he found himself drawn towards the mechanistic view of the universe as a machine. As a consequence of this obsession, unaided, he taught himself mathematics in a year. Then, again in seclusion and at the age of twenty-four, he discovered infinitesimal calculus. In so doing he had already outstripped the achievements of every other mathematician in Europe.

The following year he became a fellow of Trinity College where he was to remain for twenty-eight years. Two years later, in 1669, he became Lucasian Professor of Mathematics. Then, in 1695, he upped and left for London as Warden and then Master of the Mint. Early in the new century he became President of the Royal Society, which had been founded under the patronage of Charles II, and was knighted. He died on 2 March 1727 and was buried in great splendour in Westminster Abbey.

For a man whose intellect was to dominate his age for half-a-century, Newton's life cannot be described as anything other than dull. Much about him is summed up when it was written of his lectures at Cambridge that 'so few went to see him, and fewer that understood him, that of times he did in a manner, for want of hearers, read to the walls.' Newton, in short, was the archetypal absent-minded professor, missing meals, his head buried deep in his papers, his appearance unkempt and untidy. He never married, seemingly had no close friends, and shunned society. And yet more than any other single person, with what he wrote he shaped the coming century.

In his *Optics* he demonstrated that light, for centuries venerated as the symbol of the Godhead, was in fact composed of rays of primary colours and thus governed by mechanical laws. Even more epoch-making was his *Principia* which demonstrated for the first time that everything in the universe was subject to mechanical laws. In it he formulated the law of gravity, that the mutual attraction of two masses varies inversely with the square of the distance between them. This was a universal law which applied

A sketch by Newton in which he records one of his experiments with light using lenses. Such investigations led to his book *Optics*.

not only to the earth but also to the structure of the heavens. In one blow the organic tradition was annihilated. At the same time he reconciled the two remaining traditions, the magical one in which God was seen as an artist creating a work of art and the mechanistic one in which He was an engineer presiding over a machine. Newton made God an aesthetic engineer.

In the next century he was to be revered as the man who had vanquished the magical tradition and established the universe as a machine. In fact Newton still continued to see the universe as shrouded in esoteric mystery, one which could be unravelled by the intellectual élite whose minds were acute enough to spy God's clues. For Newton, the cosmos was still permeated by the Divine Presence much in the same way that it had been for followers of the magical tradition. But by the middle of the eighteenth century that side of his thought had been forgotten and Newton was seen as the man whose work had transformed God into a Deity detached from the world.

The collapse of the organic tradition inevitably wiped out the authority of Aristotle. The importance of this cannot be underestimated. The works of classical antiquity both Greek and Roman, or the 'Ancients' as they were called, were proved to be wrong and the 'Moderns' right. All through the Middle Ages, Western European man had been recovering the lost knowledge of antiquity. The Renaissance was an intensification of that process. Truth was seen as buried in the past, a view which was reinforced by the fact that the past was nearer to Creation. Now, for the first time, the past was scrapped. A new system of knowledge about the world had to be built through human observation and experiment. It was to lead to a golden age of medicine, agriculture, and industry. So great was the confidence and pride in the present that men no longer modelled even their style of writing on the classics but instead on the great stylists in the vernacular of the present. The magical tradition, which had embraced what until then had been seen as respected disciplines like astrology and alchemy, vanished. No more witches were burnt because men had discounted witchcraft as untrue.

This was a revolution of the human mind as gargantuan in its consequences as both the Renaissance and Reformation. And this victory of the mechanistic universe happened at precisely the moment when Spain went into terminal decline and power shifted decisively northwards to France, Holland and, as the eighteenth century progressed, increasingly to England, where the application of the discoveries consequent upon the work of Newton and his contemporaries took a practical turn, thus helping to ensure that it was in Britain, rather than other Western European countries, that the Industrial Revolution was to take place.

Chapter Forty-Six

THE RULE OF THE ÉLITE

THE great change in 1714 was the advent of a king who was politically committed to one party, the Whigs. The new dynasty were Electors of Hanover, rulers of a small state in Northern Germany. Although coming almost by accident into possession of the crown of what was fast becoming the wealthiest country in Europe and a major power, the Hanoverians continued to view affairs of state largely through the eyes not of a king of Great Britain but those of an Elector of Hanover. Hanover always had their heart, something which did not alter until the first king's great-grandson ascended the throne in 1760, but he was the first Hanoverian monarch to be brought up in England.

George I was honest, dull and diffident. Fifty-four when he became king, he was devoid of either personal charm or regal bearing and lived only for his ugly German mistresses, who were made English duchesses, and for Hanover. And, like all his family, he hated his eldest son, which created a new pattern of politics focusing on rival courts, that of the king and that of the Prince of Wales. His son, George II, who succeeded him in 1727, was no improvement on his father, although he at least had a command of English. George II was stiff and formal, a man obsessed by regularity and detail but also given to sudden bouts of ill-temper and uncontrolled passion. On the field of battle he could be courageous. Both kings, however, were sharply aware of their prerogatives, and exercised them to the full. The old picture of George II as a ruler manipulated by his wife, Caroline of Ansbach, in the interests of Sir Robert Walpole does not hold water in view of a reign of thirty-three years, over only ten of which did she exercise any influence. George II remained his own man and was a shrewd judge of abilities.

Sir Robert Walpole was the greatest political figure and fixer of the era. He took over as First Lord of the Treasury and Chancellor of the Exchequer in April 1721 when he was forty-four and was only finally forced from office over twenty years later in February 1742. No other person in this position has ever held power for so long. But Walpole was a man made for an age which had grown tired of the perpetual clash of ideologies. He was a corpulent, almost gross Norfolk squire, with coarse features

Sir Robert Walpole satirised by his opponents as the English Colossus, such was his dominance of the political scene. A quote from Shakespeare's *Julius Caesar* emphasised the point: 'Why man, he doth bestride the narrow world like a Colossus and we petty men walk under his legs and peep about to find ourselves dishonourable graves.'

and a florid complexion. His milieu was the hunting field, which he loved, and not the drawing-room, for he lacked social polish, and he revelled in the earthy and bawdy. His outlook on the world was practical, utilitarian, and dispassionate. His boyhood friend had been the leading Whig magnate in Norfolk, Viscount Townshend, who married his sister. Walpole himself married the granddaughter of a Lord Mayor of London which brought him City connections. In miniature, this set of family relationships indicated what politics was to become for much of the eighteenth century, the art of managing and sustaining a vast network of people through family and friends committed to supporting the government of the day. It was to be the age of the rule of the élite. Walpole knew the weakness of human beings and how to flatter, cajole and dominate them, which demanded of him huge reserves of patience, nerve, courage, self-control, humour and ruthlessness. Politics for him was the art of the possible. After decades of revolution, war and civil unrest, he gave the aristocratic and gentry classes what they most wanted: peace and prosperity.

The most striking feature of the country during this period is the seeming stability of the government after almost a century of turbulence, punctuated by revolutions, which first abolished the monarchy and then brought it back, accepted as monarch an armed conqueror who happened to be married to a Stuart, and then finally abandoned that dynasty altogether in favour of the ruler of a minor German state who chanced to be the only surviving Protestant descendant of James I. All of this suggested that the monarchy would be weakened even further, but that did not follow. Both George I and George II remained at the centre of the political stage as founts of honour and justice, as chief executives of the realm and makers of peace and war. They stood at the apex of a social and political hierarchy which was within their creation as they controlled all the major appointments including the civil service and church, army and navy. They also retained the right to appoint and dismiss ministers, but with one new condition, whoever the king chose as his principal minister had to be able to carry a majority in the Commons. In general the king's choice always did, as the Commons was filled with recipients of royal patronage.

That new dimension began under George I. Walpole had worked hard to gain the king's respect and indeed so closely associated had they become that when George died in 1727 everyone thought Walpole would be dismissed. But this did not happen. Walpole realised that the key to the new king was the queen and to gratify himself with both he secured for them large sums of money for their Civil List allowances, far in excess of any of their predecessors.

George II inherited Walpole but they became increasingly out of tune over foreign policy. By 1741 the king had even made overtures to members of the opposition via the Pelhams, that major configuration of Whig interest which focused around Henry Pelham and his brother the Duke of Newcastle. It was indeed the war which, in 1742, finally brought Walpole down, for he was a bad war minister and lost his hold on a majority in the House. The king now had to choose between two Whig clusters, that which centred on Lord Carteret and William Pulteney and that which looked to the Duke of Argyll and the Prince of Wales. George II opted for Carteret, soon created Earl of Granville, but the Pelhams brought him down on his handling of the war. Already, however, Henry Pelham had been given the office of First Lord of the Treasury and the Exchequer followed a year later in 1744. To begin with George was uneasy with the Pelhams who in the aftermath of the 'Forty-Five' Jacobite rebellion insisted that William Pitt, whom the king loathed, should be made Secretary of State for war. The king called on Granville and Pulteney, now Earl of Bath, to form a ministry precipitating a mass resignation of the Pelhamites. Granville and Bath were forced to resign and the Pelhams returned. Pitt was given office but only lesser posts. The king had retained the whip-hand. George II quickly discovered that the mechanics of government worked smoothly with the Pelhams, giving him what he wanted. Henceforward it was established that no administration could survive without a minister who enjoyed the confidence of both king and Commons.

So one part of what became a political system was in place, but there were other constraints within which the king had to work. These included the acceptance of regular parliamentary sessions, and the financial control of the Commons. The king met his ministers in what was called the Royal Closet but there was also a meeting of ministers called the Cabinet Council which he did not attend. This was the ancestor of our present Cabinet but it had a long way to develop. But much that we would recognise as part of the pattern of today's politics was beginning to fall into place, of which the most important was the ability of any first minister to control the Commons.

There were, however, ways and means of securing a majority. Sir Robert Walpole and Henry Pelham both knew how to make such a system work, and they were helped by the Act which extended the period of each Parliament to seven years. This meant that those in power were there long enough fully to entrench themselves. And this was achieved through a ruthless, at times bordering on corrupt, use of what was known as the patronage system or influence.

Government was stable because enough members of Parliament were, for various reasons, part of the network which brought them benefits if they voted along with the ministry of the day. Of the four hundred or so members returned by the boroughs, for example, over half were in control of either the government or private patronage. In addition, up to 30% of the House could be office-holders of the crown. Such facts indicate that the strings were already in position, and only waited for a man with the ability to begin to pull them. That is not to say they were not pulled in the previous century, but it was Walpole who realised the full potential. He recognised that the seat of political power for any chief minister was henceforth in the Commons. He therefore refused to go to the Lords and remained in the Commons, creating thereby a new office, the ancestor of our present Prime Minister, the minister for the king in the House of Commons. Walpole was the first man to play that role, succeeded in the 1740s by Henry Pelham.

In the House of Commons the leading office-holding politicians sat on one side while those out of office sat on the facing benches. Both groups were from the major political families, and it was between them that any debate raged. The role of those in

government was to secure enough votes to obtain a majority. They began by being certain of the votes of at least a hundred and eighty members by 1742 because they were men directly in the pay of government, holding offices at court or in the administration or sinecures. The problem centred on persuading enough of the remaining three hundred or so members to vote in their favour as well. And among these lurked the 'Old Corps' Whigs, those who had held Walpole in power, who were genuinely opposed to expensive foreign wars, high taxation, the growth of centralised administration, and who were also highly suspicious of the influence of the court. But the government had ways of winning these members over from actually controlling the elections to inducements such as office.

A scene from William Hogarth's series of satirical paintings, *The Election*, inspired by the notoriously corrupt Oxfordshire election of 1754. This was a contest between the Tory gentry of the county and its great Whig magnate, the Duke of Marlborough. In a highly complex scene Hogarth exposes the political corruption of the age: to the left the landlady of the Royal Oak tavern counts what she has received in bribes, in the middle a smooth Tory agent attempts to lure two ladies with gifts from a pedlar, while a sharp countryman accepts invitations from both sides.

The running of the country increasingly came to depend on the ability to manipulate a few hundred largely interconnected people, the élite. Real power was concentrated in only a few hands, those of the king and a handful of landed aristocratic families who in the main were either Whigs or converts. Between them this group could pull every lever in the book. And although those out of power lived out a fiction of being some kind of country opposition, a mixture of Whig 'outs' and Tories, bent on rescuing the king from the malign influence of evil ministers, if any were offered office with all its attendant perks they grabbed at it. From time to time this shifting opposition found a figurehead in successive Princes of Wales.

The ability of the 'Old Corps' of Whigs to hold on to power for so long was also helped by the fact that, on account of the long period of relative peace, the political scene was devoid of passion. The function of government in the hands of this interconnected circle was confined to maintaining law and order, conducting foreign policy and exerting minimum economic control. The pattern at the centre radiated downwards. In the counties the great magnates were appointed lord lieutenant by the king, as his representative in that region. The Lord Chancellor appointed the local justices of the peace who not only tried criminal cases but who also went on to cope with roads, bridges, gaols and other local amentities. The justices controlled the appointment at parish level of every officer except that of churchwarden. Only the towns might escape such pressure. There their government was usually formed by a mayor, aldermen and common councilmen being elected by the freemen of the borough.

Everything worked smoothly except when something was attempted which even the usually pro-government floating voters in the Commons really objected to. In the case of Walpole, this happened only twice. Once in 1733 when he attempted to increase taxation on commodities in an Excise Bill, but he was wise enough to withdraw it. The second time it precipitated his downfall, his failure as a war minister during the War of the Austrian Succession, but he had by then already begun to lose his touch. Walpole believed in peace, which was made with France, thus avoiding huge expense and the dislocation it brought to trade. For him the rule of the House of Hanover was not to be founded on mystique, as it had been with the Stuarts, but on sound government finance and commercial prosperity. The City financiers trusted Walpole and he built on that. To reduce the National Debt he set up a Sinking Fund to pay it off. By the 1730s confidence was such that government bonds were regarded as foolproof. He believed in low taxation, preferring to tax indirectly rather than directly on land. As a consequence he bequeathed a formidable legacy of achievement.

Henry Pelham was to attempt to emulate this in the years of peace after 1748. He was a man of very different temperament, lacking Walpole's abrasive arrogance and passion. He was far more disinterested and liberal in outlook and was, above all, a master of monetary affairs, re-structuring public finance and restoring confidence. Peace, stability and conciliation were the keynotes of his administration and when he died on 6 March 1754 the country was to enter a very different era. The ethos of the long decades of Whig dominance was summed up by one of the great commentators on the period, Horace Walpole, when he wrote of life in the House of Commons, of which he was a member: 'A bird might build her nest in the Speaker's chair, or in his peruke; there won't be a debate that can disturb them.'

All of this so far might be described as the view from the centre. The ruling élite and their system also had its downside, for it embodied an economic, social and military dominance of the two islands which was solidly English. Its sway over Scotland depended on an alliance with the Scottish Presbyterians and over Ireland on one with the Irish Anglicans. In both of these countries large percentages of the population were denied any political rights at all. The English hold was often quite fragile and ultimately depended on an ability to mobilise military force to keep the populations in subjection.

For the first fifty years of Hanoverian rule the disaffected had a living embodiment

Sir Roger Newdigate in his newly built library at Arbury Hall. Painted in 1756–58 the portrait evokes the elegant ambience of the educated landed classes. Sir Roger had been on the Grand Tour to Italy and collected antiquities. His library reflects his taste for learning and the plans in his hands celebrate his rebuilding of Arbury in the revived Gothic style, one appropriate to a man who was Tory and looked back to the Middle Ages.

for their aspirations in the man alluded to as 'The king over the water', the exiled 'James III', the 'Old Pretender', son of James II. And those who looked in that direction, either directly or covertly, multiplied rather than diminished, for the longer the Whigs were in power the greater the accumulation of those who, for one reason or another, were alienated from the new régime. If 'James III' had ever returned Protestant history may well have taken a very different course. In Ireland, the Stuarts could rely on the majority of the population who had been cruelly treated, and in Scotland on those who had seen the country's independence wiped out by the Act of Union. In England, as the Whig hegemony went relentlessly on, they could hope for Tory involvement in Jacobite plots for their restoration. But the Tories never opted out of the political system and their interest in the Jacobite cause was ambiguous and opaque. Support for the Stuarts was still strong in old Royalist parts of England, the north, the west and Wales. It extended into the middle classes in towns such as London, Bristol and Manchester. In the main, too, they could look for support from France in their various invasion attempts. Between 1689 and 1759 there were no less than fifteen Jacobite plots, some of quite major proportions. In 1715 the English end of the plot was nipped in the bud, but there was a serious rising in Scotland and in the north of England. Thirty years later came the two most significant of these challenges, the first in 1744 when the country was threatened by a fleet and a large French army which never sailed, and the second when 'James III's' son, Charles Edward Stuart, the 'Young Pretender', landed in Scotland on 25 July 1745, rapidly collecting an army which captured Perth and Edinburgh. Early in November it marched south on a promise from the prince that there would be a rising in England and aid from France. Neither happened, but it is noteworthy that the north remained neutral. The Scots were forced to retreat and were eventually savagely massacred at Culloden. The prince fled into exile and penury. As part of the peace treaty of 1748 the French withdrew their support from the Stuarts which effectively ended their hopes, although plots lingered on into the fifties. In Scotland a cruel retribution was exacted on the Highlands and the Lowlands took on the character of being an outpost of English civilisation.

What this reveals is the overwhelming dominance of the south of England over both islands. With the final defeat of the Jacobites and the advent in 1760 of a ruler who was to be billed as a truly British king, increasing efforts began to be made to bring in the disaffected and forge a new collective identity. On paper George I and George II ruled as kings of Great Britain but the reality was that they presided over a series of arranged marriages. As the century progressed these were to be replaced by the invention of the idea of a single country, Britain, and a single people, the Britons.

Chapter Forty-Seven

THE RICHEST COUNTRY

A S WHEN Walpole fell from power, a period of flux followed the death of Henry Pelham. William Pitt was his obvious successor as leader of the House of Commons but, as had been the case with Pelham, the king loathed him, regarding Pitt as factious and irresponsible. The other candidate was Henry Fox, friend both of Walpole and Pelham. The king liked Fox but unfortunately he had fallen foul of the man George II had asked to put together a new administration, the Earl of Hardwicke. As a consequence of this Hardwicke advised the king to follow the disastrous course of putting the government into the hands of the major Whig aristo-cratic grandee, Henry Pelham's elder brother, Thomas Pelham-Holles, Duke of Newcastle. Once again there was a refusal to recognise what by 1754 had become a fact, the impossibility of running government without its leading minister in the Commons able to control a majority.

Newcastle was a great political fixer, whose admirable qualities included shrewd commonsense, disinterestedness, generosity and a wide knowledge of foreign affairs. But the country was fast heading towards a major global conflict with France, one which Newcastle was incapable of leading, as he was subject to bouts of depression, jealousy and hypersensitivity, adding up to paranoia on a grand scale. His appointment was soon realised to be unworkable, which threw Pitt and Fox together. They launched a virulent attack on Newcastle, so much so that within a year he was forced to buy out Fox by admitting him to the Cabinet as Secretary of State and making him leader of the Commons as a last-ditch attempt to keep Pitt out.

On 15 May 1756 war was declared on France. Its initial phase went badly, the French taking Minorca. Then the conflict spread to the Continent when Frederick the Great of Prussia began what was to be known as the Seven Years' War by invading Saxony. The war continued to go badly, so much so that the king was ultimately forced to bring Pitt into the administration. With characteristic arrogance, Pitt would only agree to this on condition that both Newcastle and Fox were excluded from office. The war went no better, so that George II, in April 1757, dismissed Pitt and called once again on Lord Hardwicke to put together another administration. Pitt's dismissal only increased his public popularity, especially in London. It was abundantly clear that no administration could function without him, due to his ability both to command a majority in the Commons and to attract outside popular support. Equally Pitt could not function without the Duke of Newcastle who had at his disposal all the levers which worked the Whig political system. Hardwicke reconciled the two. 'I can't come in without bringing in my enemy, Mr Pitt,' Newcastle lamented to the king. 'He turned me out. But I can't serve without my enemy.'

The scene was now set for a formidable series of triumphs. Pitt took over the direction of the war while Newcastle worked the system to ensure parliamentary support and raised the money needed to pay for the global military and naval campaigns. The British war policy was a clear one, to subsidise foreign armies on the Continent with provisions and money but with a limited number of troops. The vast mass of the British army and navy was used to inflict damage on the enemy's economy and colonies. The new ministry embraced a wide range of political opinions and there was even support from many Tories. By the close of the year the tide of the war on the Continent began to change. Frederick the Great defeated first the French and Imperial armies and then the Austrian. A new leader of the allied armies was appointed, Prince Ferdinand of Brunswick, who drove the French back across the Rhine defeating them at the Battle of Krefeld in 1758.

For Britain, however, the more important theatres of war were scattered around the globe, for this was a struggle to determine who should enjoy commercial dominion of overseas markets. When war broke out, Britain already had significant colonial possessions, but by the time that peace was made in 1763 she was to emerge with the greatest empire that the world had seen since Rome. The basis of that was the territory inherited from the previous century, the old colonies along the eastern seaboard of Northern America numbering thirteen states in all, the last, Georgia, being founded only in 1732. Then there were the West Indian Islands: Bermuda, St. Kitts, Barbados, Antigua, Montserrat and Jamaica. These were the home of the sugar industry, and economies based on the importation of slave labour from Africa. In India the East India Company, established in 1600, had bases in Bombay and Calcutta. Collectively these were fast-growing markets for British products. Although textiles still dominated, the demand for metal products was rising fast. Exports to the American colonies doubled but they equally grew in East Africa and Asia and continued to increase in Europe. By 1760 British overseas possessions took 40% of English domestic products, highlighting the crucial role they occupied in the growing economy of the country. Imports from the colonies similarly rose, reflecting the

Against a distant view of a
Cornish copper mine Thomas
Daniell, merchant and mining
entrepreneur, holds a lump of
ore and meets Thomas Morcom,
who worked in the Polperro mine
of St. Agnes where the artist, John
Opie, came from.

increased demand for tea, coffee, sugar and tobacco, followed by rice, pitch, tar and timber. These commodities in their turn were re-exported to the Continent.

In response to this the mercantile marine grew from 280,000 tonnes in 1695 to 609,000 tonnes in 1760. The ports servicing the westward routes, Bristol, Glasgow, Liverpool and Whitehaven, also expanded. They, in their turn, stimulated industrial development in their hinterlands, the Severn Valley, the West Midlands, Yorkshire and Lancashire reinforcing the shift of the country's industrial base away from the south and east.

By the 1750s everyone realised the importance of these colonial markets and the necessity to cancel out the French. Future British prosperity was seen to hinge on stemming French advance in America and in India. And this is precisely what was achieved as a result of the Seven Years' War. In India, Robert Clive routed Saraj ud Dowlah at the Battle of Plassey in 1757, bringing Bengal and Orissa under the control of the East India Company. Two years later General Wolfe took Quebec in Canada. Guadaloupe was also taken, and a French invasion of England was thwarted by a bombardment of their fleet at Le Havre. Admiral Boscawen destroyed one French fleet in August and Admiral Hawke a second in November. The same year Prince Ferdinand defeated the French at the Battle of Minden. In 1760 Montreal was taken, and French Canada passed into British hands. Although peace was to be three years away what in effect was the first British Empire had been created. It owed much to William Pitt, whose stupendous energy, vision, and capability to inspire, had taken a nation with him to undreamed-of victory. But that coincided with a new sense of national unity arising from the dissolution of the Tories, the drawing together of the Whigs, and strong collective resentment of the French. Pitt, for all his genius, was a man who ruled by fear rather than affection. He was an unpleasant man, ruthless, arrogant and inconsistent, with all the symptoms of what we now recognize as a manic-depressive. In Pitt's case, his genius had luck as its firm ally. The navy had brilliant commanders, such as George Anson, and was about to enter its golden age. And Pitt did not have to cope with lingering Jacobite impulses.

Pitt was something of a new political phenomenon for he built up popular opinion outside the House. His ability to attract outside support was such that it was said of him that he was the first 'minister given by the people to the king', although the reality was the king reserved his right both to choose as well as dismiss and popular support proved all too often to be shifting sand. Henceforth that involvement of the world outside was not to diminish but grow, and any politician who ignored it did so at his peril. What was to be more sinister was that such forces could equally be cultivated by those whose aim was to destabilise existing society. And that was precisely what happened in the new reign. The unexpected death of George II on 25 October 1760 was to usher in a very different era.

During these decades of the rule of the élite, the Whig oligarchy, society began to change at a far quicker pace than ever before. Change had, of course, gone on since the sixteenth century but what was new about it in the eighteenth century was its accelerating rate. For the first time there was a sense of everyone living amidst the pressure of continuous change. And that is a feature which signals the arrival of the modern age.

In spite of this, on the surface much must have seemed unchanged. English society was still rural, with 75% of the population involved in the land. This was an era of contradictions for agriculture, for, on the one hand, it was passing through a long depression, and on the other, it was that very depression which provided the spur to innovation of a kind which was to set in motion after 1760 a new prosperity for farmers. Experimentation with new techniques had begun at the close of the previous century, but now it became far more widespread. Heroes like Jethro Tull and 'Turnip' Townshend are symbols of a general movement which developed new skills in land management, introduced new metal tools, experimented with crop rotation and new ways of fertilisation, and grew new crops. These moves forward were pioneered on the lighter soils of the south and east of the country which in the past had been given over to pasture farming but now, through the introduction of crop rotation, went over to mixed farming. The changes were aided by the sharp increase in enclosures. Enclosure not only doubled the value of the land but created far more compact farms, resulting in greater efficiency and a far better balance between arable and pasture farming. At the same time the rapid expansion of the urban population due to incipient industrialisation meant an ever-rising demand for foodstuffs, leading to regional specialisation: cheese and bacon from Gloucestershire, turkey and geese from East Anglia, hops and fruit from Kent and cider from the west country.

This was a period when the future industrial towns of the midlands and north rapidly took shape: Birmingham, Wolverhampton, Sheffield, Leeds, Manchester, Nottingham, Derby and Leicester. The Industrial Revolution lay ahead but by the 1780s the pattern of production was already there, with steel making, metalworking, the production of woollens, worsteds and cottons at the top, followed by hosiery, pottery, brewing, linen and silk. From the mid-1740s onward there was a steady small annual growth. Government firmly believed in non-intervention, seeking only to create the right conditions for expansion by freeing industry from the burdens of old-fashioned guild protectionism, internal tolls or class barriers. There was an intense interest in every form of technological innovation which would improve quality or productivity. A long series of inventions revolutionised the manufacture, above all, of textiles: John Kay's flying shuttle (1733) which increased the output of handloom weavers, James Hargreaves's spinning jenny (1768), Richard Arkwright's water frame (1769), and Samuel Crompton's mule (1779), all of which radically changed the processes of textile spinning. In 1769 James Watt patented a more energy efficient use of the steam engine. With all this dynamism, there soon emerged the men who made their fortunes from the new entrepreneurial spirit. Matthew Boulton built his Soho works just north of Birmingham. It employed five hundred men turning out a vast range of iron, bronze, copper, silver and tortoiseshell goods, using water-powered machinery. Richard Arkwright, a former barber with a sharp nose for invention and a gift for organisation, built textile mills to exploit his water frame in Derbyshire, Lancashire and Nottinghamshire. By the 1780s he was providing work for hundreds of people.

These developments called for a far more efficient transportation network to meet the demands of both passenger and freight traffic in what was a new consumer-oriented age. The roads had always been the responsibility of the parish, but before 1730 there were already a handful of what were called turnpike trusts. These took over a section of highway and maintained and improved it, but with access only by the payment of a fee, a toll. The four middle decades of the century witnessed this movement accelerate, effecting a communications revolution. The actual experience of travelling changed beyond recognition. In the 1720s it had taken over three days to

reach York or Exeter. By 1780 both could be journeyed to in twenty-four hours. Four years later the Royal Mail coach began offering a national postal service. And in the 1770s came canals, providing an alternative network for freight.

By 1760 the population was rising again. From 1660 to 1740 it had been static but then it suddenly began to go up sharply, reaching a peak in the last fifteen years of the century. This was the result of a whole complex of circumstances, increasing fertility, earlier marriages, the decline in the death rate and the absence of major epidemics. Cheaper and more plentiful food ensured a burgeoning population and one which was shifting across the country. The areas which benefited most were those of the future Industrial Revolution: the lowlands in Scotland, Yorkshire, Lancashire, and the midlands in England, and the north-east and south in Wales. More and more people lived in cities and towns. London, with half a million inhabitants, was the largest city in Western Europe. Expansion elsewhere reflected economic developments. Bristol, for instance, rose from 20,000 to 100,000 by 1760. Virtually new towns like Liverpool, Manchester and Birmingham rapidly acquired populations of between 20 and 50,000 while an old industrial centre like Norwich remained with only 20,000.

Visitors from the Continent much admired what they saw of British society. There was a degree of fluidity but the social structure as a whole remained hierarchical, male-dominated, heritable and dependent on deference. Everything from education to prevailing social attitudes reinforced the status quo. That is not to say that there was no room for movement up and down. The enterprising, intelligent and energetic could still climb upwards while those who were feckless or just unlucky slid down. Nothing was to shift the fundamental view that it was land and property which alone bestowed status. As a consequence, those who made their fortunes in either trade or commerce naturally purchased land, and along with it a position in established society.

At the top of the social pyramid stood the four hundred greatest landowners whose incomes were above £3,000 p.a. Half of these were gentry, for many gentlemen were richer than peers of the realm. Indeed the peerage increased in size very little under the first two Georges. Those who joined its ranks were from politics, the army and navy, and the law. No-one who belonged to the world of either industry or commerce received anything beyond a knighthood or a baronetcy. Together, this interconnected group of four hundred people dominated the political scene. They controlled the House of Lords through what were called 'pocket boroughs' where they were able to

Sir Richard Arkwright, the pioneer industrialist, sits with a set of cotton-spinning rollers on the polished table beside him. They not only made his fortune but transformed the industrial face of the country. The painter was Joseph Wright of Derby whose works record the early Industrial Revolution.

Commercial success brought untold riches. Sir Lawrence Dundas made a fortune as a merchant-contractor and as Commissary-General of the Army during the Seven Years' War. He became a baronet and had four splendid houses. Here he sits in the library of his London house designed by Robert Adam with furniture by Thomas Chippendale, the walls hung with some of his finest pictures. The heavy curtains and wall-to-wall carpeting catch the increasing comfort of upper class life.

control the few electors to do their bidding, thus ensuring that their younger sons sat in the Commons. Their income came not only from their estates but also from the fruits of office-holding, marrying rich heiresses, and profiting from rents from urban property. By 1780 this group of families had incomes of between £5,000 and £50,000 p.a., an 80% increase on the average peer's income in 1688. And, of course, they spent it. All over the country houses were rebuilt on a grand scale with forty rooms or more, the surrounding grounds being transformed into idyllic landscape parks. The lavish life-style was sustained by numerous servants. Monuments to conspicuous consumption, their position at the apex of society seemed unassailable.

The gentry class as a whole, of course, was far larger, some fifteen to twenty thousand of them, with incomes ranging between £200 to £3,000 p.a. According to their resources they aped the life-style of their superiors. Below them came some hundred to a hundred and fifty thousand freeholders with incomes of less than £100 p.a. These were men who were the backbone of parish administration acting as churchwardens, surveyors, overseers of the poor and constables. All of them shared in the increased general prosperity, enlarging and improving their houses. The landowning classes, in short, got richer, for there was as yet no such thing as a system of taxation which redistributed wealth within society.

The gentry overlapped with the strata below, 'the middling sort', for their younger sons made their way into the professions during the period in which that class doubled in size. They included people like attorneys, solicitors, surveyors, apothecaries, physicians and the services as well as, for example, those engaged in cultural occupations such as painters or musicians. The growing demand for professional help vividly reflected not only the advent of leisure but also the increasing complexity of day-to-day finance and administration. Professionals serviced a society which was more sophisticated, more status conscious, more comfort and amenity oriented, and more cultured than ever before. And the fees for such services could be huge. The 'middling sort' also embraced wealthy capitalists and small businessmen, people who invested their labour and profits in entrepreneurial activities. As a class they were obsessed by technological discovery, and all over the country clubs and societies sprang up dedicated to scientific advance and investigation. These were the classes whose approach to life was essentially practical and pragmatic. They had their own educational establishments outside the old-fashioned grammar schools and the slothful universities. With these people we touch Georgian society at its most dynamic.

Below all of these lay the remaining half of the population for whom not even political rights existed. They were viewed by those above them as illiterate rabble. And indeed illiteracy was rampant, particularly in the case of women and in the rural areas. This was a vast, varied, shifting and shiftless part of the population, made up of agricultural and industrial labourers, cottagers, domestic servants, ordinary soldiers and seamen, and the poor. Their conditions of life fluctuated widely but were often extremely primitive. The new mobility made possible through improved communications meant that the glaring gap between the rich and the poor was only too visible. For the lower classes life depended on their employers, and such work as they had could be temporary, seasonal or piece-work. It was inevitably subject to variations in the economy. Nonetheless until the middle of the century they too benefited from the general upward trend of the country's economic fortunes. After 1750 a steady rise in the cost of living began to threaten that, but in general diet, clothing and housing improved, and the boom meant ample work not only for men but for women and children too.

This was a society without a police force where fear of one kind or another was never far beneath the surface. The mass of the population was superstitious and prejudiced. Every so often the mob erupted and vent its wrath on unpopular groups: Roman Catholics, Jews and, above all, Dissenters and Methodists. This was accepted as a norm of life, but most riots were well-organised and well-behaved, reflecting the strong hold which deference had, as well as Christian reverence for authority. Only later in the century did the mob take on a face which began to alarm the upper classes and that was in the aftermath of the French Revolution, which violently swept away an aristocratic society. The mob then began to be viewed as dangerous, especially when under the influence of a demagogue, and increasingly the army began to be sent in.

With no police force, petty crime, and theft in particular, escalated in this first consumer society. There were simply more things to be stolen. Government fell back on extending the death penalty and transportation for more and more offences. Indeed by 1775 some 50,000 convicts had been shipped to America. After the thirteen American colonies were lost, a convict settlement was started in the new colony of Australia. But these penalties were self-defeating, for the number convicted was minimal compared with the number of cases tried.

For all its faults eighteenth century society was at heart deeply moral. The best-selling prints by the painter William Hogarth were dedicated to stories extolling virtue and condemning vice. It was a sturdily Protestant society whose common identity was still largely that forged in the reign of the first Elizabeth by such things held in common as the *Book of Common Prayer*, the *Authorised Version of the Bible* and festival days in commemoration of the monarchy: Oak Apple Day, 29 May, celebrating the

A scene from William Hogarth's moralising series of prints, *Industry and Idleness*, published in 1747, tracing the fate of two young apprentices, one idle and the other industrious. Here, in the opening scene, they are depicted at their looms, apprentice weavers in Spitalfields, the centre of the silk-weaving industry. Weavers worked in small, crowded surroundings often from twelve to sixteen hours a day.

restoration of Charles II; 1 August, which marked the Hanoverian succession; and 5 November, the Gunpowder Plot. The common reading was still Foxe's *Acts and Monuments*, casting the island's people as a new Israel, a vision celebrated in his oratorios by the great court composer, George Frederick Handel. Foreigners were still regarded with deep suspicion. Most, if not all, were Roman Catholics and that by definition cast them as enemies, a fact which was to be heightened by a hundred and thirty years of war on and off with France. That war, and the creation of an empire, were to be crucial in the gradual superimposition on to the two islands of the new identity of Great Britain. This was reflected during these decades by an ever-increasing emphasis on all things indigenous being the equal of any abroad. There was a new-found pride in every native achievement, which was to find for the first time institutional expression whether in the Society of Arts (1754), founded to encourage the 'Arts, Commerce and Manufactures of Great Britain' or the Royal Academy (1768), 'a Society for Promoting the Arts of Design'. It was an all-pervasive aura of optimism, confidence and achievement that was only to be brutally shattered by the American Revolution.

Chapter Forty-Eight

THE PURSUIT OF HAPPINESS

VIRTUALLY everyone benefited from being a citizen of the richest country, from the grandest duke to the humblest labourer. The wealth pouring in had to be spent and everywhere we look today we can see evidence of how that was done. In the country elegant houses arose, surrounded by gardens and parkland. In the towns stately squares and ordered terraces sprang up, as well as public buildings such as theatres and assembly rooms. Evidence of this wealth can also be studied in the abundance of surviving artifacts, far more than from the previous century: furniture and textiles, silver and porcelain, musical instruments and illustrated books. These form tangible evidence of a huge social revolution, for such things spoke not only of a desire for comfort but acted as status symbols for a burgeoning middle class, one which aped its betters and which subscribed to the aristocratic code of politeness as the element binding human behaviour. It was not just evidence of the country's first consumer society, but in addition, an expression of something else which was novel, leisure.

But it was leisure of a kind from which a tinge of guilt was never far absent. All forms of immorality, decadence and dissipation were, of course, firmly condemned. Money gained through hard work and enterprise should at least be seen to be spent on self-improvement. Happiness, which in the previous century had been sought primarily by man in his encounter with God and might be gained in heaven, was now found to embrace the study and the enjoyment of His creation on earth. The puritan ethic which had haunted Stuart England gave way to a joyous delight in social gatherings in coffee houses and clubs, at balls and concerts, lectures and theatres or race-meetings. This strong mutual delight in human company was not confined to the world outside but also embraced the one within. It animated the homes of the wealthy and better-off, where the husband's stern patriarchal attitude towards his wife and children was replaced by a celebration of the joys of family life captured in a new form of picture-making, the conversation piece. In such compositions the whole family across two, and sometimes three, generations come together, engaged in different aspects of the pursuit of happiness, reading, embroidering, music-making, sketching, riding, flying a kite or fishing.

All of this reflected another change. People were meeting each other across a far wider spectrum of the social hierarchy than ever before, something which happened first in London, where a season developed during the residence of the court and the sitting of Parliament, which had become annual. Members of the House of Lords and the Commons needed to be in the capital for several months of the year. They acquired town houses and brought their families with them. As a result a whole new pattern of social life emerged which engendered an abundance of new meeting places, from walking in the Mall to attending theatres.

People were more social than ever before and the promenade was one such form of gathering. In London the Mall was the great place to see and be seen. Here in the middle of the century are gathered soldiers, sailors, clergymen, milkmaids, as well as people of rank and fashion. A prominent group in the foreground centres on Frederick, Prince of Wales.

Outside London the same thing was to happen with the development of the spa, a place where people went to drink and immerse themselves in the waters for their health, to remedy the consequence of overeating and bad diet which led to skin disorders, and the cold, which resulted in chronic rheumatism. Bath quickly established itself under the aegis of 'Beau' Nash as the centre of fashion for the *beau monde*. No man dare appear wearing either boots or a sword in the splendid public rooms, nor lady wearing an apron; indeed Nash upbraided the Duchess of Queensberry for so doing by pulling at its strings. The balls and entertainments under his direction embodied a new sophistication in social life, duplicated all over the country in other spas, from Tunbridge Wells to Buxton. Later in the century the benefits of sea-bathing were discovered, and the south coast resorts of Brighton and Margate sprang to life. The future George IV, who built what he called a 'marine villa' at Brighton, attracted the whole of fashionable society. In this way the better-off of England met, gossiped, and amused themselves – and all in the name of 'improvement'.

This meant that people travelled as never before. At the beginning of the century one stage-coach a week would leave London for each of the major regional cities, such as York or Bristol. The journey would have been uncomfortable, slow and

Bath was the most fashionable of all the spas. Its elegance was owed to the developer and architect, John Wood, who saw his task to re-create the vanished Roman city. The King's Circus begun in 1754 owed its inspiration to a Roman amphitheatre and to Stonehenge, whose diameter it shares.

sometimes dangerous, not only on account of the state of the roads but also because of highwaymen. This situation changed dramatically in a revolution every bit as important as the arrival of the motor car. This was the revolution of the horse. Horses had been used for travel, industry and agricultural purposes for thousands of years, now they not only multiplied but careful breeding produced horses which had far greater strength and stamina. These drew coaches and carriages which were streamlined in their design, lighter and far more comfortable to ride in. By 1800 every town south of the Trent and east of the Severn could be reached in a day from London by regular services several times a week.

As a consequence travel, instead of being a reluctant necessity, joined the ranks of one of life's delights. Along the greatly improved road networks sped not only men and women of all sorts, but culture and fashion too: actors, musicians, painters and dancing masters, all disseminating different aspects of the newfound cult of leisure across the country.

Theatre attained a new status. Until the eighteenth century there were no theatres outside London. Plays had been acted before then in the great halls of manor houses, or in the town innyards. In 1705 the first purpose-built theatre outside London opened its doors in Bath, the forerunner of a building boom that swept the country. Soon no town of any size was without its theatre. Many, indeed, had several. In London the star system emerged with the two greatest actors of the age, David Garrick and Sarah Siddons. Garrick, through his genius

The theatre, another meeting place, underwent a renaissance. Covent Garden, depicted here by Thomas Rowlandson, and Drury Lane were the two most important London theatres. Entrepreneurs rebuilt theatres to increase audiences and hence profits. By the 1790s Covent Garden could seat 2,000. Rowlandson captures the riotous mix in an audience which includes, in the box next to the stage, George III and Queen Charlotte.

for public relations, lifted the status of both the theatre and the actor. The theatres were packed for opera, ballet, pantomime and plays; a combination of better communications and more theatres meant in addition that theatrical companies could, and did, tour.

The theatre was not the only new form of public building to mushroom. So too did assembly rooms, which enabled people to come together as never before and, by paying a subscription, dance or listen to concerts. Dancing, which had previously been the stately steps trod at court or the raffish romps of country folk, found a fresh outlet in gatherings where new measures, such as the minuet, provided a novel arena for social interplay and the marrying-off of daughters. The mass production of musical instruments and printed scores accelerated the spread of music-making as an accomplishment into vast numbers of households. Handel was the dominant composer of the age, with massed choirs singing his *Messiah* to packed audiences in the cathedrals. London became one of the musical capitals of Europe, one which both Mozart and Haydn thought it essential to visit. In the provinces music flourished, with festivals such as that of the Three Choirs, which rotated between Hereford, Worcester and Gloucester.

Reading called forth another new form of public building, the circulating library. Books had been the prerogative of the few, located in manor houses, the homes of clergy or scholars, or in the universities and schools. All that changed with the advent of the circulating library which began in London and in the fashionable spas. The demand for reading matter which could be borrowed and returned met the needs of a society bent on improving itself through the acquisition of knowledge. Children of the middle classes were expected to be able to read by the age of five or six and, for the first time, there was literature especially written for them, after which they were able to move on to a whole range of reading matter totally inaccessible in any general sense before. There were, for example, newspapers, for no provincial town was without its weekly paper, full of national and local news as well as advertisements of cultural events. And there was the novel, virtually a new genre which had all the excitement of being set in the time of the reader. Romance, horror, love and adventure opened their doors wide to whoever turned the pages of the works of such authors as Laurence Sterne, Samuel Richardson or Jane Austen.

There were those whose travels never took them beyond these voyages of the mind, but there were others for whom travel was a vivid reality. By the end of the century people were not only visiting spas but were also exploring their own country in what was virtually a discovery of England. In these journeys they came to express not only a delight in God's creation in their admiration of the world of nature, but also, increasingly, a sense of their own past. Both were viewed through eyes tinged with romance. Mountains, previously regarded as bleak obstacles, were now seen as evidence of the marvellous handiwork of God, awe-inspiring and humbling. Ruined monasteries, once looked upon as monuments to the vanished iniquity of popery and as handy quarries for stone, were now treasured as hallowed evidence of a heroic British past peopled by valiant knights and pale-faced heroines. Both inspired patriotic pride in the island. That was equally stirred by visits to factories like Josiah Wedgwood's at Etruria or Boulton and Watt's at Soho in Birmingham, where the visitors marvelled at all that was new in fashionable manufacture from vases to shoe buckles, from portrait medallions to steam engines. And all of it filled them with pride and fuelled their belief in Great Britain's glory.

That pride extended beyond their shores as the horses and coaches of the aristocracy bowled their way across the continental mainland. This was the age of what was called the Grand Tour, which no true member of the ruling élite could omit. First to France, starting off in a

Family life became a constant source of delight with the recognition of childhood as a separate period of life. Here we see the family of the great industrialist and potter, Josiah Wedgwood, in the grounds of Etruria Hall. One of his vases is proudly displayed on the table to his left. The painter was George Stubbs.

provincial town to learn what was the *lingua franca* of Europe, then to Paris to savour a refined luxury and elegance in living far exceeding anything at home. But the real mecca always remained Italy and Rome. All the paraphernalia we associate with modern tourism began to spring up: guide books, phrase books, maps and currency tables. Added to that, when the English milord reached Italy, there was no lack of guides, tutors and dealers to ensure that he missed none of the sights or any opportunity to purchase works of art to bring home. Although they toured and admired the achievements of Renaissance and baroque Italy their real attention was fixed firmly on one period, Imperial Rome.

That passion was the expression of a classically structured education, founded on a knowledge of the Greek and Roman classics. In England the élite sought to express the ideals they had read about and seen in the ruins of antiquity in what they built, and in remodelling the landscape around them. This was the golden age of the country house, seen as an antique classical villa but with every modern comfort. The country house building boom, which began with Petworth and Chatsworth in the 1680s, ran on through the decades changing the face of the countryside as aristocracy and gentry built and rebuilt their country seats in accordance with the new classical ideals. Such houses were to be monuments to civilised living with elegant reception rooms, libraries, picture galleries and studies. Nor were they closed fortresses, for they were open to be visited by members of the polite classes. And what excited such visitors most of all was everything that was new.

These houses confirmed that the English upper classes were still firmly rooted in the country, and in that they differed from their peers on the Continent, whose prime role was attendance at court. The fierce game laws were an expression of the cult of country life, epitomised by the obsession for field sports. Shooting and the newly invented fox-hunting became the life-blood of the land-owning classes, sports made the more exhilarating by improvements in gun-making so that it became possible to shoot birds on the wing, and by enclosure, which introduced hedges for the first time, so that horse and rider had to jump them in the chase.

Most other sports were not so socially divisive. Archery, bowls, boxing and horse-racing drew together the entire social spectrum. By 1700 Newmarket, Doncaster, York, Epsom and Ascot had emerged as premier race courses. Soon the whole apparatus of the sport was in place, from the Jockey Club to great classic races such as the Derby. Horses like the famous Eclipse became stars, and racing developed as mass entertainment on the grand scale.

This was a gregarious, free-ranging society unlike any other in Europe at the time. The abolition of the censorship laws opened up a vein of biting social and political satire which cut through every class and was utterly unique. And, for the first time, it was a society which produced great visual art in quantities. England which had been on the fringes of the great movements of the Renaissance and the baroque, now moved centre stage and by 1800 was to set the pace in new styles like the neo-classical and the romantic, which were to sweep Europe. Architects such as William Kent, Sir William Chambers and the Adam brothers, and painters like Hogarth, Gainsborough, Reynolds and Stubbs, acquired international reputations. They stand as monuments to the fact that art is not only a question of talent but also a response to consumer demand.

This was an urban civilisation whose activities were town-based. The old Tudor and Stuart towns with their narrow streets, cramped and higgledy-piggledy houses of timber, lath and plaster, were replaced by ones whose foremost distinguishing attributes were order, symmetry and space. They were built now of brick, stone, ashlar, tile and slate and were constructed in rows, squares and crescents with matching façades, doorways and sash windows. Piped water and drainage were introduced. Inside the rooms were airy and spacious, linked by passages and staircases. Their exterior appearance was graded to reflect the status of the owner, and they were articulated by wide streets with proper paving and lighting leading to public squares or buildings. Great local pride was taken in the construction of public buildings such as halls, churches, town halls, bridges and gaols. In addition, public parks and walks were made, where residents could stroll or ride. Some even emulated London with pleasure gardens like Vauxhall, which provided a venue for theatricals, music, dining out, balls and spectacles such as firework displays. As a consequence gentry families regularly moved into their local towns for what was the winter season, whose focus was a programme of events in the assembly rooms.

Leisure was to be a new force binding society together, for virtually every aspect was shared by all classes, whether making up a theatre audience or the crowd at a race. Happiness was seen to be found on earth as well as in heaven and everywhere life assumed a new radiance. Mind, heart and body were exercised to the full through a range of activities and artifacts hitherto unknown, or restricted only to the privileged few. There were still those, more than half the population, whose life remained one of unremitting toil in poor conditions. Their time had not yet come. But for those whose purse was full, life was an adventure to savour with new experiences at every turn, from indulgence in the latest fashion to ballooning. And savour it the Georgians did, with all their might.

Chapter Forty-Nine

REASON
AND ENTHUSIASM

ONE May evening in the year 1738 a young clergyman called John Wesley attended a meeting of committed Anglicans in Aldergate Street in the City of London. During a reading from the works of the great German reformer, Martin Luther, something extraordinary happened to him:

> '. . . about a quarter before nine, while he was describing the changes God works in the heart through faith in Christ, I felt my heart strangely warmed. I felt I did trust in Christ, Christ alone for salvation; and an assurance was given me that he had taken away my sins, even mine . . . '

In these words Wesley was describing the event which was to change his life, and that of the thousands of others the length and breadth of the country who were to find in the evangelical Christianity he and his followers taught a form of faith for which the established church was to have no place. The key word is 'felt' for, as the Archbishop of Canterbury conceded a decade later, the Church of England had 'lost its power over the heart.'

The church had entered the century diminished and embattled. With the new system of patronage firmly in place, Sir Robert Walpole did not scruple to fill ecclesiastical positions with his own nominees, all of them good Whigs. It did not necessarily follow that there were not good clerics among them, nor that poor men could no longer rise within its ranks, but the general drift was a prolonged, rapid and disastrous decline, which was to continue into the early nineteenth century. By 1801 the number of communicants at Easter had sunk to only a tenth of the population. Most facets of the eighteenth century were not likely to encourage the Church of England to arise from its spiritual torpor. The new prosperity in agriculture meant that the clerical tithes increased substantially, making livings for the first time attractive to candidates from the landed élite, and offering comfortable positions for younger sons whose elder brothers lived in the nearby manor house. As a result more and more clergy came from the gentry, and even from the aristocratic classes, leading to a greater social distancing from their parishioners. Many served their parishes well, but their response was essentially to the spiritual needs of the upper and middle classes, who looked at the world around them through the eyes of Newton, and had no place for a highly emotional religious response of the kind Wesley underwent. For them Reason ruled all. They expected their clergy to preach what amounted to a 'natural religion' in which divine revelation and miracles had a minimum place, and which focused instead on praising God the Creator as manifested in his many works. Nor were over-pious clergy welcomed in a carefree, theatre-going and card-playing society.

This was a church coming to terms with an unprecedented attack on its fundamental beliefs. It had lost the intellectual lead and was faced by headlong attacks which either undermined or rejected outright the established tenets of the Christian faith. Instead of launching a counter-offensive the Anglican church bowed before the wind and, as a result, was left in an increasing state of disarray in the face of a tide of rational and scientific scepticism. One cleric, Richard Bentley, caught the atmosphere, even if he wildly exaggerated it, when he stated that some of the clergy went so far as to believe 'that the soul is material, Christianity a cheat, Scripture a falsehood, hell a fable, heaven a dream, our life without providence, our death without hope – such are the items of the glorious gospel of those evangelists.'

Restraint, decency and seemliness were the watchwords of eighteenth century Christianity. Above all, the conventions and etiquette of polite society had no place for what they labelled 'enthusiasm', that is, any excessive form of religious piety, zeal or mysticism, all of which they dismissed as cranky and irreconcilable with Reason. And yet such a direct message to the hearts of men was to be the only way that faith was to be taken to the teeming masses of the burgeoning industrial towns and cities. The church itself had simply failed to build enough churches in these areas, let alone adjust a parish system which was medieval, bearing little if any relation to the increasing shifts in population. No wonder Wesley was to believe that 'God began His great work in England' that May evening in 1738.

But Wesley was not alone, nor was he the first, for even that meeting reflected that groups of members of the Church of England who were deeply committed to their faith were already in existence. Wesley was to be the outstanding figure among many who devoted their lives to the cause of evangelism. He himself was the son of a cleric and followed his father into the church. What was later to be labelled Methodism went back to his Oxford days when he was one of a group who formed the Holy Club. Another member was George Whitefield, also later to become famous as a preacher. In retrospect Wesley was to define Methodism as 'one that lives according to the method laid down in the Bible.' Wesley, who was deeply conservative both socially and politically, had little time for 'enthusiasm'. But he could not escape the label, for his message of salvation often produced exactly that response in his audiences. It stemmed from his own conversion experience which was based on a rediscovery of the sixteenth century reformers' belief in justification by faith alone, whereas most clergy preached a mixture of faith with good works as necessary to salvation.

This portrait of George Whitefield in the pulpit with a glimpse of members of the congregation gives an impression of his histrionic genius in action. He preached over eighteen thousand sermons during his lifetime.

For those converted in this way it was an act of revelation, producing an intensity of faith poles away from that which was disseminated in the average pulpit. The message brought by Wesley and Whitefield found no welcome with the church and so they took to preaching to vast congregations in the open air. Wesley's message was aimed at vanquishing sin and not social deprivation. It spoke to the heart rather than appealed to the intellect. And, as a consequence, fell on fallow ground in the case of the upper classes, reaping its harvest amongst the labouring poor and artisans in the newly industrialised towns and their environs. All through his life Wesley remained a member of the established church and, as he refused to take a living, was able to travel on horseback some two hundred and fifty thousand miles throughout the country, an average of eight thousand miles a year. Everywhere he went he left behind him an organisation, and these gradually formed a nation-wide network of people who committed themselves to what was an exemplary life dedicated to piety, hard work and private morality. These groups supported by subscription those who administered to them, and went on to build chapels in which to worship. Finding few clerics who would join him, Wesley proceeded to appoint lay preachers to officiate, and eventually ordained some for missionary work abroad. That action signalled the parting of the ways with the established church which was to follow Wesley's death in 1791.

Already in 1779 the standing of the lay preachers was called into question with the result that Methodist chapels were forced to obtain licences in the same way as the meeting houses of Dissenters. Both the church and society at large had their ways of freezing out enthusiasts. Laity who were attracted were ostracised. Those who sought ordination and showed any signs of Methodism were blocked. Polite society and the established church viewed Methodism with grave misgivings as a potentially subversive social force. It came under suspicion not only because it appealed to urban artisans and the workers, but also because it went on to organise them and give them voice, albeit as preachers. Methodism accorded women a role, and that was also regarded as threatening to the status quo. All of this evoked deep mistrust that the existing hierarchy of society was potentially being undermined. The self-denying lives of both the Methodist clergy and their preachers were living reprimands to a church which had become a monument to the cult of property in the form of tithes, sinecures, pluralism and lay patronage. Worse, their very existence exposed the lack of spiritual leadership of many of the clergy.

But Methodism was rent from early on by internal discord amongst its leaders. The most prominent was Selina, Countess of Huntingdon, who joined Wesley in 1739 and devoted her life to taking the cause to the upper classes. This she did by building her own chapels and staffing them with her own chaplains. When Wesley and Whitefield eventually fell out over issues of doctrine, she sided with the latter. By the time of Wesley's death, Methodism had slipped away

An early 19th century apotheosis of John Wesley who is seen preaching in the pulpit with George Whitefield below. The setting is the City Road Chapel in London and the portraits of 449 Methodist ministers stretching down to the 1820s form the congregation.

from the Church of England and was ordaining its own ministers and running an organisation which now had societies throughout what had become the United States. But the percentage of the population who became Methodists in Britain was minute, though their message reached out to many more. In 1776 their numbers totalled just thirty thousand. Nonetheless these embodied spiritual vitality in a century which was largely devoid of it.

The evangelical revival flew in the face of everything which the Age of Reason stood for. But Christianity was not alone in being ironed-out in an effort to remove or rationally explain away anything which might be regarded as inexplicable in the light of Reason. Witchcraft and superstition were subjected to exactly the same treatment. In 1736 the Witchcraft Act was repealed, bringing an end to what in the previous century had been horrendous persecutions. To any man of reason witchcraft was an aberration, a primitive survival from a darker age which, under the impact of education and economic advance, would simply vanish. The fact that this failed to happen remained as an irritant to the educated classes. The web of folklore belief and popular superstition which made up much of the minds of most ordinary country folk also refused to vanish. All of it lived on.

So, of course, did the Church of England. It was, after all, a powerful arm of the state and whatever its inertia the parish system was part of the lives of the majority of people in Georgian England. For nearly everyone came within the orbit of a white-clad cleric who baptised, married and buried them. The organisational structure of the Church of England survived intact, awaiting the renaissance that was to come in the Victorian age.

Chapter Fifty

PARADISE REGAINED: 'CAPABILITY' BROWN

THE countryside we see today was the creation of the Georgian age, the consequence of the twin pursuit of profit and pleasure: profit through new farming methods and pleasure through remodelling the landscape to give delight. This was the first time that men of wealth and position chose to express their status, power and influence by reshaping the fabric of the countryside on a huge scale. That this could be done was not only due to the vast wealth of the country in the aftermath of the Seven Years' War but also to the fact that most of the land was concentrated in large estates. The owners of these were the same men who either sat in the Commons or knew people who did, and so were able to get bills passed sanctioning enclosure, for that was often the necessary preface both to the new farming techniques and to the creation of a great landscape garden. And Parliament passed such acts by the thousand between 1750 and 1820, dramatically changing the visual appearance of the countryside.

It was change from the top, and imposed a pattern of rural society which only disintegrated in the present century, the focus of which was the great house whose purpose by the eighteenth century had considerably changed from earlier times. In the Middle Ages it had acted as the local community centre where lords of the manor entertained their tenants and where justice was rendered. It was also the administrative powerhouse of the locality. As the royal court and Parliament rose more and more to prominence from the sixteenth century onwards the function of such houses gradually changed. They were now built above all to impress others of the same class in an age when, because of easier travel, the country house visit had become a norm of upper class social life. The houses were now designed with suites of rooms in which to receive the royal family and in which to entertain their peers in splendour. Instead of living and sleeping cheek by jowl with members of the family as they had done in the past, the servants were now relegated to separate areas of the house. Even in farmhouses servants ceased to live in, and were assigned cottages close by.

The engaging face of 'Capability' Brown caught at the height of his career in 1768.

Around the great house spread parkland, an entirely artificial landscape designed to insulate the inmates from the world beyond. To achieve such elysiums often meant demolishing and moving whole villages. At the very least the humble cottages of the labouring poor had trellis and climbing plants added to them by the lord of the manor to render them suitably pretty as he and his guests rode by. Beyond the park stretched the farmland from which the old medieval strip system of cultivation finally vanished, to be replaced by the new rectangular fields enclosed by hedges or walls. As a result of this change the tenant farmers could adopt the new crop rotation systems. Those who lost out were the poorest, who now no longer had access even to common land to help eke out their meagre existence.

Such were the social realities which provided the backcloth to a revolutionary garden style, one which originated in England and was to cross not only the mainland of Europe but also travel to America.

Expressions of wealth and status such parks may have been but they were also profound statements by the owners as to how they viewed the world of nature around them. And this represented a reversal of the centuries-old belief that the natural world was the consequence of man's sin when he gave in to temptation in the Garden of Eden. Before that God had ordered nature in perfect harmony with the trees, for example, growing in ordered geometric patterns, the fruits of the earth being given spontaneously, and the animals tame. As a result of the Fall and man's transgression all that changed. Man toiled instead in the face of a hostile nature made up of impenetrable forests filled with dangerous wild beasts and with threatening mountains barring his passage. Only in the creation of a garden could man reorder nature in accordance with the Divine Will.

So the earliest gardens were divided up into geometric shapes: squares, circles and rectangles reflecting God's structure of the universe. From this arose the era of the formal garden which reached its apogee in Louis XIV's Versailles, where a vast network of canals, parterres, ponds, fountains, avenues and bosquets formed a grid which radiated out from the palace. This was the style which was taken up in England in the second half of the seventeenth century when huge gardens were carved out of the landscape, spreading out from the mansion in an elaborate series of contrasting enclosures.

That all of these were to be swept away was due not only to a change in fashion but to a rejection of the old view of nature. The one which replaced it was, however, just as artificial, for it was landscape as depicted in the poetry of classical antiquity, an arcadia inhabited by contented shepherds and shepherdesses tending their flocks in leafy glades with glimpses of temples to the pagan gods in the distance. Even more it was that vision as painters had recreated it, above all the great French artist Claude Lorraine whose landscapes were collected by the aristocracy. The desire to remodel their parks as a realisation of what they saw in these pictures accorded well with men whose education was classical and, even more, who shared a new common cultural experience, the Grand Tour. They wished to evoke on their own estates reminiscences of the Roman ruins they had seen in Italy.

Gradually the gardens of the previous century were seen as aberrations. Stiff lines gave way to serpentine ones and a cult of the wiggly walk set in. The country beyond the garden and park was no longer viewed as wild and savage. Vistas began to be opened up into it, and the line between the park around the house and what lay beyond was blurred by the invention of the ha-ha, a dry ditch with a retaining wall

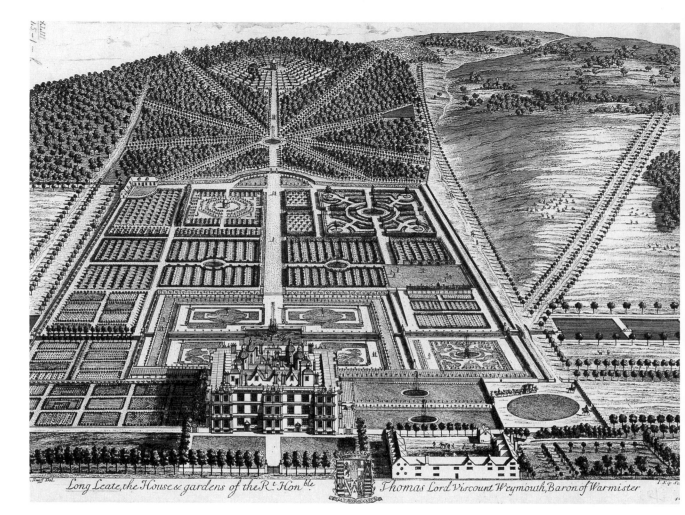

Long Leate, the House & gardens of the Rt. Honble ... Thomas Lord Viscount Weymouth, Baron of Warmister

Longleat House, Wiltshire was one of the great formal gardens of the late 17th century laid out by George London and Henry Wise in a style which looked to Louis XIV's Versailles. It is superimposed on and cut out of the surrounding landscape. This was the garden 'Capability' Brown was to sweep away.

which kept the cattle at bay but allowed the eye to run on from the park into the landscape beyond. Joseph Addison, the great writer, captured this change in an article he wrote for the magazine, the *Spectator*:

> ' . . . Fields of Corn make a pleasant Prospect; and . . . if the natural Embroidery of the Meadows were help'd and improv'd by some small Additions of Art . . . a Man might make a pretty Landscape of his own Possession.'

And this indeed is what happened.

Brown began working at Longleat in 1757 creating one of his most famous landscapes which remains to this day. Some idea of the scale of the operation can be gauged by the number of trees planted. During the 1770s between 35 to 90,000 trees a year were put in.

William Kent was the first major figure in this revolution and his most famous garden, Rousham, near Oxford, laid out around 1740, still survives. In a space defined by the river Cherwell and an estate boundary road areas were created, evoking those described by the classical poets – a valley, for instance, was laid out as the Elysian Fields and the Vale of Venus was filled with loose groves of trees, and allusions to ancient splendour in a rustic cascade. Views to the countryside around were opened up and embellished, one, for example, having a distant cottage transformed into a

William Kent's design for the
Vale of Venus at Rousham,
Oxfordshire. Rousham was one
of the earliest of the gardens in
the new landscape style designed
to evoke the arcady of the
classical world. Elegant figures
parade in, and contemplate, their
dreamworld brought to life, a
mixture of what they had seen in
paintings and what they had
experienced in Italy in reality.

Gothic mill. In such a garden the owner could stroll with his guests through scenes in which the beauties of nature had been rearranged and adorned to excite the imagination with reveries of classical antiquity and, by association, link that lost splendour with the present glories of their own country.

The greatest creator of such gardens was to be Lancelot Brown who was born in the remote hamlet of Kirkhole in Northumberland in 1716, ostensibly one of the five children of a poor family. What set him apart from the other children was that he was educated to the age of sixteen, an indication that he was probably the illegitimate son of Sir William Loraine, the local landowner, into whose service he entered immediately after his schooling. The Loraines were creating a garden in the new natural style and Brown, already proving a talented lad, became deeply involved in its planning. These early years remained wrapped in mystery and we have to assume that he was self-taught.

When he was twenty-three Brown went south via Lady Loraine's relatives and created his first garden in Kiddington in Oxfordshire. That early work already contained the essential elements of his style. He then moved on to work for Lord Cobham, one of the grandest of Whig magnates, whose garden at Stowe in Buckinghamshire was one of the greatest of the age. Brown worked there for eight years learning his craft, including inventing a tree-moving machine which could uproot and shift specimens twenty-five to thirty feet high, which meant that he could provide his patrons with instant clumps of trees. Already he began to be lent out to friends to landscape their parks and his new found status is reflected in the accounts when he suddenly began to be referred to as 'Mr'.

In 1751 he set up on his own in Hammersmith and so successful was he that thirteen years later he became royal gardener and moved to a house at Hampton Court. During a career lasting thirty-five years he landscaped about a hundred parks and made a fortune, buying a manor house and setting up as a country gentleman. He became High Sheriff of the county and sent his son to Eton. He worked not only for the king but for dukes and scores of lords. In the first half of the 1760s he was at the height of his powers. About 1760 he started Chatsworth, Ashridge and Alnwick, the year after Bowood, in 1764 followed Blenheim, Luton Hoo and Richmond Palace. To grasp the enormity of what he undertook it is only necessary to reflect that the park at Blenheim alone, his masterpiece, was over three thousand acres.

His routine was always the same. First he would visit a place, charging ten guineas a day, to determine the outlines of a scheme. He would walk around with a surveyor and a draughtsman who noted down and produced drawings of everything that was to be done. These visits were so brief and to the point that he was nicknamed

'Capability'. Brown, however, had a genius for choosing people, for he relied on a series of foremen who carried through the work on site.

This could be on a mind-boggling scale involving, if need be, rebuilding the house. His style was different from Kent's, and he had no time for classical temples and fake ruins. The formula he evolved never changed. He always created a great lake or what seemed to be a winding river by damming or diverting water, designed in such a way that the source was concealed by a bridge or a cascade suggesting that the water went on beyond. Lawns swept down to the water's edge from an undulating terrain, manufactured if need be by moving tons of earth. Clumps of trees were then carefully dotted around, different varieties ensuring contrasts of colour through the seasons. These were skilfully placed in order to frame calculated views both towards the house, the focal point of the composition, and also from it. Particular attention was paid to the approach drive, so that the visitor would glimpse the mansion from afar in a series of carefully arranged pictures. The whole park was then encompassed by a thick belt of trees through which a carriage drive wended its way so that the owner could take his guests to view the beauties of the nature he had perfected.

For twenty years Brown triumphed spawning a host of imitators and then, in the 1770s, he began to be attacked. Taste changed, his work was seen as 'desolate' and, worse, people began to appreciate the countryside as it was and were horrified at Brown's manipulation of it. In the 1780s William Cowper, the poet, summed up the shift:

> Improvement, the idol of the age,
> Is fed with many a victim. Lo! he comes,
> The omnipotent magician, Brown, appears . . .
> He speaks. The lake in front becomes a lawn,
> Woods vanish, hills subside, and vallies rise,
> And streams, as if created for his use,
> Pursue the track of his directing wand . . .

But the style 'Capability' Brown represented was to cross Europe, sweeping away the formal gardens of earlier times in favour of *le jardin anglais*. First to France, then down into Italy and across Germany and on into Russia. Brown's work epitomises the apogee of one of the few art forms whose origins were wholly English.

Chapter Fifty-One

DISINTEGRATION AND DEFEAT

A twenty-four year old young man came to the throne in 1760, the deceased king's grandson, George III. Although Hanoverian in appearance, with protruding eyes and weighty lower jaw, he regarded himself foremost as king of Great Britain rather than as Elector of Hanover. When he met his first Privy Council he referred to 'this my native country'. Unlike his predecessors he hated Hanover, and had grown up and been educated in England speaking English as his first language. In this he formed a marked contrast to his forebears, nor was that all, for he was a pious Anglican and a devoted husband. He began his reign with an idealism which made him ill-equipped to cope with the tough realities of political life. Worse, he inherited a man he hated as chief minister, William Pitt.

George III was dominated by a proud and pompous Scot, Lord Bute, who was renowned more than anything else for his handsome legs. Politically he was a disaster. The king's ambition was to make a clean sweep at his accession, allowing Bute to advance to the highest office. George had been brought up to believe that both his grandfather and great-grandfather had been reduced to ciphers by members of the Whig oligarchy, which had dominated the political scene for four decades. The fact that this was untrue did not eradicate it as a belief from the king's mind. When George came to the throne everyone longed for peace. Pitt, believing, as it turned out correctly, that France and Spain were about to sign an offensive alliance, wished instead to pre-empt this by declaring war on Spain. No one would support him so Pitt resigned in October and the king was at last rid of him.

The following year, war was indeed declared against Spain, one which went triumphantly, for the British took Martinique, Grenada, St. Lucia and St. Vincent. Bute, who was no war minister, panicked, and began negotiations for peace with France. The old Duke of Newcastle resigned over the abandonment of the alliance with Prussia, thus enabling the king to promote Bute to the summit as First Lord of the Treasury. But it was done at the huge cost of losing from the government the key figure in the long decades of Old Corps Whig rule. Newcastle was the focus of the vast network of Whig families and their connections which had been crucial to the working of any administration. For the first time since George I they found themselves fallen from power.

On 10 February 1763 the Treaty of Paris was signed in which Britain gained a vast expansion of empire at the expense of the French: the whole of Canada, Louisiana east of the Mississippi, Cape Breton and the Islands in the St. Lawrence, Tobago, Dominica, St. Vincent, the Grenadines, Senegal and Florida. This mighty triumph, whereby Britain now ruled the greatest empire since the Roman, was to prove the prelude to tragedy. And this began firstly at home, where politics entered a period of remarkable instability.

Much of the fault for that can be laid at the door of George III. His two predecessors had been shrewd enough in the main to stick with ministers who enjoyed long periods of office and who, with the aid of the old Duke of Newcastle, could work the Whig connection and sustain a majority in the Commons. That had already broken down in 1754. By the 1760s Newcastle was old and Pitt, at best, increasingly unreliable. The old framework had disintegrated so that George was to spend a decade attempting to find a minister of his own liking with whom he could work and, in turn, could command a majority in the Lower House. The resignation of the Whig oligarchs was to contribute to the emergence of an opposition party, at precisely the moment when the old one had died. The demise of the Tories began with the eclipse of the Jacobite cause, but how deep their commitment was remains open to question. Their loyalty had been transferred to the king's father, Frederick, Prince of Wales, but he also died. During the Seven Years' War the Tories had changed their stance so much that they even supported the Whig government, eroding their political identity even further. It virtually vanished entirely in 1760, when the new king appointed several Tories to positions at court and in the government. Moreover, they found in their new monarch precisely the ideals which the Tories had enshrined as their deepest principles, conservative Anglicanism and a deep reverence for established order.

The Old Corps of Whigs for all those decades had been held together by their efforts to keep the Tories out. Fallen from power, they disintegrated, and dissolved into a series of constantly shifting alliances of different groups of politicians held together around this or that leader, such as the Duke of Bedford or the Marquess of Rockingham. The result was inevitably cha-

The British monarch remains to this day Commander-in-Chief of the Army. George III took the position seriously and retained command of the American War until 1778. The portrait commemorates the summer of 1779 in which the king played an active role in meeting a threatened invasion from France.

otic as one administration succeeded another. Bute was quickly found to be a man of straw. Then came George Grenville who was an arrogant bully, followed by the Marquess of Rockingham who barely tried. Finally there was the Duke of Grafton, who was more interested in his race horses than running the government. When the king was at last driven to approach the one man he hated, Pitt, that administration collapsed through the minister's megalomania. None of this constantly shifting kaleidoscope of politicians jostling for power made for firm policy at the top, precisely what was needed as the country slowly drifted towards a major catastrophe which resulted in the loss of its North American colonies.

By the time that the Treaty of Paris was signed there were thirteen American colonies. Some had been founded over a century before, others were more recent, all of them established by royal charter. Since the reign of William III they had become answerable in practice to Parliament. Although the colonies varied widely in their system of government, in their religious preferences and in their social structure (with the differences especially marked between those in the cold north and those in the warm south), they were to all intents and purposes composed of British people who happened to have settled abroad, people who dressed and looked like anyone else in eighteenth century England, who spoke English, read books printed in London, purchased British goods and in their own artifacts imitated from afar the styles and fashions of the mother country. The vast majority of them were stoutly Protestant, for dissent from the religious situation at home had led their ancestors to emigrate in the first place. Unlike England where only a tenth of the population was dissenting, in the colonies the percentage rose to three-quarters.

In retrospect it was to prove unfortunate that no one in England had given much thought to the long-term consequences of the creation of these colonies. Each had its own locally elected assembly and crown appointed governor who was paid by the colonists but was in the last event answerable to a government which was answerable to Parliament. The administrative hold of England was therefore slender, and devoid of any formal structure which included Parliament. No immediate problems arose, because England for most of the previous century had been caught up in its own domestic crises and subsequent to that with the war against Louis XIV. During his time in office, Walpole had shown no interest in the colonies either, but by the middle of the eighteenth century the situation changed, prompted by the acquisition of Canada in 1763 from the French. In one way that removed any threat of invasion from the north but it drew attention sharply to the huge cost of defending the North American colonies during the Seven Years' War, colonies, moreover, which were known to have traded with the enemy. That had been paid for by the British tax-paying gentry classes who increasingly began to feel that the colonists should at least contribute something towards their own defence. The colonists did not share that view, arguing that as they were not represented in Parliament it had no right to impose taxes on them. Parliament, for its part, did not regard the colonists as being any different in status from the majority of the population in England, who also had no right to vote but nonetheless paid taxes as Parliament decreed.

So the scene was set for the blue touch-paper to be ignited which was slowly to smoulder and then erupt into a war and the loss of the colonies. After the peace with France, ten thousand troops were stationed in North America to defend the colonies and in 1765 Parliament decided to impose the first ever direct internal tax to help meet the cost of this. The amount levied only came to a twenty-fifth of the cost but that was beside the point. The colonial assemblies complained bitterly and there were riots in Boston. The local militia refused to put them down as they would be suppressing their own kind. Across the Atlantic Parliament saw its sovereignty being challenged by a people they viewed as little more than insolent rebels.

The colonial assemblies, finding their authority as they saw it threatened, met in the autumn in New York and declared that the British Parliament had no right to impose taxes on them: 'No taxation without representation.' The Stamp Act had succeeded in bringing to the centre of the stage a reality, that these colonial assemblies had managed until then to govern two and a half million people with a very large measure of independence from the homeland, something which they now had no intention of relinquishing. There was no sympathy, however, in Parliament for this viewpoint, although the unrest the Stamp Act had unleashed eventually forced its repeal. This was accompanied by the Declaratory Act which firmly asserted Parliament's right to legislate for the colonies. There was no gratitude for the repeal;

Benjamin Franklin, a prominent American scientist and politician (who invented the lightning conductor) was sent to England to lobby Parliament about the colonists' tax grievances. Franklin's attack on the Stamp Act, a bloody image in which Britannia's severed limbs represent the loss of her American colonies if the Act is imposed. The result would be to damage trade, indicated by the ships up for sale with brooms tied to their masts.

indeed the colonists now forcefully pressed for the right to govern themselves and began to reject parliamentary legislation. Parliament found itself still left with the problem of finding a means whereby the colonists could be taxed externally to contribute towards their own defence. The solution found was to introduce customs tariffs on paper, paint, glass, lead and tea.

In the colonies this was met by a boycott of British goods which the colonial assemblies believed would apply the necessary pressure on the home economy. Patriotic groups of objectors were formed, such as the Massachusetts Association. In January 1768 Massachusetts petitioned Parliament on the grounds of 'no taxation without representation'. In England attitudes hardened sharply, and an order was issued for the dissolution of the Association. Two regiments were sent to impose order. In October, Boston banned British imports, a ban which spread throughout the thirteen colonies. In May of the following year the British Cabinet was again forced to climb down and suspended all the tariffs, except that on tea.

And it was precisely at that point, after a decade of constantly shifting alliances and changing ministries, that the king found his equivalent of Walpole. Frederick North, Lord North, as heir to an earldom, sat in the Commons. Physically he was devoid of any attraction whatsoever, with pop eyes protruding from a swollen face atop an unwieldy body. Remarkably able and with an abundance of tact, he was also blessed with a brilliant wit and an aura of benevolence. Not for nothing were members wary of a man who seemed to slumber on the front benches only to 'awake' in time to trounce his opponent. From the king's point of view he had found a minister with whom he could work and who was able to sustain a majority in the Commons. Within a short time North attracted enough support from various groups to be able to carry the day. The truth was that he was destined to preside over the most catastrophic retreat by Britain until the years 1939 to 1979.

Worse still, the king's obsession with North contributed to the emergence for the first time of something vaguely resembling an opposition party. That found its focus in the Marquess of Rockingham and hence was known as the 'Rockingham Whigs'. Rockingham attracted intense loyalty and drew much support from members of the old Whig families who had enjoyed power earlier in the century. They also had a genius as their propagandist, Edmund Burke, who defined this nascent political 'party' as 'a body of men united for promoting by their joint endeavours the national interest upon some particular principle in which they are all agreed.' Their main contention was novel. In the past those who opposed the crown did so on the basis that the monarch needed to be rescued from the clutches of corrupt and evil counsellors. The Rockingham Whigs argued that it was the councillors who were being corrupted by the king and the court influence. They had to be removed and the king forced to submit to a policy change. In the plight of the colonists the Rockingham Whigs found a cause with which they could identify, and in adopting it they split the nation in two.

George III was personally in favour of modifying the Stamp Act and only later hardened his attitude to the colonists, but from the outset he saw it as his duty to defend the rights of Parliament. Everything on both sides of the Atlantic was in place for combustion. On 16 December 1773 the Massachusetts patriots dumped three hundred and forty chests of East India Company tea into the Boston harbour, an act known to posterity as 'The Boston Tea Party'. The effect in England was dramatic. The Boston Port Act ordered the closure of the port until the Company was compensated for its loss. Worse, the colony charter was revoked, its assembly dissolved and all rights of appointment, except for judges of the supreme court, were vested in the governor. The colony saw its freedom taken away by what they regarded as an arbitrary tyrannical power.

Their fear of what that could lead to was fuelled further by the Quebec Act, which set up a form of government for the newly acquired Canada that was to consist of a governor and a council appointed directly from Britain. Amongst its provisions was one which gave religious toleration to Roman Catholics. The colonists, the vast majority of them Dissenters, read this in the light of James II's bid for absolute rule and the restoration of England to Rome. Canada was viewed as an opening move in the imposition of a popish despotism on the thirteen colonies. In the autumn of 1774 representatives of the colonists met at a Continental Congress in Philadelphia and demanded the repeal of all legislation since 1763. An attempt to reach an accommodation with the British Parliament was defeated and the radicals took over. What were called the Suffolk Resolves were enacted, which withheld the payment of all taxes until Massachussetts had its charter re-instated. A Continental Association was formed, dedicated to the non-importation and non-consumption of British goods.

On 18 April 1775 the first shots were fired at Lexington and Concord, creating what were to be hailed as the first 'martyrs' in the cause of American freedom. The rebels were not without their sympathisers at home amongst those who sought reform. It was to take a year, however, before there was a reaction to the outbreak of what was in fact a civil war, in which each side was to depict the other as callous and cruel, much in the same way as they had in the English civil war. The British inertia worked in favour of the rebels who swiftly turned their militias into a citizen army. There was an inconclusive battle at Bunker Hill in which the British losses were huge, and General Howe, the commander, was subsequently forced to pull out of Boston.

On 24 August, George III issued a Proclamation of Rebellion but he was saddled with a minister, Lord North, who, like Walpole before him, could not handle a war. The British response was slow and disorganised, sending eventually 23,000 German mercenaries, then five Irish regiments and finally troops from Gibraltar and Minorca. But it was all too little, too late, and on 4 July 1776 the colonies issued their Declaration of Independence, a formal renunciation of allegiance, establishing the colonies as a state independent of Great Britain.

The main retaliatory British campaign of 1777 ended in disaster. It was to be two-pronged, with General Howe advancing from the south and General Burgoyne from the north. Howe made the decision to divert his troops into taking Philadelphia and failed therefore to join up with Burgoyne advancing from Canada. In October 1778 he was defeated at Saratoga. By then the British situation had worsened. In 1778 France declared war, in 1779 Spain and, finally, in 1780 the Dutch. This meant that conflict now spread around the globe, and overtures for peace began to be made on the basis of offering home rule and common citizenship to Britons and members of the empire. But it was too late for the Americans, who would settle for nothing other than independence. On 17 October 1781 the British troops under General Cornwallis surrendered at Yorktown. Lord North rightly groaned: 'Oh God! It is all over.' A year later the king was forced to accept his resignation. In 1783 peace was finally made with what had become the United States.

This was the only war Britain was to lose from 1707 to the present day. It traumatized the governing classes. At one blow, the first British Empire had been lost. The aid which the French poured into America hastened the collapse of the *ancien régime*. No one to this day has ever agreed who was at fault in what was an appalling trail of disasters and mismanagement. Once arms had been resorted to, however, the outcome was virtually inevitable. It was a civil war with all the unease of like fighting like. The Americans were Protestant English not Catholic French. The initial inertia at the British end hastened a catastrophe which was only exacerbated by trying to fight a war 3,000 miles away, over a terrain which was densely wooded and criss-crossed by unfordable rivers. The colonials knew their own country and became accomplished at guerilla warfare. Supplies took three to six months to arrive by sea and, in addition, there were all the problems of the terrible New England winters.

The British too found themselves devoid of allies. When France declared war, it was necessary to defend the island, and any troop convoys. By 1780 Britain was fighting alone in America against the colonists; in India, the West Indies, North America and Africa against the French; in the Balearics, Gibraltar, the West Indies, Central America and Florida against the Spanish; and in Ceylon, the East and West

Indies and in the North Sea against the Dutch.

This was humiliation on a tremendous scale. The ruling classes had presided over failure and defeat. It was a loss of face of such proportions that it was to lead to heavy emphasis on striving to create a new inclusive identity which was British bringing in both the Scots and Irish. In the years ahead they were to learn to unite in loyalty to the crown and to a second British Empire, one based on renewed military and naval strength and held together by a new missionary spirit. Looking back, perhaps defeat came at a salutary moment, for within six years the island was to be faced with sustaining over twenty years of war, years in which the ruling classes had seen taken from their peers on the mainland everything which they represented in the cataclysm known as the French Revolution.

The newly created United States manufactured its own patriotic mythology in this scene painted in 1820 by William Trumbull of *The Surrender of Lord Cornwallis at Yorktown*. In fact Cornwallis was 'ill' and the surrender was made on his behalf by General Charles O'Hara. In retrospect the scene has been transmuted into one of noble heroism with the flag of the newly independent country fluttering aloft in triumph.

Chapter Fifty-Two

WORLD WAR AND THE INVENTION OF BRITAIN

THE fall of Lord North brought a reversion to the political chaos reminiscent of the 1760s in which one ministry succeeded another. There were two main groups of Whigs, those who clustered around Lord Rockingham and those who followed Lord Shelburne. Each group had its up-and-coming star, in the case of Rockingham, Henry Fox's son, Charles James; in that of Shelburne, William Pitt the Younger. Both had a new political vision to take the country forward after the disaster of the American war. But it was not a shared vision for Fox and Pitt were bitter rivals. Fox, however, stole the march coming to what he believed to be power when he cemented what was viewed as an unholy alliance with his former enemy, Lord North. Rockingham had died in the summer of 1782. The victory was to be short-lived because George III, by then a highly adept political operator, plotted his downfall as much as did Pitt. All that was required was for Fox to present a bill on which Pitt and the king could appeal to the country. That came in the form of a bill proposing a radical restructuring of the East India Company which the king instructed the Lords to defeat. Pitt was called upon to form an administration and in the spring of 1784 a general election was held and the followers of Fox were routed. Pitt entered office for what was to prove a prolonged and secure tenure as Prime Minister.

Pitt was the second son of the earlier Pitt, who was created Earl of Chatham. Except for one brief period the younger Pitt was to remain Prime Minister until his death in 1806, thus dominating the political stage for twenty years. Few men have had such an unswerving belief in their own power and destiny. Together these gave him a sense of mission which was to make him arguably one of the great war ministers in the history of

James Gillray's caricature of Pitt as *The Giant-Factotum amusing himself* issued in January 1797 and reflecting his rise to political dominance. He straddles the Speaker's chair and uses the globe of the world for a game of Cup and Ball. A factotum is a servant who enjoys 'the entire management of his master's affairs'. His right foot rests on William Wilberforce and Henry Dundas, Secretary of State for War, who offer it for veneration to the Tories. His left crushes the opposition including Charles James Fox.

The GIANT-FACTOTUM amusing himself.

the country. A pragmatist by nature, he was also a brilliant organiser and administrator, carrying through reforms in the civil service, beginning to abolish, for example, the old system of sinecures and fees in favour of properly salaried posts. His reform of government finance was also to contribute significantly to the success of the war effort. Few politicians have mastered the parliamentary scene so rapidly, for although he was never to have a personal following exceeding more than fifty he was to maintain his hold over the independent members, ensuring his majority. George III came to rely on Pitt much as he had come to rely first on Bute and then on North, the difference being that this time he had alighted upon a man who actually deserved his fullest confidence.

That was to be proved in the scenario which began on 14 July 1789 when the Parisian mob stormed the Bastille, the fortress prison which symbolised the inefficient rule of the French kings which we embody in the expression the *ancien régime*. This event was to be the opening scene of a cataclysm whose consequences were to engulf the whole of Western Europe, the French Revolution. In France it swept away in a tide of bloody violence not only a centuries-old system of government, but also a centuries-old aristocratic structure of society. The opening stages of this saga were greeted with enthusiasm in England, especially by politicians like Charles James Fox, who thought that something approximating to the English parliamentary system would emerge. When events later began to take a more macabre turn the attitude swiftly changed, especially when mass public executions by the guillotine got under way and even the French king's head fell on the scaffold. It was to divide the Whig party and create what were in effect unnamed but dim ancestors of the political parties of the next century, which acted in concert not so much because they represented a network of family connection and influence, but were instead a group of men loyal to certain principles. Pitt drew into his government Whigs who defended the tradition of aristocratic government which they saw under threat, forming in effect a conservative alliance. Fox and his adherents continued to welcome the Revolution, oppose the war against France and support reform, thereby embodying a stance which was the ancestor of Liberalism. But both sides continued to act in an essentially eighteenth century way, in which the control of government and policy was seen to focus around the crown and its powers.

The general reaction in England to the Revolution was one of utter horror and revulsion. The aristocratic and propertied classes saw everything they embodied under attack. On 1 February 1793 the French declared war on Britain and Holland, signalling a struggle which was to last almost twenty-five years. The French army offered fraternal assistance to the lower orders of the countries they attacked, claiming they were throwing off the chains of monarchic and aristocratic society. As the war progressed, the full meaning of this challenge to the British ruling élite was realised and the war took on the character of a crusade for self-preservation.

In Britain it inevitably fuelled a sharp move in a conservative direction so that the slightest glimmer of any demand for change or reform was immediately suspected of revolutionary intentions. But the clock could not be put back after the events of 1789. Political debate had finally moved out of the closed arena of the privileged. The 1790s witnessed the emergence of radical movements which involved the lower orders, in particular skilled artisans in the towns, who formed Corresponding Societies calling for universal suffrage. Their cornerstone was Thomas Paine's *Rights of Man* (1791) which denounced a society founded on inherited privilege and wealth and called for equality of opportunity and rights, including universal male suffrage. In view of what had happened across the Channel these developments in England evoked a whole series of seemingly repressive measures: the suspension of Habeas Corpus in 1794, the Treasonable Practices and Seditious Meetings Acts of 1795 and Combinations Acts of 1799 and 1800. These measures went to extremes in which, for instance, anyone who so much as criticised the king or the government was guilty of treason, and any association of workers was prohibited. Collectively, their bark was worse than their bite. Few, in fact, were ever prosecuted and even fewer found guilty. By 1795, however, these radical movements had been easily suppressed and driven underground.

The war not only lasted a long time but also its geographical extent was unparalleled, embracing Europe, Asia, Africa and North and South America. England was seriously threatened with invasion several times and indeed at one point the conquest of the country came at the head of the French agenda. The nature of the fighting was also different from its predecessors for it saw the birth of the citizen army, the French mobilising vast sections of its male population. In response the British gradually had to change their military structure, evolving from an army made up of paid professionals and mercenaries to one which drew into its ranks men of all classes, from all parts of the country, and of every religious denomination. In 1789 the British army numbered just 40,000 men. By 1814 there were a quarter of a million. Add to that volunteers and part-timers and some half million of the male population was under arms. Never before had the people of the British Isles had to be forged together in martial unity on such a scale, able to face first the armies of republican France and then those of Napoleon.

This was war on a gigantic scale with vast armies criss-crossing the entire extent of Europe from the Iberian Peninsula to Russia. On the British side much of it was enacted in the New World, for the 'empire of trade' was at stake, upon which Britain's success would ultimately depend. The war opened in Europe with the French taking the Austrian Netherlands and Holland, and creating a new republic. British strength was largely naval, and in 1794 Lord Howe defeated the Brest Fleet at the battle called the Glorious First of June. Two years later Napoleon Buonaparte emerged as a military leader of genius, assuming control of the French conquest of Italy. Everywhere the French army went the old order of things crumbled, fuelling further fear at home. In 1796 Spain joined the war on the side of France; the year after that there was a brief pause in hostilities, the peace of Campo Formio.

That gave the French the breathing space they needed to prepare for the invasion of England. Mercifully, in October the British navy succeeded in destroying the French fleet at Camperdown. Napoleon and the French army invaded Egypt. By then one of the British fleets was commanded by a man of quite exceptional ability, Horatio Nelson. In August 1798 he destroyed the French Toulon fleet in the Battle of the Nile, forcing Napoleon to abandon his Egyptian campaign and hasten back to France where he was made First Consul in a *coup d'état*. Russia and Austria entered the war and with British naval aid drove the French out of Italy, but Napoleon defeated the Austrians at the Battle of Marengo in June 1800. Six months later, and after another defeat, the Austrians made peace with Napoleon, recognising the vast French satellite empire through Italy, the Netherlands, Switzerland and the Rhineland. Nelson, however, succeeded in gaining a further victory at Copenhagen in 1801, while a second commander of genius emerged in Arthur Wellesley, who destroyed the last vestiges of French power in India. In 1802 peace was signed at Amiens and the warring parties took respite before a renewal of hostilities. The treaty of Amiens came as a relief to a country which was war-weary, over-taxed and suffering from roaring inflation.

On 17 May 1803 Britain reopened the war. This second phase was to demand far more sacrifice. Income tax, introduced earlier, rose steeply. Pitt, returned to power the following year after his only short spell out of office, realised that Napoleon, who by now had crowned himself Emperor of the French, would have to be defeated on land in Europe. Napoleon on his side knew that his success depended on the conquest of Britain, and turned all his attention towards preparing a massive invasion force of some 100,000 men which assembled at Boulogne. The fact that the invasion never took place in 1804 was due to Russia, then Austria, and finally Sweden, coming into the war on the side of Britain. This meant that the French army had to march east where it defeated the Austrians at the Battle of the Ulm, Napoleon entering Vienna in triumph. Both the Austrians and the Russians were defeated a second time at the

The hero of the war on land, Arthur Wellesley, Duke of Wellington, by Goya. The artist made this drawing of Wellington in 1812 probably at the time of his triumphal entry into Madrid after his defeat of the French. From this study he made several paintings including one now in the National Gallery.

Battle of Austerlitz. At sea, the British fleet crowned its series of successes with a legendary victory which destroyed the main body of the French and Spanish fleet, the Battle of Trafalgar on 21 October 1805 in which, at the height of the battle, Horatio, now Lord Nelson, was fatally wounded. Trafalgar meant that Napoleon could no longer invade England and was the occasion of a famous speech by Pitt at the Lord Mayor's Banquet of that year:

> 'I return you many thanks for the honour you have done me; but Europe is not to be saved by the exertion of any one man. England has saved herself by her exertions, and will, as I trust, save Europe by her example.'

Pitt died on 23 January 1806 aged forty-seven, worn out by the war. He was a tremendous loss and there was no great leader to step into his shoes. Instead there followed a succession of Administrations: Lord Grenville and Fox, in the Ministry of all the Talents, then the Duke of Portland, followed by Spencer Perceval, who was assassinated in 1812, and, finally, Lord Liverpool who was to remain in power until 1827.

The funeral of the hero of the war at sea, Horatio, Lord Nelson. He was accorded a state funeral which took place in January 1806. For three days the body lay in state in the Painted Hall of Greenwich Hospital to which thousands flocked. Here the coffin begins its progress by water to the Admiralty and then, by land, to St. Paul's Cathedral. The water procession was a mile long.

The war, however, by no means slackened. In 1806 Napoleon defeated Russia at Jena and occupied Berlin. The year after he routed them again after which he made a pact with the Russian Tsar to divide Europe. By then the emperor had concluded that his only chance of vanquishing Britain was by economic means, and so he closed all European ports to British trade. This was the first major example of an economic war. (The second was with the United States in 1812–14.) As a result exports plummeted, causing industrial unrest, bankruptcies and falling prices, while the cessation of the import of grain from the mainland led to food riots. But in the end the country weathered the storm for Napoleon was forced to relax his ban because the shortages affected him adversely also. By then he had turned his attention to the Iberian Peninsula making his brother king of Spain. But this time he was to come up against strong national resistance and the fact that that could be kept supplied by British sea power via Portugal.

In April 1809 Arthur Wellesley returned to Portugal as commander-in-chief with 25,000 men and defeated the French at Talavera. For his victory he was given a peerage. Retreating behind the defensive range of the Torres Vedras mountains he bided his time until the French, cut off from any supply line, were forced to withdraw. Wellesley then captured all their fortresses and defeated them again at Salamanca. Napoleon this time turned towards Russia and in the summer of 1812 invaded it with an army of 700,000 men. The Russians retreated, so that when Napoleon reached Moscow he found no Russian army to defeat. The appalling winter then set in with no supplies and the French were forced to retreat with a loss of half-a-million men.

Meanwhile the war continued in Spain, where Wellesley crushed the French at Vittoria, wiping out their hold on the country. After his return to France, Napoleon won one battle at Dresden but lost the second at Leipzig, and was forced to withdraw beyond the Rhine. By then a huge alliance of European powers had formed against him: Britain, Prussia, Russia, Sweden, and later Austria. The allied armies advanced towards Paris which surrendered on 31 March 1814. Napoleon abdicated, and was sent into exile on the small island of Elba. The victorious allies assembled in Vienna to sort out the map of Europe in his aftermath. In May, Britain formally made peace with France but that was not quite to be the end of the saga for Napoleon escaped from Elba and landed in France on 1 March 1815, where he quickly assembled an army. Wellesley, by then Duke of Wellington, left the peace conference to lead the allied army. The British force consisted of 30,000 men. Prussia had promised to send troops, so had Austria and Russia. On 18 June 1815 the final battle of the war was fought at Waterloo in present-day Belgium. Wellington's troops withstood the repeated assaults of Napoleon's men until the Prussians arrived in time to finally rout them. The war was at last at an end.

The diplomacy carried out at Vienna was to settle the map of Europe for forty years. In that process Britain played the dominant part through Lord Castlereagh. His aim was a Europe in which France would in no way be humiliated, but one in which the territorial integrity of all its nations would be respected and stability achieved through a careful balance of forces. On the British side the territorial acquisitions may have seemed small, but they were to be of immeasurable value in forwarding her empire of trade: Malta, Guiana, Tobago and St. Lucia, the Cape of Good Hope, Singapore and Malaya. Britain's position in India was now unassailable.

It seemed that Britain was the only country to emerge from all this with her ancient institutions still intact. Elsewhere thrones had fallen and a centuries-old order of things had been done away with. Thanks to the country's naval and economic strength and to that series of great war leaders, Pitt, Nelson and Wellington, Britain had triumphed. Her many peoples had found a common identity in the face of such an enemy. Not for nothing in 1800 was a national anthem, 'God save the king', officially adopted. And, in spite of the fact that the war had taken on all the fervour of a crusade to preserve a status quo, the fact was that both the country and the ruling classes were very different in 1815 from what they had been in 1793.

These wars were the great watershed into the nineteenth century, one in which changes were forged which radically altered the nature of both the monarchy and the ruling élite. They, as it were, re-invented themselves in response firstly to the trauma of the American defeat, and then even more in response to the fear of a revolution in their own country. As far as the monarchy was concerned the scene had already been set by George III and his family, who were models of domestic propriety. The king's relapses into madness (the inherited affliction of porphyria which became permanent after 1810) only increased the nation's respect for the man they called 'Farmer George' and regarded as the father of his people. His popularity was further enhanced by the decadence of his son, George, Prince of Wales, later to be Prince Regent and George IV. Victories in the war were celebrated with festivities which focused on the crown as a symbol of national unity. These were no longer confined to the court but were organised throughout the country, the fiftieth anniversary of George III's accession in 1810 being marked by ceremonies throughout the Empire. And if the king played the role of the country's first citizen, his queen, Charlotte, was presented as a pattern for womankind. When George died in 1820 there was national mourning.

If the monarchy began to re-cast itself as an institution deserving of loyalty because it embodied virtue and patriotism, the alteration which gradually permeated the ruling élite was to be even greater. They had seen their peers obliterated on the Continent, and were aware that a hostile and critical attitude already existed in England, where writers had begun to question the rights of an élite to exercise political power based purely on birth and property. During the thirty years following 1780 the landed classes were to reassert that right, and at the same time transform themselves into people deserving of respect from below.

In 1802 the first edition appeared of a standard reference book which is issued to this day, Debrett's *Peerage*. What was startlingly novel about this publication was that for the first time it combined the aristocracies of Britain into one coherent caste. This reflected what had been happening in the second half of the century where intermarriage, particularly between the English and Scottish aristocracy, had created a new unity. That resurgence was aided by the addition of new creations which brought in the meritocracy of the war: the admirals, generals and administrators. The upper classes were not only reinforced in numbers, they were also fortunate in that the population boom caused income from land to rise dramatically because of the increasing demand for corn.

Other changes affected the nature of the upper classes, welding them as never before into a new coherence of attitude. The old means of education had been by tutor at home. This was now replaced by education at one of the public schools, Eton, Winchester, Westminster or Harrow. By 1800 70% of upper class boys went to one or other of these four schools. There they met their peers at a very young age and formed networks which lasted a lifetime. There also they were inculcated, via an education based on the study of the Greek and Latin classics, in a patriotism which set great store on the cult of heroes, men who were muscular warriors valiant on the field of battle. Along with this came a radical change in appearance. The pre-Revolutionary French fashions had emphasised class by men wearing rich fabrics lavishly embroidered and adorned with lace and jewels. By 1815 such ostentatious display was replaced by a new quiet elegance in shades of beige, grey and black for civil dress, or the wearing of a military uniform to proclaim patriotism.

Nor was that all. The 1770s were seen as an age of shocking decadence in terms of gross extravagance, gambling and sexual depravity, which was countered by a reaffirmation of the traditional view that wealth and rank entailed duty, both in terms of public service and private probity. Those, like the poet Lord Byron, who offended the new puritan ethic sought exile abroad. The upper classes were perceived as owing their status not only to birth and wealth but even more to their industry in the service of others, and their morality within the home. Instead of embodying the vices of an *ancien régime* élite awaiting a revolution, they became examples of virtue for emulation by the classes below.

These consisted in the main of the mercantile classes, whose place in the scheme of things was amply recognised by the ruling élite without allowing any great shift of political power in their direction. Trade, after all, was responsible for 60% of government revenue and contributed substantially to a war which cost one-and-a-half billion pounds. The two classes needed each other, for the class which ran the state maintained the order essential for trade to flourish, including a strong navy. The mercantile net was wide, stretching from the City and the Port of London across country and up into Scotland (where trade trebled during the second half of the century), and embraced a huge range of people, including manufacturers, middle-men, shopkeepers, and on down to pedlars. Success at war meant an expansion of Empire and with that came new markets for British goods. Patriotism and commerce were seen to march profitably hand in hand.

That sense of a new collective British identity was to impinge on the conscious-ness of the working classes, most of whom had been either directly or indirectly involved in the war effort. Moreover things like the press, popular prints, and celebrations built up a sense of nationhood into which, by 1800, Ireland was deliberately drawn. Scotland had already been assimilated in 1707 but Ireland remained with its own independent Parliament, albeit subject to the Westminster legislature. (The Welsh had legally been assimilated in an earlier century.) The revolt of the American colonies had thrown up a flare as to the potential danger Ireland embodied. For the first time demands for change came not from the subjugated Roman Catholics but from Anglo-Irish Protestants where republicanism had begun to take hold. These demands included parliamentary reform and the restoration of civil and political liberties to Roman Catholics, known as Catholic Emancipation. Moves in that direction sharpened the religious divide in the country leading to guerilla sectarian warfare in the north. There, a rising of Protestant republicans in 1798 was savagely suppressed, and one of Catholic republicans in the south was likewise put down. Pitt believed that the only solution for Ireland was to extend to the country what Scotland had undergone in 1707. In 1800 the Irish Parliament vanished and Westminster opened its doors to embrace a hundred Irish MPs, twenty-eight peers, and four bishops. Due to the implacable opposition of the king, Pitt failed to deliver the promise of Catholic Emancipation. On the surface, the result was a united Great Britain with a single legislature, but it had been achieved without any effort to solve the underlying tensions of a society which was becoming more, and not less, polarised.

In spite of the festering problem of Ireland Britain in 1815 emerged as the mother country of the greatest Empire the world has ever known. The new Empire, which by then included a new continent, Australia, replaced and exceeded in size the one which had been lost, and was this time to be held firmly in place by systems to prevent any recurrence of the American disaster. The 1784 India Act set up a system of government under the aegis of the East India Company which was to last until its power was taken over by the crown in 1858. The 1791 Canada Act established Upper and Lower Canada each with its own elective assembly, a system which was to remain until 1840. In 1770 Captain James Cook claimed New South Wales, on the east coast of Australia, as British territory. By the 1820s Britain was to govern a quarter of the world's population.

This reborn nation called for shared icons and a shared culture. That too came during those years of endeavour. The landed classes increasingly patronised and encouraged British artists who, in their turn, celebrated the nation's history and the war heroes. The death of General Wolfe at Quebec or that of Nelson at Trafalgar gave them material for pictures designed to stir popular patriotism. Through engravings, they reached virtually everyone. In 1805 the British Institution opened as a gallery for the exhibition of works by British artists. It was also used to house loan exhibitions of works from the aristocracy and gentry, thus beginning a tradition which demonstrated that a work of art could still remain private property but be shared by the community as a whole.

All of this was an astonishing renaissance. The establishment emerged in 1815 wealthier, more powerful, and more influential than ever before. But with the war now over all kinds of other problems arose on the agenda, which the long struggle against France had postponed. Many were the consequence of another very different revolution which Britain was undergoing during those same years, the one we designate as the Industrial Revolution. Its impact was to dominate the new century.

The commitment first made in 1818 to honour Nelson with a public monument was eventually fulfilled in 1843 when the massive 170 feet tall Corinthian column was erected in front of the National Gallery and the huge statue hoisted into place. The famous lions by Sir Edwin Landseer only arrived in 1867.

Chapter Fifty-Three

THE NEW MAN:
WILLIAM WILBERFORCE

I F one person had to be singled out as embodying the change which overcame the established classes between 1790 and 1820, it would be William Wilberforce. By 1790 he had already taken on many of the characteristics we now think of as quintessentially Victorian: a deep Christian piety, a devotion to family life, someone for whom wealth and social status were enabling factors in a career dedicated to good causes. His private life was beyond reproach, and a sense of fair dealing motivated his every action. The Christian life for him was one of unremitting discipline and giving. But it was also one of perpetual joy, something which he radiated to everyone he met. Wilberforce's life pivots around the central act of his conversion, which took him in one sense out of the ethos of the eighteenth century into that of the nineteenth. It was the moment when 'enthusiasm', which had been marginalised in its early stages, seized hold of members of the highest levels of society with far-reaching consequences.

William Wilberforce was born on 24 August 1759, the son of a mercantile family, based in Kingston-upon-Hull, which had made its fortune in the Baltic trade. As a child he was abnormally small and was dogged from birth with indifferent health, including weak eyesight, but he was endowed with huge physical and mental energy, a remarkable charm of manner, and a spontaneous natural generosity. Wilberforce's education followed that which was the norm for members of the prosperous classes, first to the local grammar school and afterwards to a boarding-school, in his case one close to London at Putney. His father died when he was nine and he was sent to live with an aunt and uncle who owned a villa at Wimbledon. It was there that he was exposed for the first time to people who were 'enthusiasts', being friends of the great evangelical minister, George Whitefield. This must have affected the boy, for his mother took coach south and removed him to a boarding-school in Yorkshire. To be tinged with Methodism would have spelt social ruin.

At fifteen Wilberforce went up to Cambridge, having grown into an engaging youth with a quick wit, fine singing voice and ease of manner. He was also very rich. The universities at this point acted more as a finishing school for young men of his class, the time being given over to enjoying the good things of life, including gambling, and in forming a network of friendships which would bind him into the country's ruling élite. One of these was the younger Pitt, who was to be a life-long friend. Both wished to enter politics and both were elected to the same Parliament in the same year, 1780. Wilberforce became a member of what was the Pitt set, a group which led a whirling social life dedicated to assemblies, dances, visits to the theatre and the opera, and the London pleasure gardens. Wilberforce was odd man out in one sense only for his background was trade, but his accomplished style compensated for that and opened every door, including those of the most exclusive clubs. In 1784 he was returned again as a member of Parliament, but this time with the added prestige of representing his county.

Wilberforce was by then twenty-five, and set off with his mother and sister to spend the winter on the French-Italian riviera, taking with them a clergyman of the conventional kind named Isaac Milner. Through Milner, the embers of Wilberforce's childhood encounters with the evangelicals were stirred, and he began to study the New Testament in Greek. Then, in October 1785, came what he called the 'great change', a conversion crisis in which he was engulfed by spiritual anguish. Every day he rose early to pray. 'I was,' he wrote, 'filled with sorrow.' Yet he knew that to adopt a reformed lifestyle would mean withdrawing from the fashionable and worldly circles in which he moved.

That this did not happen he owed to the advice of an old evangelical cleric, John Newton, whose counsel he sought. Newton wrote to Wilberforce: 'It is hoped and believed that the Lord has raised you up for the good of His church and for the good of the nation.' In that he was prophetic, for the norm for anyone who became 'enthusiastic' was to move within a small like-minded circle. Newton's advice to Wilberforce was for him to retain his public life and build on it. That decision was to affect not only Wilberforce but through him the behaviour of a large section of the upper classes.

Besides living a life of Christian prayer and discipline, Wilberforce began to educate himself to make up for all the wasted years. Still a member of Parliament he was as yet a man without a mission, but that came quickly. His friends in the House were two other evangelical members, Sir Charles Middleton and Sir Richard Hill. At the former's house in the country he met James Ramsay, the local rector, who, in 1784, had published an attack on the transportation and use of African slaves on the colonial sugar plantations in the West Indies. This was a large and a lucrative trade, the slaves being seized on the coast of East Africa and transported by sea in appalling conditions, so much so that a large percentage of them died on the way. They were then formed into gangs of slave labour on the plantations, subject to the most barbarous and in-human cruelty. Ramsay wrote asking how men treated like this could ever listen to the Word of God from those who kept them in such miserable servitude, arguing for an end to the trade and the emancipation of the slaves. The book produced a storm of abuse from those whose fortunes depended on its continu-ance, but there were others who were sympathetic. A second book followed, and this was the one which converted not only Wilber-force but also his friend Pitt to the cause of the Abolition of the Slave Trade.

A medallion designed for Josiah Wedgwood depicting a slave in chains. Issued in 1786 it came at the very outset of the long campaign for the abolition of slavery.

'My grand arraignment of this most detestable and guilty practice, the Slave Trade,' Wilberforce wrote, look-ing back in 1819, 'is because it is chargeable with holding in bondage, in darkness and in blood, one third of the habitable globe . . . ' In 1786 he moved to a house next to the Lords and gradually a group came together in support of the cause, but the real moment of decision came a year later on 2 May when he, Pitt and William Grenville sat under an oak on a warm May spring evening and Pitt said, 'Wilberforce, why don't you give notice of a motion on the subject of the Slave Trade? . . . Do not lose time, or the ground will be occupied by another.'

On 28 October 1787 Wilberforce wrote: 'God Almighty has set before me two great objects, the suppression of the Slave Trade and the Reformation of Manners.' By the latter he meant morals, for he had launched an attack on the decadence of the upper classes. Wilberforce, in short, determined to make goodness fashionable. He resigned from his clubs and began to create an association of his peers who would govern their lives by decency of behaviour. One of these was the playwright, Hannah More, who produced *Thoughts on the Manners of the Great*, in which she argued that the poor could only be helped by reforming the rich. In 1789 she and Wilberforce began the foundation of schools to teach reading to the rural poor. She perceptively wrote of him: 'I declare you are serving God by making yourself agreeable . . . to worldly but well disposed people, who would never be attracted to religion by grave and severe divines, even if such fell their way.'

The Abolition of the Slave Trade was to prove a lifetime's labour. It began on 22

May 1787 when a committee was formed. Two years later Pitt moved that the trade should be investigated and Wilberforce spoke eloquently for three-and-a-half hours, but they were outflanked by the opposition, which demanded more evidence. By the time that that was forthcoming the French Revolution had broken out, engendering deep unease at the idea of any change so that when the House divided on the issue in April 1791, the Abolitionists lost the vote by 163 to 88. A year later, Pitt carried a resolution that 'the Trade . . . ought to be abolished'. That indication of intent was to take over fifteen years to reach fruition.

In 1793 Wilberforce made his home in a squat Queen Anne House at Battersea Rise on a small estate at Clapham, then wholly rural. His life now pivoted between work in the House, his circle at Clapham dedicated to the reform of society, and visits to Bath for his health. Wilberforce's conversion led him to rise above party, and to take into the political mainstream a whole series of causes: public hangings, the humanising of prison life, medical aid for the poor, and their education through the Charity and Sunday School movements. In 1796 the Bettering Society was formed to investigate problems engendered by poverty. It gained an

A sketch of the library at Battersea Rise about 1824 with William Wilberforce and his family. No one is idle, the women either sewing, reading or drawing. The virtuous pattern of home life established by Wilberforce was to become a Victorian ideal.

influential ally in the father of the future Prime Minister, Sir Robert Peel, who, in 1802, pushed through with Wilberforce's help an Act to control the conditions of work, and to limit the excessive hours which children laboured in the new factories. Out of this Society arose the British Institution for 'diffusing the knowledge and facilitating the general introduction of useful mechanical inventions and improvements; and for teaching . . . the application of science to the common purposes of life.' It was to the Bettering Society that Humphry Davy was to demonstrate his miner's lamp, and Michael Faraday his discovery of electro-magnetism.

All of this activity contributed to the change of atmosphere pervading the governing classes, one hastened by the publication in 1797 of Wilberforce's A *Practical View of the Prevailing Religious System of Professed Christians, in the Higher and Middle Classes in the Country, Contrasted with Real Christianity*. It sold 7,500 copies and went through five impressions in six months, a best-seller by the standards of the age. The book took the reader on a journey, showing how Christianity should and could guide the politics, habits and attitudes of the nation. It was a book which contributed to creating the ethos of the Victorian age and for decades a copy found its place in every home. In it, Wilberforce outlined the life of the regenerate Christian as it was lived out through personal character and public acts. Penitence and spiritual anguish were counterpoints to joy and spiritual sunshine. Of Wilberforce himself a friend wrote: 'His presence was as fatal to dullness as to immorality, his mirth as irresistible as the first laughter of childhood.'

The year before the book appeared he married Barbara Spooner, the daughter of a Birmingham banker. Gradually Battersea Rise became home to a burgeoning young family and a routine of life evolved which was increasingly to become upper class society's norm, with family prayers, hard work and Sunday observance as its lynchpins. All through these years the efforts to secure Abolition went on but it was not until 1807 that the bill was at last passed with the majority of 267. The Solicitor-General spoke at length, contrasting the almost saintly figure of Wilberforce with that monster across the Channel, Napoleon. At the close of his speech the House cheered and Wilberforce sat with his head bowed, the tears streaming down his face.

Old Bishop Porteus of London wrote of that day: 'Here then after a glorious struggle of eighteen years a final period is at length put in this country to the most execrable and inhuman traffic that ever disgraced the Christian world.' On 25 March 1807 the Abolition of the Slave Trade became law. But it was one thing to pass such an act and quite another to enforce it, added to which the optimistic belief that the planters would soon emancipate their slaves proved unfounded.

Sir Thomas Lawrence's unfinished portrait of Wilberforce at the age of sixty-nine conceals the curvature of the spine he suffered from. It captures, however, his beguiling charm.

Shortly after Wilberforce and his family moved to a house in Kensington Gore. By then he had become a legend, the nation's conscience, and the house was thronged with visitors consulting the man who had come to epitomise reform. The causes he espoused read like a roll call for the values of a new age: parliamentary reform, support for Elizabeth Fry in her prison reformation, the humanisation of the criminal code, the establishment of Trustee Savings Banks, the creation of a National Gallery, involvement in the British and Foreign Bible Society, speaking in favour of Catholic Emancipation and against the evils of transportation, and taking part in founding what was to become the Royal Society for the Prevention of Cruelty to Animals.

Dogged by poor sight, weak lungs and colitis, as he got older he developed curvature of the spine, so that year by year his head fell forward a little more until it finally rested on his chest. To check this he wore 'a steel girdle cased in leather' but no one knew. They would register on encounter only a smiling and joyous presence. Wilberforce died on 29 July 1833 at the age of seventy-four, a nationally revered figure who was buried with full public honours in Westminster Abbey. With him a new age had dawned, that of reform.

Chapter Fifty-Four

REVOLUTION AVERTED: THE GREAT REFORM BILL

W AR is the harbinger of change. Suddenly three hundred thousand soldiers and sailors flooded onto the job market, bringing mass unemployment. There was a trade depression and the harvest was bad. The five years following 1815 were to bring Britain nearer to the brink of revolution from below than at any other time in her history. They were years of social turbulence and unrest, expressed in monster marches, huge open-air rallies and occasional insurrections. The radical voices, which had been suppressed in the aftermath of the French Revolution and through the long years of war, re-surfaced. In the new industrialised areas of the country working men's associations, called Hampden Clubs after the man who had challenged the absolute rule of Charles I, sprang up. These were replaced just before 1820 by the Political Unions which held open-air meetings and sent huge petitions to Parliament, signed by thousands of people. The artisans and workers in the towns demanded a reform of Parliament, universal male suffrage, lower taxation and relief from poverty. At one of these vast rallies outside Manchester the local yeomanry dispersed the crowd and eleven people were killed, immediately billed as martyrs to the cause in the 'Peterloo Massacre'. Another group, of shoemakers and silk weavers, plotted to blow up the Cabinet in what was known as the 'Cato Street Conspiracy'. They failed, but all this was evidence that a revolutionary underground was clearly active, borne out also by the scattered uprisings that occurred across the country. This was an era when the radical press was in full flood with William Cobbett's *Political Register* at the forefront. Caricaturists mercilessly ridiculed what they saw as an extravagant and corrupt ruling class led by a man whose decadence was a throwback to the previous century, the Prince Regent and future George IV. In 1819, after Peterloo, Parliament passed the Six Acts, designed to suppress any revolu-tionary movement by tightening the laws on sedition and libel, and imposing a crippling stamp duty on newspapers. It was not long before the main trouble-makers found themselves in gaol.

No revolution occurred. The radical groups were diverse and divided, but more significant was the fact that 1820 saw a sudden sharp upward turn in the economy which was to last for most of the decade. The idea that reform, and especially parliamentary reform, was desirable may have gone off the boil but it would certainly not go away. It was henceforth to be firmly on the agenda, awaiting its moment.

And that is hardly surprising, for by 1815 the parliamentary system, which went back to the Middle Ages, had become a gigantic anomaly, no longer reflecting the realities of a rapidly changing society. There were 658 MPs in the Commons but how they were elected and who they represented was to come under increasing fire. There was no independent representation, for instance, of the burgeoning new industrial and commercial centres such as Manchester, Bir-mingham, Leeds and Sheffield. In sharp contrast the long-abandoned medieval borough of Old Sarum returned two MPs. Worse, there were only seven electors and they were open to bribery. In 1830, eighteen of Cornwall's twenty-eight seats were in the control of individuals and the other ten could be purchased. Who

George Cruickshank's *Loyal Addresses and Radical Petitions* satirises the official reaction to the 'Peterloo Massacre' of 1819. The future George IV as Prince Regent receives loyal addresses from those who support 'the present order of things'. To them he graciously extends his hand to kiss while his posterior emanates a very different kind of experience to those who demand reform.

The Reformers' Attack on the Old Rotten Tree; or, the Foul Nests of the Cormorants in Danger.

had the vote also varied wildly. In thirty-nine boroughs it went with certain properties, in forty-three the electors were the town council, while in sixty-two others the freemen voted. In the counties the forty-shilling freeholders naturally cast their vote in deference to the wishes of the local landowner or else he withdrew his favours. Parliament remained one large interconnected family, the aristocracy forming the House of Lords and their sons, brothers and cousins, along with a sprinkling of gentry, making up the Commons.

Caricature showing those for and against the 1832 Reform Bill. Those against prop up a tree labelled 'Rotten Borough System' filled with birds sitting in nests, each one identified as one of the corrupt boroughs. Those for reform advance with axes while on 'Constitution Hill' William IV and Queen Adelaide stand arm in arm, receiving the salute of an Englishman, an Irishman and a Scotsman against a rising sun.

Nonetheless the system had worked well, and it was not to be until the third quarter of the previous century that anyone was to suggest that it was in any way in need of revision. The idea that reform might be desirable went back to the notorious career of an outright rogue and demagogue, John Wilkes. Although Wilkes had become an MP under aristocratic aegis he found his path to advancement blocked and turned to polemic, attacking George III's minister, Lord Bute, so violently that he was put in the King's Bench Prison. By getting his friends to apply for a writ of Habeas

Corpus, thereby implying that he had been arbitrarily arrested, the equation Wilkes and 'Liberty' was born. Later, in 1768, Wilkes was to get himself elected MP for Middlesex on a tide of public outrage on his behalf, and although he was repeatedly expelled from the House he was always re-elected back again. The fact that he was utterly pernicious, however, was neither here nor there. Looked at from the outside it seemed that the will of the electorate had been over-ruled by a corrupt élite, and that something about Parliament was in need of reform. As a result a parliamentary reform movement came into being which reached its zenith in the 1780s, coinciding with the population increase. There were many more people, some of whose fathers had had the vote which was denied to them. All of this was then to cool, firstly in response to the economic recovery following the American war, but even more in reaction to the outbreak of the French Revolution.

During the war years, however, in spite of the fact that action was ruled out, there was still a reform movement and the debate in terms of ideas continued. Jeremy Bentham was one of the many writers who gave vent to the view that a 'ruling few' dominated a 'subject many', and that an accumulation of influence and patronage controlled Parliament, the army, the church and the law. Such a view was of course attractive to the ever-growing numbers of people who found themselves outside the system but whose aspiration was to be in it. These included not only Dissenters and Roman Catholics, but also some of the new commercial and industrial classes. It was all of this which erupted in the years immediately after 1815 reaching a peak in 1820 and then suddenly falling off. But everything remained in place ready to spring to life again at the appropriate time, and that was to come quite suddenly.

In 1827 Lord Liverpool, whose greatest achievement had been to keep an administration in power for so long, resigned, dying shortly after. His successor, George Canning, died soon after his appointment and was followed by Viscount Goderich who resigned after only a few months. George IV then asked the hero of Waterloo, the Duke of Wellington, to put together a new administration. Wellington was, in fact, to be the prime cause for the collapse of the long years of Tory rule, for he split his party right down the middle, firstly in 1828 by repealing the Test and Corporation Acts, which had excluded Dissenters and Roman Catholics from holding office, and then, the following year, committing what the ultra-Tories viewed as the ultimate betrayal, Catholic Emancipation. This meant that Catholic peers could once again sit in the Lords and that Catholics could be elected to the Commons. Although the measure had been carried to avert what was an even worse scenario, unrest in Ireland, the twin props of church and state were seen to be under fire. There followed a dramatic sequence of events which suddenly brought parliamentary reform once again to centre-stage.

The 1830s opened with a severe economic crisis which precipitated industrial unrest and uprisings in the countryside, the so-called 'Swing Riots'. Abroad there was a revolution in France. Radicalism re-emerged. In April 1831 a National Union of the Working Classes was formed and political unions began to be founded in all the major manufacturing and commercial centres. The middle classes began in some instances to look towards working class radicals to help them achieve political status. This tentative alliance had the long-term possibility of a revolution erupting from below.

In 1830 George IV died, unloved and unmourned, and the country went to the polls. The Tories were in disarray and Wellington was unable to hold together an administration. The new king, William IV, found that he had no alternative but to turn to a Whig, Earl Grey, who would accept office on one condition: parliamentary

The Meeting of the Unions on Newhall Hill, Birmingham, in 1832 by Benjamin Robert Haydon. The months leading up to the passing of the Reform Bill witnessed stormy meetings of political protest in the large cities. Haydon endows the one at Birmingham with an aura of religious fervour.

reform. Grey, a Whig aristocrat endowed with extraordinary perspicacity, realised that the days of aristocratic government – the rule of the élite – could only be prolonged by major reform. Tinkering with the existing system would not be enough, for that would only leave aristocratic rule under threat. In order to reinforce it, not only did the landed interest in the counties need to be strengthened but also the new industrial and commercial middle classes needed to be given greater weight.

A committee, made up largely but not exclusively of Whig ministers, was created to draft a Reform Bill which was presented to the House by Lord John Russell in March 1831. Its contents were so radical that MPs were incredulous, but it passed its second reading in the Commons, albeit by only one vote and amidst scenes of high drama. Opponents then began to amend the bill at the committee stage against the wishes of the government, so Grey prevailed upon the king to dissolve Parliament and embark on what was in effect a plebiscite on reform. What is so extraordinary is that it was the system to be swept away which voted for its own demise in a resounding Whig victory. A second Reform Bill passed its second reading in July, this time with a majority of 136, but there was still the Lords. Overwhelmingly Tory, the Lords rejected the Bill in October, leading to riots in towns and cities. The Bill was presented a second time in December and again rejected. Government by then had serious doubts as to whether it would be able to suppress the riots and uprisings which would certainly follow a third rejection. An increasing number of peers and MPs came to believe that a further rejection would trigger revolution on the streets.

In this tense atmosphere Grey resigned in May 1832, and William IV turned once more to Wellington to form an administration. He failed, and the king was forced to call again upon Grey, whose one condition this time was that if the Lords failed to pass the Bill the king would create enough new peers to outvote the opposition. In the face of this threat the Lords crumbled, and on 7 June the Great Reform Act received the royal assent. These had been months during which many feared that the whole stability of society was at stake. What had been achieved was indeed remarkable: an unreformed Parliament had willed its own demise and its replacement by another, thus redrawing the political map of Britain. The Reform Bill remains one of the greatest events in the history of the country. Just how great was only to be revealed in retrospect, as the political calm of the Victorian age unfolded in sharp contrast to the turbulence of the continental mainland.

As Lord Grey said: 'The principle of my reform is, to prevent the necessity for revolution . . . reforming to preserve and not to overthrow.' Fear was certainly one motivating force, but it was not the only one. There was a genuine spirit of reform, a belief that the new middle classes could no longer be ignored. Their presence in terms of property and intelligence was necessary, and by 'intelligence' they meant information. The House would be richer for those who could speak with authority on behalf of the new commercial and industrial concerns. Grey also saw those new voters as potential Whigs who would help to keep his party, so long in exile, in power. Support for the changes came even from unexpected sources like reactionary Tories who actually thought that a reformed House of Commons would never allow such a thing as Catholic Emancipation to happen. Everyone believed that a reformed House would curb what was seen as an extravagant government. More than anything else, however, this was an Act by the élite to perpetuate the élite, a measure designed to silence every critic, to secure the state from any revolutionary murmur from below, and to ensure the perpetuation of aristocratic power. In that they were astonishingly successful, for it was not to begin to crumble until the 1870s.

But what did the Act do? There was never any question of universal male suffrage. Not only would the upper classes have been swamped but the general view as to what a vote meant would have been eroded. The vote was for those regarded as capable of exercising it, a privilege bestowed upon men (there was no question of women) who had a vested interest in the stability of the state. That vested interest was embodied in property. In towns, the vote was therefore given to all whose houses were valued for rates at £10 p.a., a definition which brought in shopkeepers. In the counties it remained the forty-shilling freeholders, but went on to include £10 copyholders, long leaseholders and those tenants who paid more than £50 p.a. rent. In England and Wales this gave the vote to one in every five. Separate acts were passed for Scotland and Ireland. In Ireland the effect was an increase of only 5% in the electorate but in Scotland it suddenly leapt from 4,500 to 65,000.

The Act led to the redistribution of seats. This began with a swingeing attack on pocket boroughs. Some seats with less than 2,000 voters lost their MP altogether, others with between 2 to 4,000 voters were reduced from two MPs to one. The seats thus gained were then redistributed, twenty-two to towns not previously represented. These were chosen not on the basis of their population but on the interest they embodied, such as cotton or shipping. Sixty-five more seats were allocated to the counties, many of which were divided into two. Even with all this rooting out of what was regarded as the old corruption, seventy seats still remained in the control of aristocratic patrons. Indeed such a system had its uses, for it enabled the politically brilliant to begin their careers at a very young age. Under the aegis of the Duke of Newcastle one such twenty-three-year-old was returned in the post-reform Bill election. His name was William Ewart Gladstone.

There was, however, no change in the type of person who became an MP. The landed interest remained secure, for in order to stand for Parliament there was a £300 property qualification for a borough MP and £600 for a county MP. The job was to remain unpaid until 1911. Thus rank and property was consolidated and the middle classes, who had flirted with working class radicalism, were firmly hitched to the aristocratic bandwagon. Their instincts anyway were conservative, and they had achieved what they most wanted, recognition. They were accorded a supporting role within the system, one which could not altogether be ignored, for a hugely enlarged electorate meant that more than ever Parliamentary candidates had to listen to the electorate. The House of Commons also emerged from the Reform Bill crisis with a greatly enhanced status, for although it continued to be an extension of the Lords, the upper house in the final stages had been forced to submit to them. There were, of course, more significant losers. The working classes whose rallies had earlier ignited the cause of parliamentary reform emerged empty-handed. In addition the 1832 Act effected a new polarity, for it divided the nation right down the middle between those who had property and therefore political rights, and those who possessed neither.

The Great Reform Bill must not be viewed in isolation but as the crowning glory of a series of Acts which preceded the accession of Queen Victoria in 1837. These began with the repeal of the Test and Corporation Acts and Catholic Emancipation and went on, after the Reform Bill, to include others of major importance which radically affected the whole of society. In 1833 came the Abolition of Slavery in the British Empire, and the earliest Factory Act regulating child labour and introducing factory inspectors. The first state grant towards public education was also made in 1833. The following year the Poor Law Amendment Act restructured the Elizabethan system of poor relief, creating instead larger units under the control of Boards of Guardians elected by the ratepayers. In 1835 the Municipal Corporations Act dissolved the centuries old oligarchical town corporations, in the main solidly Tory and Anglican, and replaced them with municipal councils elected by the ratepayers, thus inaugurating an era of local reform. Finally, in 1836, the Tithe Commutation Act swept away another age-old practice, the payment to the clergy in kind, one amongst a major series of changes under the aegis of the Church Commissioners reforming the Church of England.

The importance of the passing of the Great Reform Bill of 1832 can never be overestimated. Its implications still affect us today, for it demonstrated how change could be achieved through Parliament by peaceful constitutional means without resorting to violence. Although it perpetuated aristocratic power no one could deny that the aristocracy had acted against its own interests in deference to a far greater one, a reform of the constitution to avert civil war or revolution.

Chapter Fifty-Five

COUNTRY INTO TOWN: THE INDUSTRIAL REVOLUTION

1 MAY 1851 was a day of sunshine and showers. By 11 o'clock over half a million people had gathered in London's Hyde Park around the vast structure made of iron and glass known to posterity as the Crystal Palace. Along the route past the teeming crowds a thousand coaches swept, bearing some thirty thousand guests to the opening of 'The Great Exhibition of the Works of Industry of All Nations'. They assembled inside what resembled a vast cathedral of glass, so large that it was able to accommodate with ease the huge elm trees of the park. The building itself was revolutionary, Sir Joseph Paxton's engineering masterpiece, but so also were the exhibits within it. The guests, in court attire and uniforms decked with jewels and orders, awaited the arrival of their young queen, Victoria, accompanied by her husband, Prince Albert, one of the master-minds behind the exhibition. When the queen arrived, dressed in a pink crinoline sparkling with diamonds and silver embroidery, ornate iron gates were flung wide, the national anthem was sung, fol-lowed by prayers, speeches and choruses culminating in the boom of a mighty organ, trumpet fanfares, and salvoes of cannon. In this manner the Great Exhibition was declared open, an event which was to attract over six million visitors.

There were a hundred thousand objects to be seen from all over the world but the western half of the structure was devoted to British goods. There the greatest attraction by far was the machinery courts. 'Went to the machinery courts,' the queen wrote in her diary, 'where we remained two hours, and which is excessively interesting and instructive . . . what used to be done by hand and used to take months is now accomplished in a few instants by the most beautiful machinery.' There were printing presses, threshing machines, hydraulic pumps, railway carriages, locomotives and steam hammers, to name but a few. Those who went on the great day would have come away with two overwhelming impressions, one of the amazing machines, and the other of the crush of humanity. Both were to be themes dominating the decades after the end of the Napoleonic Wars.

In the thirty-six years which separated the Battle of Waterloo from the Great Exhibition something tremendous had happened which changed everything, the Industrial Revolution. That was an expression invented in the twentieth century to explain an event which those who lived through it at the time were aware of, but to which they gave no name. No one has ever been able fully to explain why this revolution, which went by fits and starts through the century, should have happened in Britain. It had roots which stretched back several centuries to the enterprise of Tudor England, and certainly the pace quickened in the eighteenth century when many of the foundations were laid: the beginnings of the use of steam and water power, huge improvements in agriculture, and the development of more efficient communications through turnpike roads and the building of canals. But none of these developments signalled the most inexplicable factor of all, the huge rise in the population.

During the first half of the nineteenth century the population rose by 73%, increasing at the rate of two million a decade. The reasons for this were various: people married younger, produced more children and were nurtured on better food. The average life expectancy also rose to forty. This sudden enormous increase in the population meant that there were more people to buy things certainly, but they would only be able to buy them if they were in work producing income to be spent. In order to find such work, people drifted in increasingly large numbers from the countryside where they were born to the towns where the new industries offered far better employment prospects and higher wages. In 1800 25% of the population lived in cities or towns. By 1881, 80%. The year of the Great Exhibition was the first time that the number of urban dwellers exceeded those who dwelt in the countryside. Nothing comparable in terms of the movement of people and the change in work had been seen since the Dissolution of the Monasteries three hundred years before.

Nearly every city and town in the country grew. Certain of them virtually exploded. The boom towns were Manchester, Birmingham, Liverpool, Leeds, Sheffield and Bristol. In 1801 Birmingham had a population of 71,000, in 1831 144,000; Manchester's figures for the same dates are 75,000 and 182,000. There was no mechanism for dealing with such an unprecedented growth and the results were

The opening of the Great Exhibition, 1 May 1851. The royal family stand in the centre at the moment when the Archbishop of Canterbury uttered a prayer, signalling mass choirs singing the *Hallelujah Chorus*. Joseph Paxton, the designer of what became called the Crystal Palace, stands in the front row to the left, third in and with his hat tucked under his arm. The Chinaman to the right had gained admission by accident, but his exotic appearance secured him a place in the official procession of foreign representatives.

LONDON going out of Town. — or — The March of Bricks & Mortar. —

George Cruikshank's biting satire *London going out of Town*. Kilns belch out bricks while prototype robots as jerry builders set to work swallowing up the countryside. The green fields of Islington and Hampstead vanished beneath the relentless march of bricks and mortar. The date of the satire is 1829 but nothing was to stop this perpetual encroachment until the creation of so-called 'green belts' in the 1930s.

often horrendous. Rows of small back-to-back houses and airless tenement blocks were built devoid of decent sanitation, thus leading to outbreaks of disease and a high infant mortality rate. Towns which in the past had been a pleasant mixture of high and low now began sharply to divide between unspeakable inner city ghettoes for workers, and comfortable airy suburbs where the superior artisans and middle classes lived in detached villas, away from the grime and filth engendered by the new factories. Such segregation, however, reflected status, not hostility, and there was always opportunity for those with talent to cross the divide and move upwards.

More people not only put appalling pressure on the urban authorities but also on agriculture, for they had to be fed. That there was no shortage of food was due entirely to a continuation of the farming improvements of the previous century. Enclosures meant far better farming, creating compact units in which tenant farmers could adopt the new crop rotation systems and experiment with the scientific breeding of stock.

Areas which had previously been wastes and commons were brought into production. It was expensive to enclose, for the Church of England had to be paid off in lieu of their ancient feudal tithes, legal bills had to be met, new hedges planted and walls built. But there were good profits to be made for the new ease of transportation meant that foodstuffs could be got to the expanding markets in the towns. There was no lack of labour either, which partly accounts for the very slow mechanisation of agriculture. Although a mechanical threshing machine had been invented in 1786 it remained a rarity in the south-east of England, even in the 1850s. Only after that date, when labour became scarcer, did machines begin to take over.

The farmers thus prospered, being well able to meet the rise in rents imposed by the landowners. They in turn ploughed money back into improving their estates, that is until later in the century when they discovered that the financial returns from banking, commerce and industry were far greater. Investment by the aristocratic and landed classes in industry set them apart from their peers on the Continent, who looked down on trade. The agricultural revolution had enriched landowners, now the Industrial Revolution was to make them richer. They exploited to the full the natural resources on their estates: lead, iron, coal and tin. To their contribution can be added that of an ever-growing band of entrepreneurs, often men of lowly origins, whose determination, ambition and downright greed was to be a major driving force behind the Revolution. These were self-made men who started small businesses, who invented new methods of manufacture, and who possessed the energy to carry through single-handed every aspect of a project which today would call for a sizeable management team. They made their fortunes, reinvested in industry, and at the same time set themselves up as landowners, ensuring that their children were suitably educated for their new status in society.

The vast sums of money engendered by the Industrial Revolution demanded a multiplication of financial services to deal with it: banks, insurance companies and stock exchanges mushroomed. Business on the London Stock Exchange doubled during the 1860s, reflecting its newfound status as a centre of national and international business. Its open character attracted investors to such an extent that by 1875 it was handling investment out of the country worth £1,000 million.

Not only was there an ever-expanding home market but British goods, being the first in the world to be mass manufactured and therefore cheap, gradually conquered the globe. By 1850 over 90% of exports were of manufactured goods and a quarter of all international trade passed through British ports, mainly in British ships. It was cotton which led the way, opening up markets in Latin America in the 1820s and in India in the 1840s. Later in the century textiles gave place to metal and coal.

All of these industries interconnected. Machinery was constructed of metals like iron and steel, and these in turn called for coal to make and often fuel them. Even so, such developments would have been nullified had it not been for the invention of the railway and the advent of the steam ship. Both required large quantities of metal for their construction, and coal to operate them. In this way a whole cycle of dependency was created. Indeed, the new railways called for so much iron that by 1851 two and a half million tons was made a year. That output never flagged for the British, the earliest railway builders in the world, went on to construct rail systems in Europe and the United States. The numbers of ships needed to cope with the soaring export trade meant that between 1840 and 1870 the overall tonnage of British ships increased by more than 180%. As a result shipbuilding became a major industry, with important yards on Clydeside and in the north-east. Coal, as the basis of steam power, became central, so that by the 1860s a hundred million tons were being produced annually for home consumption and for export.

James Nasmyth's painting of a steam hammer captures the drama of industrial production by the third quarter of the century. Men toil away as pygmies trying to satisfy the hammer's devouring jaws from which erupts a massive iron bar.

In spite of all this, the progress of mechanisation was incredibly slow. The population explosion meant that there was no lack of human power and the workers naturally resented the introduction of any machine which would render them jobless. Even as late as 1870 human hands still accounted for most of the basic processes of manufacture, with machines only doing part of the work. Where machines did make inroads production inevitably shot up. Factories, however, were far from being gargantuan monsters. Most were small-scale affairs with about a hundred workers, and the majority of people plied their skill not in a factory at all but in groups in a workshop. As the century wore on, the physical effects on the landscape became more and more visible as railways, coal mines and factories sprang up, tearing apart what had been countryside. Areas like the midlands changed beyond recognition but in the context of the country as a whole the disruption was localised.

Such developments by no means signalled a polarity between the old country and the new town way of life. Land and industry remained closely linked and indeed those in agriculture benefited from the close proximity of the industrial towns in terms both of work and markets. Women also benefited, for in the factories they enjoyed the status of full-time wage earners even though the hours could be long and arduous. The proliferation of shopkeeping and street trading gave women new opportunities, which enhanced both their position and independence. Less attractive was the exploitation of child labour. That, of course, was nothing new, for the rural economy had depended on it since time immemorial but now it was transferred to the factory floor. Children, like women, received only a third to a sixth of what a man was paid. They were fearfully overworked and abused, something which only began to be put to rights when a whole series of Factory Acts were passed from 1833 onwards and education became available through church and factory schools.

Mass production called for a very different approach to work from that prevailing in the countryside, where employment tended to be irregular and seasonal with plenty of time to accommodate local festivities. In contrast, factory work demanded discipline, set hours, good time-keeping and the need for equal quality of workmanship. What produced that attitude of mind were the virtues cultivated by the middle classes in the long puritan tradition which had been reinforced by the new evangelicalism. In this scheme of things thrift, hard work, sobriety and self-improvement went hand-in-hand with an acceptance of the woes of life. The imposition of these alien attitudes onto the shiftless lower classes took time to root, but root they did.

Unlike the landed and middle classes those who made up the work force of the Industrial Revolution were hugely diversified, forming an elaborately structured ladder. At the top were trades like tailoring, carpentry, printing, coach-building and clockmaking, all good earners, while on the bottom rungs were agricultural workers, handloom weavers and framework knitters, who were increasingly redundant in the new age of the machine. Each group of skilled workers guarded their patch fiercely and felt little if any kinship with the vast mass of the unskilled who, by 1870, made up 80% of the workforce.

Manufactured goods and markets ready to purchase them are one thing, a network of communications to get them there is another. The inheritance from the previous century was good, and continued to be improved upon. Thomas Telford and John McAdam made huge advances in road construction producing a smooth metalled surface, which meant that horses could draw three times the weight at a far greater speed. But that was as nothing compared to the railway building of Victorian England. In 1825 the Stockton and Darlington Railway opened, a landmark less in invention, for the principles of steam power were already well-known, than in the realisation of its economic potential. The cost of coal transported on that track fell by three-quarters and those who had invested money in its construction reaped high

dividends. By 1850 more than 6,000 miles of track had been laid. By 1870, 13,000. Although depleted the system remains in use to this day, a tribute to the engineering genius of men like Samuel Morton Peto and Thomas Brassey. They carried the railways the length and breadth of the country, blasting tunnels and building bridges and viaducts, let alone hundreds of stations. The new railways meant that both the raw materials and the finished products of the Industrial Revolution could be transported at high speed across country and to the ports for export abroad. Export in its turn depended on shipping where another revolution took place, as sail gave way to steam

One of the most celebrated of all Victorian narrative paintings, William Powell Frith's *The Railway Station* painted in 1862. The station was Paddington and the artist used this quintessentially Victorian phenomenon as a setting for one of his epics of modern life in which onto one canvas he provides in paint a panorama of contemporary society parallel to that Dickens gave in the novel.

power. By the last quarter of the century the latter decisively took over, as Britain's sea-going shipping became equal in size to the rest of the world's put together.

The railways meant increased communication of another kind, firstly by post and secondly by telegraph (the telegraph poles were stationed along the rail track), making the dissemination of news almost instant. More people, more money, more means whereby to transport them, and everywhere as a consequence shops and stores multiplied. Where in the previous century a town would have a few small shops now it had many, as specialisation of both goods and services set in: drapers, china shops, booksellers, chemists, milliners, hairdressers, sprang up. In 1870 the first department store opened, and by the close of the decade the chain store was launched when Jesse Boot opened the first branch of Boots the chemist in Nottingham in 1877. A wide range of people now had money in their pockets to dispose of on things other than the bare necessities of life characteristic of earlier centuries. By 1870 advertising and promotion became a part of merchandising with brand-names leading the field, employing agents and travellers on the road to sell their wares.

Even in this bustling prosperous society life could take a sudden turn for the worse when trade took a downturn. Unlike former times prosperity was such that it was possible for a far greater number of people to make provision against the evil day. Friendly Societies by the 1850s could claim over a million and a half members. They had existed before but on nothing like the same scale, for such societies became the institutional embodiment of the skilled worker, with a scope of activity extending far beyond insurance to include bargaining with employers over hours and wages and ensuring exclusivity of skill. Their importance far surpassed that of the earliest trade unions which also represented the interests of the skilled workers. At the beginning of the century they were illegal, although they grew covertly under the guise of being Benefit, or Friendly Societies. They represented the increasing solidarity of the skilled worker as against the unskilled one. But skilled workers were also vulnerable, for the newly invented machines could render certain skills redundant, and could be used to make cheaper, shoddier goods. And always the workers were subject to fluctuations in the economy, never more so than in 1812 when Napoleon attempted his economic blockade of Britain. The first two decades were ones of industrial turbulence with frequent strikes and outbreaks of violence in which workers smashed the new machines which took their work from them. Those involved in this activity were known as Luddites. No one knows how many harboured aspirations to upset the established order of things and provoke a social revolution, but by the second decade the Luddites were a spent force. So much so that in 1824 the Combination Acts were repealed, and the following year an Act gave the unions legal status and the right to collect funds. There was, however, a proviso: they were to be subject to the common law which covered conspiracy and coercion.

In October 1833 a group of farm workers in the Dorset village of Tolpuddle joined the Friendly Society of Agricultural Labourers whose aim was to secure a just regard for their work. Unfortunately the rituals and secret oaths attending their admittance brought them within an infringement of the laws governing political subversion. Six men were prosecuted and transported, in a notorious case known as that of the 'Tolpuddle Martyrs'. In the end the men were pardoned and brought back to England, but the damage was done. In the context of the growing trade unionism of the period, what was striking about the case was that it happened at all.

Indeed during the 1820s and 30s unions began to band together to form a regional and national network. They printed their own journals, giving voice to radical political views. Unity was brought about by creating a common enemy, the employer, and presenting a view of society in which the capitalist system he represented, dependent on investment by individuals in the enterprise, would be replaced by a co-operative system in which the workers would collectively own and manage their own business. Such ideas were developed by the wealthy magnate and model factory owner, Robert Owen. Under his aegis the trade union movement drew together, forming in 1834 the Grand National Consolidated Trades Union. But it was beyond Owen's abilities to hold together what were warring factions, and the whole organisation collapsed within months. In the aftermath, the unions reverted back to their craft and regional groupings dedicated to exerting pressure on employees to push up wages. Only after 1870 did the mood change. In 1871 the Trades Union Act sought to provide them with a clear status at law. Membership and organisation of the unions had developed on such a scale by now that full-time officers who were literate, numerate and well-informed were needed to run them. Gradually these unions of skilled workers, who controlled the sinews of industry in terms of raw materials and transport, began to realise their potentially enormous power.

The growing unions were the winners, but there were losers too. None more so than the agricultural workers. There were too many of them, and the labour market was glutted after 1815 with demobilised soldiers from the wars. As a consequence wages fell. The old system of living-in with the farmer gave way to part-time seasonal employment, leading to migration to where work existed. Those who lived near the new towns fared best, their women and children finding work. Enclosures made things even worse. Initially they brought work in the way of hedging and ditching, building walls and making roads, but then came the bitter reality. There was nothing to replace all the rights, which had been theirs for centuries as part of the rural way of life, and which were now taken away from them without compensation: no opportunities any more for gleaning at harvest time, no common pasture for their cattle, no sources of free fuel or ponds to fish in. Poaching therefore became a way of life in order to supplement a family's meagre diet. Parliament passed a cruel set of game laws, protecting a whole range of birds and animals for slaughter by the landowner alone. In 1803 poaching was made a capital offence. What made this so savage was that many landowners were absentees, and never hunted the game they denied their luckless estate workers.

Agricultural workers were also threatened as machines took over. One result was the series of uprisings in 1830 and 1831 called the 'Swing Riots' in the south and east of England, in which labourers smashed the new threshing machines and went on to attack leaders of the rural community. In doing so they were emitting a cry from the heart for a lost way of life, the paternalism of pre-Industrial Revolution England. The riots were put down: five hundred people were transported, six hundred imprisoned and nineteen executed. Only after about 1850 did the plight of the agricultural workers begin to take an upturn.

These were the losers, tragic victims of a massive and irreversible revolution. But by the last quarter of the century more people were better off than ever before. The initial stages of change were hard, bringing few comforts, but in the context of the age the miracle was that there was not mass starvation. On the whole, the poor did not get poorer. It only seemed that they did, for the rich certainly got richer and there was an enormous expansion at every level of the middle classes. Both domestic service and factory work gave stable full-time employment to a large section of the population whereas, if the Industrial Revolution had not occurred, there would only have been untold poverty and degradation. Those who lost out were the workers whose skills were taken over by machines, and those who laboured on the land. To them we can add the many who slaved in what were known as the sweated trades like ribbon-making. What also lost out was the physical environment in which people lived and worked. For the first time pollution occurred on a gargantuan scale, lowering standards of public health. For those who lived through the changes the psychological impact of this new way of life must have been traumatic. But the clock could never be put back.

Chapter Fifty-Six

INFORMATION AND INTERVENTION

THE Industrial Revolution together with the population explosion unleashed problems unknown to any previous century, ones which forced central government to act, albeit against its instincts. The ethos inherited from previous ages remained vigorous, based on a horror of any form of state intervention or central government. In spite of such misgivings about government action, it continued to rise on an ever-ascending curve upwards from the 1830s. The idea that the state had any role at all to play in solving social problems was in itself novel, and worked only from the negative premise that unless government intervened things would only degenerate into chaos. By such intervention, it was argued, the state was ensuring that private initiative and enterprise would flourish unimpeded. Such a line of argument came from the writings of the political economist, Jeremy Bentham. To him the test for state intervention was utility, and those who subscribed to his beliefs were known as Utilitarians. State intervention also attracted the support of the old aristocratic élite who saw it as a continuance of their paternalistic role in society. Once the door of state intervention had been pushed ajar, however, it continued to be opened wider, until in the next century virtually every aspect of daily life came under its control. In this way the modern cradle-to-grave state was born.

Towards the end of the Victorian age F. W. Maitland, the constitutional historian, wrote: 'We are becoming a much governed nation, governed by all manner of councils and boards and others, central and local, high and low, exercising powers which have been entrusted to them by modern statutes.' All of these were to sprout into existence during the long years of Queen Victoria's reign, most in response to the all-too-visible effects of the Industrial Revolution. They also came into being through another great change, the advent of extensive information based on research and statistics. From the 1830s onwards most great changes came as the result of a new form of investigative body, the Royal Commission of Enquiry. The Royal Commissions produced a mass of on-the-ground evidence which must have seemed unanswerable. What can be overlooked is that the evidence which enquiries threw up could be carefully edited to take the direction the commissioners, or indeed the government, wanted. Royal Commissions, however, were not the only new organisations producing information. A Census Office was set up, which produced every decade figures on the number, nature and location of the population. In 1837, the year in which Victoria came to the throne, the registration of births, deaths and marriages was introduced, although it was not until 1874 that it was to become compulsory. This evoked another torrent of fact. The Acts of Parliament in response to such enquiries produced yet another source of more information in a new type of official, the inspector. It took some time for the inspector to evolve his role, but one certain task he had from the very beginning was to present a report on his findings. Thus even more information piled up, leading inexorably to more government intervention.

The effect of this is seen in the steady rise in the number of government employees. In 1780 there were some 16,000, in the main collecting customs and excise duties. By 1870 there were 54,000, reflecting a radical change in government's role, for it had assumed that of regulator, co-ordinator, and director of more and more aspects of everyday life, dealing with areas as discrepant as prisons and schools, factories and lunatic asylums. The increase in what became called civil servants was to continue spiralling upwards until the 1950s. These people and the state intervention they embodied had to be paid for, and the figures here also tell the story vividly. By 1830 national taxes totalled £55 million, by 1860 £70 million, and by the early 1900s £200 million. Although initially the burden of cost was borne by the ratepayer, the increased need for money to run these new government services meant that income tax, re-introduced in 1842, rose steadily and, later in the century, death duty, a tax on inheritance was initiated. The rise in local taxation was to be even steeper. In 1850 it stood at £10 million. By 1905 it had rocketed to nearly £108 million. In local government, too, a small army of officials had sprung into being.

The huge growth in the number of civil servants was not at the outset viewed with dismay by the government. These posts were a source of patronage for them, a way to reward friends and relatives with jobs. Those in opposition naturally called for reduction and reform but it was a long time coming. Although a report in 1853 recommended a unified Civil Service and entry to it by competitive examination, it was acted upon only very slowly. Two years later competitive entry was introduced for junior posts but not till 1870 for all grades. Only gradually were the foundations laid for an

Thomas Annan's early photo-reportage of the Glasgow slums in 1868. No attempt is made to render the scene picturesque, only to record its utter squalor. The new art of photography is used here as an agent for reform.

administrative profession of real quality. For most of the century the upper reaches of the Civil Service remained a source of patronage for the government of the day.

The growth of the Civil Service was as much as anything the result of the central government's problem in persuading local government to put into practice its statutes. The 1835 Municipal Corporations Act had created borough councils elected by the ratepayers, and required to submit for Treasury approval any large capital expenditure – a defence against corruption. Ratepayers, however, did not warm to anything which increased local expenditure. To achieve its objectives therefore, government was forced by the middle of the century to offer grants as an inducement. District auditors were appointed to check up on local government expenditure. Gradually, local boards and councils multiplied, exactly as F. W. Maitland described; elected County Councils were set up in 1888, the same year in which the London County Council was created, and Urban and Rural District Councils followed in 1894. These effectively replaced the old way of governing rural areas by means of lord lieutenants and Justices of the Peace. By 1900 central government sat in the middle of a network of authorities which stretched across the entire country in a way that would have evoked consternation in 1800.

This gargantuan multiplication of the organs of government was a long-term consequence of the Industrial Revolution which produced a largely urban society for the first time, giving rise to problems which could only be met by developing Parliament's role, initiated by the Great Reform Bill, as an agent of change. One of the earliest interventions was over child labour in the factories. There was widespread concern that young children were working up to twelve and fourteen hours a day in appalling conditions. In 1833 a Royal Commission recommended action on the usual utilitarian grounds that as children were not free agents the state should intervene to protect them. The Factory Act of that year prohibited children below the age of nine from working, those aged nine to thirteen being restricted to a nine-hour day and those aged fourteen to eighteen to twelve hours. Two hours compulsory schooling was introduced for the under thirteens and, for the first time, inspectors were appointed. A decade later women were likewise categorised as being unfree agents in the workplace, the argument being used to prohibit their working in mines. Acts of Parliament regulating this or that about factory work were never altogether to disappear from the agenda.

The Church of England, which had entered the century unreformed, similarly found itself the subject of government intervention. Another commission confirmed the worst, that only half of the church's ten thousand benefices had a resident cleric and that enormous disparities of income existed between the richest bishop and the humblest parson. Criticism was fuelled too by the fact that those who did not belong to the church, the large body of Dissenters, were forced to pay church rates for the upkeep of church buildings. In 1835 the Ecclesiastical Duties and Revenues Commission, a mixture of politicians and bishops, was set up and began the long overdue process of reform. This led to the building of some two thousand new churches in response to the huge increase and shift in population. The following year, an Act swept away the historic payment to the church of a tenth of one's produce, the tithe, replacing it by the payment of money. Not since the Commonwealth in the 1650s had the state intervened so heavily in the affairs of the church to radically change it. Such interference was not to go unchallenged. In 1833 a small group of Anglican clerics, headed by John Henry Newman, began a protest which later developed into what was called the Oxford Movement. This revitalised the church but left it sharply divided between the earlier Evangelicals and the new High Church movement which was viewed as drifting Romewards. (Newman in fact became a Roman Catholic and ended a cardinal.) This had no impact, however, on the central issue, the relationship of the church and state, which went back to the sixteenth century and justified such interference in the first place. For government, the church usefully embodied a rock of traditional social values which should remain firmly yoked to it.

Interventions of this kind in the 1830s and 40s were hugely innovative. The government went on to remodel the prison system, to reform provision for the insane (both again with inspectors attached), to bring the new railway system within government regulations, to establish the primacy of the notes of the Bank of England and to introduce an inexpensive postal system, the Penny Post. These were just a handful of the areas into which the arm of the state suddenly extended itself. Three of them, however, were to have by far the greatest long term implications, those dealing with the poor, public health, and the education of the lower classes. Each was to end the century with a complete state bureaucracy around it.

Provision for the poor remained in 1830 as it had in the reign of Elizabeth I. Many viewed that system as only encouraging fecklessness and large families at public expense and the Utilitarians called for the erection of workhouses to ensure that at least the able-bodied were set to work. The rural 'Swing Riots' led firstly to a Royal Commission and then, in 1834, to the Poor Law Amendment Act. That Act was the first instance of the appearance of what was to become a new feature of modern society: the expert. The Commission collected evidence but as its members were Utilitarians its findings were a foregone conclusion and the evidence was massaged in the direction in which they wanted it to go. The country was divided into areas, each of which had a Board of Guardians elected by the ratepayers, under whose auspices

workhouses were to be built and other forms of relief provided. A central Poor Law Board was set up, signalling the advent of yet another new department of state with a bureaucracy of inspectors attached to it. The response was slow and it was not until the 1850s that workhouses began to arise in any great number. Revelations of what went on in some of them during the 1860s led to improvements, and by 1900 there

Sir Hubert von Herkomer's *Eventide* (1878) provides the only Victorian picture of the dreaded workhouse. The artist painted it from sketches made in the Westminster workhouse. Painting, like photography, was also used as a vehicle to heighten social awareness.

were even treats and outings for the inmates. The system was cost-effective, and no other state in Europe took such interest in provision for the poor. Within the workhouses the sexes were separated, uniforms were worn, and strict discipline maintained. But the fact remained that they came to symbolise an ultimate degradation, the loss of any status within society.

Poverty often as not went hand-in-hand with dirt and disease. The connection between the latter was already known in the 1830s and 40s but it took decades for the state to intervene. In 1842 Edwin Chadwick produced his famous Sanitary Report proving that illness and premature death had an environmental base and that this could be changed by government legislation. The statistics he produced were unanswerable. Death from fever, smallpox, consumption, pneumonia and other killer diseases were two or three times higher in the densely populated towns as in the rural areas. No action, however, was taken, so strong was public sentiment against any form of government interference in what was seen as essentially a local affair. In 1848 a Public Health Act set up a General Board of Health, something which was viewed with dismay, and it was wound up ten years later. In 1866 the Sanitary Act laid down that the government could overrule local authorities on matters of health but it was not to be until a Royal Commission on Public Health led to the Local Government and Public Health Acts of 1871 and 1872 that the state accepted that it had a role to play in the prevention of disease. That role was taken on with the usual reluctance and on the customary basis that inactivity would do more harm than intervention. But it had taken thirty years to come about, during which time untold thousands had died through official inertia.

Education was to be a far more complex story. Until the Industrial Revolution the state had played no role in education. Indeed any form of education for the lower orders was considered potentially dangerous, giving them ideas above their station. By the 1830s that view had shifted, in the face of ghettoes of brutalised and irreligious working class hordes in the new industrial towns. Education began to be seen as a means of taming them, ensuring that they understood their place in society and thus

Photography again used as an agent for change. From the outset in 1868 photography was an essential part of Dr Thomas Barnardo's crusade to rescue destitute and deprived children. The archive remains a remarkable testament to the poverty and degradation which made up the other side of Victorian urban life. Before and after shots like these were used as fund-raising material and for publicity.

Chapter Fifty-Seven

THE FINAL DECADES OF ARISTOCRATIC RULE

T HE passing of the Great Reform Bill in 1832 achieved what it had set out to do, prolong aristocratic rule, but it could not do so indefinitely. After 1870 it was finally to spiral downwards in a spectacular decline to the present day. But that decline was to be gradual. To all intents and purposes the aristocracy still dominated the political, social and economic scene and also the powers, such as the army and the police, which underpinned it. Only a fifth of the population had the vote and their attitudes, too, were based on land and property. At the time it must have seemed that nothing had changed, indeed that the status quo had been reinforced. In the long term that was to prove an illusion.

The forty years which followed 1832 seemed unbelievably complicated as ministries came and went. Although a two-party system was gradually emerging, no one envisaged that system as the future pattern of politics, even as late as 1860. There were confusing and shifting alliances of Whigs, Conservatives, Peelites, Irish nationalists and radicals. Regardless of these alignments, however, the majority came together, sharing certain premises as to the nature and objectives of government, in particular a strong sense of the importance of national and imperial security, which pervaded the entire political world. Government was above all to be cheap, and although it intervened, that intervention was done with reluctance and remained still essentially limited. Regardless of party, the prime aim of any government was seen as ensuring freedom of action to the individual from state interference, and creating conditions in which private enterprise and endeavour would flourish. To achieve that, ministries of different persuasions passed the long series of social and political legislation which was eventually to spell the death knell of aristocratic power.

During these decades there occurred one by one the changes which cumulatively were irrevocably to alter the power structure of the country. The reduction in the position of the monarchy with George IV and William IV, neither of whom commanded respect, accelerated. Although all acts of government continued to be carried out in the name of the sovereign (and are even to this day), this merely provided a convenient framework, giving an illusion of continuity. One by one, royal powers quietly vanished. Ever-increasing professionalism of government progressively marginalised the crown's political role in the state. Although the monarch still chose the Prime Minister and asked him to form a ministry, his choice was narrowed to someone who had the general confidence of Parliament and especially the House of Commons. In 1834 William IV granted the Prime Minister Sir Robert Peel's request for a dissolution. Henceforward such a request by a Prime Minister was never again to be refused. Peel failed to win from the electorate a Commons majority and although he enjoyed the king's support he was forced to resign. This signalled another erosion of royal power: no Prime Minister could ever again be sustained in office by the monarch. When the young and ill-educated Victoria came to the throne in 1837 the crown was to slip still further. Her open preference for Lord Melbourne and the Whigs became a danger to the monarchy even affecting her choice of the women in her service at court. The queen was saved by her marriage in 1840 to Prince

A satire in which the young Robert Peel dreams of a peerage as a reward for his part in achieving Catholic Emancipation in 1829. Its title *The Vision – the rewards of perfidy* record the views of those who opposed the motion.

THE VISION.
"And I awoke, and behold, it was a Dream!"

The eighteen-year-old Queen Victoria satirised as caught between Lord Melbourne, who was Prime Minister, on the left and Lord John Russell, on the right.

Albert who hewed out a new role for the crown as a unifying force rising above transitory demands of political party. The monarch's role in home affairs henceforth could not extend beyond one of advice and warning, however strong personal preferences might be. A diminished power over foreign policy was to linger until the 1860s.

Parliament's role too evolved from that of previous centuries into one of intervention as an agent of change. Until about 1850 most bills remained local or personal, as they had been in the past. After that date the balance decisively shifted to a preponderance of public general statutes and many more of them, indeed evermultiplying as the century wore on. Their implications, often affecting the whole population, were such that they called for meticulous drafting, and that expertise was to develop only gradually. Although members of the Lords still had immense powers of political patronage, retaining even into the 1880s control over certain constituencies, the influence of the Lords was on the decline, and was in the end to be dramatically curtailed by two further Reform Acts in 1867 and 1884 which extended the franchise to classes beyond their control. Political power now firmly lay with the Commons whose members were still drawn from the wealthier sections of the community, increasingly from those whose riches came not from the land but from commerce and industry. As the electorate widened the whole character of elections changed, leading to the development of party machines to rally the voters. That in turn gradually led to the elimination of what had been the backbone of the Commons in the previous century, the independent members. By 1870 they had vanished, and solid voting along a two-party system developed.

Ministers still had to be men of wealth, status and standing in society. They were mostly either peers by birth or were soon ennobled. What this system had in its favour was the wide age range it embraced plus the fact it contained a mixture of old and new aristocracy who, because their estates were scattered all over the country, embodied an abundance of grassroots knowledge. Any aristocratic ministry in the end remained loyal to its creed of putting country before class. This reflected the awareness of the ruling élite that although only a fifth of the population voted, it was their duty to protect and act in the interests of those who did not have the franchise. When Peel repealed the Corn Laws in 1846 he presented his action in this light, as averting starvation and famine for ordinary people, although by doing so he split his own party in two. The time had not yet come when legislation would only be attempted which had the imprimatur of the party. The gradual widening of the electorate and the rise of literacy was to mean a far more widespread knowledge and interest in political issues than ever before, leading to figures such as W. E. Gladstone and Benjamin Disraeli becoming household names in a manner up till then unthinkable.

One of the greatest statesmen of the century was Sir Robert Peel, the man who, in the aftermath of the shock of 1832, was to revive the fortunes of the Tories in a new guise, that of the future Conservative Party. Hard work and dedication to the cause, aligned to a remarkable intellectual agility and mastery of detail, ensured that he dominated the Commons through his knowledge and brainpower. A politician who was still in one sense cast in the old aristocratic mould, Peel took the bold decision that the only way to revive Tory fortunes was to accept the Reform Bill. The Tamworth Manifesto, an address to his constituents in 1834, was the first time a party had ever offered a programme to a national electorate, the progenitor of today's party manifestos. It was addressed not only to Tories but to all people of a conservative temperament who accepted the 1832 Bill, laying down the principles upon which, should they come to power, they would act. In his belief church and crown were sacrosanct but he conceded that the country's age-old institutions should be subject both to review and to change. In short, evolution rather then revolution. If the idea of a national manifesto setting out a programme for action was new, so too was the organisational drive to secure voters. That centred on local associations who searched electoral registers and recruited voters on a scale unheard of before 1832.

In 1841, owing much to such work in the constituencies as well as to fear by the landed interest of a repeal of the Corn Laws, Peel was swept to power, bringing with him one of the ablest administrations of the century. Income tax was brought back in order to obtain a freer hand for tariff reductions, and by progressively removing

export and import duties Peel was to pave the way for the heyday of free trade after 1850. He was to be looked back on as a great Prime Minister. In party terms he refashioned the Tories as the Conservatives by forging an alliance between the old traditionalists with men

A top-hatted policeman, known as a Peeler, helping people in Trafalgar Square in the early 1860s. Sir Edwin Landseer's lions had yet to be added to Nelson's Column.

attuned to the new age of industry. That reorientation was to survive even the blow dealt by his repeal of the Corn Laws.

Agriculture had stood protected by the Corn Laws since the close of the Napoleonic wars. These had guaranteed the price of corn and kept out the importation of cheap foreign grain. Such laws were increasingly an affront to the commercial and industrial classes, who believed in free trade and resented the special status thus accorded the landed rural classes. In 1839 the Anti-Corn Law League was established, sponsoring a nationwide programme of rallies, meetings and lectures. Those who supported it were largely urban and middle class, belonging to a group which also brought in Dissenters, radicals and those opposed to the establishment. Its opponents could be described as the landed interest, rural, Anglican and conservative. The League was a new form of protest movement which lacked neither money nor organisational drive. From the outset there was a realisation that in the post-1832 world the only way to achieve their objective was via the ballot box. They had to capture voters and through them MPs, and in doing this they set a precedent which other protest groups were later to emulate. The irony was that their objective was achieved not by them but by an act of aristocratic paternalism. Peel carried the Repeal of the Corn Laws in 1846 with the support of opposition Whig votes. Shortly after that the Whigs promptly allied themselves with his own backbenchers, who regarded him as having betrayed an election pledge, to bring him down.

The Anti-Corn Law League worked within the framework of how things were to be in sharp contrast to another countrywide movement, the Chartists, whose means of protest were a throwback to the years immediately after 1815. Chartism, however, was the most important political movement of the century, vividly reflected in the fact that five out of their six demands were granted by 1918. What was called the People's Charter was drawn up by a London cabinet-maker and a radical master-tailor called Francis Place in 1838. It called for universal male suffrage, the abolition of the property qualification for MPs, annual Parliaments, electoral districts of equal size, the payment of MPs and a secret ballot. None of these ideas were new but they resurfaced in a forceful way as a revival of artisan and middle class radicalism based in London and Birmingham. In the context of the late 1830s such demands would have been seen as revolutionary. In 1839 a National Convention was held in London and reconvened in Birmingham where it provoked riots and unrest which were suppressed by the army and the police. Huge petitions were presented to Parliament

The earliest photograph of a mass protest rally, the Great Chartist meeting on Kennington Common in April 1848, a daguerreotype taken by William Kilburn. It encapsulates in one image the established classes fear of revolution from below.

which promptly threw them out, one in 1839 with 1.3 million signatures and a second in 1842 with 3.3 million. In 1840, under the aegis of Feargus O'Connor, the National Charter Association was formed and meetings and demonstrations punctuated the 1840s until 1848, when they finally petered out in a vast rally on Kennington Common. The campaign, demonstrations and strikes achieved nothing in the end, but they did leave a bitter and deep legacy amongst the working classes which was to surface later in the century.

In Europe, 1848 was the Year of Revolutions, with governments facing challenges to their authority all over the Continent. In England that year was to be the preface to a decade of prosperity as the country entered its Victorian apogee. The Chartists were doomed to failure from the outset. They cast themselves in a struggle against what they viewed as a rich and indolent aristocracy allied to a perfidious middle class which had sold out to them. In a way they were right, for the Reform Bill had hitched the middle classes firmly to the aristocratic bandwagon. But the Chartists were themselves disunited, worse, they were devoid of money or weapons or even the sense to work via the electorate. Their only means of exerting pressure was by way of petition. Any unrest they caused was also easily contained in an age when both police and troops could be moved around by the new railways. Government astutely avoided making any Chartist a martyr. The movement lingered on after 1848 but it was a spent force, neutered by Victorian prosperity. It had been at its height in the years of industrial slump. After its failure radicalism was to move north to the industrial cities, where the strong egalitarian legacy of the Chartists was to pass into the labour-based politics of the working man.

After Peel's resignation came a shifting kaleidoscope of ministries for over a decade, in which party labels counted for little. What dominated the 1850s more than any other issue was the Crimean War. The popular nationalism which swept through Europe in the aftermath of the Napoleonic Wars naturally evoked strong sympathies with a country fed on the myth of British freedoms. The public supported Garibaldi in his mission to unite Italy but, at the same time, wanted to sustain the Austro-Hungarian Empire north of the Alps as a buffer against Russian expansionism. The great Foreign Minister of the period was Lord Palmerston who saw his role as guaranteeing Britain's place as the leading world power in naval and commercial terms, but not even at its apogee was Britain able to prevent Prussia's creation within Europe of a single massive German state. The consequence of that in the next century was to be momentous. Russia's expansionist policies at the expense of the disintegrating Ottoman Empire in the Near East, however, did warrant Palmerston's attention because of its repercussions on British trade in the area.

In the summer of 1853 Russia invaded what is now Romania. In the autumn a joint Franco-British force was sent to the Black Sea followed by war being declared in February of the next year. It had huge popular support from a public unaware that the country's army and navy were in a state of decay. The next two years brought nothing but sagas of ineptitude and disaster. The army laid siege to Sebastopol and there were bloody battles. What set this war apart from any other was that for the first time people at home read on-the-spot accounts of it in the newspapers. They were appalled. Although Sebastopol fell in September 1855 and peace was made the following March, the repercussions at home were tremendous. The government, headed by Lord Aberdeen, was seen to be made up of incompetent aristocrats and the war brought about its downfall. And Lord Palmerston, who succeeded, was forced to accept an enquiry into the conduct of the war. The cynical view from the street was one of disenchantment with dilettante aristocrats who had allowed the country's forces and war machine to lapse into chaos.

Three years after the close of the Crimean War the years of ever-changing ministries came to an end when the followers of Sir Robert Peel (who died in 1850), the Peelites, came together with the Whigs, Liberals and Radicals to form the future Liberal party, with Lord Palmerston as Prime Minister and William Ewart Gladstone emerging as a major force within the new party. When Palmerston died in 1865 he was succeeded by Lord John Russell and electoral reform, which had been off the agenda since 1832, returned. By the 1860s British society, with its ever-growing pop-

The first notable war reporter recorded by Roger Fenton. William Russell was correspondent for *The Times* during the Crimean War bringing its readers hitherto unknown graphic descriptions of the realities of war. His vivid reports of the appalling conditions of the troops inspired Florence Nightingale.

ulation and ever-burgeoning middle classes, was very different, calling for an extension of the franchise. The problem was how to achieve this without granting the vote, still viewed not as a natural right but a privilege bestowed, to people who might endanger the existing scheme of things. The perception was that it would be wiser to make an adjustment at a time of general prosperity and an absence of pressure rather than wait for protest to mount. The Liberal bill was defeated in 1866, however, and the Conservatives, headed by Benjamin Disraeli, were called upon to form a ministry. The Conservatives had been in the political wilderness for a generation, ever since Peel had split them down the middle over the Corn Laws. Disraeli realised that there they would dwell for as long as they were regarded as the party only of landed interest. He therefore set out to outwit Gladstone (his great rival) and the Liberals by pre-empting their role as reformers. Thus, he believed, a sure path would be laid to power. The bill the Conservatives compiled was a ramshackle, ill-thought-through affair into which Disraeli bounced his party wholly unaware of its consequences. The Act was passed in 1867 and this time granted the vote to all urban householders and to those paying £10 in rent. In the counties the occupational qualification was lowered from £50 to £15. As a result the electorate was doubled, and two people in five now had the vote. The redistribution of constituencies in response to the shifts in population was, however, minimal, thus greatly curtailing any threat to the status quo. This was in no way a landmark of the magnitude of 1832 but it was a significant marker. No one could control how that number of people would vote, especially as the secret ballot was introduced in 1872. On the surface much that was familiar remained in place. The redistribution of seats maintained a balance in favour of rural areas and an eighth of them continued to be filled by aristocratic patronage. But that was a mirage. The 1867 Act sounded the death knell of the rule of the élite. A huge electorate running into millions called for the development of party machines on an even larger scale, with a central office and active local party associations. This time the make-up of the electorate firmly reflected the changed reality of Victorian Britain in the aftermath of the Industrial Revolution, for it was urban and working. Whether Conservatives liked it or not, if they wished to remain in power in the future they would have to play to the electorate which they had created. The Liberals had to come to terms with the same dilemma and also with increasing pressure from the middle classes for a share in the control of the party. With a vast electorate, those who hoped to become MPs stood little chance of being elected without adherence to, and support from, one of the major party machines. By 1870 the monarchy had lost control of government. Now it was to be the turn of the aristocracy.

Chapter Fifty-Eight

THE LADY WITH THE LAMP

APART from the queen, Florence Nightingale remains arguably the most famous woman of the Victorian age. She was born in the first year of the reign of George IV, 1820, and died at the enormous age of ninety in 1910 in that of Edward VII. Both in her ideas and in her life she was before her time, pioneering and challenging the accepted scheme of things as laid down for a Victorian woman, demanding that she be accepted on her own terms as an equal in a man's world. Although she began with the advantages of being born into a wealthy family which had extensive connections within the establishment classes, that cannot erode the achievement of a life which defied the rules of the age. To challenge what a woman of her class could and could not do demanded great personal sacrifice, including deny-ing herself the happiness of marriage and children.

Florence Nightingale was named after the city in Italy in which she was born, one of the ten children of William Edward Nightingale, the son of a Sheffield banker, and Frances Smith. Her parents were sharply contrasted in character, her father being of a quiet and studious disposition, her mother vivacious and strong-willed. The family ethos fell within the Wilberforce evangelical tradition with its renewed religious piety and strong sense of moral commitment to the virtuous life. The Nightingales divided their time between two houses, one in Derbyshire and a second in Hampshire, punc-tuated by occasional visits to London.

In one sense Florence Nightingale's childhood was no different from that of any other girl of her class, for she was taught by a governess those accomplishments thought essential for a young lady, the ability to read and write, sew and make music and, above all, the social graces which would ensure that she would make a good marriage. In another sense her upbringing was extremely unusual, for at the age of twelve she began, with her sister Parthenope, to be educated by her father who in-structed them in subjects rarely taught to women, such as Greek and Latin, the art of composition and mathematics.

The trouble was that this only fuelled the frustration of a girl already by nature withdrawn, solitary and shy. As a young lady her place was in the home whereas, as she wrote, she longed for 'some regular occupation, for something worth doing instead of frittering time away on useless trifles.' To have been allowed that would have broken every convention in the 1830s. At seventeen she recorded: 'God spoke and called me to His service,' but what form that call was to take took sixteen years to materialise, during which time Florence grew up to be a witty, entertaining and elegant young woman who quickly attracted suitors. Chief amongst these was a handsome poet, Richard Monckton Milnes, with whom she fell in love. For seven years he waited for her to accept his proposal of marriage but, much to the fury of her family, she rejected him. Her reason strikes a modern chord: 'I could not satisfy this nature by spending a life with him in making society and arranging domestic things . . . '

Florence Nightingale as a young woman seated in the window of her parents' house, Lea Hurst.

By then she had begun to tread the path on which she was to make her name. Much to the horror of her mother she was discovered nursing sick villagers. Worse, the family had to intervene and forbid her learning nursing at the local hospital in Salisbury. That they were so opposed is hardly surprising, for hospitals then bore little resemblance to those we know today. The wards were huge, with beds jammed together. The filth was unimaginable, the floors stained with blood from operations. The patients, infected with lice and vermin, lay in sheets which were rarely washed. Surgeons walked around in clothes so stiff and soaked with blood from the operations they performed that they could sometimes stand up on their own. There was no such person as a trained nurse. As Florence Nightingale wrote, those who passed as nurses were 'women who had lost their characters' and slept either in the wards or in wooden cages just outside.

The family's decision precipitated a nervous breakdown. In 1848 two friends took Florence to Rome, where she met a rising star in the political world, Sidney Herbert, an encounter which was to prove a turning point. Both shared a passionate sense of social justice of a kind which turned her against the closed country house world she inhabited: ' . . . everything that is painful is so carefully removed out of sight, behind those fine trees, to a village three miles off. In London, at all events if you open your eyes, you cannot help seeing in the next street that life is not all as it has been made to you.'

Her determination was renewed and, defying her family who placed every obstacle in her path, she went to Germany in 1851 to learn nursing from an order of deaconesses. The contrast to her former life could not have been more dramatic. She arose at five o'clock every morning to start work. At six there was a bowl of rye gruel and then work till twelve. Then there was a ten-minute break for some broth after which she worked again until seven. Each day ended with a Bible class and then to bed. And yet she was able to write home to her mother; 'Now I know what it is to live and to love life.'

Two years later she was offered the chance to be the head of an Institution for the Care of Sick Gentlewomen in London. Her family again tried to stop her but she took the post. She had only ten days in which to set up the new hospital. There she was able to put in practice everything which had accumulated in her mind about the art of nursing. That sprang from what was then a new idea, that both patients and nurses should be comfortable. Everything was also to be spotlessly clean and the patients were to be properly fed. As there were no trained nurses, Florence set out to teach by example. From this she emerged not only as a great nurse but also a great organiser.

A year later the Crimean War began, and within months not only were there hundreds of wounded but cholera broke out. Reports were published of the terrible conditions, of the lack of a hospital let alone of any nurses to care for the soldiers. Sidney Herbert was Secretary for War. When it came to sending nurses he knew there was 'but one person in England . . . who would be capable of organising and superintending such a scheme.'

Florence Nightingale was just thirty-four when she set sail with her thirty-eight nurses, many of them women she would have to train on the spot when they arrived. Everything was against her. Her family strongly disapproved. The army doctors did not want her. No woman had ever before been employed to nurse a wounded soldier, so that she was breaking wholly new ground. The so-called hospital was in the old Turkish barracks in the village of Scutari. It was filthy, with damp oozing from the walls, the drains were clogged with rotting muck, rats were everywhere and there was nothing to cook with. Inside, several thousand soldiers lay on wooden bunks on the floors, many dying of their wounds. But the army doctors refused to let her in. Patiently Florence Nightingale and her companions waited until, after the great battle at Balaclava, the wounded came flooding in. Then the doctors were forced to capitulate. A battle of a very different kind followed, for the barracks had to be turned into a proper hospital. Her powers of organisation and energy were formidable. She wrote and wrote, reports, letters, plans to improve the way hospitals were run, others for reforming the army medical services, anything which would ameliorate the horrendous conditions in which she worked. These she wrote long into the night, for her day was filled with action in the wards. Each night she slowly toured the wards bearing a lantern in her hand. Sometimes she would pause and bend down to comfort a soldier in pain or distress. In this way the legend of 'The Lady with the Lamp' was born.

One by one the battles were won. She got the soldiers' wives to wash the bed linen so that there were clean sheets for the first time. A chef came from London and organised the kitchens, built new ovens and cooked food for the sick. The filthy walls were painted white, the rat-infested wooden platforms used as beds were replaced with iron ones, and clean water was provided. Literally tons of dirt and rubbish were carted away. Florence Nightingale saw her soldier-patients first of all as human beings, arranging for them to send money home to their families, setting up lectures and providing a room in which they could read or write. All of this was totally innovatory.

It was a tremendous achievement against equally tremendous odds for she had to fight her way through a man's world, arguing her case with people at the top who opposed her. Arrogant she could be, but no one could deny her extraordinary powers both as an administrator and as petitioner. By 1855 she had become a national heroine and the year after government accorded her total authority over running the hospital. Peace was declared a fortnight later.

These years of bitter cold, discomfort, tiredness and never-ending work had left her an emaciated figure, with her hair cut short. When she set sail for home all England wished to pay her tribute, but that was the last thing that she wanted. With her aunt, Mrs Smith, Florence Nightingale travelled back as plain 'Miss Smith', literally slipping into the country and eventually catching a train to her family in Derbyshire. She walked from the station arriving suddenly in their midst, unannounced, on 7 August 1856.

Although an invalid she was to live another half-century, dedicating it to changing the system: 'I stand at the altar of the murdered men and while I live shall fight their cause.' She sought and gained a Royal Commission on the army medical services. She enlisted and won the support of both the queen and Prince Albert. Her work embodied a revolution, recognising for the first time preventative medicine. Only one in seven in the Crimea died of wounds. The rest died of preventable diseases caused by germs being spread through bad ventilation, overcrowding, lack of drainage and proper observance of basic hygiene, in addition to the wrong clothing and diet for patients. The army fought against her but she won, and in 1859 the Army Medical School was set up according to her guidelines.

The House of Mercy. Florence Nightingale receiving the wounded at Scutari, 1856 by Jerry Barrett. Barrett painted this picture two years after the event from sketches made on the spot at the time and from sittings in London which included Florence Nightingale who stands, bathed in light, below the window. Others present include Alexis Soyer who revolutionised the army's catering.

Florence Nightingale at sixty-six enthroned amidst a group of probationer nurses. The location is her sister Parthenope's house, Claydon, where she passed much of her later life. The solitary man is her brother-in-law, Sir Harry Verney.

Florence Nightingale fought her battles from a sofa being carried from room to room. There she lay surrounded by cats, but always close to hand would be pen, paper and ink. She set about reforming the design of hospitals. Under her aegis St. Thomas's arose in London, embodying her reforms such as the need for separate units thus localising contagion, the importance of iron as against wooden bedsteads, or earthenware as against tin cups. Not one detail escaped her notice. She set out to create our modern nursing service and in 1859 wrote her most famous book, *Notes on Nursing: What it is, and what it is not*. It was full of personal experiences and was hugely in advance of its time in recognising the impact of emotional and human problems on the sick, noting how small things could affect the will to recover:

'I shall never forget the rapture of fever patients over a bunch of bright coloured flowers. I remember in my own case [she had suffered a fever while in Crimea] a nosegay of wild flowers being sent to me, and from that moment recovery became more rapid.'

In 1860 the first school for nurses in which they received technical training was opened. From that sprang a tree which was to encircle the globe and lead to the founding of the Red Cross.

In her attitudes Florence Nightingale anticipated much that was dramatically to affect women in the next century. 'Till a married woman can be in possession of her own property,' she wrote, 'there can be no love or justice.' In 1867 she declared herself for women's suffrage. What is so extraordinary about her is that she used her position of privilege to challenge the accepted social code into which she had been born. That called for bravery. The fact that she was successful was even more important, for she helped to lay the foundations not only of a revolution in nursing but also of the position of women in society.

Chapter Fifty-Nine

VICTORIAN BRITAIN: THE CLASSLESS SOCIETY

QUEEN VICTORIA reigned for over sixty years, from 1837 to 1901, and gave her name to an age which continues to make an indelible impression upon the imagination. And yet her unique imprint was achieved when the political power of the crown had finally gone into eclipse, never to recover, making the royal family in the long run seemingly redundant. That that did not happen owed as much to the nature of the woman as to the circumstances which once again made the monarchy needful to both government and people.

Victoria started her life as a headstrong, passionate young woman devoid of political sense. Her educational maturity she owed to her consort, Prince Albert, never a popular figure with the British, who began to carve out a new role for the monarchy. Returning to George III, the royal family once again became a model for private probity, indeed the court was almost middle class in its dedication to mind-improving pursuits. Interest in the arts and the sciences, in national achievements, and in good works now became the touchstone of royal activities. None of these foundations for the future popularity of the monarchy brought immediate success and, when the Prince Consort died of typhoid fever in 1861, any achievement was undermined by the twenty years of gloomy seclusion of his widow. Victoria became the familiar rotund figure encased in black, subject to attack for not fulfilling her public role as queen. That devolved on to the Prince of Wales, the genial future Edward VII, whose womanising and proximity to scandal actually damaged the royal image. But, by the time Victoria died, all of this had gone into reverse with the monarchy emerging sacrosanct as a national symbol, as potent as it had been in the days of Gloriana.

The irony was that this revival was made possible precisely because the monarchy had withdrawn from its political role. By the 1870s the queen was beginning to be viewed in a different light due to the longevity of her reign, her practice of the domestic virtues, her role through the marriages of her many children as the matriarch of Europe, as well as that of being the focus of the world's greatest empire. Indeed in 1876 she was made Empress of India. At home the extension of the franchise and the ever-increasing urban masses called for a unifying symbol whereby to hold them together and this was to be provided by a startling revival in the fortunes of the monarchy, one which was to last for a century. To the grey world created by the Industrial Revolution the crown was now destined to purvey pageantry and splendour, and that was to be deliberately built up. The process began with the celebration first of Victoria's Golden Jubilee in 1887 and then her Diamond Jubilee in 1897. Both of these were occasions for magnificent carriage processions through London of a kind which were to be multiplied by her descendants. The success of these went hand-in-hand with the advent of mass circulation newspapers such as the *Daily Mail* aimed at the newly literate. For the first time, due to railways and then trams, people could travel to enjoy spectacles, but even more they could read detailed accounts and, through photography and new reproductive processes, see pictures. This alliance of the press and the crown was only to collapse in the 1980s.

If political power had all but vanished from the monarchy, the aristocracy and gentry's hold only weakened after 1870. Both remained unassailable in terms of wealth and power, their members held together by a shared education and culture as well as by interconnection through marriage. Ownership of land was still the basis of status and social acceptance. Those who rose to join its ranks from the professions, the army, the law and commerce, all subscribed to that belief, investing heavily in estates and country houses. In 1873, 80% of the land in the United Kingdom was owned by an élite of seven thousand, out of a total population of 32 million. This élite not only dominated politics and government but every aspect of life, setting taste and style in the arts and in fashion. But they were also responsive to the new ethos of domestic probity, public duty and philanthropy, winning thereby the applause of the classes below, who accepted that such an élite was there as of right to rule them. What bound the aristocracy and gentry to the middle classes below was the possession of property and their mutual involvement in capital investment in industry. The upper classes were active in fields as varied as mines, brickworks, ports and property development. Their life-style, however, varied little from that of the previous century, centring on a large house in the country set amidst gardens and parkland and a house in London for the season. Railways made such houses accessible for weekend parties and the comfort within them far eclipsed that of the Georgian age. Some, like the Duke of Westminster at Eaton Hall, had three hundred servants. The great

The keystone of the arch of Victorian Britain, the Queen and the Prince Consort, Albert, recorded by Roger Fenton. Their domestic probity set the tone of an age.

London houses amazed every visitor to the country by their opulence and the sheer lavishness of the entertainment within them.

Aristocracy, gentry and the middle classes together embodied propertied opinion and collectively therefore were worthy of the franchise as having a stake in the security of the state. Unlike the aristocracy and gentry, however, the middle classes were a shifting indefinable kaleidoscope, embracing everyone from the entrepreneur to the skilled worker. Certain things they had in common. Two of them were that the wife did not work and that the household had at least one servant. In the main the middle classes were urban, and involved in the production and distribution of manufactures, raw materials and consumer goods: between 1850 and 1870 the number of shopkeepers rose by 54%. Together this amorphous mass of people, who formed between a fifth and sixth of the population, controlled the destiny of a country whose future was to depend heavily on the quality of its professional men. This indeed was the age of the professions, proclaimed by the roll call of organisations they formed, such as the Royal Institute of British Architects (1834), the Institute of Mechanical Engineers (1847) or the British Medical Association (1856). These bodies reflected the needs of an increasingly complex society which called for more doctors, lawyers, apothecaries, civil engineers, architects, and many other specially qualified people to meet its needs.

It was the professional and middle classes who lived in the detached and semi-detached villas built by the thousand in the suburbs of the towns and cities, each with its front and back garden, its basement and attic rooms for the servants. Within, there was the hitherto unknown clutter of the consumer age of mass manufacture together with more significant comforts, running water, indoor lavatories and bathrooms, gas light and gas stoves. Such houses were to reflect the infinite gradations within the middles classes. Moving downwards there was the terraced house, its status sharply defined by elements such as bay windows and porches and the amount of decoration on its façade.

Whereas there was more common ground binding aristocracy, gentry and middle classes, the latter firmly distanced themselves from the classes below. The working classes were also made up of a widely disparate group of people, fierce in their maintenance of an intricately graded pecking order. At the top of this highly complex hierarchy stood the skilled worker and at the bottom the unskilled labourer. There was no feeling of solidarity between them, indeed there was more to divide than to unite them. The irony was that it was the upper echelons, aspiring to practise the middle class virtues of hard work and self-discipline, which also produced the political radicals. Much of the work people were involved in was noisy, dangerous, monotonous and arduous. There was no lack either of accidents, from pit disasters to maimings by machinery. Life was hard, hardest of all between the birth of a first child, when the mother stopped working, and when that child could earn. The houses they lived in were 'two up and two down' terraced houses, often with more than one family crammed within them. There was no decoration and although there might, towards the end of the century, be running water, the lavatory was an outside closet. Inside the house, heating was by coal and lighting was by means of candles, oil or paraffin. Gradually the advent of cheap wallpaper and linoleum added some feeling of domestic comfort to the bleak interiors. Sometimes workers lived in flats called 'model dwellings', but wherever they lived it had to be within walking distance of their place of work.

At the lowest level of all was a seething unnumbered mass of the poor, unemployed and unemployable. No one knows how many there were, but the fact that three million people emigrated between 1853 and 1880 is one indication of the tide of humanity which had found no place in the social hierarchy and who wished to escape a life of destitution and state and private hand-outs. Every Victorian city and town had its slum areas where these people eked out an existence. No respectable person would ever enter such a ghetto without a police escort. Victorian society was rough at the edges but people did not actually go in fear of their lives. Whereas in the previous century and up until 1830 it had been the task of the army, as a last resort, to disperse by force of arms any unruly masses on strike or demonstrating, now it was the task of the police, bearing only truncheons. The fact that towns were divided up into living areas in this way greatly facilitated their task. Any incursion of the poor into the better-class neighbourhoods was firmly discouraged. The rich lived secure within gated and railinged streets and squares. The middle classes were a journey out to the suburbs. The turbulent and deprived elements of society were thus firmly ghettoised.

Every age has its winners and losers, the result of the ethos of the period, good

Work was apotheosised by the Victorians as being the essence of the virtuous life. The Pre-Raphaelite painter, Ford Madox Brown's *Work*, begun in 1852, was finished finally in 1863. It was inspired by the writings of Thomas Carlyle and by the latest sociological works of Henry Mayhew. The setting is Heath Street, Hampstead, and its focus is an excavator 'as the outward and visible type of Work'. To the left there is a wretch who has never learnt to work while behind are the rich who have no need to. In the foreground ragged children represent those at the bottom of the social heap. To the right stand the brainworkers, including Carlyle.

luck or ill fortune, both won or lost through hard work or fecklessness. Outside the seamless robe of the tiered classes stood the harsher facts of age and sex, which crossed all barriers. Victorian Britain was above all a sternly patriarchal society in which women at every level were subordinate. In the case of the lower classes women were looked upon as a reservoir of cheap labour, being paid only a third to two thirds of what a man was paid. Until the 1880s opportunities for women remained circumscribed, confined almost wholly to domestic service or the textile industry, plus piece-work at home. To those occupations could be added serving in a shop, tailoring, being a milliner, a governess or a teacher. But the overwhelming majority of women were in service, indeed by 1881 one in every twenty-two of the population of England and Wales was a servant, 16% of the entire labour force. From the middle class upwards no women worked, her role being that of running the home as a dutiful wife and mother, directing the household servants and, occasionally, undertaking charitable work. By 1900 fewer women were at work, an index of aspirations achieved, for it reflected the rise in income of their husbands rendering their need to work unnecessary, thus raising them to middle class status.

But change was in the air. In 1857 judicial divorce became possible, albeit the circumstances favouring the man. The Married Women's Property Act provided some independence for women in respect of their own property. This signalled the huge alteration in legal status to come. By the 1880s women could go to a university, become doctors, and take part in competitive sports such as tennis and golf. Some could vote at local elections and were also eligible to be members of School Boards or Poor Law Guardians. The suffrage movement was already under way and in 1897 the National Union of Women's Suffrage Societies was formed. Women's magazines and sections in newspapers also reflected a new collective identity and recognition.

Increasingly, intelligent women could shift for themselves. That was not so in the case of children at any level of society. They remained virtually unprotected against exploitation or physical abuse, and continued to be used in all branches of industry, sometimes with cruel effects on their physical wellbeing. Their disappearance from the factory floor was achieved less through government intervention than the fact that technological advance rendered what they did superfluous. The 1870 Education Act for the first time laid down that all children should receive compulsory education until the age of ten. That was far from welcomed by the working classes, who lost thereby a source of income. At the opposite end of the social ladder, upper class children were brought up as exhibits handed over at birth to a small army of nurses, maids, governesses and tutors, based in a separate part of the house from their parents. But, as in the case of women, change was also in the air. The foundation in

AN "UGLY RUSH!"

Mr. Bull. "NOT IF I KNOW IT!"

A *Punch* cartoon, *An Ugly Rush*, caricatures a bid in May 1870 to extend the franchise to women. Women's rights were in the air but the cartoonist, Tenniel, cruelly depicts those who demand such things as ugly harridans. 'John Bull', the embodiment of traditional Old England, resists their pressure on the door.

1889 of the National Society for the Prevention of Cruelty to Children is concrete evidence of a new awareness of the vulnerability of the young.

The eighteenth century thought and wrote in terms of the 'lower orders' or 'the middling ranks' but by 1850 the terms 'middle class' and 'working class' had become the accepted way of referring to the various strata of society. Such terms imply, however, a polarity and rigidity which did not exist. There was no group confrontation of classes in the Victorian age. The idea of hierarchy was universally accepted, nowhere more keenly than the lower down one went. The effects of the Industrial Revolution held people together as much as it seemingly divided them. But that was not the only factor which acted as cement holding this fast-changing and dynamic society (numbering by the year of the queen's death some 41.6 million) in some kind of coherence with no signs of dangerous fragmentation.

Deference held society together, meaning the acceptance by each rank of its place

within a ladder which had its summit in the monarchy, itself a symbol of national unity. Society was equally bound by the belief that a government could not pursue any moral policies which were not firmly based on Christian dogma. The basic tenets of Christianity were accepted at all levels of society, even by those who never went near a church. Christianity was woven into the fabric of the institutions of state. The fact that the various denominations waged intensive warfare did not impede this. The Church of England was split in two between the Evangelicals or Low Church and the new ritualistic High Church movement. Both streams were full of missionary zeal. So too were the dissenting churches and the Roman Catholics who re-established their episcopate in 1850, much to the alarm of Protestants. The year after that event a census revealed that 40% of the population never went to church, a blow which fuelled the missionary endeavour of every denomination towards what they saw as the pagan urban masses. Their impact was minimal. Meanwhile Charles Darwin's *The Origin of Species by Natural Selection* (1859) challenged the creation story and divided the educated classes. None of these things could remove the fact that the prevailing ethos of the age was a deeply religious one, expressed in the practice of daily prayers and Bible readings and by strict church attendance on Sunday. Government reinforced the façade by legislation creating the universal gloom of Sunday, one which amazed foreign visitors, for all shops and places of business and entertainment remained firmly shut. Only in the years following 1870 was religious fervour to begin to subside.

If the Christian religion was common ground so too was an aspiration universally shared by Victorians, that for respectability. Respectability embodied financial independence achieved through one's own efforts, self-discipline, and self-help. It brought with it a cult of work, hard work, and a veneration for home and family as a shrine. A good respectable man was a concept which cut across all social boundaries. He was the kind of man who paid his way, was never in debt, kept out of trouble and bore life's many burdens stoically. Those who were not respectable were the extravagant, the feckless, the unreliable, the drunkard, the promiscuous and those who sponged off the state. But respectability also called for a certain front which could only be achieved by those with a modicum of financial means. As a consequence, its demands could take a heavy toll on the middle classes and skilled workers who struggled to maintain such a front and avoid the slip downwards. Respectability really excluded the poor and it could also bring hypocrisy and double standards. In the context of the

Victorian Britain at its apogee encapsulated by George Cruikshank in *The British Bee Hive* published in 1867. Descending downwards from the royal family it celebrates above all the virtues of free trade resulting in the 'Bank of the Richest Country in the World'.

age it had much to say in its favour for it must have carried many people through what was still a hard life, with fortitude giving them a set of values and standards to cling to.

These values were enshrined in the home. Up and down the country there were conglomerations of small homes as never before, offering the only shelter, comfort and delight to inmates away from the workplace. For the middle classes home was sacred, a domain over which the man ruled and in which his family learnt the virtues of respectability and the moral code. Home was held together by religion, and by the common life shared within its walls of meals and sober recreation, amidst an increasing clutter of household possessions signalling the consumer age.

If the queen, deference, religion and respectability drew classes together, so too did philanthropy and good works. There was a universal horror of state provision and charity was an obligation laid by convention on every class that possessed the means whereby to practise it. In the countryside the landowners provided for their tenants. In the towns there was a never-ending proliferation of new hospitals, orphanages and asylums. By the middle of the century care was being extended to animals with the foundation of the Royal Society for the Protection of Animals (1824). The philanthropy of Victorian Britain was in excess of that of any other European country. But it was charity with an edge, for its recipients were carefully sifted in search of the deserving, nor should it obscure the fact that in one sense it implied social subordination by the recipient. By the end of the century there was increasing support for some kind of state pension.

Such were the sober principles that motivated society, but there were others of a more carefree nature. Leisure, which in the previous century had been the prerogative of the few, now extended, however sparsely, to the many. This was a direct consequence of the Industrial Revolution which sharpened the division between work and other time. By 1850 a pattern had set in, that of the five-and-a-half day week with a half-day on Saturday, Sunday off, and set holidays once a year. In the early 1870s came Bank Holidays and by 1875 there was Boxing Day, Easter Monday, Whit Monday and the first Monday in August. In the country, of course, this precipitated little change and the year remained punctuated still by age-old festivals, shearing suppers, Whitsun walks, tithe feasts, fairs and markets. But in the towns the story was a very different one. Initially those who migrated to the towns brought with them many of the crueller pastimes which the middle classes regarded with horror: cockfights, bullfights, prize fights or attending executions. Added to that there was drinking, gambling, and prostitution. Fear of the uncontrollable violence which such pursuits might unleash led the middle classes to set about the suppression of fairs as dens of vice, and the introduction of restrictions on things like opening hours. More particularly they promoted what was called 'rational recreation'.

Within every city and town sprang up public parks in which to stroll and study nature, libraries in which to read, museums in which to learn about art and history, and mind-improving exhibitions of every kind. The Mechanics Institutes provided meetings and lectures, giving the lower classes basic scientific instruction. Factory outings began, paternalistic gestures by employers aimed at encouraging a loyal workforce. Cruel sports were driven underground and new ones emerged, above all cricket and football. The Football Association was founded in 1863. Football was initially patronised by all classes, but by the 1880s it took on its working class patina proving to be a healthy and harmless means of engaging the enthusiasms of those who could easily take on the character of an uncontrollable urban mob. Local patriotism was instilled into the supporters, and the railways meant that both they and the team could travel to 'away' fixtures. Cricket in contrast maintained its upper class adherents, a sport fit for gentlemen but also appealing to a broad spectrum of the population.

Set periods of factory closure engendered the novelty of the holiday. From the point of view of the factory owner this was far better than employees just deciding not to bother to turn up. The railways meant that the holiday could develop, and the turning-point came with the cheap excursions to London in 1851 to see the Great Exhibition. Thereafter, cheap journeys to London, the seaside or some other place of interest, led millions of Victorians to move around in a way hitherto unknown. By the 1870s and 1880s what had begun as a middle class practice, a stay at a seaside resort, quickly spread down the social scale. The working classes took over certain places such as Morecambe, Blackpool and Ramsgate, and made them their own. By then, however, the upper classes were exploring the Continent in far greater number, under the aegis of the new travel company, Thomas Cook.

Most classes shared in the delights of a burgeoning urban entertainments industry. The theatre embraced all classes, which within its walls were segregated from each other both by price and by architecture. Concerts and choral societies also had universal appeal. The Henry Wood Promenade Concerts in the Albert Hall began in 1895, with the large central area filled with those who for a modest sum stood throughout the concert. Music hall, an expression of working class culture, took shape in the 1870s and 1880s attracting audiences across the social divides. And for the working classes there was the gilt and glitter of the pub and the dancing saloon, plus the pleasures of that male preserve, the Working Men's Club.

With the increasing literacy of a large proportion of the population there came a

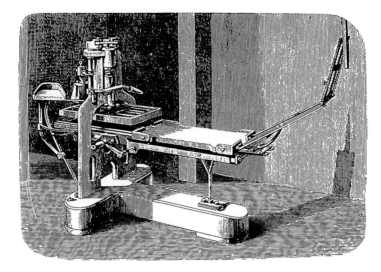

Charles Earl Stanhope's first iron printing press paved the way for the steam-driven cylinder presses which increasingly enabled mass editions and popular literacy during Victoria's reign.

shared literature beyond that of the Bible and Prayer Book. By the 1850s the middle classes were hungry for reading matter. Taxes were progressively removed from advertisements, newspapers and, finally in 1861, from paper itself. The result was a printing explosion, and a barrage of newspapers, books and periodicals. By 1880 there were no less than ninety-six dailies in the regions and the national papers also sped their way across the country. There were cheap editions of the classics and of contemporary novels. This indeed was the heyday of the serial novel, in the case of Charles Dickens holding a nation in suspense as the fate of his characters unfolded week by week. The novels of Dickens, Trollope, Thackeray, George Eliot and later Hardy, Meredith and Henry James represented to a large degree a shared culture. Only after the 1880s came the great divide between writers who received critical acclaim and those, like Ouida, whose work epitomised the rise of cheap fiction pandering to a mass audience in search of romance and sensation.

The myth of Britain, whose foundation had been laid earlier in the century, was another binding force as a national mythology was projected through best-selling history books. Macaulay's *History of England* (1849-61) and J. R. Green's *Short History of the English People* (1875) were two works which ran into edition after edition. During the 1830s history began to be taught in the public and some of the grammar schools, in order to prepare the children of the newly enfranchised classes for political responsibility. After 1870 the teaching of history was extended to the working classes with the aim of cementing national identity. History was presented as progress, as the exaltation of a political freedom which had descended from the Anglo-Saxons, was re-secured in Magna Carta, reprieved through the Civil War, and was reaching fruition in their own time. History was made to serve as the collective genealogy of the newly literate masses. Or, as the historian John Lingard put it in 1849: 'Our annals are fraught with animating scenes of national glory, with bright examples of piety, honour, and resolution, and with the most impressive and instructive lessons to princes, statesmen, and people.'

There was much indeed which held the peoples of Victorian Britain together and in their place, but mobility was not excluded. Mobility however, was complex and access to its paths was unequal. The skilled manual workers fiercely guarded, for example, any incursion into their ranks from below. The middle class expanded continually by one means or another. Ways up could be any number of means: education, family connection, money, talent, the shared membership of an organisation. Such things accounted for the shifting composition of those who entered the middle classes but the real barrier to cross was that from the middle class into the upper reaches of society. That journey hung on the passenger being deemed a gentleman and much agony attended the definition. Until the 1880s who was, or was not, a gentleman remained the decision of the classes above the aspirant. Riches, land and talent, as well as social accomplishment, were helpful attributes. Certain people could never qualify, those directly connected with factories, shopkeeping or farming, but that changed in the 1880s when an accommodation was reached that anyone who had been educated at a public school was a gentleman. That removed a possible source of conflict for it meant that even if a man failed to achieve entry himself he could achieve it for his sons. The legacy that resolution created was a hardened élitism, which was not to be undermined until after 1945.

It remains extraordinary that Victorian society held together at all, when the pressures and changes are taken into account. Britain was the first country in Western Europe to undergo such a radical transformation which others were only to begin to emulate in the 1880s. What is astonishing is how such a vast explosion and migration of population within a small island had occurred without any major social confrontation; indeed, there was instead remarkable economic and social progress. Society by 1901 was infinitely more varied and volatile, but yet it remained coherent, in spite of the fact that it was a more anonymous society. In earlier ages men had known the suppliers of their daily needs, such as transportation and fuel and water. Now people depended for such needs on small groups of workers they would never meet. Increasingly after 1870 these groups became aware of that fact, and began to realise the pressure they could exert not only on government but also on the rest of society. Increasingly, too, deference came under fire, once status could be achieved not by birth or riches but by competitive examination.

Chapter Sixty

CHARLES DARWIN AND THE ORIGIN OF SPECIES

IF the competitive examination as a means towards advancement was to undermine the established hierarchy, the theory of evolution by natural selection was to have an even more devastating effect. Give or take a little, the creation story as narrated in the Book of Genesis had gone unchallenged. Man was created in God's image as a spark of Divine Will. God had indeed taken on human form in the guise of Jesus Christ. From this sprang the whole moral and metaphysical framework of Western European civilisation. It set man apart from the brute beasts of field and forest as a unique and separate species, sharing in and aspiring to the Divine. Now all of this came under attack in the most important book to be published in the nineteenth century, Charles Darwin's *The Origin of Species* (1859). In it Darwin was to argue that species – plants, animals and other living organisms – had started as quite different creatures, undergoing over huge periods of time all kinds of changes and gradually evolving into new ones. In fact Darwin never used the word 'evolution' in his book or discussed human beings, except at the very end when he wrote: 'Much light will be thrown on the origin of man and his history.' The educated reading public, of course, realised the implications of that statement. If the theory of evolution through natural selection was accepted, it would seem to have swept away at one blow man's unique position in the scheme of things. He now took his place alongside the animals, his spark of divinity extinguished. Degradation and materialism beckoned, and indeed Darwin was to become the adopted father of the materialistic movements, such as Communism, which have dominated the twentieth century.

None of these consequences could perhaps ever have been foreseen by the blinkered amateur biologist and geologist whose book was at last prised out of him in 1859. By then he had become a recluse and a permanent invalid, but that was not how he had begun his life. Charles Darwin was descended from two great families of the previous century, his grandfathers being the doctor and biologist, Erasmus Darwin, and the entrepreneur, Josiah Wedgwood. Charles was the son of Robert Darwin and

Susanna Wedgwood of The Mount, a house which they had built outside Shrewsbury. He was born in 1809. His mother died when he was only eleven and he retained no lasting memory of her, but he worshipped his father. The reason for that idolatry has never been explained, for Robert Darwin seems to have been a repulsive man. Far from being a loving father, he was surly and domineering, striking fear into the family and imposing a rigid discipline.

When Charles was eight he was sent to a day school in Shrewsbury where his predilection for natural history and collecting specimens began to develop. A year later, in 1818, he went to Shrewsbury Grammar School and hated it: 'The school as an education for me was a complete blank,' he wrote, and was removed from it prematurely. His father decided that he should follow in his footsteps and become a doctor and so Charles was sent to the University of Edinburgh to read medicine. He had no taste for that either, and in his second year told his father he had no desire to become a doctor. The only other option open to a younger son of his class was the church and so he was packed off to Christ's College, Cambridge.

Charles had grown into a slender young man with pale blue eyes, endowed with an abundance of humour and energy, gentle and serene by nature, a man whose preferences were for country life and especially field sports, hunting and shooting. And this is how he passed most of his time at Cambridge, from which he came down with a degree of sorts in 1831. While there, he had befriended J. S. Henslow, the professor of botany, who fired him by making him read books by the German naturalist Alexander von Humboldt, and by Sir John Herschel, in particular the latter's *Introduction to the Study of Natural History*. Henslow must have sensed his pupils latent abilities, for a few months after Darwin left Cambridge, he was instrumental in his being offered the post of unpaid naturalist aboard HMS *Beagle*. His father made him refuse it but his Wedgwood relations intervened, making Robert Darwin reverse his decision. On 27 December 1831 Charles Darwin set sail from Falmouth, returning five years later on 2 October 1836. This voyage around the world, originally estimated as lasting three years, was, he recorded, 'by far the most important event in my life, and has determined my whole career.'

The purpose of the voyage was 'to complete the survey of Patagonia and Tierra del Fuego . . . to survey the shores of Chile, Peru and some islands in the Pacific; and to carry a chain of chronometrical measurements around the world.' In this quest Darwin was thrown together with a handsome aristocrat, Captain Charles FitzRoy, a man endowed with extreme authoritarianism and deep conservatism of mind. But he was a great seaman. Surprisingly Darwin was to develop a real affection for the unpredictable man.

The *Journal of Researches* which he published in 1839 was to become one of the great classic travel books, catching Darwin's release of the mind during the epic voyage. He wrote to one of his sisters in 1834: 'There is nothing like geology; the pleasure of the first day's partridge shooting or the first day's hunting cannot be compared to finding a fine group of fossil bones, which tell their story with almost a living tongue.' He was to return from these experiences a changed man, formidable, and with a fervour for all aspects of nature and a desire to discover their underlying causes. That desire was to focus on what was to become his life's passion, to explain the origin of living creatures.

In September 1835 the *Beagle* anchored off the islands of the Galapagos Archipelago, a group of craters off Ecuador. These were notable for their huge tortoises and range of flora and fauna. Darwin enthusiastically listed the many new species he found when it was pointed out to him that the birds, insects and plants varied on each island and that although they were all similar, yet they were different, and all equally related to species on the mainland. It was then that the evolution theory took hold of his mind, that wind currents had brought these species to each island where they had adapted to their new surroundings and in so doing, had altered.

The idea of evolution was not an original one. Darwin's grandfather Erasmus had

The Beagle, the ship in which Darwin made his momentous voyage, docked in Sydney harbour, 12 January 1836, nine months before its return to England.

MONKEYANA.

A contemporary cartoon from *Punch* highlights the controversy caused by Darwin's theories.

such a theory which he propounded in his book *Zoonomia* or *The Laws of Organic Life* (1794 and 1796) and, in the year in which Charles was born, J. D. Lamarck's *Philosophie Zoologique* advanced the thesis that changes in the condition of life precipitated changes in the needs of animals. Behaviour, he argued, led to alterations in the structure and shape of animals. By the time that Darwin became interested in the subject, contemporary opinion was divided into two opposing camps. Those called the Catastrophists adhered to the Biblical account, believing that there was a series of floods in the past when the earth was submerged beneath the sea and all living things had been drowned. This explained the existence of extraordinary extinct species like the mastodon, whose bones had been discovered. The opposing faction were the Uniformitarians whose beliefs stemmed from James Hutton's *The Theory of the Earth* (1785), in which it was argued that the earth as we know it was gradually formed over a very long period of time. Hutton's work was to be taken up by Charles Lyell, the volumes of whose *Principles of Geology*, were as they came out, sent to Darwin during the voyage. God had no place in Lyell's scheme of things. Water, land, valleys, even climate, changed without any kind of catastrophe. Darwin's great leap was to apply these principles to animal life. In the substratum of the pampas in South America he found one vast graveyard of strange unknown extinct monsters, whose bones he excavated and crated to be sent home. He began to ponder whether these could be the skeletons of creatures who had not been able to adapt to the changes in the environment and died out. Could others, however, have actually taken on new form and become new species?

In July 1827 he 'opened first note-book on Transmutation of Species' and this was to lead to the publication over twenty years later of *The Origin of Species*. The extraordinary phenomenon was the delay, albeit several years were spent writing a book on barnacles. The explanation for much of the delay must come from Darwin's change of character. On his return, he had married his cousin, Emma Wedgwood, a well-educated woman, and lived for a short time in London. In 1842, the Darwins moved to a house in the village of Downe, near Westerham in Kent, from which Charles rarely if ever moved for the next forty years. He now assumed not only the guise of an obsessed intellectual, but also that of a hypochondriac. He was always ailing from one thing or another, from eczema to shaking hands, from arthritis to vomiting, form catarrh to palpitations. Naturally he carefully noted down all his symptoms, providing a field day for those who came after. A wide-ranging number of explanations have been produced to explain his condition, the one now thought most likely being that he suffered from Chaga's disease, the result of being attacked in Argentina by a bug called 'Triatoma infestans'. The effects of this tally with most of what is known about Darwin's physical condition, but it cannot be proved. What all this conveniently achieved for him was the ability to retreat into his study as though prematurely senile: 'I have nothing else to record during the rest of my life, except the publication of my several books.' That was not quite true, for he went on to have no less than ten children and to be remembered as a most loving father.

He had begun to work on his theory of evolution, but that of the natural selection of the fittest had yet to come. It came as a result of reading Malthus on *Population* which traced the struggle for existence which went on in the natural world: 'It at once struck me that under these circumstances favourable variations would tend to be preserved, and unfavourable ones to be destroyed.' By 1884 Darwin had written what was effectively to be *The Origin of Species* and, although he continued to accumulate facts, he refused to publish. Then, in 1858, a man named Alfred Russell Wallace sent him a paper reaching the same conclusions. It came as a bombshell, one which was fortunately resolved by the intervention of Lyell, who had become a friend, and another who had become likewise, the great botanist Sir Joseph Dalton Hooker. Together they arranged for both papers to be read to the Linnean Society of London in

Charles Darwin in old age photographed by Julia Margaret Cameron. She was the greatest portrait photographer of the age, presenting Darwin almost in the guise of an Old Testament prophet.

July 1858. They produced no reaction whatsoever but nonetheless the advent of Wallace forced Darwin into print.

The first edition of *The Origin of Species* sold out on the day of publication. Within it we find expressions which today are commonplace but which began their life in Darwin's book, such as 'missing link', 'survival of the fittest', and 'the struggle for life'. Even by Victorian standards, Darwin's methods were surprisingly amateur. He was ruthlessly selective in his approach to evidence, including only that which would reinforce his theory. But he had a unique overriding ability to ask the right questions, often ones which seem almost naive in their simplicity, like 'What is species?' or 'How did species begin?' Although he only dealt with the origin of man by implication in the book, he was to go on to cover the topic in 1871 in his *The Descent of Man*.

These were not his only works. There were others, including an important one on the nature of coral reefs, but *The Origin of Species* was the most seminal and caused the most controversy. It turned Darwin overnight into a national icon. Its impact on mid-Victorian Protestantism was shattering, although a century later it hardly ruffles the feathers in any theological dovecote. Indeed at the time the leader of Britain's Catholics, Cardinal Newman, found no difficulty with evolution preserving always God's role as the creator of the soul. But for the decades down to 1900 the consequences of such a view of the origins of man were rightly seen as threatening the established order of society. *The Times* wrote:

> 'If our humanity be merely the natural product of the modified faculties of the brutes, most earnest-minded people will be compelled to give up those motives by which they have attempted to live noble and virtuous lives, as founded on a mistake . . .'

What has happened in the twentieth century, it could be argued, would confirm such a view.

Darwin was true to his own principles and abandoned any belief in a personal God, becoming an agnostic after he had discovered the law of natural selection. He died of a heart attack on 19 April 1882 and was buried in Westminster Abbey a few feet from Newton. The irony was that his discovery so dramatically affected all the subjects in which he had no interest: religion, society, morality and politics. The fact that today we live largely in a world of agnostic materialism descends directly from the consequences of his work.

Chapter Sixty-One

COMING TO TERMS WITH DEMOCRACY

THE half-century following the first major extension of the franchise in 1867 was to see it progressively widened, giving the vote to more and more of the population. After further reforms in 1884 and 1885 two out of every three males could vote. Although this still meant that the electorate only totalled eight million of the total population of some forty-five million, in 1914 (the year in which the First World War broke out) it now included members of the working class. The political system which had carried this revolution through, however, ostensibly remained what it had been for centuries, one of Crown, Lords and Commons in Parliament. Members of whatever persuasion all remained at heart devotees of the old rule of the élite. Their problem was to salvage as much as possible of that world, and make it work and appeal to a very different kind of society. What is so striking is that regardless as to whether a particular administration was Liberal or Conservative both henceforth channelled their energies, with enthusiasm or reluctance, into social legislation.

With the advent of a mass electorate, political parties had to present programmes for future action in order to get elected, which meant that both Liberals and Conservatives needed to clarify as far as they were able what each stood for in the eyes of voters. Both parties were fortunate in being able to enter this new age with two political giants at the helm, men whose contrasting personalities were so strong as to divide people into one camp or the other. And it was to be these leaders as much as anything who were to define what their respective parties stood for. The Liberal leader, William Ewart Gladstone, was a Scot by descent, a man of high principle and a devout churchman but with the moral zeal of a Dissenter. He also had the energy and drive to pull into coherence streams within the party's make-up which were not only Liberal but also Whig and Radical. Beneath it all, Gladstone was no revolutionary, for he revered the inherited institutions of monarchy and aristocracy. The Liberals billed themselves as devotees of economic freedom and also of the free market, believers, too, in merit as against birth as the true basis of society. That commitment to freeing the individual from constraint meant that for most Liberals the state had no role to play in controlling economic and social policy. In the end the party's fortunes were to founder on the incompatibility of these two objectives but that was not apparent in the early years. Gladstone and the Liberals together formed a group which was able successfully to cut across the social spectrum and include within its ranks Whig aristocrats, middle class businessmen, and even members of the working classes.

Gladstone's opponent was of a very different temperament. The mercurial Benjamin Disraeli, later Lord Beaconsfield, started life as a baptised Jew of uncertain financial status but he was a genius and knew it. He was also a dandy and a novelist. Ambitious and amoral, Disraeli was a great showman and, like Gladstone, nursed a romance about England and its ancient aristocracy. Indeed that reverence for things past was to become an essential attribute of a Conservatism which saw its role as the preserver of an existing order of things centred around throne, altar and empire. This was the party of the establishment, initially one of landed property but soon to become one of property alone, as its ability to win elections came to depend less and less on the shires and more and more on the 'villa vote' of burgeoning Victorian suburbia. The Conservative power-base was always to remain in the country but increasingly it built up its middle class supporters and in certain areas, like Lancashire, it attracted a working class vote as well.

We have firmly left the age of interest and entered that of party. In order for a political party to obtain power in a democracy it has to secure votes, and within a few years both sides had created party machines to rally voters to the poll when elections came. A mass electorate called also for a very different kind of politician from those of the past, men with powers of public oratory and charisma of personality. Posters, leaflets and meetings now became the vehicles whereby to promote the cause up and down the country in what became campaigns to sustain the allegiance of the faithful. In 1867 the National Union of Conservative and Constitutional Associations was formed, followed three years later by the establishment of a Central Office under the direction of the indefatigable John Gorst. He led the drive to secure the middle class vote by setting up Conservative Associations. Within the Commons a new post appeared, that of Chief Whip, whose task was to see that all Tory Members of Parliament adhered to the party line. The age of the in-dependent member had gone. The opposing party formed the National Liberal Foundation in 1877 holding what was in effect the first political party conference that year in Birmingham under the aegis of Joseph Chamberlain.

Late Victorian civic pride. This illustration of central Birmingham from 1886 shows the archetypal tableau of town hall, council house, art gallery, museum and library.

As Lord Mayor of Birmingham he had transformed that city, but he also organised the Liberal political machine within it in a way which the party was to copy elsewhere.

So the scene was set for three swathes of social legislation marking three periods more or less of dominance by one or other of the two parties, the first Liberal, the second Conservative and the third Liberal again, covering in total over fifty years. A major factor besetting any administration (which will be dealt with separately) was the increasing problem of Ireland upon whose events governments both rose and fell. But when it came to domestic issues nothing could arrest the ever-increasing flood of social reform.

Gladstone's first ministry (1868-74) introduced a competitive examination for entrance into the Civil Service and abolished the purchase of commissions in the army. The Education Reform Bill of 1870 allowed the setting-up of schools by the Education Department in any district where provision was either not efficient or suitable. His second ministry (1880-85) was less clear-sighted but went on to extend the franchise in 1884, and the year after in the Redistribution Bill to create single-member constituencies in the towns, thus further eroding what was left of landed interest. He was to return for a third (1886) and a fourth term (1892-94) but his energies were taken up with Ireland and an attack on the House of Lords ended in

failure. However, in 1894 the Liberals did introduce death duties, thus establishing the principle that the state could tax capital.

Gladstone died in 1898 and was accorded a state funeral. By then he belonged to a world that had vanished. No one, when the franchise was extended, could have imagined that a two-party system would have emerged as the norm, nor that both sides would successfully draw in voters across the classes, averting polarisation. That that did not happen may have owed much to rising living standards and the availability of cheap food, but it must also have owed something to the GOM or Grand Old Man as Gladstone was called. His government had carried through forward-looking social legislation which responded exactly to the public mood of the period. But at the same time the House of Lords remained untouched, the Church of England was not disestablished and, although he promised to introduce local government, it never happened. What he did enshrine into the new politics was a strong moral dimension which was to survive him.

Disraeli was seventy when he became Prime Minister in 1874. The Tories came to power with no real programme, but they also found themselves carrying through social reform. The Employers and Workmen Act (1875) put both employers and employees on an equal footing for the first time. The Conspiracy and Protection of Property Act (1875) freed trade unions, making a strike no longer an offence as a conspiracy. The Tories repealed the Criminal Law Amendment Act, in this way legalising peaceful picketing. The Artisan's Dwelling Act empowered local authorities to purchase land compulsorily for building and rehousing people at a reasonable rent. All of these measures and others were appeals by the old élite for the 'villa' and working class vote. Disraeli was to lose the 1880 election due to the prevailing economic depression, and to die a year later.

His successor was an aristocrat of the old school, Robert Gascoyne Cecil, third Marquess of Salisbury, a brilliant and witty man whose mission was to ensure that as much as possible of the old scheme of things survived. But even he could not stem the demand for social reform. In 1888 a Local Government Act set up sixty-two elected county councils which took over the management of roads, asylums and running the local police. The following year the London County Council was created, providing an overall authority to deal with the planning problems of what had grown into the world's greatest city. There was legislation which reflected the need to lift educational standards, essential in an age when literacy and technical skills were fast becoming a necessity. Elementary education became free in 1891. Five years after, powers were given to local councils to erect council houses. When Salisbury returned for his third term of office in 1895 he was more resistant to implementing further

change. By then demands for that within the party were embodied in Joseph Chamberlain, who had deserted the Liberals over Ireland. Salisbury succeeded in staving off Chamberlain's plan to introduce Old Age Pensions.

The old Houses of Parliament were destroyed by fire in 1834. The present building was designed by Sir Charles Barry in co-operation with Augustus Pugin in the Gothic style. The new House of Commons, depicted here by Henry Barraud, began to be used in 1850.

The marquess retired in 1902, shortly after the accession of Victoria's son as Edward VII. He was succeeded by his nephew, A. J. Balfour. Nicknamed 'Pretty Fanny', Balfour was a scintillating but bored bachelor. He was a strange combination of courage and languor and, even more than Salisbury, he found democracy distasteful. Unfortunately he showed it. He too, however, pursued the pathway of further social reform. The 1902 Education Act placed education in the hands of the recently created county and county borough councils with the aim of raising standards. Although far less ideological than the Liberals the Conservatives had to move with the times, albeit in a piecemeal and pragmatic way. Billing themselves as the defenders of time-honoured institutions, they could yet demonstrate that such a defence need not exclude adaptation and change. Balfour was to be brought down not by his own actions but those of Chamberlain who came out publicly in favour of protectionism, that is, lower duties on Empire imports which became known as the 'Imperial Preference'. Balfour resigned on this issue and the Conservatives suffered a landslide defeat by an electorate for which free trade was the sacred totem of their prosperity.

The Liberals returned to power. They came in with no master-plan but gradually, during a decade of dominance, they were to a great extent to set the agenda for the new century, one which was to embody a fundamental shift in attitude. Government may have passed an abundance of social legislation during the Victorian period but it delegated its execution to the local authorities whose response was variable. Now the state itself, bit by bit, was to take on those tasks. Already by 1914 the number of civil servants had risen to 200,000. The belief that the state could somehow miraculously provide a cure for every kind of ill in society was progressively to become an entrenched idea, unquestioned until the 1980s.

These Liberals were very different from those of the Gladstone era. Instead of being landowners they were a mixture of men of private means, trade unionists, and professional politicians drawn from occupations like law or journalism. Indeed one of the Liberals' most significant acts was to award MPs a salary of £400 p.a., thus enabling the working class to aspire to a political career. This was a time when the party was blessed with abundant intellectual vigour, epitomised less by their solid initial Prime Minister, Sir Henry Campbell-Bannerman (1905-1908), than by his successor Herbert Henry Asquith (1908-16). Although an alcoholic and womaniser, Asquith was possessed of a refined and disciplined mind, alert, to the point and efficient. He was a superb debater. His period in office was adorned by a galaxy of talent with the young Winston Churchill as President of the Board of Trade and the Welshman David Lloyd George as Chancellor of the Exchequer. Energetic and charming, Asquith abounded with fresh ideas, many of which owed their origins to another rising star, the civil servant, William Beveridge.

The Acts passed by this government read like a roll call of the foundation stones of the society in which we still live. The Trades Disputes Act (1906) granted trade unions full legal immunity, a status unequalled anywhere else in Europe and one which was not to be challenged until the 1980s. In the same year the School Meals Act enabled local authorities to provide free school meals. In 1907 probation for offenders was introduced. Then, in 1908, came a whole spate: Old Age Pensions with a government allowance of five shillings a week for those over seventy; an eight-and-a-half hour day for miners, the first time that Parliament had taken on the task of limiting the working hours of men; children under fourteen were no longer to be sent to prison and the Borstal system was set up to deal with young offenders; Labour

Cartoon by Linley Sambourne from the 5 August 1908 issue of *Punch* on Lloyd George's introduction of Old Age Pensions.

THE PHILANTHROPIC HIGHWAYMAN.

Exchanges were established as a mechanism towards finding work for the unemployed. The most important of all these Acts was the National Insurance Bill (1911), which more than any laid the foundations of what was later to take the form of the Welfare State. Part One of this Act provided for payment for workers during sickness, something to which government, worker and employer alike were to contribute. Part Two went to provide for payment during unemployment, a provision designed specifically to meet the problem of seasonal laying-off. Unemployment however, was already being recognised as potentially one of the greatest social problems of the new century. It was one which was to haunt successive governments.

In addition to these achievements the Liberals added another which directly affected the centre, the taming of the House of Lords which still had the power to block any bill from the Commons. In 1909 Lloyd George brought in a budget which introduced a super-tax for those with incomes above £2,000 p.a., besides increasing duties on tobacco and other commodities. The Lords rejected it. Asquith realised that he would require two elections in order to curb their power. The first was fought on 'the peers against the people'. When the Liberals were returned with a much reduced majority, Asquith launched a bill which curtailed the right of the Lords to oppose any money bill. In addition, any other bill which passed the Commons three times became the law, regardless of rejection by the Upper House. The life of Parliament was also shortened from seven to five years. During the crisis the old king died and was succeeded by his son, George V, who was persuaded that if it proved necessary he would flood the Lords with new Liberal peers in order to pass the bill. In December 1910 Asquith went to the country for a second time, and was returned again to power. The Lords, faced with the prospect of as many as five hundred Liberal peers, caved in. The right to oppose any money bill was lost, and in the case of other bills the Lords' power was reduced to that of delay for a period of up to two years. This battle represented more that the constitutional subjugation of the Lords to the Commons. At a deeper level it recognised that political power was no longer based on the ownership of land but sprang from a record of achievement. To both the aristocracy and the upper classes it was a bitter blow.

All of these measures were responsive to public mood and embodied a shift in perception that what had been acceptable in 1870 was no longer so in 1910. These reforming bills also averted what could have been a rapid polarisation of voting along class lines, and in a way delayed the ascent of the new Labour party. In the end, however, the Liberal government foundered. There was a sea of strikes in 1912 which forced it down the fatal road of wage regulation. The outbreak of war in 1914 forced Asquith ultimately to seek a way out by means of a coalition with the Conservatives led by Bonar Law.

In spite of all these changes, British society on the eve of the Great War must have seemed remarkably unchanged. One per cent of the population still owned sixty-six per cent of all property and only a million people paid income tax. As an era, the Edwardian period has remained enshrined in the popular imagination as a golden age, all the more so because what followed it was a dramatic contrast. Edward VII and his beautiful queen, Alexandra, reigned over a glittering court which revived monarchical pomp and splendour. The upper classes indulged in great outward show of a kind which depended on retinues of poorly paid servants. The old hierarchy of the Victorian age with its worship of respectability still seemed firmly in place. And yet beneath the surface the seeds which were to destroy that society were already there. The advent of modern plumbing, electric light and central heating, for instance, rendered much that the servant class did redundant. The *avant garde* in the arts, in theatre, literature, painting and sculpture, were already producing shock waves. Inventions like the telephone were revolutionising daily communication, while the typewriter heralded the modern office and secretary.

Perhaps the greatest change of all was to be that of the role of women, a change which affected concepts which had been held for centuries about the family, the nature of sexuality, and the role the sexes played in every sphere of human activity. Already in the 1890s women were increasingly taking jobs in nursing, teaching, or in offices. At the same time the demand for women's political rights accelerated, first with the National Union of Women's Suffrage Societies (1897) and later with the far more militant Women's Social and Political Union (1903), under the leadership of Mrs Emmeline Pankhurst. The Liberals were in favour of female suffrage, albeit treating such a measure as an appendage to some further reform of the male franchise. The violent phase of the suffragette movement which set in from 1912 in fact did more harm than good to the advancement of their cause, but it was only to be a matter of time before the vote was granted.

Although a third of the population still lived in poverty, everywhere people looked they could see tangible evidence of a new urban civilisation which had been created without revolution or bloodshed. Homes with running water and plumbing, streets which were lit, trams instead of horse-drawn buses, an efficient police force which ensured public safety, libraries, parks, art galleries and museums which provided free information and entertainment for everyone. On the whole Britain would seem to have entered the twentieth century in triumph. Sadly, this was to prove pride before the fall.

The canker was there from the onset. Britain was unique in that the vast changes caused by industrialisation had not been accompanied by either polarisation of society or a revolution. Any friction between the old and new classes had disappeared by the close of the century when a compromise was reached, one which does much to explain the failures of our own century. The aristocracy and gentry may have lost their political and even their social dominance but they held onto their cultural one. Indeed they did more than that, for they imposed it on the classes which should have replaced them. The melting-pot was the public school in which the young of both the old and new élite were educated side by side to a common code of behaviour and attitudes. The attributes which had made up the Victorian entrepreneur, hard work, money-making, inventiveness and a driving zeal for production, had to be discarded in favour of those seen as appropriate to the gentleman, the cultivation of style and the pursuits of leisure, along with those of political service. This meant turning away the reality of a massively urbanised society in favour of a cultural ideal which was rural, epitomised in the country house, the shoot and hunt, the garden, and a devotion to the past and its preservation as somehow embodying the true spirit of England. This was to have fatal consequences in the new century, contributing to the erosion of the country's economic dominance which depended precisely on the virtues which had been rejected. Technology, the new, and change, were all to be distrusted. The genius of Britain was held to lie in its innate conservatism and caution. Instead, these attitudes were to contribute dramatically to its slide downhill.

Chapter Sixty-Two

IRELAND DEPARTS

EVEN at the close of the Victorian age and with an Empire stretching around the globe Britain itself remained a conglomeration of separate countries held in allegiance to the crown. Within the island boundaries of what the Romans had designated Britannia there continued to be strong cultural, religious and linguistic differences which maintained their vigour, giving both Wales and Scotland clear identities which neither Henry VIII's administrative assimilation of Wales in 1536 nor the Act of Union of 1707 with Scotland could eradicate. In the principality of Wales that identity was reflected in the Welsh language and in the strong dissenting tradition of the chapels. Scotland had retained her own separate legal, ecclesiastical and educational traditions. But both were drawn in by other threads whereby the island was held in unity. Men from both countries were advanced to high official positions in the running of the state and of the Empire. The English political system, too, was adopted by both countries. Above all, the landed established classes had intermarried to form a cohesive élite. The Industrial Revolution drew the island even closer together, as new roads and the railways reached out to its furthest boundaries. And that Revolution also brought prosperity, averting a poverty which might have fed movements of independence.

Such should have been the scenario for the island of Ireland but it never happened. The Irish continued to be treated as a subject people upon whom an alien ruling class and religion had been imposed. Unlike the Scottish Act of Union, the Act for Ireland in 1801 brought no benefits. Indeed the reverse was the case, for it took away the Irish Parliament at precisely the period when a strong nationalistic impulse was beginning to flow. Far from stultifying that movement it intensified it. This was a society in which a small Protestant landed minority, often absent, held virtually all the land, which was farmed by a Catholic peasantry with no security of tenure. Tenants could be evicted at will for a higher rent, with no compensation of any kind for the improvements they might have made to the holding. A campaign for the repeal of the 1801 Act had been led by Daniel O'Connell in the 1840s but the British government sent in the army to suppress the movement, arresting O'Connell and the ringleaders.

The repeated use of the military by successive British governments was only to enhance their reputation as an occupying force on an alien people. Then, beginning in 1845, came the successive failures of the potato crop. Potatoes were the staple food of the Irish diet. The appalling famine halved the population either by death or through emigration. From the Irish viewpoint, despite the repeal of the Corn Laws, it seemed that the mainland had abandoned them.

That the situation could be looked upon in this way is hardly surprising for the attitude of the British government was inconsistent, uncertain as to whether to regard and treat Ireland in the same way as Wales and Scotland, or to administer the island as a colony. As a result of this irresolution no coherent policy was ever pursued. It always remained a reactive, as against a proactive, one, a patchy ramshackle affair with legislation too little, too late, and often of an ineffective and inadequate kind. The result was to fuel the movement in Ireland which eventually became that for Home Rule, one which was to reach a crescendo in the twentieth century but which need never have happened if a sustained and co-ordinated policy of reform and integration had been pursued with energy at an earlier date. All along, however, any demand for some kind of self-government was frustrated by those at Westminster who saw it as the prelude to the disintegration of the United Kingdom and Empire.

That this problem was to have such a profound impact on the workings of the British political system was precisely because the Irish MPs sat in the London Parliament. It only needed a leader to emerge who would galvanise them to act as a group for them to be able to paralyse Parliament. And that was precisely what happened when a shrewd and tenacious member of the Protestant Irish élite, Charles Stewart Parnell, entered the House in 1875.

Gladstone had come to power seven years before, stating that his mission was to pacify Ireland. The next year the Church of Ireland was disestablished, thus removing a major source of grievance, the payment by Catholics of the tithe to a Protestant ministry they did not want. The year after came a Land Act, which seemingly offered compensation to tenants unjustly evicted but in fact turned out to be so complicated that it had little impact on halting evictions. Next Gladstone attempted to establish an Irish Catholic university, much to the consternation of the Protestants. His first Irish policy ended in failure. Fatally, he had raised hopes only to dash them.

The demand for self-government grew. In 1879 the Irish Land League was formed, with Parnell as its president. Its aim was to achieve fair rents and security of tenure for tenants, leading eventually to ownership. Parnell was a revolutionary and the Land League joined forces with the nationalist movement called the Fenian Brotherhood. Exacerbated by the agricultural depression of the 1870s protest began to take active form, leading not only to rent strikes and obstructionism by tenants but worse, arson, outright violence, and assaults on landlords.

This was the situation which greeted Gladstone on his return to office as Prime Minister for a second period in 1880. A second Irish Land Act was passed in the following year with the aim of securing fair rents, freedom of sale and fixity of tenure. Although an achievement, its effect was to emphasise the emerging differences which divided the north from the south of the country. In Ulster, Protestants of a dissenting kind (as against Church of Ireland) formed the majority. In addition, that area of Ireland was the only one to experience the benefits of the Industrial Revolution, which again set it apart from the depressed Catholic agricultural south. Gladstone's Land Act worked well in the north whereas in the south it resulted in a sea of litigation and violence. In spite of its concessions, the Land League headed by Parnell still opposed the Act, and Parnell as a consequence was imprisoned.

Cartoon attacking Gladstone's Land Act of 1881 as a gesture of appeasement to the Land League. Here the League, depicted as a cudgel-wielding thug, threatens the cowering figure of Gladstone.

Then, on 6 May 1881, the new Chief Secretary for Ireland, Lord Frederick Cavendish, and the Under-Secretary, were murdered in Phoenix Park in Dublin. Such assassinations led Parnell to disassociate himself from the revolutionaries and found a new association, the National League. The British response to the murders was to pass a strongly coercive Prevention of Crimes Bill, meeting force with force. In this way during the 1880s and 90s polarity, instead of being averted, was accelerated. The terrible agricultural depression meant that half of those who reached the age of maturity emigrated, in the main to the United States where they often prospered but never forgot their tragic origins, sending home funds to finance the independence movement. In this they established a pattern of concern in which the United States somehow was always to be involved, even to the present day, in any settlement of the Irish question.

What no one had foreseen was that the further reform of the franchise in 1885 meant that the Irish Nationalist MPs led by Parnell were to hold the balance in the Commons and hence were able to dominate the workings of the British Parliament. It was at that moment that Gladstone was converted to the cause of Home Rule, the restoration of an Irish Parliament within the British Empire, which he regarded as a moral necessity. The effect on the Liberal party was catastrophic. It divided it right down the middle, and those who regarded this conversion as an act of betrayal made common cause with the rapidly emerging opponents to such a move in Ulster, known as Unionists. To Unionists in the north, Home Rule came to symbolise the opening prelude to a domination by what they regarded as popery. Gladstone's dramatic conversion paved the way for a political divide over Ireland in which Liberalism became the ally of Irish nationalism and Conservatism that of Ulster unionism.

Nonetheless, in June 1886 Gladstone introduced the first Home Rule Bill for Ireland which was defeated and led to his resignation. He lost the next election and

A contemporary cartoon, *The Scapegoat of the Family*, May 1886. Victoria, labelled as Queen Mother, attended by the countries of the Empire, sadly watches Ireland depart: 'Ireland, with all thy faults I love thee still.'

the new Prime Minister, Lord Salisbury, appointed A. J. Balfour as Secretary for Ireland. Although he sped up land sales, Balfour's rule was harsh and coercive, but in fact by encouraging land sales he paved the way for the peaceful demise of the landlord class. Meanwhile the leader of the Irish cause in the House, Parnell, was disgraced. Forged letters implied that he had been cognisant of the Phoenix Park murders, a charge which took two years in the law courts to clear. In 1890, Parnell's long liaison with a married woman, Kitty O'Shea, became public knowledge when her husband cited Parnell as co-respondent in the divorce case. In Victorian England this spelt only one thing for a man in public life, ruin. He died a year later.

Back again in power in 1892 Gladstone tried to pass a second Home Rule Bill, and again failed. By then he had nailed the Liberal party's colours firmly to the mast of Home Rule leading in the long term to the party losing its grassroots support with the English electorate, and becoming instead the voice of the Celtic fringes of Wales, Scotland and Ireland. For years the Liberals remained out of power as a consequence of Ireland, years during which speculation about what would happen should such a bill ever be passed led those in the north to assume an identity based on their Protestant faith, and the belief that their industrial prosperity would be lost if ever the union with Britain was dissolved. One bill, however, was passed by a Conservative government, the Land Purchase Act of 1903. This finally solved the land issue. The government provided long-term, low interest loans to encourage tenants to buy. By the 1920s two thirds of the land had passed into the ownership of the tenants and landlordism had become a thing of the past.

But this still did not give the Irish Home Rule. One great obstacle to achieving that objective was the House of Lords which was solidly against such a motion. To break their power of veto was to open the way for any Liberal government to pass such a bill. And this is what happened. In 1909 the Liberals under Asquith clashed with the Lords, a confrontation which was finally resolved in the Parliament Act of 1911, which stripped the Lords of its right to veto. The passing of that Act was made possible in the Commons through the support of the Irish Nationalist MPs led by John Redmond. Their reward was a Home Rule Bill introduced in May 1912 but which only became law in the year that the First World War broke out. In that Act there was provision, for a limited time, for any area of Ireland which wished to opt out by plebiscite to be able to do so. But the Act was to remain a deadletter while the war was fought.

This final move towards granting Home Rule drew those in the north in Ulster even more closely together with the support and encouragement of Conservative Unionists in England. There were huge public demonstrations and a defence corps

Postcard propaganda about 1912 by the Ulster Unionists with William III on horseback below and, ensconced at the centre above, their leader, the Dublin Tory lawyer, Sir Edward Carson.

was set up, the Ulster Volunteers. Everything in 1914 indicated that Ireland was drifting towards civil war. Instead the majority of Irish played their part in the massive allied war effort in Europe. But not everyone took that attitude. An Irish nationalist rebel, Roger Casement, opened negotiations with the Germans looking towards an uprising at Easter 1916 against the British government. Casement landed on Good Friday. For a moment it looked as though the uprising might be stillborn but then, on Easter Monday, the nationalists seized the General Post Office in Dublin and proclaimed an Irish Republic. Four days later, with a toll of some four hundred and fifty dead and well over two thousand wounded, they surrendered. Casement and the main ringleaders were executed. Martial law was imposed. In one ghastly encounter an unbridgeable chasm had been opened between the two islands. The British troops had given the Irish nationalists what they lacked, a potent patriotic mythology and a litany of martyrs to the cause. This was a point of no return.

At the 1918 election, seventy-three Irish MPs led by Éamon de Valera were elected, thirty-four of them men in jail. All of them were members of the republican movement, Sinn Féin ('ourselves'), a political identity created over a decade before in 1905, whose members wanted complete independence for Ireland. That in its turn was a reflection of something else which increased the divide, a Gaelic cultural renaissance whose aim was the de-anglicization of Ireland. The next year, 1919, Sinn Féin won every seat outside Ulster, totally replacing the Irish Nationalists and setting up what was in effect an Irish Parliament (the Dáil) in Dublin, with de Valera as the country's first president. At the same time the old administration remained in place in Dublin Castle, meaning that in effect the country had two governments. The all-too-visible drift towards civil war was accelerated by the creation of an Irish Republican Army, the IRA, which launched a campaign of terrorism against the forces of the established government, the Royal Irish Constabulary, and the soldiers of the British army. The Prime Minister, Lloyd George, authorised the recruitment of irregular contingents of soldiers demobilised from the Great War to meet the crisis. These, known as the 'Black and Tans', indulged in reprisal tactics of a kind which has remained a lasting disgrace to the traditions of the British army.

In September 1920 the British government recognised the inevitable in a Government of Ireland Act. The country was to be split in two, the twenty-six southern Catholic counties and the six northern Protestant ones. Irish MPs were to continue to sit at Westminster but there were to be two other assemblies, one in Dublin and the other in Belfast, with a Council of Ireland linking them. At the election which ensued Sinn Féin won 124 out of the 128 seats and then refused to take them or have anything to do with implementing the Act. Violence broke out, and Lloyd George realised that any attempt to impose the solution by force would mean civil war. By 1921 twenty-six of the southern counties were under martial law.

In July, a cease-fire took place and at the end of the year Ireland was accorded dominion status on a par with Canada as the Irish Free State. It still recognised the sovereignty of the crown. In the spring of 1922 the new constitution came fully into operation with a formal transfer of power from Westminster. The effect was civil war between north and south, with Ulster seceding in the spring of the following year. The Council of Ireland, designed to bring the two sides together on a regular basis, was a deadletter and was abolished in 1925.

Ireland's history has been one long saga of misman-agement from the mainland. There were moments when it seemed possible that a country whose population was in the main treated as a subject people might have been successfully drawn into the system in the same way as Scotland and Wales, both of which also had strong religious and cultural differences from England. That that never happened was a major failure of initiative by a succession of governments, especially during the Victorian period, all of which never came to grips with the fundamental problems of the country. Although Ireland was never part of Britain it had been one part of what is designated the United Kingdom. A section of that had now gone, fuelling separatist tendencies on the mainland. In 1925 Plaid Cymru (the party of Wales) was formed, promoting the Welsh language and calling for self-government, along with a radical social and economic programme. Three years later a Scottish National party was set up demanding likewise self-government for north of the border. Neither of these were to have any significant impact but they were to remain irksome and salutary reminders to those at the centre that Britain was an alliance, rather than a union, of countries. In the case of Ireland dominion status was to prove a half-way house. The advent of the Irish Free State, however, succeeded in papering over for a time what were the all-too-visible cracks beneath the surface.

The opening of the first Northern Ireland Parliament in June 1921 by King George V. Painted by William Conor, it was not a popular picture as it proved difficult to persuade any of the Members to subscribe to it.

Chapter Sixty-Three

PAX BRITANNICA

IN 1890 Queen Victoria reigned over four hundred million people inhabiting a fifth of the surface of the globe. Indeed Britain ruled over so vast a domain that virtually nothing could arise in any part of the world that would not affect her. The British Empire, then seemingly at its apogee, exerted a strong hold on the contem-porary imagination, one which cast Britain with a world-wide mission as an agent, it was believed, of good. This surge of patriotic pride was still a relatively new phenomenon. Up until the 1870s the Empire had been an administrative mechanism in the interests of commerce. Colonies were looked upon as expensive and burdensome necessities best dealt with by allowing them self-government, which was cheaper. Such a policy was summed up in 1867 when the Confederation of Canada was created. But after that date the atmosphere began to change as the age of the superpower arrived, an age in which virtually every European nation attempted to carve out a colonial empire. In the case of Britain that renewed expansion was triggered by Disraeli's purchase in 1875 of the controlling shares in the Suez Canal, vital as the lifeline to India. This was to have the effect of involving Britain first in the fate of Egypt, and gradually more and more in that of the whole of Africa. Not that there was any planned programme of British acquisition, for it was piecemeal and pragmatic. But once it began all kinds of motives were to drive the bandwagon of territorial annexation relentlessly onwards: prestige, patriotism, missionary zeal, and the need for new markets and trade routes being just some of them.

Disraeli began to extol the virtues of Empire and the queen was proclaimed Empress of India in 1876. That was followed by the great Golden and Diamond Jubilees of her reign in 1887 and 1897 when the British populace witnessed imperial cavalcades through London which made visible to them the reality of the many peoples over whom they now held sway. Such pageantry was to have an intoxicating effect in the new era of mass circulation newspapers.

The Empire was firmly linked to the economy, offering new markets and a source for raw materials to the most highly industrialised country in the world. That industrial supremacy came under threat in the last thirty years of the century during

In the 1920s a solution to Britain's post-war economic depression was seen to lie in the Empire, then at its greatest extent, with one quarter of the world's population as a potential market. The role of the Empire Marketing Board was to promote the sale of Empire goods in Britain with the belief that members of the Empire in their turn would buy British. In 1926 Empire imports only made up 30% of the total.

what was called the Great Depression. The name is a misleading one for exports were actually still rising. What it reflected was something else, the fact that other countries were becoming highly industrialised. In the 1870s Britain was overtaken by the United States and then, after 1900, by Germany. Britain's share of the world's trade dropped from 25% to 14% between 1870 and 1910. All kinds of reasons were suggested for this onset of atrophy, from the inadequacy of the British education system to the attitude of society towards those engaged in trade as somehow being inferior to the professions. Nonetheless, the Empire remained the country's market cornerstone.

The links which bound the colonies to the mother country could be very personal ones. Between 1861 and 1900 seven-and-a-half million people emigrated to Australia and New Zealand and 800,000 to Canada. These, along with Africa, were referred to as 'vacant territories', as though their indigenous population did not exist. Australia,

The Australian painter
R. Godfrey Rivers' *Under the
Jacaranda* captures the export of
English living style across the
Empire. But for the exotic tree
the picture could pass as an
English country house tea party.

claimed for Britain in 1770 by Captain Cook, had been used from the close of the eighteenth century as a dumping ground for convicts. By the 1850s it was regarded in a far different light, when first wool and then gold made it important to the British economy. Connections with Britain on the other side of the globe were to remain strong, children being sent back to be educated, the Anglican church establishing itself in the colony, and a government structure modelled on that of the homeland evolving. Such countries were self-governing and usually developed enough to send their own 'ambassador', designated High Commissioner, to London, where they established national headquarters, such as Canada House or Australia House.

India was very different and was always to form a special case. Over three-quarters of the inhabitants of the Empire lived there and it was to have a greater impact on Britain during the Victorian age than any other country, despite the Indian Mutiny (1857) when a combination of motives had led to a revolt by the native population, including a large part of the army, and the committing of appalling atrocities on both sides. The resulting reappraisal of the government of the country brought an end to the political role of the East India Company. Henceforth India had a viceroy answerable to the India Office and the British government. Indians were allowed for the first time into the administration of justice and into the civil service. But the British continued firmly to believe that they were destined to rule the country in perpetuity. Without them, the British believed India would fall apart in the face of the enormous divergences of its peoples, languages and religions. Nothing seemed to shake the hold of British rule, although as education and literacy spread it began to dawn on intelligent Indians that they were being denied their political rights.

Between 1870 and 1900 sixty million people and forty-five million square miles were added to the British Empire. Most of these can be accounted for by Africa, which began to be opened up to Europeans during the 1850s and 60s through the work of explorers like David Livingstone. Colonisation occurred in a haphazard way, beginning with coastal trading bases and then gradually spreading inland. Boundaries to such new territories were only drawn when one empire-building country came up against another. The Suez Canal signalled annexation in the north. Egypt had been temporarily occupied but that became permanent in 1882. In order to protect Egypt, neighbouring Sudan had to be conquered. Although in 1885 the British relief force failed to reach Khartoum in time to save General Charles Gordon, beleaguered there by the revolt of the Mahdi, the Sudan was eventually taken over by an army headed by General Kitchener. During the 1890s came Zanzibar, Nigeria, Gold Coast (Ghana), Gambia and Sierra Leone. The biggest problem, however, lay in the south of the continent, where the two British colonies, Cape Colony and Natal, were adjacent to two Afrikaner Boer states, Orange Free State and Transvaal, settled long before by the Dutch. These the British annexed in 1877, two years later defeating the hostile natives, the Zulus. In 1880-81 the Boers revolted, and were granted independence only a few years before gold and diamonds were discovered in the Transvaal, a discovery which changed everything. Both British and foreigners, designated by the Boers as the 'uitlanders', poured into the Transvaal, and Johannesburg sprang up almost overnight. All of this could not fail to excite the predatory Prime Minister of the British colonies, Cecil Rhodes, whose vision was of a British African Empire. Under his aegis in 1895 there took place a disgraceful attempt at a coup, an invasion of the Transvaal led by Jameson timed to coincide with an uprising by the 'uitlanders'. It was a fiasco, and any involvement by the British Colonial Office was tactfully glossed over. Inevitably it ruined the possibility of a peaceful relationship with the Boers whose two states came together under President Kruger.

War indeed finally erupted over the Boer treatment of these 'uitlanders' among whom many were British. The Boer War was to last three years (1899-1902), cost £300 million and thirty thousand men were to be killed. It began disastrously and only gradually moved towards victory with the taking of Pretoria in June 1900, but two more years of guerrilla warfare followed until peace was finally made at Vereeniging. The Boers were duly subjugated and their two states annexed to form the Union of South Africa. But the war had been a shock to the British government. It had taken half-a-million men to crush an enemy with only sixty thousand. It was an appalling indictment of the state of the British army.

After the war it became clear that some mechanism of consultation was needed to hold together the sprawling cumbrous mass which made up the Empire. Despite the fact that Empire Day was instituted in 1904 as an annual celebration, imperial authority was already on the wane and enthusiasm diminishing. The British had never quite shed their attitude that an empire was an unnecessary burden and expense. Only in the case of India was there a spectacular reassertion of the imperial role when the great Durbar of 1911 was staged in which the new king, George V, received the homage of the princes in his role as King-Emperor. Colonial and then Imperial Conferences began to be held in which the 'self-governing colonies' were referred to as 'dominions' and in which the Empire itself became interchangeable with the word Commonwealth. Increasingly these dominions began to seek for equality of status with the mother-country. As Britain paid for their defence they had no control over their foreign policy, and it was in this way the Empire entered the First World War. But after this the demand for equality accelerated. At the 1926 Imperial Conference a formula was reached which was later enshrined in the 1931 Statute of Westminster. It defined those countries as 'autonomous communities within the British Empire, equal in status . . . though united by a common allegiance to the Crown.' But this new definition took as its focus an institution which had been stripped of any political power and which relied for its potency on deference and the magic of pageantry, attributes which were gradually to cease to exert their spell.

King George V and Queen Mary setting sail for India for the Durbar in 1911, the highest point of imperial splendour.

Chapter Sixty-Four

SPLENDID ISOLATION AND WAR

WITH an Empire upon which the sun never set it was no wonder that the British at the turn of the century were complacent. The country was blessed with success, stability and abundant riches, so much so that what happened on the mainland of Europe seemed irrelevant. Its people looked across the globe rather than across the Channel. Nothing there, it was tacitly assumed, could affect what seemed to be one long saga of glory. But, like the Empire itself, that was to prove a delusion. The greatest mistake made by Lord Palmerston and his successors was to stand aside while Prussia gradually grew to be the German Empire. Suddenly in 1871 there appeared a new major power in Central Europe, with the capacity eventually to dominate the whole continent. British foreign policy since the Tudor period had been influenced by the conviction that no one nation should ever be allowed to enjoy European hegemony. In the Elizabethan age the challenge of the world-wide might of Spain had been met with the defeat of the Armada. In the two centuries that followed, the expansionist policies of France, first under Louis XIV and then under Napoleon, were curbed by Marlborough's victories and those of Nelson and Wellington. The history of the British in the twentieth century was to see re-enactments of these titanic encounters, which, like their predecessors, were to unite a nation yet again in defence of the island realm.

Lord Salisbury, who was the major influence on British foreign policy during the closing decades of the century, believed that 'it is in our interests that as little should happen as possible.' It was a policy summed up in two words: 'splendid isolation'. But it was an isolation which made a younger generation progressively more and more uneasy. Britain's relationship with Europe had left her without allies. The British cult of liberty had led successive governments to offer asylum or aid to revolutionary movements from the mainland which resulted in distrust of Britain by the European powers. On the British side the long suspicion of France remained unaltered, reinforced by clashes abroad in North Africa over the control of the Suez Canal. Two questions were at the forefront of British consideration in the 1880s and 90s: firstly, what would happen in Eastern Europe when the Turkish Empire, which still controlled the Balkans, finally collapsed; and secondly, what were the new German Empire's long term intentions?

At the outset Germany did not seem to pose a threat. The German emperor's heir was married to Queen Victoria's eldest daughter. A strong Central European state would help to keep Russia out of Europe and also to check France. That attitude only began to change in the nineties as the German economy caught up with, and then overtook, the British. There was still room in the world markets for both, but then the Germans suddenly started to build an enormous navy. Britain's navy was still the mightiest in the world, crucial for the maintenance of the Empire and for the protection of the huge imports of food and raw materials upon which the country depended, both to feed its population and to maintain the economy. The navy had had to rebuild itself as iron-clad boats took over from sail. It needed also to compete with other new navies, those created by Japan and the United States. But the German navy was something different: it was designed to be a first class battle fleet and this could imply only one thing in the long run, a confrontation with Britain. For the first time since Napoleon's invasion attempt of 1805 the country was faced with a potentially hostile force within striking distance. Britain needed peace to sustain its vast commercial empire and the diplomacy of the period strove to achieve just that. Sir Edward Grey, who was to be in charge of foreign policy from 1905 to 1916 during the crucial years which led up to war, knew that such a conflict would be unlike any that had preceded it, and could effectively wipe out a civilisation.

With the hope of averting war, relations with France were repaired by the Entente Cordiale (1904). More significantly, both the army and the navy were put into good order, the army always coming a poor second because the idea of any defence of the island from attack from the mainland seemed so infinitely remote. Although privilege had gone from the army, it did not follow that it was any more professional. Its training was old-fashioned and not even the shock of the Boer War had galvanised the government into reform. Not until R. B. Haldane became Secretary for War in 1905 did that happen. Thanks to Haldane a General Staff was set up (ensuring a far better line of command), the Territorial Army was created, and officer training corps established in many of the public and secondary schools. As a result, when war finally did break out there was a fully trained British Expeditionary Force of 100,000. Haldane's equivalent in the navy was Admiral Fisher. In 1905 the *Dreadnought* was launched, a ship surpassing every battleship yet built. By 1914 Britain was also winning the race to have the largest navy. What no one anticipated was the impact of new technological developments such as mines and the submarine and, in the case of land transportation, of motorcycles, trucks and tanks. By the last year of the war, 1918, there was a further major development, the Royal Air Force was formed.

Foreign policy was made by a small bureaucracy in the Foreign Office, which also dealt with the Empire. The decision that the country should go to war lay largely with Sir Edward Grey. The Germans gambled on the belief that Britain would wish to stay out, and it could have if the government had been prepared to accept German domination of Europe. It was, however, to be the assassination of the heir to the throne of Austria-Hungary at Sarajevo on 28 June 1914, which would trigger the war. Then the German army entered Belgium, from which there was the shortest crossing to Britain. On 4 August Grey sent an ultimatum, to which the Germans did not respond. Suddenly Britain found itself at war.

War sooner or later had been expected but when it finally came it was a surprise. The public believed it would all be over by Christmas but the Minister for War, Lord Kitchener, realised from the outset that this was going to be a long struggle. Nothing had prepared anyone for the terrible and unprecedented carnage which followed for this was a new kind of war, devoid of any swift or heroic offensive. Instead it was characterised by the grinding monotony of two armies dug into trenches facing each other across a narrow strip of land which, due to the endless bombs, came to resemble more and more the surface of the moon. The troops endured cold and isolation, feeling themselves to be locked into something from which there seemed neither escape nor an end in view.

First World War poster to encourage every class and both sexes to enter war service.

On 6 August the British Army left for France and linked up with the French Fifth Army. The German plan had been to knock them out in one massive offensive but in this they failed, the allies holding on at the river Marne. Gradually a front line snaked its way from the Belgian coastline down as far as Switzerland, and there it stayed for virtually the whole duration of the war. The town of Ypres was held, but at a price, the decimation of the British Expeditionary Force. It rapidly became clear that men would be needed in millions and Kitchener's famous poster with its slogan 'Your Country Needs You' contributed to raising a million volunteers by Christmas 1914. Similar numbers were raised in each year of the war. But the men recruited initially were inevitably untrained, devoid of proper barracks and equipment, and above all, lacked the necessary munitions with which to fight.

The war was fought on two fronts for Germany had also invaded Russia which stood in desperate need of supplies. Turkey joined the Germans and in April 1915 Italy entered the conflict on the side of Britain and France. In the same month over 40,000 Imperial troops were landed at Gallipoli in the hope of opening up a supply route to Russia. In the end they were forced to evacuate with huge losses. Meanwhile in France there was another battle in the area of Ypres and for the first time the Germans used poisoned gas to horrendous effect. The casualties kept on relentlessly mounting.

In January 1916 conscription for all adult males between eighteen and forty-one was introduced. As a consequence, women began to take on the jobs vacated by their menfolk. The number of women in domestic service suddenly fell by a quarter. In May the war's major naval engagement took place, the Battle of Jutland, which resulted in heavy losses on both sides. The German fleet escaped but never challenged the Royal Navy again. Then came the 'big push' on the Somme, an offensive which lasted from July to November with little to show for it apart from the loss of a half-a-million men mown down by German machine-

John Singer Sargent records the horrors of gas. Sargent went to the French front to record the American and British troops. Here he catches the heart-rending spectacle of blindfolded soldiers who had lost their sight, victims of mustard gas.

gun fire. This was to be the first war in which more men actually died encountering the enemy than from disease or neglect. At home the loss of Lord Kitchener, drowned on his way to Russia, led to reorganisation with Lloyd George taking over as Minister for Munitions and later as Prime Minister.

Workers at the National Shell-fitting Factory at Chilwell, Nottinghamshire in 1917. Women gained a new status during the war making up a large percentage of the munitions workforce.

Another attempt at a knockout blow against the enemy was tried in April 1917 but that too failed and in July the advance to the village of Passchendaele, close to Ypres, claimed 300,000 more lives. The battle was fought amidst a sea of mud and all that was gained was a strip four miles in width. By then the Germans had embarked on submarine warfare threatening the British merchant navy, vital for the country's food supply and for the import of raw materials. Lloyd George instituted a system of convoys. In 1917 the United States entered the war, and in Russia revolution broke out wiping out the Russian Imperial family and the rule of the tsars.

That revolution released the German army on the eastern front to move west and there was a renewed offensive in 1918 but the Germans were unable to sustain it. Marshal Foch was put in overall charge of the allied forces, and in August the Battle of Amiens was won. By then the mighty German war machine was crumbling and the German front line began to break up. At home Germany was in crisis, a blockade having strangled its supply lines so that its people began to suffer death through malnutrition. The Germans had reached the end of their capacity to endure any more. On 11 November 1918 an armistice was agreed to. The war was over.

In Britain the mood to the very end remained one of determination although the people were exhausted, the war having affected everyone in a way hitherto unknown. Peace brought a feeling of triumph mixed with a cry for vengeance. But then came the realisation of just how terrible it had been and just what those men had gone through amidst the mud of Flanders. The First World War traumatized a generation. Nothing, as Edward Grey predicted, was ever the same after it. No one, however, doubted but that the right decision had been taken, to fight. Germany's bid for domination had been squashed and that is where Britain's commitment was seen to end.

The country seemed to have learnt little from this holocaust, and wished to return in policy terms to a period of 'splendid isolation'. Once more the Empire assumed a paramount position, added to which there was now a new relationship with the United States. At the Treaty of Versailles in 1919 Britain offered a military guarantee to France but only on the condition of American participation. Britain stood back while the huge consequences which affected the whole of the mainland took place, signalling the end of the short-lived German Empire, and also of the empire of Austria-Hungary, this time after centuries. The sorting-out of so much change went on well into the 1920s. President Wilson proposed a League of Nations which was subsequently set up with the idea that it could avert a recurrence of what was viewed as 'the war to end all wars'. In 1925, at the Locarno Conference, France, Germany and Belgium mutually guaranteed each others' frontiers, a guarantee underwritten by Italy and Britain. By 1930 Britain had successfully succeeded in getting back to where she had been at the opening of the century, her face firmly averted from the European mainland and turned instead towards her Empire. In that year France proposed that the European nations should form some kind of federal link primarily of an economic character. The idea was firmly rejected.

Chapter Sixty-Five

TWO UNCERTAIN DECADES

FOR the majority of the population peace meant going back to normal and by normal they meant 1914. Few recognised that the war had made such a return impossible. So much had changed that the clock could not be put back. The desire to do so inhibited the pressing need to move forwards to a world which was changing faster than ever before. Democracy as a means of running a country was to prove both a means of accelerating change but also of impeding it. In 1918 the Franchise Act, responding to the post-war mood of expectancy, gave the vote to every man over twenty-one and every woman over twenty-eight, thus trebling the electorate to 22 million. Ten years later the age qualification for women was equalised, thus adding five million more to the electorate. The vote ceased to be a privilege bestowed upon those deemed to have a vested interest in the state and became a birthright. After 1918 the working classes could tip the electoral balance decisively one way or the other for the first time. Bidding for the votes of this vast new electorate began to be the dominating factor for all political parties. In response to this the parties not only developed their inherited Victorian party machines, but also embraced the new media, first the mass circulation newspapers and then, in the mid-1920s, broadcasting. Naturally such an electorate welcomed advantageous social reform. What it did not warm to was government action which brought home sharp truths. In some ways, therefore, a democracy was more difficult to handle and a less effective means of government than the monarchical and aristocratic systems which had preceded it. Henceforward a government could only do what public opinion would tolerate.

This fact soon emerged during the two decades which spanned the end of the First World War and the beginning of the Second in 1939. Already, after two centuries of expansion caused by the world's first Industrial Revolution, decline and decay had set in. It had begun earlier in the case of agriculture during the 1870s: by 1938 only 4.2% of the workforce remained on the land. But after 1918 it became far more

George V broadcasts to Britain and the Empire on Christmas Day 1934. Popular monarchy combining public pageantry and domestic probity was born with George V and Queen Mary and aided by the new mass media, first newspapers, then radio, and later television.

serious when coal, cotton, shipbuilding, iron and steel, areas which had made up the aristocracy of Victorian productivity, also began to decline. That was inevitable, for countries like Germany and Sweden, for example, now built ships and India produced her own textiles, added to which new countries like China and Japan launched themselves into the world market. Not only was British decline not recognised internally but industry itself was blighted by inefficiency, failing to respond to new product requirements, modern technology and management. In addition, it was deeply resistant to change and innovation. The results of industrial decline escalated unemployment levels to what Victorians would have regarded as a crisis point. For two decades it remained over a million, soaring up higher in 1920-21 and again in 1931-33. This prolonged consistency was a new phenomenon, for in the previous century unemployment was cyclical in a boom-and-bust rotation. What it registered was something irreversible, the first signs of a post-industrial Britain. Those out of work in the twentieth century, however, had the vote and could therefore no longer be ignored. But the effect across the country was by no means uniform, rather made up of a series of isolated pockets of misery in places like Northern Ireland, Clydeside, the north-east and Lancashire. Nor was every part of the industrial landscape cast into darkness, for the inter-war years witnessed the rise of the south-east with a whole new range of industries: motor car manufacture, machine tools, electrical appliances, aircraft and the new synthetics like plastic and artificial silk. The trouble was that no one would come to terms with the fact that the old industries were in terminal decline.

Nor did governments respond to what these new industries called for, a far better-educated workforce. Instead there were twenty years of official inertia following the raising of the school leaving age to fourteen in 1918. There it was to remain, in spite of a major report recommending that it should be raised to fifteen in 1926. That was to be implemented in 1939, but the war intervened. This failure in education policy sprang from a fear that if the working classes were educated they would not want to work hard at long boring jobs. Indeed, it was believed that it would erode their will to work at all. And, again looking backwards, their education would only exacerbate the servant problem for the upper classes.

The idea that a government should be involved in industry at all, let alone have an economic policy, was still a novelty in the 1920s. After the war everyone believed that all that was called for was the restoration of sound currency by returning to the Gold Standard (measured by an exchange rate for the pound of $4.86); properly balanced budgets and a free market would do the rest. As for a slump, the only way out of that was to cut government expenditure. That actually did not square, as it produced further unemployment which called for more state money in the form of benefits. As the inter-war years passed governments opted more and more for protectionism, defending, through the introduction of tariffs, the home market. This not only marked the end of the long reign of free trade but also something else of significance: the state was becoming progressively more involved in the running of the economy, an activity which was to continue in an ever-ascending curve.

That involvement had begun during the war when government had been forced to take over whole areas of the economy for the first time, anticipating what was to happen after 1945, nationalisation, which lay in the future, but the seeds were already there, sown, ironically, by the Conservatives. In 1926 the government acquired the British Broadcasting Company making it into a Corporation which was in effect a state monopoly. In the same year the Central Electricity Board was established with the aim of providing a nation-wide power grid. Both proved to be precedents upon which to build.

But what was to propel such a notion right into the centre of the arena was the arrival of a new political party for whom the nationalisation of the means of production was to be a fundamental tenet. The meteoric rise of the Labour Party and the equally catastrophic descent of the Liberals was to be the greatest political phenomenon between 1918 and 1939. The speed with which Labour assumed a position as the official opposition and then went on to hold office in what was a new two-party system can only be described as astonishing.

The Labour Party's roots lay back in the previous century. Until the 1880s the unions had remained not only diverse but divided; although they may have harboured the odd politically motivated revolutionary group their concern had been with trade and craft protection. The change came with the advent of a new type of union, the bulk of whose membership was unskilled, but who collectively, through strikes, could hold an urbanised and industrialised society to ransom. During the same period there also emerged intellectual groups who were to provide the ideological framework for such a new party. In 1881 the Democratic Federation was formed, inspired by the teachings of Karl Marx and dedicated therefore to the destruction of capitalism. Three years later they merged with another group, the Labour Emancipation League, to form the Social Democratic Federation. In the same year, 1884, Sidney and Beatrice Webb founded the Fabian Society whose message was nationalisation: 'The emancipation of Land and Industrial Capital from individuals and class ownership, and the vesting of them in the community for general benefit.' The Fabians tended to be armchair visionaries, certainly not revolutionaries, an attribute they shared with movements in the arts, like that led by William Morris, who yearned for a return to the worker-craftsman living in a romantic medieval utopia. The general drift of all these groups was to replace profit-mongering capitalism with collective ownership and co-operative management of the means of production and distribution.

Until the 1890s working class voters had supported the Liberals, but in 1891 a particularly bitter strike triggered the emergence of an independent labour political organisation with links to the Fabian Society. A year later three of their members, including Keir Hardie, were elected MPs, and in 1893 the Independent Labour Party was born. Keir Hardie was a self-taught socialist thinker who found himself leading what was in the early days a small, poor, and weak party but one whose objectives were to become those of the future parliamentary Labour Party, and were radically to affect the direction of the country and of society for much of the century. They proposed a long list of social reforms including the abolition of overtime, piecework and child labour, the introduction of an eight hour day, benefits for the sick, disabled, old, widowed and orphaned, as well as unemployment benefit. They also demanded a further extension of the franchise, the abolition of indirect taxes, the 'taxation, to extinction, of unearned incomes', and a 'graduated income tax'. The most important clause of all was Clause 4, which called for the state 'to secure the collective ownership of all the means of production, distribution and exchange'.

The failure of the Liberals to respond to many of these currents within working class aspirations heralded their eventual demise. By 1895 there were six hundred Labour councillors and in 1898 there was the first Labour local authority. But any real bid for political power called for far wider support and for finance, which only arrived when Labour became allied to the trades unions. In 1899 the Trades Union Congress voted to increase the number of Labour MPs and the next year set up a Labour Representative Committee. The real change, however, followed a legal judgment in 1901, the Taff Vale judgment, which laid down that funds of a union could be drawn upon if its officials were found liable in an action brought for damages. Suddenly a hundred and twenty unions decided to affiliate themselves to the Committee and the unions proceeded to instigate a political levy on their members to finance its MPs.

In 1903 the Liberals entered into a secret agreement with Labour, promising, in return for Labour's support of certain Liberal measures, a free hand in thirty constituencies. In the 1906 Parliament there were thirty MPs who took for the first time the name of the Labour Party. The Liberals reversed the Taff Vale judgment in the Trade Disputes Act. When a judge in 1909 ruled that unions should not make use of funds to finance MPs, the Liberals reversed this in the Trade Unions Act of 1913, which went on to sanction the collection of a political levy. But although the Labour Party travelled far, even in 1918 it was still a minority.

Meanwhile the Conservative Party had managed to adapt to the new democratic age in a way which was also to hasten the demise of the Liberals. The trebling of the electorate in 1918, far from being a disaster, ushered in an era of Conservative victories. Although Prime Ministers like Lord Salisbury had regarded the arrival of democracy with horror, by 1918 the Conservative Party was well on the way to becoming the party of the ever-burgeoning middle classes of suburbia. Nor did it lack working support in places like Liverpool and Birmingham. All in all, the Conservatives had succeeded in adapting to the twentieth century with remarkable ease. The party had ceased to be the party of the landed gentry and became instead one dominated by business and industry. Unlike the Labour Party, it had no driving ideology, preferring to present itself simply as efficient government of a kind which defended property rights, stood up for conventional morality, and cultivated patriotism to king and country. Conservatism abhorred any socialistic idea of a gigantic redistribution of wealth and, as the excesses of the Russian Revolution became known, drew to its ranks those who feared any form of Bolshevism securing a foothold in Britain.

The war had ended with a Coalition Government in power, headed by Lloyd George, which went to the country and was returned. After an initial flurry of commercial activity there followed an horrendous slump, producing massive unemployment. The coalition broke up, and in 1922 there was another election, the results of which began to spell out the collapse of the Liberals, for the party was split between those who were loyal to Lloyd George as against those who still adhered to Asquith. This division was to make Labour the opposition party for the first time, in what was a Conservative victory. A year later the Prime Minister, Bonar Law, resigned and was succeeded by Stanley Baldwin. Baldwin was typical of the new Conservatism. The son of a midland ironmaster, he rose through his gifts of oratory rather than those of intellect. He had been an indifferent Chancellor of the Exchequer and was generally viewed as indolent. However, in a period of industrial strife he had perhaps the most essential attributes: the ability and will to heal and ease tensions, and a firm belief in the middle ground. These he framed in a highly romanticised view of England, casting it, in clear contradiction to the reality, as a nation rooted in the rural landscape. Through his mastery of the new art of broadcasting this approachable man was able to weave his spell upon the public. His long-term political objectives were to obliterate the Liberals, above all Lloyd George, replacing them with Labour, aiming to establish a two-party system in which what the two sides had in common was greater than their differences.

As Baldwin wished to embark on a protectionist policy he felt bound to seek a mandate by holding another election on the issue of tariff reform. Although the Conservatives won the election they were outnumbered by the combined forces of Liberal and Labour, with the consequence that the king, George V, sent for the leader of the Labour Party to form a government. James Ramsay MacDonald was the illegitimate son of Scottish peasants but he was born with huge powers of oratory and with a will to rule. This first Labour government only held office for ten months, but it was long enough to establish in the eyes of the electorate that far from carrying through revolutionary measures Labour acted with responsibility, and could govern within the established scheme of things. The Liberals and Lloyd George were finished. Labour's major problem was how to distance itself from any taint of Bolshevist extremism. What brought them down was an attempt to make a treaty with Russia and the publication of a letter from the Comintern to the British Communists asking them to overthrow the Labour government. Baldwin and the Conservatives were returned with a huge majority, but Labour also increased its vote.

Baldwin was Prime Minister again with Winston Churchill, who had deserted the Liberals, as Chancellor of the Exchequer. A return to the Gold Standard and to the old exchange rate for the pound of $4.86 contributed to spiralling unemployment. In the midst of the ensuing sharp downturn in the economy the miners threatened to strike. Baldwin bought time by granting a nine-month subsidy until a Royal Commission could present its findings. When it did, both the miners and their employers rejected them. The unions called for a General Strike on 4 May 1926. Although the government had prepared itself for a dramatic flare-up of class tension, Baldwin did everything he could to minimise its divisive potential, refusing to use force and always discriminating between what he regarded as two separate disputes.

The General Strike he saw as a challenge to democracy, in which the will of four million union members was being forced onto a population of forty-two million. He came forward with proposals which broke the alliance and on 12 May the General Strike was called off. In this way a cycle of working class militancy which had gone on for a decade-and-a-half came to its end. The miners, however, continued to strike for a further nine months until they were forced to give in. The following year, the Trades Disputes Act declared general and sympathy strikes illegal. All of this was to overshadow what was the Conservatives biggest achievement, a reorganisation of local government in 1928-29 in which the old Poor Law was at last swept away and its responsibilities transferred, together with those for health and roads, to the counties and county boroughs. The Conservatives lost the 1929 election on the issue of unemployment. Nonetheless, a new two-party system was in place and something approaching consensus politics had emerged.

A Labour government was returned, which quickly had to cope with realities and not ideals. During the three years it held office the world collapsed by half its cash value. The Labour government did precisely what a Conservative one would have done, put up taxes and reduced government expenditure, thereby adding yet fur-

Conservative Party poster for the 1929 General Election, the year after the vote was extended to women. The sun radiates topics on which any government would henceforth have to deliver if they were to be elected.

ther to unemployment. By 1933, 23% of the workforce was unemployed, and the Cabinet set about finding ways to cut £78 million in the face of what was an international flight from sterling. On 23 August the Cabinet voted in favour of swingeing cuts, although Ramsay MacDonald felt that he was duty-bound to proffer the king his resignation. He returned from the palace having agreed to head a National Government. No one knows how this came about, he consulted none of his Cabinet colleagues and the party regarded his action as a betrayal. Reacting to cuts in pay to those in public service the fleet mutinied, and Britain came off the Gold Standard, the pound being devalued.

In response to such an appalling financial crisis the National Government called an election and was returned with a massive 556 seats. Ramsay MacDonald remained as Prime Minister with the Conservative Neville Chamberlain as Chancellor of the Exchequer, presiding over what was an economy gradually on the upturn. Protectionist tariffs were introduced, signalling the end of that bastion of Victorian prosperity and enterprise, free trade. In 1935 Ramsay MacDonald made way for the Conservative Baldwin, who was by now too old for office. His last act was to see through the abdication of Edward VIII. In this age of democracy, the monarchy had found a new role with George V, in which it combined private probity with public service and grandeur. The crown in 1936 passed to a man quite unsuited to maintaining such a dull role. Worse, he did little to conceal his pro-German sympathies and was in love with an American divorcée whom he intended to marry. Edward abdicated, and Baldwin resigned after the coronation of Edward VIII's brother as George VI, a name he took to reflect the return of monarchy to the dutiful role carved out for it by his father.

The genial Baldwin was succeeded by the distant and aloof figure of Neville Chamberlain. Cold and unsympathetic, Chamberlain had been a brilliant Minister of Health and Chancellor of the Exchequer, but it was his ill fortune to hold the premiership during a period when the whole focus was on the events which led up to war with Germany. When that finally came in August 1939 it brought the curtain finally down on what had been two tempestuous decades. No one, however, had solved the most fundamental problem: unemployment.

But beneath these intricacies of political life other more far-reaching changes were taking place. The years 1918-21 witnessed the greatest shift in land ownership since the dissolution of the monasteries four hundred years before. Land was no longer a basis for political power, nor, with agriculture in decline, was it profitable. Faced by 40% death duties (a tax introduced first in 1894) and ever-rising taxes the upper classes got rid of their estates, holding on to them only in urban areas. The ever-increasing business and professional classes bought up land, reinforcing Baldwin's vision of the rural ideal as the British way of life. Aristocratic power had gone, but the external façade of aristocracy was maintained. Much to the horror of the old nobility, Lloyd George did a lively trade in giving honours to tycoons and industrialists, starting off with an asking price of £10,000 for a knighthood and thereon upwards.

In reality the enormous discrepancies in life-style so evident before 1914 were fast disappearing. Fewer and fewer people had servants, which removed the greatest social divide. Fashion in clothes and better diet meant that people could be far less easily placed in terms of class by their physical appearance than before. Although there was no diminution in differences of incomes, such differences were far less visibly perceptible. Everyone bought the same things, the rich merely buying a superior version. Even the advent of the BBC hastened this levelling, introducing to the public for the first time a universally accepted voice for speech. Levelling, of course, went up as well as down, as the progress towards an ever-larger middle class continued.

It was the middle classes who really held political power in the age of suburbia. House building boomed as never before, homes which for the first time had the new comforts of electricity and modern plumbing. In 1914 only 10% of the population were home-owners. By 1939 that number had risen to 31%. Families were smaller. The birthrate began to fall from the 1870s onwards, but in the post-war period control of the size of families through the use of contraceptives became customary for the middle classes. Life expectancy rose sharply: in 1921 it was fifty-six for men and sixty for women. This was due to medical progress and the conquest of centuries-old killer diseases, allied to improvements in diet. Much that had dimmed the lives of ordinary people in the past was now taken care of by the state. In 1925 the provision of pensions was extended to widows and orphans, and the age for the old age pension was dropped from seventy to sixty-five. Gradually the state was taking to itself roles until then regarded as the responsibility of the family, such as looking after the old, sick, orphaned and bereaved.

Better housing, longer life span, smaller family units, and for those in work more leisure and more money than ever before. Consumerism was to be one of the major themes of the century. Chain stores such as Woolworths and Marks & Spencer became the norm in every city high street. What was regarded as the average necessary equipment for the ordinary home multiplied to embrace the vacuum cleaner, the gas stove, the radio and even the refrigerator and gramophone. The motor car, which before 1914 had been the plaything only of the rich, became a middle class necessity. By 1939 there were half-a-million holders of driving licences.

Not only did people accumulate more things, they also had more time at their disposal. After 1918 the working week was reduced from fifty-six to forty-eight hours. By 1939, eleven million manual workers had at least a week's paid holiday a year. Mass entertainment arrived in the form of the cinema and the dance hall. Public libraries in 1939 lent two hundred and fifty million books; four years before that the paperback book was born. Sport was enjoyed by every level of society: hunting by the upper classes, cricket and rugby football by the middle classes, greyhound racing and association football by the working classes.

Suburbia arrives, the epitome of the huge rise in living standards by the lower middle class between the wars: a semi-detached house with garden and garage and a car.

The tide turned sharply against many of the attitudes which bound together

Victorian society. Sex ceased to be an unmentionable activity. Religious observance, which had never had a hold on the urban masses, continued to decline sharply. Nonetheless the state showed no willingness to relinquish its hold over the Church of England, vetoing in Parliament attempts in 1928 to revise the *Book of Common Prayer*, unchanged since 1662.

Sexual equality for women continued to make further strides but the ingrained attitudes of centuries were not easily shed. Acts in 1919 and 1923 gave women rights equal to those of men in cases of divorce. Women gained the vote fully in 1928, but the reality of their new status was slow to gain ground. Few made any headway in the professions and women's pay remained inferior to that of men.

The advent of the British Broadcasting Corporation, the BBC, in 1926 probably did more to create a new national sense of common identity then anything else. The first Director General, the future Lord Reith, was a dour Scot but he had all the abilities needed to understand this new invention and take it into the lives of everyone. He was a cultural dictator who believed in the rule of taste and rectitude, but that did not mean he lacked imagination. The potential of the new medium for education and entertainment was enormous. Music alone was suddenly accessible to all. Even more importantly broadcasting opened the doors of people's minds as never before.

In spite of unemployment and poverty leading to mass marches and demonstrations, there was no increase in crime. Events like the famous hunger march from Jarrow in 1936 were orderly, civilised, non-violent affairs. Throughout Western Europe liberal democracies had been threatened by the slump. In the case of Germany, democracy was swept away. But extremes never took hold in Britain. On the far left were the Communist Party and the Unemployed Worker's Union. On the far right there was, from 1932, the British Union of Fascists. The following for such movements was small, and they were treated humanely. The Public Order Act of 1936, however, prohibited the wearing of uniforms for political purposes (the British Fascists had donned black shirts), and put a limit to paramilitary forces. Chief Constables were also given the power to ban processions likely to lead to public disorder.

These were the two decades when government failed to face up to the bitter truth of the terminal decline of some of the country's major industries. Instead they fudged and fumbled, instituting welfare payments to salve the situation. The initial 1911 Insurance Act was hugely developed and extended. By 1931 unemployment was costing £125 million. In 1934 the Unemployment Act brought the administration of relief under government aegis by means of Public Assistance Committees. The

Thomas Campbell Dugdale captures the sometimes cruel social division of the 1930s. A decadent couple lean out of a window of the luxurious Ritz Hotel to watch the arrival of out-of-work miners from Jarrow in 1936.

introduction of a means test, however, was bitterly resented. Nonetheless, by 1939 Britain had one of the most advanced unemployment welfare systems in the world.

The Conservatives had held office for eighteen of those twenty-one years. They did so because the Liberals were split and also because Labour was viewed by the electorate with suspicion as to their true intent. But this was Conservatism of a very different kind from that at the opening of the century; in fact it was semi-socialist, certainly moderate and progressive, with men like Neville Chamberlain dedicated to improving the lot of everyone. That is not to deny that poverty existed, for it certainly did, but the definition of the poverty level had gone up considerably from what it had been in 1900. Society increasingly believed that the state had a role to play in running the economy. When war broke out again, government could at least work from the basis of a secure and unchallenged parliamentary democracy.

Chapter Sixty-Six

ALONE

OSTENSIBLY Britain had emerged from the First World War triumphant. Her navy remained the greatest in the world, enhanced by Germany's decision to scuttle hers rather than surrender it. The Empire was larger than ever, with new British protectorates in the Middle East such as Iraq and Palestine. Britain could return to her proud isolation as the island mother country of an Empire and Commonwealth that circled the globe. As far as the mainland of Europe was concerned the League of Nations could get on with sorting out the problems of what was now a redrawn map containing several new nation states such as Czechoslovakia, Hungary and Poland. The Foreign Office concluded that there would be no war in Europe for at least a decade as its two major powers, France and Germany, had both suffered such devastation.

In one sense this was right. There was no war. In another, the government was incredibly short-sighted, refusing to recognise that it dwelt in a world of illusions. The financial centre of the world's gravity was no longer London but New York and it was henceforth to be the dollar and not the pound which called the tune. Soon even the American navy was to eclipse the British. In the Far East Japan was rapidly emerging not only as a major economic, but also as a military, power. That held implications for the Empire, many of whose countries, such as Canada, Australia and South Africa, were demanding more and more independence. In effect the Empire was beginning to break up. Although 1918 brought an extension of British influence, that influence had to be maintained with men and money, and people began to question the wisdom of such expense during a period of crippling recession.

Britain stood back from Europe. Relations with France swiftly deteriorated and, as in 1914, Britain seemed oblivious as to Germany's true situation. Germany may have lost the war but her economy eventually emerged from it as the strongest in Europe. And German markets had always been important for exports, which certainly coloured British attitudes. Within the British political establishment there was a current in favour of a more lenient treatment of the defeated enemy, a belief that what was extracted as compensation at Versailles had gone just too far.

With war regarded as distant, all sides of the political spectrum supported disarmament. Every political party was committed to it, above all the Labour Party, and so was a public which could not countenance any repetition of the toll of the war years. So the British army was reduced to a series of small units to act as a colonial police force, and the navy was also run down. The military machinery essential for modern armoured warfare was abandoned completely. In the case of the air force, planes were just not replaced.

All through the inter-war years the Foreign Office was far more preoccupied with the danger of two very distant powers who were both seen as potential major threats to British interests. Russia was a communist state whose avowed mission was to export revolution across the world. At home she evoked fear of subversion and abroad concern, for she was uncomfortably close. Japan was also seen as a threat to the Empire after 1921 and her expansionist ambitions were revealed when the Japanese invaded Manchuria in 1931. In this light, it is hardly surprising that Germany's rehabilitation was so swift. By 1926 she had joined the League of Nations. Such a policy might have had much to commend it if the dramatic recession of 1929 to 1931 had not fuelled an extreme nationalism within Germany, which brought Adolf Hitler and the Nazis to power in January 1933.

With hindsight Hitler's unbalance is all too apparent, but no one at the time recognised his rise as the advent of another Napoleon bent on dominating the Continent. Neville Chamberlain was one of those who believed that Germany had been ill-treated in 1918, and looked to pacify her. That process has been called 'appeasement', condemned in retrospect as weakly giving in, but in fact it can also be seen as an honest attempt to reach a settlement which would avert another catastrophe. Even with this attitude it is significant that in precisely the same year in which Hitler set about re-arming Germany, Chamberlain began covertly to step up British rearmament. Covertly because public opinion would have been against it and so politically was the Labour Party.

That attitude by the British public was not to shift until the close of 1938 by which time war was seen to be almost inevitable. The change was brought about by a series of events which cumulatively affected people's perception, beginning in March 1936 when Hitler sent German troops into the Rhineland and occupied it, an action which violated both the Versailles and Locarno Treaties. It went unchallenged. Belgium declared herself neutral which meant that the French had to extend their line of defence northwards. Both these moves were enough to trigger a rapid expansion of British air defences. Any future war was seen to depend on air and sea forces, leaving the French to cope with those on land.

The effect of such moves was to make the British government nervous. In Italy a Fascist dictator, Mussolini, was in power and attempts were made to court him away from any alliance with Hitler. Not that there was an indication as yet that Hitler intended to invade Britain. But it was known in 1937 that should he have decided to do so, the country had not the means whereby to resist him. Time was needed in order to build up the island's defences, above all its air force. With this in mind it was indicated in November that Britain had no objection to Germany settling her territorial disputes on her eastern frontier. One of these seemed reasonable, for in the post-war settlement after 1918, 3.2 million people of German origin in the Sudetenland area of Bohemia had been made part of Czechoslovakia.

In March 1938 Hitler marched in triumph into Vienna and Austria became part of a fast-emerging new German Empire. Chamberlain realised that still more time was needed for Britain to build up her strength. He still hoped that some kind of accommodation might yet be reached. Unfortunately Hitler was a stranger to reason. What on the British side was

Neville Chamberlain's return from his meeting with Hitler in Munich in 1938 with his message of 'Peace in our time' formed television's first outside broadcast.

diplomacy was read on the German as weakness. In September Chamberlain flew to meet Hitler, agreeing German annexation of the Sudetenland. He persuaded both the French and his own Cabinet to go along with it. Chamberlain then flew immediately to meet Hitler a second time in Munich, conveying this message but with the proviso that Czechoslovakia itself should not be touched. When he returned proclaiming 'Peace in our time', he was accorded a hero's welcome.

This was to prove a turning point for everything from now onwards went into a spectacular reverse. By the opening of 1939 it was clear that Britain was faced with war. The government decided to re-arm whatever the consequences. From the point of view of an imminent confrontation the monoplanes, which were superior to anything in the German Luftwaffe, were ready. All of this action was coloured by the fact that Hitler's intent to invade Belgium and the Netherlands became known. The control of that area of the mainland had always been crucial to Britain. From it in 1588 sailed Parma's soldiers of invasion; in the following century it had been the field upon which Marlborough's victories over Louis XIV were fought. Once again the security of the island was seen to be at stake.

On 15 March Hitler broke the Munich agreement and marched into Prague, taking Czechoslovakia. Every signal sent to Hitler was ignored. He turned his attention next to Poland. On 21 March Chamberlain declared Britain's support for Poland, a futile gesture at that distance. Russia remained unaligned but fear of Bolshevism made Britain's approach tardy, so much so that by the time an approach was made, Russia had agreed a pact with Germany to divide Poland. On 1 September 1939 that country was invaded by Germany, and two days later Britain declared war. Historians have been divided ever since these events, seeing them either as a shameful indictment of a craven policy of giving in to brutal force, or as an attempt bravely to reach a solution and avert a global catastrophe. It can also be claimed that if Chamberlain had failed to buy time Britain would have been annihilated.

Things were not as they were in 1914. The country's huge commitments to maintaining the Empire and Commonwealth had been viewed as precluding Britain from taking part in any European war. Such a conflict would have to be paid for, and it could lead to bankruptcy. There was as yet no indication that aid would be forthcoming from the United States which had gone into isolation. The resources of the Empire could, however, still be counted upon. The viceroy of India had the right to commit the country to war, which he did. Canada and Australia, both still deeply tied to the mother country, offered their support, as did South Africa, where General Smuts overthrew the Prime Minister who opposed the move. Even with this support, Britain was pathetically weak in 1939. The Expeditionary Force which crossed to

The cartoonist David Low's comment on Neville Chamberlain in 1939. The Nazi tiger has devoured him, tossing his moustache and top hat to one side, and is about to munch the umbrella of 'Appeasement'.

France was put together in a hurry. The navy's ships were old and its aircraft carriers inferior. The Royal Air Force offered the country's only possible salvation. Nothing could obscure the bitter truth that Britain was about to embark on a war which could not be afforded.

For ten months, labelled the 'phoney war', nothing much seemed to happen. Britain had no alternative but to stand by while Russia and Germany carved up Eastern Europe without much opposition. Germany took Poland while Russia took over Finland, Latvia, Estonia and Lithuania. Then in April 1940 Germany invaded Denmark, moving on after to Norway. The navy was sent and there was a confused sea battle which for the British was a disaster. Chamberlain was forced to resign. (He died two years later.)

On 10 May 1940 Winston Churchill, a formidable and maverick politician, who knew more about the war than any other minister, became Prime Minister. This was to be one of those rare moments when events and the man were to be perfectly matched. Indeed Churchill, then aged sixty-four, saw himself as destined for the part. Here was not only dogged determination and genial ebullience but a mind imbued with a deep sense of the country's history and a tongue blessed with rare rhetorical powers, passionate and powerful enough to hold a people together. A Coalition Government was formed with a War Cabinet. The Labour Leader, Clement Attlee, became Deputy Prime Minister. Among those who held office the Labour politician Ernest Bevin, as Minister for Labour, was to prove crucial in ensuring the support of the unions.

On that day, 10 May, the German armies swept into Belgium and the Low Countries. The French army and the British Expeditionary Force moved northwards to Belgium to meet them but the Germans made a lightning thrust through the Ardennes and as a result the French and British forces found themselves cut off. The decision was taken to evacuate. This was a terrible and humiliating defeat. The navy, aided by a flotilla of any kind of sea-worthy vessel, rescued some 224,00 British and

95,000 French troops from Dunkirk. On 14 June Paris surrendered and a week later France fell.

Britain stood alone. Never before in the history of the island had there been a crisis quite like this one. Hitler, like Napoleon before him, had taken most of Western Europe with an army which had proved unstoppable. The barges began to assemble at Boulogne to carry the German troops across the Channel to invade England. But they could only sail if the victory of the skies was won. All that Britain had was her navy, her Spitfire planes, and the rhetoric of Churchill to inspire her people. In a speech which ranks alongside that of Gloriana at Tilbury, Churchill exhorted the island people with these words:

'Let us therefore brace ourselves to our duties, and so bear ourselves that, if the British Empire and its Commonwealth last for a thousand years, men will still say: "This was their finest hour."'

The battle of the skies, the Battle of Britain, began and was to rage on through the summer and early autumn of 1940. The Luftwaffe had met its match in the RAF, which was aided both by radar, which warned of the enemy's approach, and ultrasound, which enabled German signals to be read and thus their strategy to be known. The enemy, however, was to make a fatal mistake. It turned from bombing airfields to bombing London in the hope of shattering public morale and producing panic. That decision gave the RAF space to recoup and on 15 September it repulsed a huge raid in which sixty German planes were shot down. Two days later Hitler postponed the invasion of Britain and then in January it was delayed indefinitely. The Battle of Britain had been won and morale soared. Churchill was to sum up the achievement, saying 'Never in the field of human conflict was so much owed by so many to so few.'

The island had been saved but that battle only proved to be the prelude to a mighty conflict which was to spread around the globe. The Luftwaffe turned its attention next to Britain's ports and industrial centres and from November to May some 36,000 tons of bombs were dropped on them. In the latter month, however, Hitler turned his attention eastwards to the state he hated most, Russia, and invaded it. The British, always fearful of the Soviet Union, now entered into an alliance. Across the Atlantic the American people had been both shocked and moved by the heroism of the British, stirring them out of their isolation. President Roosevelt offered unlimited credit, Lend-Lease. That meant that the war could be paid for but it also meant an ever-growing mountain of debt which would have to be dealt with at a later date.

The skies may have been won but Britain could only survive if the Atlantic sea

routes were kept open, ensuring the supply of food and raw materials for her people and her factories. More than once starvation was closer than the population ever realised as German U-boat submarines took their toll. A third of British merchant shipping was sunk and 30,000 lives were lost at sea. This was a grinding, seem-

The sculptor Henry Moore sketching in the London Underground during the Blitz of 1940. Night after night Londoners sought refuge below ground from the unrelenting bombing of their city by the Germans.

ingly unending battle, which went on for three years until, by 1943, the U-boat losses suffered by the Germans became so great that victory came to the allies.

It was a complicated war because the defeat of her land forces meant that Britain could only attack her inland foe by air. The attacks began in 1941 but it was not until the following year that there were enough planes to launch what was a mass terror bombing of Germany, flattening whole areas of Cologne, Hamburg and Berlin. It took a huge toll on the RAF, as hundreds of planes were shot down. It was not until the Americans produced a new long-range escort fighter in 1944 that the raids really became devastating. But their effect on the German people was the same as such raids had on the British, it only served to strengthen morale.

War in the Atlantic, war over German skies, and then came war in the Mediterranean and North Africa. Italy under Mussolini entered the conflict on the side of Germany, a decision which gave Britain some early victories. In November 1940 half of the Italian fleet was destroyed at Taranto. The Italians then advanced into British-administered Egypt only to be faced by a counter-attack which virtually took over North Africa. Meanwhile the Germans invaded the Balkans. A British force was sent to Greece, but in April 1941 was forced to evacuate. Worse was to follow in Africa, where Hitler sent Rommel and the crack Afrika Corps. The British were driven back and forced to surrender at Tobruk.

The war continued to escalate throughout 1941. In June the Germans invaded Russia reaching the outskirts of Moscow in December. The bitter winter did to the German troops what it had done to Napoleon's. They were forced for the first time to retreat. In the same month of December the Japanese bombed the American fleet in Pearl Harbor, and the United States entered the war. The Japanese armies then proceeded to sweep through the Far Eastern parts of the British Empire. On Christmas Day Hong Kong surrendered. Two months later one of the Empire's lynchpins, Singapore, fell. Malaya was lost and the Japanese pushed on through Burma to the Indian frontier.

At last in 1942 the tide began to turn in favour of the allies. The Germans were locked from July to November in the battle for Stalingrad, where they lost a quarter-of-a-million men. In Africa the British Eighth Army, under generals Montgomery and Alexander, defeated Rommel and his troops at El Alamein. By the summer of 1943 the Germans had abandoned North Africa and the allies turned their attention to Italy, landing in Sicily in July and taking Naples in October. Mussolini fell from power, and the new Italian government sought an armistice only to find themselves occupied by the Germans. A long-drawn-out war of attrition was then fought over the mountain ranges which divided the peninsula.

Much pressure had be exerted on the allies to invade Europe in 1943 but it was too early. During the year which followed Britain acted as an aircraft carrier for a massive build-up of land forces. Operation Overlord as it was called proved to be an organisational triumph as, in a period of two days in June 1944, 185,000 men and 19,000 vehicles were landed on the beaches of Normandy. A reflection of Britain's future status in the world was the fact that the commander-in-chief was an American, Eisenhower. The British engaged the German troops in a long battle around Caen while, at the end of July, the Americans broke out of Avranches and in one vast sweep trapped most of the German army. On 21 August the remnant surrendered. Three days later, Paris was liberated.

The Americans pressed on through Alsace while the British liberated Belgium but a failure to open the port of Antwerp for supplies enabled the German army to regroup. On 16 September the allies made a small bridgehead over the Rhine at Arnhem which proved to be a disaster and they were obliterated. The German counter-attack swept into the Ardennes but then petered out. By then Germany was grinding to a halt due to the lack of raw materials such as oil and aviation spirit with which to continue the war. Weariness was setting in, as indeed it was in Britain, where the population found itself exposed to waves of a new terror, V1 and V2 weapons, falling from the skies. But the end was in sight. From the east the vast Soviet armies were advancing, swallowing up Eastern Europe on their way. Montgomery wanted the allies to make a dash for Berlin but Eisenhower opted for a uniform advance. On 4 May 1945 German forces surrendered to Montgomery. From the east the Russians had reached Berlin the previous month. Hitler and his cronies had committed suicide in a bunker. The war in Europe officially ended on 8 May.

But the war in the Far East still went on. Success there came as a result of a decision which had been made by Roosevelt and Churchill in the summer of 1942, to pour resources into making the first atomic bomb. The cost was gargantuan. Although the British regained Burma, defeat for the Japanese only followed the dropping of the atomic bomb on Hiroshima on 6 August. On 14 August the war in the East was also at an end.

This had been a war unlike any other. Although far fewer people had been killed than during the First World War, the effects of the war on the British were cataclysmic. For the first time, war had affected every single person on the island. The psychological, physical, emotional and mental impact cannot be over-estimated. For six years Britain was to all intents and purposes a totalitarian state, albeit preserving the veneer of democracy. The Emergency Powers Act of May 1940 had given the government unlimited authority over both people and property. The British people

Winston Churchill inspecting bomb damage resulting from the blitz. Air raids brought the devastation of war to ordinary people as never before.

were taken over, and regimented as never before. Children were evacuated to the country away from the bombing, identity cards were mandatory for everyone, labour was directed, work was classified into essential and non-essential. Food rationing was introduced, something which was to last until 1954. Clothes were also rationed. Luxuries had a 100% tax imposed upon them. Everyone of fighting age was conscripted into the forces, and those left behind either joined Air Raid Precautions or the Home Guard. The ARP watched the night skies and saw that every house was blacked out, that windows were taped and underground shelters maintained. The Home Guard was a body of 1.5 million volunteers who relieved the military of routine tasks and trained to meet an invasion.

Women were central to the war effort. They served in the forces in the Women's Royal Naval Service, the Women's Royal Air Force and the Auxiliary Territorial Service. They also ran the Women's Voluntary Service, coping with every kind of task that the war threw up on the home front. And, even more, they were the work force, keeping the munitions factories at the peak of production. It was to take a heavy toll, for women were not only workers but wives and mothers as well.

The comforts were few, the hardships many. Double, even triple, shifts were put in. When the miners went on strike it was through exhaustion, and Bevin met it by conscripting young men to the mines. The country was taxed as never before, in the case of unearned income at the rate of 94% in the pound. Even so people gave what they could in war bond contributions. The war demanded from everyone unremitting hard work and discipline. And it levelled out society. Servants virtually vanished.

Everyone ate the same food and wore the same utility clothes. Classes, hitherto segregated, were thrown together in the countryside or Home Guard. Everyone knew that they either had to stand or fall together. In retrospect, the war was to be looked back upon with a certain nostalgia as being almost enjoyable. All classes shared a unity of spirit and purpose which still casts a radiance decades later.

Victory, but of what kind? The Second World War was to prove to be a far greater turning point in the nation's fortunes than its predecessor. The international settlement was being worked out while the war was in progress in a series of meetings between the allied leaders. Stalin, Roosevelt and Churchill. Already in such meetings Britain was relegated to third place, for power had now passed to Russia and the United States. In February 1945 an agreement was made at Yalta, which was the one put into effect at the war's end. Russia swallowed the whole of Eastern Europe including Poland, imposing on those countries what was a brutal dictatorship. Germany was divided into three major zones of occupation: the British, the Russian and the American. Berlin, in the Russian zone was likewise divided.

In the West democracy had survived, but Britain was reduced to being a client state of America. It has been argued recently that the United States was well aware that it was asset stripping Britain, but without aid from the United States, both during and after the war, the British people would have endured untold hardship. Britain's subsequent collapse from a major power to an offshore island was to be a rapid one. The war had in fact reinforced insularity in the minds of the British people making them, as in 1918, wish to turn their backs on the European mainland. During the war London had been the capital of free Europe, with every political and military leader at some stage established there. Britain could have played the leading role in creating a new Europe after 1945. A great opportunity was missed.

Nonetheless, but for Britain, Europe would have become one vast German Empire. She had stood alone, going to war in defence of international law and honour. Along with the defeat of the Spanish Armada and of Napoleon this has become one of the great icons of the island's history. But it has now begun to be questioned, as documents have revealed that negotiating a peace with the Germans after the Battle of Britain was seriously considered. Only in the aftermath of the war, however, did the full horror of the Nazi régime come to light, above all the appalling concentration camps and the liquidation of some six million Jews. That knowledge was to endow the struggle in retrospect with a moral dimension of good triumphing over evil. No wonder that the British people believed that the age of Utopia was about to dawn for them.

Chapter Sixty-Seven

UTOPIA
COMES AND GOES

THE world had changed in 1945 far more than people realised. The middle classes naturally thought, as they had in 1918, that the end of the war would signal a return to the time before the war, to an age of servants and people accepting their place in a graduated social order. For the majority of the population there was no question of returning to such an ethos. Instead there was a determination to secure what had so far been denied them: full employment, adequate wages and increased social provision. The tide moreover was flowing that way, for the population had been led to believe throughout the war that peacetime would usher in a new and more just age. Political equality had been granted but social and economic equality had yet to come. The British people had in fact already experienced such equality during the war, under the aegis of the state, so that it was hardly surprising that no one questioned the state's ability to achieve it in more permanent form once the war was over. Government had solved problems during the war, so it could now continue to solve them in peacetime, with housing, health and employment at the top of everyone's agenda.

Already by 1945 the ground had been laid for that massive swing to the left which would bring the Labour party into power. Labour was viewed as the party which would carry through what people had been promised in Sir William Beveridge's 1942 Report, which was the blueprint for what we know as the Welfare State. Beveridge had been asked to produce a post-war plan for social welfare.

Labour poster for the General Election of 1945. The V for Victory hovers over suburbanised England.

Its foundation stone was to be the weekly insurance stamp which was to provide against unemployment, sickness and other contingencies. The Report included proposals for a national health service by placing everyone, again by way of the stamp, into an insurance scheme which would provide medical treatment free of charge. There were other far-reaching measures, such as family allowances and benefits on birth, death and marriage. The Beveridge Report, which came out in the depths of the war, was that rare thing, a government document which was a bestseller, fuelling a universal expectation that things would be different when the war came to an end.

A foretaste of just how different came in 1944 with the passing of the Education Act. Although not implemented until 1946, it raised the school leaving age to fifteen, with the Minister of Education having the discretion to raise it another year. Henceforward the state was bound to provide free education for everyone, education of a kind which was divided into three categories: primary, secondary and further. Everyone had the first and then, just after the age of eleven, there was a competitive examination. Those who passed it went on to the grammar schools for an academic training. Those who did not went to secondary modern schools, where the stress was on manual skills. The old fee-paying public schools and those which were called 'direct-grant' from government were left untouched. This Act was of fundamental importance for the future structure of British society, which was to be transformed within a generation into a meritocracy dependent on talent. What it also signalled was that education would become a perennial fixation with governments of whatever political persuasion. In a democratic age education formed the minds of potential voters, and ensured which party remained in power. Education was thus regarded as fair game for economic, political and social engineering, motivated by the unproven belief that education was the panacea for all ills.

All of this prepared the ground for May 1945, when the Labour Party rejected the offer of going to the country to prolong a national government in favour of an open election. On 5 July Labour swept to power, leaving the war leader, Churchill, devastated at the people's ingratitude. The feeling of a new start was emphasised by the fact that out of the four hundred Labour MPs over two hundred were first-timers. The Labour war-time ministers, Arthur Greenwood, Hugh Dalton, Ernest Bevin and Stafford Cripps, headed by Clement Attlee as Prime Minister, took over the government. Attlee, ostensibly a dull, taciturn little man, had an unrivalled knowledge of the workings of government. In addition he possessed the elusive quality of being able to hold together a party which attracted people of widely differing viewpoints, ranging from militant unionists to middle class intellectuals. For once the party was not only united on its objectives but also on the means to achieve them.

At the top of the list came full employment. In 1944 a White Paper had committed government to maintaining a high level of employment which in the wake of the Beveridge Report was seen to be the state's major policy priority. By 1948 there were a million less unemployed than there had been in 1938. That million was accounted for by 400,000 in the services and 600,000 in the civil service, for Labour's measures for social provision inevitably meant an escalation of bureaucracy. Full employment was to remain an article of belief for all governments until it began to be questioned in the middle of the 1970s. By then its negative aspects had come glaringly to light for it meant turning a blind eye to over-manning and permitting restrictive practices to multiply, both of which had serious effects on industry.

In the forefront of Labour's programme came the implementation of that central article of socialist faith, Clause 4, through nationalisation. This began in 1946 with the Bank of England and civil aviation. Neither presented a problem. Most capitalist countries had a state bank and no one then believed that civil aviation was viable without public subsidy. The following year came the railways and the mines, both of which had been state controlled during the war, nationalisation merely acknowledging a reality. The reality that was not acknowledged was that both industries were already ailing, even in the 1930s. Coal was well past its zenith not only because other countries had developed their own mines but also because it was shortly to be overtaken by oil as an energy source. The nationalisation got off to a very bad start. 1947, the winter that the new National Coal Board took over, was the worst winter for sixty years, but the mines were unable to deliver. Factories closed and homes were without light and heat. This was to set in motion in the mind of the public what was to become an ever-growing sense of grievance against state-run enterprises. The railways, too, were a mirage. They had enjoyed a renaissance during the war when petrol had been rationed, masking again a reality, that in the post-war era road transport would take over. So it was not long before the railways began to spiral downwards, becoming monuments to dirt and unreliability and a byword among the public for inefficiency.

Gas and electricity were nationalised in 1948, neither contentious, the same year that the National Health Service became operable. The National Health Act was passed in 1946, this time only with difficulty. The need for such social provision had been recognised for decades and indeed promised in the Beveridge Report. But the medical profession were aghast at the contents of the Minister of Health Aneurin Bevan's sweeping bill which took over all hospitals including voluntary ones, put general practitioners onto basic salaries, and introduced controls over the sale of practices. All hospital and specialist service, all care and treatment by local doctors and dentists, was to be free. The British Medical Association resisted and in order to gain their co-operation Bevan was forced to concede the right of members of the profession to practise privately. If one single institution may be said to epitomise the Welfare State, the National Health Service was it. It was hugely beneficial to everyone and utterly unique, regarded by many as perhaps the single most enlightened piece of legislation of the century.

The government pressed on with its programme through into 1949, nationalising iron and steel, which again were declining industries. It was inevitable that the results were to prove unsatisfactory. The system devised for running these new state enterprises was by way of public corporations answerable to government. Within four years of Labour rule 20% of the economy was taken out of private hands and placed in those of the state. To socialists, nationalisation was a moral imperative, a magic wand to be waved with, it was believed, limitless powers of transformation. Alas, too little thought had been given to the practical implications, and the magic of the miracle-working wand was found to lack potency.

This was, however, a great reforming government, comparable with that which followed the Reform Bill of 1832. Its legislation set upon the stage the scenery, or rather permanent set, against which successive governments were to act for the next thirty years. The nationalisation programme went hand-in-hand with other equally significant pieces of legislation. The National Insurance Act of 1946 ensured that the entire population paid compulsory contributions in return for cash benefits covering old age, sickness, unemployment, widowhood, and other circumstances of deprivation, and introduced benefits for birth, marriage and death as promised by Beveridge. In 1948 the Criminal Justice Act virtually abolished flogging and attempted, but failed, to abolish hanging. In the same Act an extension to the legal aid

HERE HE COMES, BOYS!

Harley Street doctors put up a trip wire as Aneurin Bevan, the architect of the National Health Service, approaches, in a cartoon by Vicky, *News Chronicle*, 7 August 1945.

system increased the divorce rate, a recognition of the shift from the centuries-old view that marriage was an institution only to be dissolved in exceptional circumstances. The Labour Party also further curtailed the power of the House of Lords, reducing their ability to delay a bill to a year. One more blow to privilege was to end all forms of plural voting, such as the second vote given to graduates, in favour of 'one man one vote'.

Not everything was so successful. Some two million homes had been devastated, gutted, or damaged in the war but the re-building programme failed to take off. In 1945 only three thousand new homes were built. The demand for houses inevitably accelerated the rape of the countryside, begun in the thirties, when already 60,000 acres of land a year were being swallowed up for building. After the war, that figure continued to go sharply upwards as the country found itself at the mercy of urban requirements as never before. The New Towns Act of 1946 created fourteen new towns between 1947 and 1950. These were formed by taking people out of the congested inner city areas of London and Glasgow and re-housing them. The government gave power to local authorities to designate development areas in the countryside and countered its spoliation by the creation of national parks, embracing Dartmoor, the Peak District, Snowdonia, the Lake District, and the North Yorkshire moors. Even what was called a 'green belt', a band of land which could not be built upon, was created to prevent London from becoming a solid built-up mass.

All of this change cost money, and that was where the problems quickly began to surface. Initially, it seemed that British industry after the war got off to a flying start, for its two main competitors, Japan and Germany, were suffering from the aftermath of war. For a few years British exports did well, but when its rivals returned to production in the fifties Britain's shortcomings began to emerge. Other countries were not only able to produce more, but the quality was far better. This was to present successive governments with a profound dilemma for an expensive social revolution had been carried through on borrowed money, on the assumption that any loans would quickly be repaid by a booming British economy, a boom which failed to materialise. In 1945 American Lend-Lease came to an end. Interest on the debts run up by Britain during the war ate up £73 million p.a. It was clear that the repayment of these debts – or sterling balances as they were called – would be a long-delayed process. To pay for the war foreign investments had to be sold off. It was reckoned that Britain needed to raise exports to 175% of their pre-war volume to cover the deficit that used to be covered by the income from those investments, known as invisible exports. To help the initial period of post-war recovery the United States lent Britain £1,100 million with the modest interest rate of 6%. But the loan had strings attached to it, the most important one being that within a year, owners of sterling outside Britain could convert their currency if they so wished. In July 1947 that convertability clause came into operation. Foreign gold and currency reserves began to be withdrawn from Britain at such a rate that a month later convertability was suspended. By then the loan had been spent, thanks largely to the substantial rise in the cost of raw materials which followed the end of the war. What saved the British situation was the decision of the United States to aid the recovery of Europe. Under the Marshall Plan Britain received £700 million with no obligation to repay it. Nonetheless the reality of the situation was that American dominance of world trade and the financial markets had pushed Britain down into the role of a second class power. The devaluation of the pound from $4.03 to $2.80 recognised this new scheme of things. Although viewed with horror by the public as a bitter blow to prestige, in fact the move had beneficial economic effects. By 1950 the clouds were gathering thick and fast in what had once seemed the cloudless sky of the new Socialist Utopia. Following the sterling convertability crisis Sir Stafford Cripps became Chancellor of the Exchequer, ushering in an era of austerity with tight price controls, a wages freeze, cuts in imports, as well as continuing shortages and rationing. The Welfare State had been set up on borrowed money and its costs were soaring. By 1951 the National Health Service cost £365 million a year to run. American debts needed repaying and it gradually became clearer that principles would have to be sacrificed in order to meet the bills. Controversy about principles surfaced with the proposed introduction of prescription charges in what had been started as a free health service. By 1950 the government was already running out of steam but the very idea of charges opened wide the gap in the ranks between the utopians and the realists in a way which was to prove fatal.

In 1950 there was an election and Labour was returned but with only a narrow majority of six, which meant that no contentious legislation could be passed. Prescription charges were, however, introduced and Aneurin Bevan and Harold Wilson, a future Labour Prime Minister, resigned. Financially things began to get worse. War broke out between North and South Korea, and Britain, via the United Nations, was committed to supporting the United States' policy towards that war. Fear of the intentions of Russia contributed to escalating defence costs which rose to 14% of national income. Wage restraint came to an end and the unions began to strike for more money. In October 1951 Attlee called another election. The Conservatives mounted their campaign, working from an acceptance of the Welfare State but going on to call for the nation to be set free, free from rationing, never ending queues, restrictions and controls, let alone the utter drabness of it all. The

Conservatives came to power with a majority of seventeen and the great socialist experiment was at an end.

Every change brings its losers as well as its winners. In this one the majority won but those who lost were left with a deep feeling of bitterness and hostility towards the emergence of what they saw as an omnipotent state. The middle classes felt betrayed, subjected as they were to taunts by Labour politicians like Sir Hartley Shawcross who told them, 'We are the masters now.' Those who wished to return to a 1930s lifestyle did so by emigrating to Africa where they could find the servants which had vanished in the new Britain. But most of the middle classes stayed put. They consisted in the main of the literate clerical class which had sprung into existence in order to keep the books engendered by the Industrial Revolution. With the advent of free education, more people were around who could now do these tasks, an inescapable change which meant loss of status for the old guard. The middle classes also felt acutely the rise of the skilled manual worker, men at a premium in the post-war era, who could demand the same or more money as those who used to be their literate superiors.

Not every aspect of the Welfare State was bad news for the middle classes, for their ability to understand and cope with the paperwork of bureaucracy meant that they were quick to turn the system to their own advantage. But even that was a waning asset in the face of the greatest blow of all, the Education Act. In the past the middle classes who could not afford to send their children to public schools had paid modest fees to gain them a kind of exclusivity in the grammar schools. The Act abolished fee-paying and introduced entry by examination. Grammar schools now took in the brightest children regardless of their social background, and middle class children suddenly found themselves rubbing shoulders with those of the working class. Children who failed to reach the grammar school were assigned to the secondary school, in the eyes of the middle classes a stigma of failure.

These were not the only rumblings of discontent, for the Welfare State ushered in the era of 'Whitehall knows best'. Government restrictions undoubtedly inhibited the entrepreneur. He was faced with restrictions on raw materials, and with refusals to grant building licences, besides being subjected to detailed investigation into any proposed initiative. In this way the state instead of being seen to move the economy forward was seen to be holding it back.

We are still living with the consequences of 1945-51. Inevitably historians are divided in their conclusions. One group sees it as an era of unparalleled enlightenment, a supreme legislative achievement lifting the whole of society. In this scenario it can also be seen as inevitable, a culmination of events already set in train before 1939. But even among those who sing its praises there are reservations. In their view its long term failure was because the Labour Party was not socialist enough and what was done was a kind of botched-up half-way house which could never be satisfactory, as indeed became very rapidly apparent. Others look back and see the creation of the Welfare State as ushering in a delusion built on debt, an expensive socialist experiment which only accelerated Britain's decline. The utopian dreams and visions its wand conjured up would fade as one by one everything vanished – the Empire and Commonwealth, the country's role as a world power, the genius which made Britain into an industrial giant. All would be as dust leaving a subliterate, unhealthy and institutionalised proletariat dependent on state hand-outs. But there was to be no turning back. Both the main political parties accepted the Welfare State as a point of departure for any government. Twenty-five years were to pass before anyone began to question its right to exist.

Aerial view of the Festival of Britain, 1951. Ostensibly to celebrate the centenary of the Great Exhibition of 1851, it offered people a vision of the Socialist Utopia to be, after years of war and austerity. The Dome of Discovery was the largest ever constructed but it was demolished along with the rest of the Festival by the incoming Tory government. The Royal Festival Hall alone remains today.

Chapter Sixty-Eight

CONSENSUS AND THE MISMANAGEMENT OF DECLINE

THE twenty-five years after 1950 are usually referred to as the era of consensus. However stormy the political, social, or economic waters, no one challenged the fundamental tenets upon which late twentieth century Britain stood. These stemmed from the Beveridge Report and from the economic theories of John Maynard Keynes. Indeed any attempt to alter the system, let alone suggest that some of it might be questionable, was viewed as being positively unpatriotic and got nowhere. What people failed to grasp was that there were actually some things government could not do. The state instead was seen as being capable of ushering in a golden age and politicians, who in a democracy depend on votes, naturally did nothing to disabuse the electorate of this idea. Irrespective of political party, for over twenty years there were certain shared assumptions and objectives which were to remain constant until they came under fire in the mid 1970s.

With memories of the twenties and thirties still vividly in people's minds full employment remained top of any political agenda. Throughout the fifties and sixties unemployment never exceeded more than 3% of the workforce, and to allow it to rise beyond that was considered dangerous to the country's social stability. To achieve this figure meant ignoring over-manning, restrictive practices and resistance to change. Ironically, no objections were raised to the growth of automation, as jobs were so plentiful. Such a policy, however, bore within itself the seeds of its own destruction. Full employment meant bidding for workers and so wages spiralled ever upwards, in the end reaching unaffordable heights, fuelling a deadly inflation and pricing British goods out of the world markets. For twenty years the policy just about worked through the state managing demand in the economy. Then, in the 1970s, full employment began to vanish. Attempts to achieve it again by the usual method of inducing growth failed, and produced exactly the opposite effect, more unemployment. No government, whether Labour or Conservative ever dared to admit that a policy of full employment should be abandoned; to do so would have meant confronting the unions.

The unions were, of course, deeply committed not only to full employment but also to nationalisation. As the revival of Britain depended on its economy and therefore its workforce, the co-operation of the unions was regarded as crucial to any government. By the mid-1950s a new generation of trade union leaders had emerged. They took full employment for granted, and now saw their role as one of pressing for better conditions and higher and higher wages, irrespective of the state of the economy. No government was prepared to outface them. When, in 1956, the Conservatives passed their Monopolies and Restrictive Practices Act, for example, the unions were excluded, meaning that a golden opportunity to sweep away restrictive practices was lost. If the Conservatives dared not cross the unions, Labour's ability to do so was even more constricted for the party was actually enmeshed in a system which depended on the unions for its funds via the political levy. Progressively the electorate became aware of this link, and saw how it impaired the ability of any Labour government to take independent action. Nonetheless the first moves towards union reform were taken by the Socialists in the 1960s, but they were forced to draw back. It was not until the 1970s, when strikes soared out of control that a Conservative government determined to make a stand, but they, too were defeated.

These were the decades when the state was omniscient. There was intervention into every aspect of society, including areas in which it had no knowledge at all, where interference in the end often made a problem worse. No

By the close of the 1970s union militancy had lost them the sympathy of the voters. Strikes such as that by the refuse collectors resulted in scenes like this one in February 1979, in which piles of uncollected garbage lay rotting in a street in Victoria, London.

one questioned the state's role as the problem solver, a role which was valid just as long as the state could come up with solutions. When that increasingly failed to happen, as it did in the 1970s, the result was collapse. Inevitably such an ever-expanding government demanded an equally ever-expanding bureaucracy to sustain it. Not that more civil servants necessarily meant greater efficiency, indeed often quite the reverse. This was to be the age of the mega-department. In 1956 there were twenty-six government departments. By 1972 there were just seventeen including three major creations reflective of the state's burgeoning interventionist role: the Department of Trade and Industry, the Department of Health and Social Security, and the Department of the Environment. Those who staffed these huge departments changed too as the old Civil Service generalist gave way, in the aftermath of a government report in 1968, to staff with more specialised skills, including those of management. Civil servants multiplied but so did those who feared the state's ever-growing powers. Its competence gradually began to be questioned but it was not until the 1970s that actual disillusion set in.

On the whole the Welfare State was welcomed as it brought huge advantages across a broad spectrum of society. The problem was that people thought its cornucopia to be a never-ending one. The Welfare State became more and more expensive to maintain, so too did the taxation whereby to sustain it. As income tax gradually began to impinge, thanks to inflation, onto the wage-packets of even the working classes, blind adherence to the tenets of the Welfare State began to be questioned.

In the final analysis everything depended on the success of the economy and both parties accepted that the economy henceforth should be a mixed one. Most industry remained in private hands, but government acted as a planning agent, influencing business decisions without imposing direct controls. No one questioned the state's ability to manage the economy successfully. The state after all, had run the economy during the war which had been won; it was but the shortest of steps to accepting that the state should therefore intervene in the running of the economy in peacetime, in order to achieve its social and economic ends. What was not fully appreciated was that the economy was in decline. Already by 1950 the long era of effortless superiority had gone. Textiles were in continuous decline. Steel might double its output between 1950 and 1966 but in the rest of the world output was quadrupled. Shipbuilding began to lose out to the Japanese and by 1975 even the British car industry went into insolvency. The running of industry was not helped by party politics, as successive governments nationalised and de-nationalised, deflated and reflated the economy. Neither was it aided by the small army of media economists who were forever analysing and pronouncing upon its performance, resulting in industrial paranoia. As the years passed the British economy became a subject of universal fascination both inside the country and abroad. Unfortunately those who examined its workings applied to it a medical term: 'the British disease'.

If preserving full employment, placating the unions and intervening in the economy were fixed points of reference for the government of the day, so too was education. Both main parties had a passionate belief that education was the key to curing any British economic malaise. Education multiplied, not only in quantity but also in the age to which people were educated. In the 1960s eight new universities were founded and the old ones were encouraged to expand. It was hoped that these new students would pursue the sciences, but instead they opted for the social sciences, above all sociology with its concern for curing the problems of society. In the case of the Labour Party education had another dimension, for through it they believed a new social equality could be achieved. Even the middle classes realised that the eleven plus examination was a means whereby only a quarter of the population received a good education, so they did not oppose the socialist introduction of the comprehensive system which progressively did away with the old grammar schools. Indeed some of the major drives to introduce comprehensive schools occurred under the Conservative governments. The aim was to undermine privilege, and the old teaching method of learning verities was replaced by that of 'discovery', with an abundant use of tape-recorders, television, and other technology. By the 1970s this educational revolution was seen not to be working, as literacy and numeracy declined. Parents then began to make huge financial sacrifices in order to send their children to one of the untouched fee-paying private schools. At the same time the belief that education could solve the country's economic woes was also seen more and more to be a delusion, and, like other aspects of a burgeoning Welfare State, the growth of education ate up more and more of tax payers' money.

These were some of the major issues which made up the agenda for any government, whether Labour or Conservative. The Labour Party had a new leader in Hugh Gaitskell, who in fact never came to power as Prime Minister. Under him, the party moved to the right, although he failed in an attempt to re-write Clause 4. The fact that he attempted it at all signalled increasing division between left and right, intensified after 1960 when the left of the Labour Party became committed to unilateral nuclear disarmament. Not only was Labour beset by never-ending internal wrangles but it lacked any cohesive vision as to where to go next. Increasingly the militant left set the agenda, demanding a battery of social legislation dealing with issues such as racial discrimination and equal opportunities, in a manner which often had little if any support from the party's grassroots. By then the working class vote was being eroded by affluence.

If Labour occupied the consensus ground by conviction the Conservative Party stood there with reluctance, acknowledging that the times had changed. They accepted that people expected as of right jobs, housing, health provision, better education, and more equality and justice. They were, however, a party which had always been remarkably successful at swimming with the tide and quickly emerged during the fifties as the natural party of government, winning three consecutive general elections. This was what was called One Nation Conservatism whose aim was not equality but rather that all men should have an equal chance to be unequal. It stood for freedom in a less state-dominated economic system and still clung to the old pillars of crown, church and Christian morality.

The two major parties dominated the political scene leaving the Liberals and the Welsh and Scottish Nationalist parties to surface only in elections, when the public became dissatisfied with the main parties. This was a democratic system whose weaknesses were inbuilt. As both major parties wanted power, intervention in the economy became geared around election dates. Neither side had any taste for telling the electorate what was often the bitter truth for fear of affecting their ratings at the polls, an arrangement which worked smoothly as long as the economy was more or less healthy. Problems only surfaced when circumstances demanded that the unions be curbed. Confrontation surfaced over wage demands, which had followed a set pattern established during the fifties. Wages rose annually as of right. What is so extraordinary in retrospect is that these annual settlements carried with them no obligation at all by the workforce to greater productivity or efficiency in return. This meant that by 1961 wages were rising 50% faster than industrial output. Nothing was done to confront this problem, or to face the fact that the cost of the Welfare State continued to spiral upward so that by the middle of the 1970s public expenditure ate up more than 50% of the entire national income. It was an age of cosmetic solutions, whose only outcome could be disaster.

Few periods in British history have been more complex, although a division into three, covering the decades, seems accurately to reflect its phases. The fifties passed smoothly with the economy apparently on the upturn, and the government avoiding any action on what were clearly to be in the future major problems, transport and immigration. The sixties began to press alarm bells as the country was forced to turn to the International Monetary Fund to be baled out of financial difficulties and unemployment reached over three-quarters of a million. It was during these years that Britain's declining industrial heritage came home to roost with a vengeance. The seventies saw the breakdown of consensus amidst a sea of acrimony and recrimination as both political parties struggled to reach a working relationship with union power, which ended in catastrophe.

The fifties, however, seemed to be an optimistic sunny decade. Winston Churchill, although in poor health, came back as Prime Minister and apart from denationalising steel and road transport left the work of his predecessors intact. There was no attempt to cross the unions. Indeed government policy was not far different from that which would have been pursued by Labour with an emphasis on a house-building programme which was hugely successful. In 1952 George VI died and his daughter came to the throne as Elizabeth II. Her accession was hailed as the

Churchill visits his old school, Harrow, in 1954 to join in the annual school sing-song.

beginning of a new Elizabethan age. The last of the war-time rationing ended in 1954 and building restrictions ended soon after, leading to a boom. The pattern of annual wage rises was set, with prices always lagging slightly behind. That should have been a warning as should also have been the return of Germany and Japan to production. By 1955 these two countries were manufacturing goods of such high quality that they quickly showed up their British equivalents as shoddy. Germany and Japan had the advantage of new post-war machinery and in the case of Japan, to which can be added India, that of cheap labour. For the first time for two centuries Britain began to import textiles. Nothing was done to stem that tide, nor the tide of Commonwealth immigrants which in the late fifties reached 26,000 a year.

In April 1955, in his eighties and ill, Churchill resigned and was succeeded by the urbane and charming Anthony Eden. There was another election and the Conservatives were returned. Eden's premiership was to be entirely dominated by the crisis over the Suez Canal which contributed to his breakdown in health and his resignation in 1957. Harold Macmillan became the new Prime Minister, 'Supermac', as he came to be called. Macmillan was a man of keen intelligence, a patrician and very much the opposite of the Labour leader, Hugh Gaitskell. As under Churchill there was no question of crossing the unions, and this was precisely the period during which the militant extreme left seized power on the workshop floor. Unofficial strikes began to multiply. Macmillan can be said to have inaugurated the era of spend, spend, spend. He overruled his Chancellor of the Exchequer and the estimates for government expenditure went £50 million in excess. He also relaxed credit. The result was a consumer boom during which most people bought cars, television sets, washing machines and refrigerators. In July 1957 he made a remark which has passed into history when he said that people had 'never had it so good'.

Such a policy had its inevitable consequences and in August 1961 the government, faced by rising deficits, turned to the International Monetary Fund, which had been created in 1944, its members contributing a quota upon which they could draw to redress temporary problems. The government was lent £714 million. This ushered in a decade in which, despite the fact that one cruel economic reality followed another, nothing seemed to impinge upon the impulse of government to spend. There was the cost of keeping troops around the globe in Germany, Kenya, Borneo and in the Persian Gulf, all seen as potential British markets, a point of view which also conditioned commitment to overseas aid to developing countries. Conscription to the armed

The coronation of Queen Elizabeth II in 1953 was the apogee of the monarchy's use of antiquarian pageantry to lighten a grey democratic age. The photographer, Cecil Beaton, responded exactly to this mood of nostalgia for an age which had gone in this image of the young queen in her coronation robes.

forces ended which meant that the army had to be paid properly for the first time since the war. Defence costs continued to rise, so much so that in the end it was thought cheaper to abandon a British nuclear deterrent in favour of buying an American one. As roads replaced rail the cost of building new motorways rocketed. The state found itself left with propping up an uneconomic Victorian railway system, a third of which it proposed to axe in 1963 in order to make it viable. Instead of carrying that policy through the government drew back, fearing the social consequences if they left places cut off, thus causing population movement which would engender yet more demands on state funding. With unemployment rising again, and immigration now running at 100,000 a year, government had no alternative but to act in an attempt to curb both. The 1962 Commonwealth Immigration Act imposed restrictions but it was already too late. The ghettos and social tensions were already there, not to mention the demands on the social services. Britain began to be billed as 'the sick man of Europe'.

The reaction to any problem during this period was to set up yet another government quango, in this instance a National Economic Council which was to consult with industry and produce a financial plan. The result of that investigation was the conclusion that a 4% annual growth in the economy was needed to sustain the country. A National Incomes Commission was set up, but the unions refused to co-operate. In the end it was not the state of the economy but scandal which brought the government down. That took the form of a minister lying to the Commons about his affair with a call girl who was also involved with a Russian diplomat, thus creating a security risk. Amidst a haze of sleaze Macmillan, by then ill, left a government in disarray. The Conservative Party, after consultation, chose the Scottish peer, the Earl of Home, as its leader. Home had to renounce his title in order to take on the role but he could not save his party from electoral defeat in 1964.

By then Hugh Gaitskell had died and the Labour Prime Minister was Harold Wilson. Wilson had much in common with his predecessor, Macmillan. Both continued to overestimate Britain's role in the world, both were to undergo the process of realising that change, and both in the end were unable to come to terms with it. Although not by any means patrician, Wilson was also a politician of considerable tactical skill. What started in his favour was the note of modernity which he set out to strike. That was not to last long and was dispelled when the state of the economy came fully to light. There was an £800 million trade deficit, allied to the fact that the advent of a Labour

Coventry Cathedral was bombed in November 1940. The new cathedral, designed by Sir Basil Spence, was completed in 1962, the first major public building since 1939. In the background, rising as a backcloth to the high altar, is the vast tapestry of Christ in Majesty designed by the painter, Graham Sutherland.

With the advent of television politicians had to take on the guise of actors and conquer the new art, one which could publicly make or break them. Harold Wilson, seen here giving an interview in 10 Downing Street in 1974, was a master of the common touch.

government always led people to move their money out of the country, fearful as to what Labour would do. Labour began by making dividends subject to income tax, and taxing all capital gains. Both moves were inimical to investment. Following in the wake of Macmillan another loan was negotiated, this time from the United States. The amount was £2 billion, and the government embarked on a spending spree. A whole rash of new ministries was set up ranging from one for the Arts to another for Land and Natural Resources. Prescription charges were abolished and old age pensions and other state benefits were increased.

Wilson's modernising thrust was to be expressed by a National Plan whose prime objective was to expand the national income. A Prices and Incomes Board was established to monitor tendencies to inflation and persuade both management and unions to accept its deliberations. In an effort to conciliate the unions the new Board made no real attempt to hold down wage settlements, which of course ran counter to its long term aim. Then the government dared to embark on union reform. In 1965 a Royal Commission on Industrial Relations called for all unions to be registered, and only those would henceforth have the right to strike. That, it was hoped, would eliminate unofficial strikes which now made up 95% of union action. When it came to the crunch the government retreated, and the Commission's work remained a dead letter.

Restricted by Labour's small majority in the House, Wilson had no choice but to choose a moment for another election which took place in March 1966. The Labour government returned with an enhanced majority. By then the Conservatives had acquired a new and equally unpatrician leader in Edward Heath. Once in power, the Wilson government gave up trying to face realities and went instead for easy and cheap options, social legislation which reflected the growing libertarianism of the period. These included lowering the age for the vote to eighteen, the establishment of the Open University, the Sexual Offences Act, which permitted homosexual acts between consenting adults over twenty-one, and the Abortion Act, which laid down the guidelines for abortion. At the same time half the grammar schools went over to the comprehensive system. The only piece of legislation which attempted to cope with a deepening social problem was the 1968 Race Relations Act. Two years before, immigration had reached 600,000 with little sign of any assimilation of those who came into the existing population.

Meanwhile the Prices and Incomes Board attempted to stem inflation. Dividend increases in 1966 were made illegal for a year, wage increases were also made illegal for six months and thereafter were to be granted only in special circumstances. Prices were held down. The following year a massive dock strike forced the devaluation of the pound to $2.40, leading to the severest tax increases since 1939. The public was enraged. For the devaluation to achieve anything it had also to be accompanied by deflation, which meant unemployment, or prices would rise. Deflation was embarked upon. Once more the Labour government tried to turn its attention to the unions as the result of the 1969 Donovan Report. A bill was introduced into the House to curb union power. The unions forced its withdrawal. Wilson, ever optimistic, and also sensing that the deflationary policy was working, decided to call an election but this time Labour lost.

The ten years following 1969 were to be even more catastrophic. Just about everything seemed to come home to roost. By 1975 consumer prices were two-and-a-half times what they had been twenty years earlier. Of the world's major industrial countries in the seventies, Britain alone had declining exports. There was a 25% deterioration in the country's terms of trade and the value of the pound fell 30%. Meanwhile wage increases spiralled ever upwards, reaching 29.4% in 1974. The deflationary policy set in motion by the Wilson government called for three to four years to take effect, as in the meantime industrial profits fell. To stay the course called for enormous political resolution. This was the decade which truly marked the end of the Industrial Revolution. It also witnessed the irony of a Conservative administration rescuing ailing companies by nationalising them. The only glimmer on the horizon was an unexpected stroke of luck, oil was discovered beneath the North Sea and began to come to the rescue as the seventies reached their close.

Already by the middle of the 1960s attitudes towards politicians had begun to change. Instead of being seen as benign agents ushering in Utopia they were blamed for failing to deliver. The new Prime Minister, Edward Heath, was a grammar school meritocrat who entered office with the determined intention of tackling the unions and a strong conviction that Britain should join the European Economic Community. In the latter endeavour he was successful. What his new government failed to grasp was that its predecessor's policy was beginning to have salutary effects. So instead of persevering with deflation, however painful, the Heath government reflated the economy, reducing taxes and relaxing credit control. Until then the Bank of England had laid down guidelines for credit, but these were now swept away with a mandate to lend money to whatever seemed to be a good risk. The result within three years was that the money supply had multiplied by 84%. This triggered a surge of speculative buying of shares and property so that in one year, 1971-72, the price of houses in London doubled. Unemployment naturally fell, but in 1972 the cost of that was prices increasing by 10% and wages by 18%. This coincided with massive increases in commodity prices in the international markets. As a result, firms began to fail and go bankrupt. Against all Conservative principles the government saved both Rolls Royce and the Upper Clyde Shipyard by nationalising them. In 1972 government expenditure crossed the 50% margin to become 52% of national income.

In 1971, in fulfilment of its pledge to face up to the unions, Parliament passed the Industrial Relations Act. Henceforth unions would have to register in order to have legal status. The government could impose strike ballots and delays of up to sixty days before strike action could be taken. Unions which broke the rules were to be subject to fines, and an Industrial Relations Court was set up to implement the Act. Few measures have evoked such embittered resistance. In 1970 10 million days had been lost through strikes; in 1971 that rose to over 13 million. The Trades Union Conference passed a resolution instructing its members not to register. Government now found that it was one thing to pass an Act, and quite another to enforce it. The battle lines were drawn.

In the autumn of 1972 a three-month pay freeze was introduced after which the maximum increase was to be a pound a week plus 4% of existing wages. That year 24 million days were lost in strikes. The most spectacular was the miners' strike for they went on to arbitration which found in their favour. This opened the floodgates. The railways worked to rule for three months. Then the dockers followed. The government bravely embarked on a statutory wages policy along with a ban on all strikes. This policy was to go in three stages and involved freezes on prices, rents and dividends. The third phase of that policy began in October 1973. The fact that strikes were banned was completely ignored. The gas workers and the Civil Services went on strike, the miners refused to work overtime, and the railways again worked to rule. The government was forced to introduce a three-day working week to save energy. There were swingeing cuts in public expenditure and the minimum lending rate soared to 13%. Britain was reduced to being a twilight zone. Then, on 5 February 1974, the miners voted once more to strike. Heath decided to call a general election, hoping for a mandate from the population to outface the unions but he failed to get it. The election revealed a deeply divided country and Labour under Harold Wilson was returned with a majority of three, despite the fact that the Conservatives got more votes. Disillusionment with both sides found expression in a surge of Liberal and Nationalist MPs.

The Heath government had ended in failure but at least it had faced up to the unions even though it lost the fight. In the midst of all this industrial unrest and turmoil it had carried through a massive reorganisation of local government, creating forty-five counties and six metropolitan areas. It had also introduced selective eligibility for welfare benefits. Heath's greatest achievement, however, was Britain's entry into the European Common Market. But his government remained a failure. The unions had brought it down. Also, contrary to Conservative principles, it had epitomised state intervention on a gargantuan scale. As it left office the full impact of an external circumstance beyond its control began to be dramatically felt. In 1973 the Organisation of Petroleum Exporting Countries (OPEC) began sharply to push up the price of oil in the aftermath of a war in the Middle East between the Arabs and the Israelis. The oil price not only quadrupled, but the Arab countries also imposed a restriction on supplies. The implications for every Western European country, all of which had gone over to oil as an energy source, was to be massive, both in economic and political terms. But this was to be Harold Wilson's inheritance.

In `1973 the balance of payments deficit had stood at £1½ billion. The increased oil and commodity prices would force that up to £4 billion. Worse, the advent of a Labour government, always associated with prodigality, meant that investors began selling, so much so that the secondary banks which had financed the previous government's speculative boom had to be baled out by the Bank of England and the large clearing banks, in order to avoid bankruptcy. The incoming Wilson administration had no choice but to give way to the miners. The Industrial Relations

Act was repealed and any form of pay restraint was dismantled. The government then went on to spend on increased old age pensions and other benefits, to subsidise food, and allow loss-making nationalised industries to run up deficits. Within six months prices rose by 8% and wages by 16%. In order to meet the rising balance of payments deficit the government had to pay 17% interest on long-dated bonds. The Chancellor of the Exchequer embarked on reflation, triggering a mass of bankruptcies in the private sector. To avert even more unemployment government was forced to step in to save them. By the middle of 1975 inflation was running at 25%, wages were going up at a rate of 35% and public expenditure was swallowing 60% of national income. Wilson had come in with the promise of some kind of 'social contract' with the unions but it is hardly surprising it proved a dead issue. The economics of Maynard Keynes were finally seen not to work, when soaring labour costs went hand in hand with rising unemployment and low productivity. Inflation was worse in Britain than anywhere else, and the country was viewed as being in absolute decline.

At this point Harold Wilson decided to retire, passing on his premiership to James Callaghan. He was a man with union credentials and sterling straightforward qualities. The unions proffered him co-operation, but only on condition that there would be no income policy imposed by law. It was an appalling inheritance. The rest of the world looked on askance as Britain slipped ever downwards, and the international money markets, investors and financiers began to lose faith in the pound. What the country needed was wage restraint, public spending cuts, and the acceptance of some unemployment. By 1976 its debts were greater than ever. The sterling balances of other countries, which had remained at £4 billion for twenty-five years, in the 1970s rose to £12 billion. Money flowed out of Britain in a torrent. The value of the pound fell to $1.63. Unemployment reached 1.5 million with inflation running at 17%. There was no alternative but to call in the International Monetary Fund and suffer the ignominy of whatever conditions would be imposed.

The loan was of £2.3 billion on the basis of dramatic cuts in the money supply. Those who for years had advocated budget deficits to stimulate demand were criticised for the impact of the amount of money in circulation and its effect on the economy. The government, whether it liked it or not, had to embrace a monetarist policy based on a belief that the amount of money in circulation at any given time was important. Added to that was the necessity of imposing, and keeping to, cash limits on spending. Callaghan summed it up in a speech which heralded the Conservatism of his successor, Margaret Thatcher, when he denounced the idea that:

> '. . . you just spend your way out of recession and increase employment by cutting taxes and boosting spending . . . that option no longer exists . . . it

worked by injecting inflation into the economy. And each time that happened the average level of employment has risen. Higher inflation followed by higher unemployment. That is the history of the last twenty years.'

This signalled the end of an era, for there were to be no more stimulative deficits. Unemployment was taken on board as a necessary evil to the running of an economy. Ever since 1945 even 2% unemployment had been regarded as politically and socially dangerous. Heath blanched when it reached a million and did a U-turn to bring it down and Wilson had the irony of presiding over 1.4 million unemployed.

Such conditions could only signal industrial anarchy. The government itself was reduced to a majority of one, and was kept going only by a pact with Liberal MPs. It pushed on with social legislation which led to the establishment of a Police Complaints Board and a Race Relations Commission, but the focus of attention was never really to shift from the economy and the unions. In 1978 the government wanted four years of wage restraint with no cuts in income tax as compensation (by then inflation had brought the vast majority of workers into the tax bracket). The unions rejected it; the car workers struck, and got a rise of 17%. The next year the lorry drivers claimed 25% followed by a litany of claims from the public sector workers in the winter of 1978-79. Six weeks of strikes closed schools, saw the rubbish pile up in the streets and even, in Liverpool, the dead lie unburied. Callaghan had the misfortune on returning from abroad and, on being asked about the crisis, to reply 'What crisis?' The government then proceeded to settle for a 9% increase in the public sector which left their policy in ribbons. On 28 March a vote of no confidence in the Commons was carried by just one vote, 311 to 310. The Conservatives swept to power with their new leader, Margaret Thatcher, on a programme which promised to curb the unions, cut taxes and government spending and to bring an end to constant government intervention in the management of the economy. Such a programme would mean not just an adjustment in the role of the state but a radical change in its very function.

In many ways this was a most extraordinary period, turbulent at times and just short of outright mob violence. What is remarkable is that Britain in 1979 seemed intact, its social hierarchy untouched, still stretching down from the monarchy through the aristocracy to the middle and working classes. This facade concealed, however, what was constant change, with the upper classes being levelled downwards and the working classes moving up. Together, they formed a massive middle class. In 1960, 1% of the population owned 38% of the private capital. In 1974, that had dropped to 25%. And in spite of all the traumas nothing could conceal the stupendous overall rise in the working class standard of living. In fact the Welfare

State had made everyone in one sense better off, for people no longer had to make their own provision for the services the state provided.

What is also striking is that so many of the fundamental tenets upon which successive governments founded their policies during these years proved to be delusory. A budget deficit had been seen as an almost magically effective instrument of policy. The continuing failure to create conditions to encourage investment had accelerated decline. It was investment which had been the key to the Industrial Revolution in the past and which had given the country its financial strength and political prestige which other nations had envied and copied. Alas, both had gone, along with the Victorian virtues which had maintained them, now looked upon as dull and constraining. These had been the first decades in the nation's history when power was concentrated not in the hands of the landed classes or even the businessmen, but instead in those of a group of specialised politicians who depended for their existence on the electorate. Much that subsequently occurred raises the question as to whether these politicians were in fact qualified effectively to run an economy, affected as they always were by their desire to be re-elected.

What cannot be denied is that things began to go wrong in the sixties and radically in the seventies. It is still too early to pinpoint the cause. Certainly the country was still living off the moral and financial heritage of its Victorian forebears. Two world wars had also left their devastating imprint upon the whole of society. But no one can deny that there had been crass mismanagement. By the close of the 1970s Britain had lost status and was seen both by those within it and outside as in decline and decay. Doubts began to cross people's minds as to whether everything which had been built up since 1945 was indeed right for the country. As far back as 1966 Edward Heath had expressed enthusiasm for the free play of the market-place and went on to dare to question the ever-escalating cost of the Welfare State. When Margaret Thatcher came to power in 1979 she was faced with two options, either to continue to manage decline more successfully than it had been so far by her predecessors, or to attempt to sweep away the lumber of the past in such a way as would not lead the country into polarity, thereby hoping to usher in a new order.

David Hockney's *Mr and Mrs Ossie Clark and Percy* painted in 1970 catches the atmosphere of the period known as 'The Swinging Sixties' with its emphasis on youth, sartorial elegance, and relaxed living style.

Chapter Sixty-Nine

EMPIRE TO EUROPE

I N 1945 Britain was one of the 'Big Three', together with Russia and the United States, and had a thousand warships, a huge air force, and bases and troops scattered around the globe. Maintaining that global power and those troops depended on the country's wealth, a quarter of which had gone in the war, and on its future economic performance. The exercise of authority ultimately depends on economic power and the graph for that shows one long downward slide. In 1953 Britain still had 8.6% of the world's manufacturing production, only slightly less than in 1939. By the close of the 1950s the world's other economies were beginning to move up the league table. West Germany passed Britain in the 1960s, France and Japan in the 1970s. By 1980 Britain only held 4% of world manufacture and figured as sixth in the world's league of manufacturing nations. Although that decline was arrested for a time in the eighties, by the close of that decade it had moved one further step downwards to seventh place below Italy.

With that catastrophic backdrop there was no way that an Empire could ever be sustained. By 1945 the idea of an Empire, even if re-labelled Commonwealth, was seen as wrong, as a hangover from a vanished Imperial age. The granting of independence to the many countries which had once formed the British Empire was always presented as a moral gesture concealing the fact that British withdrawal was a hard economic necessity. The country could simply no longer afford its Empire. However, in sharp contrast to the internal political history of Britain, the handling of decline abroad was done with great skill, avoiding both extensive human suffering and national humiliation. In the case of the dissolution of the Empire consensus was seen to work in the best possible way. Gradually a set pattern emerged, a pattern which always began in London with an initiative to grant independence and ended with a royal visit, the ceremonial hauling-down of the Union Jack, and the handing over of power to some kind of democratic system based on Parliament. The fact that Westminster was unexportable to places like Africa was glossed over. And by the time that any political system which had been set up on departure collapsed, the British had long gone.

Even before the war India, 'the jewel in the crown', had been promised independence. The difficulty was to withdraw without a bloody confrontation between the Hindu Congress party and the Moslem League. In 1947 the British announced that they would withdraw on 1 June 1948. That announcement forced the issue of partition between what was to become Moslem Pakistan and Hindu India. By the time the last viceroy, Lord Mountbatten, arrived, the structure of government was already in a state of dissolution. Mountbatten had no choice other than to pull back the independence day to 15 August 1947. Although they attempted to draw the partition boundaries it was already a hopeless task. The two states were created but only after a million people had been killed fleeing from one side to the other. Despite that, and the fact that India became a republic two years later, India together with both Pakistan and Ceylon, remained proud to be members of the Commonwealth.

In 1948 Burma became independent and opted not to join the Commonwealth. The same year the British also withdrew from Palestine. That was to be far more complicated. In 1917 Britain had declared that Palestine should become a national home for the Jewish people, in spite of the fact that it was occupied by Arabs. During the 1930s, due to the Nazi persecutions, the immigration of Jews to Palestine escalated so that by 1939 they formed 29% of the population. After the war Britain realised that a continuation of this open-door policy would alienate the Arabs and vitiate the supply of oil to the West. Restriction was therefore imposed, but the pressure from the United States to lift this was instant. Meanwhile, open conflict involving Jews, Arabs and occupying British forces erupted and in 1947 the problem was referred to the United Nations, which declared that Palestine should be partitioned and a state of Israel created. The British refused to implement the decision and withdrew when their mandate expired in May 1948. They left behind what was to be a major problem in the Middle East.

Those tensions were accentuated by the rise of Arab nationalism which was also to affect the British occupation of Sudan, Egypt and the Suez Canal Zone. In 1954 Britain withdrew from the Sudan and agreed also to withdraw from Egypt. The Canal was still vital to British interests as the route to India and Australia and also as the passage for oil imports. In the middle of the 1950s the Empire still seemed formidable, occupying large areas of Africa and the Far East, as well as bases in the Near East. Then in July 1956 the new Egyptian nationalist leader, Colonel Nasser, suddenly nationalised the Suez Canal which was owned by a French company. There was huge outrage both in France and Britain who together demanded that the Canal be internationalised. Egypt refused, and at that point the decision was taken to regain it by force. The strategy devised for that operation was to remain as a lasting shame, for

Israel was persuaded to attack Egypt, giving Britain and France the excuse to intervene to prevent further conflict. In that way the moral order of international law was used to camouflage naked aggression.

On 20 October Israel attacked Egypt according to plan. Britain and France called on both sides to withdraw while their troops occupied the Canal. Egypt refused and on 5 November paratroopers were dropped, followed the day after by the arrival of the fleet from Malta. Port Said was taken and the troops set off on a hundred-mile trek to Suez. Then suddenly Britain and France caved in to a ceasefire demanded by the United Nations Security Council. It was all over.

But the issue was far more complex and humiliating for Britain than even the surface events indicated. From the outset the United States had been against the use of force. At home the Labour Party and many Conservative MPs were also appalled at an action which was redolent of the age of Lord Palmerston. But it was American power which in fact determined the British withdrawal, for the attack had put British gold reserves under intense pressure. The oil supply was also seen to be under threat as the move had offended the Arab countries. The only other source for both money and oil was the United States, who were opposed to the action.

A last imperial gesture. British troops dig in along the banks of the Suez Canal in 1956. World opinion, and much of that at home, was to force withdrawal.

In one devastating denouement Britain was seen no more to be a world power. Suez was an act of gross miscalculation, for it established in the eyes of the world that Britain no longer had the resources to mount an overseas action if the United States disapproved. The economic resources to sustain an Imperial role had gone and the government stood universally condemned. It was a huge turning point. Members of the Commonwealth were henceforth not to be susceptible to British guidance. It alienated the Arab states in the Middle east, turned Nasser into a world figure, and allowed Russia to extend its influence into Egypt. It also imposed a strain on British relations with the United States. The French, co-partners in the enterprise, regarded the British with withering contempt. Even after such a major disaster it is astonishing that successive governments continued to behave as though Britain still had world status. It had gone.

Nationalism was not only sweeping through the Middle East, its tide was engulfing Africa. So fast was the political and social change there that the British withdrawal, conceived initially as a protracted one, had to be accelerated. Nor was Britain alone in making an exit for other European countries were also pulling out of Africa. In many instances it was either get out, or be drawn into an expensive armed conflict which Britain could certainly not afford. So one by one the countries of the Empire were granted independence in carefully stage-managed ceremonies, making Britain seem magnanimous in the hand over. In this way a number of wholly politically created countries emerged which often fell apart shortly after, due to tribal rivalries. Real problems over withdrawal were only to occur in countries where there were significant numbers of white settlers.

The evacuation began in West Africa with Ghana in 1957, followed by Nigeria in 1960, Sierra Leone in 1961, and Gambia in 1965. East Central Africa presented far greater problems. Kenya was devolved along tribal lines in 1963 but it was complicated by a white minority and the problem of how to set up an independent multi-racial state in which an African majority in the assembly had the political power, while much of the economic power was still held by a relatively small wealthy white minority. Tanzania became independent in 1964,

Stamps commemorating independence by three former colonies: Uganda, 1962, Ghana, 1957 and Nigeria, 1960. All remained members of the Commonwealth.

Harold Macmillan as Prime Minister touring Africa in 1960 when he made his famous 'wind of change' speech. Here he is welcomed to eastern Nigeria, a country which was granted its independence the same year.

Uganda in 1962, Zambia and Malawi in 1954. The real problem was Southern Rhodesia, later to be called Zimbabwe, which had a dominant white population to which Britain could not be seen to hand over power. That was to take twenty years to resolve. In 1965 the Rhodesian Prime Minister, Ian Smith, issued a Unilateral Declaration of Independence. Britain could only respond with ineffective economic sanctions. It was not to be until the close of the 1970s that the situation was cleared up and a system whereby to guarantee black majority rule was worked out. In 1980, at long last, the British were able to withdraw gracefully from their last African outpost.

By 1964, the year in which Harold Wilson came to power, the Empire had gone. Although British governments still laboured under the delusion that the country had a world role, its only power base henceforth was to be its possession of a nuclear deterrent. Already, by the close of the 1950s, that was seen as a cheap means of maintaining some kind of global status. Conventional defence began to be radically cut by successive governments. In May 1957 the first British hydrogen bomb was exploded. There was, however, a fatal weakness to this scenario for delivery systems for atomic weapons were ruinously expensive and Britain could not compete with either Russia or the United States. In 1960 'Blue Streak' was cancelled and the American 'Sky Bolt' V-bombers were purchased. Two years later Americans cancelled the bombers, leaving Britain devoid of a delivery system for its nuclear weapons. Macmillan, the Prime Minister at the time, persuaded the American president to sell Britain their new Polaris submarine missile. The truth of the matter was that the technological change in the nature of warfare was so enormous that the economy could no longer afford it.

That became even clearer as the sixties advanced. In 1965 the Labour government cancelled the projected TSR2 low-level bombers deciding to buy instead the American FB111A. But that order too was cancelled. More defence cuts followed in 1967, the same year in which British troops were withdrawn from Malaya and Aden, with Singapore to follow in 1971. During the 1970s, in terms of defence, Britain was an American dependency which certainly did not help the country's negotiations with the European Community. Nor did that change under Mrs Thatcher when Britain became the base for the deployment of ninety-six US Cruise missiles aimed at Russia. The country's defences were strengthened in 1979 by the purchase of the Trident missile from the Americans, an enhanced nuclear delivery system which would maintain Britain's nuclear status into the twenty-first century.

In this context the Falklands war surfaces almost as an aberration. The Falkland Islands are eight thousand miles south of Britain off the coast of Argentina where some eighteen-hundred settlers of British descent live. For years the Foreign Office had sought to reach an agreement with Argentina whereby to hand the islands over. Then in 1982 the ruling Argentinian military junta invaded the Falklands. Mrs Thatcher refused to compromise, securing support not only from the United States but also from the European Economic Community. The United Nations also condemned Argentina's act of aggression. A British task force sailed, lacking both air cover and air warning systems, but luck held. At a cost of £1,500 million the islands were retaken and national honour and international law were seen to be upheld. Not only that, but the will of the British people had been met.

Virtually all that is now left of the Empire are a few scattered outposts like the Falklands, Gibraltar and Hong Kong. The latter, however, after complex negotiations, is to revert to China in 1997 when the colony's lease expires. The ghost of the Empire lives on in the Commonwealth, which had shown some effectiveness in 1961 when it expelled South Africa for its policy of racial discrimination, apartheid, but otherwise remains a disparate group of states, from democracies to one-party régimes whose role seems progressively more and more opaque. Nonetheless, the Empire left its mark even if only in the form of the English language circling the globe. Ties of affection between the mother country and Canada, Australia and New Zealand still exist although as time passes the links binding even these become ever more vestigial, and republican movements surface.

Historians have not reached any agreement as to what the British Empire represented. Was much of it acquired as a cosmetic to the onset of decline at home? Did it embody captive markets for British goods? It had been built up over the centuries by unscrupulous adventurers and was used as a dumping-ground for the wayward. It had been brutal and exploitative and it had embodied unashamed racial superiority. There is no doubt that Britain owed much of her success in both world wars to the fact that the troops of the Empire could be called upon. One million African soldiers and labourers fought in the First, while well over half a million Indians, Australians and Canadians were killed or severely wounded in the Second. These men had fought for democracy and freedom and yet must have wondered why it had not been granted to them at home. At least in the end it was, and the British departure was a graceful one. It left Britain with a major problem, one which was pin-pointed in 1962 by a former American Secretary of State, Dean Acheson, when he remarked that 'Britain had lost an Empire and not yet found a role'. Whether that role was to be in Europe was to be the question to occupy the minds of the British government and people for the closing decades of the century.

Immigration changed the make-up of the workforce from the middle of the 1950s onwards. A worker at Bilston steel works, Birmingham, 1982.

Europe presented the British with a continuing problem. The psychological adjustment it was to demand still remains unresolved almost half-a-century on. Britain cast itself in 1945 as a major power on a level with Russia and the USA. To admit anything else was to come to terms with a very hard reality, that the country was a middle-ranking European state divided from the mainland by the Channel. That was a concept difficult to swallow. For five centuries Britain had only involved itself in Europe to defeat any power which threatened to dominate it. After achieving that objective it had then always retreated behind its watery frontiers. What happened after 1945 was progressively to make that stance more and more untenable. There were those who accepted it as inevitable and who embraced the European ideal but there were also those who rejected it, looking for any way forward whereby they might avert what they regarded as the demise of a proud nation state.

In 1945 the Potsdam Conference of the 'Big Three' saw Russia extend her grip across Eastern Central Europe by creating a series of police states to act as buffers between it and the West. No one could guess whether Stalin had ambitions or not to move further in that direction. The new political geography of Europe was summed up by Churchill in a speech he made in 1946: 'From Stettin in the Baltic . . . to Trieste in the Adriatic an iron curtain has descended across the continent.' With large Communist parties in both Italy and France and a shattered economy the West was more than vulnerable. Ernest Bevin, who was Attlee's tough Foreign Secretary, realised that its survival depended on America not retreating into isolation but maintaining her commitment to what remained of free Europe. Britain could certainly no longer play such a role. In 1947 its troops were withdrawn from Greece and Turkey. In response to Russia's consolidation of its massive power block the American president, Truman, announced his doctrine that free peoples should not be subjugated by minorities or outside pressure.

In June 1947 the Marshall Plan followed, whereby the United States extended aid for the economic recovery of Europe; thanks to it the capitalist economies of the West revived and thrived. Again with Russia in mind Britain and France, two years before, had already drawn together with Belgium, the Netherlands and Luxembourg in the Treaty of Brussels, pledging mutual and collective military aid against any aggressor. That fear of what Russia might do was heightened when Russia blockaded Berlin which had been divided between the victors but which was in the Russian zone. An air-lift of supplies from the West was set in motion and it was made clear that any interference with it would bring war. As America had the monopoly of atomic weapons, that did not occur.

In 1949 Bevin's hopes reached fulfilment in the North Atlantic Treaty Organisation (NATO), in which America and the states of Western Europe joined in a defensive alliance which was to bring peace for four decades. On the Continent the idea of a united Europe began to take off, and in May the Council of Europe was formed. Significantly, the British did not attend. Britain also refused to join a European defence force, agreeing instead and at huge expense to maintain four divisions within Europe, a permanent drain on the country's foreign exchange. Then, in 1950, the French and Germans came together to establish the European Coal and Steel Community. Although the British were invited they declined, trying instead to obstruct its creation.

This decision to stand apart not only meant that the focus of the new Europe was to be Paris and Bonn but also, when eventually Britain did gain admittance, that the country was joining an association to whose shaping and development it had made no contribution. In 1955 an Action Committee for a United States of Europe was formed. Britain this time was represented, albeit in only a minor way and declining to go any further. Six major European states, however, went on to consult as to how they could form a Common Market. Macmillan, then Prime Minister, witheringly referred to one of their meetings as some 'archeological excavation'.

In 1957 the Treaty of Rome established the European Economic Community (EEC). After a transitional period there was to be a free movement of people, services and capital between France, West Germany, Italy, Belgium, the Netherlands and Luxembourg. There would be no tariffs against each other and a single uniform tariff against the imports of all other countries. A Social Fund was set up to cope with any adjustments that might arise. All of this was totally unacceptable to the British government as it was regarded as being prejudicial to Commonwealth imports, the main source of Britain's cheap food. The new Community's Common Agricultural Policy would mean that the existing way of supporting farmers would change from being one of subsidies to one of customs duties and, as a consequence, the price of food would rise.

In response the British set up a rival organisation, the European Free Trade Association (EFTA), which included Austria, Denmark, Sweden and Portugal, with the aim of establishing a free trade area among its members in a decade. Naturally it looked to the EEC as a market, but it refused to join. The Treaty of Rome had stated that any European state could apply for membership and by 1961 Harold Macmillan decided that perhaps Britain should, after all, join, providing both EFTA and the Commonwealth interest were safeguarded. Alas, that was not to be so easy, for in January 1963 the French president, General de Gaulle, vetoed British entry. In the eyes of the French, Britain was a satellite of the United States and that was incompatible with being a member of the EEC.

With the ever-sliding state of the British economy a market of 250 million people could no longer be sniffed at, so that Harold Wilson now applied for entry in 1967. British entry was once again vetoed by de Gaulle. By then the EEC was beginning to be looked upon longingly as the means whereby the British economy might be rejuvenated. Its appalling state was given by de Gaulle as the main reason for rejection. By 1970 de Gaulle had gone, and a committed European, Edward Heath, was now the British Prime Minister. He applied a third time, and it was thanks largely to his skilled diplomacy that the French were persuaded to accede. The decision to enter Europe was the subject of a free vote in the Commons and the bill was passed in July 1972, the country officially entering the EEC on 1 January 1973.

The negotiations had been extremely complex allowing for a transitional period for adjustments. But the irony was that Britain joined the EEC the year when the consequences of the oil crisis were forcing Europe into recession. In fact the EEC was no quick panacea. It, together with the oil crisis, only made the underlying weakness of the British economy even more glaring. The majority of the Labour Party had always been against joining, and when returned to power in 1974, Labour held a referendum as to whether the country should opt out. In a unique event in the country's democratic history 67.2% of the two-thirds of the population who voted were in favour of staying in. But that decision needed to be reflected in the actions of an enthusiastic pro-European government which Labour was not. It opposed any moves towards federalism, fought against monetary union, and disliked the new elections of British representatives to the European Parliament.

Those attitudes were shared by the Conservative Mrs Thatcher. When she came to power she found the country committed to large financial contributions to the Economic Community when Britain was, in fact, poorer than six out of the nine Community members. In 1984 she won a battle about Britain's contribution and the payments were reduced by half. Two years later

Edward Heath watches votes being counted at Earl's Court after the referendum on Britain's entry into the Common Market in 1975.

came the Single European Act adopted by the Community in which its Parliament in Brussels was to have sovereign power on a wide range of issues. The idea that sovereignty was divisible was unknown to the British constitution and foretold future battles. Another was to be over the European Exchange Rate Mechanism whereby no single currency dominated the market and an agreement bound each member state to keep the exchange value of its currency from moving too far above the lowest-valued, or below the highest-valued, currencies at any time. Each sovereign state retained the right to make a fundamental change to its exchange rate of the existing value where appropriate. Although Mrs Thatcher wanted Britain to stay out of this arrangement her Chancellor wanted the country to enter and in October 1990, a month before Mrs Thatcher's fall, that happened. The results were to be such that it was not long before Britain was forced to withdraw.

The debate about Britain and Europe is still current. On the one side there are those who view the Community (now formally called the European Union) as the final erosion not only of Britain's sovereignty but its links with the countries of her former Empire. Both political parties have ebbed and flowed in their attitude to it and indeed been split in their own ranks. Labour began by regarding the EEC as a den of capitalism while the Conservatives saw it as an agent for promoting socialism by the back door. There were many who embraced the new European ideal seeing Britain as having the possibility of playing a major role in a visionary endeavour, albeit one which would demand a major political, social and cultural adjustment from the people.

And who were those people? If the Empire had gone and Europe was viewed as a necessary evil, Britain itself was undergoing internal pressures which were pulling it apart. And that tendency to fragment was not the consequence of the substantial post-war immigrant community which failed to integrate as their predecessors had done, but rather the resurfacing of ancient historic identities. After the middle of the 1950s the relationships of the component parts of Britain were never again to be so tranquil. In 1967 the Scottish National Party won a seat in the Commons reflecting an increasing desire north of the border for an independent Scottish voice to be heard. In 1974 eleven National Party MPs were elected. During the same period in Wales Plaid Cymru gained ground, and in 1966 an MP was elected. In Wales the concern was different being one rather for the survival of a cultural identity expressed in the Welsh language. But both movements gained strength in the 1970s, particularly after 1973 when both Edinburgh and Cardiff could see advantages in having direct links with the administrative capital of the EEC in Brussels. The English began to realise what they had long forgotten, that they were members of an artificial nation which they had forged. During the late 1970s devolution bills to establish regional assemblies were introduced and a referendum was held in 1979 as to whether they should be implemented. There was no massive endorsement but the sentiment remains. If devolution had proceeded, it would have meant not only the dismemberment of the island but also left England devoid of its own assembly. In England, too, regional identities like those in the north or south-west were beginning to have their own strong voices.

Eclipsing all of this by far was the problem of Northern Ireland. In 1949 the Irish Free State became the Republic of Ireland. Northern Ireland remained part of Britain. Indeed that event was to make sharper the line of division between north and south and there was a commitment by government that severance between Britain and Northern Ireland could only take place with the agreement of the Parliament in Stormont. Northern Ireland was a province, in which two-thirds of the population were Ulster Protestants or Unionists and a third Catholics. The latter were inevitably reduced to the status of being an underclass for the Unionists worked the system in their favour through plural voting, gerrymandered constituencies, and discrimination in local government, housing and social benefits. The Catholics naturally had no alternative but to look south to Dublin.

It was hoped economic prosperity would solve the problem but, in spite of efforts to bring in middle class Catholics during the sixties, that did not happen. Then in 1965 the civil rights movement reached Northern Ireland from America, and two years later the Civil Rights Association was formed, beginning a long series of non-violent demonstrations to draw attention to the plight of Catholics. In 1968 a march at Londonderry was banned leading to a violent confrontation with the police which was seen on every television screen. The movement then took off so strongly that the following year the Northern Ireland Prime Minister lost the election and Britain was forced to send in troops to protect the Catholic minority. That year the Irish Republican Army, the IRA, split, one half adhering to the peaceful non-violent approach of the civil rights movement and the other half committed to defending the Catholic minority against the British troops, viewed by them as an army of repressive occupation. The result was an acceleration of polarisation. Catholics and Protestants moved house, forming ghettoes, and there followed more and more assaults and skirmishes.

A Prevention of Incitement to Hatred Act was passed in 1970 but to little effect and the next year the first British soldier was killed. Protestant paramilitary groups then sprang up in response to the IRA and internment of suspected terrorists was introduced, which only further alienated the Catholic community. Then, on 30

January 1972, British soldiers killed thirteen people during a demonstration in Londonderry. 'Bloody Sunday' was a turning point. Two months later devolved government at Stormont ceased and direct rule from Westminster began. Attempts to restore some form of

Bloody Sunday, 30 January 1972, when British troops opened fire on a civil rights march through Derry, killing fourteen unarmed men.

devolved government only ended in failure and as the seventies advanced the IRA believed that if they took their activities to the mainland of Britain it would lead in the end to the troop evacuation of Northern Ireland. Successive governments struggled to find a solution to a situation where clashes of belief and ideology were of a kind which belonged to the seventeenth, rather than the late twentieth, century. In 1973 the Sunningdale Agreement produced a new scheme to re-establish devolved government but with some involvement by the south by way of a Council of Ireland. The idea of even co-operating with the south produced strikes. The terror the IRA brought to the mainland only emphasised the need to find a solution and in 1981 Mrs Thatcher launched the Anglo-Irish Inter-Government Council. Once again there were plans for a new Northern Ireland assembly and elections actually took place, but produced only candidates from the two extremes, Sinn Féin and the Democratic Unionists. The scheme proved a non-starter.

If anything, the situation only deteriorated in the eighties. In 1984 the IRA bombed the Tory Party conference hotel in Brighton, coming perilously close to murdering the Prime Minister, Mrs Thatcher. This led to an angry government response, which included gagging the IRA and Sinn Féin in the media. But both the British and the Irish Republican governments recognised that each had a role to play in whatever settlement was eventually reached. They were faced, however, with a people who had not only been polarised but brutalised by twenty years of hate, fear, suspicion, and terrible violence. No one in 1990 was any nearer a solution.

By that date Britain was number seven, and the least important of the western economies. The decline in the economy had been the key factor in the country's reduction to the level of a middle-ranking European state. What is surprising is how long, and with what reluctance even now, that fact has taken to sink in. As late as 1964 Harold Wilson could still say: 'We cannot afford to relinquish our world role', when it had already vanished. Britain has returned in a sense to where she was in 1603, but is far less independent, for the country is now a satellite of two empires, the American and the European. The former is reflected in a countryside dotted with US bases and the latter in membership of a group of European states whose headquarters is in Brussels. The EC is the lineal descendent of earlier European empires, the Roman, medieval Christendom, or the Habsburg Empire. England in the middle ages had itself presided over such a continental domain, but from the sixteenth century onwards it looked firmly westwards. In the Act of Uniformity of 1534 England had cut itself off from the Universal Church, an assertion of Imperial status which came to an end with accession to the Treaty of Rome in 1972. History had come full circle and Britain has to learn to look eastwards again, for the commercial markets upon which the future depends are those of medieval England. It had been an era of lost opportunities for Britain could have taken the lead in Europe after 1945, but chose not to. It was an age dominated by the uncertainties of what was called the Cold War, waged across the Iron Curtain and dividing east from west. What that curtain ensured was that the centre of gravity of the new Europe had been in the west. When the Iron Curtain crumbled in 1989 it signalled a profound geographical shift. The heart of Europe became a newly-united Germany with the former eastern bloc countries now wishing to become members of the European Community. The old enemy Russia internally disintegrated. That shift has pushed Britain onto the geographical margins. It has also made the country of far less importance to American strategy. With the disappearance of the Iron Curtain the old parameters have gone and Britain looks across the Channel at a Europe which resembles that before 1939, bringing with it troubles long thought buried.

Chapter Seventy

A NEW BEGINNING?

THE period 1979 to 1990 was to be encapsulated in one person, Margaret Thatcher. Her impact on the direction the country was to go in exceeded even that of Winston Churchill, whose role was essentially confined to one of leading a nation to victory in war but not of actually changing its internal course. In sharp contrast Mrs Thatcher was to be the vehicle whereby everything which everyone had taken for granted since 1945 was to come under sudden and devastating attack. Indeed during her eleven years in power, government was, for the first time since the 1830s, to attempt to draw back and not to extend the influence of the state into yet more areas of daily life. Ever-escalating state intervention had only resulted in a limping economy and slow growth. For decades governments had oscillated between expansionist and deflationary policies. For decades, too, it had been accepted that government's prime role was to spend more and more taxpayer's money. Margaret Thatcher, the daughter of a Grantham grocer, was quite unlike any other Prime Minister since 1945. Down-to-earth and with no time for the intellectual theorising which had dominated politics, her prime guide was her instinct and what she regarded as common-sense. That was the key to her initial success, the fact that her message was a very simple one: reduce the role of the state, stop inflation, and create a society which rewarded the effort of the individual. Tough, determined, ruthless, and ultimately divisive as a political personality, Mrs Thatcher was a Prime Minister whose era stands apart for another reason: the policies never changed. There was pragmatism, but on the whole there were no concessions. However rough the ride, and much of it was, the journey was to be endured to the bitter end.

This was a new brand of Conservatism, one which had emerged during the 1970s under the aegis of the Centre for Policy Studies and Mrs Thatcher's mentor, Sir Keith Joseph. The scenario outlined by the New Right read like a programme of revenge on two generations of social engineers, setting out to replace what they viewed as the dead-hand of state-directed corporatism with the doctrine of the free market. The stranglehold of the unions, which made the country virtually ungovernable during the 1970s, had to be broken. The money supply had to be controlled. Labour had already tried a monetarist policy and failed. To achieve such a policy successfully would call for nerves of steel, for curbing inflation would entail not only mass bankruptcies but also soaring unemployment. That had to be endured, so that in the future, growth in the money supply would only match that in productivity. Such a policy in its initial stages could never be popular and it would take time to see its effects. Fortunately the Prime Minister was not only resolute but lucky.

The Conservatives were to win four elections in succession, providing the government with a period of time long enough to see their policies through, unrivalled in the post-war period. Mrs Thatcher was shrewd at choosing election dates, sweeping back to power on the euphoria of the Falkland triumph, in 1983; and finally, having brought down inflation, in 1987, just before the onset of a damaging recession. Such longevity meant that enormous changes could be made and from the outset it was assumed that any strategy had to be a long-term one. Although the longevity could not have been predicted, it welds the Thatcher era into an unusual whole, which opened quite cautiously in 1979 and reached a crescendo

Mrs Thatcher as Prime Minister cultivated a forceful public image which earned her the sobriquet of the Iron Lady. Here she arises out of a tank during a visit to British troops in Germany in 1986.

in 1987. At the outset the New Right were in a minority but were nonetheless placed in control of the purse-strings, with Sir Geoffrey Howe as Chancellor of the Exchequer. Gradually politicians Mrs Thatcher labelled as 'wet' were got rid of, and those she designated 'dry' or 'one of us' were brought into office. In this way the old style Conservatism with its paternalistic grandees and devotees of the Welfare Sate were swept aside. The old 'one nation' Conservatism of the consensus era met only with scorn as increasingly the New Right's policies, like privatisation, were set in motion.

What the programme was to be was first glimpsed in the area of taxation and public expenditure. Henceforward indirect taxation was preferred to direct. The standard rate of income tax was reduced from 33% to 30% and for the richest it was brought down from 83% to 40%. For the first time there was a government which believed that cutting people's taxes was better than spending their money. Cash limits were also imposed on government spending. What took time to sink in was that this policy had come to stay. Indeed in later budgets it was taken even further, with huge increases in indirect taxation and a reduction of the standard rate of income tax by 1987 to 27%. For the first time for nearly eighty years the idea that the electorate would welcome taxing the better off was thrown out. The effect for many was a far greater prosperity but it undoubtedly widened the gulf between the richest and the poorest.

These tight financial restraints, which included a high interest rate at between 14% and 17%, had a dramatic effect. The worst recession since 1931 set in, with a 100,000 people a month rendered unemployed in 1981. There was de-industrialisation on a vast scale and inflation running at 20%, not helped by having to meet huge wage increases which were inherited from the government's predecessors. The fact was that however appalling the level of unemployment (and ultimately it was to reach over three million) the majority remained in work with their standard of living unimpaired. Fear of job loss led to moderate pay settlements and increased productivity, so that by 1983 inflation had fallen to only 5%. Unemployment cost money in benefits, a bill which was met by cuts in expenditure and income from North Sea oil. It also contributed to social unrest with inner city riots occurring both in 1981 and 1985.

The expression which gained currency was to refer to 'real jobs', meaning not those hedged round with restrictive practices nor those concerned with the thousands supporting central and local government bureaucracy, a particular disdain was reserved for them. Early on, businessmen were brought in to scrutinise government structure with a view to reforms in efficiency and hiving off. Local government was looked upon as a bloated monument to the old consensus corporatism with one in eight in the country working in the structure. They also made up the Labour heartland with extreme left wing councils squandering ratepayers' money. In 1980, controls were imposed on their expenditure and ability to borrow. Their reply was to levy a supplementary rate, but that was stopped by ratecapping. Value for money was to be achieved by the introduction of competitive tendering for local services like collecting refuse. The 1986 Local Government Act abolished the Greater London Council and six metropolitan authorities wiping out a structure which went back to the 1880s. In this way those seen as the worst offenders were obliterated, and the wings of local government by bureaucracy began to be clipped overall.

Similar considerations permeated the government's attitude to the Health Service and to education. The idea of state provision was not challenged but in the case of the former money was placed directly into the hands of the doctors and hospitals to exercise their own financial housekeeping. Hospitals were also given the opportunity of opting out of the Health Service, and many began to fear that what was still regarded as the glory of the Welfare State was about to be dismantled. In the case of education it was the universities which felt the full blast of government disapproval, being looked upon as complacent enclosed communities, which had eaten up money and failed to produce wealth creators. Stern monetary discipline was imposed with injunctions to adopt new managerial techniques. The 1986 and 1988 Education Acts applied the same rigours to schools. New-style examinations were introduced, results providing a means of assessing a school's success, which was then made public. A National Curriculum was laid down, and participation on governing bodies involved parents for the first time in a school's decision-making and accountability. This too was an attack on local authority management, which was taken further when schools were given the chance to opt out, be funded directly from the centre, and run their own affairs.

All of these actions irrevocably changed things which had seemed immutable to the majority. So too did the sale of council houses to their tenants in 1980, which was an immensely popular measure. Some 800,000 houses were sold by the end of 1984 and by 1990 it was to mean that two-thirds of the population were owner-occupiers. Britain had become a property-owning democracy on a scale inconceivable in 1900.

In this enormous shake-up there had to be losers as well as winners. Welfare benefits, although also unchallenged as a state obligation, were never satisfactorily dealt with. Poverty was still to be relieved as a right, and indeed it was accepted that extra payments should be made in particular circumstances. This process was

The downside of the years of Conservative rule, mass unemployment. Here the unemployed await their call in a Department of Health and Social Security Office in North London in 1984.

institutionalised in an act of 1970 but due to inflation, problems began to arise. By the 1980s even low-paid workers were paying income tax. Benefits were paid but a worker would find that 80% or 90% of any increase to his gross take-home pay was taken away at source. The result was to create a 'poverty trap' into which many people became inexorably caught.

These activities were tangential to the New Right's two central objectives: to humble the unions and to dismantle the collectivist state by privatising the nationalised industries. Neither was attempted until the government was in a position of strength. The unions stood by their old creed: full employment, Clause 4, and high wages. During the early years government steered clear of confrontation. The earliest sign of what was to come was a total freeze-out of the unions from government after forty years of dialogue. Proposals to close uneconomic mines in 1981 were abandoned, the same year in which the National Union of Mine Workers elected a new and uncompromising president, Arthur Scargill. Government spent its time preparing the ground for the clash to come. Two Employment Acts in 1980 and 1982 ate into union power. These involved secret ballots for strikes, the outlawing of secondary picketing and sympathy strikes, besides making unions legally responsible for their own actions. As a result the balance shifted back in favour of the employer. By 1984 the government could actually deny those who worked in its Intelligence Headquarters in Cheltenham the right to belong to a union at all.

Police surrounding Easington Colliery, County Durham, in August 1984, to protect any miner who wanted to work from intimidation. The miners' strike finally broke union power but it was to leave a legacy of embitterment.

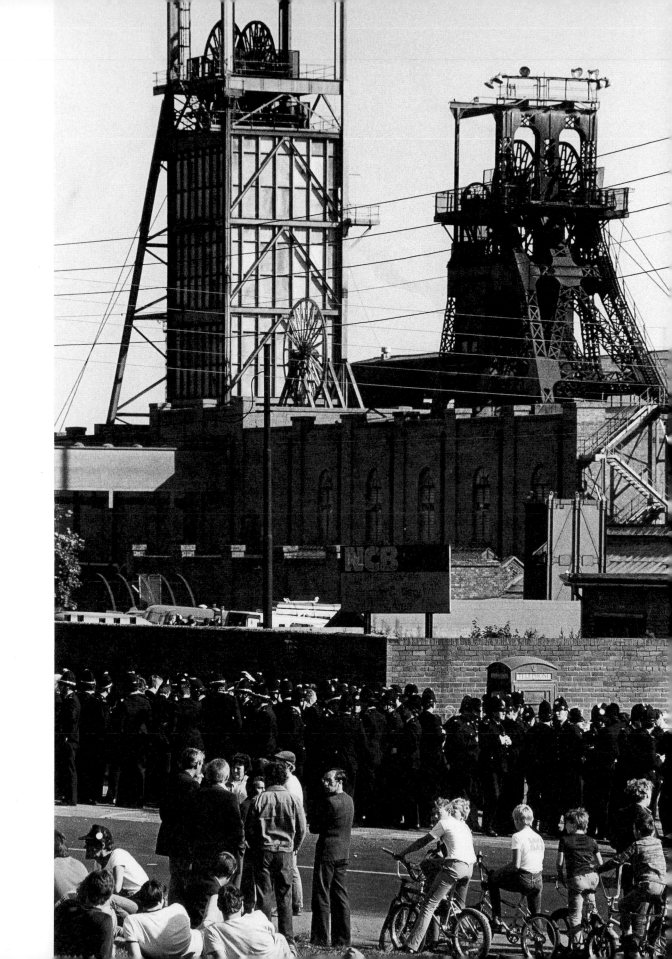

Only after her triumphant return to power in 1983 was Mrs Thatcher prepared for the battle. By then not only was the necessary legislation firmly in place but union membership, due to unemployment, had dropped substantially. More to the point, the power stations had a six months' supply of coal after which many could go over to oil (which had largely replaced coal as an energy source). Already a 1982 report had said the coal industry was uneconomic and pits should close. Then in 1984 the Coal Board announced the closure of twenty pits, knowing what would follow. Apart from a group in Nottinghamshire, the miners voted to strike. The subsequent strike lasted 362 days from 5 March 1984 to 3 March 1985. It was to be a bloody strike, with violence and intimidation rending whole communities apart. Scargill sent his 'flying pickets' all over the country, while the government moved the police around to protect those who wanted to work. In the end the men were forced to go back out of sheer necessity, as well as disillusionment with their leadership. There was no settlement, just a return to work on a narrow majority vote. The government won, and the guts were knocked out of the union movement. Between 1984 and 1987 the number of miners fell by over 70,000 and forty-two pits were closed.

An equally violent strike by printworkers followed in 1986. A group who worked for a major newspaper magnate refused to move to Wapping in the Docklands, and to operate the new computerised print technology which elsewhere in the world had been in use since the 1960s. Once again the police were heavily involved in protection, this time of members of the electricians' union who had taken on the job. These uses of the police to handle what were deemed 'riotous assemblies' led to them being seen as agents of the government rather than law enforcers. That view was also reinforced for many by their role in suppressing the inner city riots which were made up in the main of black youths. As a result the police began also to be thought of as racist.

Union power had been broken after almost a century. The dismantling of the mixed economy was another reversal of a long-lived phenomenon over which again few tears were shed. The call was to 'roll back the state' by sweeping aside the infra-structure of the era of consensus. The nationalised industries made losses which were subsidised by the taxpayer. Not only would government shed a loss-maker and all the problems such an industry involved, but they would also end its bureaucracy. As in the case of the unions, the problem was cautiously approached until the time was right and it could be accelerated. From 1979 to 1983 only £1.4 billion of publicly owned enterprises was sold off. In the first fifteen months following the 1983 election £1.7 billion went, followed by the massive £4 billion sell-off of the telephone system, British Telecom. That sale was designed to spread share-owning through the

The Docklands were the flagship of the Thatcher free enterprise era. Nine square miles were open for redevelopment by the private sector, the crowning glory of which was Canary Wharf with its towering skyscraper symbolising the new age.

community as never before. British Airways followed and then British Steel, Britoil, Britgas, British Airports, in 1989 water, and in 1990 electricity. In this way a major objective was achieved whereby government withdrew from being directly involved in running major sections of the economy, letting market forces take over.

The sell-off of the nationalised industries, which expanded share-holding across the land, went hand-in-hand with a reform of the City, starting with the abolition of exchange controls. Ever since the Second World War it had been difficult to invest abroad. That policy was now reversed, releasing huge investment funds. In five years the amount invested abroad rose from £12½ billion to £70 billion. On 26 October 1986, 'big bang', as it was nicknamed, occurred – a reform of the stockmarket, bringing an end to restrictive practices, and going over fully to the new technology of computerisation, in an effort to make London a global trading centre along with New York and Tokyo, able to cope not only with the orders of large institutional finance but also with the needs of the small share-holder. All of this reflected the fact that the focus of money-making had shifted from industry to financial services: banks, unit trusts, pension funds and insurance companies. At the same time the old established rules governing credit were relaxed so that 100% mortgages, for example, were given. In the end this activity only fuelled an expansion whose foundation was debt, and on 19 October 1987 there was a stockmarket crash. This signalled the onset of a recession which hit all of Europe, but Britain worst of all.

This coincided with the decline in Mrs Thatcher's fortunes. In her fourth term of office she seemed to become increasingly imperious, but, more significantly, things like privatisation were carried through without sufficient regard to making out the case to the public. The government's refusal to listen meant that the measure to reform the antiquated rating system was to end in disaster. The flat-rate tax which assessed the value of houses, other buildings and landed property was the main source of local government revenue. 18 million of the 35 million voters in the country paid rates, albeit 6 million of those had them paid by the social services. The existing system was unjust but to transform it into a poll tax based on the number of adult occupants of a property was to extend disaffection with the government through a huge swathe of the population. The only other poll tax in the country's history had led to the Peasants' Revolt. This time there were riots in Scotland where it was introduced first in 1989, and then in the following year there were similar and violent demonstrations in England and Wales.

As 1990 progressed the Prime Minister's style attracted more and more criticism. There were also internal disagreements in the government. The Chancellor, by then Nigel Lawson, had resigned over her opposition to joining the European Exchange

Rate Mechanism and then, in November, her Foreign Secretary, Geoffrey Howe, resigned. He followed his resignation with a devastating attack on Mrs Thatcher in the Commons. The Conservatives, with an election looming, feared that they might be carrying an electoral liability, and began to cast around for a new leader. In the contest which followed Mrs Thatcher lost in the first round, and rather than face the humiliation of defeat she resigned. By then there were enemies on all sides but her exit needs to be placed in the context of a biting recession. She had come to power promising prosperity and had for a time given it. Now it was seen to have ebbed. Her last gesture was to throw her weight behind John Major as her successor.

One of the brilliant posters which contributed to the sweeping Conservative victory of 1979. The irony was that not long after unemployment, far from falling, was dramatically to rise to three million.

For a decade it had seemed as though no other political party existed and those that struggled to oppose were incalculably affected by the impact of Mrs Thatcher. As the 1980s progressed, Labour was rendered an anachronism still adhering to viewpoints which belonged to the past, those of statism, centralisation and planning. Any appeal which it had evaporated as the party moved further to the left when Callaghan went in 1980 and was replaced by Michael Foot, a pacifist and ardent supporter of nuclear disarmament. The Labour manifesto for the 1981 election was described as 'the longest suicide note in history'. Soon after, Foot was replaced by Neil Kinnock, elected by a newly created electoral college which was biased towards the left. The party also continued to be riven by dissensions in its ranks but in spite of this, gradually managed to drop one by one its vote-losing policies. By 1990 it had embraced the European Community and adopted multi-lateral disarmament. There was no hint either that it would re-nationalise privatised industries nor repeal Conservative union legislation. If those changes had been taken on board earlier they would have averted the split which happened when a group on the right of the party defected, and founded the Social Democratic Party. For a short time they bid for the middle ground, and for a period worked in tandem with the Liberals under the name of an Alliance. But in the end they were marginalised. Labour's problem was that its voting base was in the old declining industrial areas like the north and north-east, Scotland, Wales and Northern Ireland. Their supporters were workers in the public sector, and council house tenants. Labour had no message for a society which was now firmly based in the new technology and on the idea of wealth creation.

To come to power Labour needed to win the votes of the classes which had prospered in the 1980s. The pattern of that across the country marked another big shift. It was the areas which had seen the first Industrial Revolution which were hardest hit. They belonged to a world that had finally gone. The new prosperity was now firmly entrenched in the east and south-east in proximity to the European mainland. There, during the eighties, an unprecedented boom in the good life occurred, with shopping and leisure centres mushrooming everywhere, signalling the heyday of the consumer society.

The aim of the Thatcher era had been to reverse the main lines of the country's development since 1945. From a mood of resignation to decline there had been a sharp shift towards welcoming the attempt to clear away the debris of the past and start afresh. For most of the century those who took part in government had been men of intellect and independent means who were appalled at the consequences of the industrialisation and urbanisation of Britain. Their reaction was a state of mind which accepted the need for reform even if it was at their own financial expense (as indeed it was) and culminated in the setting up of the Welfare State. That milieu foundered in the 1970s. The left despised it for being paternalistic and patronising. The right felt no sympathy for what they regarded as the able-bodied poor, and revived and lauded the long-suppressed basic human instinct that individual effort should reap its rewards. There was therefore a visible lack of compassion for those swept onto the heap of failure. All that was vaguely hoped was that the vacuum caused by the era's demolitions would somehow be filled by the free market. This was not always so. On every side there was a move away from what was left of the old community values in favour of the more competitive ones of the enterprise age.

There were, however, ironies. The creed which began with the cry to draw back the state and release the individual eventually became in many areas an agent of greater centralisation. That was because the only means which government found of achieving its aim was by axing the intermediary bureaucracy scattered across country and replacing it with direct ties to the centre. Nonetheless, after Mrs Thatcher nothing would be the same again. Consensus might be assumed to be at an end. The Social Democratic Party's attempt to revive it seemed to have failed, and the only remaining opposition appeared to be a Labour Party in the grip of terminal decline. The truth of the matter was that everyone recognised that many of the changes made were changes which should not be gone back on. No one wanted to return to the era of the unions. No one wanted to return to nationalisation. No one desired to resurrect the manipulation through fiscal machinery of equality of income. Privatisation indeed proved to be such a success that it began to be copied across Western Europe and then, in the aftermath of the dissolution of the Communist empire, in the East, where it was taken up as a remedy to the failed socialist economies.

Was this a new beginning or not? It is still too early to know. A decade dominated by the philosophy of the market place had changed people's perception and their way of working, permeating not only the social services and education but also all of the professions. It is too soon to know what the long-term effects of this will be. Meanwhile, Britain will continue to live with the consequences of what some have described as the Thatcher revolution for the foreseeable future.

Chapter Seventy-One

THE CONSUMER SOCIETY

THE twentieth century has been a period of enormous change but nothing approaching that lived through by the Victorians, who visibly saw the surface of the island change far more dramatically in response to the Industrial Revolution. Then, the population had quadrupled. In this century it had only doubled, reaching 54 million in 1981. That is due to a number of factors from falling fertility rates to the decline in infant mortality, from the practice of birth control to the lack of need for children as wage-earners. Nonetheless, Britain still remains the third most populous country in Western Europe. And, as in the previous century, the population has migrated. One person in three now lives in the south-east, and as long as the economic orientation of the country looks towards the European mainland that shift seems likely to remain for the present, reinforcing developments already taking place in which towns like Felixstowe boom and those like Liverpool become heritage centres, handsome historic monuments to an era which has gone. Indeed the opening of the Channel Tunnel in 1994, providing a direct link both by road and rail with the Continent, can only emphasise that geographical swing of the pendulum.

Urbanisation has been replaced by suburbanisation as cities sprawl outwards in what are conurbations, forming vast built-up areas like Birmingham and Tyneside and, in the case of London, an overall expanse of 610 square miles with some 7 million inhabitants. New modes of transport enable people to travel unheard-of distances to work, by road and rail. Car ownership trebled in the decade following 1958, leading to the huge road-building programme of M-motorways criss-crossing the country, with major consequences for accessibility, commerce, and the environment, besides sounding the death knell of the railways. By 1985 nearly 65% of households owned a car. To meet the pressure of this massive increase, the centres of cities and towns were sacrificed to the automobile as ring roads and fly-overs were constructed. This went hand-in-hand with what was supposed to be inner city renewal, schemes which were firmly in the hands of the planners as the hearts of cities were torn out, and replaced by tower blocks of flats and shopping centres. By the middle of the 1970s the results of this were already seen to be catastrophic. To add to

the problem the 1980s were marked by the arrival of the out-of-town shopping mall and leisure complex, rendering the city centres ever more redundant. Immigration also added to the urban problem for, unlike earlier immigrants, those who came from India, Pakistan or Bangladesh wished to form their own communities without integrating into the cultural habit of their adopted country. As a result certain cities became ghetto-ised.

If the country was increasingly at the mercy of the town, the face of Britain itself was visibly altering under the impact of a renewed wave of industrialisation in the 1960s. The landscape, which had last been formed in the eighteenth century in response to an earlier Agrarian Revolution, now had to respond to farming methods

The end of the island, 1994. The Waterloo terminal of the Channel Tunnel providing a daily train service linking Paris, Brussels and London.

in which new types of machinery demanded the removal of hedges, footpaths and woods, and in which an abundant use of chemical fertilisers multiplied the yield. Factory farming of chickens, eggs, pork and bacon was introduced providing in abundance products previously thought of as luxuries. Farming boomed, but at the cost of destroying the inherited environment, which led to protest movements in the 1980s against both the methods and the visible result. Although 60% of the land was held by only 0.5% of the population, the owners in the main were no longer individuals but institutions. They, of course, had no desire to live there, but merely to exploit the land as a source of revenue. As a consequence country houses were demolished or converted to institutional use, while the élite landscapes around them disintegrated. Occasionally estates passed into the hands of conservation bodies such as the National Trust, to be preserved as time-capsules from other centuries, still sometimes housing the descendants of the families which had built them. As rural buildings such as barns and labourers' cottages ceased to relate to the new economic reality, they were colonised by the newly affluent middle classes, who restored and prettified them in accord with a romanticised view of times past. Land, however, no longer bestowed status. But a house in the country still could, a fact reflected in the spread of second homes in the 1980s.

This reflects the fact that despite the appalling economic saga since 1945, on the whole most of the population now lived in a style undreamt-of by their grandparents. The average national income doubled between 1948 and 1976. During the 1950s a car, a holiday abroad, and a raft of consumer domestic comforts like central heating gradually became commonplace. In 1986 no less than 20 million people went on holiday abroad. By the 1990s house ownership was the rule rather than the exception, followed by an ever rising share-ownership. As a result British life is now dominated by a consumer-led white-collar middle class, within which the pecking order is as complex as at any other time in the country's history. It is a society of integrated inequality, whose dominant force is the professional person. The old landed upper classes have virtually vanished, to be replaced by a new upper class, recruited as much from above as from below, of employers, businessmen, politicians, administrators and academics. Status within society is no longer determined by birth or wealth so much as by education, intelligence and cultural aspiration.

The result is a very complex, fluid society in which families can rapidly rise and fall. The stabilising function of a defined hierarchy which had governed earlier ages has gone, even though the cosmetic of the earlier realities is sustained in the bestowal of peerages and titles. The decisive move therefore is not only away from an aristocratic society, but from a proletarian one too. That is caught in the decline of the

The consumer society of the 1980s in action. This was the golden age of the shopping mall and the galleria.

manual worker. By 1985 only a third of the workforce was manual and even within that group there was a skilled élite which would think of itself as middle class. That shift to non-manual work opened up jobs to women, whose change in status remains crucial to any understanding of the transformation of late twentieth century British society. By the mid 1960s over 38% of women worked and by 1990 they were moving up the ladder of professional achievement, aided by the feminist movement of the 1970s. Women now spent less of their life child-bearing and running the home, which ceased to be patriarchal, moving over towards equality of the sexes in its structure.

The family itself, as a unit of society, has progressively demanded redefinition as the divorce rate soared and the institution of marriage began to be abandoned. A third of all marriages ended in failure adding to a rising under-class of one-parent families, to which can be added the other losers in society: the old, the unemployed, and those caught in the poverty trap. With the ever-pervading libertarian ethos, couples began to avoid forming any contract either legal or religious, and just lived together. The result has been that births out of wedlock present a statistic unparalleled in the country's recorded history. If the disintegration of the family

Britain becomes a heritage theme park. Visitors ride through Shakespeare's Stratford-upon-Avon in 1987, catching a glimpse of the playwright's birthplace.

The Conservative government saw future prosperity as depending on service industries such as tourism.

presents an ongoing problem, so too does the burden of the multiplication of the old. In the 1990s over 20% of the population is over sixty and to live beyond eighty is now common. Segregation of a new kind has arrived, one in which the old are no longer integrated in the community.

This seemingly more equal society, however, masks all kinds of divisions. Education is divided between private and the state. In spite of the fact that education has largely been a disaster area, and that Britain has fewer people being educated beyond the age of sixteen than any other country in Western Europe, it still remains the prime agent of social mobility. Those who aspire for their children understand this, and will make any sacrifice in order to advance their chances through education. Although the dominance of the university intellectual on government thinking has passed, a degree remains an essential attribute for any form of social advancement. But not only is education divided, so too is health care. For the more affluent, insurance schemes to make provision for private medical treatment have become increasingly attractive. Inequalities in terms of income, capital, and social opportunity are still inevitably there, but not on the scale of earlier periods, although perhaps slightly more so since the 1980s. Such inequalities are disguised by a new classlessness of dress, speech, and social manner by the young. It is no longer easy to place someone by their speech and dress. But the age has also seen the emergence of new self-inflicted inequalities, like those between swathes of the working class who smoke, take no exercise and eat the wrong foods, and the middle class health fanatics who live off organic produce and dedicate themselves to exercise.

It has become an age of universal leisure. People spend as much time looking at television as they do working. Television itself binds society together in its way far more than radio; it was virtually universal by the middle of the 1970s and its greatest effect has been to privatise domestic life and make it more isolated. Entertainment and information are within the four walls of the home. Television was revived by the BBC in 1946 but the real turning point came with the advent of commercial television in 1955. This had a salutary effect on the BBC but an even greater effect on the viewers, for it took into every home a view of society which was orientated firmly to the marketplace and the ownership of things. Children no longer made toys, they consumed them.

By 1980 the average hours of work came down to 43 a week. Paid holidays of up to four weeks became normal and mass tourism exploded. Greater affluence, bringing more disposable income and along with it greater mobility, has engendered a gargantuan entertainment industry from theme parks to pop concerts.

That obsession with consumerism and the pursuit of pleasure, with no moral

overtones attached, epitomises the secular materialism of the period. The infra-structure of universally ac- cepted Christian ethical values has vanished, with philosophers providing no new moral structure. By 1980

One of the new cathedrals of the financial services era, Richard Rogers' Lloyds insurance building which opened in 1986.

only 5% of the population regularly attended a place of worship. Religion became marginal and churches began to close or be demolished. Gradually any restriction on a person's behaviour, especially sexual, now had to be justified, as values became privatised. Indeed the age of the minority interest arrived with ever-escalating provision made to meet the needs of groups in society as discrepant as the disabled and witches. All kinds of social behaviour, which once put people beyond the pale, were now accommodated. Only outright violence and extreme forms of perversion were regarded as reprehensible. In this way society could be said to have become more unsettled and fragmented than in previous ages when there had been a firm structure and definite boundaries beyond which no one should overtly trespass in the wider interests of coherence and stability.

Despite Mrs Thatcher's call to roll back the state, its presence continued to mark every stage of life, from birth certificate, through enforced schooling, the health service, finding and training for a job, insurance against illness, accident and unemployment, maybe a council house and welfare allowances, winding up with the old age pension and the death certificate. All of this was looked upon less with a sense of gratitude, which had marked its inception, than as a right. This was an age of bitter disillusion with the state and those who guided it, first with the patrician planners of the 40s and 50s, then with those who ran the quangos and unions of the 60s and 70s, and finally with the businessmen who called the tune in the 80s. A social hierarchy was dismantled in the 1960s, deference and status going along with it. This happened at every level, until it finally eroded any authority a parent or a teacher might have over a child. A chain of command had disappeared but no new source of authority was put in its place.

From the 1960s onwards every established institution, one by one, was held up to ridicule and derision. Nothing any more was untouchable, until by the 1990s even the monarchy was deconstructed. The monarchy had survived remarkably intact as a symbol of national unity around which the country could rally, as indeed it did on the occasion of the Queen's Silver Jubilee in 1977, and on that of the Prince of Wales's marriage in 1981. But the behaviour of the younger generation of the royal family began to bring it into disrepute, and the long-held mystery was subjected to the scalpel. The monarchy found itself increasingly isolated, as the political creeds of both left and right espoused either equality or meritocracy as the basis for society, neither logically accommodating monarchy.

If the monarchy remains in place with some of its senior members still held in respect, so too do the age-old institutions of Lords and Commons. By 1990 the presence of hereditary peers and the bishops in the Lords was a glaring anomaly offset by the arrival of over three hundred life-peers, either political appointees or people of real distinction in the life of the nation. Members of Parliament, now paid, were much diminished in status, their role largely confined to trotting into the appropriate lobby whenever the party whip was cracked. As the century draws to its close the power of Parliament can be seen to have been gradually reduced, not only by adhesion to the European Community with its own Parliament but due to the new pattern of things.

The House was once the focus of major debates but now they are rarely of significance, the real issues being debated in the press, on radio and television. The politician as statesman and hero has become a figure of the past. Difference in background of members has also narrowed. All parties are now largely made up of members of the professional classes, most are graduates. Although Labour members tend to be state educated and Conservative private, their class background can often be identical. Politics and class are now further apart than they were in 1890 or 1945. Efforts to reform the system have all failed, whether it be to change the structure of the upper house, obtain a Bill of Rights, or go over to a system of proportional representation.

The real seat of power resides in the Cabinet which consisted in the Victorian period of about fifteen, and is now made up of some twenty ministers heading the great departments of state. It is the Cabinet which dictates legislation, although even that role can be eroded by a dominant Prime Minister such as Mrs Thatcher, who made extensive use of outside advisers. Nor should the power of those in control of the enormous government machine at the centre be underestimated. Although local government is much diminished, there remain thousands of civil servants, and beyond them 5 million workers in the public sector. No party which wishes to remain in power can afford to ignore controlling the major appointments in that machine, or alienate its overall voting potential.

But late twentieth century Britain lacks the energy of earlier ages. The initiative and ambition that changed not only the island but, in some instances, whole parts of the globe, is absent. There is an exhaustion, a weariness, and an almost visible yearning for the quiet life. And that in spite of the fact that most British people have yet to come to terms with their greatly reduced status in the world. Apart from short distant conflicts like the Falklands war, the country has enjoyed since 1945 a prolonged period of peace almost unparalleled in its history. Dreams are now realised not in the next world nor in the world of empires, but in that of more and more material things. Real income has trebled since 1900 and the average Briton is better fed, better clothed, better housed, longer-lived and more leisured than at any time in the nation's history. On the positive side it can be said that this, more than any other previous century, is truly the age of the common man.

Chapter Seventy-Two

POSTSCRIPT: BEYOND 1990

Most readers will by now have placed themselves within the time span of these final chapters. Already events have moved on, for example, in Northern Ireland and in our dialogue with the European Union, and perhaps by the time this book has been published there may have been a change of government. But the central problems and dilemmas facing the country will be the same. Until recently, the story of Britain has been seen by historians as one in which a ruling minority has survived both an agrarian and industrial revolution into a post-industrial age with remarkable continuity, achieved by an ability to concede and incorporate. Such a survival was also brought about by a deep native distrust of ideas and ideologies, a devotion to freedom and tolerance, and a basic preference for pragmatism and common sense. Virtually no other European country has shown such an amazing capacity to change, and yet outwardly preserve an apparently seamless robe of continuity. Historians used to argue that this was because we had our revolution in the mid-seventeenth century, but more recently there have been those who have suggested that we have never really had a revolution, and that this may account for the ailing nature of some of our institutions. At the close of the twentieth century it is those institutions – the crown, Parliament, the church and the forces of law and order – seen as responsible for this bloodless evolution which now stand under fire. Perhaps for the first time we have an inability to self-reform. On the mainland of Europe, war, invasion, occupation and bloody revolutions have taken their toll in every country, bringing convulsions and instability of a kind we have been fortunate never to have experienced. But, one can now see, those dislocations have had their beneficial side because the basic principles of government, society and great institutions have had to be re-thought and re-formed. That has been particularly true of the period following the last war. Europe in the aftermath of 1945 had to reinvent itself whereas we, seemingly the winners, perpetuated ideas and systems which were already showing signs of strain and becoming progressively irrelevant in the fast-changing world at the close of the century. The British, however, remain fervently patriotic but it is a patriotism whose make-up belongs largely to the past. It is essentially backward-looking and therefore presents enormous problems of reconciliation with the European idea; in addition, the very concept of Britain is now being deconstructed by historians as an invention elaborated over the centuries to persuade those who live here that they share a common identity. Perhaps if this drift to regionalism prevails, the story of Britain will in future no longer be able to be told, but rather the separate stories of England, Wales, Ireland and Scotland. History alone will tell.

As I lay down my pen I am suddenly conscious of the title of this book, *The Story of Britain*. A story presupposes a beginning but it also implies an ending. The former we have but the latter has yet to come, for that is the nature of history. History never ends but merely unfolds further chapters. Looking back over the centuries I am struck that there is no single prolonged unfolding to the present. Rather I see a succession of differently structured societies succeeding one another as the ideas which created them formulate, reach an apogee and then go into decline. There is no discernible single pattern to that process either. Sometimes it is extremely slow-moving, like the gradual erosion of Romano-British society or the gentle cadence making up the rise and fall of the medieval world. At other times it can be quite sharp and dramatic, like republicanism in the seventeenth century which came and went in a few years, or the social levelling brought about by the First World War which finally ended the rule of the aristocracy.

It is essential to understand that it is impossible to read the past except through the eyes of the present. We are the prisoners of the perception of our own age. But it is important to try to be non-judgmental and assess each society on its own terms. None has been perfect. All have brought losers as well as winners. Through the centuries whole ethnic groups have been subjugated; the Celts by the Romans, the Romano-British by the Anglo-Saxons, the Anglo-Saxons by the Normans, the Welsh and the Irish by the English. Other groups also suffered: in the Middle Ages there were slaves devoid of any status and between the Reformation and the Victorian age dissenters and Roman Catholics were deprived of their rights as citizens. In every age there has been a litany of the deprived: the poor, the illiterate, the immigrant, the disabled, women, homosexuals and children. It is difficult not to conclude that to be successful any society must inevitably work from a premise of the exclusion of those who do not adhere to its tenets, in order for it to function and protect the identity and coherence of the majority. Today we would judge as successful those forms of society which gathered most within their orbit. But that is a verdict of hindsight formed by the values of a libertarian age.

So each era calls for assessment on its own merits, for they are all transitory. Medieval society was universal, the mirror of heaven come down to earth. It sought to be a just and binding one in which each person had his place and role to fulfil within the divine scheme of things. Each day heaven came down to earth and was glimpsed in every cathedral and parish church. Everyone passionately believed that the real life was the one to come beyond the grave. In the secular state of post-Reformation Tudor and Stuart England a reordered hierarchy fanned downwards from the God-ordained ruler. Each layer of society had its part to play, some to command, others to obey, each accorded his niche bowing to the will of order and authority. Church and state were coeval, therefore those who could not accept membership of the Church of England, like Roman Catholics or Dissenters, had no right to be members of the commonwealth. Universalism gave way to a national identity in which the harmony of the state reflected the harmony of the cosmos. As regal rule gradually passed into aristocratic hands in the Georgian and Victorian ages, it was property which above all determined a person's status in society. To possess it meant that an owner had a stake in the country, and in ensuring its stability and commercial prosperity in the face of both threats from below and those from foreign powers. To extend the franchise beyond those who thus qualified was regarded with abhorrence as giving power to the feckless and irresponsible. Eyes continued to be on the next world but increasingly the present one was seen to contain its delights. In our own democratic age hierarchy cosmetically remains but in reality it has gone. Every member of the population is now regarded as having an inalienable right by birth alone to take part in decisions, via the ballot box, as to which direction the country should go. Aristocracy based on birth and possessions has been replaced by meritocracy, the rule of the talented, regardless of belief or gender. For the vast majority there is now only one life, the present, and that must be savoured to the full. We are still in the midst of that phase of society but whether we are at its apogee or witnessing its decline it is too early to say. One thing is certain, it too will pass away as yet another chapter unfolds in the unending story of Britain.

KINGS AND QUEENS

Reproduced from *Whitaker's Almanack 1996* with the permission of the publishers, J. Whitaker and Sons Ltd.

HOUSES OF CERDIC AND DENMARK

REIGN

927–939 ATHELSTAN
Second son of Edward the Elder, by Ecgwynn, and grandson of Alfred
Acceded to Wessex and Mercia *c*.924, established direct rule over Northumbria 927, effectively creating the Kingdom of England
Reigned 15 years

939–946 EDMUND I
Born 921, fourth son of Edward the Elder, by Eadgifu
Married (1) Ælfgifu (2) Æthelflæd
Killed aged 25, *reigned* 6 years

946–955 EADRED
Fifth son of Edward the Elder, by Eadgifu
Reigned 9 years

955–959 EADWIG
Born before 943, son of Edmund and Ælfgifu
Married Ælfgifu
Reigned 3 years

959–975 EDGAR I
Born 943, son of Edmund and Ælfgifu
Married (1) Aethelflæd (2) Wulfthryth (3) Ælfthryth
Died aged 32, *reigned* 15 years

975–978 EDWARD I (the Martyr)
Born c.962, son of Edgar and Æthelflæd
Assassinated aged *c*.16, *reigned* 2 years

978–1016 ETHELRED (the Unready)
Born c.968/969, son of Edgar and Ælfthryth
Married (1) Ælfgifu (2) Emma, daughter of Richard I, count of Normandy
1013–14 dispossessed of kingdom by Swegn Forkbeard (king of Denmark 987–1014)
Died aged *c*.47, *reigned* 38 years

1016 EDMUND II (Ironside)
Born before 993, son of Ethelred and Ælfgifu
Married Ealdgyth
Died aged over 23, *reigned* 7 months (April–November)

1016–1035 CANUTE
Born c.995, son of Swegn Forkbeard, king of Denmark, and Gunhild
Married (1) Ælfgifu (2) Emma, widow of Ethelred the Unready
Gained submission of West Saxons 1015, Northumbrians 1016, Mercia 1016, king of all England after Edmund's death
King of Denmark 1019–35, king of Norway 1028–35
Died aged *c*.40, *reigned* 19 years

1035–1040 HAROLD I (Harefoot)
Born c.1016/17, son of Canute and Ælfgifu
Married Ælfgifu
1035 recognized as regent for himself and his brother Harthacanute; 1037 recognised as king
Died aged *c*.23, *reigned* 4 years

1040–1042   HARTHACANUTE
*Born c.*1018, son of Canute and
Emma
Titular king of Denmark from
1028
Acknowledged king of England
1035–7 with Harold I as regent;
effective king after Harold's death
Died aged *c.*24, *reigned* 2 years

1042–1066   EDWARD II (the Confessor)
Born between 1002 and 1005, son
of Ethelred the Unready and Emma
Married Eadgyth, daughter of
Godwine, earl of Wessex
Died aged over 60, *reigned* 23 years

1066   HAROLD. II (Godwinesson)
*Born c.*1020, son of Godwine, earl
of Wessex, and Gytha
Married (1) Eadgyth (2) Ealdgyth
Killed in battle aged *c.*46, *reigned* 10
months (January–October)

THE HOUSE OF NORMANDY

1066–1087   WILLIAM I (the Conqueror)
Born 1027/8, son of Robert I, duke
of Normandy; obtained the Crown
by conquest
Married Matilda, daughter of
Baldwin, count of Flanders
Died aged *c.*60, *reigned* 20 years

1087–1100   WILLIAM II (Rufus)
Born between 1056 and 1060, third
son of William I; succeeded his
father in England only
Killed aged *c.*40, *reigned* 12 years

1100–1135   HENRY I (Beauclerk)
Born 1068, fourth son of William I
Married (1) Edith or Matilda,
daughter of Malcolm III of
Scotland (2) Adela, daughter of
Godfrey, count of Louvain
Died aged 67, *reigned* 35 years

1135–1154   STEPHEN
Born not later than 1100, third son
of Adela, daughter of William I,
and Stephen, count of Blois
Married Matilda, daughter of
Eustace, count of Boulogne
1141 (February–November) held
captive by adherents of Matilda,
daughter of Henry I, who contested
the crown until 1153
Died aged over 53, *reigned* 18 years

THE HOUSE OF ANJOU (PLANTAGENETS)

1154–1189   HENRY II (Curtmantle)
Born 1133, son of Matilda,
daughter of Henry I, and Geoffrey,
count of Anjou
Married Eleanor, daughter of
William, duke of Aquitaine, and
divorced queen of Louis VII of
France
Died aged 56, *reigned* 34 years

1189–1199   RICHARD I (Coeur de Lion)
Born 1157, third son of Henry II
Married Berengaria, daughter of
Sancho VI, king of Navarre
Died aged 42, *reigned* 9 years

1199–1215   JOHN (Lackland)
Born 1167, fifth son of Henry II
Married (1) Isabella or Avisa,
daughter of William, earl of
Gloucester (divorced) (2) Isabella,
daughter of Aymer, count of
Angoulême
Died aged 48, *reigned* 17 years

1215–1272   HENRY III
Born 1207, son of John and Isabella
of Angoulême
Married Eleanor, daughter of
Raymond, count of Provence
Died aged 65, *reigned* 56 years

1272–1307   EDWARD I (Longshanks)
Born 1239, eldest son of Henry III
Married (1) Eleanor, daughter of
Ferdinand III, king of Castile (2)
Margaret, daughter of Philip III of
France
Died aged 68, *reigned* 34 years

1307–1327   EDWARD II
Born 1284, eldest surviving son of
Edward I and Eleanor
Married Isabella, daughter of Philip
IV of France
Deposed January 1327, *killed*
September 1327 aged 43, *reigned* 19
years

1327–1377   EDWARD III
Born 1312, eldest son of Edward II
Married Philippa, daughter of
William, count of Hainault
Died aged 64, *reigned* 50 years

1377–1399	RICHARD II *Born* 1327, son of Edward (the black Prince), eldest son of Edward III *Married* (1) Anne, daughter of Emperor Charles IV (2) Isabelle, daughter of Charles VI of France *Deposed* September 1399, *killed* February 1400 aged 33, *reigned* 22 years

THE HOUSE OF LANCASTER

1399–1413	HENRY IV *Born* 1366, son of John of Gaunt, fourth son of Edward III, and Blanche, daughter of Henry, duke of Lancaster *Married* (1) Mary, daughter of Humphrey, earl of Hereford (2) Joan, daughter of Charles, king of Navarre, and widow of John, duke of Brittany *Died* aged *c*.47, *reigned* 13 years
1413–1422	HENRY V *Born* 1387, eldest surviving son of Henry IV and Mary *Married* Catherine, daughter of Charles VI of France *Died* aged *c*.34, *reigned* 9 years
1422–1471	HENRY VI *Born* 1421, son of Henry V *Married* Margaret, daughter of René, duke of Anjou and count of Provence *Deposed* March 1461, *restored* October 1470 *Deposed* April 1471, *killed* May 1471 aged 49, *reigned* 39 years

THE HOUSE OF YORK

1461–1483	EDWARD IV *Born* 1442, eldest son of Richard of York, who was the grandson of Edmund, fifth son of Edward III, and the son of Anne, great-granddaughter of Lionel, third son of Edward III *Married* Elizabeth Woodville, daughter of Richard, Lord Rivers, and widow of Sir John Grey *Acceded* March 1461, *deposed* October 1470, *restored* April 1471 *Died* aged 40, *reigned* 21 years

1483	EDWARD V *Born* 1470, eldest son of Edward IV *Deposed* June 1483, *died* probably July–September 1483, aged 12, *reigned* 2 months (April–June)
1483–1485	RICHARD III *Born* 1452, fourth son of Richard of York and brother of Edward IV *Married* Anne Neville, daughter of Richard, earl of Warwick, and widow of Edward, Prince of Wales, son of Henry VI *Killed* in battle aged 32, *reigned* 2 years

THE HOUSE OF TUDOR

1485–1509	HENRY VII *Born* 1457, son of Margaret Beaufort, great-granddaughter of John of Gaunt, fourth son of Edward III, and Edmund Tudor, earl of Richmond *Married* Elizabeth, daughter of Edward IV *Died* aged 52, *reigned* 23 years
1509–1547	HENRY VIII *Born* 1491, second son of Henry VII *Married* (1) Catherine, daughter of Ferdinand II, king of Aragon, and widow of his elder brother Arthur (divorced) (2) Anne, daughter of Sir Thomas Boleyn (executed) (3) Jane, daughter of Sir John Seymour (died in childbirth) (4) Anne, daughter of John, duke of Cleves (divorced) (5) Catherine Howard, niece of the Duke of Norfolk (executed) (6) Catherine, daughter of Sir Thomas Parr and widow of Lord Latimer *Died* aged 55, *reigned* 37 years
1547–1553	EDWARD VI *Born* 1537, son of Henry VIII and Jane Seymour *Died* aged 15, *reigned* 6 years
1553	JANE *Born* 1537, daughter of Frances, daughter of Mary Tudor, the younger sister of Henry VIII, and Henry Grey, duke of Suffolk *Married* Lord Guildford Dudley, son of the Duke of Northumberland *Deposed* July 1553, *executed* February 1554 aged 16, *reigned* 14 days

1553–1558 MARY I
Born 1516, daughter of Henry VIII
and Catherine of Aragon
Married Philip II of Spain
Died aged 42, *reigned* 5 years

1558–1603 ELIZABETH I
Born 1533, daughter of Henry VIII
and Anne Boleyn
Died aged 69, *reigned* 44 years

THE HOUSE OF STUART

1603–1625 James I (VI OF SCOTLAND)
Born 1566, son of Mary, queen of
Scots and granddaughter of
Margaret Tudor, elder daughter of
Henry VII, and Henry Stewart,
Lord Darnley
Married Anne, daughter of
Frederick II of Denmark
Died aged 58, *reigned* 22 years

1625–1649 CHARLES I
Born 1600, second son of James I
Married Henrietta Maria, daughter
of Henry IV of France
Executed 1649 aged 48, *reigned* 23
years

COMMONWEALTH DECLARED 19
May 1649
1649–53 Government by a council
of state
1653–8 Oliver Cromwell, *Lord
Protector*
1658–9 Richard Cromwell, *Lord
Protector*

1660–1685 CHARLES II
Born 1630, eldest son of Charles I
Married Catherine, daughter of
John IV of Portugal
Died aged 54, *reigned* 24 years

1685–1688 JAMES II (VII of Scotland)
Born 1633, second son of Charles I
Married (1) Lady Anne Hyde,
daughter of Edward, earl of
Clarendon (2) Mary, daughter of
Alphonso, duke of Modena
Reign ended with flight from
kingdom December 1688
Died 1701 aged 67, *reigned* 3 years

INTERREGNUM 11 December 1688
to 12 February 1689

1689–1702 WILLIAM III
Born 1650, son of William II, prince
of Orange, and Mary Stuart,
daughter of Charles I
Married Mary, elder daughter of
James II
Died aged 51, *reigned* 13 years

and
1689–1694 MARY II
Born 1662, elder daughter of James
II and Anne
Died aged 32, *reigned* 5 years

1702–1714 ANNE
Born 1665, younger daughter of
James II and Anne
Married Prince George of
Denmark, son of Frederick III of
Denmark
Died aged 49, *reigned* 12 years

THE HOUSE OF HANOVER

1714–1727 GEORGE I (Elector of Hanover)
Born 1660, son of Sophia (daughter
of Frederick, elector palatine, and
Elizabeth Stuart, daughter of James
I) and Ernest Augustus, elector of
Hanover
Married Sophia Dorothea, daughter
of George William, duke of
Lüneburg-Celle
Died aged 67, *reigned* 12 years

1727–1760 GEORGE II
Born 1683, son of George I
Married Caroline, daughter of John
Frederick, margrave of
Brandenburg-Anspach
Died aged 76, *reigned* 33 years

1760–1820 GEORGE III
Born 1738, son of Federick, eldest
son of George II
Married Charlotte, daughter of
Charles Louis, duke of
Mecklenburg-Strelitz
Died aged 81, *reigned* 59 years

REGENCY 1811–20
Prince of Wales regent owing to the
insanity of George III

1820–1830   GEORGE IV
             Born 1762, eldest son of George III
             Married Caroline, daughter of
             Charles, duke of Brunswick-
             Wolfenbüttel
             Died aged 67, *reigned* 10 years

1830–1837   WILLIAM IV
             Born 1765, third son of George III
             Married Caroline, daughter of
             George, duke of Saxe-Meiningen
             Died aged 71, *reigned* 7 years

1837–1901   VICTORIA
             Born 1819, daughter of Edward,
             fourth son of George III
             Married Prince Albert of Saxe-
             Coburg and Gotha
             Died aged 81, *reigned* 63 years

THE HOUSE OF SAXE-COBURG AND GOTHA

1901–1910   EDWARD VII
             Born 1841, eldest son of Victoria
             and Albert
             Married Alexandra, daughter of
             Christian IX of Denmark
             Died aged 68, *reigned* 9 years

THE HOUSE OF WINDSOR

1910–1936   GEORGE V
             Born 1865, second son of Edward VII
             Married Victoria Mary, daughter of
             Francis, duke of Teck
             Died aged 70, *reigned* 25 years

1936   EDWARD VIII
             Born 1894, eldest son of George V
             Married (1937) Mrs Wallis Warfield
             Abdicated 1936, *died* 1972 aged 77,
             reigned 10 months (20 January to 11
             December)

1936–1952   GEORGE VI
             Born 1895, second son of George V
             Married Lady Elizabeth Bowes-
             Lyon, daughter of 14th Earl of
             Strathmore and Kinghorne
             Died aged 56, *reigned* 15 years

1952–   ELIZABETH II
             Born 1926, elder daughter of
             George VI
             Married Philip, son of Prince
             Andrew of Greece

KINGS AND QUEENS OF SCOTS 1016 TO 1603

1016–1034   MALCOLM II
             Born c.954, son of Kenneth II
             Acceded to Alba 1005, secured
             Lothian c.106, obtained Strathclyde
             for his grandson Duncan c.1016,
             thus forming the Kingdom of
             Scotland
             Died aged c.80, *reigned* 18 years

1034–1040   DUNCAN I
             Son of Bethoc, daughter of
             Malcom II, and Crinan
             Married a cousin of Siward, earl of
             Northumbria
             Reigned 5 years

1040–1057   MACBETH
             Born c.1005, son of a daughter of
             Malcolom II and Finlaec, mormaer
             of Moray
             Married Gruoch, granddaughter of
             Kenneth III
             Killed aged c.52, *reigned* 17 years

1057–1058   LULACH
             Born c.1032, son of Gillacomgan,
             mormaer of Moray, and Gruoch
             (and stepson of Macbeth)
             Died aged c.26, *reigned* 7 months
             (August–March)

1058–1093   MALCOLM III (Canmore)
             Born c.1031, elder son of Duncan I
             Married (1) Ingibiorg (2) Margaret
             (St Margaret), granddaughter of
             Edmund II of England
             Killed in battle aged c.62, *reigned* 35
             years

1093–1097   DONALD III BÁN
             Born c.103. second son of Duncan I
             Deposed May 1094, *restored*
             November 1094, *deposed* October
             1097, *reigned* 3 years

1094   DUNCAN II
             Born c.1060, elder son of Malcolm
             III and Ingibiorg
             Married Octreda of Dunbar
             Killed aged c.34, *reigned* 6 months
             (May–November)

1094–1107   EDGAR
             Born c.1074, second son of
             Malcolm III and Margaret
             Died aged c.32, *reigned* 9 years

1107–1124   ALEXANDER I (The Fierce)
*Born c.*1077, fifth son of Malcolm
III and Margaret
Married Sybilla, illegitimate
daughter of Henry I of England
died aged *c.*47, *reigned* 17 years

1124–1153   DAVID I (The Saint)
*Born c.*1085, sixth son of Malcolm
III and Margaret
Married Matilda, daughter of
Waltheof, earl of Huntingdon
Died aged *c.*68, *reigned* 29 years

1153–1165   Malcolm IV (The Maiden)
*Born c.*1141, son of Henry, earl of
Huntingdon, second son of David I
Died aged *c.*24, *reigned* 12 years

1165–1214   WILLIAM I (The Lion)
*Born c.*1142, brother of Malcolm IV
Married Ermengarde, daughter of
Richard, viscount of Beaumont
Died aged *c.*72, *reigned* 49 years

1214–1249   ALEXANDER II
Born 1198, son of William I
Married (1) Joan, daughter of John,
king of England (2) Marie,
daughter of Ingelram de Coucy
Died aged 50, *reigned* 34 years

1249–1286   ALEXANDER III
Born 1241, son of Alexander II and
Marie
Married (1) Margaret, daughter of
Henry III of England (2) Yolande,
daughter of the Count of Dreux
Killed accidentally aged 44, *reigned*
36 years

1286–1290   MARGARET (The Maid of Norway)
Born 1283, daughter of Margaret
(daughter of Alexander III) and Eric
II of Norway
Died aged 7, *reigned* 4 years

FIRST INTERREGNUM 1290–2
Throne disputed by 13
competitors. Crown awarded to
John Balliol by adjudication of
Edward I of England.

THE HOUSE OF BALLIOL

1292–1296   JOHN (Balliol)
*Born c.*125, son of Dervorguilla,
great-great-granddaughter of
David I, and John de Balliol

Married Isabella, daughter of John,
earl of Surrey
Abdicated 1296, *died* 1313 aged *c.*63,
reigned 3 years
SECOND INTERREGNUM 1296–1306
Edward I of England declared John
Balliol to have forfeited the throne
for contumacy in 1296 and took
the government of Scotland into
his own hands.

THE HOUSE OF BRUCE

1306–1329   ROBERT I (Bruce)
Born 1274, son of Robert Bruce and
Marjorie, countess of Carrick, and
great-grandson of the second
daughter of David, earl of
Huntingdon, brother of William I
Married (1) Isabella, daughter of
Donald, earl of Mar (2) Elizabeth,
daughter of Richard, earl of Ulster
Died aged 54, *reigned* 23 years

1329–1371   DAVID II
Born 1324, son of Robert I and
Elizabeth
Married (1) Joanna, daughter of
Edward II of England (2) Margaret
Drummond, widow of Sir John
Logie (divorced)
Died aged 46, *reigned* 41 years

1332 Edward Balliol, son of John
Balliol, crowned King of Scots
September, expelled December
1333–6 Edward Balliol restored as
King of Scots

THE HOUSE OF STEWART

1371–1390   ROBERT II (Stewart)
Born 1316, son of Marjorie,
daughter of Robert I, and Walter,
High Steward of Scotland
Married (1) Elizabeth, daughter of
Sir Robert Mure of Rowallan (2)
Euphemia, daughter of Hugh, earl
of Ross
Died aged 74, *reigned* 19 years

1390–1406   ROBERT III
*Born c.*1337, son of Robert II and
Elizabeth
Married Annabella, daughter of Sir
John Drummond of Stobhall
Died aged *c.*69, *reigned* 16 years

1406–1437	JAMES I	
	Born 1394, son of Robert III	
	Married Joan Beaufort, daughter of John, earl of Somerset	
	Assassinated aged 42, *reigned* 30 years	
1437–1460	JAMES II	
	Born 1430, son of James I	
	Married Mary, daughter of Arnold, duke of Gueldres	
	Killed accidentally aged 29, *reigned* 23 years	
1460–1488	JAMES III	
	Born 1452, son of James II	
	Married Margaret, daughter of Christian I of Denmark	
	Assassinated aged 36, *reigned* 27 years	
1488–1513	JAMES IV	
	Born 1473, son of James III	
	Married Margaret Tudor, daughter of Henry VII of England	
	Killed in battle aged 40, *reigned* 25 years	
1513–1542	JAMES V	
	Born 1512, son of James IV	

Married (1) Madeleine, daughter of Francis I of France (2) Mary of Lorraine, daughter of the Duc de Guise
Died aged 30, *reigned* 29 years

1542–1567 MARY
Born 1542, daughter of James V and Mary
Married (1) the Dauphin, afterwards Francis II of France (2) Henry Stewart, Lord Darnley (3) James Hepburn, earl of Bothwell
Abdicated 1567, prisoner in England from 1568, *executed* 1587, *reigned* 24 years

1567–1625 JAMES VI (and I of England)
Born 1566, son of Mary, queen of Scots, and Henry, Lord Darnley
Acceded 1567 to the Scottish throne, *reigned* 58 years
Succeeded 1603 to the English throne, so joining the English and Scottish crowns in one person. The two kingdoms remained distinct until 1707 when the parliaments of the kingdoms became conjoined

PRIME MINISTERS

Sir Robert Walpole	*April*	1721	Viscount Palmerston	*June*	1859
Earl of Wilmington	*February*	1741	Earl Russell	*October*	1865
Henry Pelham	*August*	1743	Earl of Derby	*June*	1866
Duke of Newcastle	*March*	1754	Benjamin Disraeli	*February*	1868
Duke of Devonshire	*November*	1756	William Ewart Gladstone	*December*	1868
Duke of Newcastle	*July*	1757	Benjamin Disraeli	*February*	1874
Earl of Bute	*May*	1762	William Ewart Gladstone	*April*	1880
George Grenville	*April*	1763	Marquess of Salisbury	*June*	1885
Marquess of Rockingham	*July*	1765	William Ewart Gladstone	*February*	1886
Earl of Chatham	*July*	1766	Marquess of Salisbury	*July*	1886
Duke of Grafton	*October*	1768	William Ewart Gladstone	*August*	1892
Lord North	*January*	1770	Earl of Rosebery	*March*	1894
Marquess of Rockingham	*March*	1782	Marquess of Salisbury	*June*	1895
Earl of Shelburne	*July*	1782	Arthur James Balfour	*July*	1902
Duke of Portland	*April*	1783	Sir Henry Campbell-Bannerman	*December*	1905
William Pitt	*December*	1783	Herbert Henry Asquith	*April*	1908
Henry Addington	*March*	1801	David Lloyd George	*December*	1916
William Pitt	*May*	1804	Andrew Bonar Law	*October*	1922
William Wyndham Grenville	*February*	1806	Stanley Baldwin	*May*	1923
Duke of Portland	*March*	1807	James Ramsay MacDonald	*January*	1924
Spencer Perceval	*October*	1809	Stanley Baldwin	*November*	1924
Earl of Liverpool	*June*	1812	James Ramsay MacDonald	*June*	1929
George Canning	*April*	1827	Stanley Baldwin	*June*	1935
Viscount Goderich	*August*	1827	Neville Chamberlain	*May*	1937
Duke of Wellington	*January*	1828	Winston Churchill	*May*	1940
Earl Grey	*November*	1830	Clement Attlee	*July*	1945
Viscount Melbourne	*July*	1834	Winston Churchill	*October*	1951
Duke of Wellington	*November*	1834	Sir Anthony Eden	*April*	1955
Sir Robert Peel	*December*	1834	Harold Macmillan	*January*	1957
Viscount Melbourne	*April*	1835	Sir Alec Douglas-Home	*October*	1963
Sir Robert Peel	*August*	1841	Harold Wilson	*October*	1964
Lord John Russell	*June*	1846	Edward Heath	*June*	1970
Earl of Derby	*February*	1852	Harold Wilson	*March*	1974
Earl of Aberdeen	*December*	1852	James Callaghan	*April*	1976
Viscount Palmerston	*February*	1855	Margaret Thatcher	*May*	1979
Earl of Derby	*February*	1858	John Major	*November*	1990

PICTURE CREDITS

The author and publishers wish to thank all private owners, museums, galleries, libraries, agencies and other institutions for permission to reproduce works in their collection.

American Philosophical Society, Philadelphia 363; Lord Annan 383; Arcaid Photo Library 551, 557 563; Ashmolean Museum, Oxford 254; Barnardos Publicity Services, 413; The City of Bayeux 43, 44, 45, 46, 47 48; The Duke of Beuccleuch, K.T. 207, 275; Birmingham Reference Library 455; Bodleian Library, Oxford, 269(Hatton 20 1r), 37(Auct F 4 32 1r), 105(Douce 313 f394v), 106(New College Ms 288), 167(Douce 363), 317(New College Ms 361/2), 487 & 504(Conservative Party Archive); Bridgeman Art Library, 192, 264, 283, 285, 304, 310, 352, 387, 402, 429, 451, 390(Birmingham Art Gallery), 323(Soane Museum), 299(Blenheim), 300(Blenheim), 301(Blenheim); British Library 35(Cotton Vespasian A viii f2), 40(Additional 33241 1b, 58(Cotton Claud D11 f45v), 67(Harley 5102 f37), 74(Cotton Aug II. 106) 83(Royal 2Axxii), 98(Additional 42130 f202v), 101(Nero D vi), 111(Royal 20 E 1), 120(Royal 18E11 f41 6v), 122(Royal 16Fii f73), 129(Arundel 38), 132(Cotton Julius Eiv f22), 134(Cotton Julius E1V art6 f22v), 135(Add.48976- Rous roll), 139(Royal 15Ef14r), 175(Titus D IV); British Museum, 10, 17, 21, 71, 96, 137, 212, 293, 341, 354, 373, 388; Burrell Collection, Glasgow 68; Cambridge Univ Aerial Photo/MOD 27; Cambridge University Library 77(Ee 50 f30); Camera Press 519, 534; Chatsworth Settlement 245, 246; City of Bayeux 43, 44, 45, 46, 47, 48; Colchester Museum 13; Corinium Museum, Gloucester 9; Corpus Christi College, Cambridge 93,(Ms171 f265r) 125(Ms61); Cottrell-Dormer/Courtauld Institute of Art 356;Dean & Canons of Windsor 165; ET Archive 2, 21, 24, 32, 62, 112, 122, 131; Fotomas 127, 151, 153, 172, 177, 197, 202, 215, 217, 219, 223, 225, 229, 236, 237, 238, 241, 256, 258, 260, 262, 273, 275, 277, 279, 294, 320, 369, 457; Geffrye Museum, London 492; Gernsheim Collection, University of Texas at Austin 418; Paul Graham 548; Granada TV 522; Guildhall Library 307; Sonia Halliday 140, 141; Nick Hedges 536; Hulton Picture Library 417, 423, 482, 490, 495, 502, 520, 532, 553; Illustrated London News 379; Imperial War Museum 477, 478; John Rylands Library 349, 350; AFKersting 7, 15, 52, 55, 61, 65, 81, 88, 91, 102, 157, 160, 340; Kunstmuseum Basle 174; Lee Miller Archive 499; Magdalene College, Cambs 282; Magnum 542(Gilles Peress), 559 & 560(Martin Parr); Manchester Art Gallery 436; Mansell Collection, 185, 337, 409, 420, 440, 449, 465; Mary Evans Picture Library 398; Museum of London 69; National Army Museum 251; National Gallery, London 116, 117; National Library of Ireland 464; National Maritime Museum 204, 239, 374, 448; National Portrait Gallery 147, 187, 289, 313, 348, 385; National Trust 426; Network, 545,(Peter Jordan) 549(John Sturrock); Newdegate Settlement, 325; Nightingale Museum, St Thomas Hospital, 430, 548; Northern Ireland Assembly/K Dalzell 469; A Poignant, 31; Popperfoto 511, 513, 517; Press Association, 474; Private Collection, 332; Public Record Office, 54, 471; Punch 439, 459; Queensland Art Gallery, 472; Reunion des Musees Nationaux, 253; RIBA, 249; Royal Archives © 1995 Her Majesty Queen Elizabeth II, 162, 180, 221, 227, 231, 245, 268, 339, 361, 421; Royal Institution, Cornwall, 329; Eddie Ryle Hodges, 12; Science & Society Library, 315, 400; Science Photo Library, xii; Sherbourne Castle, 194; Skyscan, 3, 7, 355; Edwin Smith, 23; Society of Antiquaries, 149; Solo Syndication, 497, 507; Suffolk Record Office, Ipswich Branch 414; Tate Gallery, 529 © David Hockney 1970-1; Thomas Photos, 84, 85, 86, 87, 88, 89; Trinity College, Cambridge, 316(Ms R 4 48c); Ulster Museum, 203, 298, 467; Victoria & Albert Museum, 74, 86, 200, 209, 396, 433; Vindolanda Trust, 17; Walker Art Gallery, Liverpool, 412; Wedgwood Museum, Staffordshire, 343, 382; Westminster Abbey 114; Westminster Cathedral, 188; Winchester Cathedral, 183; Worshipful Company of Wax Chandlers, 148; Yale University Art Gallery 367; Yorkshire Museum, 107; The Marquess of Zetland 334;

The publishers also acknowledge with thanks the following for permission to include copyright material: Penguin Books for permission to use 39 lines from *The Canterbury Tales* by Geoffrey Chaucher, translated by Nevill Coghill, copyright © Nevill Coghill, 1958, 1960, 1975, 1977; Faber and Faber Ltd for 5 lines from Little Gidding from *Four Quarters* by T. S. Eliot.

INDEX